Cessna
Pilot
Center

Manual
of Flight

ii

CE315490C

PREFACE

Congratulations on taking the first step toward learning to fly. The Cessna Private Pilot *Manual of Flight* contains the answers to many of the questions you may have as you begin your training program. It is based on the "study/review" concept of learning. This means detailed material is presented in an uncomplicated way, then important points are summarized through the use of bold type and color. The manual incorporates many design features that will help you get the most out of your study and review efforts. These include:

- **Margin Notes** — The margin notes, which are printed in color, summarize key points from the text. They emphasize material contained in the FAA tests, as well as other important data. You are encouraged to add your own study notes in the wide margins provided on each page.

- **Illustrations** — Illustrations are carefully planned to complement and expand upon concepts introduced in the text. Color in the illustrations and the accompanying captions flag them as items that warrant your attention during both initial study and review.

- **Bold Type** — Important new terms in the text are printed in bold type, then defined.

- **Checklist** — A checklist appears at the end of each section to help you verify your understanding of principal concepts.

- **Glossary** — The glossary defines commonly used aeronautical terms.

- **Abbreviations** — Abbreviations explains the most frequently used aviation acronyms and abbreviations.

- **Federal Aviation Regulations** — Appropriate FARs are presented in a separate booklet, which includes exercises designed to test your understanding of pertinent regulations.

The manual is the key element in the training materials. Although it can be studied alone, there are several other components which we recommend to make your flight training as complete as possible. These include the *Private Pilot Workbook*, *Private Pilot Training Syllabus*, and *FAA Practical Test Study Guide*. You also may refer to the video presentations which go along with each Flight Prep. These video programs are designed to enhance and complement your study. When used together, these various elements provide an ideal framework for you and your instructor as you prepare for the FAA computer and practical tests.

TABLE OF CONTENTS

flight prep 1

AIRPLANES

One of the first things you are likely to notice during a visit to your local airport is the wide variety of airplane styles and designs. Although, at first glance, you may think that airplanes look quite different from one another, you will find that their major components are quite similar. [Figure 1-1]

THE FUSELAGE

The fuselage serves several functions. Besides being a common attachment point for the other major components, it houses the cabin, or cockpit, which contains seats for the occupants and the controls for the airplane. The fuselage usually has a small baggage compartment and may include additional seats for passengers.

THE WING

When air flows around the wings of an airplane, it generates a force called "lift" that helps the airplane fly. Wings are contoured to take maximum advantage of this force, as you will see in Section B. Wings may be attached at the top, middle, or lower portion of the fuselage. These designs

Figure 1-1. Typically, an airplane is made up of five major parts. The fuselage is considered to be the central component, since the powerplant, wings, empennage (tail section), and landing gear are attached to it.

Figure 1-2. You can move the ailerons by turning the control wheel in the cockpit. When you turn the wheel to the left, the left aileron moves up and the right moves down. During flight, this is how you start a turn to the left. Turning the wheel to the right has the opposite effect. You can operate the flaps using a switch or handle located in the cockpit. They are used primarily for takeoffs and landings.

are referred to as high-, mid-, and low-wing, respectively. The number of wings can also vary. Airplanes with a single set of wings are referred to as **monoplanes**, while those with two sets are called **biplanes**.

To help you fly the airplane, the wings have two types of control surfaces attached to the rear, or trailing, edges. They are referred to as ailerons and flaps. **Ailerons** extend from about the midpoint of each wing outward to the tip. They move in opposite directions — when one aileron goes up, the other goes down. **Flaps** extend outward from the fuselage to the midpoint of each wing. They always move in the same direction. If one flap is down, the other is down. [Figure 1-2]

The wings have two types of control surfaces called the ailerons and flaps.

THE EMPENNAGE

The empennage consists of the **vertical stabilizer**, or fin, and the **horizontal stabilizer**. These two surfaces are stationary and act like the feathers on an arrow to steady the airplane and help you maintain a straight path through the air. [Figure 1-3]

The horizontal and vertical stabilizers help you maintain a straight path through the air.

Figure 1-3. Besides the two fixed components, the empennage has two important movable surfaces called the rudder and the elevator.

Figure 1-4. You operate the rudder with your feet, using pedals located in the cockpit. When you press the left rudder pedal, the nose moves left, while the right pedal moves the nose right.

The **rudder** is attached to the back of the vertical stabilizer. You use it to move the airplane's nose left and right. Actually, you use the rudder and ailerons in combination during flight to initiate a turn. You will learn the details about this later. [Figure 1-4]

The **elevator** is attached to the back of the horizontal stabilizer. During flight, you use it to move the nose up and down so you can direct the airplane to the desired altitude, or height. [Figure 1-5]

Figure 1-5. The elevator is moved by using the control wheel. When you pull back on the wheel, the nose moves up; when you push forward, the nose moves down.

Most airplanes have a small, hinged section at the back of the elevator called a **trim tab**. Its purpose is to relieve the pressure you must hold on the control wheel to keep the nose in the desired position. In most small airplanes, you control the trim tab with a wheel or crank in the cockpit. Your flight instructor will direct you in the proper use of the trim control for the airplane you are flying.

STABILATOR

Some empennage designs vary from the type of horizontal stabilizer just discussed. They have a one-piece horizontal stabilizer that pivots up and down from a central hinge point. This type of design, called a **stabilator**, requires no elevator. You move the stabilator using the control wheel, just as you would the elevator. When you pull back, the nose moves up; when you push forward, the nose moves down. An antiservo tab is mounted at the back of the stabilator, to provide you with a control "feel" similar to what you experience with an elevator. Without the **antiservo** tab, control forces from the stabilator would be so light that you might "over control" the airplane or move the control wheel too far to obtain the desired result. The antiservo tab also functions as a trim tab. [Figure 1-6]

The stabilator is a variation of the standard horizontal stabilizer. It does not require an elevator.

LANDING GEAR

The landing gear absorbs landing loads and supports the airplane on the ground. It typically is made up of three wheels. The two **main wheels** are located on either side of the fuselage. The third may be positioned either at the nose or at the tail. If it is located at the tail, it is called a **tailwheel**. In this case, the airplane is said to have **conventional landing gear**.

Landing gear usually consists of two main wheels and a third wheel mounted on either the nose or the tail.

Figure 1-6. The stabilator pivots up and down as you move the control wheel. The antiservo tab moves in the same direction as the trailing edge of the stabilator.

Conventional gear is common on older airplanes, as well as on some newer ones. It is desirable for operations on unimproved fields, because of the added clearance between the propeller and the ground. However, airplanes with this type of gear are more difficult to handle during ground operations.

When the third wheel is located on the nose, it is called a **nosewheel**. This design is referred to as **tricycle gear**. An airplane with this type of gear has a steerable nosewheel, which you control through use of the rudder pedals.

Landing gear can also be classified as either fixed or retractable. **Fixed gear** always remains extended, while **retractable gear** can be stowed for flight to reduce air resistance and increase airplane performance.

SHOCK STRUTS

Just as you need shock absorbers on your car, you need some shock-absorbing device on the landing gear. **Shock struts** are designed for this purpose. They absorb bumps and jolts, as well as the downward force of landing. [Figure 1-7]

BRAKES

Airplane brakes usually are located only on the main wheels and may be operated independently from one another.

Airplane brakes operate on the same principles as automobile brakes, but they do have a few significant differences. For example, airplane brakes usually are located only on the main wheels, and are applied by separate

Figure 1-7. There are two primary shock-absorbing systems in use. The oleo strut consists of an enclosed cylinder which houses a piston, oil, and air. It absorbs pressure rapidly and then slowly releases it. The spring steel strut, as its name implies, is made of steel that is designed to "give" as pressure is applied.

pedals. Because of this, you can operate the brake on the left independently of the brake on the right, or vice versa. This capability is referred to as **differential braking**. It is important during ground operations when you need to supplement nosewheel steering by applying the brakes on the side toward the direction of turn. In fact, differential braking is extremely important on conventional gear airplanes, since some do not have a steerable wheel.

THE POWERPLANT

In small airplanes, the powerplant includes both the engine and the propeller. The primary function of the engine is to provide the power to turn the propeller. It also generates electrical power, provides a vacuum source for some flight instruments, and, in most single-engine airplanes, provides a source of heat for the pilot and passengers. A **firewall** is located between the engine compartment and the cockpit to protect the occupants. The firewall also serves as a mounting point for the engine. [Figure 1-8]

> The engine drives the propeller which, in turn, produces thrust. It also provides electrical power, a vacuum source, and heat for the cabin.

AIRCRAFT CERTIFICATION

So far, we have only talked about airplanes. Actually, there is a much broader grouping called "aircraft" which contains not only airplanes, but such things as helicopters, gliders, and balloons. These various aircraft, with their wide range of size, complexity, and capability, must all share the same skies.

Figure 1-8. The engine compartment is enclosed by cowling, which is also called a nacelle. Besides streamlining the nose of the airplane, the cowling helps cool the engine by ducting air around the cylinders. The propeller, mounted on the front of the engine, translates the rotating force of the engine into a forward-acting force called "thrust" that helps the airplane fly.

The FAA uses category, class, and type for both aircraft and pilot certification.

To help divide these aircraft into similar groupings, the Federal Aviation Administration (FAA) has established two systems of category, class, and type. One applies when aircraft designs are approved, or certified, for flight. The other is used to describe certification of pilots.

For aircraft certification, **category** relates to the intended use of an aircraft and sets strict limits on its operation. The **normal** and **utility** categories are common to most small airplanes. You will find that many airplanes used in flight training are certified for both of these categories, depending on how they are loaded. When loaded for the utility category, the airplane can withstand heavier stresses than it can in the normal category. **Acrobatic** aircraft have the fewest operating limitations because their design requirements demand more strength than those of the normal or utility category. **Commuter** aircraft are designed to carry passengers, but they are limited to 19 seats and 19,000 pounds or less. **Transport** usually refers to airliners and other large aircraft that exceed certain weight limits or passenger-carrying capacity. [Figure 1-9]

The **restricted** category is for special-purpose aircraft such as agricultural spray planes or slurry bombers used to fight forest fires. **Limited** refers to military aircraft that are now allowed to be used only for limited purposes in civil aviation. The **provisional** category is really an interim measure for newly designed aircraft which have not met all requirements for initial certification, but still can be operated for certain purposes. **Experimental** refers to a wide range of aircraft such as amateur-homebuilt and racing planes, as well as research and development aircraft used to test new design concepts.

AIRCRAFT CERTIFICATION			
Category		**Class**	**Type**
Normal	Restricted	Airplane	Specifies make and model such as:
Utility	Limited	Rotorcraft	
		Glider	C-172
Acrobatic		Balloon	Hughes 500
Commuter	Provisional	Landplane	Boeing 747
Transport	Experimental	Seaplane	

Figure 1-9. For aircraft certification purposes, the FAA establishes broad categories first. These are further broken down into classes, then into types, which are essentially the make and model.

PILOT CERTIFICATION		
Category	**Class**	**Type**
Airplane	Single-Engine Land Multi-Engine Land Single-Engine Sea Multi-Engine Sea	Specifies make and model such as: C-172 Hughes 500 Boeing 747
Rotorcraft	Helicopter Gyroplane	
Glider	- - - - - - - - - - - - -	
Lighter-Than-Air	Airship Balloon	

Figure 1-10. For purposes of pilot certification, category is the broadest grouping and contains only four entries. With the exception of gliders, each category is further broken down into classes. Finally, the type designates the make and model. When you complete your training, your pilot certificate will probably specify "airplane single-engine land." The type normally is not listed for small airplanes.

For pilot certification, aircraft are again broken down into category, class, and type. In this case, though, category and class have different meanings than when used for aircraft certification. [Figure 1-10]

CHECKLIST

After studying this section, you should have a basic understanding of:

✓ **Major airplane components** — What they are and what functions they serve.

✓ **Control surfaces** — Where the major control surfaces are attached, how they work, and what they do.

✓ **Landing gear** — What the difference is between conventional and tricycle gear.

✓ **Brakes** — How airplane brakes differ from those found on an automobile.

✓ **Powerplant** — What the powerplant does and what functions the cowling and the firewall serve.

✓ **Aircraft certification** — How aircraft are classified and how the system differs between aircraft certification and pilot certification.

FOUR FORCES OF FLIGHT

The four aerodynamic forces are lift, weight, thrust, and drag. They are in equilibrium during straight-and-level, unaccelerated flight; lift equals weight and thrust equals drag.

During flight, the four forces acting on the airplane are lift, weight, thrust, and drag. **Lift** is the upward force created by the effect of airflow as it passes over and under the wings. It supports the airplane in flight. **Weight** opposes lift. It is caused by the downward pull of gravity. **Thrust** is the forward force which propels the airplane through the air. It varies with the amount of engine power being used. Opposing thrust is **drag**, which is a backward, or retarding, force that limits the speed of the airplane. [Figure 1-11]

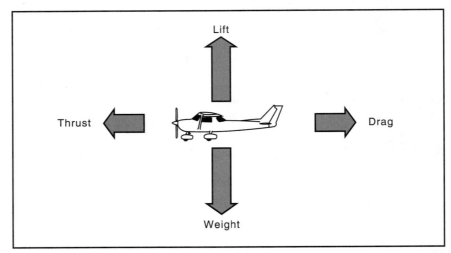

Figure 1-11. In straight-and-level, unaccelerated flight, the four forces are in equilibrium. Weight is equal to and directly opposite lift; thrust is equal to and directly opposite drag. Notice that the arrows which represent the opposing forces are equal in length, but all four arrows are not the same length. For example, the lift arrow is longer than the drag arrow.

The arrows which show the forces acting on an airplane are often called **vectors**. The magnitude of a vector is indicated by the arrow's length, while the direction is shown by the arrow's orientation. When two or more forces act on an object at the same time, they combine to create a resultant. [Figure 1-12]

These basic examples of vector diagrams will be helpful during the following discussion. Now let's consider the four forces in greater depth, starting with lift.

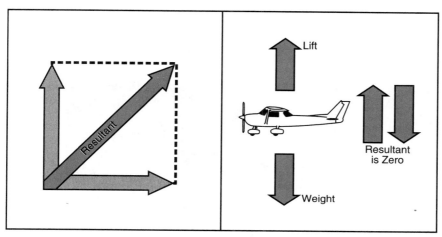

Figure 1-12. When vertical and horizontal forces are applied, as shown on the left, the resultant acts in a diagonal direction. When two opposing vertical forces are applied, as shown on the right, they tend to counteract one another. If the forces are equal in magnitude, the resultant is zero.

LIFT

Lift is the key aerodynamic force. It is the force that opposes weight. In straight-and-level, unaccelerated flight, when weight and lift are equal, an airplane is in a state of equilibrium. If the other aerodynamic factors remain constant, the airplane neither gains nor loses altitude.

When an airplane is stationary on the ramp, it is also in equilibrium, but the aerodynamic forces are not a factor. In calm wind conditions, the atmosphere exerts equal pressure on the upper and lower surfaces of the wing. Movement of air about the airplane, particularly the wing, is necessary before the aerodynamic force of lift becomes effective.

During flight, however, pressures on the upper and lower surfaces of the wing are not the same. Although several factors contribute to this difference, the shape of the wing is the principal one. The wing is designed to divide the airflow into areas of high pressure below the wing and areas of comparatively lower pressure above the wing. This pressure differential, which is created by movement of air about the wing, is the primary source of lift. Later, you will see that several other factors influence total lift.

BERNOULLI'S PRINCIPLE

The basic principle of pressure differential of subsonic airflow was discovered by Daniel Bernoulli, a Swiss physicist. **Bernoulli's Principle**, simply stated, says, "as the velocity of a fluid (air) increases, its internal pressure decreases."

Bernoulli's Principle explains how air pressure decreases as velocity increases.

Figure 1-13. As the air enters the tube, it is traveling at a known velocity and pressure. When the airflow enters the narrow portion, the velocity increases and the pressure decreases. Then, as the airflow continues through the tube to the wider portion, both the velocity and pressure return to their original values.

One way you can visualize this principle is to imagine air flowing through a tube that is narrower in the middle than at the ends. This type of device is usually called a **venturi**. [Figure 1-13]

It is not necessary for air to pass through an enclosed tube for Bernoulli's Principle to apply. Any surface that alters airflow causes a venturi effect. [Figure 1-14]

When air flows over the curved upper surface of a wing, it increases in velocity. This increase reduces the pressure above the wing and produces the upward force of lift.

The wing of the airplane is shaped to take advantage of this principle. The greater curvature on the upper portion causes air to accelerate as it passes over the wing. The resulting pressure differential between the upper and lower surfaces of the wing creates an upward force. This difference in pressure is the main source of lift. [Figure 1-15]

Figure 1-14. Even after the upper portion of the tube is removed, the venturi effect applies to air flowing along the lower section of the tube. Velocity above the curvature is increased and pressure is decreased. You can begin to see how the venturi effect works on a wing, or airfoil, if you picture an airfoil inset in the curved part of the tube.

Figure 1-15. Air flowing over the top of an airfoil reaches the trailing edge in the same amount of time as air flowing along the relatively flat bottom. Since both the upper and lower surfaces pass through a block of air at the same speed, the air flowing over the curved upper surface travels farther. This means it must go faster, resulting in lower pressure above the airfoil than below.

NEWTON'S THIRD LAW OF MOTION

The remaining lift is provided by the wing's lower surface as air striking the underside is deflected downward. According to Newton's Third Law of Motion, "for every action there is an equal and opposite reaction." The air that is deflected downward also produces an upward (lifting) reaction.

Since air is much like water, the explanation for this source of lift may be compared to the planing effect of skis on water. The lift which supports the water skis (and the skier) is the force caused by the impact pressure and the deflection of water from the lower surfaces of the skis.

Under most flying conditions, the impact pressure and the deflection of air from the lower surface of the wing provide a comparatively small percentage of the total lift. The majority of lift is the result of the decreased pressure above the wing rather than the increased pressure below it.

There are many other factors that determine the lifting capacity of a wing. Before we look into these, let's first discuss some basic terminology.

AIRFOILS

An airfoil is any surface, such as a wing, which provides aerodynamic force when it interacts with a moving stream of air. Remember, an airplane's wing generates a lifting force only when air is in motion about it. Some of the terms used to describe the wing, and the interaction of the airflow about it, are listed here. [Figure 1-16]

Leading edge — This part of the airfoil meets the airflow first.

Trailing edge — This is the portion of the airfoil where the airflow over the upper surface rejoins the lower surface airflow.

Chord line — The chord line is an imaginary straight line drawn through an airfoil from the leading edge to the trailing edge.

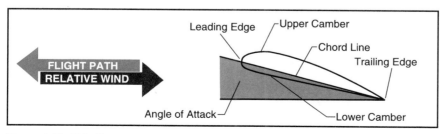

Figure 1-16. **This figure shows a cross-section of a wing in straight-and-level flight. Chord and camber are terms which help to define the wing's shape, while flight path and relative wind help define the movement of the wing with respect to the surrounding air. Angle of attack is determined by the wing's chord line and the relative wind.**

Camber — The camber of an airfoil is the characteristic curve of its upper and lower surfaces. The upper camber is more pronounced, while the lower camber is comparatively flat. This causes the velocity of the airflow immediately above the wing to be much higher than that below the wing.

The flight path and relative wind are always parallel to and opposite each other.

Relative wind — This is the direction of the airflow with respect to the wing. If a wing moves forward horizontally, the relative wind moves backward horizontally. Relative wind is parallel to and opposite the flight path of the airplane.

You shouldn't confuse the actual flight path with the flight attitude of the airplane. For example, the airplane's fuselage may be parallel to the horizon while the aircraft is descending. [Figure 1-17]

The angle formed by the wing chord line and relative wind is called the angle of attack.

Angle of attack — This is the angle between the chord line of the airfoil and the direction of the relative wind. It is important in the production of lift. [Figure 1-18]

Figure 1-17. This airplane is in a level flight attitude, while the actual flight path is forward and down. Notice that the relative wind is upward and back, parallel to and opposite the flight path.

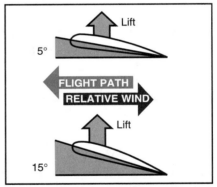

Figure 1-18. As the angle of attack increases, lift also increases. Notice that lift acts perpendicular to the relative wind, regardless of angle of attack.

AIRFOIL DESIGN FACTORS

Wing design is based on the anticipated use of the airplane, cost, and other factors. The main design considerations are wing planform, camber, aspect ratio, and total wing area.

Planform refers to the shape of the airplane's wing when viewed from above or below. Each planform design has advantages and disadvantages. [Figure 1-19]

Camber, as noted earlier, affects the difference in the velocity of the airflow between the upper and lower surfaces of the wing. If the upper cam-

Figure 1-19. The straight wing has excellent slow-flight characteristics, and it is economical to build. However, it is inefficient from a structural, weight, and drag standpoint. The elliptical wing is more efficient in terms of weight and drag, but it has less desirable slow-flight characteristics and is more expensive. The tapered wing is relatively efficient with reasonable weight, drag, and construction costs, as well as good slow-flight capability. The sweptback and delta wings used on higher performance aircraft are efficient at high speeds, but not at low speeds.

ber increases and the lower camber remains the same, the velocity differential increases.

There is, of course, a limit to the amount of camber that can be used. After a certain point, air will no longer flow smoothly over the airfoil. Once this happens, the lifting capacity diminishes. The ideal camber varies with the airplane's performance specifications, especially the speed range and the load-carrying requirements.

Aspect ratio is the relationship between the length and width of a wing. It is one of the primary factors in determining lift/drag characteristics. At a given angle of attack, a higher aspect ratio produces less drag for the same amount of lift. [Figure 1-20]

Figure 1-20. Aspect ratio is the span of the wing, wingtip to wingtip, divided by its average chord. In general, the higher the aspect ratio, the higher the lifting efficiency of the wing. For example, gliders may have an aspect ratio of 20 to 30, while typical training aircraft have an aspect ratio of about seven to nine.

Wing area is the total surface area of the wings. Most wings don't produce a great amount of lift per square foot, so wing area must be sufficient to support the weight of the airplane. For example, in a training aircraft at normal operating speed, the wings produce only about 10.5 pounds of lift for each square foot of wing area. This means a wing area of 200 square feet is required to support an airplane weight of 2,100 pounds during straight-and-level flight.

You can see that design has a lot to do with a wing's lift capability. Planform, camber, aspect ratio, and wing area are some of the major design factors. When we discuss drag, you'll see how design factors also affect drag.

Angle of incidence is the angle between the chord line and a line parallel to the longitudinal axis of an airplane. You cannot control this angle.

Once the design of the wing is determined, the wing must be mounted on the airplane. Usually it is attached to the fuselage with the chord line inclined upward at a slight angle, which is called the **angle of incidence**. [Figure 1-21]

Figure 1-21. Angle of incidence refers to the angle between the wing chord line and a line parallel to the longitudinal axis of the airplane. A slight positive angle of incidence provides a positive angle of attack while the airplane is in level flight at normal cruising speed. It also improves over-the-nose visibility when the airplane is in a level flight attitude.

PILOT CONTROL OF LIFT

Changing angle of attack or airspeed are the two primary ways to control lift.

Thus far in our discussion of lift, we have looked at only those factors which are controlled by aircraft design. Now, we'll examine the actions you can take to control lift. For example, you can change the angle of attack and the airspeed. You can also change the shape of the wing by lowering the flaps. Keep in mind that anytime you do something to change lift, drag is affected. If you increase lift, drag increases. Drag is always a by-product of lift.

CHANGING ANGLE OF ATTACK

You have direct control over angle of attack. During flight at normal operating speeds, if you increase the angle of attack, you increase lift. Anytime you move the control column fore or aft during flight, you change the

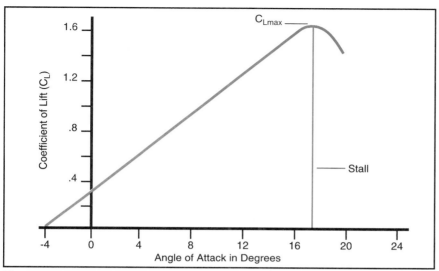

Figure 1-22. As angle of attack increases, C_L also increases. This continues to a point where C_L peaks. This point of maximum lift is called C_{Lmax}. In this example, C_{Lmax} occurs at about 17°. If the maximum lift angle is exceeded, lift decreases rapidly and the wing stalls.

angle of attack. At the same time, you are changing the coefficient of lift. The **coefficient of lift** (C_L) is a way to measure lift as it relates to angle of attack. C_L is determined by wind tunnel tests and is based on airfoil design and angle of attack. Every airplane has an angle of attack where maximum lift occurs. [Figure 1-22]

A **stall** is caused by the separation of airflow from the wing's upper surface. This results in a rapid decrease in lift. For a given airplane, a stall always occurs at the same angle, regardless of airspeed, flight attitude, or weight. This is the stalling or critical angle of attack. Since training airplanes normally do not have an angle of attack indicator, the important point to remember is that you can stall an airplane at any airspeed, in any flight attitude, or at any weight. [Figure 1-23]

An airplane can be stalled at any airspeed and in any flight attitude.

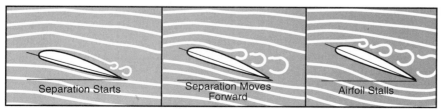

Figure 1-23. Increasing the angle of attack beyond C_{Lmax} causes progressive disruption of airflow from the upper surface of the wing. At first, the airflow begins to separate at the trailing edge. As angle of attack is further increased, the airflow separation progresses forward until the wing is fully stalled.

Stall characteristics vary with different airplanes. However, in training airplanes during most normal maneuvers, the onset of a stall is gradual. The first indications may be provided by a stall warning device or a slight buffeting of the airplane.

To recover from a stall, you must decrease the angle of attack.

All you have to do to recover from a stall is to restore the smooth airflow. The only way to do this is to decrease the angle of attack to a point below the stalling or critical angle of attack.

An airplane always stalls when the critical angle of attack is exceeded, regardless of weight or airspeed. The indicated airspeed of a stall, however, varies with weight and configuration. Maneuvering can also affect stall speed.

Although the stalling or critical angle of attack does not vary with weight, the stalling speed does. It increases slightly as the weight of the airplane increases and decreases as weight decreases. This means you need slightly more airspeed to stay above the stalling speed in a heavily loaded airplane. If you want to fly an airplane at a given weight, there are many combinations of airspeed and angle of attack which will produce the required amount of lift. Later you will see how maneuvering, such as during a turn, also affects the stalling speed.

CHANGING AIRSPEED

Lift is proportional to the square of the airplane's velocity. If an airplane's speed is doubled, lift increases fourfold.

The faster the wing moves through the air, the greater the lift. Actually, lift is proportional to the square of the airplane's speed. For example, at 200 knots, an airplane has four times the lift of the same airplane traveling at 100 knots if the angle of attack and other factors are constant. On the other hand, if the speed is reduced by one-half, lift is decreased to one-quarter of the previous value.

Although airspeed is an important factor in the production of lift, it is only one of several factors. The airspeed required to sustain an aircraft in straight-and-level flight depends on the flap position, the angle of attack, and the weight.

ANGLE OF ATTACK AND AIRSPEED

The relationship between angle of attack and airspeed in the production of lift is not as complex as it may seem. Angle of attack establishes the coefficient of lift for the airfoil. At the same time, lift is proportional to the square of the airplane's speed. Since you can control both angle of attack and airspeed, you can control lift.

Total lift depends on the combined effects of airspeed and angle of attack. When speed decreases, you must increase the angle of attack to maintain the same amount of lift. Conversely, if you want to maintain the same amount of lift at a higher speed, you must decrease the angle of attack.

USING FLAPS

When properly used, flaps increase the lifting efficiency of the wing and decrease stall speed. This allows you to fly at a reduced speed while maintaining sufficient control and lift for sustained flight. Remember, though, that when you retract the flaps, the stall speed increases.

The ability to fly slowly is particularly important during the approach and landing phases. For example, an approach with full flaps permits you to fly slowly and at a fairly steep descent angle without gaining airspeed. This allows you to touch down at a slower speed. In addition, you can land near the approach end of the runway, even when there are obstacles along the approach path.

Flaps allow you to steepen the angle of descent on an approach without increasing airspeed.

In training airplanes, **configuration** normally refers to the position of the landing gear and flaps. When the gear and flaps are up, an airplane is in a clean configuration. If the gear is fixed rather than retractable, the airplane is considered to be in a clean configuration when the flaps are in the up position. During flight, you can change configuration by raising or lowering the gear, or by moving the flaps. Flap position affects the chord line and angle of attack for that section of the wing where the flaps are attached. This causes an increase in camber for that section of the wing and greater production of lift and drag. In contrast, landing gear position normally has little or no effect on chord line or angle of attack. [Figure 1-24]

There are several common types of flaps. The **plain flap** is attached to the wing by a hinge. When deflected downward, it increases the effective camber and changes the wing's chord line. Both of these factors increase the lifting capacity of the wing. The **split flap** is hinged only to the lower portion of the wing. This type of flap also increases lift, but it produces greater drag than the plain flap because of the turbulence it causes. The **slotted flap** is similar to the plain flap. In addition to changing the wing's camber and chord line, it also allows a portion of the higher pressure air

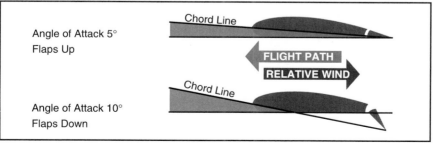

Angle of Attack 5°
Flaps Up

Chord Line

FLIGHT PATH
RELATIVE WIND

Angle of Attack 10°
Flaps Down

Chord Line

Figure 1-24. Flaps increase lift (and drag) by increasing the wing's effective camber and changing the chord line, which increases the angle of attack. In some cases, flaps also increase the area of the wing. Most flaps, when fully extended, form an angle of 35° to 40° relative to the wing.

Figure 1-25. Flap types include plain, split, slotted, and Fowler. Although some flaps increase the wing's surface area, most change only the effective camber and the chord line.

beneath the wing to travel through a slot. This increases the velocity of the airflow over the flap and provides additional lift. Another type of flap is the **Fowler flap**. It is attached to the wing by a track and roller system. When extended, it moves rearward as well as down. This rearward motion increases the total wing area, as well as the camber and chord line. The Fowler flap is the most efficient of these systems. As you might expect, it also is the most expensive. [Figure 1-25]

Although the amount of lift and drag created by a specific flap system varies, we can make a few general observations. As the flaps are extended, at first they will produce a relatively large amount of lift for a small increase in drag. However, once the flap extension reaches approximately the midpoint, this relationship reverses. Now, a significant increase in drag will occur for a relatively small increase in lift. Because of the large increase in drag beyond the half-flap position, most manufacturers limit the takeoff setting to half flaps or less.

WEIGHT

Weight varies with aircraft equipment, cargo, fuel, expendable loads, and flight maneuvers. It acts downward toward the center of the earth.

The weight of the airplane is not a constant. It varies with the equipment installed, passengers, cargo, and fuel load. During the course of a flight, the total weight of the airplane decreases as fuel is consumed. Additional weight reduction may also occur during some specialized flight activities, such as crop dusting, fire fighting, or sky diving flights. You will see later in this chapter that weight is also affected by airplane maneuvering.

In contrast, the direction in which the force of weight acts is constant. It always acts straight down toward the center of the earth.

THRUST

The airfoil shape and angle of attack of the spinning propeller create a pressure differential which is similar to that created by the wing.

Thrust is the forward-acting force which opposes drag and propels the airplane. In most airplanes, this force is provided when the engine turns the propeller. Each propeller blade is cambered like the airfoil shape of a wing. This shape, plus the angle of attack of the blades, produces reduced pressure in front of the propeller and increased pressure behind it. As is the case with the wing, this produces a reaction force in the direction of the lesser pressure. This is how the propeller produces thrust, the force which moves the airplane forward.

During straight-and-level, unaccelerated flight, the forces of thrust and drag are equal. Later you will see that thrust and drag also are equal in stabilized turns, climbs, and descents.

You increase thrust by using the throttle to increase power. When you increase power, thrust exceeds drag, causing the airplane to accelerate. This acceleration, however, is accompanied by a corresponding increase in drag. The airplane continues to accelerate only while the force of thrust exceeds the force of drag. When drag again equals thrust, the airplane ceases to accelerate and maintains a constant airspeed. However, the new airspeed is higher than the previous one.

When you reduce thrust, the force of drag causes the airplane to decelerate. But as the airplane slows, drag diminishes. When drag has decreased enough to equal thrust, the airplane no longer decelerates. Once again, it maintains a constant airspeed. Now, however, it is slower than the one previously flown.

DRAG

As you have seen, drag is associated with lift. It is caused by any aircraft surface that deflects or interferes with the smooth airflow around the airplane. A highly cambered, large surface area wing creates more drag (and lift) than a small, moderately cambered wing. If you increase airspeed, or angle of attack, you increase drag (and lift). Drag acts in opposition to the direction of flight, opposes the forward-acting force of thrust, and limits the forward speed of the airplane. Drag is broadly classified as either parasite or induced.

PARASITE DRAG

Parasite drag includes all drag created by the airplane, except that drag directly associated with the production of lift. It is created by the disruption of the flow of air around the airplane's surfaces. Parasite drag normally is divided into three types: form drag, skin friction drag, and interference drag.

Form drag is created by any structure which protrudes into the relative wind. The amount of drag created is related to both the size and shape of the structure. For example, a square strut will create substantially more drag than a smooth or rounded strut. Streamlining reduces form drag.

Parasite drag increases with an increase in airspeed. It consists of all drag not associated with the production of lift.

Skin friction drag is caused by the roughness of the airplane's surfaces. Even though these surfaces may appear smooth, under a microscope, they may be quite rough. A thin layer of air clings to these rough surfaces and creates small eddies which contribute to drag.

Interference drag occurs when varied currents of air over an airplane meet and interact. This interaction creates additional drag. One example of this type of drag is the mixing of the air where the wing and airframe join.

Each type of parasite drag varies with the speed of the airplane. The combined effect of all parasite drag varies proportionately to the square of the airspeed. For example, a particular airplane at a constant altitude has four times as much parasite drag at 160 knots as it does at 80 knots. [Figure 1-26]

INDUCED DRAG

Induced drag is associated with the production of lift. It is directly related to angle of attack and increases as angle of attack increases. Normally, induced drag decreases as airspeed increases.

Induced drag is the main by-product of the production of lift. It is directly related to the angle of attack of the wing. The greater the angle, the greater the induced drag. Since the wing usually is at a low angle of attack at high speed, and a high angle of attack at low speed, the relationship of induced drag to speed also can be plotted. [Figure 1-27]

TOTAL DRAG

Total drag for an airplane is the sum of parasite and induced drag. The total drag curve represents these combined forces and is plotted against airspeed. [Figure 1-28]

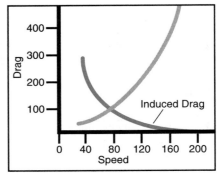

Figure 1-26. If airspeed is doubled, parasite drag increases fourfold. This is the same formula that applies to lift. Because of its rapid increase with increasing airspeed, parasite drag is predominant at high speeds. At low speeds, near a stall, parasite drag is at its low point.

Figure 1-27. Induced drag is inversely proportional to the square of the speed. If speed is decreased by half, induced drag increases fourfold. It is the major cause of drag at reduced speeds near the stall; but, as speed increases, induced drag decreases.

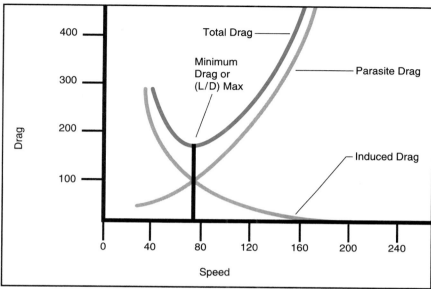

Figure 1-28. The low point on the total drag curve shows the airspeed at which drag is minimized. This is the point where the lift-to-drag ratio is greatest. It is referred to as L/D$_{max}$. At this speed, the total lift capacity of the airplane, when compared to the total drag of the airplane, is most favorable. This is important in airplane performance.

CHECKLIST _____

After studying this section, you should have a basic understanding of:

✓ **The four forces** — What they are, how they act, and their relationships during straight-and-level, unaccelerated flight.

✓ **Lift** — The key aerodynamic force, how it is created (including Bernoulli's Principle and Newton's Third Law of Motion), and how it acts.

✓ **Airfoil terminology** — The meanings of camber, chord, flight path, relative wind, angle of attack, angle of incidence, and other basic aerodynamic terms.

✓ **Airfoil design** — How lift is affected by basic design considerations, including aspect ratio, camber, planform, and wing area.

✓ **Pilot control of lift** — How you control lift during flight by changing the airspeed, angle of attack, or the airplane's configuration (including the use of flaps).

✓ **Stalls** — How an airplane stalls, exceeding the maximum lift angle of attack, the stalling or critical angle of attack, stall recovery.

✓ **Angle of attack and airspeed** — How angle of attack establishes the coefficient of lift for the airfoil, and how angle of attack and airspeed combine to produce lift.

✓ **Weight** — How it changes during flight, and the direction in which it acts.

✓ **Thrust** — How it is produced, how it acts, and the relationship between thrust and drag.

✓ **Drag** — How it acts, what causes it, the main classifications, and the relationships between drag, angle of attack, and airspeed.

PREFLIGHT AND ENGINE STARTING

Safe flying begins on the ground. The attitudes and habits established in the initial stages of training greatly influence the standards you will follow throughout your flying career. Observe your instructor carefully as the preflight and engine-starting procedures are explained for the first time.

Perform the preflight inspection prior to each flight to ensure the aircraft is in a safe condition for the flight. As the pilot in command, you will be entirely responsible for making this decision. Any defects discovered during this inspection should be evaluated and, if required, corrected prior to that flight. Your flight instructor should point out the various components to be inspected and explain how to evaluate the airworthiness of an aircraft.

USE OF CHECKLISTS

Regardless of the number of times you repeat a procedure, follow a step-by-step checklist to ensure that all necessary items are accomplished in a logical sequence. Written checklists are used because of variations in types and models of airplanes and because it is unwise to rely on your memory. Use of checklists is also stressed in the Practical Test Standards (PTS).

Always use a written checklist to ensure all steps are completed.

PREFLIGHT INSPECTION

The preflight inspection is only the first of many procedures you will carry out according to a written checklist. The following discussion presents the proper sequence for a typical preflight inspection. [Figure 1-29]

In the cabin (position 1), check the aircraft papers to see that all items are included. The memory aid **ARROW** may be used as follows to help you remember the required documents:

A — Airworthiness certificate (required by FAA)
R — Registration certificate (required by FAA)
R — Restricted radiotelephone operator's permit (required outside the U.S.)
O — Operating instructions, pilot's operating handbook, or approved aircraft flight manual (required by FAA)
W — Weight and balance data, as well as equipment list (required by FAA)

Engine and airframe logbooks must be available, but not necessarily on board the aircraft. You also should be aware of the **minimum equipment list (MEL)** concept and how it applies. When using an approved Part 91 MEL, you need to know what instruments and equipment are required, how to operate the airplane with inoperative instruments/equipment, and procedures for obtaining a Special Flight Permit.

If an MEL is applicable to your aircraft, you should understand the procedures for its use.

Figure 1-29. During the preflight inspection, you methodically check the airplane in a planned sequence. The steps for a typical airplane are outlined in the text with a numbered callout for each position.

FAR Part 91 stipulates that an airplane must be operated in compliance with the operating limitations set forth in the approved flight manual and, if applicable, the MEL. In addition to the required flight manual, often referred to as the pilot's operating handbook, or POH, specific placards and markings prescribed by the airworthiness standards for the particular airplane type must also be available.

Remove the control lock so the controls can be checked for freedom of movement. Then, as a safety precaution, make sure no one is standing near the propeller and turn the master switch ON. Next, check the fuel quantity gauges to ensure proper operation and to note the amount of fuel in each tank. Then, place the wing flaps in the full-down position, so you can examine the internal components, and turn the master switch OFF.

Next, check the windshield, or windscreen, and cabin windows for cleanliness and general condition. Inspect the instrument panel for any irregularities, such as cracked glass, and for any instruments or radios which have been removed for maintenance.

When all cabin checks are completed, verify that the magneto switch, master switch, mixture control, and throttle are in the appropriate OFF positions. Then, continue with the exterior part of the preflight check.

Inspect the left portion of the fuselage (position 2) for skin wrinkles, dents, and loose rivets. Examine the lower surface of the fuselage, which is especially susceptible to rock damage, for dents, cleanliness, and evidence of excessive engine oil leakage. If the static air source is located on the fuselage, examine it for obstructions. During cleaning or waxing of the airplane, the small static port can be plugged with wax. It is important that the static source be open so the airspeed, altimeter, and vertical speed indicators function properly.

You will need to inspect several items on the tail section (position 3). Remove the control surface lock, if installed, before you check the tail assembly. External locks are often used if gusty wind conditions are anticipated. Inspect the tail surfaces for general condition, looking closely for dents, skin wrinkles, and loose rivets. The underside and leading edge of the horizontal stabilizer (or stabilator) are easily damaged by rocks thrown up during takeoffs and landings on unimproved runway surfaces. Examine the elevator (or stabilator) and rudder for damage, loose hinge bolts, and freedom of movement. Inspect the control cables and stops for damage and the surface skin for dents and wrinkles. At this time, inspect the trim tab for security and general condition, the tail and beacon lights for damage, and the VOR navigation antenna. Finally, remove the tail tiedown chain or rope. If the airplane is equipped with a tailwheel, check the steering arms, cables, and springs for wear. In addition, inspect the tire for wear, proper inflation, cuts, and abrasions.

Go over the right portion of the fuselage (position 4), repeating the same procedures used at position 2. Next, inspect the right wing flap and aileron (position 5). Remove the control surface locks, if installed. Inspect the wing flap completely. Check the flap hinges for security, wear, and freedom of movement. Look over the aileron for security, damage, and freedom of movement. In addition, check the aileron pushrods or control cables for security, damage, and tension. Check the right wingtip (position 6) for damage and secure attachment. Then, inspect the right navigation light. Examine the leading edge of the right wing (position 7) for dents or other damage. Check the upper wing surface for frost or snow accumulation. Next, inspect the fuel tank vent opening and check the fuel drains, vents, and fuel quantity.

Check the fuel tank drain for obstructions, security, and leakage. If the airplane is equipped with a quick-drain device, drain a few ounces of fuel into a clear container and examine it for the presence of water and other contaminants. You can detect water, because it is heavier than avgas and settles to the bottom of the container. It contrasts clearly with the color of the avgas. Since fuel contamination is possible at any time, you should do this check before every flight.

Check for fuel contamination before each flight.

Inspect the fuel quantity level by removing the filler cap and looking into the tank. The quantity in the tank should agree with the fuel gauge reading you observed on the associated fuel gauge. After you have checked the fuel level, replace the filler cap and tighten it securely. Finally, remove the tiedown chain or rope.

Inspect the attachment points of the main landing gear (position 8) for dents and wrinkles. Check the tire for wear, cuts, abrasions, and proper inflation. Inspect the wheel fairing, if installed, for cracks, dents, and general security. Look at the hydraulic brake and brake lines for security and leaks. Give particular attention to proper inflation of the gear strut.

Check the front cowl openings (position 9) for obstructions. Inspect the engine compartment, which is accessible through the cowl access door, for loose wires and clamps, worn hoses, and oil or fuel leaks. Determine the oil quantity by removing and reading the dipstick. Add oil if the level is below the minimum recommended by the manufacturer. Then, replace the dipstick, tighten it securely, and check the oil filler cap for security. Drain the fuel strainer (if located within the engine compartment) for several seconds to eliminate any water or other contaminants that may have collected in it. Water can form in the fuel tanks from condensation of moisture in the air, or it may be present in fuel added to the tanks. Finally, close the access door.

The cowl flaps, if installed, should be checked for security. Then, inspect the propeller and spinner, and check the propeller blades and tips for nicks and scratches. Propeller nicks can cause excessive stress in the metal of the propeller. They should be repaired by a certificated mechanic prior to flight. If your airplane has a constant-speed propeller, check it for oil leakage. You can generally detect leakage by the presence of oil streaks along the backsides of the propeller blades. In cold weather, you should carefully pull the propeller through two or three revolutions in the direction of normal propeller rotation. This procedure loosens the congealed oil and makes engine starting easier.

Check the windshield and cabin windows (position 10) for cleanliness and general condition. Do not use a dry rag to clean the windshield, because it can scratch the surface. Only a cloth and cleaning compound specifically designed for airplane windshields should be used.

Check the communications antenna for general condition and security. Use the same procedure to check the left main landing gear as was used at position 8.

Inspect the left wing structure (position 11) in the same manner you used on the right wing. Then, remove the tiedown chain or rope. Next, inspect the fuel tank vent opening. Perform the checks of the fuel tank drains, vents, and fuel quantity in the same manner described in position 7.

Remove the pitot tube cover, if installed, and check the tube opening for obstructions. A plugged pitot tube opening causes the airspeed indicator to malfunction. In addition, the pitot tube itself should show no signs of damage and should not be bent out of alignment. Also, be sure to check the static port if it is located on the pitot tube. Check the stall warning vane on the leading edge of the wing for freedom of movement. It is a good practice to turn on the master switch just prior to the stall warning vane inspection. This enables you to check the stall warning signal when the vane is deflected upward. Remember to turn the master switch OFF immediately after making this inspection. If your airplane is equipped with a pneumatic stall warning device, check the leading edge opening for obstructions.

Examine the left wingtip (position 12), using the same procedure you used for the right. Inspect the left wing flap and aileron (position 13), using the same steps that were used for the right. After loading the baggage, close the door and make sure it is secure (position 14).

STARTING PROCEDURES

After you have completed the preflight inspection, you are ready to begin the prestarting checklist. Since there are a number of different procedures used to start airplane engines, it is important to use an appropriate written checklist. [Figure 1-30]

Although the starting procedure can vary from airplane to airplane, there are certain common safety precautions and suggestions that apply universally. You should avoid starting the engine with the tail of the airplane pointed toward parked automobiles, spectators, or an open hangar. In addition to being discourteous, wind blast and debris could injure persons and damage property.

STARTING THE ENGINE

1. Prime — AS REQUIRED (2 to 6 strokes; none if engine is warm).
2. Carburetor Heat — COLD.
3. Throttle — OPEN 1/8 INCH (CLOSED if engine is warm).
4. Mixture — RICH.
5. Propeller Area — CLEAR.
6. Master Switch — ON.
7. Ignition Switch — START (release when engine starts).
8. Oil Pressure — CHECK (30 seconds summer, 60 seconds winter).
9. Starter — CHECK DISENGAGED (if starter were to remain engaged, ammeter would indicate full scale charge with engine running at 1000 RPM).
10. Avionics Power Switch — ON.
11. Navigation Lights and Flashing Beacon — ON as required.
12. Radios — ON.

Figure 1-30. This checklist is typical for a single-engine airplane. Follow the recommendations of the Pilot's Operating Handbook for the best engine-starting method.

If you are using an unimproved surface, inspect the ground under the propeller before you start the engine. Rocks, pebbles, or any other loose debris can be picked up by the propeller and hurled backward. Remove any such particles to avoid damaging the propeller and other parts of the airplane. If this is not possible, move the airplane to another location before you start the engine.

The following discussion is based on a typical starting sequence for a training airplane. Always use a checklist appropriate to the airplane you are flying. [Figure 1-31]

First, prime as required (item1). This will help you to start the engine in cold weather. The number of primer strokes required depends on the length of time the engine has been shut down and the temperature of the outside air. If the engine has been shut down for less than an hour or it is a warm day, it will probably start without priming. Most light airplane operator's handbooks recommend that you use from two to six strokes. Colder temperatures require the greater number of strokes. Place the carburetor heat control (item 2) in the COLD position. When the control is placed in this position, the air entering the engine is filtered to remove dust and dirt. Open the throttle (item 3) one-eighth of an inch so that when the engine starts it is operating at a low speed which lessens engine wear. Next, set the mixture control (item 4) to RICH.

Figure 1-31. Before you begin the starting sequence, make sure you are familiar with the location and operation of each of the controls. The numbered callouts in the art correspond to the items referenced in the text.

Now, clear the area. To do this, you should open a window or door, look for anyone in the area, then shout, "Clear!" to warn anyone near the airplane that the propeller is about to rotate. You should then listen for a reply to ensure that there is no one in the immediate area. When you are sure that the area is clear, turn the master switch ON (item 5) to supply electrical power to the ignition switch. Then, rotate the ignition switch to supply power to the starter motor (item 6). It is important to release the starter as soon as the engine starts to avoid damage to the starter motor.

After the engine is running smoothly, adjust the throttle to a low power setting. This prevents undue friction within the engine before the lubricating oil has had a chance to coat the engine's internal parts thoroughly. It is important to check immediately that the oil pressure gauge is in the green arc (item 7). If the oil pressure does not register properly within 30 seconds in warm weather or 60 seconds in cold weather, shut down the engine. This will prevent possible damage and will allow you to determine the nature of the problem.

POSITIVE EXCHANGE OF FLIGHT CONTROLS

During flight training, there must always be a clear understanding of who has control of the aircraft. Prior to your first flight, your instructor should brief you on the correct procedure for exchange of flight controls. A positive three-step process is recommended by the FAA.

When your instructor wants you to take control, he/she will say, "You have the flight controls." You should acknowledge immediately by saying, "I have the flight controls." Then, your instructor again says, "You have the flight controls." During this procedure, a visual check is recommended to see that the other person actually has the flight controls. When returning the controls to your instructor, you should follow the same procedure. Stay on the controls and keep flying the aircraft until your instructor says, "I have the flight controls."

There should never be any doubt as to who is flying the aircraft.

CHECKLIST

After studying this section, you should have a basic understanding of:

✓ **Checklist** — The importance of written checklists.

✓ **Preflight** — The purpose of a preflight inspection, including a general understanding of what items are checked and why.

✓ **Starting** — Procedures used in starting an airplane, including general safety procedures.

✓ **Positive exchange of flight controls** — How to make sure there is complete understanding about who is in control of the aircraft.

TAXIING, ENGINE SHUTDOWN, AND TIEDOWN

In this section, you are introduced to some of the techniques and procedures used during taxi operations. Next, you will learn procedures and cautions for engine shutdown and for securing the airplane.

TAXIING

You usually begin learning about taxiing on the first training flight. During taxi practice, you learn directional control techniques and proper throttle usage. Later in the training program, you will learn which control positions to use during crosswind takeoffs and landings. Airplanes which have tricycle landing gear and steerable nosewheels are relatively easy to taxi. However, there are techniques which you must learn, and some precautions that you should observe.

USE OF THE THROTTLE

In general, good throttle use is based on smooth, precise adjustments of power. Erratic throttle movement can cause directional control difficulties. To help you make proper adjustments, a friction adjustment is incorporated in the throttle assembly. [Figure 1-32]

Correct taxi techniques require correct power control. For example, more power is required to start the airplane moving than to keep it moving. You should add power slowly until the airplane starts rolling, then reduce it.

Figure 1-32. The friction control adjusts the throttle's resistance to movement, so your natural arm movements do not overcontrol the throttle. In addition, the friction adjustment prevents the throttle from moving because of engine vibration.

You also will find that you need a greater amount of power to start and sustain an airplane in motion on a soft surface than on a hard surface.

Control taxi speed primarily with the throttle and secondarily with the brakes. Use the brakes only when a reduction of engine r.p.m. is not sufficient to slow the airplane. Using the brakes to control the airplane's speed causes excessive wear and overheating of the braking system. Light airplanes usually have brakes on only two wheels, and the brakes are relatively small. For this and other reasons, many flight instructors recommend operating at a taxi speed that is no faster than a brisk walk. When you are operating in confined areas, however, keep your speed slow enough to allow you to stop safely without using the brakes. You should be able to stop by reducing power or by shutting down the engine. A useful suggestion for developing proper taxi speed control is for you to assume that the brakes are inoperative. This will help you learn proper use of power to control taxi speed.

Control taxi speed with the throttle, and use the brakes only when needed.

ENGINE COOLING DURING TAXIING

Many air-cooled engines are tightly enclosed by the cowling. Because of the slow speeds associated with taxiing and ground operations, only small amounts of cooling air flow into the engine compartment and over the engine cylinders. Prolonged ground operations, particularly in warm weather, can cause overheating in the engine cylinders even before the oil temperature gauge indicates a pronounced rise in temperature. If your airplane has a cylinder head temperature gauge, use it to monitor engine temperature. You should refer to the airplane's POH for the recommended power settings for engine warmup to provide the optimum flow of cooling air through the engine compartment.

DIRECTIONAL CONTROL DURING TAXI

On most airplanes, the nosewheel is linked to the rudder pedals, and you steer during taxi operations by using rudder pressure. When you depress the right rudder pedal, the nosewheel turns to the right, causing the airplane to turn right. If you depress the left rudder pedal, the nosewheel turns to the left, causing the airplane to turn left. The amount that you can turn the nosewheel varies with different makes and models of airplanes.

During ground operations, you normally depress the left rudder pedal to turn left and the right pedal to turn right.

In addition to turning the nosewheel in the direction of the turn, depressing the rudder pedal also causes the rudder to move. Therefore, airflow over the rudder from propeller slipstream may provide a small additional force which assists you in turning the airplane. To make a turn of a smaller radius than you can accomplish through nosewheel steering alone, depress the rudder pedal fully in the direction of the turn, then lightly apply the

To make tight turns, apply full rudder pressure, then apply the brake on that rudder pedal.

individual toe brake on that rudder pedal. This procedure applies braking in the direction of the turn and produces a smaller turn radius.

EFFECTS OF WIND ON TAXI TECHNIQUES

The basic skills just discussed allow you to taxi effectively in calm or light wind conditions. However, when wind speed is moderate or strong, you must use special techniques. In a strong wind, there is a tendency for the wind to get under the upwind wing and tip the airplane toward the downwind side. You can counteract this tendency by using the flight controls properly. The aileron, rudder, and elevator (or stabilator) controls are relatively ineffective at slow speeds. However, as the speed of air over the controls increases, control effectiveness also increases. The flight controls respond the same, whether you are taxiing at five knots with no wind or sitting still with a five-knot headwind. However, if you taxi the airplane at 15 knots into a 15-knot wind, the controls have a 30-knot airflow over them and respond to that velocity of airflow.

On the other hand, if you taxi the airplane at five knots with a tailwind of five knots, the taxi speed and the wind speed are canceled, and the controls respond as though no wind exists. If you slow the airplane, the controls respond as though there were an increasing tailwind component. When you stop the airplane completely, the control surfaces are subjected to the direct effects of a five-knot tailwind.

TAXIING IN HEADWINDS

When you taxi an airplane directly into a headwind, the wind flows over and under both wings equally and has no tendency to tip the airplane. Under these conditions, you should hold the elevator (or stabilator) control near neutral, or slightly forward of neutral, to exert normal pressure on the nose gear.

If you hold the control wheel full forward in a strong headwind, the wind striking the downward deflection of the elevator (or stabilator) forces the tail section up and the nose down. This condition places more than the normal weight on the nose gear, compresses the nose strut, and brings the propeller tips closer to the ground. Normally, this is not hazardous. On rough terrain, however, this procedure can cause the propeller to be damaged by contact with the ground. [Figure 1-33]

TAXIING IN TAILWINDS

When you are taxiing in a strong tailwind, place the control wheel in the full-forward position. This causes the wind to strike the upper surface of

Figure 1-33. When taxiing over rough ground into a strong headwind, you should hold back the control wheel so the elevator (or stabilator) is raised. This procedure forces the tail down and increases propeller clearance.

the elevator (or stabilator) and to exert a downward force on the tail. [Figure 1-34]

TAXIING IN CROSSWINDS

Crosswinds cause a lifting effect on one wing. Normally, the wind is not strong enough to actually overturn the airplane. With a strong wind and improper control placement, though, the airplane could be upset, resulting in serious damage.

QUARTERING HEADWIND

To counteract the tipping tendencies of a left quartering headwind, apply neutral elevator (or stabilator) pressure and turn the control wheel full left.

Figure 1-34. With a tailwind, full forward control wheel pressure is used to prevent the wind from raising the tail and causing the airplane to nose over.

Figure 1-35. As wind velocity increases, the tipping tendency becomes more pronounced. However, with a strong wind, the ailerons are more effective and tend to compensate for this effect.

Then, the wind flowing over the left wing exerts pressure against the raised aileron, tending to force that wing down. Be sure to move the aileron control to its full deflection. The controls are less effective at slow taxi speeds, and a small amount of deflection may be of little value. [Figure 1-35]

With a quartering headwind from the right, the tipping tendency is to the left. Therefore, right aileron is required. [Figure 1-36]

Taxiing with a quartering headwind is similar to the conditions you encounter in a crosswind takeoff or landing. Your understanding of the effects of wind on taxiing will help you develop your crosswind takeoff and landing techniques.

QUARTERING TAILWIND

When the wind is striking the airplane from behind, you must position the ailerons to counteract the tipping tendency and rotate the control wheel away from the wind. When the wind is from the left rear (a left quartering tailwind), turn the aileron control to the right. Since quartering tailwinds also have a tendency to flow beneath the elevator (or stabilator) and lift the

Figure 1-36. In a right quartering headwind, apply neutral elevator (or stabilator) and turn the control wheel full right to raise the right aileron and lower the left aileron.

tail, the airplane may tip over on the nosewheel and one main wheel. To counteract this tipping force, move the control wheel full forward to lower the elevator (or stabilator). The tailwind then applies an aerodynamic force on the top of the elevator (or stabilator) and tends to push the tail down. [Figure 1-37]

You must be particularly cautious when you are slowing down and beginning a turn in a quartering tailwind. The increasing tailwind component, combined with the normal tendency of the airplane to tip during the turn, makes the airplane especially vulnerable to being overturned. Slow taxi speeds and slow turns minimize this danger.

Use extra care when slowing down or turning in a quartering tailwind.

PRACTICING PROPER CONTROL POSITIONING

During much of the time that you spend taxiing, the winds probably will be at a level where control positioning is not critical. However, proper control placement requires practice. Therefore, you should practice proper control positioning on every flight. When there are light winds, assume

While taxiing, you should practice proper control wheel placement.

Figure 1-37. A left quartering tailwind requires full right aileron deflection and full forward elevator (or stabilator) pressure. In a right quartering tailwind, full left aileron deflection and full forward elevator (or stabilator) is used.

that the winds are strong and from whichever direction the windsock indicates. In this way, you can practice correct placement of the aileron and elevator (or stabilator) controls as if it were necessary.

The benefits of this practice will be evident later in the flight training program when you actually encounter strong winds. In addition, you will develop a constant awareness of wind direction early in the program. By the time you reach the takeoff position on any given flight, you already will have evaluated wind speed and direction.

HAND SIGNALS

As pilot in command, you are always responsible for the safe operation of your airplane.

You should be familiar with the standard hand signals used by ramp personnel for directing you during ground operations. However, keep in mind that, even when you are being directed, you continue to be responsible for the safe operation of your airplane. [Figure 1-38]

ENGINE SHUTDOWN AND PARKING

At the completion of a flight, taxi the airplane into the parking area, using a safe taxi speed and proper control procedures. After you reach the desired parking area, you may wish to check for accidental activation of the ELT by tuning 121.5 MHz just before you shut down the radios. This helps eliminate false ELT alarms and preserves the ELT's batteries until they may be needed. Then, proceed with the engine shutdown according

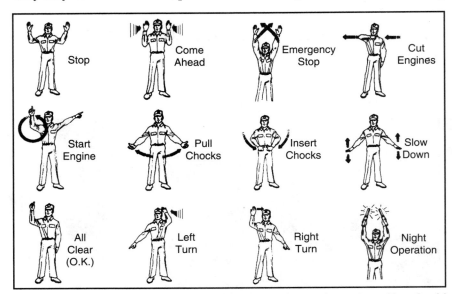

Figure 1-38. Some of the more common hand signals are shown here. You should review them periodically, especially during the early portion of your flight training program.

to the appropriate checklist. Your postflight procedures should include making sure your passengers deplane safely (after engine shutdown), and you also should perform a postflight inspection. As an extra precaution, remove the key from the ignition.

MOVING THE AIRPLANE

You can safely and easily maneuver most light tricycle-gear airplanes by using a towbar attached to the nosewheel. The towbar normally is stowed in the baggage compartment and should be used when available. Fixed-base operators usually have an assortment of towbars for use if you do not have one in the airplane. When you use a towbar, be sure the nose gear is not turned beyond its steering radius limits.

MOVING THE AIRPLANE WITHOUT A TOWBAR

Since an airplane is composed of lightweight materials, only certain points may be used for pushing or pulling it. Your instructor will show you the location of bulkheads and ribs located under the skin of the airplane. Normally, these are the points you will use when a towbar is not available.

PIVOTING THE AIRPLANE

It is possible to pivot a tricycle-gear airplane by applying downward pressure on the tail section. With the tail depressed, the nosewheel will clear the ground, and you will be able to turn the airplane in either direction. However, with some airplanes, and particularly older aircraft, this practice is discouraged (except in an emergency). In some cases, the practice is prohibited, since structural damage may occur. If the procedure is permitted, follow all applicable precautions and limitations. Keep in mind, pivoting an airplane in this way causes one wingtip to move forward while the other moves backward. [Figure 1-39]

Figure 1-39. You can apply downward pressure on the tail by pushing on the fuselage directly over a bulkhead (A) and/or by pushing down on the front spar of the horizontal stabilizer adjacent to the fuselage (B).

It is easy to pivot a tailwheel-type airplane, because the tailwheel usually pivots 360°. One person can turn the airplane around by pushing on the side of the fuselage over a bulkhead.

PUSHING THE AIRPLANE

Pushing on the leading edge of the horizontal and vertical stabilizers is acceptable if you are cautious. Apply pressure only to the leading edge near the fuselage.

The leading edge of the wing is also a good push point on low-wing airplanes. Apply pressure only at rib locations. When the wing is used as a push point, more than one person is needed to maintain directional control of the airplane. On high-wing airplanes, wing struts make good push points.

You can also push or pull the airplane by its propeller. However, only apply pressure near the propeller hub. If you apply pressure to the propeller tip, it may be permanently bent and produce a serious vibration problem in flight. The nosecap, engine cowling, and the trailing edges of wings and control surfaces are not designed for moving the airplane, and you should not use them for this purpose.

SECURING THE AIRPLANE

Proper tiedown procedures are the best precaution against damage to a parked airplane from strong or gusty winds. When the airplane is in the proper tiedown area, place chocks in front of and behind the main wheels and release the parking brake (if set).

Secure all flight controls to prevent the control surfaces from striking their stops. Most airplanes are equipped with internal control locks. Others may require you to use external padded battens (control surface locks). Even if the airplane is equipped with internal control locks, it may be necessary to use external locks to prevent gust loads from being fed back into the control system during extremely strong or gusty wind conditions. When you use external control locks, you should fasten streamers or tiedown lines to the locks. This alerts you and airport ramp personnel to remove the external locks prior to flight.

Before you leave the airplane, secure it with tiedown ropes or chains. Secure the tiedowns without slack, but not tight. Too much slack allows the airplane to jerk against the ropes or chains, while too little slack may permit high stresses to be placed on the airplane. The tail tiedown should be secure, but not so tight that it raises the nose of the airplane. In a headwind, a raised nose increases the angle of attack of the wing and creates additional lifting force, causing more pressure on the wing tiedown restraints.

CLEANUP

After the airplane is secured, you should make a careful check of the interior of the airplane. Make sure all switches are off and that trash, papers, and flight planning items are cleaned from the cabin area. On the exterior of the airplane, install the pitot tube cover, if applicable. Place the propeller in a horizontal position to lessen the possibility of damage to another taxiing aircraft's wingtip. Placing the propeller in a horizontal position also permits the spinner to offer more protection to the prop hub from rain, snow, and ice. This is especially important if an aircraft is equipped with a constant-speed propeller.

CHECKLIST

After studying this section, you should have a basic understanding of:

✓ **Taxiing** — The procedures and proper control placements to use when taxiing an airplane in various wind conditions, including headwinds, tailwinds, crosswinds, and quartering tailwinds.

✓ **Hand signals** — Some of the more common hand signals used by ground personnel to direct airplanes while taxiing.

✓ **Shutdown** — Procedures to follow when shutting down the airplane, including checking for activation of the airplane's ELT.

✓ **Moving the airplane** — How to move the airplane by hand without damaging the skin or internal components of the airframe.

✓ **Securing the airplane** — How airplane controls are secured and how to tie down the airplane to the ramp by the use of chains or ropes.

STRAIGHT-AND-LEVEL FLIGHT

Your flight training will normally begin with instruction in the techniques of straight-and-level flight. The objectives of this maneuver are to point the airplane in a particular direction, maintain that direction, and fly at a predetermined altitude.

LEVEL FLIGHT

For a given power setting, there is a fixed nose and wing position which result in level flight.

You control the airplane's direction and altitude by controlling the nose and wing positions with reference to the natural horizon. This is called **attitude flying**. During training in attitude flying, you learn that there is a fixed nose position (pitch attitude) and a fixed wing position (bank attitude) for each flight condition. With a constant power setting and the aircraft's attitude adjusted to these fixed positions, the aircraft will maintain the selected flight conditions.

You should be aware of the difference between visual flying and instrument flying. **Visual flying** simply means that the natural horizon is used as a reference point. **Instrument flying** requires you to use the flight instruments for airplane attitude reference. The attitude indicator, altimeter, and the heading indicator give you most of the information you need to maintain straight-and-level flight. [Figure 1-40]

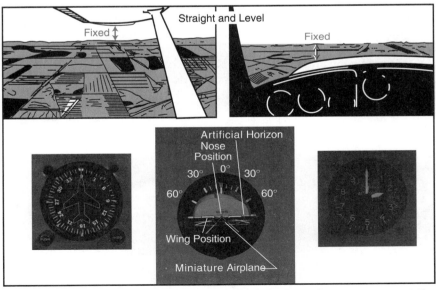

Figure 1-40. The visual and instrument presentations shown here are representative of what you will see when the airplane is established in straight-and-level flight.

Figure 1-41. As you look out the left window of the cockpit, this is how the level flight attitude appears in a low-wing or high-wing airplane.

CONTROLLING BANK ATTITUDE

In straight-and-level flight, the wings remain level with the horizon, and the flight path is parallel to the earth's surface. To maintain this configuration, it is necessary to fix the relationship of the airplane to the horizon. To do this, pick a point on the wingtip for a reference; the wings-level position is maintained by keeping the wingtips a given distance above or below the horizon. [Figure 1-41]

CONTROLLING PITCH ATTITUDE

To control pitch attitude, or nose position, select a point on the airplane's nose or a spot on the windshield as a reference point. This point should be directly in front of you. [Figure 1-42]

Figure 1-42. When viewed from the pilot's seat, this is how straight-and-level flight will appear.

The exact appearance of the wingtips and nose in reference to the horizon depends on the type of airplane being flown, your height, and how you position your seat. A key element in attitude flying is determining the wing and nose positions that result in level flight.

CONTROLLING HEADING AND ALTITUDE

Cross-check the flight instruments to verify heading and altitude.

In practicing straight-and-level flight, you learn to maintain a specific heading and altitude by establishing the wing and nose attitudes for level flight. Then, you periodically refer to the heading indicator and altimeter to verify that you are on the desired heading and at the preselected altitude.

ATTITUDE FLYING

To fly by instrument reference, you will need to learn the techniques of scanning. Develop the habit of keeping your eyes moving continuously between outside reference points and the instruments, always remaining alert for other air traffic in your vicinity. At no time should you concentrate entirely on any one reference. [Figure 1-43]

Several forces may cause the airplane to drift from the desired attitude. Power changes, turbulence, wind gusts, and brief periods of inattention to wing position can all cause changes in heading or altitude.

When you notice a variation from the selected heading or altitude, first reestablish straight-and-level flight, then apply necessary corrections.

Since flying is a continuous series of small adjustments, you must learn to maintain a desired attitude as closely as possible and make smooth, prompt corrections as necessary. Abrupt changes can result in over-correcting. Each correction should be made in two steps. First, if the heading or altitude has changed, apply control pressure to return to a straight-and-level flight attitude. Second, adjust the attitude reference points to return the airplane slowly to the desired heading and altitude, and adjust the power setting, if required. The nose position helps you to know when the wings are not level. The position of the wingtip also provides a small clue when the nose is high or low. [Figure 1-44]

Figure 1-43. Your eyes should move from one wing to the nose, to the appropriate instruments, and then to the other wing.

Figure 1-44. Here is an example of an airplane (high-wing and low-wing) in a nose-high right bank. The left wing and nose are above their normal straight-and-level positions. Notice also how the wing is slightly inclined to the horizon, indicating a nose-high attitude.

ATTITUDE AND ELEVATOR MOVEMENT

Changes in pitch attitude, caused by movement of the elevator (or stabilator), result in altitude changes during cruising flight. The elevator (or stabilator) also affects the rate of climb or descent during altitude changes. Since it controls the pitch position of the nose, we can say that altitude is controlled primarily by the elevator (or stabilator) in straight-and-level flight.

AIRSPEED AND POWER

After you gain reasonable control over the airplane attitude, you will be able to control airspeed primarily with power. The throttle is used mainly to control airspeed and the elevator (or stabilator) to control altitude. After cruise airspeed has been established and power is constant, it is possible to use airspeed variations to detect pitch attitude changes. [Figure 1-45]

| Climb | Level Flight | Descent |

Figure 1-45. If power remains constant, any change in pitch will be reflected as an increase or decrease in airspeed.

TRIM

Trim adjustments eliminate the need for continuous forward or backward pressure on the wheel to maintain attitude. If the airplane feels nose-heavy, you are holding back pressure to maintain a given attitude. Likewise, if forward pressure is required, the airplane will feel tail-heavy. When it is properly trimmed, you will not have to apply either forward or back pressure to maintain a constant pitch attitude. [Figure 1-46]

Use the trim to relieve control wheel pressure.

Use the trim tab only to remove control wheel pressure; do not use it to fly the airplane. The proper procedure is to set the airplane in the desired pitch attitude and at the selected airspeed, then trim away any control pressure necessary to hold that attitude. With a few exceptions, trim tab adjustments should be made whenever you must apply a continuous forward or rearward force to the control wheel.

EFFECTS OF RUDDER USE

Airplanes are designed to remain in stable, aerodynamic balance during cruising flight. Therefore, aileron or rudder pressures are not constantly required. This balanced condition is sometimes referred to as flying "hands off," meaning that you can remove your hands and feet from the controls and the airplane will continue to maintain straight-and-level flight.

During normal flight, the rudder is streamlined with the airflow over the airplane. The ball of the turn coordinator should remain in the center of

Trim Tab

Figure 1-46. In this example, back pressure is being applied to maintain a constant pitch attitude (top left). By rotating the trim wheel in the nose-up direction (right), the trim tab will move down (bottom left) and deflect air passing over the elevator, causing a reduction in required back pressure. Rotate the trim wheel until all pressure is eliminated.

| Ball to Left | Apply Left Rudder Pressure |

Figure 1-47. A rule you can use for rudder correction is, "When the ball is out of center, step on the ball." Here the ball is to the left of center, and you must apply left rudder pressure to center it.

the inclinometer. If the ball moves out of the center when you are maneuvering, the airplane is skidding or slipping. Apply rudder pressure to return the ball to the center. [Figure 1-47]

STRAIGHT-AND-LEVEL FLIGHT BY INSTRUMENT REFERENCE

After practicing straight-and-level flight using visual references, your instructor will have you repeat this practice using only instrument references. You will find that the airplane responds just as it does when it is flown visually. During flight by instruments, the attitude indicator is your primary flight instrument, since it is the only instrument that displays both pitch and bank information. [Figure 1-48]

Figure 1-48. As shown on the left, a typical instrument panel is arranged in what is called the basic "T" configuration. In this arrangement, the attitude indicator is at the center of the "T," and supporting instruments are beside and below it. On the right, you can see that the attitude, airspeed, and vertical speed indicators, as well as the altimeter, are used to control the pitch attitude of the airplane. Bank is controlled by use of the attitude indicator, heading indicator, and turn coordinator.

Deviation from desired altitudes and headings is caused by the same forces, whether you are flying by instrument references or visual references. Corrections also are made in the same way. When the bank attitude and heading have changed, or are changing, first return to a straight-and-level flight attitude. Next, look at the altimeter and heading indicator to determine the amount of correction needed to return to the original altitude and heading. Finally, make small attitude corrections to return to the desired altitude and heading.

KINESTHETIC SENSE

Kinesthetic sense is generally defined as the feel of motion and pressure changes through nerve endings in the organs, muscles, and tendons. This is the feeling pilots describe as the "seat of the pants" sensation. If you rely solely on this sense when flying by instrument references, it is possible to experience **spatial disorientation**. This is an incorrect mental image of your position, attitude, or movement in relation to what is actually happening to your airplane. It can cause an inexperienced pilot to make incorrect control movements. Therefore, during instrument flight, it is extremely important to believe only what your instruments tell you and not respond to your physical sensations.

CHECKLIST

After studying this section, you should have a basic understanding of:

✓ **Straight-and-level flight** — How to establish and maintain straight-and-level flight using visual references.

✓ **Attitude flying** — What scanning is, how to apply it, and the differences between visual and instrument flying.

✓ **Maintaining heading and altitude** — What the procedures are for correcting deviations in heading and altitude.

flight prep 2

AERODYNAMICS OF MANEUVERING FLIGHT

This section takes you beyond straight-and-level flight to the aerodynamics of maneuvering flight. You will find that specific aerodynamic principles apply to climbs, descents, and turning maneuvers. These concepts will help you understand the performance limitations of your airplane. At the same time, you will learn important safety-of-flight considerations related to these performance limitations.

THREE AXES OF FLIGHT

The three axes of flight pass through the airplane's center of gravity.

All maneuvering flight takes place around one or more of three axes of rotation. They are called the **longitudinal**, **lateral**, and **vertical axes** of flight. The common reference point for the three axes is the airplane's **center of gravity** (CG), which is the theoretical point where the entire weight of the airplane is considered to be concentrated. Since all three axes pass through this point, you can say that the airplane always moves about its CG, regardless of which axis is involved. The ailerons, elevator, and rudder create aerodynamic forces which cause the airplane to rotate about the three axes. [Figure 2-1]

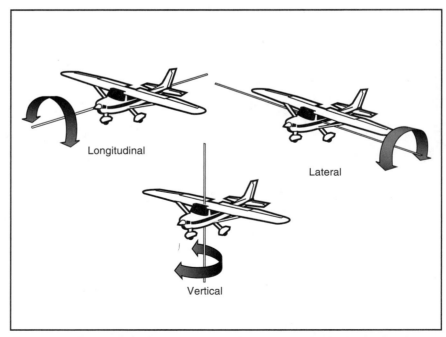

Longitudinal

Lateral

Vertical

Figure 2-1. Ailerons control roll movement about the longitudinal axis; the elevator controls pitch movement about the lateral axis; and the rudder controls yaw movement about the vertical axis.

Figure 2-2. Deflected ailerons alter the chord line and change the effective camber of the outboard section of each wing. In this example, the angle of attack increases for the right wing, causing a corresponding increase in lift. At the same time, you can see that the left wing will lose some of its lift because of a decrease in its angle of attack. The airplane will roll to the left, because the right wing is producing more lift than the left wing.

LONGITUDINAL AXIS

Now consider what happens when you apply control pressure to begin a turn. When you deflect the ailerons, they create an immediate rolling movement about the longitudinal axis. Since the ailerons always move in opposite directions, the aerodynamic shape of each wing and its production of lift is affected differently. [Figure 2-2]

Roll movement about the longitudinal axis is produced by the ailerons.

One of the first things you will learn during flight is that the rolling movement about the longitudinal axis will continue as long as the ailerons are deflected. To stop the roll, you must relax control pressure and return the ailerons to their original, or neutral, position. This is called neutralizing the controls.

LATERAL AXIS

Since the horizontal stabilizer is an airfoil, the action of the elevator (or stabilator) is quite similar to that of an aileron. Essentially, the chord line and effective camber of the stabilizer are changed by deflection of the elevator. [Figure 2-3]

Pitch movement about the lateral axis is produced by the elevator (or stabilator).

Figure 2-3. When you lower the elevator, the angle of attack of the stabilizer increases, and it produces more lift. The lifting force created by the stabilizer causes the airplane to pivot forward about its lateral axis. The net result is a decrease in the angle of attack of the wings, and an overall decrease in the pitch attitude.

Movement of the control wheel fore or aft causes motion about the lateral axis. Typically, this is referred to as an adjustment to pitch, or a change in pitch attitude. For example, when you move the control wheel forward, it causes movement about the lateral axis that decreases the airplane's pitch attitude. A decrease in pitch attitude decreases the angle of attack. Conversely, an increase in pitch attitude increases the angle of attack.

VERTICAL AXIS

Yaw movement about the vertical axis is produced by rudder.

When you apply pressure on the rudder pedals, the rudder deflects into the airstream. This produces an aerodynamic force that rotates the airplane about its vertical axis. This is referred to as yawing the airplane. The rudder may be displaced either to the left or right of center, depending on which rudder pedal you depress. [Figure 2-4]

FORCES ACTING ON A CLIMBING AIRPLANE

When you transition from level flight into a climb, you must combine the change in pitch attitude with an increase in power. If you attempt to climb just by pulling back on the control wheel to raise the nose of the airplane, momentum will cause a brief increase in altitude, but airspeed will soon decrease.

The amount of thrust generated by the propeller for cruising flight at a given airspeed is not enough to maintain the same airspeed in a climb.

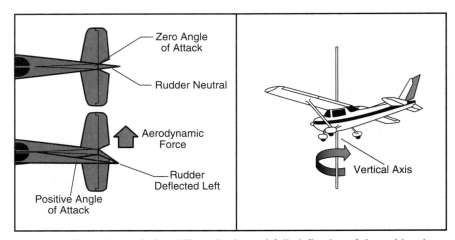

Figure 2-4. Since the vertical stabilizer also is an airfoil, deflection of the rudder alters the stabilizer's effective camber and chord line. In this case, left rudder pressure causes the rudder to move to the left. With a change in the chord line, the angle of attack is altered, generating an aerodynamic force toward the right side of the vertical fin. This causes the tail section to move to the right, and the nose of the airplane to yaw to the left.

Figure 2-5. The forces of weight, lift, thrust, and drag are in equilibrium during a stabilized climb, just as they are during straight-and-level flight. When an airplane is
climbing, though, the force of weight consists of two components. The first opposes
lift and is perpendicular to the flight path. The second is called the rearward component of weight and acts in the same direction as drag, opposite to the direction
of thrust.

Excess thrust, not excess lift, is necessary for a sustained climb. In fact,
during a true vertical climb, the wings supply no lift, and thrust is the only
force opposing weight. [Figure 2-5]

An airplane climbs
because of excess thrust,
not excess lift.

FORCES ACTING ON A DESCENDING AIRPLANE

Let's continue our discussion by considering the forces of weight, lift,
thrust, and drag as they affect a descending airplane. If you are using
power during a stabilized descent, the four forces are in equilibrium.
During the descent, a component of weight acts forward along the flight
path. As speed increases, this force is balanced by an increase in parasite drag.

In a descent, a compo-
nent of weight acts for-
ward along the flight
path.

During a power-off glide, the throttle is placed in an idle position so the
engine and propeller produce no thrust. In this situation, the source of the
airplane's thrust is provided only by the component of weight acting forward along the flight path. In a steady, power-off glide, the forward component of weight is equal to and opposite drag.

CONSTANT AIRSPEED DESCENT

Once you have established a state of equilibrium for a constant airspeed
descent, the efficiency of the glide will be affected if you increase drag. For
example, if you lower the landing gear, both parasite and total drag

increase. To maintain the airspeed you held before the landing gear was extended, you have to lower the nose of the airplane.

You also can increase drag by descending at a speed that creates more drag than necessary. Any speed, other than the recommended glide speed, creates more drag. If you descend with the speed too high, parasite drag increases; and if you descend with speed too slow, induced drag increases. [Figure 2-6]

GLIDE ANGLE AND GLIDE SPEED

During a descent, the angle between the actual glide path of your airplane and the horizon usually is called the **glide angle**. Your glide angle increases as drag increases, and decreases as drag decreases. Since a decreased glide angle, or a shallower glide, provides the greatest gliding distance, minimum drag normally produces the maximum glide distance.

The way to minimize drag is to fly at an airspeed that results in the most favorable lift-to-drag ratio. This important performance speed is called the **best glide speed**. In most cases, it is the only speed that will give you the maximum gliding distance. However, with a very strong headwind, you may need a slightly higher glide speed, while a slower speed may be recommended to take advantage of a strong tailwind.

LIFT-TO-DRAG RATIO

The higher the value of L/D_{max}, the better the glide ratio.

The lift-to-drag ratio (L/D) can be used to measure the gliding efficiency of your airplane. The airspeed resulting in the least drag on your airplane will give the maximum L/D ratio (L/D_{max}), the best glide angle, and the maximum gliding distance.

Figure 2-6. In a constant-airspeed, power-off descent, weight is balanced by the resultant of lift and drag. Notice that the angle between the lift vector and the resultant is the same as the angle between the flight path and the horizon. This is the glide angle of the airplane. If drag increases, the angle between the lift vector and the resultant vector increases and, consequently, the glide angle steepens.

GLIDE RATIO

The glide ratio represents the distance an airplane will travel forward, without power, in relation to altitude loss. For example, a glide ratio of 10:1 means that an airplane will descend one foot for every 10 feet of horizontal distance it travels. Since the throttle is closed in a power-off glide, the pitch attitude must be adjusted to maintain the best glide speed.

In the event of an engine failure, maintaining the best glide speed becomes even more important. This is especially true for a power failure after becoming airborne. Promptly establishing the correct gliding attitude and airspeed is critical. For a loss of power during flight, using the right speed could make the difference between successfully gliding to a suitable area or landing short of it.

If a power failure occurs after takeoff, immediately establish the proper gliding attitude and airspeed.

EFFECT OF WEIGHT ON THE GLIDE

Variations in weight do not affect the glide angle, provided you use the correct airspeed for each weight. Normally, optimum, or best, glide speeds are given in the pilot's operating handbook (POH) for typical weight ranges. A fully loaded airplane requires a higher airspeed than the same airplane with a light load. Although the heavier airplane sinks faster and will reach the ground sooner, it will travel the same distance as a lighter airplane as long as you maintain the correct higher glide speed for the increased weight.

An airplane's maximum gliding distance is unaffected by weight, but the best glide airspeed increases with weight.

FORCES ACTING ON A TURNING AIRPLANE

From our discussion about the three axes of rotation, you learned that ailerons control roll movement about the longitudinal axis, and the rudder controls yaw movement about the vertical axis. Coordinated turns require you to use both of these flight controls. You use the ailerons to roll into or out of a bank and, at the same time, you use the rudder to control yaw.

Before your airplane turns, however, it must overcome inertia, or its tendency to continue in a straight line. You create the necessary turning force by banking the airplane so that the direction of lift is inclined. Now, one component of lift still acts vertically to oppose weight, just as it did in straight-and-level flight, while another acts horizontally. To maintain altitude, you will need to increase lift by increasing back pressure and, therefore, the angle of attack until the vertical component of lift equals weight. The horizontal component of lift, called **centripetal force**, is directed inward, toward the center of rotation. It is this center-seeking force which causes the airplane to turn. Centripetal force is opposed by **centrifugal force**, which acts outward from the center of rotation. When the opposing

The horizontal component of lift causes an airplane to turn.

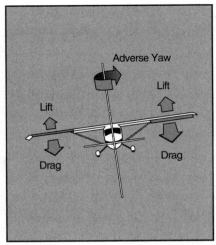

Figure 2-7. The resultant of the horizontal component (centripetal force) and the vertical component of lift is the total lift provided by the wings. The resultant of centrifugal force and weight is the total load the wings must support.

Figure 2-8. If you roll into a turn without using rudder to help establish the turn, the airplane will yaw about its vertical axis opposite to the direction of the turn. Adverse yaw is caused by higher induced drag on the outside wing, which is producing more lift.

forces are balanced, the airplane maintains a constant rate of turn, without gaining or losing altitude. [Figure 2-7]

ADVERSE YAW

When you roll into a turn, the aileron on the inside of the turn is raised, and the aileron on the outside of the turn is lowered. The lowered aileron on the outside increases the angle of attack and produces more lift for that wing. Since induced drag is a by-product of lift, you can see that the outside wing also produces more drag than the inside wing. This causes a yawing tendency toward the outside of the turn, which is called **adverse yaw**. [Figure 2-8]

The basic purpose of the rudder on an airplane is to control yawing.

The coordinated use of aileron and rudder corrects for adverse yaw when you roll into or out of a turn. For a turn to the left, you depress the left rudder pedal slightly as you roll into the left turn. Once you are established in the turn, you relax both aileron and rudder pressures and neutralize the controls. Then, when you want to roll out of the turn, you apply coordinated right aileron and rudder pressure to return to a wings-level attitude.

OVERBANKING TENDENCY

During your initial flight training, you will learn how to maneuver the airplane through coordinated use of the controls. As you enter a turn and increase the angle of bank, you may notice the tendency of the airplane to continue rolling into an even steeper bank, even though you neutralize the ailerons. This **overbanking tendency** is caused by the additional lift on the outside, or raised, wing. The outside wing is traveling faster than the inside wing. This adds to the lift, and the combined effects tend to roll the airplane beyond the desired bank angle.

The overbanking tendency is most pronounced at high angles of bank. To correct for this tendency, you will have to develop a technique of coordinated use of opposite aileron, away from the turn, to maintain your desired angle of bank. Overbanking tendency exists, to some degree, in almost all airplanes.

LOAD FACTOR

So far in this discussion, you have looked at the combination of opposing forces acting on a turning airplane. Now it's time to examine load factors induced during turning flight. To better understand these forces, picture yourself on a roller coaster. As you enter a banked turn during the ride, the forces you will experience are very similar to the forces which act on a turning airplane. On a roller coaster, the resultant force created by the combination of weight and centrifugal force presses you down into your seat. This pressure is an increased load factor that causes you to feel heavier in the turn than when you are on a flat portion of the track.

The increased weight you feel during a turn in a roller coaster is also experienced in an airplane. In a turning airplane, however, you must compensate for the increase in weight and loss of vertical lift, or you will lose altitude. You can do this by increasing the angle of attack with back pressure on the control wheel. The increase in the angle of attack increases the total lift of the airplane. Keep in mind that when you increase lift, drag also increases. This means you must also increase thrust if you want to maintain your original airspeed and altitude. An airplane in a coordinated, level turn is in a state of equilibrium, where opposing forces are in balance. This is similar to the state of equilibrium that exists during unaccelerated, straight-and-level flight.

During turning maneuvers, weight and centrifugal force combine into a resultant which is greater than weight alone. Additional loads are imposed on the airplane, and the wings must support the additional load factor. In other words, when you are flying in a curved flight path, the wings must support not only the weight of the airplane and its contents, but they also must support the load imposed by centrifugal force.

The load factor imposed on an airplane will increase as the angle of bank is increased.

Load factor is the ratio of the load supported by the airplane's wings to the actual weight of the aircraft and its contents. If the wings are supporting twice as much weight as the weight of the airplane and its contents, the load factor is two. You are probably more familiar with the term "G-forces" as a way to describe flight loads caused by aircraft maneuvering. "Pulling G's" is common terminology for higher performance airplanes. For example, an acrobatic category airplane may pull three or four G's during a maneuver. An airplane in cruising flight, while not accelerating in any direction, has a load factor of one. This one-G condition means the wings are supporting only the actual weight of the airplane and its contents. [Figure 2-9]

A positive load occurs when centrifugal force acts in the same direction as weight. Whenever centrifugal force acts in a direction opposite weight, a negative load is imposed. For example, if you abruptly push the control wheel forward while flying, you would experience a sensation as if your weight suddenly decreased. This is caused by centrifugal force acting upward, which tends to overcome your actual body weight. If the centrifugal force equaled your actual body weight, you would experience a "weightless" sensation of zero G's. A negative G-loading occurs when the centrifugal force exceeds your body weight. In rare instances, you may experience a rapid change in G-forces. For example, in extremely turbulent air, you might be subjected to positive G's, then negative G's, and sometimes sideward G-forces. Sideward G's are called transverse G-forces.

LOAD FACTOR AND STALL SPEED

Earlier you learned that you can stall an airplane at any airspeed and in any flight attitude. You can easily stall an airplane in a turn at a higher-than-normal airspeed. As the angle of bank increases in level turns, you must increase the angle of attack to maintain altitude. As you increase the angle of bank, the stall speed also increases. [Figure 2-10]

Increasing the load factor will cause an airplane to stall at a higher speed.

Actually, stall speed increases in proportion to the square root of the load factor. If you are flying an airplane with a one-G stalling speed of 55 knots, you can stall it at twice that speed (110 knots) with a load factor of four G's. Stalls that occur with G-forces on an airplane are called **accelerated stalls**. An accelerated stall occurs at a speed higher than the normal one-G stall speed. These stalls demonstrate that the critical angle of attack, rather than speed, is the reason for a stall. Stalls also can occur at unusually high speeds in severe turbulence, or in low-level wind shear.

LIMIT LOAD FACTOR

When the Federal Aviation Administration certifies an airplane, one of the criteria they look at is how much stress the airplane can withstand. The **limit load factor** is the number of G's an airplane can sustain, on a continuing basis, without causing permanent deformation or structural

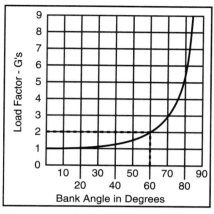

Figure 2-9. During constant altitude turns, the relationship between load factor, or G's, and bank angle is the same for all airplanes. For example, with a 60° bank, two G's are required to maintain level flight. This means the airplane's wings must support twice the weight of the airplane and its contents, although the actual weight of the airplane does not increase.

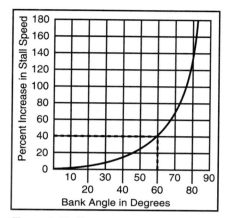

Figure 2-10. If you attempt to maintain altitude during a turn by increasing the angle of attack, the stall speed increases as the angle of bank increases. The percent of increase in stall speed is fairly moderate with shallow bank angles — less than 45°. However, once you increase the bank angle beyond 45°, the percent of increase in the stall speed rises rapidly. For example, in a 60°, constant-altitude bank, the stall speed increases by 40%; a 75° bank increases stall speed by 100%.

damage. In other words, the limit load factor is the amount of positive or negative G's an airframe is capable of supporting.

Most small general aviation airplanes with a gross weight of 12,500 pounds or less, and nine passenger seats or less, are certified in either the normal, utility, or acrobatic categories. A normal category airplane is certified for nonacrobatic maneuvers. Training maneuvers and turns not exceeding 60° of bank are permitted in this category. The maximum limit load factor in the normal category is 3.8 positive G's, and 1.52 negative G's. In other words, the airplane's wings are designed to withstand 3.8 times the actual weight of the airplane and its contents during maneuvering flight. By following proper loading techniques and flying within the limits listed in the pilot's operating handbook, you will avoid excessive loads on the airplane, and possible structural damage.

In addition to those maneuvers permitted in the normal category, an airplane certified in the utility category may be used for several maneuvers requiring additional stress on the airframe. A limit of 4.4 positive G's or 1.76 negative G's is permitted in the utility category. Some, but not all, utility category airplanes are also approved for spins. An acrobatic category airplane may be flown in any flight attitude as long as its limit load factor does not exceed six positive G's or three negative G's.

A key point for you to remember is that it is possible to exceed design limits for load factor during maneuvers. For example, if you roll into a steep, level turn of 75°, you will put approximately four G's on the airplane. This is above the maximum limit of 3.8 G's for an airplane in the normal category. You also should be aware of the conditions specified for the maximum load limit. If flaps are extended, for instance, the maximum load limit normally is less. The POH for the airplane you are flying is your best source of load limit information.

MANEUVERING SPEED

An important airspeed related to load factors and stall speed is the **design maneuvering speed** (V_A). This limiting speed normally is not marked on the airspeed indicator, since it may vary with total weight. The POH and/or a placard in the airplane are the best sources for determining V_A. Although some handbooks may designate only one maneuvering speed, others may show several. When more than one is specified, you will notice that V_A decreases as weight decreases. An aircraft operating at lighter weights is subject to more rapid acceleration from gusts and turbulence than a more heavily loaded one.

The amount of excess load that can be imposed on an airframe depends on the aircraft's speed.

Any airspeed in excess of V_A can overstress the airframe during abrupt maneuvers or turbulence. The higher the airspeed, the greater the amount of excess load that can be imposed before a stall occurs. V_A represents the maximum speed at which you can use full, abrupt control movement without overstressing the airframe. If you are flying at or below this speed, any combination of pilot-induced control movement, or gust loads resulting from turbulence, should not cause an excessive load on the airplane. This is why you should always fly at or below V_A during turbulent conditions.

The design maneuvering speed also is the maximum speed at which you can safely stall an airplane. If you stall the airplane above this speed, you will generate excessive G-loads. At or below this speed, the airplane will stall before excessive G-forces build up. By staying at or below V_A, you avoid the possibility of overstressing or even damaging the airplane.

STALLS

All pilots should be knowledgeable about the causes and effects of stalling. This knowledge is a training requirement and it is especially important during flight at slow airspeeds where the margin above the stall speed is small. Keep in mind, slow airspeeds are necessary for every take-off and landing.

CAUSES OF STALLS

As indicated earlier, a stall occurs when the maximum lift angle of attack (C_{Lmax}) is exceeded. If you do not recover promptly by reducing the angle of attack, a secondary stall and/or a spin may result.

A forward CG causes a higher stalling speed than a more rearward CG. Besides CG position, load factor, flap setting (configuration), weight, and other factors can affect the actual stalling speed. Turbulence, lack of coordination, and snow, ice, or frost on the wings are examples. As you might expect, these factors can increase the stalling speed.

STALL RECOGNITION AND RECOVERY

There are any number of ways to recognize that a stall is imminent. Ideally, you should be able to detect the first signs of an impending stall and make appropriate corrections before it actually occurs. If you have a good understanding of the types of stalls, recognition is much easier. Recovery at the first indication of a stall is quite simple; but, if you allow the stalled condition to progress, recovery becomes more difficult.

Knowing the flight characteristics of the airplane you are flying and being aware of the specific phases of flight where stalls are most likely to occur are additional factors in stall recognition. For example, power-on, turning stalls often occur during a departure or climb after takeoff, and power-off, turning stalls are common during the turn to the final approach for a landing.

A typical indication of a stall is a mushy feeling in the flight controls and less control affect as the aircraft's speed decreases. The reduction in control effectiveness is primarily due to reduced airflow over the flight control surfaces. In fixed-pitch propeller airplanes, a loss of revolutions per minute (r.p.m.) may be noticeable as you approach a stall in power-on conditions. Also, a reduction in the sound of air flowing along the fuselage is usually evident. Just before the stall occurs, buffeting, uncontrollable pitching, or vibrations may begin. Finally, your kinesthetic sense (ability to recognize changes in direction or speed) may also provide a warning of decreased speed or the beginning of a sinking feeling. These preliminary indications serve as a warning for you to decrease the angle of attack and add power to increase the airspeed.

Figure 2-11. In a single-engine airplane, you will experience the greatest effect of torque during takeoff or climb when you are in a low-airspeed, high-power, high angle of attack flight condition.

LEFT-TURNING TENDENCIES

Propeller-driven airplanes are subject to several left-turning tendencies caused by a combination of physical and aerodynamic forces — torque, gyroscopic precession, asymmetrical thrust, and spiraling slipstream. You will need to compensate for these forces, especially when you are flying in high-power, low-airspeed flight conditions following takeoff or during the initial climb. If you know what is happening to the airplane, you will have a better idea of how to correct for these tendencies.

TORQUE

Torque effect is greatest in a single-engine airplane during a low-airspeed, high-power flight condition.

In airplanes with a single engine, the propeller rotates clockwise when viewed from the pilot's seat. **Torque** can be understood most easily by remembering Newton's third law of motion. The clockwise action of a spinning propeller causes a torque reaction which tends to rotate the airplane counterclockwise about its longitudinal axis. [Figure 2-11]

Generally, aircraft have design adjustments which compensate for torque while in cruising flight, but you will have to take corrective action during other phases of flight. Some airplanes have aileron trim tabs which you can use to correct for the effects of torque at various power settings.

GYROSCOPIC PRECESSION

The turning propeller of an airplane also exhibits characteristics of a gyroscope — rigidity in space and precession. The characteristic that produces a left-turning tendency is precession. **Gyroscopic precession** is the resultant reaction of an object when force is applied. The reaction to a force

Figure 2-12. If the pitch attitude of an airplane is changed from a nose-high to a nose-level position, a force will be exerted near the top of the propeller's plane of rotation. A resultant force will then be exerted 90° ahead in the direction of rotation, which will cause the nose of the airplane to yaw to the left.

applied to a gyro acts in the direction of rotation and approximately 90° ahead of the point where force is applied. [Figure 2-12]

ASYMMETRICAL THRUST

When you are flying a single-engine airplane at a high angle of attack, the descending blade of the propeller takes a greater "bite" of air than the ascending blade on the other side. The greater bite is caused by a higher angle of attack for the descending blade, compared to the ascending blade. This creates the uneven, or **asymmetrical thrust**, which is known as P-factor. **P-factor** makes an airplane yaw about its vertical axis to the left. [Figure 2-13]

P-factor results from the descending propeller blade on the right producing more thrust than the ascending blade on the left.

Figure 2-13. Asymmetrical thrust occurs when an airplane is flown at a high angle of attack. This causes uneven angles of attack between the ascending and descending propeller blades. Consequently, less thrust is produced from the ascending blade on the left than from the descending blade on the right. This produces a tendency for the airplane to yaw to the left.

You should remember that P-factor is most pronounced when the engine is operating at a high-power setting, and when the airplane is flown at a high angle of attack. In level cruising flight, P-factor is not apparent, since both ascending and descending propeller blades are at nearly the same angle of attack, and are creating approximately the same amount of thrust.

P-factor causes an airplane to yaw to the left when it is at high angles of attack.

A good way to learn more about asymmetrical thrust is to take a look at a tailwheel-type airplane the next time you're on an airport ramp. Its high angle of attack is quite apparent, and you can easily see the difference between the ascending and descending blade angles.

SPIRALING SLIPSTREAM

As the propeller rotates, it produces a backward flow of air, or slipstream, which wraps around the airplane. This **spiraling slipstream** causes a change in the airflow around the vertical stabilizer. Due to the direction of the propeller rotation, the resultant slipstream strikes the left side of the vertical fin. [Figure 2-14]

GROUND EFFECT

An airplane is usually in ground effect when it is less than the height of the airplane's wingspan above the surface.

Another significant aerodynamic consideration is the phenomenon of **ground effect**. During takeoffs or landings, when you are flying very close to the ground, the earth's surface interferes with the airflow and actually alters the three-dimensional airflow pattern around the airplane. This causes a reduction in wingtip vortices and a decrease in upwash and downwash.

Wingtip vortices are caused by the air beneath the wing rolling up and around the wingtip. This causes a spiral or vortex that trails behind each

Figure 2-14. As the slipstream produced by the propeller rotation wraps around the fuselage, it strikes the left side of the vertical fin. A left-turning tendency is created as the air "pushes" the tail of the airplane to the right and yaws the nose left.

wingtip whenever lift is being produced. Wingtip vortices are another factor contributing to induced drag. Upwash and downwash refer to the effect an airfoil exerts on the free airstream. **Upwash** is the deflection of the oncoming airstream upward and over the wing. **Downwash** is the downward deflection of the airstream as it passes over the wing and past the trailing edge.

If you remember how angle of attack influences induced drag, it will help you understand ground effect. During flight, the downwash of the airstream causes the relative wind to be inclined downward in the vicinity of the wing. This is referred to as the **average relative wind**. The angle between the free airstream relative wind and the average relative wind is the **induced angle of attack**. In effect, the greater the downward deflection of the airstream, the higher the induced angle of attack and the higher the induced drag. Since ground effect restricts the downward deflection of the airstream, both the induced angle of attack and induced drag decrease. When the wing is at a height equal to its span, the decline in induced drag is only about 1.4%; when the wing is at a height equal to one-tenth its span, the loss of induced drag is about 48%. [Figure 2-15]

Ground effect reduces induced angle of attack and induced drag.

 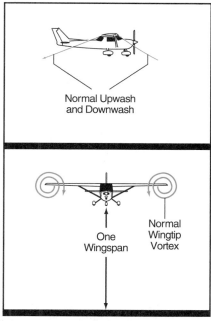

Figure 2-15. When you are flying in ground effect, the effects of upwash, downwash, and wingtip vortices decrease. This results in a reduction of induced drag. Ground effect is most noticeable near the surface, and it decreases rapidly until it becomes negligible at a height approximately equal to the wingspan of the aircraft.

Ground effect allows an airplane to become airborne before it reaches its recommended takeoff speed.

With the reduction of induced angle of attack and induced drag in ground effect, the amount of thrust required to produce lift is reduced. What this means is that your airplane is capable of lifting off at lower-than-normal speed. Although you might initially think that this is desirable, consider what happens as you climb out of ground effect. The power (thrust) required to sustain flight increases significantly as the normal airflow around the wing returns and induced drag is suddenly increased. If you attempt to climb out of ground effect before reaching the speed for normal climb, you might sink back to the surface.

In ground effect, induced drag decreases, and excess speed in the flare may cause floating.

Ground effect is noticeable in the landing phase of flight, too, just before touchdown. Within one wingspan above the ground, the decrease in induced drag makes your airplane seem to float on the cushion of air beneath it. Because of this, power reduction usually is required during the flare to help the airplane land. Although all airplanes may experience ground effect, it is more noticeable in low-wing airplanes, simply because the wings are closer to the ground.

CHECKLIST

After studying this section, you should have a basic understanding of:

✓ **Three axes of flight** — What they are and how control surface deflection creates movement about them.

✓ **Center of gravity** — Where an airplane's entire weight is considered to be concentrated and where the three axes of flight intersect.

✓ **Forces acting on a climbing airplane** — Why a sustained climb requires excess thrust, and how the four forces are in equilibrium during a stabilized climb.

✓ **Forces acting on a descending airplane** — The significance of glide angle, glide speed, glide ratio, and the effect of weight on a glide.

✓ **Forces acting on a turning airplane** — What causes an airplane to turn, how forces are balanced in a stabilized turn, and how to compensate for adverse yaw.

✓ **Load factor** — What it is, and how it relates to angle of bank, stall speed, and maneuvering speed.

✓ **Stalls** — Their causes, how to recognize them, and recovery techniques.

✓ **Left-turning tendencies** — How the forces of torque, gyroscopic precession, asymmetrical thrust, and spiraling slipstream affect propeller-driven airplanes.

✓ **Ground effect** — How an airplane is affected when it is less than the height of its wingspan above the surface.

STABILITY

An airplane that is said to be inherently stable will require less effort to control.

In this section, you will learn about the various aspects of stability that are designed into an airplane. Although no airplane is completely stable, all airplanes must have desirable stability and handling characteristics. An inherently stable airplane is easy to fly, and it reduces pilot fatigue. This quality is essential throughout a wide range of flight conditions — during climbs, descents, turns, and at both high and low airspeeds. You will see that handling characteristics are directly related to stability. In fact, stability, maneuverability, and controllability are all interrelated design characteristics.

Stability is a characteristic of an airplane in flight that causes it to return to a condition of equilibrium, or steady flight, after it is disturbed. For example, if you are flying a stable airplane that is disrupted while in straight-and-level flight, it has a tendency to return to the same attitude. **Maneuverability** is the characteristic of an airplane that permits you to maneuver it easily and allows it to withstand the stress resulting from the maneuvers. An airplane's size, weight, flight control system, structural strength, and thrust determine its maneuverability. **Controllability** is the capability of an airplane to respond to your control inputs, especially with regard to attitude and flight path.

Large transport aircraft are normally designed to be very stable, since passenger comfort is a primary consideration. On the other hand, light training aircraft are designed to be more maneuverable, and somewhat less stable. The two major categories of stability are static and dynamic. Within each of these, there are subcategories called positive, neutral, and negative stability. In addition, since stability applies to all three axes of rotation, it may be classified as longitudinal, lateral, or directional.

STATIC STABILITY

Static stability is the initial tendency that an object displays after its equilibrium is disrupted. When you fly an airplane with **positive static stability**, it tends to return to its original attitude after displacement. A tendency to move farther away from the original attitude following a disturbance is **negative static stability**. If an airplane tends to remain in its displaced attitude, it has **neutral static stability**. [Figure 2-16]

Positive
Static Stability

Negative
Static Stability

Neutral
Static Stability

Figure 2-16. Positive static stability is the most desirable characteristic, because the airplane attempts to return to its original trimmed attitude. Almost any airplane you fly exhibits this characteristic. Both negative and neutral static stability are undesirable characteristics.

DYNAMIC STABILITY

Dynamic stability describes the time required for an airplane to respond to its static stability following a displacement from a condition of equilibrium. It is determined by its tendency to oscillate and damp out successive oscillations after the initial displacement. Although an airplane may be designed with positive static stability, it could have positive, negative, or neutral dynamic stability.

Assume the airplane you're flying is displaced from an established attitude. If its tendency is to return to the original attitude directly, or through a series of decreasing oscillations, it exhibits **positive dynamic stability**. If you find the oscillations increasing in magnitude as time progresses, **negative dynamic stability** is exhibited. **Neutral dynamic stability** is indicated if the airplane attempts to return to its original state of equilibrium, but the oscillations neither increase nor decrease in magnitude as time passes. [Figure 2-17]

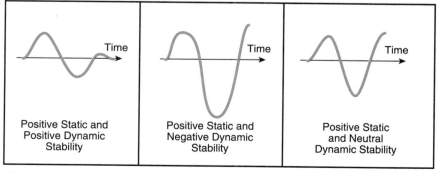

Positive Static and
Positive Dynamic
Stability

Positive Static and
Negative Dynamic
Stability

Positive Static
and Neutral
Dynamic Stability

Figure 2-17. The most desirable condition is a combination of positive static stability with positive dynamic stability. In this situation, you need less effort to return the airplane to its original attitude because it "wants" to return there.

LONGITUDINAL STABILITY

When you consider the overall stability of an airplane, remember that the airplane moves about three axes of rotation. **Longitudinal stability** involves the pitching motion or tendency of the airplane about its lateral axis. An airplane which is longitudinally stable will tend to return to its trimmed angle of attack after displacement. This is good, because an airplane with this characteristic tends to resist either excessively nose-high or nose-low pitch attitudes. If an airplane is longitudinally unstable, it has the tendency to climb or dive until a stall or a steep dive develops. As a result, a longitudinally unstable airplane is dangerous to fly.

BALANCE

To achieve longitudinal stability, most airplanes are designed so they're slightly nose heavy. This is accomplished during the engineering and development phase by placing the center of gravity slightly forward of the center of pressure.

The location of the center of gravity with respect to the center of lift determines the longitudinal stability of an airplane.

The **center of pressure** is a point along the wing chord line where lift is considered to be concentrated. For this reason, the center of pressure is often referred to as the **center of lift**. During flight, this point along the chord line changes position with different flight attitudes. It moves forward as angle of attack increases and aft as angle of attack decreases. As a result, pitching tendencies created by the position of the center of lift in relation to the CG vary. For example, with a high angle of attack and the center of lift in a forward position (closer to the CG) the nose-down pitching tendency is decreased. The position of the center of gravity in relation to the center of lift is a critical factor in longitudinal stability. If the CG is too far forward, the airplane is very nose heavy; if the CG is too far aft, the airplane may become tail heavy.

The horizontal stabilizer is set at a negative angle of attack. This offsets the nose-down pitching tendency caused by the CG being located forward of the center of lift.

When the airplane is properly loaded, the CG remains forward of the center of lift and the airplane is slightly nose heavy. The nose-heavy tendency is offset by the position of the horizontal stabilizer, which is set at a negative angle of attack. This produces a downward force, or negative lift on the tail, to counteract the nose heaviness. The downward force is called the **tail-down force**. It is the balancing force in most flight conditions. [Figure 2-18]

With the exception of T-tail airplanes, additional downward forces are exerted on horizontal tail surfaces by downwash from the propeller and the wings. The strength of the downward force is primarily related to the speed of the airplane, but the position of the stabilizer in relation to the wings and the propeller also affects it. T-tail designs are not subject to the same downwash effect, simply because the horizontal tail surface is above most, or all, of the downwash. [Figure 2-19]

Figure 2-18. To sustain level flight, the lift produced by the wings must support the weight of the airplane plus the tail-down force that results from the negative angle of attack on the stabilizer.

Power changes also affect longitudinal stability. If you reduce power during flight, a definite nose-down pitching tendency occurs due to the reduction of downwash from the wings and the propeller. This decreases the associated downward force on the tail, and reduces elevator effectiveness. Although this is a destabilizing factor, it is a desirable characteristic, because it tends to result in a nose-down attitude during power reductions. The nose-down attitude helps you maintain, or regain, airspeed.

On airplanes other than T-tails, a power reduction decreases the downwash on the horizontal stabilizer from the wings and propeller slipstream. This is what causes the nose to pitch down after a power reduction.

Figure 2-19. As the downwash from the propeller and the wings passes over the horizontal stabilizer, it "pushes" the tail section down. This tail-down force helps to balance the airplane about its lateral axis, and it influences the longitudinal stability of the airplane.

Increasing power has the opposite effect. It causes increased downwash on horizontal tail surfaces and tends to force the nose of the airplane to rise. The influence of power on longitudinal stability also depends on the overall design of the airplane. Since power provides thrust, the alignment of thrust in relation to the longitudinal axis, the CG, the wings, and the stabilizer are all factors. The **thrustline** is determined by where the propeller is mounted and by the general direction in which thrust acts.

In most light general aviation airplanes, the thrustline is parallel to the longitudinal axis and above the CG. This creates a slight pitching moment around the CG. If thrust is decreased, the pitching moment is reduced and the nose heaviness tends to decrease. An increase in thrust increases the pitching moment and increases nose heaviness. Notice that these pitching tendencies are exactly the reverse of the pitching tendencies resulting from an increase or decrease in downwash. This thrustline design arrangement minimizes the destabilizing effects of power changes and improves longitudinal stability. [Figure 2-20]

Although the tail-down force is excellent for longitudinal stability and balance, it is aerodynamically inefficient. The wings must support the negative lift created by the tail, and the negative angle of attack on the stabilizer increases drag. If an airplane design permitted two lifting surfaces, both the wings and the horizontal stabilizer, aerodynamic efficiency would be much greater.

CANARD

The canard design utilizes the concept of two lifting surfaces. A **canard** is a stabilizer that is located in front of the main wings. Canards are something like miniature forward wings. They were used in the pioneering

Figure 2-20. Airplanes with the thrustline parallel to the longitudinal axis and above the CG produce a pitching moment about the CG which partially counteracts downwash effects on the stabilizer. An increase in power, or thrust, increases downwash on the stabilizer and produces a nose-up pitching tendency. At the same time, the increased thrust also creates a nose-down pitching tendency because the thrustline is above the CG.

days of aviation, most notably on the Wright Flyer, and are now reappearing on several original designs. [Figure 2-21]

Since both the main wings and the canard produce positive lift, the design is aerodynamically efficient. A properly designed canard is stall/spin resistant. The canard stalls at a lower angle of attack than the main wings. In doing so, the canard's angle of attack immediately decreases after it stalls. This breaks the stall and effectively returns the canard to a normal lift-producing angle of attack before the main wings have a chance to stall. Ailerons remain effective throughout the stall because they are attached to the main wings. In spite of its advantages, the canard design has limitations in total lift capability. Critical design conditions also must be met to maintain adequate longitudinal stability throughout the flight envelope.

CENTER OF GRAVITY POSITION

The position of the center of gravity (CG) is another key factor in longitudinal stability. Distribution of weight in an airplane determines the position of the center of gravity. This weight includes the basic weight of the airplane itself, as well as the weight of fuel, passengers, and baggage. Since the weight of the airplane and the distribution of that weight normally are fixed, the CG location is largely determined by what you put into the airplane, and where you put it. For example, if you load heavy baggage into an aft baggage compartment, it might cause the CG to shift to an unfavorable position. This could be critical, so let's look briefly at what happens when the position of the CG shifts beyond acceptable limits.

As you might expect, for an airplane to be controllable during flight, the CG must be located within a reasonable distance forward or aft of an optimum position. All airplanes have forward and aft limits for the position of the CG. The distance between these limits is the **CG range**. [Figure 2-22]

Figure 2-21. With its location in front of the wings, the canard is actually a small, forward wing, as well as a stabilizer. It provides longitudinal stability about the lateral axis by lifting the nose of the airplane.

Figure 2-22. An airplane must be loaded so the effect of weight distribution does not adversely affect longitudinal balance. The CG will remain within the approved CG range if the distribution of weight is acceptable.

When the CG is within the approved CG range, the airplane not only is controllable, but its longitudinal stability also is satisfactory. If the CG is located near the forward or aft limit of the approved CG range, a slight loss of longitudinal stability may be noticeable. However, elevator (stabilator) effectiveness is still adequate to control the airplane during all approved maneuvers.

CG TOO FAR FORWARD

If you load your airplane so the CG is forward of the forward CG limit, it will be too nose heavy. Although this tends to make the airplane seem stable, adverse side effects include longer takeoff distance and higher stalling speeds. The condition gets progressively worse as the CG moves to an extreme forward position. Eventually, elevator (stabilator) effectiveness will be insufficient to lift the nose. [Figure 2-23]

CG TOO FAR AFT

An airplane loaded to its aft CG limit will be less stable at all speeds.

A CG located aft of the approved CG range is even more dangerous than a CG that is too far forward. With an aft CG, the airplane becomes tail heavy and very unstable in pitch, regardless of speed. [Figure 2-24]

An airplane becomes progressively more difficult to control as the CG moves aft. If the CG is beyond the aft limit, it will be difficult to lower the nose to recover from a stall or a spin.

CG limits are established during initial testing and airworthiness certification. One of the criteria for determining the CG range in light airplanes is a spin recovery capability. If the CG is within limits, a normal category airplane must demonstrate that it can be recovered from a one-turn spin; and a utility category airplane that is approved for spins must be recoverable from a fully developed spin. The aft CG limit is the most critical factor. As the CG moves aft, elevator effectiveness decreases. When the CG is at the aft limit, elevator effectiveness is adequate; but, when the CG is beyond the aft limit, the elevator may be ineffective for stall or spin recovery.

Figure 2-23. If the CG is well forward of the approved CG range, elevator effectiveness will be insufficient to exert the required tail-down force needed for a nose-high landing attitude. This may cause the nosewheel to strike the runway before the main gear.

Figure 2-24 If the CG is too far aft, you will not have enough elevator effectiveness to raise the tail and lower the nose of the airplane. As a result, you will be unable to recovcer form a stalled condition and a spin may develop.

As a pilot, there are certain actions you can take to prevent an aft CG position. You can make sure the heaviest passengers and baggage, or cargo, are loaded as far forward as practical. Lighter passengers and baggage normally should be loaded in aft seats or compartments. The main thing you must do is follow the airplane manufacturer's loading recommendations in the POH. If you do this, your airplane will be loaded so the CG is within the approved range where longitudinal stability is adequate and, at the same time, where you can control the airplane during all approved maneuvers. Two important points to remember are that a CG beyond acceptable limits adversely affects longitudinal stability, and the most hazardous condition is an extreme aft CG position. You will learn more about the effects of adverse loading in the section on weight and balance.

LATERAL STABILITY

Stability about an airplane's longitudinal axis, which extends nose to tail, is called **lateral stability**. If one wing is lower than the opposite wing, lateral stability helps return the wings to a wings-level attitude. This tendency to resist lateral, or roll, movement is aided by specific design characteristics of an airplane. Four of the most common design features that influence lateral stability are dihedral, keel effect, sweepback, and weight distribution. Two of these, keel effect and sweepback, also help provide directional stability about the vertical axis.

DIHEDRAL

The most common design for lateral stability is known as wing dihedral. **Dihedral** is the upward angle of the airplane's wings with respect to the horizontal. When you look at an airplane, dihedral makes the wings appear to form a spread-out V. Dihedral usually is just a few degrees.

If an airplane with dihedral enters an uncoordinated roll during gusty wind conditions, one wing will be elevated and the opposite wing will drop. This causes an immediate side slip downward toward the low wing. The side slip makes the low wing approach the air at a higher angle of attack than the high wing. The increased angle of attack on the low wing produces more lift for that wing and tends to lift it back to a level flight attitude. [Figure 2-25]

Wing Dihedral

Figure 2-25. Wing dihedral contributes to lateral stability. Low-wing airplanes commonly have more dihedral than high-wing airplanes. The center of gravity is well below the wing in a high-wing airplane. Because this CG position has a stabilizing effect, very little dihedral is necessary.

KEEL EFFECT

Lateral stability is also provided by keel effect. During flight, the vertical fin and side area of the fuselage react to the airflow very much like the keel of a ship. This **keel effect** is the steadying influence exerted by the side area of the fuselage and vertical stabilizer. When the airplane rolls to one side, a combination of the pressure of the airflow against the keel surface, along with the airplane's weight, tends to roll the airplane back to a wings-level attitude. [Figure 2-26]

SWEEPBACK

In many airplanes, the leading edges of the wings do not form right angles with the longitudinal axis. Instead, the wings taper backward from the root of the wing to the wingtips. This is called **sweepback**. In higher performance airplanes with pronounced sweepback, the design helps maintain the center of lift aft of the CG. In light training airplanes, sweepback helps improve lateral stability. [Figure 2-27]

Sweepback also may aid slightly in directional stability. If an airplane rotates about its vertical axis or yaws to the left, the right wing has less sweep and a slight increase in drag. The left wing has more sweep and less drag. This tends to force the airplane back into alignment with the relative wind.

WEIGHT DISTRIBUTION

You have no control of the design features that help maintain lateral stability, but you can control the distribution of weight and improve lateral stability. For example, most training airplanes have two fuel tanks, one inside each wing. Before you take off on a long flight, you normally fill both tanks. If you use fuel from only one tank, you will soon notice that

Figure 2-26. Laterally stable airplanes are designed so that a larger portion of the keel area is above and behind the center of gravity. Since more of the keel area is aft of the CG, the keel area also acts as a weather vane about the vertical axis. This helps maintain vertical (directional) stability.

Figure 2-27. If an airplane with sweepback inadvertently rolls about its longitudinal axis and a side slip occurs, the leading edge of the lower wing meets the relative wind more nearly perpendicular than the higher wing. This increases lift and drag on the lower wing and decreases them on the higher wing, which tends to restore the wings to a level position.

Figure 2-28. An airplane must have more surface area behind the CG than it has in front of it. The same is true for a weather vane; more surface aft of the pivot point is a basic design feature. This arrangement helps keep the airplane aligned with the relative wind, just as the weather vane points into the wind.

the airplane wants to roll toward the wing with the full tank. The distribution of weight is uneven and lateral stability is affected. In this case, you can easily correct the imbalance in weight by using an equal amount of fuel from the full tank.

DIRECTIONAL STABILITY

Stability about the vertical axis is called **directional stability**. Essentially, an airplane in flight is much like a weather vane. You can compare the pivot point on the weather vane to the center of gravity pivot point of the airplane. The nose of the airplane corresponds to the weather vane's arrowhead, and the vertical fin on the airplane acts like the tail of the weather vane. [Figure 2-28]

EFFECTS OF LATERAL AND DIRECTIONAL STABILITY

Although airplanes are designed with stabilizing characteristics which lighten your workload while you are flying, there are normally some undesirable side effects. Two of the most common ones are Dutch roll and spiral instability.

Dutch roll is a combination of rolling/yawing oscillations caused either by your control input or by wind gusts. In a typical case, when equilibrium is disturbed, the rolling reaction precedes the yaw, and the roll motion is more noticeable than the yaw motion.

When the airplane rolls back toward level flight in response to the dihedral effect, it continues to roll too far and side slips the other way. Each oscillation overshoots the wings-level position because of the strong dihedral effect. Dutch roll actually is the back-and-forth, rolling/yawing motion. If the Dutch roll tendency is not effectively dampened, it is considered objectionable.

The alternative to an airplane that exhibits Dutch roll tendencies is a design that has better directional stability than lateral stability. If directional stability is increased and lateral stability is decreased, the Dutch roll motion is adequately suppressed. However, this design arrangement tends to cause spiral instability.

Spiral instability is associated with airplanes that have strong directional stability in comparison with lateral stability. When an airplane with spiral instability is disturbed from a condition of equilibrium, a side slip is introduced. In this case, the strong directional stability tends to yaw the airplane back into alignment with the relative wind. At the same time, the comparatively weak dihedral effect lags in restoring lateral stability. Due to the yaw back into the relative wind, the outside wing travels faster than the inside wing and, as a result, more lift is generated by the outside wing. The yaw forces the nose of the airplane down as it swings into alignment with the relative wind. The net result is an overbanking and nose-down tendency which generally is considered less objectionable than Dutch roll.

As you can see, even a well-designed airplane may have some undesirable characteristics. Generally, designers attempt to minimize the Dutch roll tendency, since it is less tolerable than spiral instability. Because of this, many airplanes have some degree of spiral instability which generally is considered acceptable.

The overall stability characteristics of an airplane are closely related to its tendency to enter a spin after stalling. A stable airplane tends to resist spin entry, while an unstable airplane is less spin resistant.

STALL AND SPIN AWARENESS

No discussion of the aerodynamics of flight would be complete without considering spins. Your awareness of what causes spins, and how you can avoid them, is very important. You also need to know how to recover from a spin, if necessary. Since private pilot applicants are not required to demonstrate flight proficiency in intentional spins, this discussion is primarily concerned with fundamental concepts and relationships associated with unintentional spins.

For many years, stall and spin related accidents have accounted for approximately one-quarter of all fatal general aviation accidents. National Transportation Safety Board (NTSB) statistics indicate that most stall/spin accidents result from incidents where a pilot is momentarily distracted from the primary task of flying the aircraft. Because of these factors, regulations stress stall and spin awareness training which is intended to emphasize recognition of situations that could lead to an unintentional stall and/or spin. This is accomplished by use of instructional exercises that include realistic distractions during flight at slow airspeeds. The practice of intentional stalls and recovery techniques is also included in this training. However, only flight instructor candidates are required to demonstrate proficiency in actual spin entry, spins, and spin recovery techniques as a requirement for certification.

Stall and spin awareness is emphasized during flight training. The use of realistic distractions during flight at slow airspeeds is part of this required training.

SPINS

The spin is the most complex of all flight maneuvers. There are actually hundreds of factors that contribute to the spinning of an airplane. In a light, training airplane a **spin** may be defined as an aggravated stall which results in autorotation. During the spin, the airplane descends in a helical, or corkscrew, path while the angle of attack is greater than the critical angle of attack.

PRIMARY CAUSES

A stall must occur before a spin can develop. However, a stall is essentially a coordinated maneuver where both wings are equally or almost equally stalled. In contrast, a spin is an uncoordinated maneuver with the wings unequally stalled. In this case, the wing that is more completely stalled will often drop before the other, and the nose of the aircraft will yaw in the direction of the low wing.

To enter a spin, an airplane must first be stalled. In a spin, both wings are in a stalled condition.

Typically, the cause of an inadvertent spin is exceeding the critical angle of attack while performing an uncoordinated maneuver. The lack of coordination is normally caused by either too much or not enough rudder control for the amount of aileron being used. The result is a cross-controlled condition. If you do not initiate the stall recovery promptly, the airplane is more likely to enter a full stall that may develop into a spin. The spin that occurs from cross controlling usually results in rotation in the direction of the rudder being applied, regardless of which wing is raised. In a skidding turn, where both aileron and rudder are applied in the same direction, rotation will be in that direction. However, in a slipping turn, where opposite aileron is held against the rudder, the resultant spin will usually occur in the direction opposite the aileron that is being applied.

When an airplane is in a stalled or nearly stalled condition, uncoordinated use of the flight controls (aileron and rudder) can easily cause a spin. In most cases, the spin rotation will be in the direction of rudder deflection.

Coordinated use of the flight controls is important, especially during flight at slow airspeeds. Although most pilots are able to maintain coordination of the flight controls during routine maneuvers, this ability often deteriorates when distractions occur and their attention is divided between important tasks. Distractions that have caused problems include preoccupation with situations inside or outside the cockpit, maneuvering to avoid other aircraft, and maneuvering to clear obstacles during takeoffs, climbs, approaches, or landings. These kinds of distractions are another causal factor in stall/spin accidents. Because of this, you will be required to learn how to recognize and cope with these distractions by practicing "flight at slow airspeeds with realistic distractions" during flight lessons under the guidance of your instructor.

PHASES OF A SPIN

Many different terms may be used to describe a spin. The **incipient spin** is that portion of a spin from the time the airplane stalls and rotation starts until the spin is fully developed. A **fully developed** spin means the angular rotation rates, airspeed, and vertical speed are stabilized from turn to turn and the flight path is close to vertical. In light, training airplanes, a complete spin maneuver consists of three phases — incipient, developed, and recovery. [Figure 2-29]

Normally, the recovery from an incipient spin requires less time (and altitude) than the recovery from a fully developed spin. Higher altitudes tend to prolong a recovery. The less dense air is not as responsive to anti-spin controls as the heavier air at lower altitudes.

While some characteristics of a spin are predictable, every airplane spins differently. In addition, the same airplane's spin behavior changes with variations in configuration, loading, and several other factors.

WEIGHT AND BALANCE

Airplanes with an aft CG tend to be less stall/spin resistant than airplanes with a forward CG.

Even minor weight and balance changes can affect an aircraft's spin characteristics. Heavier weights generally result in slow spin rates initially; but, as the spin progresses, heavier weights tend to cause an increasing spin rate and longer recovery time. Distribution of weight is even more significant. Forward center of gravity positions usually inhibit the high angles of attack necessary for a stall. Thus, an airplane with a forward CG tends to be more stall and spin resistant than an aircraft with an aft CG. In addition, spins with aft CG positions are flatter than ordinary spins. A **flat spin** is characterized by a near level pitch and roll attitude with the spin axis near the CG of the airplane. Recovery from a flat spin may be extremely difficult or even impossible.

In a training airplane, the addition of a back seat passenger or a single suitcase to an aft baggage compartment can affect the CG enough to change the characteristics of a spin. Instead of an ordinary spin, a flat spin could easily occur. You also should be aware of other unfavorable loading possibilities. A concentration of weight, or unbalanced weight distribution, a long way from the CG is undesirable. This type of loading may occur with tip tanks or outboard wing tanks. If the fuel in these tanks becomes unbalanced, an asymmetrical condition exists. The worst asymmetric condition is full fuel in the wing on the outside of the spin and no fuel in the tanks

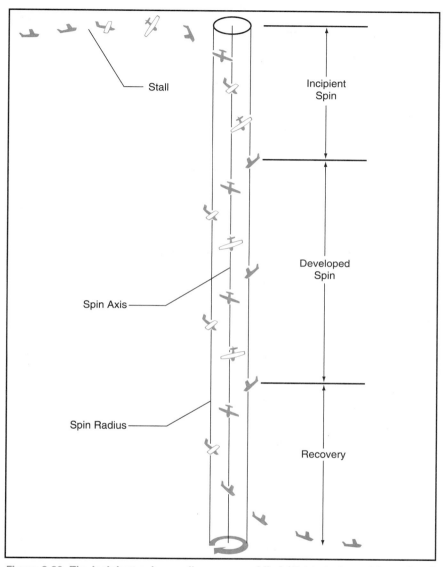

Figure 2-29. The incipient spin usually occurs rapidly in light airplanes (about 4 to 6 seconds) and consists of approximately the first two turns. At about the half-turn point, the airplane is pointed almost straight down but the angle of attack is usually above that of the stall because of the inclined flight path. As the one-turn point approaches, the nose may come back up and the angle of attack continues to increase. As the airplane continues to rotate into the second turn, the flight path becomes more nearly vertical, and the pitching, rolling, and yawing motions become more repeatable. This is the beginning of the fully developed spin. The last phase, recovery, occurs when anti-spin forces overcome pro-spin forces. During recovery, the angle of attack on both wings decreases below the critical angle and the rotation rate slows. This phase can range from one quarter of a turn to several turns.

on the inside of the turn. Once the spin is developed, the momentum (inertial force) makes recovery unlikely under these conditions.

From this discussion, it is apparent that observing weight and balance limitations is essential. In fact, all operating limitations are imposed for safety purposes. This is particularly important for limits concerned with spins.

There is no guarantee that a normal category airplane will recover from a fully developed spin.

Single-engine, normal category airplanes are prohibited from intentional spins. This is indicated by a placard with words such as "No acrobatic maneuvers, including spins, approved." However, during aircraft certification tests, normal category airplanes must demonstrate recovery from a one-turn spin or a three-second spin, whichever takes longer. The recovery must take place within one additional turn with normal control inputs. Since airplanes in the normal category have not been tested for more than one-turn/three second spins, their performance characteristics beyond these limits are unknown. The one-turn margin of safety only provides a check of the airplane's controllability in a delayed or aggravated stall which is early in the incipient phase of a spin. This does not provide any assurance that recovery is possible from a fully developed spin.

Acrobatic category airplanes must fully recover from fully developed spins within one and one-half additional turns. Certification in this category also requires six turns or three seconds, whichever takes longer, before the recovery controls are applied.

Utility category airplanes may be tested under the one-turn (normal) criteria or they may satisfy the six-turn (acrobatic) spin requirements. However, spins in utility category airplanes may be approved only with specific loading, such as at a reduced weight and with a forward CG position. It is extremely important for you to understand all of the operating limitations for your airplane. Applicable limitations are placarded and/or included in the POH.

SPIN RECOVERY

It should be clear that you, as an applicant for a private pilot certificate, are not required to demonstrate flight proficiency in spin entries or spin recovery techniques. Even though your flight instructor may demonstrate a spin at some point during your training, you should never intentionally enter a spin. As already mentioned, the emphasis in stall/spin awareness training for private pilots is awareness of conditions that could lead to an unintentional stall or spin. You also need to have a basic understanding of how to recover from a spin.

Spin recovery techniques vary for different aircraft; therefore, you must follow the recovery procedures outlined in the POH for your airplane. The following is a general recovery procedure, but it should not be applied arbitrarily without regard for the manufacturer's recommendations.

Since an airplane must be in a stalled condition before it will spin, the first thing you should do is try to recover from the stall before the spin develops. If your reaction is too slow and a spin develops, move the throttle to idle, neutralize the ailerons, and raise the flaps. Next, apply full rudder deflection opposite to the direction of the turn. When the rotation rate slows, briskly position the elevator forward to approximately the neutral position to decrease the angle of attack. As the rotation stops, neutralize the rudder and smoothly apply back pressure to recover from the steep nose-down pitch attitude. During recovery from the dive, make sure you avoid excessive airspeed and high G-forces. This could cause an accelerated stall, or even result in structural failure.

CHECKLIST

After studying this section, you should have a basic understanding of:

✓ **Stability** — What it is and how it causes the airplane to return to a condition of equilibrium after it is disturbed.

✓ **Static stability** — What it is, and the difference between positive, negative, and neutral static stability.

✓ **Dynamic stability** — What it is, and the difference between positive, negative, and neutral dynamic stability.

✓ **Longitudinal stability** — How a longitudinally stable airplane tends to return to its trimmed angle of attack after displacement.

✓ **Balance** — How the location of the center of gravity with respect to the center of lift affects longitudinal stability.

✓ **Tail loads** — How tail-down forces caused by the angle of attack of the horizontal stabilizer, downwash, and the location of the thrust-line affect longitudinal stability.

✓ **Center of gravity position** — How a CG location beyond approved limits can alter an airplane's controllability and adversely affect its longitudinal stability.

✓ **Lateral stability** — How dihedral, keel effect, sweepback, and weight distribution affect an airplane's lateral stability about its longitudinal axis.

✓ **Directional stability** — How Dutch roll and spiral instability affect the aircraft.

✓ **Stall and Spin Awareness** — Why training is required, what a spin is, what causes a spin, what the phases of a spin are, and how to recover from a spin.

CLIMBS AND DESCENTS

For straight-and-level flight, the objective was to maintain altitude. In this section, you will learn how to change altitude by precisely controlling airplane pitch and power. When practicing climbs, your objectives are to become proficient in establishing the proper climb attitude, to apply the appropriate control pressures, and to trim the airplane correctly to maintain the climb attitude. During practice climbs, it is important to learn the relationships between attitude and power, as well as between climb speed and climb performance.

CLIMBS

A climb is established by adjusting both pitch and power.

Enter a climb by adding power smoothly to establish the recommended climb power setting and increasing back pressure on the control wheel. The back pressure raises the nose of the airplane smoothly until the desired climb attitude is established. [Figure 2-30]

As the climb attitude is established, the airspeed gradually slows and stabilizes on or near the desired climb speed. The combination of the climb attitude and the climb power setting determines the airplane's performance.

The airspeed indicator provides an indirect indication of pitch attitude. If you see that the airspeed is lower than you desire, use the pitch attitude references to lower the airplane's nose position. Conversely, if the airspeed is higher than you desire, you must raise the airplane's nose position. Then, retrim slightly when the new attitude produces the desired climb speed. Use the position of the wingtips and the angle which they make with the horizon to establish the proper climb attitude, just as you used them to establish level flight attitudes. [Figure 2-31]

Figure 2-30. The climb attitude represented by the nose position and the attitude indicator should resemble these.

Figure 2-31. The left side shows the left wingtip as it appears when the airplane is flying level for both high- and low-wing airplanes. The right side shows the same wingtip when the airplane is in a climb attitude.

LEFT-TURNING TENDENCY DURING THE CLIMB

As the airplane climbs, it tends to turn to the left, and the ball of the turn coordinator tends to move off center to the right. Use right rudder pressure to maintain coordination and return the ball to the center of the inclinometer. A combination of forces such as P-factor, torque, and spiraling slipstream causes this left-turning tendency. The effects are most pronounced at high power settings and low airspeeds, such as those used during climbs.

Manufacturers design airplanes to compensate for the left-turning tendency during cruising flight. However, at other power settings or speeds, you must apply rudder pressure to counteract this tendency. Rudder trim tabs are used to counteract the left-turning tendency on more powerful airplanes.

Right rudder pressure is required during a climb.

MAINTAINING THE CLIMB

Refer to the airspeed indicator, altimeter, and the ball of the turn coordinator to monitor the climb. If changes are necessary, make small adjustments after looking at the nose and wingtip positions or the attitude indicator. Then, allow the airplane to stabilize in the new attitude and remove control pressures by trimming.

CLIMB SPEEDS

Early in your flight training, your instructor will introduce you to several specific climb speeds. Each of these speeds has a difference effect on the airplane's climb performance and, therefore, is used at different times.

The **best rate-of-climb** speed is an important performance speed. It provides the most gain in altitude in the least amount of time. The **best angle-of-climb** speed results in a steeper climb. It is used to clear obstacles in the takeoff path, such as trees or powerlines at the end of the runway. It is generally the slowest of the specified climb speeds. [Figure 2-32]

Use **cruise climb speed** to achieve a higher groundspeed while climbing to cruising altitude during cross-country flight. This speed usually is higher than the other climb speeds and provides better engine cooling. It also improves forward visibility over the nose of the airplane. You can determine the cruise climb speed, as well as the best rate-of-climb and angle-of-climb speeds, by referring to the pilot's operating handbook.

LEVELOFF FROM A CLIMB

Lead your leveloff by 10% of the established rate of climb.

To return to straight-and-level flight from a climb, begin the transition before you reach the desired altitude. The amount of lead for the leveloff depends on the rate of climb. Generally, a 10% lead is sufficient. For example, if the rate of climb is 500 f.p.m., you should begin to level off approximately 50 feet (10% of 500) below the desired altitude. Maintain climb power until you accelerate to cruise speed, then reduce power to the cruise setting. Finally, trim control pressures to hold the aircraft in a level flight attitude.

DESCENTS

You will practice descents to learn the techniques used for losing altitude without gaining excessive airspeed, controlling the rate of descent with

Figure 2-32. The best rate-of-climb airspeed allows you to gain altitude faster than any other speed. The best angle-of-climb speed results in the greatest altitude gain in the shortest distance.

power and attitude, and converting altitude into as much distance as possible without the use of power. Initially, you will practice descents at the airspeed used for approaches to landings. After you learn this type of descent, you will practice the cruise descent. Since a cruise descent is flown at cruise airspeed, you will maintain a higher groundspeed.

ESTABLISHING THE DESCENT AT APPROACH SPEEDS

Usually you apply carburetor heat as the first step in establishing a descent. Many airplane manufacturers recommend using carburetor heat when you fly for long periods at low power settings. Next, reduce power to a predetermined setting or to idle. As you reduce power, apply back pressure gradually to the control wheel until the airplane slows to the desired descent speed. When you reach the descent airspeed, lower the nose attitude to the descent attitude that holds this airspeed. After you have established the proper descent attitude, trim the airplane. In many airplanes, the descent attitude is nearly the same as that used for straight-and-level cruising flight. [Figure 2-33]

Descents usually require an adjustment to both pitch and power.

Because the airflow over the controls is less rapid than at cruise airspeed and there is little propeller slipstream over the empennage, the controls tend to feel soft or mushy and less positive in response. You can learn to use this "feel" to help determine when the airplane is flying slowly. The feel you will develop in practicing descents is important to approach and landing practice.

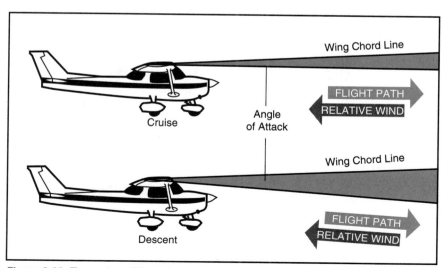

Figure 2-33. **To produce lift at slower airspeeds, the wing must be at a higher angle of attack. To attain the higher angle of attack during a descent, maintain a near-level attitude.**

MAINTAINING THE DESCENT

Use the airspeed indicator, altimeter, heading indicator, turn coordinator, and vertical speed indicator during the descent, as in other maneuvers. After you have established the desired descent attitude and trimmed the airplane properly, you should refer to these instruments to confirm that the airspeed, heading, and rate of descent are correct. If adjustment is required, make an attitude adjustment (either visual or instrument), permit the attitude to stabilize, and then refer to the appropriate instruments to confirm that you are descending as desired.

CONTROLLING THE RATE OF DESCENT

In a constant airspeed descent, use power to control the rate of descent.

If you wish to maintain a constant airspeed descent, control the rate of descent with power. You will need to hold the pitch attitude slightly higher as you add power. On the other hand, if you have reduced power, you must lower the pitch attitude slightly to maintain a given airspeed. When power is added, propeller slipstream over the elevator (or stabilator) increases; therefore, a small trim adjustment is necessary. You can monitor the rate of descent by referring to the vertical speed indicator when your descent is well established and the instrument has settled to an accurate indication.

USE OF FLAPS

You can increase the angle of descent by using flaps. You may also need to make moderate trim adjustments. Make descents with flaps retracted when you need maximum range or distance. When you wish rapid dissipation of altitude, use a full-flap, power-off glide. [Figure 2-34]

Figure 2-34. At a constant power setting, as flap deflection increases, the angle of descent also increases.

LEVELOFF FROM THE DESCENT

To return to straight-and-level flight, begin the transition before you reach the desired altitude. As with a climb, begin the leveloff at an altitude equal to 10% of the rate of descent by adjusting the nose position to level flight and simultaneously adding power to the cruise setting. Refer to wing and nose positions in order to maintain the proper attitude throughout the transition from descent to straight-and-level flight. Since adding power and increasing airspeed produce a moderate tendency to pitch upward, adjust the trim to relieve forward control pressures as you attain straight-and-level flight.

Lead your descent leveloff by 10% of the rate of descent.

CHECKLIST _____

After studying this section, you should have a basic understanding of:

✓ **Climbs** — How to establish, maintain, and level off from a climb.

✓ **Climb speed** — The meaning of best rate-of-climb, best angle-of-climb, and cruise climb speeds.

✓ **Descents** — How to establish, maintain, and level off from a descent.

✓ **Constant airspeed descents** — How to control the rate of descent when airspeed must be held constant.

✓ **Flaps** — Why flaps are beneficial during a descent.

TURNS

Turns generally are described by the number of degrees of bank necessary to produce them. A medium bank turn is one in which the airplane tends to hold a constant bank angle without control force on the ailerons. For training airplanes, 20° to 40° is a typical medium bank range, with 30° being most common.

ENTERING THE TURN

The ailerons control the roll rate, as well as the angle of bank.

To roll into a bank, you apply aileron control pressure in the direction of the desired turn. For example, to execute a left turn, you turn the control wheel left to place the left aileron up and the right aileron down. How fast the airplane rolls depends on how much aileron control pressure you apply. How far the airplane rolls (the steepness of the bank) depends on how long you deflect the ailerons, since the airplane continues to roll as long as the ailerons are deflected. When the airplane reaches the desired angle of bank, neutralize the ailerons. [Figure 2-35]

ELEVATOR CONTROL PRESSURES

During a turn, increased elevator back pressure is required to increase total lift.

When performing a turn, you must increase the pitch attitude slightly to increase the total lift. Therefore, the nose position you use to maintain the desired altitude is slightly higher in a turn than in level flight. The pitch attitude adjustment required for a medium bank turn is slight. However, steeper banks require a higher pitch attitude. [Figure 2-36]

COORDINATION OF CONTROLS

Apply sufficient rudder pressure to keep the ball of the inclinometer centered.

When you roll into a turn, the aileron on the inside of the turn is raised, and the aileron on the outside of the turn is lowered. As discussed in an earlier section, the lowered aileron on the outside increases the angle of

Figure 2-35. Turning the control wheel to the left causes the right wing to produce more lift and the left wing less. This causes the airplane to roll to the left.

Figure 2-36. The proper reference for a medium bank turn is shown on the left. Notice how much higher the nose is for the steep bank turn shown on the right.

attack and produces more lift for that wing. Since induced drag is a by-product of lift, the outside wing also produces more drag than the inside wing. This causes a yawing tendency toward the outside of the turn, called adverse yaw. You use rudder pressure to counteract this tendency. [Figure 2-37]

You will hear the term "coordination" used when discussing turning techniques. This means you apply rudder pressure and aileron pressure simultaneously to properly counteract adverse yaw. The ball of the turn coordinator assists you in determining how much pressure is necessary. For a coordinated turn, the ball should remain in the center of the inclinometer. If the ball is not in the center, you should apply enough rudder pressure to center it. [Figure 2-38]

Figure 2-37. When the airplane is rolling to the left, adverse yaw attempts to move the nose to the right. Apply sufficient left rudder pressure to counteract this force.

Figure 2-38. In this example, the ball is located left of center. Therefore, apply sufficient left rudder pressure to center the ball.

Figure 2-39. Both of these banks are approximately 15°. The nose position appears different during left and right turns because you sit to the left side of the centerline of the airplane.

While the turn is in progress, you should occasionally check the altimeter, vertical speed indicator, and airspeed indicator to determine if corrections are necessary. If corrections are required, you should make necessary adjustments in steps. For example, if the nose is low, the airspeed high, and the altitude decreasing, increase pitch attitude to stop the descent and airspeed increase. When the airspeed has stopped increasing and the altitude has stabilized, make a slight nose-up pitch attitude adjustment to return to the desired altitude.

VISUAL REFERENCES IN THE TURN

When you make turns by visual reference, first apply coordinated aileron and rudder pressures in the direction you wish to turn. Notice that the nose of the airplane appears to move in an arc with respect to the horizon. You can determine when you have reached the proper bank angle by observing the angle of the cowling and instrument panel with respect to the horizon. [Figure 2-39]

ROLLING OUT OF THE TURN

Lead your roll-out by an amount equal to one-half your bank angle. For example, in a 20° bank turn, begin your roll-out approximately 10° before you reach the desired heading by applying coordinated aileron and rudder pressure. At the same time, begin releasing the back pressure on the control wheel so aileron, rudder, and elevator pressures are neutralized when the airplane reaches the wings-level position.

TURNS BY INSTRUMENT REFERENCE

For turns by instrument reference, simply substitute the attitude indicator for the natural horizon.

After practicing turns by visual reference, you will learn to perform turns using instrument reference. Control pressures are applied in the same manner as when you use visual references, and the indications of the instruments are interpreted in the same way.

PERFORMING THE TURN

To establish a 15° turn, bank the airplane and apply coordinated rudder pressure until the 15° position is aligned with the bank index at the top of the attitude indicator. Then, neutralize aileron and rudder pressures and adjust the pitch attitude slightly upward, using additional back pressure on the control wheel. [Figure 2-40]

Make corrections in the same manner as when you are using visual references. However, adjust the attitude by using the attitude indicator and scan the other instruments to verify that the turn is progressing as you desire. One advantage of performing turns by instrument reference is that the nose position on the attitude indicator looks the same during left and right turns. Recover from the turn by applying coordinated aileron and rudder pressure, releasing the back pressure, and reestablishing straight-and-level flight by reference to the attitude indicator.

STANDARD-RATE TURNS

The angle of bank frequently used in making turns by instrument reference is one that results in a standard-rate turn. A **standard-rate turn**

A standard-rate turn is a turn of 3° per second.

Figure 2-40. This is how your instruments appear once you are established in a level 15° banked turn to the left. Notice how the nose of the miniature airplane is elevated slightly above the horizon line.

produces a turn rate of three degrees per second. These turns are made by referring to the turn coordinator. [Figure 2-41]

ANGLE OF BANK REQUIRED FOR STANDARD-RATE TURN

The angle of bank necessary to produce the standard-rate turn is strictly a function of the true airspeed — the greater the airspeed, the greater the angle of bank needed to maintain a standard-rate turn. Training airplanes typically maintain cruise true airspeeds of approximately 100 to 110 knots. The angle of bank required for a standard-rate turn is approximately 15° to 17° at these speeds. The following list shows some typical speeds and the required bank angles for standard-rate turns:

True Airspeed	Approximate Bank Angle
100 knots	15°
110 knots	17°
120 knots	18°
130 knots	20°

TIMED TURNS

By using a standard rate, you can determine the amount of time required to make a turn before you initiate it. First, determine the number of degrees to be turned and divide by three. Then, note the time according to the second hand on the airplane clock and roll into the turn using the proper angle of bank for a standard-rate turn. Roll out to level flight when the predetermined amount of time has elapsed. [Figure 2-42]

Figure 2-41. When the wing of the miniature airplane is aligned with the index, you will be turning at a rate of 3° per second and will complete a standard-rate turn of 360° in two minutes. If the wing of the miniature airplane is midway between the level flight position and the standard-rate position, you are performing a one-half standard-rate turn, or a turn of 360° in four minutes.

Figure 2-42. To determine the time it will take to make a 180° turn, divide 180° by 3. It takes 60 seconds to perform this turn.

COMBINATIONS OF FUNDAMENTAL MANEUVERS

As discussed earlier, straight-and-level flight, climbs, descents, and turns are the four fundamental flight maneuvers upon which you base all others. If you develop a thorough understanding of these basic elements and maintain effective and precise control of the airplane when you are performing each maneuver, you will develop a high level of proficiency as you continue your flight training.

As soon as you are proficient in climbs, descents, and turns, you will be introduced to climbing and descending turns to predetermined headings and altitudes. You will practice these combination maneuvers using both visual and instrument references.

CLIMBING TURNS

The objective of practicing climbing turns is to smoothly combine the techniques of climbs with those of turns. To perform a climbing turn, establish the climb as previously discussed. When climb power and attitude are set, roll to the desired bank angle. This is a two-step procedure initially; however, as you gain experience and proficiency, you will enter the maneuver by simultaneously establishing the climb attitude and the proper bank.

You should use the same airspeed for straight climbs and climbing turns. However, your rate of climb will be less for climbing turns than straight climbs. Generally, you perform climbing turns using shallow bank angles, because steep bank angles divert more of the vertical component of lift, which causes a reduction in rate of climb.

During maneuvers, you will find that you rarely reach the desired heading and altitude at the same time. If you reach the desired heading first, level the wings and maintain the climb until you reach the desired altitude. On the other hand, if you reach the altitude first, lower the nose to a level flight attitude and continue the turn to the desired heading. If you reach both the desired heading and altitude at the same time, you can perform these procedures simultaneously.

DESCENDING TURNS

Descending turns to preselected headings and altitudes combine the procedures for straight descents with those used in turns. Enter the decent using either visual or instrument references in the manner previously outlined for the straight descent. When you have established the descent attitude, roll to the desired angle of bank. As with climbing turns, initially perform the procedure in two steps. As you gain proficiency, you will learn to establish the descent attitude and bank simultaneously. As in any maneuver, you should trim off control pressures as required to maintain the selected attitude.

Use power to control the rate of descent. Make the initial power setting for the desired rate of descent and allow the pitch attitude and the rate of descent to stabilize. If you desire a higher rate of descent, reduce power. In contrast, you must add power if you desire a lower rate of descent.

Maintain the same airspeed in descending turns as in straight descents. However, your rate of descent will be higher in a descending turn than in a straight descent with a comparable power setting, because the vertical lift component is less when the airplane banks. You can compensate for this with a slight addition of power.

CHECKLIST _____

After studying this section, you should have a basic understanding of:

✓   **Turn entry and roll-out** — How to use the ailerons, elevator, and rudder in a coordinated manner when entering and exiting turns.

✓   **Standard-rate turn** — What it is and how to determine when the airplane is making a standard-rate turn.

✓   **Climbing and descending turns** — How to combine turns, climbs, and descents smoothly to enter and level off from climbing and descending turns.

MANEUVERING DURING SLOW FLIGHT

Slow flight may be broadly defined as flight at an airspeed below the normal cruise speed. However, during training you will normally practice this maneuver at airspeeds well below the normal cruise speed. This helps you develop a feel for the controls and an understanding of how load factor, pitch attitude, airspeed, and altitude control relate to each other under these conditions. Knowledge of these relationships will aid you in maintaining proper airspeeds and pitch attitudes for changing flight conditions. It also helps you assess the reduction of control effectiveness during flight at slower-than-normal speeds and determine the power required for flight at different airspeeds.

While maneuvering during slow flight, you should fly the airplane slightly above the stall speed. This speed must be sufficiently slow so any significant reduction in speed or power, or increase in load factor, results in stall indications.

The procedures for entering the maneuver from cruise flight help develop smoothness and coordination of elevator (or stabilator), rudder, and power controls. The initial objective is to perform a smooth transition from cruise flight to slow airspeeds while maintaining altitude. Enter at an altitude that will allow you complete the maneuver no lower than 1,500 feet AGL.

Before you begin any maneuver which is not necessary for normal flight, you should execute a clearing turn. A **clearing turn** usually consists of at least a 180° change in direction. A typical method of executing this maneuver is to make two 90° turns in opposite directions. The clearing turn allows you to scan the local area for traffic which may be hidden by blind spots on your airplane.

Use a clearing turn to scan for traffic in your area.

ENTRY PROCEDURES

To enter the maneuver, first execute a clearing turn. Once the area is clear of traffic, apply carburetor heat if it is normally used when power is reduced, then reduce power several hundred r.p.m. (or several inches of manifold pressure) below the power setting required to maintain altitude. After reducing power, apply any necessary back pressure to the control wheel to maintain altitude as the airspeed decreases. If you apply back pressure too fast, the airplane climbs; if you apply it too slowly, the airplane descends. During this transition, use the trim to remove excess control wheel pressure.

When the airplane nears the desired pitch attitude and airspeed, increase power to a setting which will maintain altitude. Then make small power

Figure 2-43. These are the approximate visual and instrument pitch attitudes required in a wings-level position while maneuvering during slow flight.

adjustments to maintain a constant altitude and retrim the airplane, as necessary, to remove control wheel pressures. [Figure 2-43]

Use right rudder pressure to compensate for torque and P-factor.

As the airplane slows, you will also notice that the rudder pressure requirements change. Right rudder pressure becomes necessary for proper coordination and heading control. The high angle of attack, high torque, and pronounced P-factor create left-turning tendencies. If you do not apply right rudder, these tendencies will cause the airplane to turn to the left. You should refer to the ball of the turn coordinator to help determine the amount of rudder required.

While you are maneuvering during slow flight, you will get a sensation of insufficient control response. The controls feel "mushy," and it is necessary to use greater control movements for corrections than are normally required. The response of the airplane to control movements is also slow.

ALTITUDE AND AIRSPEED CONTROL

If you attempt to climb by applying back pressure during flight at slow airspeeds, you will not be successful. Instead, the airspeed will decrease, stall indications will occur, and the altitude will decrease.

If you lose altitude by lowering the nose, the airspeed will increase beyond acceptable limits. The correct procedure for regaining lost altitude is to apply power. When you do this, it will also be necessary to make a small increase in pitch attitude to maintain the desired airspeed. To lose altitude, reduce power and, at the same time, reduce pitch attitude slightly.

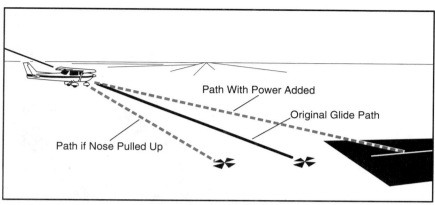

Figure 2-44. During final approach, if you apply control wheel back pressure in an attempt to extend the glide, the airspeed decreases and an even steeper glide angle is created. The correct procedure is to add power and adjust pitch to maintain the proper approach speed.

The approach-to-landing phase of flight gives a practical application of the relationship of power and airspeed. Assuming a stabilized approach, if the airplane appears to be low while on final approach at a constant airspeed, you must apply additional power and adjust pitch attitude as necessary. [Figure 2-44]

CLIMBS, DESCENTS, AND TURNS

When you are flying at slow airspeeds, altitude is controlled by power. To climb, add power; to descend, reduce power and adjust pitch attitude as necessary to maintain a constant airspeed. To execute turns at slow airspeeds, you must use a slightly different technique. As in any turn, part of the total lift force is diverted to make the airplane turn. For example, during a turn at normal cruise airspeed, you must apply slight control wheel back pressure to gain the extra vertical lift needed. This requirement results in a slight decrease in airspeed. However, during flight at minimum airspeeds, the loss of airspeed brings the airplane closer to the stall. The steeper the turn, the greater the load factor and the higher the stall speed. Therefore, you should make shallow turns and add power to maintain sufficient airspeed to prevent a stall. Even when you apply full power, a stall may occur because you have exceeded the critical angle of attack while trying to maintain altitude.

USE OF FLAPS

You will also practice maneuvering during slow flight using flaps and landing gear, if the airplane has retractable gear. During practice, the instructor will tell you to lower the flaps. You should do this a small

Extend and retract flaps in small increments.

Figure 2-45. According to the indicator on the left, the airplane may have a safe margin of airspeed with the flaps extended. However, the airspeed indicator on the right shows that sudden or complete retraction of the flaps at that speed may place the airplane near the stall speed in a no-flap condition.

amount at a time. At each position, pause to adjust the attitude to correct airspeed, adjust power to maintain altitude, and retrim to relieve control wheel pressures.

Addition of flaps to the first position (10° to 15°) normally causes small changes in pitch attitude, power, and trim. However, with flaps extended beyond this amount, large changes may be required. When you extend the flaps completely, the pitch attitude change and power requirement usually are quite pronounced. With the wing flaps fully extended, drag is very high, and a large percentage of available power is required to maintain altitude. Full power will probably produce only a very slow rate of climb, if any.

RETURN TO CRUISE FLIGHT

To return to cruise airspeed from slow flight, first apply full power while maintaining a constant altitude, then raise the flaps slowly, one position at a time. This technique is recommended to allow the speed to increase gradually as you retract the flaps. [Figure 2-45]

CHECKLIST

After studying this section, you should have a basic understanding of:

✓   **Altitude and airspeed control** — How to use power and pitch to control the altitude and airspeed of the airplane while maneuvering during slow flight.

✓ **Climbs, descents, and turns** — How to establish and maintain a climb, descent, or turn during flight at slow airspeed.

✓ **Recovery** — The procedures used to accelerate the airplane to straight-and-level flight.

TRAFFIC PATTERNS

The purpose of the standardized traffic pattern is to improve both the safety and efficiency of operations conducted at airports not served by a control tower. Normally, turns in a traffic pattern are made to the left. This pattern is called a **left-hand pattern**. You will find variations from the described pattern at different localities and at airports with control towers. For example, a **right-hand pattern** may be designated to expedite the flow of traffic when obstacles or concentrations of population make the use of a left-hand pattern undesirable.

TRAFFIC PATTERN LEGS

A normal traffic pattern is rectangular and has five named legs; downwind, base, final, upwind, and crosswind. Each traffic pattern also has a designated altitude at which the pattern is to be flown. [Figure 2-46]

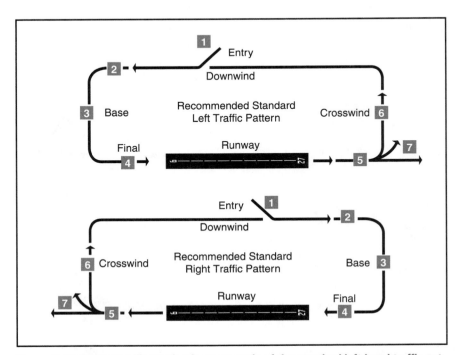

Figure 2-46. The upper illustration is an example of the standard left-hand traffic pattern. The lower one depicts a right-hand pattern. The numbered callouts in this illustration are fully explained in the following text.

PATTERN ENTRY

Traffic pattern entry procedures at an airport with an operating control tower are specified by the tower operator. At uncontrolled airports, traffic pattern altitudes and entry procedures may vary according to established local procedures. Usually, you enter the pattern at a 45° angle to the downwind leg, abeam the midpoint of the runway, and at a pattern altitude which is normally 1,000 feet above the ground (item 1). It is important to use the appropriate advisory frequency to obtain local weather, traffic, and landing information prior to entering the pattern. (Communications are covered later in this section.) At an uncontrolled airport, you may be the one to determine which runway to use, depending on the type of services available. In many cases, your decision will be based on the wind direction indicator.

DOWNWIND LEG

Fly the downwind leg (item 2) parallel to the runway and at the designated traffic pattern altitude. For most training airplanes, the appropriate distance from the runway is about one-half to one mile. If it becomes necessary to maneuver to maintain spacing with another airplane, only shallow "S" turns should be used, since traffic following you cannot anticipate major maneuvers such as a 360° turn. Normally, you begin the descent for landing when the airplane is abeam the touchdown point. However, you may need to delay the start of the descent if the downwind leg must be extended to follow traffic.

BASE LEG

Normally, you turn onto the base leg when the touchdown point is approximately 45° behind the inside wing tip. However, the base leg (item 3) must be adjusted according to other traffic and wind conditions. For example, if the wind is very strong, begin the turn sooner than normal. One important objective of the base leg is to allow the airplane to roll out on final approach at a distance no closer than one-quarter mile from the end of the runway, at an altitude appropriate to the glide path being flown.

The base leg should allow you to turn final no closer than one-quarter mile from the end of the runway.

FINAL APPROACH

The final approach (item 4) is the path the airplane flies immediately prior to touchdown. Since it is flown along an imaginary extension of the centerline of the runway, you must compensate for any crosswind conditions. If the approach does not terminate in a full-stop landing, climb out straight ahead, then follow the procedures outlined for the takeoff leg.

TAKEOFF LEG

The takeoff leg (item 5) normally consists of the airplane's flight path after takeoff. This leg is also called the upwind leg. Fly the airplane directly above an imaginary extension of the runway centerline and do not permit it to drift to one side or the other. Normally, you continue along this leg, without turning, until you reach an altitude within 300 feet of pattern altitude. Under certain conditions, such as high density altitudes or the existence of special airport procedures, you may need to start a turn at a somewhat lower altitude. Never start a turn at an altitude which, in your opinion as the pilot in command, is unsafe.

CROSSWIND LEG

Begin the crosswind leg (item 6) after you pass the departure end of the runway and have achieved a safe altitude. Also, be sure to check for other traffic in the pattern before starting your turn to crosswind, since you may have to extend your upwind leg to follow another aircraft. Ideally, as you turn from crosswind to downwind, the airplane is once again at the appropriate traffic pattern altitude.

A common misconception is that an airplane may stall when it turns downwind, since the wind shifts from a headwind to a tailwind. Although the groundspeed of the airplane is increased when turning downwind, the airspeed does not change. A stall that occurs during a turn to downwind, or to any other leg, is usually due to a pilot becoming distracted and failing to properly monitor the instruments and fly the airplane.

TRAFFIC PATTERN DEPARTURE

Always comply with the published departure procedures for any uncontrolled airport.

When a control tower is in operation, you can request and usually will receive approval for just about any type of departure. For example, you might request a straight-out, downwind, or right-hand departure. As a courtesy to the tower operator, make your departure request when you ask for takeoff clearance. At airports without an operating control tower, you must comply with the departure procedures established for that airport. These procedures usually are posted by airport operators so you can become familiar with the local rules. The standard procedure is either to fly straight-out or to make a 45° turn in the direction of the pattern after you reach pattern altitude (item 7).

COMMUNICATIONS

At airports with operating control towers, you are required by regulations to establish contact with the tower and obtain a clearance prior to entering the Class D airspace. Likewise, a clearance must be obtained prior to taxiing onto the runway for takeoff.

When you are within 10 miles of an uncontrolled airport, monitor the published CTAF, if your aircraft is radio equipped.

At airports without control towers, you are not required to have or use a radio. However, if you are radio equipped, using your radio greatly enhances safety. When inbound and about 10 miles out, obtain the local weather, runway conditions, and traffic information from the FSS located at the field or from the UNICOM operator, as appropriate. Then, switch to the published common traffic advisory frequency (CTAF) for that airport. This frequency is usually, but not always, the same frequency used to obtain airport information.

Monitor CTAF for a short period of time before you transmit to get a picture of the traffic situation and determine the best procedure for entering the pattern. Then, report your aircraft identification, position, and intentions. Always remember to include the name of the airport in your broadcasts, since more than one airport may be assigned the same CTAF.

When you depart, obtain airport information first, then monitor CTAF. Finally, when the runway and approach path are clear, announce your intentions and take off. On departure, monitor CTAF until you are about 10 miles from the airport.

COLLISION AVOIDANCE

The primary responsibility for collision avoidance rests with you, the pilot in command. Although several systems have been designed as safety aids, nothing can replace vigilance. Airport operations require a constant effort to see and avoid other aircraft. You should make a point of checking both the approach and departure paths prior to takeoff or landing.

Here are some other procedures you can use at both controlled and uncontrolled airports to enhance your visibility. Use anticollision and landing lights in the pattern and within a 5- to 10-mile radius of the airport. During climbout, accelerate the airplane to cruise climb speed as soon as you reach a safe altitude. The higher speed results in a lower pitch attitude and increased forward visibility. In addition, avoid turns of more than 90° while you are in the traffic pattern. Also, prior to commencing any turn, check for traffic.

RUNWAY INCURSION AVOIDANCE

The official definition of a runway incursion is, "Any occurrence at an airport involving an aircraft, a vehicle, person, or object on the ground that creates a collision hazard or results in loss of separation with an aircraft taking off or intending to take off, landing, or intending to land."

Runway incursions are primarily caused by errors associated with clearances, communications, airport surface movement, and positional awareness. The problem is compounded by the fact that any aircraft or pilot can cause a runway incursion. There are over 200,000 registered aircraft in the United States and approximately 675,000 pilots. In addition, an incursion may be caused by a tower controller or almost any person on an airport.

In spite of the extent of this hazard, there are a number of things you can do to avoid it. The first is preflight planning. Make sure you review and understand all Notices to Airmen (NOTAMs) dealing with airport construction or lighting. Then, after you are in your aircraft, remember the following recommended procedures.

1.   Strive for clear and unambiguous pilot-controller communications. Read back (in full) all clearances involving active runway crossing, hold short, and taxi into position and hold instructions.

2.   While taxiing, concentrate on your main responsibilities. Don't become absorbed in other tasks, or conversation, while the aircraft is moving.

3.   Complete as many checklist items as possible before taxi or while holding short.

4.   If unsure of your position on the airport, stop and ask for assistance. At a controlled airport, you can request progressive taxi instructions.

5.   When possible, while in a run-up area or waiting for a clearance, position your aircraft so you can see landing aircraft.

6.   Monitor the appropriate radio frequencies for information on other aircraft cleared onto your runway for takeoff or landing. Be alert for other aircraft which may be on other frequencies or without radio communications.

7.   After landing, stay on the tower frequency until instructed to change frequencies.

8.   During periods of reduced visibility, or at night, use your exterior taxi/landing lights, when practical, to help others see your aircraft.

9.   If you fly into or out of an airport where Land and Hold Short Operations or Simultaneous Operations on Intersecting Runways are used, make sure you understand the required procedures.

10. Report deteriorating or confusing airport markings, signs, and lighting to the airport operator of FAA officials. Also report confusing or erroneous airport diagrams and instructions.

CHECKLIST

After studying this section, you should have a basic understanding of:

✓   **Traffic pattern legs** — What they are and how they are flown.

✓   **Traffic pattern entry** — What the proper procedures for entering the traffic pattern are.

✓   **Traffic pattern departure** — What the procedures for departing the traffic pattern are.

✓   **Communications** — Who you should contact and when you should establish contact.

✓   **Runway incursion avoidance** — What it means and how to minimize the risks.

flight prep

3

SAFETY OF FLIGHT

In this section, we will discuss various aspects of the flight environment that you will encounter each time you fly. These include scanning, collision avoidance, blind spots in aircraft design, right-of-way rules, altitude rules, and special safety considerations. You will also be introduced to some of the Federal Aviation Regulations, and you will receive an overall view of important factors related to the safety of flight.

VISUAL SCANNING

The most effective way to scan during daylight is through a series of short, regularly spaced eye movements in 10° sectors.

One of the primary factors involved with safety of flight is your ability to see and avoid other aircraft. When you are flying, you should spend at least 70% of your time **scanning**, or looking outside your airplane. For scanning to be effective, though, you must develop a pattern that is compatible with how your eyes function. For example, your eyes require time to refocus when switching from the instrument panel to distant objects outside the airplane. Another characteristic of your eyes is that only a very small area in the back of the eye can send clear, sharply focused images to the brain. Since the eyes require time to focus on this narrow viewing area, scanning is most effective when you use a series of short, regularly spaced eye movements. This will help to bring successive areas of the sky into the central visual field. The FAA recommends that your eye movements not exceed 10°, and that you focus for at least one second on each segment. Be sure that the scan pattern you develop covers all of the sky you can see from the cockpit, both horizontally and vertically.

Effective scanning habits help you compensate for a phenomenon called **empty field myopia**. This condition usually occurs when you are looking at a featureless sky that is devoid of objects, contrasting colors, or patterns. Flying in haze or reduced visibility is an example. In this situation, your eyes tend to focus at only 10 to 30 feet. At this distance, spots on the windshield may look like airplanes and aircraft further away may go undetected. With empty field myopia, an aircraft must be two or three times larger (closer) before you are able to see it. If you feel that you are experiencing empty field myopia, you should consciously increase your scan rate and focus your eyes alternately far and near.

Focusing on the different sectors as you scan can be difficult when flying into the sun, just as driving a car into the sun is a problem. You may want to consider a different route or departure time that will minimize the sun's effects. Also, you know from experience that a clean windshield and sunglasses improve your ability to see objects more clearly in bright sunlight. Keep in mind that when two aircraft are flying on a head-on collision course and both are traveling at 150 knots, they will travel one quarter of a mile toward each other in the three seconds that it usually requires for the pilots to take action. This makes early detection of other aircraft very important.

Your peripheral vision also plays an important role in spotting other aircraft because it is especially effective in detecting relative movement. This movement becomes apparent only during the moments when your scan is stopped. Relative movement usually is your first perception of a collision threat as you stop to focus on successive sectors of the sky. Remember, however, that you should be especially alert for an aircraft which shows no movement in relation to your airplane. It is likely to collide with you unless you take evasive action. When you are considering evasive action, you will need to estimate the other airplane's relative altitude. [Figure 3-1]

If there is no apparent relative motion between another aircraft and yours, you are probably on a collision course.

Remember that the other pilot may be occupied with tasks other than scanning and may not react in the manner that you anticipate. As you take evasive action, watch the other aircraft to see if it makes any unusual maneuvers and, if so, plan your reaction accordingly. You should also be aware that there may be more than one potential collision hazard in an area at the same time. The more time you spend on developing your scan in the early part of flight training, the more natural it will become later. The scanning techniques described here will help you to see potential conflicts earlier and allow you to take the proper action to avoid a collision. Also, being aware of the blind spots in your aircraft's design will improve your awareness of potential hazards.

Figure 3-1. To determine if you are at about the same altitude as another aircraft, use the horizon as a reference. If the aircraft appears to be above the horizon, the aircraft is probably at a higher altitude than you are. If the aircraft appears to be below the horizon, the aircraft is probably at a lower altitude than you. If the aircraft is on the horizon, it may be at your altitude. You must decide quickly if it poses a threat and, if so, take the appropriate evasive action.

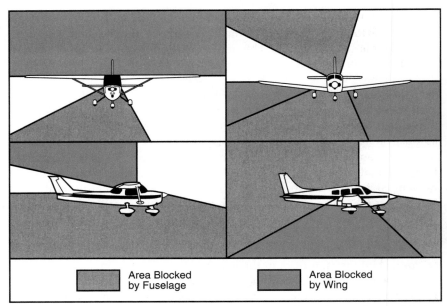

Figure 3-2. In both high-wing and low-wing designs, portions of your view are blocked by the fuselage and wings. This can make it difficult to see conflicting traffic.

BLIND SPOTS AND AIRCRAFT DESIGN

Airplanes, like automobiles, have problems associated with **blind spots**. Due to the nature of airplane design, blind spots are of special concern. High-wing airplanes make it difficult to see above the airplane, but it is very easy to see below the airplane. On the other hand, it is very easy to see above a low-wing aircraft and difficult to see below it. This is important to remember while climbing or descending, particularly when operating in the area around an airport. [Figure 3-2]

Turns require special consideration, too. Before you initiate a turn, always look in the direction of your turn. In a low-wing airplane, this presents no difficulty. In a high-wing airplane, your view is blocked as soon as you lower the wing to start a turn. By gently lifting that wing and looking before you start the turn, you can "clear" the area of other aircraft.

AIRPORT OPERATIONS

Any operation in the vicinity of an airport warrants extra caution. Even airports with control towers may be hazardous because of the large amount of air traffic. A controlled environment does not relieve you of the responsibility to see and avoid other traffic. In some cases, you may need to be even more vigilant. At airports without control towers, which are referred to as uncontrolled airports, you have other concerns. At these airports, you may see a combination of experimental aircraft, ultralight aircraft, gliders, and aircraft both with and without radios. This variety of aircraft increases the chance that conflicting traffic can be blocked by blind spots in aircraft design. This can develop into a serious problem, particularly during the approach and landing phases of flight. [Figure 3-3]

If you are flying a high-wing aircraft that is climbing out on departure, the blind spot created by the wing will not allow you to see above the airplane. At the same time, it is possible that a low-wing aircraft may be descending for a landing and the pilot cannot see below the wing.

A good way to reduce the possibility of a collision during extended climbs or descents is to make shallow S-turns and avoid climbing or descending at steep angles. Climbing at a faster airspeed permits a shallower angle. This, in turn, enables you to see better over the engine cowling. Making shallow S-turns as you are climbing increases your range of vision, too. If

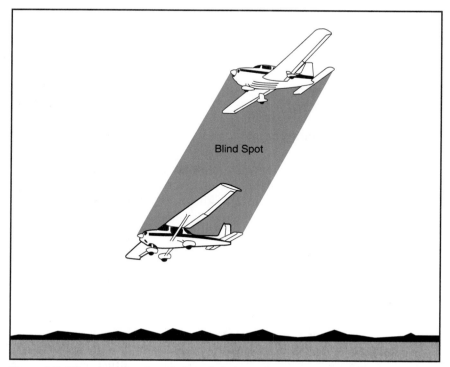

Figure 3-3. When a high-wing airplane is below a low-wing airplane on approach to landing, both airplanes can easily remain out of sight of each other. Similar problems can occur during departures.

you are flying a low-wing airplane, plan your descent so that it won't have to be steep, and make S-turns as you descend.

MANEUVERS IN THE TRAINING AREA

Prior to starting any maneuvers, make clearing turns and carefully scan the area for other aircraft.

As you continue your flight training, your instructor will teach you to make **clearing turns** when you are in the practice area, which is the area used to practice flight maneuvers. It is important not only to clear the area for traffic, but to maintain your scan while practicing the maneuvers. Your instructor will demonstrate the various types of clearing turns for you. They usually consist of at least a 180° change in direction. These turns allow you to see the areas blocked by the blind spots of your aircraft, and they make it easier to maintain visual contact with other aircraft in the practice area. Remember to make clearing turns and carefully scan the entire area for other traffic before you begin each maneuver.

In cases where traffic conflicts arise, it is necessary for you to know what action to take. This usually is based on who has the right-of-way.

RIGHT-OF-WAY RULES

Throughout your training, you will become more and more familiar with **Federal Aviation Regulations**, or FARs. FARs are the rules that the FAA asks you to follow when you are in the flight environment. They are very specific about right-of-way rules. First, the regulations state very clearly that the pilot in command is responsible for seeing and avoiding all traffic in visual flight conditions. This is a big responsibility, and one that you and every pilot must fulfill in the interest of safety.

An aircraft in distress has the right-of-way over all other aircraft.

The regulations also specify that an aircraft in distress has the right-of-way over all other air traffic. You can think of an aircraft in distress as one that may not be able to maneuver as well as it could in normal conditions.

Additional rules apply when similar aircraft are approaching each other. For instance, if your airplane and another airplane are on a collision course, both pilots should take the proper action to avoid each other. Primarily, there are three situations where these rules apply: aircraft approaching from the side, or converging; approaching each other head-on; and overtaking, or passing, another aircraft. [Figure 3-4]

If two aircraft are approaching each other head-on or nearly so, both aircraft will give way to the right. In other converging situations, airplanes and helicopters need to give the right-of-way to airships, gliders, and balloons. [Figure 3-5]

Figure 3-4. When aircraft are approaching from the side, or converging, the aircraft to the other's right has the right-of way. The aircraft to the left must give way to the one on the right. If you are flying the aircraft on the left and need to give way, make a turn away from the other aircraft in a manner that will not interfere with its flight path.

In a situation where you are going fast enough to overtake a slower aircraft, pass the other aircraft to the right and stay well clear. Watch the other airplane carefully until you are safely beyond it. [Figure 3-6]

Figure 3-5. In the event that you see an aircraft coming straight at you, or head-on, both of you are required to alter course to the right. If there is safe altitude separation, this action is not necessary.

Figure 3-6. There will be situations where you will be overtaking another aircraft traveling in the same direction. The aircraft being overtaken has the right-of-way, so you must pass well clear on the right.

In general, the least maneuverable aircraft normally has the right-of-way.

The FARs also state that when aircraft are converging (except head-on or nearly so), a balloon has the right-of-way over all other aircraft. A glider has the right-of-way over any airship, airplane, or rotorcraft; and an airship has the right-of-way over any airplane or rotorcraft. Finally, an aircraft that is towing or refueling another aircraft has the right-of-way over all other engine-driven aircraft. The general rule concerning right-of-way is that the least maneuverable aircraft usually has the right-of-way over all other air traffic.

If two or more aircraft are approaching an airport for landing, the aircraft at the lower altitude has the right-of-way, but the pilot should not take advantage of this to cut in front of another aircraft.

The last right-of-way rule concerns your actions at an airport when you intend to land. An aircraft on final approach or an aircraft that is landing has the right-of-way over other traffic in the pattern and those on the ground. If you are entering the traffic pattern at the same time as other aircraft that are also preparing to land, the aircraft at the lowest altitude has the right-of-way. However, this is not intended to allow you to enter the pattern below the specified traffic pattern altitude and disrupt or cut in front of those already established in the pattern.

MINIMUM SAFE ALTITUDES

For safety reasons, there are minimum altitudes that you must maintain during flight. These rules apply at all times except during takeoffs and landings.

The minimum safe altitude anywhere must allow an emergency landing, following an engine failure, without undue hazard to persons or property on the surface.

The lowest altitude at which you can fly anywhere is one which allows an emergency landing without undue hazard to persons or property on the surface. The FAA wants you to have enough altitude so that you have more options for emergency landing sites in the event your engine fails.

Over a congested area, such as a city or metropolitan area, you are required to fly 1,000 feet above any obstacle within a horizontal radius of 2,000 feet of the aircraft. If you keep in mind that 1,000 feet is a minimum altitude and fly at altitudes higher than that over congested areas, you will have more time to troubleshoot any problems and can choose a better landing site if you have to make an emergency landing.

When flying over an uncongested area, you must fly at least 500 feet above the surface. The minimum safe altitude is slightly different for sparsely populated or open water areas. There, you cannot fly within 500 feet of any person, vessel, vehicle, or structure. Remember to observe these rules and to stay at an altitude high enough so that you can make a safe landing if your engine fails. [Figure 3-7]

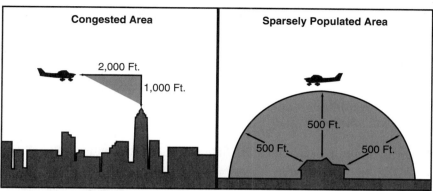

Figure 3-7. Minimum safe altitudes over congested areas are based on obstruction clearance. A congested area may be a city, town, settlement, or an open air assembly of people. Notice that obstacle clearance over sparsely populated areas is reduced significantly.

VFR CRUISING ALTITUDES

Along with minimum safe altitudes, the FAA also has regulations to keep aircraft separated. These are called **VFR cruising altitudes**.

VFR is a term you will see and hear often during your training. It means **visual flight rules**, which are frequently referenced in FARs. These rules apply to contact, or visual, flying where you navigate by maintaining visual contact with objects on the surface. Cruising altitudes are one example of these rules.

To apply the rules for cruising altitudes, you need to know your altitude above mean sea level (MSL), as well as your altitude above ground level (AGL). This can be done accurately only with a current altimeter setting. If you fly out of an airport that has weather reporting capabilities, you can get the current pressure setting and dial it into your altimeter before you take off or before you enter the traffic pattern to land. If the airport has no weather reporting equipment or your aircraft has no radio, you can set your altimeter to the field elevation before you take off.

When you are enroute, you must set your altimeter to the current reported setting of a weather station within 100 n.m. of the aircraft. This is neces-sary because the barometric pressure can change significantly over a 100 n.m. distance, which will have an effect on both your indicated and true altitudes. If no station is within 100 n.m., you can use the setting from an appropriate available station. If you are not equipped with a radio, you can use the elevation of the departure airport or an appropriate altimeter set-ting obtained before departure. This last situation is rarely used, since most airplanes today are radio equipped. The important thing is to keep resetting your altimeter as new reports become available. The main reason for this is so all aircraft in the area will be using the same setting for altitude reference.

Anytime you fly in level cruising flight above 3,000 feet AGL, you must follow the VFR cruising altitudes, which are also referred to as east/west cruising altitudes. Aircraft flying on instruments and aircraft flying under visual flight rules have different cruising altitudes, which are assigned to separate aircraft.

For a magnetic course of 0° — 179°, fly odd thousands plus 500 feet; for a magnetic course of 180° — 359°, fly even thousands plus 500 feet.

If you are flying a magnetic course of 0° through 179°, you must fly an odd thousand-foot altitude plus 500 feet. This will give you cruising altitudes of 3,500 feet MSL, 5,500 feet MSL, 7,500 feet MSL, or higher. If you are flying a magnetic course of 180° through 359°, you will need to fly even thousand-foot altitudes plus 500 feet: 4,500 feet MSL, 6,500 feet MSL, 8,500 feet MSL, or higher. As a safety precaution, it is customary to fly at a VFR cruising altitude, when practical, even if you aren't above 3,000 feet AGL. [Figure 3-8]

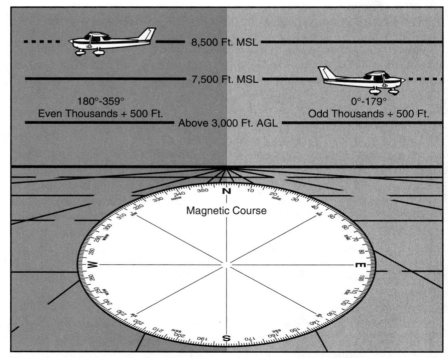

Figure 3-8. Cruising altitude rules are designed to provide a minimum of 1,000 feet vertical separation between VFR aircraft. An eastbound aircraft might be at 7,500 feet while a westbound aircraft could be at 8,500 feet. The rules officially apply above 3,000 feet AGL and below 18,000 feet MSL, and the altitudes are based on magnetic course.

SPECIAL SAFETY CONSIDERATIONS

So far, we have discussed many aspects of scanning, collision avoidance, right-of-way, FARs, obstruction clearance, and cruising altitudes. This final discussion covers some aspects of the flight environment which require special safety considerations and development of good personal flying techniques.

We've already discussed the need for extra care in the vicinity of airports. You also face the potential for heavy traffic on airways and around navigational aids. Airways are similar to highways for cars. They represent routes from one place to another, and they tend to attract air traffic. Therefore, it is important to maintain your scan, use the correct VFR cruising altitude, and make shallow S-turns if you need to climb or descend while on an airway. Airways intersect above navigational aids, or navaids. With the increase in air traffic around navaids, you must be especially alert for other aircraft.

If you need to climb or descend while on an airway, make shallow turns to look for traffic.

If you find yourself spending more time than necessary looking for charts or at your instruments, you should consider organizing the cockpit a little better before your flight. Take some time to plan your flight and be sure you have everything you need. This should include a check of the windshield to be sure it is clean. Remember, if the outside visibility is good, you have a better chance of spotting a hazard than if you are flying in haze or other low visibility conditions. Haze tends to make traffic and terrain features appear farther away than their actual distance. Think about the blind spots that exist in the airplane and plan to compensate for them. Mentally review the safety information you learned in this section.

Objects typically are closer than they appear when you view them through haze.

Finally, there are two suggestions to help make your flight a safer one. **Operation Lights On** is a voluntary program that encourages you to use your landing lights during departures and approaches, both day and night. This practice is recommended especially when operating within 10 miles of an airport, or in conditions of reduced visibility. It is recommended that you check the pilot's operating handbook for your aircraft for any limitations on the use of the lights.

You are also encouraged to turn on anticollision lights whenever the engines are running, day or night. However, anticollision lights need not be turned on when they might interfere with safety. For example, strobe lights should be turned off when their brightness might be detrimental to the vision of others.

CHECKLIST _____

After studying this section, you should have a basic understanding of:

✓   **Scanning** — The best method for scanning, and how much time you should spend looking outside.

✓   **Empty field myopia** — When it may occur, and how you can recognize and correct for it.

✓   **Blind spots** — What areas of vision are blocked by blind spots and what you can do to increase your visibility during climbs and descents.

✓   **Clearing turns** — Why and when they are done, and how many degrees you should turn.

✓   **Right-of-way** — Which aircraft have the right of way when converging, approaching head-on, and overtaking.

✓   **Minimum safe altitudes** — What your minimum safe altitude is over congested areas, over uncongested areas, and over sparsely populated areas.

✓   **VFR cruising altitudes** — When they must be used and what the east/west cruising rules are.

✓   **Operation Lights On** — What the concept is and when you use it.

You have learned that developing an awareness of safety factors is an important step in understanding the flight environment. In this section, you will become familiar with several new terms and concepts related to operations in the airport environment. Knowing how to determine the correct runway to use and understanding the markings on taxiways and runways will be essential every time you fly. The various types of lighting used at airports is another important area for study, which will have direct application when you begin flying at night.

CONTROLLED AND UNCONTROLLED AIRPORTS

Air traffic controllers direct operations at controlled airports from the tower. At uncontrolled airports, you are responsible for determining the active or favored runway and following local procedures. There are two types of airport environments that you will operate in — controlled and uncontrolled. A **controlled airport** has an operating control tower. All aircraft in the vicinity, as well as those on the ground, are subject to instructions issued by air traffic controllers. In order for you to operate in the controlled airport environment, a two-way radio is required for contact with the controllers. At an **uncontrolled airport**, control of VFR traffic is not exercised. Although you are not required to have a two-way radio, most pilots use radios to transmit their intentions to other pilots. You are also responsible for determining the active runway and how to enter and exit the traffic pattern.

RUNWAY LAYOUT

Because airplanes are directly affected by wind during takeoffs and landings, **runways** are not arbitrarily placed by builders. If there is only one runway at an airport, it is placed so that you can take off and land in the direction of the prevailing wind. If there is more than one runway, the main runway is aligned with the prevailing wind and the remaining runway or runways are placed so that they are aligned with other common wind directions.

The numbers that you see on runways are not arbitrary, either. First of all, you normally fly magnetic courses and headings, as opposed to true courses and headings. Secondly, since the wind direction at airports is also given to you in degrees relative to magnetic north, the number on the runway correlates to a magnetic north reference. The runway's magnetic

Runway numbers are derived from the runway's direction in degrees relative to magnetic north.

Figure 3-9. Even though there are numbers on both ends of a runway, they are different because the runway designators are 180° apart. A runway labeled "9" on one end is labeled "27" on the opposite end. The runway may be referred to as either 9 or 27, depending on the direction you are using for takeoff or landing. You will use runway 9 if you are taking off or landing to the east and runway 27 if you are taking off or landing to the west.

direction is rounded off to the nearest 10°, with the last zero omitted. So, a runway with a magnetic heading of 268° is rounded off to 270° and, with the zero dropped, becomes runway 27. A runway with a magnetic heading of 088° becomes runway 09. To further simplify runway numbers, any runway that is between the headings of 010° and 090° is designated with a single-digit runway number, so runway 09 is marked as runway 9. [Figure 3-9]

At some airports, there may be two or three parallel runways with the same runway number. If there are two parallel runways, one is labeled the left runway and the other is the right; for example, "36L" and "36R." If there is a third parallel runway, the one in the middle is the center runway and the respective runways are marked "36L," "36C," and "36R." [Figure 3-10]

AIRPORT ELEVATION

In the previous section of this chapter, we mentioned setting your altimeter to the airport elevation prior to takeoff if an altimeter setting isn't available. The official **airport elevation** is the highest part of usable runway surface, measured in feet above mean sea level. The airport elevation is available from several sources, including aeronautical charts.

TAXIWAYS

Your link between the airport parking areas and the runways are the **taxiways**. They are easily identified by a continuous yellow centerline stripe. Sometimes, the edges of the taxiway, as well as the centerline, will be marked by double yellow stripes. Many times, taxiways are labeled "Taxiway A," "Taxiway B," and so on, to help you identify routes to and from runways.

Figure 3-10. At large airports with heavy air traffic, it is common to have parallel runways. When assigning runways for takeoffs and landings, air traffic controllers will refer to these runways as "three-six-left," "three-six-center," or "three-six-right."

Figure 3-11. Holding position markings consist of hold lines painted across the taxiway and a sign identifying the runway. They may be painted wherever taxiways and runways intersect. ILS hold lines are placed farther away from the runway.

As you transition from the taxiway to the runway, you will see hold lines. **Hold lines**, which are generally 125 feet to 250 feet from the touchdown area, keep you clear of the runway in use. Normally, there will be a sign nearby to identify the associated runway. Larger airports may have additional taxiway/runway location signs, as well as direction, destination, and information signs. At an uncontrolled airport, you should stop and check for traffic and cross the hold lines only after ensuring that no one is on an approach to land. At a controlled airport, the controller may ask you to hold short of the runway for landing traffic. In this case, you should stop before the lines and proceed only after you are cleared to do so by the controller, and you have checked for traffic. [Figure 3-11]

For your safety at an uncontrolled airport, stop and check for traffic before crossing the hold lines.

At airports equipped with an instrument landing system (ILS), it is possible for aircraft near the runway to interfere with the ILS signal. If this is the case, you will find the hold lines placed farther from the runway to prevent any interference. This means you may find two hold lines for some runways. The one closest to the runway is the normal hold line, while the one farthest away is the ILS hold line. At other locations only an ILS hold line may be used. When ILS approaches are in progress, you may be asked by the controller to ". . . hold short of the ILS critical area."

RUNWAY AND TAXIWAY MARKINGS

Runway markings vary between runways used solely for VFR operations and those used in conjunction with IFR operations. **Instrument flight rules** (IFR) apply to flights conducted by reference to the aircraft instruments when visibility is reduced. This often requires the pilot to conduct an instrument approach at the destination. You must have an instrument rating to fly in IFR conditions.

Instrument approaches are classified according to whether or not they use an electronic glide slope for guidance to the landing runway. If they do, they are called precision approaches, such as an "ILS." If they don't, they are called nonprecision approaches, and the corresponding runway markings vary accordingly.

Runway markings differ, depending on whether the runway is used only by VFR traffic or by both VFR and IFR traffic.

A basic VFR runway will have the runway number and a dashed white centerline. When a basic VFR runway is used in conjunction with a nonprecision instrument approach, threshold markings are added. Touchdown zone markers, fixed distance markings, and side stripes are added when the runway is used in conjunction with a precision approach. Occasionally, you may see fixed distance markings and side stripes on a nonprecision runway.

A **STOL runway**, or short takeoff or landing runway, is built for specially designed aircraft that require shorter distances for takeoff and landing. It is not advisable to use this type of runway unless you are flying an aircraft that has these short-field capabilities. [Figure 3-12]

At airports with a displaced threshold, the beginning portion of the landing zone is marked with a solid white line with white arrows leading up to it.

It is not uncommon to fly into an airport that has a runway with another type of marking called a **displaced threshold**. Usually, if the threshold is

Figure 3-12. The common types of runway markings for VFR, precision, nonprecision, and STOL runways are shown here. As a VFR pilot, you are not restricted from using the precision and nonprecision instrument runways. The threshold marker, touchdown zone marker, fixed distance marking, and side stripes on the precision instrument approach runways are there to aid pilots who are making instrument approaches. STOL runways are clearly marked to avoid any confusion.

displaced, it is because of an obstruction off the end of the runway. This might prohibit you from making a normal descent and landing on the beginning portion of the pavement. Trees, powerlines, and buildings are typical examples of such obstructions. The beginning of the landing portion of the runway, or threshold, is marked by a solid white line. Arrows and arrowheads used in a displaced threshold area are white. Arrowheads used on a taxiway prior to a runway threshold are yellow. Even though the first few hundred feet of pavement may not be used for landing, it may be available for taxiing, the landing rollout, and takeoffs.

A **blast pad/stopway area**, sometimes referred to as an overrun, is different from the area preceding a displaced threshold because it cannot be used for either takeoffs or landings. The blast pad is an area where propeller or jet blast can dissipate without creating a hazard to others. The stopway area is paved so that, in the event of an aborted takeoff, an aircraft can use it to decelerate and come to a stop. The pavement strength may be able to support the weight of an airplane, but not be strong enough for continuous operations. Because of its reduced weight-bearing capabilities, no one is allowed to use a blast pad/stopway area for landing or departing. The beginning of the landing portion of the runway is marked with a solid white line, just as it is with the displaced threshold. [Figure 3-13]

> A blast pad/stopway area should be used only as an overrun; it is not designed for taxi, takeoff, or landing.

Figure 3-13. You will recognize a displaced threshold by the white arrows leading up to a solid white line. The line is the displaced threshold and indicates the beginning of the landing zone. The blast pad/stopway area is painted with yellow chevrons, which indicate the structure of the pavement is unusable for normal operations. Because of this, taxiways will not extend into the area. There also may be areas with yellow diagonal stripes on each side of the runway where the pavement strength is reduced. Operations are not permitted on these areas, either.

AIRPORT SIGNS

Major airports usually have complex taxi routes, multiple runways, and widely dispersed parking aprons. In addition, vehicular traffic in certain areas may be quite heavy. As a result, airfield signs are standardized to promote safety in ground operations by making it easy for you to identify taxi routes, mandatory holding positions, and boundaries for critical areas. Another benefit, in case you fly outside the United States, is that the U.S. standards are practically the same as those which are promoted by the International Civil Aviation Organization (ICAO). The standards include specifications such as size, height, location, and illumination requirements.

Altogether there are six types of airport signs — mandatory, location, direction, destination, information, and runway distance remaining. A brief explanation of the six types is included in the following paragraphs. The numbers preceding each paragraph are keyed to the accompanying illustration. [Figure 3-14]

1 **Mandatory Instruction Signs** denote an entrance to a runway, a critical area, or an area prohibited to aircraft. These signs are red with white letters or numbers.

2 **Location Signs** identify either the taxiway or runway where your aircraft is located. They also identify the boundary of the runway safety area/obstacle free zone (OFZ) or ILS critical area for aircraft exiting the runway. These signs are black with yellow inscriptions and a yellow border and do not have arrows.

3 **Direction Signs** indicate directions of taxiways leading out of an intersection. They have black inscriptions on a yellow background and always contain arrows which show the approximate direction of turn.

4 **Destination Signs** indicate the general direction to a remote location such as for inbound or outbound traffic. They have black inscriptions on a yellow background and always contain an arrow.

5 **Information Signs** advise you of such things as areas that cannot be seen from the control tower, applicable radio frequencies, and noise abatement procedures. These signs use yellow backgrounds with black inscriptions.

6 **Runway Distance Remaining Signs** are used to provide distance remaining information to pilots during take-off and landing operations. The signs are located along the sides of the runway, and the inscription consists of a white numeral on a black background. The signs indicate the distance remaining in thousands of feet. These runway distance remaining signs are recommended for runways used by turbojet aircraft.

Sometimes the installation of a sign may not be practical. In this event, if the requirement for information or guidance exists, a surface painted sign may be used. Surface painted signs may include directional guidance or

Figure 3-14. Several examples of all six airport signs are depicted in the *Aeronautical Information Manual* (AIM). For additional details, you also may refer to AC 150/5340-18C, *Standards for Airport Sign Systems.*

location information. For example, the runway number may be painted on the taxiway pavement near the taxiway hold lines.

Another surface marking you will need to become familiar with is the one associated with a closed runway or taxiway. For one reason or another, a runway or taxiway may not be usable, so there will be a large "X" painted on both ends. Although the surface may appear to be usable, this runway or taxiway cannot be used safely.

Large "Xs" painted on runways or taxiways indicate that they are closed.

WIND DIRECTION INDICATORS

During takeoffs and landings, you need to know which runway to use. At a controlled airport, there are various methods of obtaining the current airport information, including the "active runway," or runway in use. At an uncontrolled airport, you may be the one to determine which runway to use, depending on the type of services available. In many cases, your decision will be based on what you see when looking at a wind direction indicator.

There are two types of wind direction indicators usually located near the runway. The most common is the **wind sock**, which is used at both controlled and uncontrolled airports. Although a wind sock may not be your initial source of wind information at a controlled airport, there will still be a wind sock positioned near the runway. It will tell you the wind conditions near the touchdown zone of the runway. In gusty conditions, the wind sock moves back and forth. Also, the stronger the wind, the straighter the extension of the wind sock. [Figure 3-15]

The other type of wind direction indicator is a **wind tee**. The tail of the tee aligns itself like a weather vane into the wind. However, it does not indicate wind intensity or gusty conditions. In some cases, a wind sock and tee may be at the same location. If so, the tee may be manually aligned to show which runway is active. [Figure 3-16]

Figure 3-15. A wind sock may be your key to choosing the correct runway at an uncontrolled field. The sock aligns itself into the wind because the wind blows into the large end and out the small end. The small end of the wind sock points downwind. When possible, you should select the runway that is the closest to paralleling the sock, and take off or land into the wind.

Figure 3-16. The wind tee on the left is not as common as the wind sock. However, it is still effective in helping you to determine the wind direction and favored runway. Because the wind tee is similar to an airplane, it will weathervane into the wind. You need to take off or land into the wind on the runway that most closely parallels the direction of the tee. In contrast, the tetrahedron, shown on the right, is typically used as a landing direction indicator. The tetrahedron may swing around with the small end pointing into the wind, or it may be manually positioned to show landing direction. In either case, you are cautioned not to use it solely as a wind direction indicator, but to use it in conjunction with a wind sock.

A **tetrahedron** is a landing direction indicator, usually located near a wind direction indicator. It may swing freely, as the wind sock does, or it may be manually positioned to show the direction of landing. [Figure 3-16]

SEGMENTED CIRCLE

When installed at uncontrolled airports, a wind sock, wind tee, or wind cone is usually placed in the middle of a **segmented circle** at a central location on the airport. The segmented circle has a two-fold purpose. First, it helps to identify the location of the wind direction indicator. Second, there will be extensions on the segmented circle if the traffic pattern is other than left-hand traffic as the FARs require. [Figure 3-17]

At uncontrolled airports, unless otherwise specified, all turns in the traffic pattern should be made to the left.

Figure 3-17. At this airport, the segmented circle with the wind sock is located on the north side of runway 9/27. The wind sock shows that the wind is coming from the northeast and that runway 9 should be the active runway. A check of the "L" extensions on the segmented circle shows that runway 9 has a left-hand turn from base leg to final, so you will fly a standard pattern. However, runway 27 has a nonstandard traffic pattern, since a right-hand turn is required from base to final.

A traffic pattern with right-hand turns, called a nonstandard pattern, may be necessary due to noise abatement procedures, terrain, or obstructions. The "L-shaped" extensions are placed so they indicate the direction you should turn in the traffic pattern for a given runway. You can think of the "L" as your base and final legs to the runway. If it is a right turn from "base" to "final" on the "L," then you need to make a right-hand pattern on your approach. If right-hand turns are required for the approach, they normally will be used for departure as well.

When approaching an uncontrolled airport that you are not familiar with, it is recommended that you overfly the airport at 500 to 1,000 feet above the traffic pattern altitude to observe the flow of traffic and to locate the segmented circle. If no traffic is observed, follow the directions indicated by the "L" extensions and land on the runway indicated by the wind direction indicator. If there are no extensions for the runways, they all have standard left-hand traffic patterns. At night, the segmented circle is normally illuminated by overhead lights that allow you to see both the wind direction indicator and the segmented circle.

Some uncontrolled airports also have radio operators who are able to tell you the wind direction and speed, and advise you of the runway in use. Usually, airports have a designated calm-wind runway. This runway is used whenever the wind is five knots or less. However, you must still watch carefully for other traffic that may be using other runways. Also, remember that even though there may be someone at an uncontrolled airport to advise you of the current winds and active or favored runway, you must make the final decision as to which runway to use.

TAXIING IN WIND

Takeoffs and landings are not the only times you are concerned about wind. Taxi operations can become critical in high winds or gusty conditions, too. Strong winds passing over and around the wings and horizontal stabilizer during taxi can actually lift the airplane. In the most adverse conditions, it is possible for the airplane to flip or roll over.

When taxiing into a quartering headwind, hold the aileron up on the side from which the wind is blowing and maintain neutral elevator.

Proper use of the aileron and elevator controls normally will counteract the wind and help you maintain control of the airplane. For example, if the wind is blowing from the left front quarter, you should hold the left aileron up to counteract the lifting tendency of the wind. In a tricycle-gear airplane, the elevator should be in a neutral position to prevent the wind from exerting any lifting force on the tail. [Figure 3-18]

While taxiing a tailwheel airplane, hold the elevator up in a headwind and down in a tailwind.

Tailwheel airplanes are taxied with the ailerons held the same as for a tricycle-gear airplane. However, the elevator must be positioned to help keep the tailwheel on the ground. In a headwind, you will hold the elevator control aft (elevator up). In a tailwind, hold the elevator control forward (elevator down).

Figure 3-18. Your knowledge of proper control use during windy conditions will help you control the airplane while taxiing. With a quartering headwind, you position the control wheel as if you want to turn into the wind and maintain level flight. With a quartering tailwind, you position the control wheel as if you want to turn away from the wind and descend.

The most critical situation is when you are taxiing a tricycle-gear airplane with a high wing in a strong quartering tailwind. The high wing is susceptible to being lifted by the wind. In extreme conditions, a quartering tailwind can cause the airplane to nose over and flip on its back. [Figure 3-19]

A quartering tailwind is the most critical wind condition when taxiing a tricycle-gear, high-wing airplane.

Figure 3-19. Taxiing with strong quartering tailwinds is the most critical situation. In the most severe conditions, the flow of air beneath the horizontal stabilizer and wing can lift the airplane and tip it over. With a tailwind from the left side, position the control wheel full forward and to the right. The correct flight control positions are: left aileron down, right aileron up, and elevator (or stabilator) down.

You will find a difference between taxiing tricycle versus conventional, or tailwheel, airplanes. Weathervaning, or turning into the wind in direct crosswinds, is a tendency of tailwheel airplanes. Weathervaning also is possible in tricycle airplanes, but it normally is not a problem. This is due to the ground friction caused by the nosewheel and the more aft position of the main gear. When you turn while taxiing, the flow of air around the airplane changes direction, and you will have to compensate by altering the position of the control surfaces.

RAMP AREA

The area where airplanes are parked and tied down is called the **ramp area**, or parking area. The airport terminal and maintenance facilities are often located near the ramp area. Aircraft refueling is also done there, so you should be alert for fuel trucks driving on the ramp and trucks in the process of refueling. When you are taxiing through the ramp area, you should be especially alert for people who are walking to or from their aircraft. The prop blast generated by your airplane can blow dust and gravel at them. This is a good reason to avoid starting your aircraft when someone is walking behind it. You should also use low idling r.p.m.'s just after starting your engine. As you proceed to the taxiway, your taxi speed should be only as fast as a brisk walk. At this speed, you can stop the aircraft in time to avoid conflicts with people or vehicles on the ramp.

Also, remember to tie the airplane down whenever you leave it for any length of time. This will prevent the aircraft from rolling into other aircraft on the ramp or being turned over by wind in the event of gusty conditions.

NOISE ABATEMENT PROCEDURES

The FAA, in conjunction with airport proprietors and community leaders, is now using **noise abatement** procedures to reduce the level of noise generated by aircraft departing over neighborhoods that are near airports. The airport authority may simply request that you use a designated runway, wind permitting. You also may be asked to restrict some of your operations, such as practicing landings, during certain time periods. There are three ways to determine the noise abatement procedure at an airport. First, if there is a control tower on the field, they will assign the preferred noise abatement runway to you. Second, you can check the *Airport/Facility Directory*, which will be discussed in Flight Prep 8, for information on local procedures. Third, there may be information for you to read in the pilot's lounge, or even signs posted next to the runway that will tell you what to do.

AIRPORT LIGHTING

Your flying experiences will soon take you from flying only in the daytime to flying at night, as well. You will notice that airport lighting is similar from one airport to the next. Airports that are lighted for nighttime operations use FAA-approved colors, so there is continuity from airport to airport.

AIRPORT BEACON

At night, **airport beacons** are used to guide pilots to lighted airports. Airport beacons may be of the older rotating type, or the newer flashing variety which produces the same effect. If you have enough altitude, beacons can be seen at great distances in good visibility conditions. The combination of light colors from an airport beacon indicates the type of airport. As a routine measure, you are not permitted to operate at military airports. [Figure 3-20]

For seaplane pilots, a water airport is marked with a beacon that has flashing white and yellow lights. Heliport beacons alternate between green, yellow, and white lights.

Generally, you will find that an airport's beacon is on from dusk until dawn. The beacon usually isn't on during the day unless the ceiling is less than 1,000 feet and/or the ground visibility is less than three statute miles, the normal VFR minimums. Remember, though, the airport beacon may not always be turned on when the weather is below VFR minimums.

If an airport beacon is on during the day, the weather is probably below VFR minimums.

APPROACH LIGHTING SYSTEMS

Some airports have complex lighting systems to help instrument pilots transition to visual references at the end of an instrument approach. These **approach lighting systems** can begin as far away as 3,000 feet along the

Figure 3-20. Airport beacons that indicate civilian land airports use alternating white and green lights. Beacons at military airports have two flashes of white that alternate with a single green light.

extended runway centerline, and can aid VFR pilots operating at night. The most complex systems are for precision instrument runways. Usually, these systems have sequenced flashing lights that look like a ball of light traveling toward the runway at high speed. Closer to the runway, more lights guide you to the touchdown zone. For nonprecision instrument runways, the approach lighting is simpler and, for VFR runways, the system may consist only of visual glideslope indicators.

VISUAL GLIDESLOPE INDICATORS

These are light systems that indicate your position in relation to the desired glideslope to the runway. The indicator lights are located on the side of a basic or instrument runway and they can be used for day or night approaches. One of the most frequently used installations is the **visual approach slope indicator** (VASI).

You should remain on or above the glide path when approaching a runway served by VASI.

VASI configurations vary and may have either two or three bars. Two-bar systems have near and far bars and may include 2, 4, or 12 light units. The VASI glide path provides safe obstruction clearance within 10° of the extended runway centerline out to four n.m. from the threshold. You should not begin a descent using VASI until your aircraft is aligned with the runway. When landing at a controlled airport that has a VASI, regulations require you to remain on or above the glide path until a lower altitude is necessary for a safe landing. [Figure 3-21]

At larger airports, there may be a three-bar VASI system that incorporates two different glide paths. The lower glide path is normally set at 3°, while the higher one is usually one-fourth of a degree above it. The higher glide path is specifically for certain transport category aircraft with high cock-

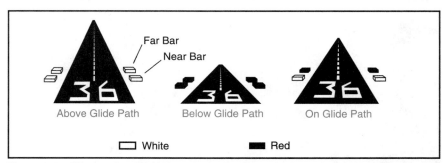

Figure 3-21. The two-bar VASI shows whether or not you are on a glide path that will take you safely to the touchdown zone of the runway. The lights are either white or red, depending on the angle of your glide path, and may be visible from 20 miles at night. If both light bars are white, you are too high; if you see red over red, you are below the glide path. If the far bar is red and the near bar is white, you are on the glide path. The memory aid, "red over white, you're all right," is helpful in recalling the correct sequence of lights.

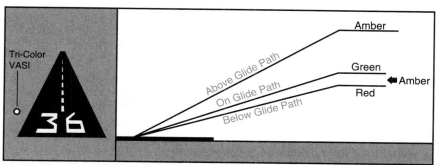

Figure 3-22. The tri-color system also gives you information as to whether or not you are on a safe glide path. If you see amber, you are too high; and if you see red, you are too low. If the light is green, you are on the glide path. As you descend below the glide path, you may see dark amber during the transition from green light to red, so you should not be deceived into thinking that you are too high.

pits. This ensures they will have sufficient altitude when crossing the threshold. If you encounter a three-bar VASI system, use the two lower bars as if it were a standard two-bar VASI.

A **tri-color system** uses a single light unit to project a three-color visual path. It has some similarity to the two-bar VASI because you will see a red light if you are too low. [Figure 3-22]

Some airports may have a **pulsating system** which projects a two-color visual approach path into the final approach area. A pulsating red light normally indicates below glide path; above glide path is normally pulsating white; and the on-glide path indication is a steady white light. The useful range is about four miles during the day and up to 10 miles at night.

With a pulsating system, the below-glide-path indication is normally a pulsating red light.

Another system is the **precision approach path indicator** (PAPI). It has two or four lights installed in a single row instead of far and near bars. The PAPI is normally located on the left side of the runway and can be seen up to five miles during the day and 20 miles at night. [Figure 3-23]

Figure 3-23. If all of the PAPI system lights are white, you are too high. If only the light unit on the far right is red and the other three are white, you are slightly high. When you are on the glide path, the two lights on the left will be white and the two lights on the right will be red. If you are slightly low, only the light on the far left will be white. If you are below the glide path, all four of the lights will be red.

THRESHOLD LIGHTS

If your destination airport has a VASI system, it will lead you down to the touchdown zone on the runway. At night, there are three ways to tell where the runway begins. If the runway has a displaced threshold, there will be a set of green lights on each side of the white threshold line to indicate the beginning of the landing portion of the runway. If the threshold is not displaced, the beginning of the runway pavement will have a row of green lights across it. These lights are two-sided. If you were taking off or landing on the opposite end, they would appear red to mark the end of the usable portion of the runway. Because they are different colors when viewed from opposite directions, you will see green lights designating the approach end of the runway and red lights for the departure end.

Sometimes high intensity white strobe lights are placed on each side of the runway to mark the threshold. These are called **runway end identifier lights** (REILs) and can be used in conjunction with the green threshold lights.

RUNWAY EDGE LIGHTS

You may already be familiar with runway edge lights. They consist of a single row of white lights bordering each side of the runway. Runway edge lights can be classified according to three intensity levels. **High intensity runway lights** (HIRLs) are the brightest runway lights available. **Medium intensity runway lights** (MIRLs) and **low intensity runway lights** (LIRLs) are, as their names indicate, dimmer in intensity. At some airports, you will be able to adjust the intensity of the runway lights from your cockpit by using your radio transmitter. At others, the lights are preset or are adjusted by air traffic controllers.

Some runway edge lights incorporate **runway-remaining lights** on the last half of the runway (or last 2,000 feet of runway, whichever distance is less). They have yellow edge lights to inform you of the amount of runway left. The lights are two-sided, so they appear white when viewed from the opposite end of the runway.

Some airports may have flush-mounted centerline lighting. This system helps instrument pilots determine the amount of runway remaining in very low visibility situations. These lights are placed on the last 3,000 feet of the runway. From the 3,000-foot point to the 1,000-foot point, alternating red and white lights appear, with the last 1,000 feet of lights changing to red only.

TAXIWAY LIGHTING

As you taxi off the active runway, blue taxiway lights guide you from the runway to the ramp area. Because they can be seen from any direction, they are said to be omnidirectional lights. The lights line both edges of the taxiway. At some airports, green taxiway centerline lights may also be installed. These lights are located along the taxiway centerline in both straight and curved portions of the taxiway. They also may be located along designated taxiing paths in portions of runways, ramps, and apron areas. [Figure 3-24]

Taxiway edges are identified at night by blue lights that can be seen from all directions.

PILOT CONTROL OF AIRPORT LIGHTING

For practical and economic reasons, the approach, runway, and taxiway lights at some unattended airports may be on a timer that will turn off the lights 15 minutes after they have been activated. If this is the case, you need to be able to turn them on again as you prepare to depart or approach

1	Runway Lights	8	Taxiway Turnoff Lighting
2	Taxiway Lights	9	Touchdown Zone Lighting
3	Airport Beacon	10	Runway Centerline Lights
4	Threshold Lights	11	Runway End Identifier Lights
5	VASI Installation	12	High Intensity Runway Lights
6	Obstruction Lights	13	Displaced Threshold Lights
7	Approach Light System		

Figure 3-24. This pictorial summary shows the various types of airport marking and lighting typically found at large, controlled airports.

to land. **Pilot-controlled lighting** is the term used to describe systems that you can activate by keying the aircraft's microphone on a specified radio frequency. Keep in mind that other types of airport lighting may be pilot controlled, not just approach and runway lighting. For example, VASI and REIL lights may be pilot controlled at some locations.

After three-step runway lights are initially turned on, you can select medium intensity by keying your microphone five times.

The following example shows the general procedures you would use at an airport with three-step pilot-controlled runway lights. Initially, you should key your microphone seven times on the specified frequency to turn all the lights on at maximum intensity. If conditions dictate a lower intensity, key your microphone five times for medium-intensity lighting and three times for the lowest intensity. For each adjustment, you must key the microphone the required number of times within a period of five seconds. Remember though, using the lower intensity lighting on some installations may turn the REILs completely off. The *Airport/Facility Directory* contains a description of the type of pilot-controlled lighting available at individual airports.

OBSTRUCTION LIGHTING

You will see obstruction lighting both on and off the airport, during the day and at night. The purpose of this type of lighting is to give you advanced warning of obstructions. For example, obstruction lights are installed on prominent structures such as towers, buildings and, sometimes, even powerlines. Bright red and high intensity white lights are typically used and may flash on and off. Remember that there may be guy-wires extending from the top of the tower to the ground, so be sure that you are well clear of the object.

CHECKLIST

After studying this section, you should have a basic understanding of:

✓ **Runways and Taxiways** — How they are marked, and what the different markings indicate.

✓ **Wind direction indicators** — The types of indicators and what information they provide.

✓ **Tetrahedron** — What it is primarily used for.

✓ **Taxiing in wind** — What wind situations are most critical and how to position your controls.

✓ **Airport lighting** — What the various types are, how they are used, and which can be pilot-controlled.

The checklists and takeoff procedures outlined in this section are provided as general guidelines only. Be sure to consult the pilot's operating handbook for your airplane for the proper checklists and procedures.

PRETAKEOFF CHECK

Before each takeoff, it is important for you to perform a pretakeoff check of the airplane equipment and systems to ensure proper operation. Use a written checklist provided by the airplane manufacturer or operator. This ensures that each item is checked in the proper sequence and that nothing is omitted.

Use a written checklist whenever possible.

After you taxi the airplane to the runup area, position it so the propeller blast is not directed toward other aircraft. If possible, point the nose into the wind to improve engine cooling. To prevent damage to the propeller and other parts of the airplane, avoid engine runups on loose gravel and sand.

During the pretakeoff check, which is sometimes referred to as the runup, divide your attention between the cockpit and the area around the airplane. If the parking brake slips, or you do not hold the toe brakes firmly, the airplane can move forward while your attention is inside the cockpit.

Usually, the engine will have warmed sufficiently before the pretakeoff check so it will accelerate smoothly when you apply power. All engine instrument indications must be normal before takeoff. If you observe any abnormal condition during the runup, return the airplane for maintenance, since even minor malfunctions can affect the safety and efficiency of the flight. Let's follow through a typical pretakeoff checklist.

If you notice an abnormal condition prior to flight, delay the flight until the problem is resolved.

1. Check that the cabin doors are securely closed and latched.

2. Check the flight controls to determine that they move correctly, freely, and easily throughout their total travel. A small movement of the controls is not sufficient; move each control through its full range of travel while noting the direction of movement.

3. Set the elevator trim to the TAKEOFF position.

4. Set the throttle to the r.p.m. recommended by the manufacturer for the power check.

   a. Move the carburetor heat to the ON position and note the power loss, then return it to the OFF position. With hot air entering the carburetor, the engine r.p.m. should decrease, indicating the carburetor heat is functioning.

b. Test the magnetos by noting the r.p.m with the magneto switch in the BOTH position, then move the magneto switch to the RIGHT position and note the r.p.m drop. Next, return the magneto switch to BOTH, then switch to the LEFT position and again note the r.p.m drop. Finally, return the magneto switch to the BOTH position for takeoff. The airplane manufacturer specifies the maximum permissible r.p.m. reductions for each magneto, as well as the maximum differential. For example, a manufacturer may specify that each magneto may not drop more than 150 r.p.m., and that the maximum difference between the two may not exceed 75 r.p.m.

c. Check the engine instruments. With the exception of the oil temperature gauge, they should register operation in the green arcs. Oil temperature may not indicate in the normal range until after takeoff. However, the airplane is considered ready for takeoff if the engine accelerates normally, the oil pressure remains steady and normal, and other engine instruments continue to register normally.

d. Check the suction gauge for a normal indication. A low reading may indicate a dirty air filter. Unreliable gyro indications may result if sufficient suction is not maintained.

5. Check and set the flight instruments, systems, and radios.

a. Set the altimeter to the altimeter setting supplied by the tower controller, or to the correct field elevation if you are operating from an uncontrolled field.

b. Set the heading indicator to coincide with the magnetic compass.

c. Check all gyro instruments for stable operation.

d. Check the ammeter or loadmeter for proper indication.

e. Set the radios to the desired frequencies.

f. Set the course selectors to the desired courses or radials.

When the checklist is complete, you are ready for takeoff. Before you taxi onto the runway, be sure to check both the approach and departure paths for traffic. At an uncontrolled field, be sure to check the entire area for other traffic as well. When the runway is clear, taxi the airplane into the takeoff position. At controlled airports, you must obtain a takeoff clearance from the control tower prior to taxiing onto the runway.

TAXIING INTO TAKEOFF POSITION

When you are ready for takeoff, taxi onto the runway, line up with the runway centerline, center the nosewheel, and neutralize the ailerons. After checking the windsock to determine the wind position in relation to the runway, you are ready to begin the takeoff roll.

Place your right hand on the throttle and keep it there throughout the takeoff. This assures that the throttle does not vibrate back during the takeoff roll. It also allows you to close the throttle quickly if you decide to abort the takeoff. Your feet should be resting on the floor with the balls of your feet on the bottom edges of the rudder pedals. This places your feet in a position where they have no tendency to press the toe brakes inadvertently.

Proper placement of your hands and feet during the takeoff roll improves airplane control and safety.

TAKEOFF PROCEDURES

Begin the takeoff roll with a smooth application of power. As soon as you apply power and the airplane begins to roll, select a point on the cowl through which the runway centerline passes and use it as a reference for directional control. In addition, check the engine instruments to ensure the engine is developing full power and operating within limits. Slow acceleration or any hesitation in power is sufficient reason to discontinue the takeoff.

During the takeoff roll, maintain directional control with the rudder pedals; use the neutral aileron position if the wind is straight down the runway. The rudder pedals control the steerable nosewheel and are usually sufficient to maintain directional control; however, the rudder itself becomes more effective as you increase speed. Because of this, the amount of rudder deflection required for directional control changes throughout the takeoff roll. Before you add power, the rudder is neutral. As you add power, apply right rudder pressure to counteract engine torque. As speed increases and the controls become more effective, reduce rudder pressure to maintain directional control and apply slight back pressure to the control wheel. Establish the takeoff attitude at the speed specified in the pilot's operating handbook. In most training airplanes, this attitude is similar to the normal climb attitude.

The takeoff attitude is important because it is a compromise between holding the nose on the ground and selecting an attitude which is too nose-high. If the nosewheel is held on the ground too long, the airplane tends to build excess airspeed, which increases the length of runway required for takeoff. With an excessively nose-high attitude, the airplane may be forced into the air prematurely and then settle back to the runway. Also, it may be at such a high angle of attack (high drag condition) that it cannot accelerate to the liftoff airspeed. With the proper attitude, the airplane attains a safe speed and becomes airborne near the proper climb speed. If you hold that attitude after liftoff, the airplane accelerates to climb speed. Another advantage of maintaining this attitude is that the airplane will be in the best attitude to accelerate to climb speed if it is lifted into the air prematurely by a wind gust.

The speed used for initial climb after takeoff varies with local conditions.

The initial climb speed varies, based on flap position and obstacles in the departure path. You may need to fly at the obstacle clearance speed, best angle-of-climb speed, or best rate-of-climb speed. The correct speed for each airplane and operating condition is specified in the pilot's operating handbook. When the airplane reaches the correct climb speed, adjust the pitch attitude to maintain this speed. During the climb, fly the takeoff leg of the traffic pattern straight out on an extension of the runway centerline without drifting to one side or the other.

CROSSWIND TAKEOFF

During practice of takeoffs, one of the factors which you must consider is the effect of a crosswind. The term **crosswind component** refers to that part of the wind velocity that acts at a right angle to the airplane's path on takeoff or landing. Most airplanes have a maximum demonstrated crosswind component listed in the POH. Of course, your personal crosswind limit is based on your skill level as well as any limitation set forth by your instructor during training. A crosswind component chart is used to calculate the crosswind component under a given set of conditions. It also allows you to calculate the **headwind component**, which may be used to adjust takeoff and landing performance figures. [Figure 3-25]

Ailerons and rudder are used to counteract the effect of a crosswind during takeoff and landing.

During the takeoff and landing rolls, a crosswind tends to push and roll the airplane to the downwind side of the runway. To compensate for this effect, use the ailerons the same way you do for crosswind taxiing. For slow airspeeds at the beginning of the takeoff roll, you should use full aileron deflection. The wind flow over the wing with the raised aileron tends to hold that wing down, while airflow under the wing with the lowered aileron tends to push that wing up. These factors counteract the rolling tendency caused by the crosswind. As the airplane accelerates, the ailerons become more effective. Reduce the deflection gradually, so it is just sufficient to counteract the rolling tendency.

The wind also attempts to weathervane the airplane. You can counteract this effect by rudder application. The weathervaning tendency is a result

Sample Problem
Wind Direction . . . . 050°
Wind Speed . . . 25 knots
Runway in Use 9

WIND COMPONENTS

HEADWIND COMPONENT - KNOTS

WIND SPEED ~ KNOTS

ANGLE BETWEEN WIND DIRECTION AND FLIGHT PATH

CROSSWIND COMPONENT - KNOTS

Figure 3-25. First, determine the angle between the wind and runway (090° – 050° = 40°). Enter the crosswind component chart at the point where the angle of 40° meets the wind speed of 25 knots. Proceed horizontally to the left and read the headwind component of 19 knots, or move vertically down and read the crosswind component of 16 knots.

of the wind striking the vertical stabilizer and rudder surfaces which are a considerable distance from the center of gravity. This causes the nose of the airplane to turn into the wind. The amount of crosswind correction necessary depends on the crosswind component. With moderate crosswind components, the airplane is sensitive to side loads as it approaches liftoff speed. If your corrections are improper, they will place side loads on the landing gear.

It takes practice to determine how much aileron and rudder deflection is required to compensate for a crosswind. When you use the right amount, you feel no side load and the airplane tracks straight down the runway. Hold the airplane on the runway until you attain a slightly higher-than-normal liftoff speed. At this point, lift the airplane off the runway promptly and establish a normal climb attitude. This technique reduces the chance of the airplane being lifted off the runway prematurely by a sudden gust of

Figure 3-26. As speed increases during takeoff and ailerons become effective, reduce aileron pressure until there is just enough to counteract the crosswind. When the airplane is airborne and you have established a positive rate of climb, enter a crab by making a coordinated turn into the wind. This technique allows the airplane to track straight out on an imaginary extension of the runway centerline.

wind before it has attained sufficient airspeed to remain airborne. [Figure 3-26]

TURBULENCE

Turbulence, caused by high winds or other atmospheric conditions in the vicinity of an airport, can decrease takeoff maneuverability and climb performance. Essentially, this is because it can increase the possibility of a stall. Therefore, increased climb speeds must be maintained after a takeoff in rough air.

SIMULATED TAKEOFF EMERGENCIES

Although an engine malfunction on takeoff is rare, the possibility does exist. Therefore, you will learn ways to handle this situation during flight training. The simulated emergency situation occurs when your instructor reduces engine power by smoothly closing the throttle. The objective of this practice is to prepare you to meet the problems of an engine failure on takeoff. It helps you develop judgment, technique, confidence, and the ability to respond quickly and accurately to situations requiring prompt action.

One emergency you might encounter is an engine malfunction on the takeoff roll or just after liftoff. If you suspect a malfunction during the takeoff roll, abort the takeoff quickly by moving the throttle to the idle position. Use the brakes as necessary to stop the airplane, and use the rudder to maintain directional control.

If your airplane has become airborne when the simulated emergency occurs, you should reduce the pitch attitude slightly and allow the airplane to settle back to the ground. Generally, if the airplane is low and power is lost, you have no choice but to continue straight ahead, making only small changes in direction to avoid obstacles. This technique is necessary because insufficient altitude is available to make a power-off 180° turn to return to the airport for a landing.

Should an engine fail at low altitude after takeoff, you must land straight ahead, making only small turns.

CHECKLIST _____

After studying this section, you should have a basic understanding of:

✓ **Pretakeoff check** — What the procedures are to ensure a properly operating airplane prior to flight.

✓ **Takeoff procedures** — What the procedures are to initiate takeoff and to control the airplane during the takeoff roll and initial climbout.

✓ **Crosswind takeoffs** — What the effects of a crosswind are on takeoff and how to compensate for these effects.

NORMAL AND CROSSWIND LANDINGS

The approach and landing is the phase of flight most pilots look forward to, because it represents a high degree of accomplishment. Proper execution of landings is important because it gives an indication of your ability to perform basic maneuvers, plan ahead, and divide your attention among several tasks.

EFFECTS OF WIND

Initially, your instructor will probably have you practice landings on calm days. In a no-wind situation, you can simply fly perpendicular or parallel to the runway to maintain a uniform traffic pattern. As your skill level increases, you will begin to fly in windy conditions. In order to maintain the desired path around the traffic pattern, you will need to make adjustments for the wind. These adjustments will vary for each leg of the traffic pattern. [Figure 3-27]

The effects of wind on turns and on the final approach are covered, as appropriate, in the following discussion. Later, you will practice ground reference maneuvers, which will allow you to perfect your wind correction techniques.

APPROACH AND LANDING

A landing is nothing more than the transition of the airplane from being an airborne vehicle to being a ground vehicle. When you have mastered

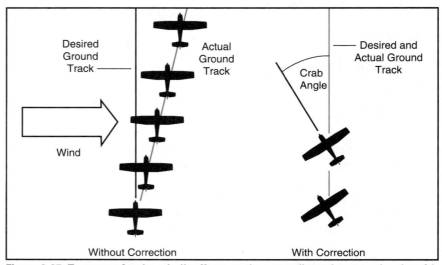

Figure 3-27. To correct for the wind's effects, make a coordinated turn so the aircraft's nose is directed into the wind. The angle between the airplane's nose and the desired path over the ground is called the crab angle. As the wind tends to blow you away from your desired ground track, the crab angle allows you to maintain it.

the procedures and techniques of landing, you will be able to land the airplane consistently and safely on the area you have selected. This requires a high degree of planning that begins on the downwind leg.

If you use a different traffic pattern size, airspeed, flap setting, or rate of turn to base and final on each approach, you have a new problem to solve. Your chances of touching down consistently at the appropriate spot on the runway are much lower. Fly the traffic pattern so the distance of the downwind leg from the runway does not vary. In addition, your altitude, point of power reduction, and approach airspeed should be the same for each approach. The turns to base and final should be consistent. Then, you can use flaps and power to make minor corrections for position and to compensate for wind.

Throughout training, you should practice consistency and precise control of the airplane to reduce the number of variables in the landing approach. The following paragraphs describe a typical approach and landing in a training airplane.

Each traffic pattern and approach should be flown in a consistent manner.

DOWNWIND LEG

Fly the downwind leg at a distance appropriate to your airplane and local traffic requirements. For most training airplanes, this distance is about one-half to one mile from the runway in use. The airplane's ground track should parallel the runway, with no tendency to angle toward or drift away from it. Angling or drifting causes the traffic pattern to have an abnormal shape, which greatly influences the length of the base leg. When you approach the 180° point, or the point opposite the intended landing area, your airspeed should be near cruise in most training airplanes. In addition, your altitude should be at the designated traffic pattern altitude. This is usually 1,000 feet AGL, unless specified otherwise. [Figure 3-28]

Figure 3-28. At the 180° point, reduce the power to the descent power setting, maintain altitude, and allow the airspeed to slow to approach speed.

Use the approach speed recommended in the POH or, if none is given, use 1.3 V_{S0}.

When the airplane reaches approach airspeed, you normally maintain that speed and initiate the descent. However, you may need to delay the start of the descent if the downwind leg must be extended to follow traffic. The transition from cruise speed on downwind to descent speed is a practical application of the transition from cruise to descent that you learned earlier. The POH normally specifies the recommended approach speed. When an approach speed is recommended, you should maintain the speed as precisely as possible. If an approach speed is not recommended, use a final approach speed that is 1.3 times the power-off stall speed in the landing configuration (V_{S0}).

BASE LEG

You usually begin the turn to base leg when the touchdown point is approximately 30° to 45° behind the wing. However, before beginning the turn, be sure to check for other traffic. [Figure 3-29]

With practice, this perspective becomes so familiar that you can detect the need for small corrections at this position. Vary the start of the turn to base leg to compensate for variations in conditions. Throughout the approach, you must be alert for other traffic in the pattern, especially on final approach. As you turn base, the wind tends to push the airplane farther away from the runway. Therefore, it is usually necessary to execute a turn of more than 90° to apply the necessary crab angle. Then, monitor your ground track, since further adjustments may be required.

When the airplane rolls out on base leg, it is at the point called the key position. When you reach this spot on each approach, you must assess your position and determine whether or not to make corrections in the approach pattern. [Figure 3-30]

Figure 3-29. From the downwind perspective, the runway will look similar to this view when it is time to begin your turn from downwind to base.

Figure 3-30. At the key position, evaluate your altitude, airspeed, distance from the runway, and wind. Then make any corrections needed to adjust the approach.

For example, if the airplane is high, it will land beyond the desired touch-down point. In this situation, there are two possible corrections— you can reduce power or extend additional flaps. You can use one or both, depending upon the amount of correction needed.

If the airplane is low or wide on base leg, or the wind is stronger than nor-mal, you will also need to make corrections. Otherwise, the airplane will land short of the desired point. There are two actions that you can take to avoid this situation. You can begin the turn to final sooner than normal, or you can add power. You can use either one or both, depending on the amount of correction necessary. Retracting the flaps is not considered an acceptable correction. Normally, once you extend the flaps, they are not retracted until you have completed the landing or abandoned the landing approach.

Make corrections for position anytime you recognize a need. The signifi-cance of the key position is that it is an early decision point where you can easily make major adjustments. This ensures a smooth approach and avoids large or abrupt last-minute corrections. Throughout the approach, you should continue to assess your position relative to the runway to determine the need for additional corrections. Through the process of assessing your position, making corrections, and then reevaluating the touchdown point, you are able to judge your touchdown point accurately.

FINAL APPROACH

Before you turn to the final approach leg, always look in all directions for other traffic. If the area is clear, make the turn to final. The turn to final is usually completed at a distance of at least one-quarter mile from the run-way threshold. Normally, your altitude is about 300 to 400 feet AGL as you roll out on final. This may vary with the particular airplane or because of adjustments for other traffic in the pattern.

Complete the turn to final no closer than one-quarter mile from the runway.

Based on existing wind conditions, you may have to begin the turn to final sooner or later than in a no-wind situation. Your objective is to complete the turn and roll out on the extension of the runway centerline. Maintain the approach airspeed as specified in the POH, or 1.3 V_{S0}, as appropriate. Monitor the approach speed until you begin the landing transition.

The recommended approach speed is an indicated airspeed that should not be adjusted for various temperature and altitude combinations. Although temperature and pressure changes will change air density, and therefore lift, a given indicated airspeed will continue to ensure the same amount of lift.

Do not adjust approach speed for nonstandard temperature or pressure.

Throughout the landing approach, your ability to use visual attitude references to control speed is the key to a good landing. You must be able to scan outside references while controlling the speed accurately. The pitch attitudes should look familiar, since they are the ones you used when you practiced straight descents and descending turns.

Your required rate of descent on final approach is directly affected by the headwind component. As the wind speed increases, your groundspeed decreases. This means you will need to decrease your rate of descent in order to reach the runway.

If you maintain a constant approach angle, the apparent shape of the runway will remain fixed. If your approach becomes shallower, the runway will appear to shorten and become wider. Conversely, if your approach is steepened, the runway will appear to be longer and narrower. Therefore, if you maintain a constant approach angle, the sides of the runway will maintain the same relationship and the threshold will remain in a fixed position in relation to the airplane's nose. [Figure 3-31]

During early landing practice, it is common to overcontrol the airplane. To avoid this, make smooth, positive corrections back to that pattern, whenever you notice a deviation. If you are low, for example, it is usually not necessary to make an abrupt correction and climb back to the standard pattern. Instead, you can add power and reduce the rate of descent and/or level off for a short period until you regain the correct approach angle.

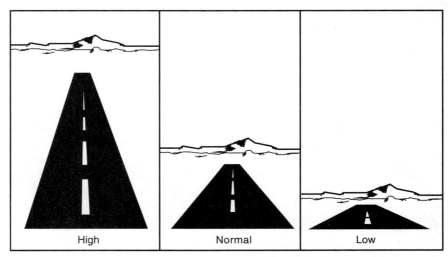

| High | Normal | Low |

Figure 3-31. This illustration shows how the apparent length and width of the runway vary with approach angle. By monitoring the shape of the runway, you can maintain a constant approach path.

Frequently, approach speed is near the best angle-of-glide speed. This means that any other airspeed results in a steeper angle of descent. If the airplane is short of the desired touchdown spot, you cannot stretch a glide by raising the nose and slowing the airspeed; instead, you must add power.

If the approach is extremely high, there is very little value in entering a steep descent. Although it appears the airplane will reach the chosen point of touchdown, the dive causes an increase in airspeed which must be dissipated in the flare. The result is that a greater distance is covered as the airplane floats down the runway, usually well beyond the selected touchdown point.

LANDING

The landing consists of three elements — the flare, the touchdown, and the roll-out. The term **flare** refers to the process of changing the attitude of the airplane from a glide or descent attitude to a landing attitude. Its purpose is to reduce speed and decrease the rate of descent.

You can estimate the point at which the airplane will actually touch down. Find the point where the glide path intersects the ground and add the approximate distance to be traveled in the flare. The glide path intersection point, also called the aiming point, is the spot on the ground that has no apparent relative movement. As the airplane descends, all objects beyond the glide path intersection point appear to move away from the airplane, while objects closer appear to move toward it. The approximate distance traveled in the flare varies, depending on the approach speed and wind. [Figure 3-32]

> The actual point at which the airplane will land is located some distance beyond the "aim" point used on final approach.

Figure 3-32. During the final approach, you will touch down several hundred feet beyond the aiming point. This allows the airplane to stabilize in the flare prior to touchdown.

Figure 3-33. In preparation for landing, adjustments are made to the airplane's attitude, speed, and rate of descent during the flare.

The flare begins at different altitudes for airplanes of varying weights and approach speeds. However, for most training airplanes, it begins at approximately 10 to 20 feet above the ground. Initiate the flare with a gradual increase in back pressure on the control wheel to reduce speed and decrease the rate of descent. Ideally, the airplane reaches a rate of descent near zero, approximately one foot above the runway at about 8 to 10 knots above stall speed with idle power. [Figure 3-33]

Next, attempt to hold the airplane just off the runway by increasing back pressure. This causes the airplane to settle slowly to the runway in a slightly nose-high attitude as it approaches stall speed. The pitch attitude at touchdown should be very close to the pitch attitude at takeoff, with the nosewheel held clear of the runway. The main wheels should touch down beyond and within 500 feet of a point specified by your instructor. After touchdown, maintain back pressure and allow the nosewheel to touch down gently.

The cues you make use of in the flare and landing are a combination of visual and kinesthetic feelings. You have practiced descents and power-off stalls to build sensitivity to control responses and smoothness in preparation for the flare and landing. Generally, kinesthetic sensitivity is not developed fully at the time you begin landing practice; therefore, vision is the most important sense.

The altitude for the flare and the height throughout the flare are determined by your depth perception. **Depth perception** is the visual comparison of the size of known objects on the ground; therefore, the area where you focus your vision during the approach is important. If you focus too close to the airplane or look straight down, the airspeed blurs objects on the ground. This causes your actions to be delayed or too abrupt. When you focus too close to the airplane, the tendency is to overcontrol and level off too high.

If you focus too far down the runway, you will be unable to judge height above the ground accurately. Consequently, your reactions will be slow. In this situation, you will generally allow the airplane to fly onto the runway without flaring. Thus, it becomes obvious that you must focus at some intermediate point. A guideline is to focus about the same distance ahead of the airplane as when you are driving a car at the same speed. However, you must look to one side of the airplane, since its nose may block your view ahead during the flare and landing. [Figure 3-34]

During the roll-out, maintain directional control with rudder pressure. As the airplane touches down, your feet should be in the same position on the rudder pedals as they were during the flare. With your heels on the floor, there is no tendency to use the brakes inadvertently, but you will be able to reach them, if necessary.

GO-AROUND

A general rule of thumb in landing practice is that, if the airplane has not touched down in the first one-third of the runway, you should abandon the landing by flying around the traffic pattern and setting up another landing approach. This go-around procedure may also be required when an aircraft or some other obstacle is on the runway or when you feel the approach is uncomfortable, incorrect, or potentially dangerous.

Figure 3-34. The flare and landing are made easier when you focus at the correct distance ahead of the airplane.

The decision to make a go-around should be positive; initiate the maneuver before a critical situation develops. Once you have made the decision, carry it out without hesitation. In many cases, the go-around is initiated with the airplane at a slow airspeed and in a nose-high attitude. In this situation, your first response is to apply all available power, then accelerate the airplane to the best angle-of-climb speed and adjust the pitch attitude. Once you reach a safe speed and altitude, retract the flaps. If another aircraft is on the runway during the go-around, make a gentle turn to the right side of the runway, if possible. [Figure 3-35]

Continue the climb on the takeoff leg parallel to the runway until you reach the crosswind leg. If another airplane is ahead, allow proper spacing and join the traffic pattern.

BOUNCED LANDING

At times, you may perform landings that cause the airplane to bounce into the air. Usually, it is wise not to attempt to salvage these landings. Instead, you should make an immediate go-around. Except when lowering flaps or trimming the airplane, you should have your hand on the throttle throughout the approach and landing. When a landing is bad, make a prompt decision to go around and add all available power. Adjust the pitch attitude to a normal climb attitude and complete the go-around procedures.

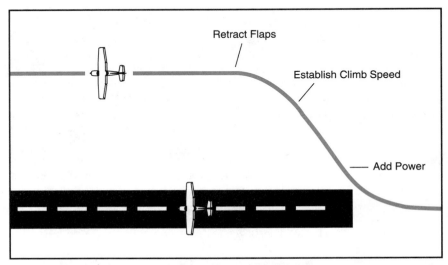

Figure 3-35. When you initiate a go-around with another airplane on the runway, adjust your flight path to be far enough to the side of the runway that it does not interfere with an airplane taking off. In this position, you can see the runway clearly. Special cases, such as use of parallel runways, may prevent you from making this slight turn or may require you to make a slight left turn.

If the airplane bounces only a small amount and gains just a few feet of altitude, hold the nose in the landing attitude while the airplane settles back to the runway. Use a similar procedure if the airplane "balloons" because the elevator has been pulled back too rapidly. After stopping the resulting climb, return the nose to the landing attitude and hold it in that attitude until the airplane settles on the runway. However, if you balloon too high or there is any question about the successful outcome of the landing, the best procedure is to go around.

When any doubt exists as to the successful outcome of an approach and landing, execute an immediate go-around.

USE OF WING FLAPS DURING LANDING

You can make landings with no flaps, partial flaps, or full flaps. The procedures used with various flap settings are generally the same; however, there are specific differences. With no flaps, the rate of descent usually is less than with partial flaps. To avoid this situation, you must adjust power and the traffic pattern. Since the stall speed with no flaps is higher than it is with full flaps, the airplane touches down at a faster speed and the landing roll-out is longer.

When you use full flaps for landing, you will typically extend the first increment of flaps on the downwind leg and the next on base leg. Usually, you will extend full flaps on the final approach leg. At the full-flap setting, the rate of descent increases, so the tendency is to land short. The touchdown speed is slower, since the full-flap stall speed is less than the no-flap or partial-flap stall speed. This results in a shorter ground roll.

If a go-around with full flaps is required, follow the procedures recommended in the pilot's operating handbook. After adding all available power, retract the flaps to an intermediate setting, if required, but do not attempt to enter a normal climb attitude immediately. Instead, use the straight-and-level, slow flight attitude which allows the airplane to maintain its present altitude. As you approach the best angle-of-climb speed, maintain that speed until all obstacles are cleared. Then, accelerate to the best rate-of-climb speed, slowly retract remaining flaps, and continue the departure just as you would a normal takeoff. During the initial stages of a go-around, be extra cautious. An attempt to raise the nose immediately may result in a stall. In addition, suddenly raising all of the flaps can cause the airplane to descend onto the ground.

CROSSWIND LANDING TECHNIQUE

The approach to landing in a crosswind is essentially the crosswind takeoff process in reverse. The turn to final should be completed on an extension of the runway centerline, with the airplane in a crab to correct for wind drift.

On final, lower the wing into the wind and use opposite rudder pressure to keep the nose pointed straight down the runway. This is referred to as a **side slip**. When you perform the slip properly, the airplane has no tendency to drift from one side of the runway to the other. Beginning pilots usually place the airplane in the wing-low condition at altitudes of 100 to 200 feet AGL while on final, but as they become more experienced, they tend to wait until just before they begin the flare. [Figure 3-36]

The airplane must contact the runway without drifting to either side. You must align both the ground track and the longitudinal axis of the airplane with the runway. If you do not, side loads will be imposed on the landing gear and tires, resulting in damage. As the airplane slows, the downwind wing will lower and the other wheel will touch the ground. As the airplane continues to slow, add more aileron, since the ailerons become less effective with speed loss.

In moderate and light crosswinds, the nose attitude for liftoff and touchdown is the same as in normal takeoffs and landings. In a strong crosswind, place the nose on the ground with positive elevator pressure to allow the nosewheel to assist in directional control. Take care not to lift the main landing gear off the runway as a result of excessive airspeed and

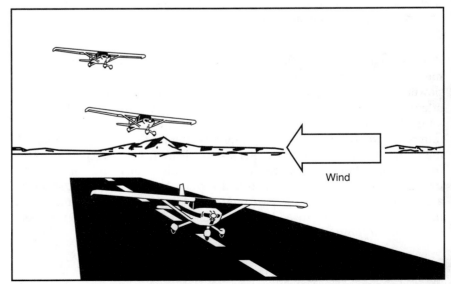

Figure 3-36. Start the flare at the normal altitude and hold the wing down throughout the flare and touchdown. This causes the airplane to touch down initially on one main wheel.

Figure 3-37. During the landing flare and roll-out, use the rudder to keep the nose of the airplane aligned with the centerline, and use the ailerons to control drift.

control wheel pressure. In addition, aileron controls should be fully into the wind, not neutralized, at the end of the landing roll. [Figure 3-37]

In gusty wind conditions, you may use a slightly different landing technique. You can maintain better control if you fly the airplane onto the runway at an airspeed slightly higher than normal, then hold it on the runway with slight forward control wheel pressure. In a left-hand traffic pattern, when the wind is from the right side of the runway, the wind tends to distort the pattern by pushing the airplane wide on the downwind leg and slowing the groundspeed on the base leg. If you do not correct this condition, it will result in angling turns to final and approaches that are shallower or short of the runway.

When the wind is from the left of the landing runway, it tends to push the airplane closer to the runway and increase groundspeed on base leg. This situation may cause you to overshoot the final and results in approaches that are high and long. If you recognize these tendencies, you can take corrective action in the traffic pattern.

SLIPS

The slip is a flight attitude used to increase the angle of descent without causing an increase in airspeed. You accomplish this by exposing as much of the airplane surface to the oncoming air as possible, so the airplane's frontal area produces considerable drag. This allows a steeper angle of descent without acceleration. Flaps serve the same purpose, but they cannot always be used because of crosswinds or gusts. The two types are side slips and forward slips. They are aerodynamically the same, but they differ in the way you maneuver the airplane with respect to the ground.

SIDE SLIP

A side slip is used to compensate for drift during crosswind landings. To maintain a constant heading and a straight flight path, balance the aileron and rudder control pressure. Too much aileron or too little opposite rudder causes a turn in the direction of bank. In contrast, too much rudder or too little opposite aileron causes a yaw away from the bank. To steepen the descent, increase both aileron and rudder in a coordinated manner. [Figure 3-38]

FORWARD SLIP

The **forward slip** can be valuable when you are landing in fields with obstructions. In an airplane with side-by-side seating, you will usually slip to the left, since this provides you with an excellent view of the land-

Figure 3-38. During a side slip in a no-wind condition, the nose of the airplane remains on the same heading throughout the maneuver, but the ground track is sideways in the direction of the low wing. However, when you perform a side slip into a crosswind, the resulting ground track is a straight line which is parallel to the longitudinal axis of the airplane.

Figure 3-39. To initiate a forward slip, lower one wing by using aileron control. At the same time, apply opposite rudder to keep the airplane from turning in the direction of the lowered wing. This procedure keeps the airplane's ground track in alignment with the extended centerline of the runway, but allows the nose of the airplane to angle away from the runway. To prevent the airspeed from increasing, raise the nose slightly above the normal gliding position. In this attitude, the glide path steepens, even though the airspeed remains constant.

ing area during the entire slip. However, if a crosswind is present, execute the slip into the wind. [Figure 3-39]

As soon as you lose sufficient altitude, begin the recovery. Raise the low wing and simultaneously ease rudder pressure as you level the wings and adjust pitch attitude to the normal glide attitude. The only difference between the control application in right and left slips is that the control pressures are reversed. You should perform forward slips with the engine at idle power, since using power decreases the rate of descent.

CHECKLIST _____

After studying this section, you should have a basic understanding of:

✓ **Key position** — What the importance of the key position is and how to adjust the approach from that point.

✓ **Landing** — How control of the airplane is maintained during the landing flare and roll-out, and the influence of ground effect.

✓ **Flaps** — How flaps are used in an approach and during a go-around.

✓ **Crosswind landings** — How to compensate for a crosswind in the traffic pattern and during final approach, landing, and roll-out.

POWER-OFF STALLS

Stalls are practiced to accomplish two main objectives. First, they enable you to become familiar with the stall warnings and handling characteristics of an airplane as it transitions from cruise to slow airspeeds and approaches a stall. Second, if you inadvertently enter a stall, you will be conditioned to recover promptly and effectively with a minimum loss of altitude.

CERTIFICATION REGULATIONS

FAR Part 23 prescribes the airworthiness standards for light airplanes. It contains the regulations pertaining to flight performance and handling characteristics, structure, powerplant, equipment, and operating limitations. Before a manufacturer can offer an airplane for sale, it must meet the specifications of this regulation, including flight testing and stall demonstrations. You should find the following points of particular interest:

1. You must be able to correct a roll or yaw up to the stall. This means that you must have effective use of the controls up to actual stall occurrence.

2. You must be able to prevent more than 15° of roll or 15° of yaw through normal use of controls during the recovery from a stall. In short, the controls must be effective during the recovery.

3. There must be a clear and distinct stall warning with the landing gear and flaps in any position you choose and in either straight or turning flight. The stall warning must begin between 5 and 10 knots before the stall occurs, continue into the stall, and end with the recovery. The acceptable stall warning can be buffeting or vibration of the airplane just prior to the actual stall or a visual or aural stall warning instrument.

4. If the airplane loses more than 100 feet or pitches more than 30° nose down during the stall demonstration, this information must be listed in the aircraft flight manual.

CAUSES OF THE STALL

Simply stated, a stall is caused by an excessive angle of attack, which causes the smooth airflow over the upper wing surface to break away, resulting in a loss of lift. However, the stall does not occur over the entire wing area at once. For example, consider a wing planform that begins to stall first at the wingtips and then spreads inward toward the root. This is an undesirable characteristic, since the disrupted airflow near the wingtip can reduce aileron effectiveness to such an extent that it may be impossi-

Figure 3-40. When wing twist is incorporated into the wing design, the wingtip has a lower angle of incidence than the wing root (usually two or three degrees). This results in the wingtip having a lower angle of attack than the root during the approach to a stall. Thus, the wingtip and ailerons will still be flying and providing positive control when the wing root has stalled.

ble to control the airplane about its longitudinal axis. One method often used by airplane designers to prevent this problem is to incorporate a slight twist or washout in the wing. [Figure 3-40]

Another method sometimes used to assure positive control during the stall is installation of **stall strips**, which consist of two metal strips attached to the leading edge of each wing near the fuselage. These strips disrupt the airflow at high angles of attack, causing the wing area directly behind them to stall before the wingtips stall.

Remember, the airplane will stall whenever the critical angle of attack of the wing is exceeded. The stall can occur at any airspeed and in any flight attitude. The indicated airspeed at which the stall occurs varies with the airplane's weight, G-loading, and power and flap settings. Flight Prep 2, Section A contains a complete discussion of the aerodynamics of stalls.

STALL PRACTICE

Practice stalls in an area away from other air traffic at an altitude that will allow you to recover from a stall at least 1,500 feet above the ground. Before stall practice, as well as prior to other maneuvers, remember to make clearing turns to ensure there are no other airplanes in the area. If there are airplanes nearby, wait until they are well clear before performing the maneuver.

You will do the first stall from a power-off, wings-level glide, such as the one you use when you land the airplane. This is called a power-off stall. To enter the stall, apply carburetor heat (if required), reduce power to idle, apply full flaps (once a safe flap extension speed has been attained), establish a normal glide, and trim the airplane. Next, start to slow the airplane by applying back pressure on the control wheel.

Near the stall, the controls feel mushy and the engine and slipstream noises are reduced.

One objective of the maneuver is to gain a "feel" for the control pressures and responses as the airplane approaches the stall. As speed slows, the airplane's response to control pressures becomes slower, and it is necessary to use greater displacement of the controls to achieve the desired results. The feeling is sometimes called "mushy" or "soft," as compared to the more solid feel of the controls at cruise speed. As you approach the stall, there are other cues that tell you the airplane is slowing. For example, the engine sound decreases, as does the tone and intensity of the slipstream noise. The stall warning begins 5 to 10 knots before the stall. The warning indications may be a light, buzzer, horn, buffeting, or any combination of these. One of the purposes of stall practice is to recognize the indications applicable to your airplane.

As part of your stall/spin awareness training, you will be required to recognize signs of an impending stall. For example, buffeting and decay of control effectiveness are good aerodynamic indications of an approach to a stall. This flight condition, just before a stall occurs, is sometimes called the incipient stage of a stall, or an imminent stall. If you react promptly with the correct control response, recovery from an approach to a stall is easy. [Figure 3-41]

After you add power, move the carburetor heat control (if in use) to the COLD or OFF position. Normally, flaps are then retracted to an intermediate setting; however, the retraction procedures for stall recovery vary widely from one airplane to another. As the airplane accelerates, you should initiate a climb and continue to retract the remaining flaps.

Begin Recovery at First Buffeting

Figure 3-41. Your first action to recover from an approach to a stall is to decrease the angle of attack by releasing back pressure while simultaneously applying power. Move the throttle promptly and smoothly to obtain all available power. In addition, apply appropriate rudder pressure to center the ball of the turn coordinator.

Figure 3-42. During stall practice, the airplane may tend to roll to one side as the nose pitches down. If this occurs, use coordinated aileron and rudder pressures to level the wings at the same time you apply power and adjust pitch attitude.

During an approach to a stall, you have control of the airplane. This means you can still maintain attitude, heading, and altitude. However, when the airplane does stall, lift is lost, and you can no longer maintain full control of the aircraft. In fact, typical indications of the stall include wing drop, nose drop, and loss of altitude. Buffeting also may occur. The first sign of the stall varies with airplanes, control input, and flight conditions. Normally two conditions are evident: the nose drops and a loss of altitude follows.

The recovery for the stall is the same as for the approach to a stall; release back pressure and simultaneously apply full power. Normally, you should retract the flaps to an intermediate setting. As the airspeed begins to increase following the recovery, readjust the pitch attitude gently and smoothly. [Figure 3-42]

SECONDARY STALL

The increase in stall speed which accompanies an increase in G-loading is an important consideration during stall recoveries. As the nose of the airplane is raised after stall recovery, you will be increasing the G-loading on the airplane. This causes a corresponding increase in stall speed. If the increase in stall speed exceeds the airspeed, the airplane will immediately enter a secondary stall. [Figure 3-43]

Too Rapid – Secondary Stall

Too Late – Excessive Speed

Figure 3-43. It is important for you to apply the correct amount of back pressure during stall recoveries. Applying back pressure too rapidly may result in a secondary stall, while not applying it rapidly enough may cause the airplane to build excessive airspeed and lose a significant amount of altitude.

TURNING FLIGHT STALLS

Once your instructor is satisfied that you can properly execute power-off stalls straight ahead, you will be asked to perform them during turning flight. The entry procedure is exactly the same as that used for stalls performed straight ahead, except your instructor will have you enter a turn using approximately 20° of bank. Initially, you normally begin with imminent stalls, then progress to full stalls.

Recovery, as with all stalls, begins by lowering the nose and applying full power. Then, bring the wings to a level flight attitude by coordinated use of the ailerons and rudder, and retract the flaps to an intermediate setting. As the airplane accelerates, begin a climb and retract the remaining flaps.

CHECKLIST

After studying this section, you should have a basic understanding of:

✓   **Stalls** — Why an airplane stalls and how the wing is designed to provide you with positive control throughout the stall entry and recovery.

✓   **Stall entry and recovery** — What the procedures are for entering and recovering from a stall.

✓   **Approach to a stall and stalls** — What the difference is between the two and how to recognize each.

✓   **Secondary stalls** — What a secondary stall is and how to avoid one.

✓   **Turning flight stalls** — What the basic procedures are for practice of turning stalls.

POWER-ON AND ACCELERATED STALLS

Once you have gained proficiency in power-off stalls, your instructor will demonstrate and allow you to practice power-on stalls. At first your instructor may have you practice power-on approaches to a stall before you proceed to more fully developed stalls. Once you are proficient in power-on stalls, your instructor may introduce the accelerated maneuver stall. However, the accelerated stall is not a required maneuver in the Private Pilot PTS and should not be practiced routinely or in solo flight.

POWER-ON STALLS

The power-on, straight-ahead stall is the type most frequently encountered shortly after takeoff. This stall can occur if you attempt to lift the airplane from the runway at too slow an airspeed and apply excessive back pressure to the control wheel. This produces an extreme nose-high attitude and high angle of attack. This type of stall also can occur when you are flying at a low altitude over terrain which increases in elevation faster than the airplane is able to climb. The power-on, turning stall normally occurs during the departure turn following takeoff. This type of stall generally results from distractions that divert your attention from flying the airplane. During practice of these stalls, you should select an altitude that allows the recovery to be completed at an altitude of no less than 1,500 feet AGL.

STRAIGHT-AHEAD STALL

Although you will use a high power setting during this stall, do not enter it from a high airspeed. If you use a high airspeed, the pitch attitude you will encounter is extremely nose high. After you complete your clearing turns, reduce power and slow the airplane to near liftoff speed while maintaining a constant altitude. Then, add back pressure to increase the angle of attack, while simultaneously increasing power to the takeoff or recommended climb setting.

The power-on stall is entered near liftoff speed.

In order to maintain directional control and coordination, increase right rudder pressure continually as you increase the power and pitch attitude. Throughout the approach to the stall and the recovery, you should maintain coordinated flight.

INDICATIONS OF THE APPROACHING STALL

You should develop an awareness of the various indications of the approaching stall as the airspeed decreases. For example, the noise of the slipstream passing over the airplane and the engine noise level decrease

Figure 3-44. The pitch attitude in a power-on, straight-ahead stall resembles the visual relationship of the nose and horizon shown on the left. The instrument indications are pictured on the right. The angle created by the wingtips and the horizon can also provide a useful indication of the airplane's pitch attitude.

as the engine begins to labor during the climb. In addition, the flight controls feel mushy and soft. [Figure 3-44]

RECOVERY PROCEDURES

The procedures for recovery from the power-on stall are basically the same as for the power-off stall. Decrease the angle of attack while you simultaneously apply full available power (if you are not already at full power), and use coordinated aileron and rudder pressures to return the airplane to straight-and-level flight or establish a climb, as appropriate.

STALLS

Maintain coordinated flight throughout stall entry and recovery.

After you become familiar with the characteristics of the power-on approach to a stall, you will begin practicing stalls. You enter in the same manner as an approach to a stall. Clear the area and reduce power and airspeed. Just above liftoff speed, increase power to the recommended takeoff or climb power setting. Observe the indications of the approaching stall, maintain directional control, and continue to increase the angle of attack until the stall occurs. When the stall has developed fully, pronounced buffeting usually becomes evident and the nose normally pitches down, even though you hold full back pressure. There is a tendency for the airplane to pitch more steeply and rapidly and exhibit more right- or left-rolling tendencies in the stall than in an approach to a stall. However, by maintaining coordinated flight throughout the entry and recovery, you can minimize this rolling tendency. [Figure 3-45]

The main objective in stall recovery is to maintain positive and effective control of the airplane while losing minimum altitude. A common error made during stall recovery is using an excessive nose-down pitch attitude. The ideal recovery should be to a near-level attitude that results in minimum altitude loss and does not cause a secondary stall.

Figure 3-45. To recover from a power-on stall, decrease the angle of attack by releasing control wheel back pressure to lower the nose. You simultaneously add all available power and use the rudder and ailerons in a coordinated manner to return the airplane to straight-and-level flight or to establish a climb, as appropriate.

TURNING STALLS

The power-on turning stall is just a variation of the power-on, straight-ahead stall. After clearing the area, enter a power-on turning stall in the same way you enter a straight-ahead stall, but add a 20° banked turn to the left or right.

As you approach the stall, the angle of bank tends to steepen in a left turn and become shallower in a right turn. This occurs because of the tendency of torque and P-factor to roll the airplane to the left. When you practice stalls in each of these variations, you should try to identify the indications of the approaching stall and use coordinated ailerons and rudder throughout the entire maneuver.

The recovery is the same as for the power-on, straight-ahead stall. Lower the nose while simultaneously applying full power, then use coordinated ailerons and rudder pressures to return the airplane to straight-and-level flight or a climb, as appropriate.

ACCELERATED MANEUVER STALLS

Although not included in the Private Pilot PTS or the Syllabus, your instructor may introduce you to the accelerated maneuver stall. The term "accelerated" refers to a stall which occurs at a higher-than-normal airspeed because of an additional load factor. This increased load factor is normally induced during a steep turn.

To avoid extremely high structural loads, perform accelerated maneuver stalls only when you are operating below the airplane's maneuvering speed. Also, avoid abrupt pitch changes because of the high gyroscopic loads produced by the propeller. The stall speed increase during an accelerated

Accelerated stalls must be performed only when you are below maneuvering speed.

maneuver stall can be substantial. Stall speed is approximately equal to the one-G stall speed of the airplane multiplied by the square root of the load factor. For example, if you place the airplane in a 60° bank and maintain level flight, you are imposing a load factor of two G's. Since the square root of two is 1.4, the one-G stall speed is multiplied by 1.4 to obtain the two-G stall speed. Assuming the airplane used in this example has a one-G stall speed of 55 knots, placing it in a 60° bank will increase the stall speed to 78 knots ($\sqrt{2} = 1.4 \times 55 = 78$).

To begin the accelerated maneuver stall, check the area for other traffic by making clearing turns and select an entry altitude that allows you to complete the maneuver at an altitude no lower than 1,500 feet AGL. Then, while maintaining straight-and-level flight, reduce the airspeed of the airplane below its published maneuvering speed. Next, roll the airplane into a 45° level turn and firmly apply back elevator pressure to initiate a stall. Normally, you start your recovery at the first indication of a stall by releasing sufficient back pressure to eliminate all indications of the stall and simultaneously applying all available power. Finally, use coordinated ailerons and rudder pressure to return the airplane to straight-and-level flight.

SPINS

The airplane must be in a stalled condition before it can spin, and an uncoordinated flight maneuver is usually involved.

A spin is typically caused by exceeding the critical angle of attack during an uncoordinated maneuver. When this occurs, one wing stalls before the other and, as lift on the stalled wing is lost, it begins to drop. If the other wing is still producing some lift, the lifting forces are out of balance. The imbalance between the unequally stalled wings leads to rotation approximately about the vertical axis. A **spin** can, therefore, be defined as an aggravated stall which results in autorotation. The key word for you to remember in this definition is "stall." In order for a spin to develop, a stall must occur first.

Since an airplane must be in a stalled condition before it will spin, the first thing you should do as you approach an inadvertent spin is try to recover from the stall before the spin develops. If your reaction is too slow and the spin develops, move the throttle to idle, retract the flaps, if they are extended, and neutralize the ailerons. Next, apply full rudder deflection opposite the direction of rotation. Just after the rudder reaches the stop, briskly position the control wheel forward of the neutral position to decrease the angle of attack (break the stall) and hold these control inputs. As the rotation stops, neutralize the rudder and smoothly apply back pressure to recover from the steep nose-down pitch attitude. During recovery from the dive, make sure you avoid excessive airspeed and high G-loadings. The recovery procedure can vary from airplane to airplane; therefore, be sure you are familiar with the spin recovery technique published in the pilot's operating handbook for the airplane you fly.

Most airplanes manufactured today are not required to demonstrate their ability to recover from a fully developed spin. Intentionally entering a spin in these airplanes can be extremely dangerous. However, if an airplane approved for spins is available, your instructor may demonstrate one for you. Keep in mind that, even when using an airplane approved for spins, recovery techniques vary.

Never spin an airplane which has not been specifically approved for spins.

As an applicant for a private pilot certificate, you are not required to demonstrate flight proficiency in spin entries or spin recovery techniques. Even though your flight instructor may demonstrate a spin at some point during your training, you should never intentionally enter a spin without an experienced instructor on board. The emphasis during private pilot training is on stall/spin awareness. This means an awareness of conditions that could lead to an unintentional stall or spin. You also need to have a basic understanding of how to recover from a spin.

CHECKLIST

After studying the section, you should have a basic understanding of:

✓ **Entry and recovery procedures** — How to enter and recover from power-on stalls.

✓ **Rudder usage** — What the importance of the rudder is during the entry and recovery from power-on stalls.

✓ **Accelerated maneuver stalls** — What this type of stall is and how to enter and recover from it.

✓ **Spins** — Why an airplane spins and how to recover from a spin

flight prep 4

PITOT-STATIC INSTRUMENTS

Since an airplane operates in a three-dimensional atmosphere, you need several special instruments to provide you with necessary flight information. One group of these instruments operates on the principle of pressure differential to provide you with your speed, rate of climb or descent, and altitude. This group is referred to as the pitot-static instruments. [Figure 4-1]

EFFECTS OF ATMOSPHERIC CONDITIONS

Since pressure differential is so important in the operation of the pitot-static instruments, let's consider some basic information about atmospheric pressure and how it varies. The atmosphere is heavier near the earth's surface than it is at higher levels. In fact, at sea level, air exerts an average pressure of 14.7 pounds per square inch (p.s.i.). At 18,000 feet, the pressure decreases to approximately half that much. As pressure decreases, air density also decreases. In addition, since air expands when it is heated, warm air is less dense than cold air. This means that air density varies with changes in both pressure and temperature.

Figure 4-1. The three pitot-static instruments are the airspeed indicator, the altimeter, and the vertical speed indicator (VSI). The other instruments and gauges will be discussed later.

Humidity also affects the density of the air, but to a lesser degree. Humid air is less dense than dry air.

Think of how often these conditions change. Variations are most apparent between seasons, and hourly changes routinely occur. This continuous process of change is one of the most common characteristics of the atmosphere.

INTERNATIONAL STANDARD ATMOSPHERE

To provide a common reference for temperature and pressure, the **International Standard Atmosphere** (ISA) has been established. These standard conditions are the basis for certain flight instruments and most airplane performance data. At sea level, the standard atmosphere consists of a barometric pressure of 29.92 in. Hg (1013.2 mb.) and a temperature of 15°C (59°F). Since both of these values change with altitude, **standard lapse rates** have been established to help you calculate the temperatures and pressures you can anticipate at various altitudes. In the lower atmosphere, the standard pressure lapse rate for each 1,000 feet of altitude change is approximately 1.00 in. Hg, and the standard temperature lapse rate is 2°C (3.5°F). Pressure and temperature normally decrease as altitude increases. For example, the approximate standard pressure and temperature at 2,000 feet MSL are 27.92 in. Hg (29.92 − 2.00) and 11°C (15°C − 4°C).

ISA at sea level equals 29.92 in. Hg, or 1013.2 millibars, and has a temperature of 15°C. Temperature decreases approximately 2°C for each 1,000-foot increase in altitude.

PITOT-STATIC SYSTEM

Pressure-sensitive devices convert pressure supplied by the pitot-static system to instrument indications in the cockpit. The airspeed indicator, altimeter, and vertical speed indicator all use static pressure, but only the airspeed indicator uses pitot pressure.

The static system provides surrounding, or ambient, air pressure to the airspeed indicator, altimeter, and VSI.

Pitot pressure, also called **impact** or **ram** air pressure, is supplied by the pitot tube or head. The **pitot tube** is usually mounted on the wing or on the nose section, so the opening is exposed to the relative wind. This arrangement allows ram air pressure to enter the pitot tube before it is affected by the airplane's structure. Since the pitot tube opening faces forward, an increase in speed increases ram air pressure.

The pitot system provides impact, or ram, air pressure to the airspeed indicator.

Static pressure enters the pitot-static system through a **static port**, which is located in an area of relatively undisturbed air. It is common to have the static port flush-mounted on the side of the fuselage, or it may be combined with the pitot tube. An airplane may have one or two static ports,

Figure 4-2. Ram air pressure enters the system through a hole in the forward end of the pitot tube. Electrical heating elements may be installed to remove ice from the pitot head, and a drain opening normally is located near the aft portion of the pressure chamber. Ram air pressure is supplied only to the airspeed indicator, while static pressure is used by all three instruments.

depending on its design. For simplicity, this discussion references a single port. [Figure 4-2]

AIRSPEED INDICATOR

The airspeed indicator measures the difference between impact and static air pressure and displays the result as an airspeed. The colored arcs denote safe operating ranges for various flight conditions.

The airspeed indicator displays the speed of your airplane through the air by comparing ram air pressure with static air pressure — the greater the differential, the greater the speed. The airspeed indicator is divided into color-coded arcs that define speed ranges for different phases of flight. If you know the significance of each color code, you can easily identify the safe speed ranges for use of flaps, for normal operations, for smooth-air operations (caution range), and for maximum speed. [Figure 4-3]

Color	Meaning
White	Flap Operating Range
Green	Normal Operating Range
Yellow	Caution Range
Red	Never-Exceed Speed

Figure 4-3. Besides delineating various speed ranges, the boundaries of the color-coded arcs also identify airspeed limitations.

AIRSPEED LIMITATIONS

Several airspeed limitations, called **V-speeds**, are shown on the airspeed indicator. They are V_{S0}, V_{S1}, V_{FE}, V_{NO}, and V_{NE}. **V_{S0}** is defined as the stalling speed or the minimum steady flight speed in the landing configuration. In small airplanes, this is the power-off stall speed at the maximum landing weight in the landing configuration (gear and flaps down). **V_{S1}** is defined as the stalling speed or the minimum steady flight speed obtained in a specified configuration. For small airplanes, this is the power-off stall speed at the maximum takeoff weight in the clean configuration (gear up, if retractable, and flaps up). You should check the POH for specific information on your airplane. **V_{FE}** indicates the maximum speed with the flaps extended, while **V_{NO}** is the maximum structural cruising speed. Finally, **V_{NE}** denotes the never-exceed speed.

V-speeds denote important airspeed limitations.

The lower limit of the **white arc** is V_{S0}, and the upper limit is V_{FE}. This arc is commonly referred to as the flap operating range, since its lower limit represents the full flap stall speed and its upper limit provides the maximum flap speed. You will usually fly your approaches and landings at speeds within the white arc. The lower limit of the **green arc** is V_{S1}, and the upper limit is V_{NO}. This is the normal operating range of the airplane. V_{NO} is considered to be the **maximum structural cruising speed**. You should not exceed it except in smooth air. Most of your flying will occur within this range. The **yellow arc**, or caution range, is bounded by V_{NO} and V_{NE}. You may fly within this range only in smooth air, and then, only with caution. Finally, the **red line** is V_{NE}, or the never-exceed speed. Operating above this speed may result in damage or structural failure.

The white arc is the flap operating range, the green arc is for normal operations, the yellow arc is the caution range, and the red line marks the never-exceed speed.

Although the airspeed indicator presents important airspeed limitations, not all V-speeds are shown. For example, one very important speed not displayed is **V_A**, or maneuvering speed. This represents the maximum speed at which you can stall an airplane or apply full and abrupt control movement without the possibility of causing structural damage. It also represents the maximum speed that you can safely use during turbulent flight conditions. V_A is included in the pilot's operating handbook and is usually on a placard in the cockpit. You should be aware that V_A changes at different aircraft weights for some airplanes. For instance, V_A may be 100 knots when an airplane is heavily loaded and 90 knots when the load is light.

V_A is the maximum speed for full and abrupt use of the controls without risk of structural damage. It also is the maximum speed for flight in turbulent conditions.

Two additional speeds of importance to you when you are flying a retractable-gear airplane are V_{LO} and V_{LE}. **V_{LO}** is the maximum speed you can safely use while raising or lowering the landing gear. **V_{LE}** is the maximum speed you can safely use with the landing gear in a fully extended position. These speeds are not displayed on the airspeed indicator.

V_{LO} is the maximum landing gear operating speed, while V_{LE} is the maximum gear extended speed.

Now that you are familiar with airspeed limitations, let's consider the four types of speed you will deal with during flight. They are indicated airspeed, calibrated airspeed, true airspeed, and groundspeed.

As altitude increases, the indicated airspeed at which a given airplane stalls in a specific configuration remains the same.

Indicated airspeed (IAS) is the reading you get directly from the airspeed indicator. Since the airspeed indicator is calibrated to indicate true airspeed under standard sea level conditions, IAS does not reflect variations in air density as you climb to higher altitudes. For example, your indicated stall speed remains the same even though your true airspeed normally increases with altitude. IAS also is uncorrected for installation (position) and instrument errors.

CAS is IAS corrected for installation and instrument errors.

Calibrated airspeed (CAS) is indicated airspeed corrected for installation and instrument errors. Although attempts are made to minimize these errors, it is not possible to eliminate them entirely throughout the full range of operating speeds, weights, and flap settings. To determine calibrated airspeed, read indicated airspeed and then correct it by using the chart or table in the pilot's operating handbook.

TAS is the actual speed of your airplane through the air.

True airspeed (TAS) represents the true speed of your airplane through the air. It is calibrated airspeed corrected for altitude and nonstandard temperature. As altitude or air temperature increase, the density of the air decreases. For a given IAS, this means TAS increases with altitude.

Groundspeed is your actual speed over the ground.

Groundspeed (GS) represents the actual speed of your airplane over the ground. It is true airspeed adjusted for wind. A headwind decreases groundspeed, while a tailwind increases it.

ALTIMETER

The altimeter indicates your flight altitude by measuring ambient air pressure.

The altimeter senses pressure changes and displays altitude in feet. It usually has three pointers, or hands, to indicate the altitude. The longest pointer shows hundreds of feet, the middle-sized pointer indicates thousands of feet, and the shortest pointer shows tens of thousands of feet. It also has an adjustable barometric scale for changes in pressure. [Figure 4-4]

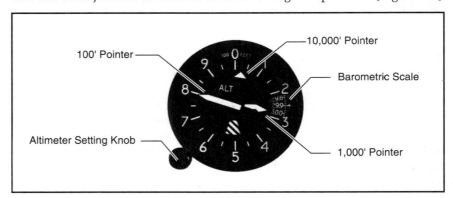

Figure 4-4. This altimeter shows an altitude of 2,800 feet. The barometric scale in the window on the right is set at 29.90 inches of mercury.

Although the altimeter is one of your key flight instruments, it has certain limitations. The basis of its calibration is the International Standard Atmosphere, where pressure, temperature, and lapse rates have fixed values; however, actual atmospheric conditions seldom match these standard values. In addition, local pressure readings within a given area normally change over a period of time, and pressure frequently changes as you fly from one airport to another. As a result, altimeter indications are subject to errors. The extent of the errors depends on how much the pressure, temperature, and lapse rates deviate from standard, as well as how recently you have reset your altimeter.

The best way to minimize altimeter errors is to update your altimeter setting frequently. Then, adjust the barometric scale in the altimeter setting window by turning the knob. In most cases, you use the current altimeter setting of the nearest reporting station along your route of flight. While you can minimize altimeter errors, you cannot entirely eliminate the common inaccuracies caused by nonstandard atmospheric conditions.

A current altimeter setting for the area you are flying over is essential for reliable altitude indications.

ALTITUDE DEFINITIONS

The altimeter measures **altitude**, which is the vertical elevation of an object above a given reference point. The reference may be the surface of the earth, sea level, or some other point. There are several different types of altitude, depending on the reference point used. The five most common types are: indicated, pressure, density, true, and absolute.

Indicated altitude is the altitude you read directly from the altimeter when it is correctly adjusted to the local altimeter setting. This is the altitude you will use most often during flight.

Pressure altitude is displayed as the height above the standard datum plane when you adjust the altimeter to the standard sea level atmospheric pressure of 29.92 in. Hg. The **standard datum plane** is a theoretical plane where the air pressure is equal to 29.92 inches of mercury. Pressure altitude is used with existing temperature to compute density altitude and other values.

Density altitude is pressure altitude corrected for nonstandard temperature. It is really a theoretical value which is computed from existing temperature, and it is an important factor in determining airplane performance. Performance charts for many older aircraft are based on density altitude. When the outside air temperature is above standard, density altitude is higher than pressure altitude, and aircraft performance is reduced.

When the air temperature is warmer than standard for a given altitude, the density altitude will be higher than the pressure altitude.

True altitude is the actual height of an object above mean sea level. On aeronautical charts, the elevation figures for fixed objects, such as airports, towers, and TV antennas, are true altitudes. You can calculate approximate true altitude with a flight computer, but the computation is based on the assumption that pressure and temperature lapse rates match ISA values. Normally, these lapse rates vary from those in a perfectly standard atmosphere. In two cases, however, true and indicated altitude are equal. One occurs during flight, when you have the correct altimeter setting and atmospheric conditions match ISA values. The other occurs on the ground. When you set the altimeter to the local pressure setting, it indicates the field elevation, which is a true altitude. [Figure 4-5]

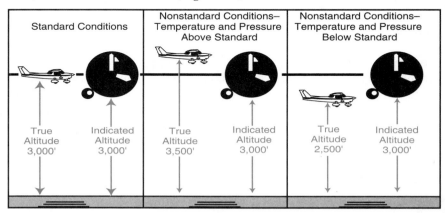

Figure 4-5. During flight, indicated and true altitude are equal only in standard atmospheric conditions. When nonstandard conditions exist, true altitude may be higher or lower than indicated altitude. When atmospheric pressure or temperature is higher than standard, your true altitude is higher than your indicated altitude. When pressure is lower or temperature is colder than standard, your true altitude is lower than your indicated altitude.

Absolute altitude is the actual height of the airplane above the earth's surface over which it is flying. This altitude varies with the height of the airplane, as well as the height of the surface. Absolute altitude is commonly referred to as height above ground level (AGL). [Figure 4-6]

Figure 4-6. Your absolute altitude can change rapidly as you pass over varying terrain elevations.

ALTIMETER ERRORS

The most common altimeter error is also the easiest to correct. It occurs when you fail to keep the altimeter set to the local altimeter setting. For example, assume your altimeter is set to 30.00 in. Hg. and you are flying at a constant altitude of 3,500 feet. If you fly into an area where atmospheric pressure is 29.50 in. Hg, the altimeter will sense this decrease in pressure as an increase in altitude and will display a higher reading. Your response will be to lower the nose of the airplane and descend to maintain your "desired" altitude. [Figure 4-7]

Since you know that atmospheric pressure decreases approximately one inch of mercury for each 1,000-foot increase in altitude, you can compute the error. In this example, the altimeter setting decreased from 30.00 to 29.50, a change of 0.50 in. Hg. Since one inch equals 1,000 feet, 0.50 inches equals 500 feet (1000 × .50 = 500). Next, you need to know if you are flying higher or lower than the desired altitude. Since you are flying from an area of higher pressure to an area of lower pressure, your indicated altitude will result in a lower altitude than you intended. A good memory aid is, "When flying from high to low or hot to cold, look out below." The accuracy of altimeters is affected by extreme variations from standard atmospheric pressure and temperature conditions. The *Aeronautical Information Manual* (AIM) emphasizes the

Figure 4-7. If you fly from an area of higher pressure to an area of lower pressure without resetting your altimeter, you will fly at a lower altitude than you had intended. If you reset the altimeter to the correct setting, you will maintain the desired altitude.

need to exercise caution during flight in conditions with extremely low pressure (below 28.00 in. Hg) or unusually high pressure (above 31.00 in. Hg).

VERTICAL SPEED INDICATOR

The VSI measures the change in ambient air pressure as the aircraft climbs or descends. It displays the change as a rate of climb or descent in feet per minute.

The vertical speed indicator (VSI), which sometimes is called a vertical velocity indicator (VVI), is connected to the static system. This instrument measures how fast the ambient air pressure is increasing or decreasing when the aircraft climbs or descends. It then displays the air pressure changes as a rate of climb or descent in feet per minute. [Figure 4-8]

The VSI is capable of displaying two different types of information. One is called trend, and the other is called rate. **Trend** information shows you an immediate indication of an increase or decrease in the airplane's rate of climb or descent. **Rate** information shows you a stabilized rate of change. For example, if you are maintaining a steady 500 f.p.m. climb, and you lower the nose slightly, the VSI will immediately sense this change and display a decrease in the rate of climb. This first indication is called the trend. After a period of six to nine seconds, the VSI will stabilize and display the new rate of climb, which, in this example, would be something less than 500 f.p.m.

BLOCKAGE OF THE PITOT-STATIC SYSTEM

Although pitot-static instruments have some accuracy limitations, usually they are very reliable. Gross errors almost always indicate blockage of the pitot tube, the static port, or both. Blockage may be caused by moisture (including ice), dirt, or even insects.

Figure 4-8. The vertical speed indicator tells you how fast you are climbing or descending. The VSI on the left shows a 300 f.p.m. descent, while the VSI on the right reflects a 300 f.p.m. climb.

During preflight, you should make sure the pitot tube cover is removed. Then, check the pitot and static port openings. If they are clogged, the openings should be cleaned by a certificated mechanic. It is also possible for the pitot tube to become blocked during flight through visible moisture when temperatures are near the freezing level. If you are flying in visible moisture and your airplane is equipped with pitot heat, you should turn it on to prevent pitot tube icing.

A clogged pitot tube only affects the accuracy of the airspeed indicator, but blockage of the static port affects the altimeter, vertical speed, and airspeed indicators. If the static system clogs and the airplane is equipped with an alternate static source, you should open the alternate source. In most cases, the alternate source is vented inside the cockpit where static pressure is lower than outside static pressure. As a result, its use causes slight errors in pitot-static instrument indications. For example, the airspeed and the altimeter read higher than normal and the vertical speed indicator momentarily shows a climb. Check your pilot's operating handbook for information on use of the alternate static source.

Blockage of the pitot tube affects only the airspeed indicator, but a clogged static system affects all three pitot-static instruments.

Now consider the specific errors caused by pitot-static system blockages, beginning with the airspeed indicator. If the pitot tube clogs and its associated drain hole remains clear, ram air will no longer be able to enter the pitot system. Air already in the system will vent through the drain hole, and the remaining pressure will drop to ambient (outside) air pressure. Under these circumstances, the airspeed indicator reading decreases to zero, because the airspeed indicator senses no difference between ram and static air pressure. In other words, the airspeed indicator acts as if the airplane is stationary on the ramp. The apparent loss of airspeed is not usually instantaneous. Instead, the airspeed generally drops slowly to zero.

If the pitot tube is blocked and its drain hole remains open, the airspeed reading will drop to zero.

If both the pitot tube and the drain hole become clogged in flight, ram air will no longer enter the pitot system, and air in the system will be trapped. This means that no change in ram air pressure occurs as actual airspeed changes; therefore, no change is apparent on the airspeed indicator. If the static port remains clear, however, the airspeed changes with altitude.

If both the pitot tube and the drain hole clog, the airspeed indicator will react like an altimeter.

As altitude increases above the level where the pitot and drain hole clogged, static pressure decreases. This causes an apparent increase in the ram air pressure relative to static pressure, so the airspeed indicator shows an increase in speed. The opposite effect occurs when the airplane descends below the altitude where the blockages occurred.

If the static port clogs and the pitot tube remains clear, the airspeed indicator continues to operate, but it is inaccurate. Airspeed indications are

If the static port clogs, the indicated airspeed increases as the airplane descends and decreases when it climbs.

slower than the actual speed when the airplane is operated above the altitude where the static ports clogged. This is because the trapped static pressure is higher than normal for that altitude. Conversely, the airspeed indicates faster than the correct value when you are operating at a lower altitude. This results because the trapped static pressure is lower than normal for that altitude. Remember, if you suspect the static ports are clogged, you can switch to the alternate static system, if one is available. A blockage of the static system also affects the altimeter, which operates on ambient air pressure. In this case, air pressure in the system will not change and neither will your indicated altitude.

Finally, since the vertical speed indicator is connected to the static system, any blockage of the static system also affects the VSI. When the static system is completely blocked, the VSI continually indicates zero.

CHECKLIST

After studying this section, you should have a basic understanding of:

✓ **International Standard Atmosphere (ISA)** — What ISA values at sea level are and what the standard temperature and pressure lapse rates are.

✓ **Pitot-static system** — How the pitot-static system operates and what instruments are affected.

✓ **Airspeed indicator** — How the airspeed indicator functions; what the differences are between IAS, CAS, TAS, and GS; what V-speeds are; and what the airspeed indicator color codings mean.

✓ **Altimeter** — How the altimeter functions and what the differences are between indicated, pressure, density, true, and absolute altitudes.

✓ **Vertical speed indicator** — How the VSI functions and what the differences are between trend and rate indications.

GYROSCOPIC INSTRUMENTS

In the previous section, you were introduced to the pitot-static instruments. The next group of instruments uses gyroscopic principles to provide you with a pictorial view of the airplane's rate of turn, attitude, and heading. These three instruments are the turn coordinator, attitude indicator, and heading indicator. A fourth instrument, the magnetic compass, is not a gyroscope, but it is used in conjunction with the heading indicator. [Figure 4-9]

Gyroscopic instruments have unique operating principles and power sources. Let's begin by briefly discussing two fundamental concepts that apply to gyroscopes — rigidity in space and precession.

RIGIDITY IN SPACE

Any rotating body exhibits certain gyroscopic properties. One of these properties — **rigidity in space** — means that once a gyroscope is spinning, it tends to remain in a fixed position in space and resists external forces

A spinning mass tends to remain in a fixed position.

Turn Coordinator   Heading Indicator   Attitude Indicator

Figure 4-9. As you climb, descend, or turn, you can cross-check the gyroscopic instruments to confirm your attitude and direction.

Figure 4-10. Regardless of the position of its base, a gyro tends to remain rigid in space, with its axis of rotation pointed in a constant direction.

applied to it. A gyro which is freely, or universally, mounted is set on gimbal rings, which allow the gyro to rotate freely in any direction. [Figure 4-10]

Some gyros, such as those used in turn indicators and some heading indicators, have semirigid mountings and use only two gimbal rings. These gyros have only two planes of rotation.

PRECESSION

A force applied to a gyroscope causes a reaction in the direction of rotation, 90° ahead of the point where the force was actually applied.

Another characteristic of the gyro is **precession**, which is the tilting or turning of a gyro in response to pressure. Unfortunately, it is not possible to mount a gyro in a frictionless environment. A small force is applied to the gyro whenever the airplane changes direction. The reaction to this force occurs in the direction of rotation, approximately 90° ahead of the point where the force was applied. This causes the slow drifting and minor erroneous indications in the gyro instruments. We discussed gyroscopic precession in Flight Prep 2, with respect to the spinning propeller.

SOURCES OF POWER

The turn coordinator usually is driven by electrical power, while the attitude and heading indicators generally use a vacuum system.

Gyroscopes may be operated either by electrical power or by a vacuum (suction) system. Most small airplanes use a combination of both systems to provide a backup in case one system fails. The turn coordinator typically uses electrical power and may incorporate a small warning flag to indicate a loss of power. The vacuum system includes an engine-driven vacuum pump which powers the attitude and heading indicators. [Figure 4-11]

It is important for you to monitor vacuum pressure during flight, because the attitude and heading indicators may not provide reliable information when suction pressure is low. The vacuum or suction gauge generally is marked to indicate the acceptable range. Some airplanes are equipped

Figure 4-11. Air is first drawn into the vacuum system through a filter assembly. It then moves through the attitude and heading indicators where it causes the gyros to spin. After that, it continues to the vacuum pump where it is expelled. A relief valve prevents the vacuum pressure or suction from exceeding prescribed limits.

with a vacuum warning light which illuminates when the vacuum pressure drops below the acceptable level. These airplanes also may be equipped with an electrically driven, standby vacuum pump.

TURN COORDINATOR

The turn coordinator senses yaw and roll movement about the vertical and longitudinal axes. It has two main elements — a miniature airplane to indicate the rate of turn and an inclinometer to indicate coordinated flight [Figure 4-12]

The turn coordinator shows yaw and roll movement about the vertical and longitudinal axes.

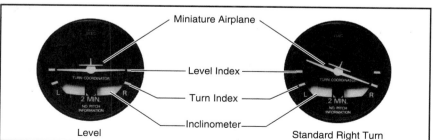

Figure 4-12. When the miniature airplane is level, as shown on the left, the airplane is neither turning nor rolling. When you establish a bank, the miniature airplane also banks. The indicator on the right shows a turn to the right. If the ball is centered in the inclinometer, the turn is coordinated.

In a standard-rate turn, your airplane will complete a 360° turn in two minutes.

When you are rolling into or out of a turn, the miniature airplane banks in the direction the airplane is rolled. A rapid roll rate causes the miniature airplane to bank more steeply than a slow roll rate. You can use the turn coordinator to establish and maintain a **standard-rate turn** by aligning the wing of the miniature airplane with the turn index. This means the turning rate is three degrees per second. At this rate, you will complete a 360° turn in two minutes. You should remember that the miniature airplane of the turn coordinator does not indicate angle of bank. It only indicates the rate at which the airplane is rolled into or out of a turn. After the turn is stabilized, it indicates the rate of the turn itself.

The inclinometer is used to establish and maintain coordinated flight.

The inclinometer is another important part of the turn coordinator. It consists of a liquid-filled, curved tube with a ball inside. The ball actually is a balance indicator, which is used to determine coordinated use of aileron and rudder.

During coordinated, straight-and-level flight, the force of gravity causes the ball to rest in the lowest part of the tube, centered between the reference lines. During a coordinated turn, forces are balanced, which also causes the ball to remain centered in the tube. If forces are unbalanced, such as during a slip or skid, the ball moves away from the center of the tube.

The position of the ball defines the quality of the turn, or whether you have used the correct angle of bank for the rate of turn. In a **slip**, the rate of turn is too slow for the angle of bank, and the ball moves to the inside of the turn. In a **skid**, the rate of turn is too great for the angle of bank, and the ball moves to the outside of the turn.

You maintain coordinated flight by keeping the ball centered. If the ball is not centered, you usually apply enough rudder pressure to center it. To do this, you apply rudder pressure on the side where the ball is deflected. The simple rule, "Step on the ball," may help you remember which rudder pedal to depress. You also may vary the angle of bank to help restore coordinated flight from a slip or skid. To correct for a slip, you should decrease bank and/or increase the rate of turn. To correct for a skid, increase the bank and/or decrease the rate of turn.

Besides maintaining coordination in turns, the inclinometer helps you recognize the need to compensate for engine torque and adverse yaw. For example, when you enter a climb, the nose of the airplane tends to move to the left due to P-factor. This is indicated by the ball of the turn coordinator moving to the right of center. When this occurs, you know the airplane is in uncoordinated flight. To correct this condition, "Step on the ball." In this case, you must depress the right rudder pedal until the ball centers; then, you must maintain sufficient rudder pressure to keep it centered.

ATTITUDE INDICATOR

The attitude indicator is a vacuum-powered instrument which senses pitching and rolling movements about the airplane's lateral and longitudinal axes. It provides you with a substitute horizon, and it is especially useful when the natural horizon is obscured by clouds, reduced visibility, or darkness. The attitude indicator is the only flight instrument that provides both pitch and bank information. It uses an artificial horizon and miniature airplane to depict the position of your airplane. Since it is an extremely precise instrument, you can detect very small changes in pitch and bank. [Figure 4-13]

The attitude indicator displays pitch and roll movement about the lateral and longitudinal axes.

Modern attitude indicators normally are very reliable instruments as long as the correct vacuum pressure is maintained. Some function properly during 360° of roll or 85° of pitch. Gyros in older indicators, however, will "tumble" from their plane of rotation beyond approximately 100° of bank or beyond 60° of pitch.

Although the attitude indicator is a reliable flight instrument, you should remember to cross-check it against outside visual references and other flight instruments. Occasionally, attitude indicators fail gradually without providing obvious warning signals.

Figure 4-13. The attitude indicator presents you with a view of the airplane as it would appear from an aft position. Prior to flight, you should set the miniature airplane symbol so that it is level with the horizon bar. The angle of bank is shown both pictorially by the relationship of the miniature aircraft to the deflected horizon bar and by the alignment of the pointer with the banking scale at the top of the instrument. Pitch is indicated by the position of the "nose," or center, of the miniature airplane with respect to the horizon bar.

HEADING INDICATOR

The heading indicator
displays yaw movement
about the vertical axis.

The heading indicator, also called a directional gyro (DG), is a vacuum-powered instrument which senses yaw movement of the airplane about the vertical axis. It displays headings based on a 360° azimuth, with the final zero omitted. In other words, "6" indicates 60°, "21" indicates 210°, and so on. When properly set, it is your primary source of heading information. Heading indicators in most training airplanes are referred to as "free" gyros. This means they have no automatic, north-seeking system built into them.

Due to precession, the
heading indicator must
be aligned periodically
with the magnetic com-
pass.

Due to internal friction within the gyroscope, precession is common in heading indicators. Precession causes the selected heading to drift from the set value. For this reason, you must regularly realign the indicator with the magnetic compass and consider the deviation shown on the compass correction card. [Figure 4-14]

Like attitude indicators, the vacuum-powered heading indicator has operating limits in both pitch and roll. If you exceed these limits, the gyro may tumble, which may damage the instrument. If the indicator has tumbled, you must reset it by aligning it with a known heading or with a stabilized indication from the magnetic compass.

MAGNETIC COMPASS

The magnetic compass is
the only direction seek-
ing instrument in most
light airplanes.

The magnetic compass was one of the first instruments to be installed in an airplane, and it is still the only direction seeking instrument in many airplanes. If you understand its limitations, the magnetic compass is a reliable

Figure 4-14. You should align the heading indicator with the magnetic compass before flight and check it at 15-minute intervals during flight. When you do an in-flight alignment, be certain you are in straight-and-level, unaccelerated flight, with the magnetic compass showing a steady indication.

Figure 4-15. The compass doesn't work on gyroscopic principles, but you will use it frequently to help correct for gyroscopic precession in the heading indicator. To use it properly, you need to understand some of the unique characteristics of magnetism.

source of heading information. It is a self-contained unit which does not require electrical or suction power. [Figure 4-15]

The only source of power for the magnetic compass is magnetism. It is a simple **bar magnet**, consisting of a metal bar with two poles. Lines of magnetic force flow out from each pole in all directions, and eventually return to the opposite pole. The bar magnet in the compass is mounted so it can pivot freely and align itself automatically with the earth's magnetic field. [Figure 4-16]

VARIATION

When you fly under visual flight rules, you ordinarily navigate by referring to charts which are oriented to true north. Because the aircraft compass is oriented to magnetic north, you must make allowances for the difference between these poles in order to navigate properly. You do this by applying a correction called variation to convert a true direction to a magnetic direction. **Variation** at a given point is the angular difference between the true and magnetic poles. The amount of variation depends on where you are located on the earth's surface. [Figure 4-17]

Variation is the angular difference between magnetic and true direction, as measured at any point on the earth.

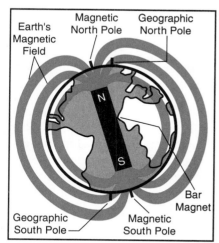

Figure 4-16. The geographic north and south poles form the axis for the earth's rotation. These positions are also referred to as true north and south. Another axis is formed by the magnetic north and south poles, which are referred to as magnetic north and south. A freely mounted bar magnet will align itself with the magnetic axis formed by the north/south magnetic field of the earth.

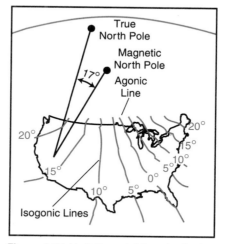

Figure 4-17. Variation at this point in the western United States is 17°. Since the magnetic north pole is located to the east of the true north pole in relation to this point, the variation is easterly. When the magnetic pole falls to the west of the true pole, variation is westerly. Isogonic lines connect points where the variation is equal, while the agonic line defines the points where the variation is zero.

FOR (MH)	0°	30°	60°	90°	120°	150°	180°	210°	240°	270°	300°	330°
STEER (CH)	359°	30°	60°	88°	120°	152°	183°	212°	240°	268°	300°	329°
RADIO ON [X]						RADIO OFF ☐						

Figure 4-18. On this compass correction card, the deviation varies between 0° and 3°. For example, if you want to fly a magnetic heading (MH) of 060°, the compass heading (CH) also is 060°; to fly 180° magnetic, you must fly a compass heading of 183°.

DEVIATION

Deviation is the error caused by the magnetic fields of the airplane and its electronic equipment.

Disturbances from magnetic fields produced by metals and electrical accessories within the airplane itself also produce an error in compass indications. This is referred to as deviation. Although the error cannot be completely eliminated, deviation error can be decreased by manufacturer-installed compensating magnets located within the compass housing. As a pilot, you correct for deviation by using a compass correction card, which is mounted near the compass. The card normally indicates whether the corrections apply with the radio on or off. [Figure 4-18]

COMPASS ERRORS

Although you can apply the appropriate corrections for variation and deviation, additional errors are characteristic of the compass. These errors occur during flight in turbulent air or while you are turning or changing speed. Because of this, your primary heading reference during flight is the heading indicator. The magnetic compass is considered a backup source of heading information.

For the compass to orient itself to magnetic north, it must be able to swing freely within the compass housing. However, this freedom of movement, makes the compass sensitive to in-flight turbulence. In light turbulence, you may be able to use the compass by averaging the readings. For example, if the compass swings between 030° to 060°, you can estimate an approximate heading of 045°. In heavier turbulence, however, the compass is almost useless.

MAGNETIC DIP

Magnetic dip results in turning and acceleration errors.

As we discussed earlier, the compass determines direction through use of a bar magnet which aligns itself with the magnetic field of the earth. These lines of magnetic force are parallel to the surface of the earth at the magnetic equator; however, they deflect increasingly downward as they approach the magnetic poles. Since the compass seeks alignment with these lines, the closer it is to the magnetic poles, the more it deflects downward. This **magnetic dip** results in turning and acceleration/deceleration errors. [Figure 4-19]

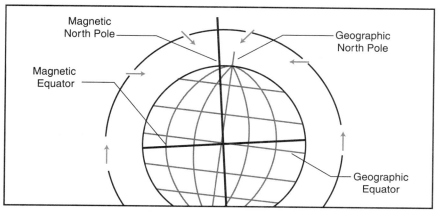

Figure 4-19. The compass is not subject to magnetic dip near the equator, so compass errors are not a factor. Magnetic dip increases gradually as the compass moves closer to the poles, so compass errors increase. Within approximately 300 miles of either magnetic pole, these errors are so great that use of the compass for navigation is impractical.

ACCELERATION ERROR

Acceleration error is influenced by the amount of magnetic dip. The greater the dip, the greater the error. As you accelerate the airplane, the compass indicates a turn to the north. The compass returns to its previous heading as the acceleration subsides. Conversely, as you slow the airplane, the compass shows a turn to the south. Again, when you stop decelerating, the compass returns to an accurate indication. The acceleration/deceleration error is most pronounced when you are flying on headings of east or west, and it decreases gradually as you fly closer to north/south headings. The error doesn't occur when you are flying directly on a north or south heading. The memory aid, ANDS (Accelerate North, Decelerate South), may help you recall this error.

> If you accelerate the aircraft in the northern hemisphere, the compass shows a turn to the north; if you decelerate, it indicates a turn to the south.

TURNING ERROR

Turning error is directly related to magnetic dip; the greater the dip, the greater the turning error. It is most pronounced when you are turning to or from headings of north or south. In the northern hemisphere, when you begin a turn from a heading of north, the compass initially indicates a turn in the opposite direction. When the turn is established, the compass begins to show the turn, but it lags behind the actual heading. The amount of lag decreases as the turn continues, then disappears as the airplane reaches a heading of east or west.

> Turning error causes the magnetic compass to lead or lag the actual magnetic heading of the airplane during turns.

When turning from a heading of east or west to a heading of north, there is no error as you begin the turn. However, as the heading nears north, the compass increasingly lags behind the airplane's actual heading. When you turn from a heading of south, the compass initially indicates a turn in the proper direction but leads the airplane's actual heading. This error also cancels out as the airplane reaches a heading of east or west. Turning from east or west to a heading of south causes the compass to indicate the heading correctly at the start of a turn, but then it increasingly leads the actual heading as the airplane nears a southerly heading. [Figure 4-20]

The amount of lead or lag is approximately equal to the latitude of the airplane. For example, if you are turning from a heading of south to a heading of west while flying at 40° north latitude, the compass will rapidly turn to a heading of 220° (180° + 40°). At the midpoint of the turn, the lead will decrease to approximately half (20°), and upon reaching a heading of west, it will be zero.

The lead and lag errors presented here are only valid for flight in the northern hemisphere. These same types of errors exist in the southern hemisphere, but they act in opposite directions.

MINIMIZING ERRORS

The magnetic compass provides accurate indications only when you are flying in smooth air and in straight - and - level, unaccelerated flight.

If your heading indicator fails and you understand the errors of the magnetic compass, you should still be able to navigate properly. When you are

Figure 4-20. The left portion of the figure shows that a right turn from a heading of north initially causes the compass to indicate a left turn. The right portion shows that a turn from a heading of south causes the compass to indicate a turn in the correct direction, but at a much faster rate.

referring to the compass for heading information, remember that it is accurate only when your airplane is in smooth air and in straight-and-level, unaccelerated flight. At other times, you can still minimize compass errors. When you are flying in an area of turbulence, attempt to find smoother flight conditions. Keep in mind that turning errors only exist when you are making a turn; acceleration errors only exist when you are changing speed.

CHECKLIST _____

After studying this section, you should have a basic understanding of:

✓   **Gyroscopic principles** — What rigidity in space and precession are and how these principles affect gyroscopic instruments.

✓   **Turn coordinator** — What the instrument displays and what is meant by a standard-rate turn and coordinated flight.

✓   **Attitude indicator** — What its function is and how it reflects the pitch and bank attitude of an aircraft.

✓   **Heading indicator** — What its function is, why it precesses, and how to keep it properly aligned.

✓   **Magnetic compass** — What its basic operating principles are and how to compensate for its inherent errors.

ENGINE AND PROPELLER

The engine and propeller work in combination to provide thrust. You will often hear an airplane's engine called the **powerplant**. This is an appropriate term, because it not only provides the power to propel the airplane, but it also powers most airplane accessory systems. For example, the electrical system, cabin heating, and windshield defrosting all rely on the energy produced by the engine.

THE ENGINE

There are several types of aircraft engines in use today. This discussion will concentrate on the engines you are most likely to encounter. Training airplanes are normally powered by **reciprocating engines**, which get their name from the back-and-forth movement of their internal parts.

PRINCIPLES OF OPERATION

You can consider each cylinder in a reciprocating engine as a pump for air and fuel. The more air and fuel that is pumped through it in a given time, the more energy it produces. [Figure 4-21]

FOUR-STROKE OPERATING CYCLE

The back-and-forth, or reciprocating, motion of the piston is caused by the ignition and controlled burning of the fuel/air mixture within the cylinder's combustion chamber. This produces mechanical energy by a series of events that occur in a repetitive cycle known as the **four-stroke operating cycle**. [Figure 4-22]

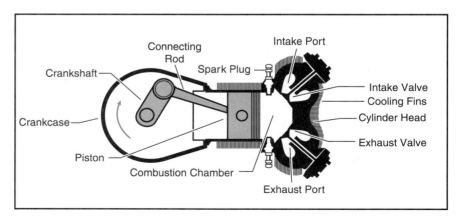

Figure 4-21. The movable piston is attached to the crankshaft by a connecting rod. The crankshaft and the connecting rod change the back-and-forth motion of the piston to rotary, or turning, motion which drives the propeller.

Figure 4-22. The arrows in this illustration indicate the direction of motion of the crankshaft and piston during the four-stroke cycle.

When the piston moves away from the cylinder head on the intake stroke, the intake valve opens and the fuel/air mixture is drawn into the combustion chamber. As the piston moves back toward the cylinder head, the intake valve closes and the fuel/air mixture is compressed. When compression is nearly complete, the spark plugs fire and the compressed mixture is ignited to begin the power stroke. This is the whole reason for the series of events. The rapidly expanding gases from the controlled burning of the fuel/air mixture drive the piston away from the cylinder head. This provides the power that rotates the crankshaft. Finally, the exhaust stroke expels the burned gases from the chamber through the opened exhaust valve.

Even when the engine is operated at a fairly slow speed, the four-stroke cycle takes place several hundred times each minute. In a four-cylinder engine, each cylinder operates on a different stroke. Continuous rotation of the crankshaft is maintained by the precise timing of the power strokes in each cylinder.

ABNORMAL COMBUSTION

As you might expect, the correct timing of the four-stroke cycle is not the only thing that determines how well the engine operates. Your actions can have a direct impact on its operation. You must be sure the engine is properly serviced and maintained. You also must follow the manufacturer's recommendations for such items as using the recommended fuel grade and keeping engine pressures and temperatures within the specified limits. If you do not observe the recommended procedures, abnormal combustion in the form of detonation or preignition may result.

Detonation occurs when fuel in the cylinders explodes instead if burning smoothly.

With normal combustion, the fuel/air mixture burns in a very controlled and predictable manner. Although the process occurs in a fraction of a second, the mixture actually begins to burn at the point where it is ignited by the spark plugs, then burns away from the plugs until it's all consumed. This type of combustion causes a smooth buildup of temperature and pressure and ensures that the expanding gases deliver the maximum force to the piston at exactly the right time in the power stroke. **Detonation**, on the other hand, is an uncontrolled, explosive ignition of the fuel/air mixture within the cylinder's combustion chamber. It causes excessive temperatures and pressures which, if not corrected, can quickly lead to failure of the piston, cylinder, or valves. In less severe cases, detonation causes engine overheating, roughness, or loss of power.

Detonation may result if you allow the engine to overheat or if you use an improper grade of fuel.

Detonation can happen anytime you allow the engine to overheat. It also can occur if you use an improper grade of fuel. The potential for engine overheating is greatest under the following conditions: use of fuel grade lower than that recommended, takeoff with an engine that is already overheated or is very near the maximum allowable temperature, operation at high r.p.m. and low airspeed, and extended operations above 75% power with an extremely lean mixture. If detonation is suspected on climbout, you can help cool the engine by retarding the throttle and by climbing at a slower rate.

Preignition is the uncontrolled combustion of fuel in advance of normal ignition.

In a properly functioning ignition system, combustion is precisely timed. In contrast, **preignition** takes place when the fuel/air mixture ignites too soon. In extreme cases, it can cause serious damage to the engine in a short period of time. Preignition is caused by residual hot spots in the cylinder. A hot spot may be a small carbon deposit on a spark plug, a cracked ceramic spark plug insulator, or almost any damage around the combustion chamber.

Preignition and detonation often occur simultaneously, and one may cause the other. Inside the aircraft, you will be unable to distinguish between the two, since both are likely to cause engine roughness and high engine temperatures. To avoid these problems, maintain engine temperatures within the recommended limits, maintain a sufficiently rich mixture, and use only the proper grade of fuel.

ENGINE SYSTEMS

Now that you have an idea of how the basic components of an engine work, let's look at the systems that help you control and monitor the engine. These include the throttle and mixture control, as well as the ignition, induction, lubrication, and cooling systems.

ENGINE CONTROLS

In a typical training airplane with a fixed-pitch propeller, there are only two primary engine controls — the **throttle** and the **mixture**. Later in this section we'll discuss a third control, the propeller control, which applies to airplanes with constant-speed propellers. [Figure 4-23]

| Throttle | Mixture | Tachometer |

Figure 4-23. The throttle controls engine speed by regulating the amount of fuel and air that flows into the cylinders, while the mixture controls the ratio of the fuel-to-air mixture. A mixture that is too rich contains too much fuel for the existing conditions, and a mixture that is too lean does not contain enough fuel. Engine speed is expressed in revolutions per minute (r.p.m.) and is displayed on the tachometer. The window in the lower part of the instrument keeps a record of engine running time.

IGNITION SYSTEM

The ignition system provides the spark that ignites the fuel/air mixture in the cylinders. It is made up of the magnetos, spark plugs, interconnecting wires, and the ignition switch. [Figure 4-24]

Figure 4-24. Before flight, you use the ignition switch to check each magneto separately. During flight, you use both magnetos. Notice the wires from each magneto are connected to one of the spark plugs in all four cylinders. The numbers in the cylinders indicate firing order.

A **magneto** is a self-contained, engine-driven unit that supplies electrical current to the spark plugs. It uses permanent magnets to generate an electrical current completely independent of the aircraft's electrical system. The magneto generates sufficiently high voltage to jump a spark across the spark plug gap in each cylinder. The system begins to fire as soon as you engage the starter and the crankshaft begins to turn. It continues to operate whenever the crankshaft is rotating.

The dual ignition system on an airplane engine provides improved engine performance.

Use of two magnetos enhances safety and increases reliability of the ignition system. The magnetos operate independently of each other; each fires one of the two spark plugs in each cylinder. The firing of two spark plugs improves combustion of the fuel/air mixture and results in a slightly higher power output. If one of the magnetos fails, the other is unaffected. The engine will continue to operate normally, although you can expect a slight decrease in engine power. The same is true if one of the two spark plugs in a cylinder fails.

You control the operation of the magnetos with the **ignition switch** on the instrument panel. The first four positions are: OFF, RIGHT, LEFT, and BOTH. Some ignition switches also include a START position. When you select the LEFT or RIGHT position, only one magneto is activated. When you select BOTH, the system operates on both magnetos.

You can identify a malfunctioning ignition system during the pretakeoff check by observing the decrease in r.p.m. that occurs when you first move the ignition switch from BOTH to RIGHT, and then from BOTH to LEFT. A small decrease in engine r.p.m. is normal during this check. The permissible decrease is listed in your pilot's operating handbook. If the engine stops running when you switch to one magneto or if the r.p.m. drop exceeds the allowable limit, don't fly the airplane until the problem is corrected. The cause could be fouled plugs, broken or shorted wires between the magneto and the plugs, or improperly timed firing of the plugs.

An engine that continues to run after the ignition switch is turned to OFF may have a disconnected ground wire in the ignition switch.

Although the ignition system is usually trouble free, you still need to be alert for the special problems associated with a magneto. Because the magneto requires no outside source of electrical power, be certain that you turn the ignition switch to the OFF position following engine shutdown. Even with the battery and master switches OFF, the engine can fire and turn over if you leave the ignition switch ON and the propeller is moved. The potential for serious injury in this situation is obvious. In addition, if the ignition switch ground wire is disconnected, the magneto may continue to fire even if the ignition switch is OFF. If this occurs, the only way to stop the engine is to move the mixture lever to the idle cutoff position, then have the system checked by a qualified mechanic. Finally, if you encounter static on the airplane's communications radio, a loose connection in the ignition system or a break in the shielding around the ignition wiring may be the cause.

INDUCTION SYSTEM

The purpose of the induction system is to bring outside air into the engine, mix it with fuel in the proper proportion, and deliver it to the cylinders where combustion occurs. Since it is critically important that an uninterrupted mixture of fuel and air reach the engine, you should be thoroughly familiar with the operation of this system in your airplane.

Outside air enters the induction system through an **intake port** at the front of the engine compartment. This port normally contains an air filter that inhibits the entry of dust and other foreign objects. Since the filter may occasionally become clogged, an alternate source of air must be available. Usually, the alternate air comes from inside the engine cowling where it bypasses a clogged air filter. Some alternate air sources operate automatically, while others operate manually.

The **carburetor** mixes the incoming air with fuel and delivers the fuel/air mixture to the combustion chamber. A float-type carburetor system is used on most light aircraft. When the air enters the carburetor it passes through a venturi. This increases its velocity and decreases its pressure. Fuel enters the carburetor from a float chamber where it is maintained at a nearly constant level by a float device. The float chamber is vented to the outside so that pressure inside remains equal to the atmospheric pressure, even during climbs and descents. [Figure 4-25]

The operating principle of float-type carburetors is based on the difference in pressure at the venturi throat and the air inlet.

Figure 4-25. Fuel is drawn from the float chamber past a mixture needle and into the venturi where it mixes with the incoming air. Since the discharge nozzle is located in an area of low pressure created by the venturi, the fuel is forced through the discharge nozzle by the higher atmospheric pressure in the float chamber.

When you lean the mixture, you decrease the fuel flow to compensate for decreased air density.

Carburetors are calibrated at sea level, and the correct fuel-to-air mixture ratio is established at that altitude with the mixture control set in the FULL RICH position. However, as altitude increases, the density of air entering the carburetor decreases while the density of the fuel remains the same. This means that at higher altitudes, the mixture becomes progressively richer. To maintain the correct fuel/air mixture, you must be able to adjust the amount of fuel that is mixed with the incoming air. This is the function of the mixture control. This adjustment, often referred to as **leaning the mixture**, varies from one airplane to another. Refer to the POH to determine specific procedures for your airplane.

You may be able to correct engine roughness during runup at a high-elevation airport by leaning the mixture.

Most mixture adjustments are required during changes of altitude or during operations at airports with field elevations well above sea level. A mixture that is too rich can result in engine roughness. The roughness normally is due to spark plug fouling from excessive carbon buildup on the plugs. This occurs because the excessively rich mixture lowers temperature inside the cylinder, inhibiting complete combustion of the fuel. This condition may occur during the pretakeoff runup at high elevation airports and during climbs or cruise flight at high altitudes. Usually, you can correct the problem by leaning the mixture according to POH instructions.

If you do not adjust the mixture control during descents from high to low altitudes, the fuel/air mixture will be too lean.

If you fail to enrich the mixture during a descent from high altitude, it normally will become too lean. High engine temperatures can cause excessive engine wear or even failure. The best way to avoid this type of situation is to monitor the engine temperature gauges regularly and follow POH guidelines for maintaining the proper mixture.

Carburetor Icing

You should expect carburetor ice when temperatures are below 21°C (70°F) and the relative humidity is high.

The effect of fuel vaporization and decreasing air pressure in the venturi causes a sharp drop in temperature in the carburetor. If the air is moist, the water vapor in the air may condense. When the temperature in the carburetor is at or below freezing, **carburetor ice** may form on internal surfaces, including the throttle valve. Because of the sudden cooling that takes place in the carburetor, icing can occur even on warm days with temperatures as high as 38°C (100°F) and humidity as low as 50%. However, it is more likely to occur when temperatures are below 21°C (70°F) and the relative humidity is above 80%. The likelihood of icing increases as temperature decreases down to 0°C (32°F) and as relative humidity increases. Below freezing, the possibility of carburetor ice decreases with decreases in temperature.

Although carburetor ice can occur during any phase of flight, it is particularly dangerous when you are using reduced power, such as on descents or in the traffic pattern. You may not notice it during a descent until you try to add power. [Figure 4-26]

Figure 4-26. Carburetor ice reduces the size of the air passage to the engine. This restricts the flow of the fuel/air mixture and reduces power.

Figure 4-27. When you turn the carburetor heat ON, a valve cuts off air flow from the normal air intake and allows heated air from an alternate source to enter the carburetor.

In an airplane with a fixed-pitch propeller, your first indication of carburetor icing is a decrease in engine r.p.m., followed by engine roughness and possible fuel starvation. In an airplane with a constant-speed propeller, as discussed later in this section, the power changes are reflected by shifts in manifold pressure. The **carburetor heat** system eliminates the ice by routing air across a heat source before it enters the carburetor. [Figure 4-27]

Generally, you should use full carburetor heat whenever you reduce engine r.p.m. below the normal operating range for your airplane or when you suspect the presence of carburetor ice. Carburetor heat tends to decrease engine output and increase the operating temperature of the engine. Normally, you do not use it continuously when full power is required, particularly during takeoff. Be sure to check your pilot's operating handbook for specific recommendations.

The use of carburetor heat causes a slight decrease in engine power, because the heated air is less dense than the outside air that had been entering the engine. This enriches the mixture. When ice is present in an airplane with a fixed-pitch propeller and you use carburetor heat, there is a slight decrease in r.p.m., followed by a gradual increase in r.p.m. as the ice melts. If ice is not present, the r.p.m. will decrease slightly, then remain constant. Remember that in an airplane with a constant-speed propeller, these power changes are reflected by manifold pressure.

The first indication of carburetor ice in an airplane equipped with a fixed-pitch propeller is a loss of r.p.m.

If carburetor ice is present in an airplane with a fixed-pitch propeller, the decrease in r.p.m. caused by the enriched mixture will be followed by an increase in r.p.m. as the ice melts.

Fuel Injection and Turbocharging

Fuel injection and turbocharging are common induction system features for high-performance aircraft used in general aviation. Chances are good that you will encounter both of these systems early in your flying career. Fuel injection is more precise than a float-type carburetor in metering fuel and distributing the fuel/air mixture. Lower fuel consumption, increased horse-power, lower operating temperatures, and longer engine life are some of the advantages of this system. The system also is generally considered less susceptible to icing than a carburetor system. However, starting procedures usually are more complex than for carburetor systems, especially when the engine is hot.

When you operate a reciprocating engine at high altitudes, efficiency of the engine diminishes as a result of lower air density even though the volume of airflow into the engine remains the same. This is a characteristic of any non-turbocharged engine, where the fuel/air mixture is not compressed. A turbocharger may be added to the engine to compress the mixture before it enters the cylinders. This compression increases air density so the engine can operate at high altitudes and still produce the same amount of power as it would at sea level. However, turbocharged engines, which usually are also fuel injected, have tight operating parameters, and require careful mixture adjustments and monitoring. Since both turbocharging and fuel injection have unique operating characteristics, try to arrange a checkout with an experienced flight instructor before flying an airplane equipped with these systems.

OIL SYSTEM

Airplane engines depend
on circulation of oil for
lubrication of internal
parts and cooling.

The engine oil system performs two important functions. It lubricates the engine's moving parts and aids in cooling of the engine by reducing friction and removing some of the heat from the cylinders. [Figure 4-28]

The oil filler cap and dipstick for measuring the oil quantity are accessible through a panel in the engine cowling. You should check the oil quantity before each flight. See your pilot's operating handbook or placards near the access panel for the minimum operating quantity, as well as the recommended oil type and weight for your airplane. After engine start, you should use the oil pressure and oil temperature gauges to monitor the system.

Immediately after start-
ing the engine, adjust
r.p.m. and check engine
instruments for the
proper indications.

The oil pressure gauge provides a direct indication of the oil system operation. A below-normal pressure may mean that the oil pump is not putting out enough pressure to circulate oil throughout the engine, while an above-normal pressure may indicate a clogged oil line. You should consider any abnormal indication to mean that vital engine parts are not receiving the necessary lubrication. Under these circumstances, your best course of action is to follow the appropriate instructions in your POH. Most manufacturers recommend that you shut down the engine if the oil pressure

Figure 4-28. The heart of the system is the oil pump, which draws oil from the sump and routes it to the engine. After the oil passes through the engine, it returns to the sump. In some airplanes, additional lubrication is supplied by the rotating crankshaft, which splashes oil onto portions of the engine.

does not begin to rise within 30 seconds after an engine start in the summer, or 60 seconds in the winter. [Figure 4-29]

The oil temperature gauge is usually located next to the oil pressure gauge. This allows you to check both at the same time. Unlike the oil pressure gauge, which usually reacts quickly to changes in pressure, changes in oil temperature occur more slowly. This is particularly noticeable after starting a cold engine, when it may take several minutes or longer for the gauge to show any increase in temperature. [Figure 4-30]

Excessive engine temperatures can result in loss of power, high oil consumption, and possible engine damage.

Figure 4-29. This gauge measures the pressure in pounds per square inch (p.s.i.) of the oil supplied to the engine. Green typically indicates the normal operating range, while red indicates the minimum and maximum pressures.

Figure 4-30. The oil temperature gauge measures the temperature of oil as it enters the engine. The green area shows the normal operating range and the red line indicates the maximum allowable temperature.

High engine oil temperatures may be caused by an oil level that is too low.

You should check the oil temperature periodically to see if it remains within the normal operating range. This is particularly important when you are using a high power setting, since this tends to increase oil temperatures. Abnormally high indications may also indicate a plugged oil line, a low oil quantity, or a defective temperature gauge.

COOLING SYSTEM

The burning fuel within the engine's cylinders produces intense heat. While the engine oil system is essential to internal cooling of the engine, additional cooling is required to maintain normal temperatures. Much of the remaining heat is dissipated in the exhaust gases, but outside air is also used for cooling. [Figure 4-31]

Airplanes equipped with cowl flaps may have a **cylinder head temperature gauge** that provides a direct temperature reading from one of the cylinders. The cowl flaps are opened when the cylinder head temperature indicates the engine requires increased cooling. This usually is necessary during ground operations, when airflow across the engine is at a minimum, and any time during flight when power settings are high and airspeeds are low. [Figure 4-32]

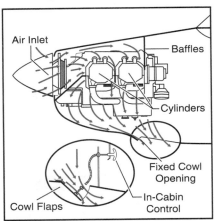

Figure 4-31. Outside air usually enters the engine compartment through an inlet behind the propeller hub. Baffles direct it to the hottest parts of the engine, primarily the cylinders, which have fins that increase the area exposed to the airflow. Some airplanes have fixed openings in the cowling so outside air can exit the engine compartment. On others, cowl flaps provide an adjustable opening to regulate the airflow around the engine and to reduce drag.

Figure 4-32. Like the other engine gauges, the normal range for the cylinder head temperature gauge is marked in green. You should compare the readings from the cylinder head temperature and oil temperature gauges. A disparity between the two may indicate a malfunction in one of the instruments. Oil and cylinder head temperatures above the normal operating range may indicate that you are using too much power with the mixture set too lean.

Besides using cowl flaps, you can reduce high engine operating temperatures by enriching the mixture. A richer mixture burns at a slightly lower temperature. Other methods for reducing engine temperatures include reducing the rate of climb, increasing the airspeed and, when conditions permit, decreasing the power setting.

Engine temperature may be reduced by enriching the mixture, reducing the rate of climb, increasing the airspeed, or reducing power.

PROPELLER

Although the engine produces the power, the propeller provides the thrust to propel the airplane through the air. The propeller consists of a central hub with two or more blades attached. Each blade is an airfoil that acts like a rotating wing. Since it is an airfoil, the propeller blade is subject to the same aerodynamic factors that apply to any airfoil. [Figure 4-33]

When the propeller rotates through the air, it creates a low pressure area in front of the blade, much like the wing's curvature creates a low pressure area above the wing. However, unlike the wing, which moves through the air at a uniform rate, the propeller sections near the tip rotate at a much greater speed than those near the hub. To compensate for this, each small section of the propeller blade is set at a different angle to the plane of rotation. The gradual decrease in blade angle resulting from this gives the propeller blade its twisted appearance. Blade twist allows the propeller to provide a fairly constant angle of attack and more nearly uniform thrust throughout most of the length of the blade.

The overall angle of a propeller's blades affects its operating efficiency. A propeller with a low blade angle, known as a **climb propeller**, provides the best performance for takeoff and climb, while one with a high blade angle, known as a **cruise propeller**, is more adapted to high speed cruise and high altitude flight.

Figure 4-33. The cross sections of this propeller blade illustrate the well-defined airfoil shape. One surface of the blade is cambered, or curved, while the other is comparatively flat. The leading edge is the thick, cambered part of the blade that meets the air during rotation. Notice how the twist of a propeller blade causes the shape of the airfoil cross-sections to change as they move toward the tip of the propeller.

FIXED PITCH

Light airplanes may have either a fixed-pitch or a constant-speed propeller. With a fixed-pitch propeller, blade angle is selected on the basis of what is best for the primary function of the airplane. You cannot change this angle. You shouldn't confuse the term **pitch** as it applies to propeller blades with pitch as it relates to an aircraft's attitude. A propeller's pitch is the number of inches that it would move forward in one revolution if it were moving through a solid medium and did not undergo any slippage or loss of efficiency as it does in air. Pitch is proportional to blade angle (the angle between the chord line of the blade and the propeller's plane of rotation). Because of its direct connection to the crankshaft, the only power control for a fixed-pitch propeller is the throttle, and the only power indicator is the tachometer. [Figure 4-34]

CONSTANT SPEED

A constant-speed propeller allows you to select the blade angle that provides the most efficient performance.

Compared to a fixed-pitch propeller, the constant-speed propeller is much more efficient. It is often referred to as a variable-pitch or controllable-pitch propeller, since you can adjust the blade angle for most efficient operation. The main advantage of a constant-speed propeller is that it converts a high percentage of the engine's power into thrust over a wide range of r.p.m. and airspeed combinations.

With a constant-speed propeller, the propeller control regulates engine r.p.m. and the throttle controls engine power output, as indicated on the manifold pressure gauge.

An airplane with a constant-speed propeller has two power controls — the propeller control and the throttle. The propeller control changes the pitch of the propeller blades and regulates the r.p.m. of the engine and the prop, as indicated on the tachometer. The throttle adjusts the power output of the engine, which is directly indicated on the manifold pressure gauge. [Figure 4-35]

Figure 4-34. A fixed-pitch propeller is connected directly to the engine's crankshaft. Engine power rotates the crankshaft as well as the propeller, and the propeller converts the rotary power into thrust.

Green—Normal Operating Range

Figure 4-35. The manifold pressure gauge shows the pressure inside the engine in inches of mercury (in. Hg). It usually has color-coded markings to help you identify the normal operating range.

When the engine is not running, the manifold pressure gauge registers atmospheric pressure. When a normally aspirated engine is running, the gauge senses the reduced pressure in the manifold and indicates less than atmospheric pressure. During a climb with a constant power setting, manifold pressure gradually decreases as you gain altitude.

The propeller control permits you to select a low blade angle and high r.p.m. setting for maximum thrust on takeoff. After you reach cruising flight conditions, you can use a higher pitch and a lower r.p.m. setting to maintain adequate thrust for the desired airspeed. This is comparable to using a low gear in your car to accelerate, then using a high gear for cruising speed. Most hydraulic pitch-change mechanisms found on single-engine airplanes use high-pressure oil to oppose the aerodynamic twisting forces acting on the blades. [Figure 4-36]

The governor regulates the oil pressure sent to the pitch-change mechanism to maintain an equilibrium between aerodynamic and hydraulic pitch-changing forces at the selected r.p.m. For a given r.p.m. setting, there is always a maximum allowable manifold pressure. Operating above this level may cause internal stress within the engine. Specific operating instructions are contained in your pilot's operating handbook. As a general rule, you should avoid high manifold pressures with low r.p.m. settings.

With constant-speed propellers, you should avoid low r.p.m. settings with high manifold pressure.

PROPELLER HAZARDS

The propeller is the most dangerous part of the airplane, and you should treat it with caution at all times. You should routinely provide your

Figure 4-36. A hydraulic piston in the hub of the propeller is connected to each blade by a piston rod. This rod is attached to forks that slide over the pitch-change pin mounted in the root of each blade (item 1). High-pressure oil enters the cylinder from the governor through the center of the propeller shaft and piston rod (item 2). The oil pressure moves the piston toward the rear of the cylinder, moving the piston rod and forks aft (item 3). The forks push the pitch-change pin of each blade toward the rear of the hub, causing the blades to twist toward the high-pitch position.

passengers a thorough briefing regarding propeller hazards and how they can be avoided, stressing the need to stay well clear of the propeller area at all times.

When hand-starting an airplane, a competent pilot must be at the controls.

Occasionally, you may find it necessary to turn the propeller by hand to start the engine. Be sure you have seen a demonstration of the correct procedure before attempting this yourself, since it can be extremely dangerous if done improperly. Always ensure that a qualified pilot is at the controls, and remember that the person hand-propping the airplane is in charge of the starting procedure.

CHECKLIST

After studying this section, you should have a basic understanding of:

✓ **Engine** — What type of engine is used in a typical training airplane and what its general operating principles are.

✓ **Abnormal combustion** — What the causes and indications of detonation and preignition are and what the recommended corrective actions are.

✓ **Ignition system** — What its major components are and how the magnetos operate.

✓ **Carburetor** — What the fuel/air mixture is and how it is controlled, and what hazards are associated with carburetor ice.

✓ **Engine oil system** — How the oil system provides lubrication and cooling for the engine.

✓ **Propeller** — How it produces thrust, and what the differences are between fixed-pitch and constant-speed propellers.

FUEL AND ELECTRICAL SYSTEMS

In previous sections, you were introduced to a variety of instrument and powerplant systems. This section concludes the equipment discussion with a presentation of the airplane's fuel and electrical systems. As you read this section, you will see why correct system operation is so important.

FUEL SYSTEMS

Fuel systems are actually quite complex and include a number of individual components such as tanks, lines, vents, valves, drains, and gauges. There are two general types of fuel systems found in light airplanes — those that require a fuel pump and those that operate on gravity feed. Regardless of the system on the airplane you use for training, you will eventually encounter both systems. [Figure 4-37]

The **fuel-pump system** is usually found in low-wing airplanes, where the fuel tanks may be located below the engine. It is also used in most high-performance airplanes with fuel-injected engines. An engine-driven pump provides fuel under pressure from the fuel tanks to the engine. Because the engine-driven pump operates only when the engine is running, an electrically operated **boost pump** provides fuel under pressure for engine starting and as a backup, should the engine-driven pump malfunction. The

Figure 4-37. A typical fuel-pump system contains the components shown here. Fuel-pump and gravity-feed systems are similar, except the gravity system does not include engine-driven or electric boost pumps and fuel pressure gauges.

boost pump is operated by a switch in the cockpit. You should refer to your POH for the correct operating procedures.

If an airplane is equipped with a fuel pump, it will have a **fuel pressure gauge** that allows you to monitor the fuel system. If fuel pressure drops below the normal operating range, indicating a possible malfunction of the engine-driven fuel pump, turning on the fuel boost pump will ensure a steady flow of fuel to the engine.

In a **gravity-feed system**, fuel flows by gravity from the fuel tanks to the engine. It works well in high-wing airplanes where the difference in height between the wing-mounted fuel tanks and the engine allows the fuel to flow under sufficient pressure to meet the requirements of the engine. The gravity-feed system is very common on high-wing airplanes with carbureted engines in the lower horsepower range.

FUEL SYSTEM COMPONENTS

The fuel tanks are usually located in the wings. They are replenished with fuel through a filler cap on top of the wing using a fuel nozzle and hose similar to the one you use to refuel an automobile. However, with airplanes, you should be especially careful not to allow the fuel nozzle spout to project very far into the tank, since you can damage the tank.

Filling fuel tanks after the last flight of the day prevents moisture from condensing by eliminating air in the tanks.

The condensation of moisture in partially filled fuel tanks can result in water entering fuel lines and restricting engine operation. You can minimize this by refilling the tanks following the last flight of the day. Since water and other sediments are heavier than fuel, any foreign material will collect at the bottom of the tank where it can be removed when you open a drain valve during the preflight inspection.

Fuel tanks contain a vent that allows air pressure inside the tank to remain the same as that outside the tank. This prevents the formation of a vacuum which would prevent fuel from flowing out of the tank. The vents may be located in the filler caps, or the tank may be vented through a small tube extending through the wing surface. The tanks also contain an overflow drain that prevents the rupture of the tank due to fuel expansion. The overflow drain may be combined with the fuel tank vent or it may have a separate opening. On hot days, it is not unusual to see a small amount of fuel coming from the overflow drain.

The fuel quantity gauges are located on the instrument panel, where they are usually grouped with engine monitoring gauges such as oil pressure and temperature. The gauges show the amount of fuel measured by a sensing unit in each fuel tank. Newer gauges show the tank capacity in both gallons and pounds. [Figure 4-38]

The fuel selector valve allows you to select fuel from various tanks. A common type of selector valve contains four positions: LEFT, RIGHT, BOTH, and OFF. Selecting the LEFT or RIGHT position allows fuel to feed only from that tank, while selecting the BOTH position feeds fuel from both tanks. Normally, you operate this type of fuel selector in the BOTH position. The LEFT or RIGHT position may be used to balance the amount of fuel remaining in each wing tank. [Figure 4-39]

Another common type of fuel selector switch has three positions: LEFT, RIGHT, and OFF. With this type of system, you must monitor fuel consumption closely to ensure that you don't run a tank completely out of fuel. For one thing, this will cause the engine to stop running. Also, running for prolonged periods on one tank causes an unbalanced fuel load between tanks. Regardless of the type of fuel selector in use, if the airplane is equipped with an engine-driven fuel pump or electrical boost pump, running a tank completely dry may allow air to enter the fuel system and cause a condition known as **vapor lock**. When this situation develops, it may be difficult, or impossible, to restart the engine.

On an airplane equipped with fuel pumps, running a tank completely dry may cause vapor lock.

Proper fuel management requires that you have a detailed knowledge of the airplane's fuel system. Therefore, you should become thoroughly familiar with the specific procedures established in the POH by the manufacturer of your airplane.

After the fuel selector valve, the fuel passes through a strainer before it enters the carburetor. This strainer removes moisture and other sediments

Figure 4-38. Do not depend solely on the accuracy of your fuel quantity gauges. Always observe the fuel level in each tank visually during the preflight inspection and then compare it with the corresponding fuel quantity indication.

Figure 4-39. Placards near the fuel selector may show the tank capacity in gallons of usable fuel. There also may be limitations on single tank operations, such as level flight only. Usually, you will find that the BOTH position is required for takeoffs and landings or maneuvering.

that might be in the system. Since these contaminants are heavier than aviation fuel, they settle in a sump at the bottom of the strainer assembly.

It is generally recommended that you drain the fuel strainer before each flight. If the system design will allow it, you should also check the fuel visually to ensure that no moisture is present. Moisture in the sump is hazardous because in cold weather it can freeze and block fuel lines. In warm weather, it can flow into the carburetor and stop the engine. If moisture is present in the sump, it probably means there is more water in the fuel tanks, and you should continue to drain them until there is no evidence of contamination. In any event, never take off until you are certain that all moisture has been removed from the engine fuel system. If you are in doubt, have the system inspected by a qualified mechanic.

The fuel system contains a small hand-operated pump called a primer. It is used to pump fuel directly into the cylinders prior to engine start. The primer is useful in cold weather when fuel in the carburetor is difficult to vaporize. You can often start a cold engine by priming it when it would not start otherwise.

REFUELING

There may be occasions when you will refuel your airplane yourself. Even when it is done by someone else, you should be on hand to ensure it is done properly. While airplane fuel is a hazardous substance, refueling can be safely accomplished if you follow a few simple procedures.

The major refueling hazard is the possible combustion of the fuel by a spark that causes fumes to ignite. The most probable cause of a spark is from static electricity that discharges between refueling equipment and the airplane. The possibility of sparking can be greatly reduced if you make sure that a ground wire from the fuel truck is attached to the airplane before the fuel cap is removed from the tank. The airplane should be grounded throughout the refueling procedure and the fuel truck should be grounded to the airport surface.

FUEL GRADES

In addition to using the proper refueling technique, you must also ensure that you are using the proper grade of fuel. Using an incorrect grade may seriously affect engine performance and it may result in engine damage or failure. This is another reason it is highly recommended that you be present during refueling.

Airplane engines are designed to operate with a fuel that meets certain specifications. The recommended fuel grade and authorized substitutes are in the pilot's operating handbook for your airplane. Fuel grades are identified according to octane, or performance number, and all fuel of the same grade has been dyed a standard color to assist in identification. [Figure 4-40]

In an emergency, using the next higher grade of fuel for a short period of time is not considered harmful, provided the manufacturer authorizes it. On the other hand, using a lower rated fuel may be extremely harmful. If it becomes necessary to mix various grades of fuel, the fuel may lose its characteristic color and become clear. This may cause confusion because turbine fuel also is colorless and reciprocating engines cannot operate on it. You should always use the fuel specified in the POH.

Using a fuel grade lower than specified causes cylinder head and engine oil temperatures to exceed normal operating limits.

If the recommended fuel grade is not available, you may substitute the next higher grade, if approved by the manufacturer.

ELECTRICAL SYSTEMS

The electrical systems found in light airplanes reflect the increased use of sophisticated avionics and other electrical accessories. Since most operations in today's flight environment are highly dependent on the airplane's electrical system, you need to familiarize yourself with basic features.

ALTERNATORS

On light airplanes, electrical energy is supplied by a 14- or 28-volt direct-current system, which usually is powered by an engine-driven alternator. Some older airplanes may be equipped with generators, but alternators have many advantages for airplanes, just as they do for automobiles. Light weight, lower maintenance, and uniform output, even at low engine r.p.m., are the principal advantages.

Grade	Color
80	Red
100LL	Blue
100	Green
Turbine Fuel	Colorless

AVGAS ONLY

Grade 100LL   Grade 100

Figure 4-40. Color coding of fuel and placement of decals near fuel tank filler caps helps ensure that you use the proper grade of fuel.

Alternators actually produce **alternating current** (AC) first, and then convert it to **direct current** (DC) for use in the system. Direct current is delivered to a **bus bar** which serves to distribute the current to the various electrical components on the aircraft. [Figure 4-41]

Figure 4-41. An electrical system schematic like this sample is included in most POHs. Notice that the various bus bar accessories are protected by circuit breakers. However, you should still make sure all electrical equipment is turned off before you start the engine. This protects sensitive components, particularly the radios, from damage which may be caused by random voltages generated during the starting process.

Another essential part of the electrical system is the storage battery. Its main purpose is to provide a means of starting the engine. It also permits limited operation of electrical components, such as the radios, without starting the engine. Finally, the battery is a valuable source of standby or emergency electrical power in case of alternator malfunction.

AMMETER

An ammeter is used to monitor the electrical current in amperes within the system. Actually, there are two types of ammeters. One reflects current flowing to or from the battery. The other type simply displays the load placed on the alternator and is often referred to as a loadmeter. [Figure 4-42]

A charging ammeter (needle on the plus side) is normal following an engine start, since the battery power lost in starting is being replaced. After the battery is charged, the ammeter should stabilize near zero and the alternator will supply the electrical needs of the system. A discharging ammeter means the electrical load is exceeding the output of the alternator, and the battery is helping to supply system power. This may mean the alternator is malfunctioning, or the electrical load is excessive. In any event, you should reduce your electrical load to conserve battery power and land as soon as practicable.

With a loadmeter, you can tell immediately if the alternator is operating normally, because it should reflect the amount of current being drawn by the electrical equipment. The POH will tell you the normal load to expect. Loss of the alternator will cause the loadmeter to indicate zero.

Figure 4-42. When the pointer of the ammeter on the left is on the plus side, it shows the charging rate of the battery. A minus indication means more current is being drawn from the battery than is being replaced. The loadmeter type on the right reflects the total load placed on the alternator by the system's electrical accessories. When all electrical components are turned off, it reflects the amount of charging current demanded by the battery.

MASTER SWITCH

The master switch controls the entire electrical system. Turning on the master switch is like turning on the ignition in an automobile. The airplane's ignition system is independent of the electrical system, since magnetos supply current to the spark plugs. However, the engine's starter won't operate unless the master switch is ON because power for the starter comes from the electrical system, not the magnetos. [Figure 4-43]

During normal operations, both sides of the master switch are on. In case of alternator malfunction, it can be isolated from the system. Another use for the split-type master switch is when you want to check equipment on the ground before you start the engine. In this situation, you can select only the battery side.

CIRCUIT BREAKERS AND FUSES

As the electrical system schematic shows, circuit breakers or fuses are used to protect various components from overloads. With circuit breakers, resetting the breaker usually will reactivate the circuit, unless an overload or short exists. If this is the case, the circuit breaker will continue to pop, indicating an electrical problem. [Figure 4-44]

Manufacturers usually provide a holder for spare fuses in the event you need to replace one in flight. In fact, FARs require you to carry extra fuses for night flight. Be sure to familiarize yourself with the electrical system for the airplane you fly. Many airplanes are equipped with low-voltage

Figure 4-43. Most airplanes use a split-rocker type master switch. The right half is labeled "BAT" and it controls all power to the electrical system. The left half is labeled "ALT" and it controls the alternator.

Figure 4-44. As a pilot, you are expected to know the location of the circuit protection device for each electrical component. Normally, the component's name is printed on the circuit breaker panel.

warning lights which indicate the need for specific corrective actions. The POH provides a thorough description of normal and emergency operations for the electrical system.

CHECKLIST

After studying this section, you should have a basic understanding of:

✓ **Fuel systems** — What the major types are, what components are included, and how they function.

✓ **Fuel grades** — How to recognize fuel grades by color and how to check for fuel contamination.

✓ **Electrical systems** — What the major components are and how they function.

✓ **Master switch** — What it does and how it controls the entire electrical system.

STEEP TURNS

The constant altitude, steep turn is an excellent maneuver for developing coordination, planning, and precise airplane control. The following discussion applies primarily to steep turns required for private pilot certification. This maneuver consists of a coordinated 360° turn performed at a bank angle of 45°, ± 5°. For simplicity, 45° banks are used in this text. The PTS requires turns in both directions.

As in all training maneuvers, you must be aware of other traffic in the area. Therefore, before beginning the maneuver, make clearing turns to ensure the practice area is free of conflicting traffic. As you perform the maneuver, it is your responsibility to remain vigilant and avoid any traffic flying through the area.

To enter a steep turn, stabilize the altitude, airspeed, and heading of the airplane. If you begin the maneuver from a stabilized condition, you can fly it more precisely. Use section lines or prominent land features to establish an entry heading and aid in orientation. As with most in-flight maneuvers, select an entry altitude that will allow you to complete the maneuver no lower than 1,500 feet AGL.

TURN ENTRY

Enter at the speed recommended in the pilot's operating handbook. If no recommendation is given, use cruise speed or maneuvering speed, whichever is less. As you enter the turn, establish the bank at a moderate rate. If you roll the airplane into the bank too rapidly, you often will have difficulty establishing the pitch attitude necessary to maintain level flight.

As you establish the turn, increased power and back pressure are required.

Normally, you add power as the bank angle approaches 45°. Even when you apply power, the airspeed usually decreases and you must apply considerable back pressure to maintain altitude. You can use the trim to help relieve control wheel pressure in the turn, but you must remember to change the trim again as you complete the turn and roll out to straight-and-level flight.

VISUAL AND INSTRUMENT REFERENCES

As you roll into a steep turn, establish the correct pitch and bank attitudes by referring to the natural horizon. Use the attitude indicator to confirm the correct attitudes. Once you are established in the turn, maintain proper pitch and bank by referring to both the natural horizon and attitude

Figure 4-45. Here are the visual and instrument indications you will see when established in a level, steep turn to the left and right. In a stable turn, the only instrument which shows a continual change is the heading indicator.

indicator. Use the altimeter and vertical speed indicator to show when you must change pitch. [Figure 4-45]

ALTITUDE CONTROL

Altitude corrections in turns of 45° or more deserve special consideration. If you lose altitude because of a nose-low attitude, simply pulling back on the control wheel may not provide a satisfactory correction. The force created by back pressure on the control wheel raises the nose, but it also tightens the turn. This procedure simply increases the load on the airplane and does little to correct for altitude. The proper response is to reduce the angle of bank temporarily and simultaneously increase the pitch attitude. When you have made this correction, return to the desired angle of bank and apply slightly more back pressure than you used previously.

When you lose altitude in a steep turn, decrease the angle of bank, increase pitch, then roll back into the turn.

ROLL-OUT TECHNIQUE

Perform the roll-out procedures for steep turns in the same manner as those for medium bank turns. However, you should begin the roll-out approximately 20° before reaching the desired heading. Generally, less rudder pressure and aileron movement are required during the roll-in than during the roll-out. This is because the control pressures exerted during the roll-out must overcome the airplane's overbanking tendency.

The elevator (or stabilator) control pressures you use during the roll-out are the reverse of those used during the roll-in. As the bank decreases, you must decrease back pressure and pitch attitude gradually to avoid gaining altitude and to reduce power back to the cruise power setting.

When you gain proficiency in steep turns in both directions, you will learn to perform them first in one direction, then in the other, with no hesitation between the turns. To accomplish this, you must apply back pressure during the first turn, reduce it during the roll-out, then reapply it as the angle of bank increases in the opposite direction.

OVERBANKING TENDENCY

When an airplane is in a level, steep turn, an **overbanking tendency** exists because the wing on the outside of the turn travels farther than the inside wing. Because it is traveling farther, the outside wing has a faster airflow over its surface. The higher airflow results in more lift on the outside wing. [Figure 4-46]

In addition, rudder pressure is required throughout the turn. The tail section, because of its distance aft of the center of gravity of the airplane, does not track in the same arc. Therefore, you need rudder pressure to streamline the fuselage in the arc of the turn.

Figure 4-46. The increase in lift on the outside wing tends to increase bank. To counteract this tendency, you must apply slight aileron pressure opposite to the turn.

TORQUE AND P-FACTOR

You will notice less overbanking tendency in a right turn than in a left turn. This is due to torque and P-factor, which tend to roll the airplane to the left and work against the overbanking tendency in a right turn. However, these factors increase the overbanking tendency during left turns.

CHECKLIST

After studying this section, you should have a basic understanding of:

✓ **Entry and recovery procedures** — How to enter and recover from a steep turn.

✓ **Altitude recovery** — The correct procedure to use in the event altitude is lost in a steep turn.

✓ **Overbanking tendencies, torque, and P-factor** — How these affect the airplane when it is established in a turn, as well as during turn entry and recovery, and how to compensate for them.

EMERGENCY LANDING PROCEDURES

Since modern airplane engines are extremely reliable, actual mechanical malfunctions are rare. However, inadvertent fuel exhaustion or an actual engine component malfunction may require you to make an emergency descent and landing. Five general steps used to cope with this type of situation are listed in sequence.

1. Maintain control of the airplane and establish the best glide speed.

2. Scan the immediate area for a suitable field.

3. Turn to a heading that will take the airplane to that field.

4. Attempt to determine the cause of the power failure and restart the engine, if possible. Follow an appropriate emergency checklist and declare an emergency.

5. Set up a landing approach to the selected field.

Emergency landing practice puts the airplane in a precarious position in the event of unforeseen circumstances. For this reason, you should practice these procedures only when the instructor is in the airplane.

ESTABLISHING ATTITUDE AND GLIDE SPEED

The first step after an engine failure is to establish the best gliding attitude and airspeed.

If the engine fails during the climb or while cruising, you should attempt to conserve altitude. Apply back pressure on the control wheel as you slow the airplane to the appropriate gliding attitude and airspeed. This speed is normally specified in the POH and is the speed which provides the greatest horizontal travel from a given altitude. As you reach the best glide speed, trim the airplane to relieve the control pressures and to aid in maintaining the proper attitude and airspeed. If the airspeed is below the best glide speed at the time of power failure, lower the nose immediately to obtain this speed and retrim the airplane. If the flaps are extended, increase the airspeed to a safe flap retraction speed, retract the flaps, establish the best glide speed, and retrim the airplane.

SELECTING A FIELD

Select a field within the immediate area. As a general guideline, select a field that can be evaluated easily for obstructions and terrain, and one that is within gliding distance from your present altitude. If you select a field several miles from your present position, you may arrive to find it covered with rocks and trees and crisscrossed with several ditches or fences. You would have been better off to have selected a field within your immediate area.

There are many variables to consider in selecting a suitable field, including the wind direction and speed, length of the field, obstructions, and the surface condition. You must evaluate all these factors and decide which field provides the greatest possibility of a successful landing.

A long field positioned into the wind, with a firm, smooth surface that is free of obstructions, is the most desirable. However, all of these features are seldom available. On one occasion, it may be better to accept a cross-wind landing on a long field, rather than attempt to land into the wind on a very short field. On another occasion, a downwind landing with light winds and no obstructions may be preferable to a landing into the wind with numerous obstructions.

MANEUVERING TO A FIELD

If you follow the previous suggestions, the field you select should be within easy gliding distance. This means the airplane should be headed directly toward the field, and any excess altitude should be dissipated near the field. From that vantage point, you are in a good position to observe the field carefully for wires, fences, holes, tree stumps, ditches, or other hazards that you did not observe clearly from a greater distance.

It is inadvisable to circle away from the field, then try to make a long, straight-in glide to the field. The estimation of glide distance from a far-away point is difficult, even for experienced pilots. A circling approach over the field allows you to make adjustments for altitude and keeps you in a position from which you can reach the field.

It is better to circle over a field than away from it.

DETERMINING CAUSE OF FAILURE

After you have set up the glide, selected the field, and headed the airplane for the field, you should attempt to find the cause of the malfunction and restart the engine, if possible. Loss of engine power that occurs suddenly is often caused by a fuel problem. Therefore, check to make sure the fuel selector is on and is set to a tank that has fuel.

Next, check the mixture to see that it is in the RICH position and, if the airplane is equipped with an auxiliary fuel pump, that it is turned ON. Apply carburetor heat early in the procedure to determine if ice has formed and to attempt to remove it. Then, check the magneto switch to see that it is in the BOTH position.

After a quick check for obvious problems, you should carefully follow the appropriate emergency checklist. This serves two purposes. First, a check-list makes sure you have checked each item which may be responsible for

Always use an emergency checklist when one is provided.

the engine failure. Second, if you are still unable to restart the engine, a checklist will make sure you have the airplane properly configured for the emergency landing.

Be methodical, perform your checks in a definite sequence, and take time to be thorough. It may seem as though it takes minutes to accomplish this, but it requires only a few seconds to make an unhurried check. If you discover the cause of the power failure and remedy it, you will not need to use the starter to restart the engine, since the propeller continues to turn, or windmill, in a power-off glide.

Once you have prepared for the landing, use your radio to declare an emergency. Be sure to give your position as accurately as possible, as well as the type of airplane and number of persons on board.

EMERGENCY LANDING APPROACH

If you have planned correctly, the airplane should be at the 180° point when you reach a normal traffic pattern altitude. From that point, the approach is like a normal power-off approach. The value of this procedure is that it places you in a position where you have familiar points from which to judge glide angle, speed, and distances. [Figure 4-47]

Unfortunately, it is not always possible to reach the ideal position. You may have to use a right-hand pattern instead of a left-hand pattern because of your position. If the altitude at which power failure occurs is too low or the distance to a suitable landing field is too great, you may not be able to arrive at either a left or a right 180° position. If this situation occurs, the alternative is to plan the approach so the airplane can intercept the normal traffic

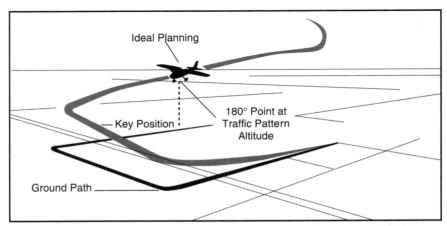

Figure 4-47. If you are able to maneuver the airplane to a normal downwind position, you should be able to use all of the normal cues to turn base leg, judge position, and turn to final.

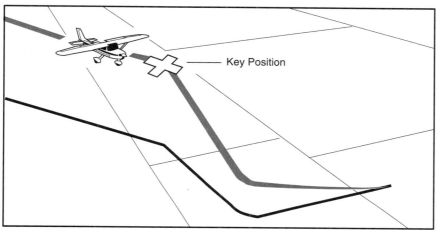

Figure 4-48. When the ideal pattern cannot be flown, you should try to visualize a normal traffic pattern overlying the chosen field. Then, consider the altitude and your position so you can plan to intercept the traffic pattern at the earliest point.

pattern. For example, the next best place for interception may be the key position. [Figure 4-48]

Use flaps as required during the approach. Full flaps should be used only after the turn to final is completed and you are assured of reaching the intended field.

During the landing, you must remember the distance traveled in the landing flare. For example, if the desired landing point is just beyond a ditch, the aiming point must be on the near side of the ditch. [Figure 4-49]

Figure 4-49. In this example, it appears that the airplane will touch down short of the intended point. During the flare, however, the airplane will glide across the ditch and land at the desired spot.

EMERGENCY LANDING PRACTICE

Since most practice emergency landing approaches terminate in a go-around, it is possible for you to fall into the habit of considering the procedure as just another training exercise. To avoid this, assume that each simulated emergency landing will actually result in a landing. Careful cultivation of this assumption will prepare you for the possibility that you may be required to perform an actual emergency landing.

If the selected field is an approved landing area, your instructor may require you to proceed and land. If the field is not approved, initiate a go-around when the instructor specifies. The altitude for the go-around will be low enough so the outcome of the simulated emergency landing is apparent and high enough that safety is not compromised.

To initiate the go-around, apply all available power, place carburetor heat in the COLD position, and establish an airspeed at or above the best angle-of-climb. When you are well clear of all obstructions, retract the flaps and resume a normal climb. In order to conform with normal traffic pattern procedures, do not begin turns below 400 feet AGL.

PARTIAL POWER MALFUNCTIONS

In addition to practicing emergency landings, you must know how to cope with certain other situations. To practice these procedures, the instructor simulates or states a given problem, then demonstrates or explains the best corrective actions. These problems may include partial loss of power, rough engine operation, carburetor ice, fuel starvation, and fire in the engine compartment.

OTHER EMERGENCY PROCEDURES

In addition to partial or complete power malfunctions, you should become familiar with other system or equipment malfunctions. These should include inoperative electrical system, fire or smoke in the cabin, gear or flap malfunctions, door opening in flight, and inoperative elevator trim tab. You should be able to explain the causes, indications, and remedial actions for these and other malfunctions. You should also be familiar with the proper course of action in the event you become lost, are trapped on top of an overcast, lose radio communications, or encounter unanticipated adverse weather. Finally, whenever an emergency or abnormal situation develops, remain calm. Also, check to see if the manufacturer has a published checklist for the conditions. If one exists, it should be followed in a calm, methodical manner.

The procedures described in this section generally apply to the more common inflight emergencies in a typical training airplane. Different procedures may apply to a specific emergency situation or airplane. For example, loss of pressurization while cruising at high altitude in a pressurized airplane would require a rapid emergency descent, instead of a descent at best glide speed. As pilot in command, you should be thoroughly familiar with all emergency procedures relevant to your airplane.

CHECKLIST

After studying this section, you should have a basic understanding of:

✓ **Engine failure or loss of power in flight** — What the possible causes of an engine failure are and the use of an appropriate emergency checklist.

✓ **Emergency landing field selection** — What factors to consider in selecting a suitable landing site.

✓ **Maneuvering to an emergency field** — What factors to consider to ensure a safe approach to and arrival at an emergency field.

✓ **Takeoff emergencies** — What procedures to follow in the event the engine fails during or shortly after takeoff.

✓ **Other emergencies** — How to determine the possible cause and remedial action for each condition.

GROUND REFERENCE MANEUVERS

The maneuvers described in this section are rectangular courses, S-turns, and turns around a point. They are collectively called ground reference maneuvers. To some degree, you execute these maneuvers each time you fly in the traffic pattern or proceed to and from the practice area.

DETERMINING WIND

You can prepare for flying ground reference maneuvers by determining the direction of the wind before you leave the airport. Then, verify the direction and velocity of the wind as you approach the practice area. [Figure 4-50]

Another method you can employ to determine wind direction is to fly a 360° constant airspeed, constant bank turn. Your path over the ground will provide valuable information about the wind. [Figure 4-51]

RECTANGULAR COURSE

As you fly a rectangular course, you will quickly notice its similarity to the traffic pattern. In fact, this maneuver helps you develop the skills needed to fly a uniform traffic pattern, because it requires you to compensate for the effects of wind.

The instructor normally selects a field well away from other traffic and populated areas with sides not more than one mile nor less than one-half mile in length. These dimensions are rough guidelines, but the shape

Figure 4-50. The runway in use, wind sock indication, and movement of smoke or dust are valuable indications of wind direction. Wind also produces advancing wave patterns on water and grain fields, and leans rows of trees away from the wind.

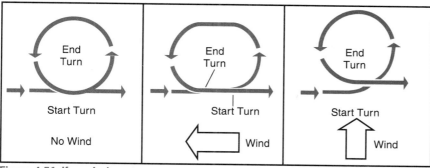

Figure 4-51. If an airplane turns at a constant speed and angle of bank in a calm wind condition, as shown on the left, the track over the ground is circular and the airplane completes the turn over the point where it began. In a headwind, as shown in the center, the turn is completed on the original track, but behind the point where it was started. In a direct crosswind, as shown on the right, you complete the turn abreast of, but on the downwind side of, the point where you started.

should be square or rectangular within the approximate limits given. The maneuver is flown at an altitude of approximately 600 to 1,000 feet above ground level. The bank angle in the turning portions of the pattern should not exceed 45°.

This maneuver requires you to combine several flight techniques. First, you may need to use varying crab angles throughout the straight flight segments. Second, you must track an imaginary line parallel to a fixed line. Third, you need to plan ahead and use different angles of bank in order to roll out of the turns at the proper distance from the field boundary. Finally, you must maintain a constant altitude throughout the maneuver. [Figure 4-52]

Figure 4-52. Notice that this pattern has two legs in which no crab angle is needed, since the airplane will have either a direct headwind or tailwind. It also has two legs which require crab angles in different directions. The bank angles required to make the turns symmetrical are functions of the airplane's groundspeed.

The flight path should not be directly over the edges of the field, but far enough away so the boundaries can be observed as you look out the side windows of the airplane. If you attempt to fly over the edges of the field, the required turns will be too steep or the maneuver will result in an oval-shaped course. The closer the track of the airplane is to the edges of the field, the steeper the bank required. Typically, the distance from the field boundary will be approximately one-quarter to one-half mile.

Start each turn as you arrive abeam each corner and roll out equidistant from the next side.

This maneuver may be entered from any direction. For the purposes of this discussion, though, assume that you enter the maneuver downwind. To begin, fly the airplane parallel to the field until you approach the corner. Start a turn at the exact time the airplane is abeam the corner. As you complete the turn, the airplane should be following a ground track that is parallel to and equidistant from the next side of the field. In determining the amount of bank to use, you will discover it to be a function of the airplane's groundspeed; the greater the groundspeed, the greater the angle of bank required. As you proceed through the first turn, your groundspeed decreases. Therefore, you will gradually decrease the bank to maintain your distance from the field. In addition, you will need to turn more than 90°, since a crab is usually required on the crosswind leg. Continue around the field, adjusting bank and crab angles as required to maintain a constant distance. After several circuits around the field, you may be asked to reverse your direction of flight.

The complexity of the rectangular course maneuver is increased when the wind blows across the course diagonally. In this situation, use a crab on all four legs. Practice this maneuver until you can fly correct ground tracks at the specified altitudes and distances. You may also be requested to alternately glide on a simulated final approach leg and climb back to the simulated traffic pattern altitude. This provides more realistic practice of an approach and climbout from an airport.

S-TURNS

As you discovered when flying the rectangular course, the angle of bank required during a symmetrical turn varies with the airplane's groundspeed. The practice of flying S-turns is designed to help you further develop this skill.

Normally, your instructor will select a straight ground reference line or a road that lies perpendicular to the wind. The objective on this maneuver is to fly two perfect half-circles of equal size on opposite sides of the road at a constant altitude. As with most ground reference maneuvers, you enter the S-turn on a downwind heading at an altitude of approximately 600 to 1,000 feet AGL. The maximum bank for this maneuver also should be limited to 45°. As you cross the road, roll immediately into a left turn.

Since the airplane is flying downwind, it is at its highest groundspeed, so the bank angle is the steepest you will use throughout the maneuver. As you continue through the turn, gradually reduce the bank to trace a symmetrical half circle. Time the roll-out so the airplane is rolled level, headed directly upwind, and is perpendicular to the road just as you cross it. [Figure 4-53]

At the completion of the first 180° of turn, the airplane should recross the road, then smoothly and gradually roll into a turn in the opposite direction. Since the airplane is headed upwind, this portion of the maneuver has the slowest groundspeed and requires the shallowest bank. Steepen the bank gradually throughout the turn to continue tracing a half-circle the same shape and size as the one on the opposite side of the road. You attain the steepest bank just before roll-out as you reach the road. The "S" is completed as the airplane crosses the road on a perpendicular flight path with the wings level.

TURNS AROUND A POINT

The final ground reference maneuver is called turns around a point. This maneuver further refines your skills in making constant radius turns around an object on the ground while maintaining a constant altitude.

Do not confuse the techniques for performing turns around a point with the steep turns performed at altitude with a constant angle of bank. This maneuver requires you to perform constant radius turns around a preselected point on the ground. Your objective is to maintain a constant altitude and roll out

Figure 4-53. The shallowest angle of bank occurs just before and after the airplane crosses the road into the wind. The steepest bank occurs just before and after the airplane crosses the road downwind.

on the initial entry heading after completing the number of turns specified by your instructor. The maneuver is flown at an altitude of 600 to 1,000 feet AGL, and the bank is normally limited to a maximum of 45°.

Select a reference point away from obstructions for added safety.

Select a reference point that is prominent and easily distinguished, yet small enough to establish a definite location. It should be in the center of an area away from livestock, buildings, or concentrations of people on the ground. This prevents annoyance and undue hazard. You should also select an area that affords the opportunity for a safe emergency landing.

You can use trees, isolated haystacks, or other small landmarks, but they are not as effective as the intersections of roads or fence lines. The latter items are more effective, because the wing may momentarily block your view of the reference point during the maneuver. By selecting a road or fence line intersection, you can mentally project these lines to their logical intersection and maintain your orientation.

The correct way to enter this maneuver is from a downwind position with the first turn to the left. Fly downwind at a distance from the reference point equal to the radius of the desired turn. As you arrive exactly abeam the selected point, enter a 45° bank turn to the left. Then, carefully plan the track over the ground and vary the bank, as necessary, to maintain that track. [Figure 4-54]

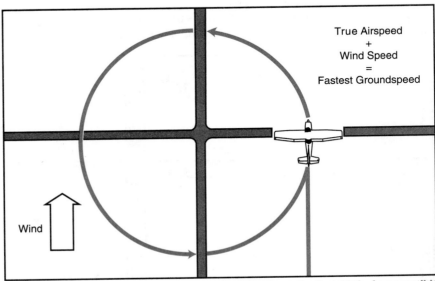

Figure 4-54. Decrease the bank continuously throughout the first 180° of turn until it reaches a minimum value (normally at or near level flight) as the airplane crosses the road into the wind. Throughout the next 180° of turn, steadily increase the angle of bank to its maximum value.

Normally, you will complete two consecutive 360° turns in one direction and then roll out on the entry heading, altitude, and airspeed. You also will be required to reverse the turn direction after completing a specified number of turns.

As you gain experience, you may practice entering the maneuver at any point. Remember that the angle of bank at any given point is dependent on the radius of the circle being flown, the wind velocity, and the groundspeed. When you enter the maneuver at a point other than directly downwind, you must carefully select the angle of bank and the radius of the turn in terms of wind velocity and groundspeed. Also, you normally limit your maximum angle of bank to 45°, which occurs when the airplane is flying directly downwind.

CHECKLIST

After studying this section, you should have a basic understanding of:

✓ **Rectangular course** — What the objectives of this maneuver are, including the correct use of crab angles and the proper method for making symmetrical turns at each corner of the maneuver.

✓ **S-turns** — How this maneuver is flown, and when the angle of bank is at its steepest and shallowest points.

✓ **Turns around a point** — What the purpose of this maneuver is, including an understanding of when to increase the angle of bank and when to decrease it.

flight prep 5

AIRSPACE

In this section, you will learn about the various airspace segments and classifications that are designated throughout the country. Of equal importance are the operational requirements that might affect you within the different airspace segments. You also need to know which flight restrictions or aircraft equipment requirements apply in certain situations and what areas you should avoid altogether.

Another reason for being familiar with the airspace structure is that visual flight rules require you to maintain certain minimum flight visibilities and safe distances from clouds. Since these rules vary from one type of airspace to another, you need to know which rules to apply in each situation. In general, there are two broad classifications of airspace — controlled and uncontrolled. Additional classifications of airspace include special use airspace and other airspace areas.

CONTROLLED AIRSPACE

You will soon realize that the major portion of airspace that covers the conterminous U.S. is controlled. Actually, **controlled airspace** is airspace of defined dimensions within which air traffic control, or ATC, service is provided to controlled flights. It includes the following subdivisions which are designated by regulation — Class A, Class B, Class C, Class D, and Class E. Each of these classifications will be covered in the following discussion. Uncontrolled airspace is designated as Class G, which is covered later in this section. There is no airspace designation for Class F in the United States.

The important thing to know about operating in controlled airspace is that you may be subject to air traffic control. **Air traffic control** (ATC) is a service provided by the FAA to promote the safe, orderly, and expeditious flow of air traffic. As a routine measure, IFR flights are controlled from takeoff to touchdown, since they are permitted to operate in all kinds of weather. As a VFR pilot, your contact with ATC typically is limited to terminal areas. For example, when you take off or land at controlled airports, you must contact the control tower, and you will often use radar approach and departure control services.

Separation of air traffic is the primary function of air traffic control, and radar is one of the controller's principal tools. Because of this, FARs require you to use the aircraft transponder (if your aircraft is so equipped) whenever you fly in controlled airspace. A **transponder** is an electronic device aboard the airplane that enhances your aircraft's identity on an

ATC radar screen. An air traffic controller may assign an individual code to your transponder to help distinguish your aircraft from others in the area. Transponders carry designations appropriate to their capabilities. For example, those used in general aviation have Mode A capability. Usually they can be set to any of 4,096 codes, and many are able to indicate, or encode, your altitude on the controller's radar screen. A Mode A transponder with altitude encoding equipment is referred to as having Mode C capability. Another type of transponder which uses advanced technology is the Mode S transponder, which also is compatible with Mode C altitude reporting equipment. FARs require that, if you are flying at or above 10,000 feet MSL, excluding the airspace at and below 2,500 feet AGL, your transponder must have altitude encoding capability. This requirement applies in all airspace (controlled or uncontrolled) within the 48 mainland states and the District of Columbia. Transponders and radar are discussed in more detail later in this chapter.

> A transponder with altitude encoding equipment is required when flying at or above 10,000 feet MSL, except when at or below 2,500 feet AGL.

To provide you with an overview of the kinds of airspace you may encounter, the next two pages present a comprehensive diagram of the airspace system. This diagram includes the operational requirements, as well as the cloud clearance and visibility minimums, appropriate to the various airspace classifications. [Figure 5-1]

As you read through the entire section, you may find it helpful to refer back to this diagram to see how the various segments interrelate. In practice, the airspace structure is not as limiting to flight operations as it may seem. After you become familiar with the system, you will see that it is possible to fly under visual flight rules, or VFR, with comparatively few restrictions.

CLASS A AIRSPACE

The airspace extending from 18,000 feet MSL up to and including 60,000 feet MSL is defined as the **Class A airspace**. It covers the majority of the conterminous U.S. and extends 12 nautical miles out from the U.S. coast. Within Class A airspace, all pilots must be instrument rated. In addition, all aircraft must be transponder equipped, operated under IFR, and controlled directly by ATC. Because of the overall increase in speed of aircraft operating in Class A airspace and the corresponding increase of the closure rates between these aircraft, VFR flight is not allowed.

Also, because aircraft in Class A airspace operate at such high speeds, it would be impractical for the pilots to reset their altimeters every 100 n.m. So, within Class A airspace, pilots are required to set their altimeters to the standard setting of 29.92 in. Hg. This means that all pilots will be maintaining their assigned altitudes using the same altimeter reference.

> At and above 18,000 feet MSL, pilots must set their altimeters to 29.92 in. Hg.

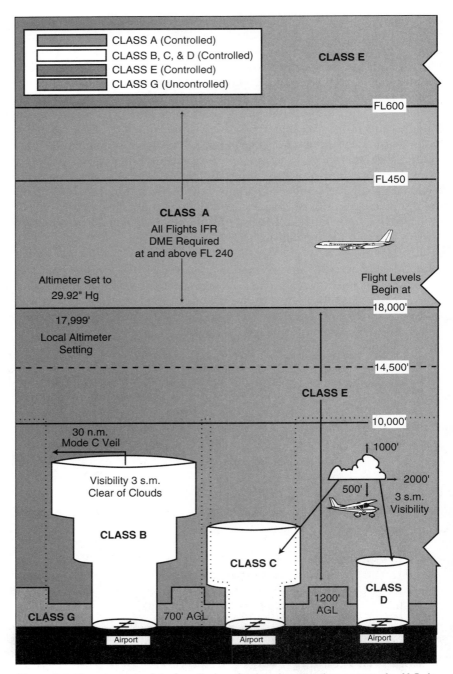

Figure 5-1. To enhance safety for all aircraft, the airspace that covers the U.S. is divided into controlled and uncontrolled airspace. Operational requirements depend on the type of airspace you are flying in, as well as your altitude.

Aircraft operating in all airspace of the 48 contiguous States and the District of Columbia at and above 10,000 feet MSL must be equipped with an operable transponder with Mode C except when operating at and below 2,500 feet AGL. FAR Part 91 also requires a Mode C transponder when operating in Class C airspace and when within 30 n.m. of the primary airport of a Class B area. The dotted line in the airspace diagram shows where these requirements prevail.

Along with these requirements, you also must be aware of the minimum flight visibilities and cloud clearance requirements that apply at various altitudes in controlled and uncontrolled airspace.

Altitudes within Class A airspace are expressed differently. At 18,000 feet MSL and above, altitudes are prefaced by the letters "FL," meaning flight level, with the last two zeros omitted. As an example, 35,000 feet is referenced as FL 350.

CLASS B AIRSPACE

At some of the country's major airports, **Class B airspace** has been designated to separate all arriving and departing traffic. While each Class B area is usually designated for a major terminal, it typically serves several airports in the area. A Class B area has different levels of airspace that are portrayed as a series of interconnected circular patterns around the airport. You may notice that it looks something like an upside-down wedding cake. [Figure 5-2]

Each Class B area is individually designed to serve the needs of the particular airport that it surrounds. Terrain, the amount and flow of air traffic, and the location of other airports all influence each design. Generally, you will find that Class B airspace surrounds the busiest airports in the country.

A transponder with Mode C is required for operations within a Class B area, and when flying within 30 n.m. of the primary airport, from the surface to 10,000 feet MSL.

To operate within Class B airspace, your aircraft must have two-way radio communications capability and a transponder with Mode C. With certain exceptions, the transponder is required within 30 nautical miles of the

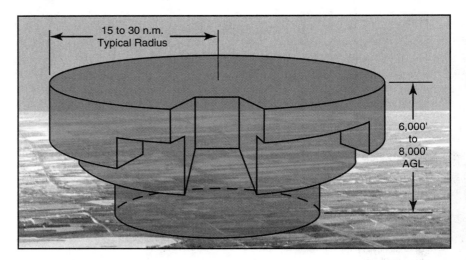

15 to 30 n.m.
Typical Radius

6,000'
to
8,000'
AGL

Figure 5-2. Each Class B airspace layer is designated by an upper and lower altitude, commonly referred to as the ceiling and floor for that segment. Each layer is a building block for controlling the airspace in the area and for funneling air traffic into the terminal area.

Class B area's primary airport from the surface to 10,000 feet MSL. In addition, a VOR or TACAN is required for IFR operations.

In order to fly within Class B airspace, or to take off or land at an airport within that airspace, each pilot-in-command of a civil aircraft must possess at least a private pilot certificate. An exception is made to allow student pilots to operate in certain Class B areas. Student pilots may be permitted to conduct flight operations within these Class B areas by obtaining specified training and a logbook endorsement from a certified flight instructor. However, student pilot operations are prohibited at designated major airports within the nation's busiest Class B areas. You should refer to FAR Part 91 for specific rules pertaining to student pilot operations within Class B airspace.

A private pilot certificate is required for operations at some major airports in the nation's busiest Class B areas.

Before entering any part of Class B airspace, you are required to contact ATC on the appropriate frequency. Before departing an airport in a Class B area, you must advise ATC of your intended altitude and route of flight. ATC permission is required before you can fly through the Class B airspace, even after a departure from an airport that is other than the primary airport. You will find that some Class B areas have VFR corridors which have been designated to permit you to fly through the area without contacting ATC. Within a VFR corridor, you are not actually in the Class B airspace, so you do not have to meet the operational and equipment requirements. However, most Class B areas don't have designated VFR corridors. Another concern you should have when operating in the vicinity of a Class B area is flying too close to the boundaries. Aircraft within the Class B area may be assigned altitudes at or near the floor of that airspace. If you do not give yourself an extra margin of clearance when you are circumnavigating a Class B area, you are actually increasing the potential for a collision. Also, keep in mind that regulations specify a speed limit of 200 knots (230 statute miles per hour) indicated airspeed when flying in the airspace underlying Class B airspace or in a designated VFR corridor for a Class B area. The FAA encourages aircraft which are not required to operate in a Class B area to avoid it whenever practical. The boundaries of Class B areas are clearly shown on sectional and terminal area charts, which are covered in Flight Prep 8.

Authorization from ATC is required before you may operate an aircraft within a Class B area.

CLASS C AIRSPACE

Factors considered in designating controlled airspace include safety, users' needs, and the volume of air traffic. Because of these considerations, many busy airports are surrounded by **Class C airspace** areas. Within a Class C area, ATC services are provided to ensure traffic separation for all IFR and VFR aircraft.

Participation in this service is mandatory. You will find that Class C areas usually have very similar physical dimensions from one location to another,

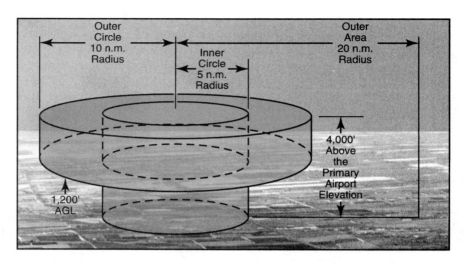

Figure 5-3. A Class C area consists of two circles of airspace extending upward from the primary airport. The first circle usually begins at the surface and has a five nautical mile radius from the center of the airport. The second typically begins at 1,200 feet AGL and has a 10 n.m. radius. Both circles have an upper limit of 4,000 feet above the elevation of the primary airport. The outer area usually extends out to 20 n.m. from the primary airport. A Class C area may have one or more satellite airports.

although some may be modified to fit unique aspects of a particular airport's location. [Figure 5-3]

Normally, the radius of the outer area of Class C airspace is 20 n.m. from the primary airport.

The "outer area" associated with a Class C area extends 10 n.m. beyond the outer circle. VFR pilots are not required to contact ATC prior to entering the outer area, but it is helpful to do so. For approach, departure, or overflights, ATC normally provides the same radar services for you in the outer area as it does within the Class C airspace.

The minimum radio equipment required to take off or land at an airport within a Class C area is a two-way radio and a transponder with encoding altimeter.

Within a Class C area, all aircraft are subject to FAA operating rules. One of these rules applies to arrivals and overflights. Prior to entering the area, you must establish two-way communications with the ATC facility having jurisdiction and maintain it while you are operating within the airspace. When you are departing the primary airport, you must maintain radio contact with ATC until you are clear of the area. In addition to the two-way radio requirement, all aircraft operating in a Class C area and in all airspace above it, from its ceiling up to 10,000 feet MSL, within the lateral boundaries of that Class C area, must be equipped with an operable transponder with encoding altimeter (Mode C). Aircraft operating in the airspace beneath a Class C area are not required to have a transponder with Mode C. An airspeed limit of 200 knots applies in Class C airspace when operating at or below 2,500 feet above the surface within 4 nautical miles of the primary airport.

There may be times when you fly into a satellite airport located within a Class C area. If so, you must be in contact with ATC while you are in the Class C airspace. The radar service provided to you will be discontinued early enough for you to change to the appropriate tower or airport advisory frequency at your destination. When departing a satellite airport, you should contact ATC as soon as practicable after takeoff.

Keep in mind that ATC facilities may not operate full time at some Class C locations, so radar service may not be available at all times. If the ATC facility is closed, the operating rules for the Class C area are not in effect either. Hours of operation for ATC facilities are listed in the *Airport/Facility Directory*.

> **If you are departing a satellite airport within a Class C area, you must establish two-way communications with ATC as soon as practicable after departure.**

CLASS D AIRSPACE

Airports which have operating control towers, but are not associated with Class B or C airspace, are surrounded by **Class D airspace**. Air traffic control is exercised by the control tower within the area to provide separation between aircraft and an orderly flow of traffic in and out of the airport. The airspace at an airport with a part-time control tower is designated as Class D only when the tower is in operation. [Figure 5-4]

> **The purpose of a Class D airspace area is to provide a smooth flow of aircraft landing and taking off from an airport with an operating control tower.**

If the control tower is operating, you must establish two-way communications with the tower prior to entering the Class D airspace and for all operations to, from, or on that airport. You also must comply with the prescribed speed limitation of 200 knots maximum when at or below 2,500 feet AGL within 4 nautical miles of the primary airport, as well as any established approach/departure procedures applicable to the airport. As a general rule, you should avoid Class D airspace areas except to take off or land at an airport within the area.

At airports where the tower operates part time, the airspace changes to Class E, or a combination of Class E and Class G when the tower is closed.

2,500' AGL

Figure 5-4. A typical Class D area consists of the airspace surrounding an airport with an operating control tower. It normally extends up to and including 2,500 feet above the airport elevation. Due to requirements unique to each airport, extensions for instrument approaches and departures may be included. The lateral limits of Class D airspace areas vary widely. Vertical dimensions may also vary.

For these airports, check the *Airport/Facility Directory* for the tower's hours of operation and the airspace designation.

In some Class D airspace areas, a satellite airport may be located within the airspace designated for the primary airport. If a control tower is in operation at the satellite airport, you would contact them for arrival and departure. When the satellite airport is a nontower field, you must establish contact with the primary airport's control tower. When departing a nontower satellite airport in Class D airspace, contact the controlling tower as soon as practicable after takeoff. To the maximum extent practical and consistent with safety, satellite airports have been excluded from Class D airspace. For instance, airspace may be carved out of a Class D area to allow traffic to arrive and depart from a nontower satellite airport.

CLASS E AIRSPACE

A large segment of Class E airspace includes that extending from 14,500 feet MSL up to 18,000 feet MSL, excluding restricted and prohibited areas and airspace within 1,500 feet of the surface.

Much of the remaining controlled airspace is designated as **Class E airspace**, which includes several different segments. One portion of Class E consists of the airspace covering the 48 contiguous states, District of Columbia, and the area of Alaska east of 160° west longitude. Also included is the airspace out to 12 n.m. from the coastlines. This Class E airspace begins at 14,500 feet MSL and extends up to, but not including, the base of the Class A airspace at 18,000 feet MSL. The only exceptions are restricted and prohibited areas and airspace within 1,500 feet of the surface.

During flight in Class E airspace between 14,500 and 18,000 feet MSL, you have no additional operating requirements beyond those mentioned previously. For example, you must operate the Mode C feature of your transponder when at or above 2,500 feet AGL and apply the appropriate cloud clearance and visibility requirements. Remember that you cannot fly VFR above FL 180, which is Class A airspace.

Federal airways normally begin at 1,200 feet above the surface, extend upward to 18,000 feet MSL, and include the airspace within four nautical miles each side of the airway centerline.

Another segment of Class E airspace is the low altitude airway system. When you begin flying cross-country, you will notice that aeronautical charts depict a network of routes connecting one navaid to another. These routes are used by VFR, as well as IFR aircraft, and are called Federal airways, or Victor airways. These airways are based on VOR or VORTAC navigation aids and are identified by a "V" and the airway number. A few airways are based on L/MF (low/medium frequency) navigation aids, or NDBs. These airways are referred to as colored airways and are designated by a color and a number. The only colored airways still in use are in Alaska and coastal North Carolina. Airways are usually eight nautical miles wide, begin at 1,200 feet AGL, and extend up to but not including

18,000 feet MSL. Some airway segments, such as those over mountainous terrain, may have a floor greater than 1,200 feet, which is designated on sectional charts. VFR cloud clearance and visibility requirements on an airway depend on your cruising altitude. [Figure 5-5]

The links between airports and the airway route system are also designated Class E airspace. These portions extend controlled airspace closer to the ground. This allows IFR traffic to remain in controlled airspace while transitioning between the enroute and airport environments. These segments of Class E airspace usually begin at 1,200 feet AGL if they are associated with an airway. This airspace is not outlined on sectional charts unless it borders uncontrolled airspace.

Some airports located in Class E or Class G airspace areas have operating control towers. You are required by FARs to establish radio communications prior to 4 n.m. from the airport (up to and including 2,500 feet AGL) and to maintain radio contact with the tower while in the area.

At nontower airports which have an approved instrument approach procedure, Class E airspace often begins at 700 feet above the surface. At some nontower airports, Class E airspace extends upward from the surface, and usually encompasses airspace surrounding the airport, in addition to

Figure 5-5. Federal airways are part of the airway route system that you can use to navigate across the country. They are commonly called Victor airways.

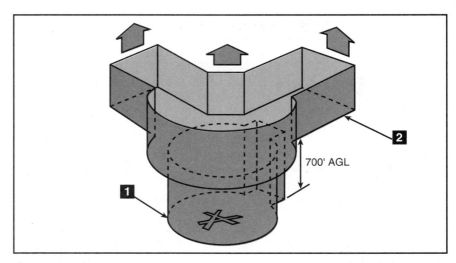

Figure 5-6. This nontower airport is surrounded by Class E airspace which extends from the surface (item 1) and adjoins Class E airspace which begins at 700 feet AGL (item 2).

extensions to accommodate arrivals and departures. Both of these types of Class E airspace are depicted on aeronautical charts. [Figure 5-6]

CLOUD CLEARANCE AND VISIBILITY REQUIREMENTS

As clouds lower and flight visibility is reduced, it soon becomes impractical and unsafe to fly under VFR. VFR cloud clearance and visibility requirements are specified in regulations. These regulations also prohibit you from flying when conditions are below basic VFR weather minimums. When this occurs, all aircraft in controlled airspace must be flown by instrument rated pilots in accordance with IFR clearances issued by ATC.

VFR cloud clearance and visibility requirements are designed to help you avoid flying into clouds, as well as to maintain adequate forward visibility in flight. They are also designed to meet other practical requirements, such as seeing and avoiding other air traffic and navigating to your destination. The type of airspace and the altitude at which you fly are the determining factors. [Figure 5-7]

Keep in mind that these values are legal minimums. You may need to establish higher personal minimums until you have acquired more practical experience. Your instructor can advise you in this area.

SPECIAL VFR

In the vicinity of an airport, while in Class B, C, D, or E airspace, you may conduct normal VFR operations, such as traffic pattern entry, takeoffs, and landings, only when the ground visibility is at least three miles and the

VFR IN CONTROLLED AIRSPACE		
Altitude	**Flight Visibility**	**Distance From Clouds**
Class A	Not Applicable	Not Applicable
Class B	3 statute miles . . .	Clear of Clouds
Class C and Class D	3 statute miles . . .	500 feet below 1,000 feet above 2,000 feet horizontal
Class E: Less than 10,000 feet MSL	3 statute miles . . .	500 feet below 1,000 feet above 2,000 feet horizontal
At or above 10,000 feet MSL	5 statute miles . . .	1,000 feet below 1,000 feet above 1 statute mile horizontal

Figure 5-7. Basic VFR weather minimums which apply in Class A, B, C, D, and E controlled airspace are listed in FAR 91.155. Notice VFR flight is not authorized in Class A airspace.

cloud ceiling is at least 1,000 feet. If ground visibility is not reported, you can use flight visibility. When the weather is below VFR minimums and there is no conflicting IFR traffic, a **special VFR clearance** may be obtained from the ATC facility having jurisdiction over the affected airspace if the visibility is a minimum of one mile and you can remain clear of clouds. As a private pilot, you may obtain a special VFR clearance only during the daytime. Because of the difficulty in seeing clouds at night, special VFR in not permitted between sunset and sunrise unless you have a current instrument rating and the aircraft is equipped for instrument flight. Since three miles is the minimum visibility for student pilots, they are not authorized to request a special VFR clearance. At certain major airports special VFR clearances are not issued to fixed-wing aircraft. These airports are annotated on sectional charts with the phrase "NO SVFR."

A special VFR clearance requires you to have a visibility of at least one mile and to remain clear of clouds. Requests for special VFR should be made to the ATC facility responsible for the affected airspace. For example, in Class D airspace you would request special VFR from the control tower.

AIRSPEED LIMITATIONS

Since the airspace at lower altitudes, and especially in the vicinity of airports, tends to be congested, the FAA has established aircraft speed restrictions. In general, flights below 10,000 feet MSL are limited to a maximum indicated airspeed of 250 knots. When operating in Class C or D airspace, at or below 2,500 feet above the surface and within 4 nautical miles of the primary airport, you must not exceed 200 knots indicated airspeed. This 200-knot restriction also applies in airspace underlying a Class B area and in VFR corridors through Class B airspace.

Do not exceed 200 knots IAS when at or below 2,500 feet AGL within 4 n.m. of the primary airport of Class C or D airspace.

VFR IN CLASS G AIRSPACE (UNCONTROLLED)		
Altitude	**Flight Visibility**	**Distance From Clouds**
1,200 ft. or less above the surface (regardless of MSL altitude)	Day : 1 s.m.	Clear of clouds
	Night: 3 s.m.	500 ft. below 1,000 ft. above 2,000 ft. horizontal
More than 1,200 ft. above the surface, but less than 10,000 ft. MSL	Day: 1 s.m. Night: 3 s.m.	500 ft. below 1,000 ft. above 2,000 ft. horizontal
More than 1,200 ft. above the surface and at or above 10,000 ft. MSL	Day and night: 5 s.m.	1,000 ft. below 1,000 ft. above 1 s.m. horizontal

Figure 5-8. For day flights in uncontrolled (Class G) airspace within 1,200 feet of the surface, you are required to remain clear of any clouds and maintain one statute mile visibility. Above 1,200 feet AGL during the day, cloud clearance increases significantly. At and above 10,000 feet MSL, the requirements are the same as they are in controlled airspace.

CLASS G AIRSPACE (UNCONTROLLED)

Airspace which has not been specified as Class A, B, C, D, or E, is designated as **Class G, or uncontrolled airspace**. ATC has neither the authorization nor the responsibility to exercise control of air traffic in Class G airspace. The amount of uncontrolled airspace has continued to decrease due to the need to coordinate the movement of air traffic. Uncontrolled airspace typically extends from the surface to the base of the overlying Class E airspace, which is normally 700 or 1200 feet AGL. In some areas of the western U.S. and Alaska, uncontrolled airspace may extend upward to 14,500 feet MSL. An exception to this rule occurs when 14,500 feet MSL is lower than 1,500 feet AGL. In that event, uncontrolled airspace continues up to 1,500 feet above the surface. Day cloud clearance and visibility requirements are somewhat less stringent than they are in controlled airspace. However, night visibility and cloud clearance rules are the same as they are in controlled airspace. [Figure 5-8]

Whether flying in controlled or uncontrolled airspace, it is important to know the rules for operating in each class of airspace. Prior to entering an airspace segment, be sure you can comply with the pilot certification and radio equipment requirements for that class of airspace. [Figure 5-9]

SPECIAL USE AIRSPACE

Large segments of controlled and uncontrolled airspace have been designated as **special use airspace**. Operations within special use airspace are considered hazardous to civil aircraft operating in the area. Consequently, civil aircraft operations may be limited or even prohibited, depending on the area. To help you determine the type of operations and the rules for the

AIRSPACE REQUIREMENTS FOR VFR OPERATIONS			
Requirement	Class B	Class C and D	Class E and G
Entry prerequisites	ATC clearance	Radio contact	None
Two-way radio communications	Yes	Yes	No (with some exceptions)
Minimum pilot certification	Private or Student	Student	Student

Figure 5-9. Apart from weather minimums, this chart summarizes the requirements for operating VFR in the different classes of airspace. In addition, two-way communications are required between aircraft and operating control towers located within Class E and G airspace.

various areas, special use airspace is divided into prohibited, restricted, warning, military operations, alert areas, and controlled firing areas.

PROHIBITED AREAS

Prohibited areas contain airspace of defined dimensions identified by an area on the surface of the earth within which the flight of aircraft is prohibited. Such areas are established for security or other reasons associated with the national welfare. These areas are published in the *Federal Register* and are depicted on aeronautical charts.

RESTRICTED AREAS

In certain areas, the flight of aircraft, while not wholly prohibited, is subject to restrictions. These designated **restricted areas** often have invisible hazards to aircraft, such as artillery firing, aerial gunnery, or guided missiles. Permission to fly through restricted areas may be granted by the controlling agency. The dimensions of many of these areas may be such that you can avoid them altogether. In any case, extra caution is appropriate, even when you are flying near a restricted area.

> You may fly through a restricted area only if permission is granted by the controlling agency.

WARNING AREAS

A **warning area** is airspace of defined dimensions, extending from three nautical miles outward from the coast of the United States, that contains activity that may be hazardous to nonparticipating aircraft. The purpose of such warning areas is to warn nonparticipating pilots of the potential danger. A warning area may be located over domestic or international waters or both.

> Unusual, often invisible, hazards such as aerial gunnery and guided missiles may be encountered in a warning area.

MILITARY OPERATIONS AREAS

Another area that warrants extra caution is a **military operations area** (MOA). MOAs are blocks of airspace in which military training and other military maneuvers are conducted. MOAs usually have specified floors and ceilings for containing military activities. VFR aircraft are not

> If you must fly through an MOA when it is in operation, use extreme caution.

prevented from flying through MOAs while they are in operation, but it is wise to avoid them when possible. [Figure 5-10]

ALERT AREAS

Areas shown on aeronautical charts to inform you of unusual types of aerial activities or high concentrations of student pilot training are **alert areas**. You should be especially cautious when flying through them. Pilots of participating aircraft and pilots transiting the area are equally responsible for collision avoidance.

CONTROLLED FIRING AREAS

The distinguishing feature of a **controlled firing area**, compared to other special use airspace, is that its activities are discontinued immediately when a spotter aircraft, radar, or ground lookout personnel determine an aircraft might be approaching the area. Since nonparticipating aircraft are not required to change their flight path, controlled firing areas are not depicted on aeronautical charts.

OTHER AIRSPACE AREAS

As indicated in the *Aeronautical Information Manual,* **other airspace areas** mainly consist of airport advisory areas and military training routes. Other segments in this category may be designated by temporary flight restrictions or flight limitations/prohibitions. Parachute jump areas and terminal radar service areas (TRSA's) are also classified as other airspace areas.

18,000' MSL

9,000' MSL

Sheppard 3
Military Operations Area
9,000' to 18,000' MSL
1 Hr. Before SR
1 Hr. After SS, Mon-Fri
Ft. Worth ARTCC

Figure 5-10. FSSs within 100 n.m. of an MOA are provided with information regarding the hours of operation. When MOAs are not in operation, there should be no problem in flying through them. If you need to fly through an MOA, contact the controlling agency for traffic advisories.

AIRPORT ADVISORY AREA

Another type of airspace surrounding certain airports is an **airport advisory area**. This airspace extends 10 s.m. from airports where there is a nonautomated **flight service station** or (FSS) located on the field and no operating control tower. You will normally contact the FSS on the published CTAF frequency prior to entering the airport advisory area. The FSS provides **local airport advisory** (LAA) service, which includes advisories on wind direction and velocity, favored runway, altimeter setting, and reported traffic within the area.

An airport advisory area includes the airspace within 10 s.m. of an airport with an FSS but without an operating control tower.

Most airport advisory areas and the associated services have gradually been phased out as automated flight service stations replace existing nonautomated facilities. Currently, pilots who fly into an airport with an automated FSS normally will not be able to receive local airport advisory service on the advisory frequency, 123.6 MegaHertz. However, the airspace and the service will continue to be provided by approximately 26 nonautomated or auxiliary FSS facilities which have been designed to supplement 61 automated sites. Provisions for these auxiliary FSSs also include five additional sites in Alaska that operate on a seasonal basis.

MILITARY TRAINING ROUTES

Low-level, high-speed military training flights are conducted on **military training routes** (MTRs). Generally, MTRs are established below 10,000 feet MSL for operations at speeds in excess of 250 knots. Routes at and below 1,500 feet AGL are generally designed to be flown under VFR; routes above 1,500 AGL are developed primarily to be flown under instrument flight rules (IFR). MTRs are classified as "VR" where VFR operations apply and "IR" where IFR operations apply. Operations on IRs are conducted under IFR regardless of the weather conditions.

Regardless of weather conditions, military training flights on MTRs may be conducted at speeds in excess of 250 knots.

Even though you are not restricted from flying through MTRs, you need to check with an FSS within 100 n.m. to obtain the current information regarding MTR activity in your area. MTRs are marked on sectional charts.

TEMPORARY FLIGHT RESTRICTIONS

Temporary flight restrictions apply to a specific hazard or condition. When necessary, these restrictions are imposed by the FAA to protect persons or property on the surface or in the air. The objectives are to provide a safe environment for rescue/relief operations and to prevent unsafe congestion of sightseeing or other aircraft above an incident or event which may generate high public interest. The FAA will issue a Notice to Airmen (NOTAM) designating the area in which a temporary restriction applies. Situations which warrant these restrictions include toxic spills, volcano eruptions, nuclear incidents, aircraft hijackings, forest fires, and so forth.

For rescue/relief aircraft operations, the restricted airspace is normally limited to 2,000 feet above the surface within a two nautical mile radius. Incidents within Class B, C, or D airspace are handled through existing procedures, and usually they do not require issuance of a NOTAM. In other cases, the FSS nearest the incident site is normally the coordination facility.

When a NOTAM is required, the format will include the facility establishing the temporary restriction, location, effective times, the area defined in statute miles, and the affected altitudes. The NOTAM also will contain the FAA coordination facility, the reason for the restriction, the agency directing any relief activities, commercial telephone numbers, and other information considered appropriate by the issuing authority.

FLIGHT LIMITATIONS/PROHIBITIONS

Limitations in proximity to space flight operations are designated by NOTAM. These limitations provide protection for space flight crews and prevent costly delays. A NOTAM also may be issued to create flight restrictions in the proximity of the President, Vice President, foreign heads of state, and other persons who may attract large numbers of people. When such NOTAMs are issued, they are considered to be regulatory.

PARACHUTE JUMP AREAS

Parachute jumping sites are tabulated in the *Airport/Facility Directory*. The busiest periods of activity are normally on weekends and holidays. Sites that have been used on a frequent basis and that have been in use for at least one year are depicted on sectional charts. Times of operation are local, and MSL altitudes are listed unless otherwise specified.

EMERGENCY AIR TRAFFIC RULES

Other situations may arise when the FAA needs to issue emergency air traffic rules. These rules are issued immediately after determining that, without such action, the air traffic control system cannot operate at the required level of safety and efficiency. If this happens, a NOTAM is issued to communicate information about the emergency rules governing flight operations and the use of navigation facilities. It designates the airspace in which these rules apply. When a NOTAM is issued with this information, no one may operate an aircraft in conflict with it.

ADIZ/DEWIZ

All aircraft entering domestic U.S. airspace from outside must provide identification prior to entry. **Air Defense Identification Zones** (ADIZs) are established to facilitate this identification in the vicinity of U.S. international airspace boundaries. Generally, you must file an IFR or defense VFR (DVFR) flight plan for all operations that enter or exit an ADIZ. In addition, you normally are required to have a two-way radio and make periodic position reports. A transponder, with Mode C (or Mode S) capability is required, and the transponder must be transmitting pressure altitude information. Failure to follow these rules may result in your aircraft being intercepted by U.S. security.

The **distant early warning identification zone** (DEWIZ) is the same as an ADIZ, except that it lies along the coastal waters of Alaska. The DEWIZ and the ADIZ have somewhat different operating rules. If you are thinking of flying into either of these areas, you should refer to the *Airman's Information Manual* for detailed procedural information.

During a defense emergency or during air defense emergency conditions, special security instructions may be issued in accordance with the Security Control of Air Traffic and Air Navigation Aids (SCATANA) plan. Under the provisions of this plan, the military will direct the necessary actions to land, ground, divert, or disperse aircraft and take over control of navaids in the defense of the U.S. If SCATANA goes into effect, ATC facilities will broadcast instructions over available frequencies.

CHECKLIST

After studying this section, you should have a basic understanding of:

✓ **Controlled airspace** — What the major divisions are, the operating requirements for each type, and what purposes they serve.

✓ **Uncontrolled airspace** — What the definition is.

✓ **VFR cloud clearance and visibility requirements** — What they are, where they apply, and how they change with altitude.

✓ **Airspeed limitations** — What the indicated airspeed restrictions are and where they apply.

✓ **Special use airspace** — What the types are and what restrictions apply to each type.

✓ **Other airspace areas** — What these areas include, and what rules and procedures apply within each type.

✓ **Emergency air traffic rules** — When these rules may be put into effect and what flight operations may be restricted.

✓ **ADIZ/DEWIZ** — Why these zones are established, and general rules for operations within them.

RADIO COMMUNICATIONS

In previous sections, you became aware of a number of situations that require you to be in two-way radio contact with controllers, flight service stations, and other facilities. In fact, nearly any service you obtain during flight requires radio communications. In this section, you will learn about radio communications equipment and how you should talk on the radio. You will need to become familiar with a number of unique words and phrases which are commonly used in aviation. Depending on your background, talking on the radio may be a new way of communicating, but it will soon become as natural to you as flying the airplane.

VHF COMMUNICATIONS EQUIPMENT

Communications radios in general aviation aircraft use a portion of the **very high frequency** (VHF) range, which includes the frequencies between 118.0 MegaHertz (MHz) and 135.975 MHz. Communications radios are classified according to the number of channels they were designed to accommodate. Most radios of current manufacture have either 360- or 720-channel capability. A 360-channel radio uses 50 kHz (.05 MHz) spacing between channels, such as 118.05, 118.10, 118.15, 118.20. A 720- channel radio doubles the frequencies available by using 25 kHz (.025 MHz) spacing, such as 118.025, 118.050, 118.075, 118.100.

Most VHF radios you will encounter have both communications and VOR navigation receiver capability in one unit. Use of the VOR receiver for navigation is discussed in Flight Prep 9. [Figure 5-11]

Figure 5-11. Radios normally have frequency selectors and a frequency display, along with the on/off/volume and squelch controls. The switch in the center permits selection of .05 or .025 MHz fractions for communications frequencies. Because communications radios usually include a combination transmitter and receiver, they are called transceivers.

You will find that 720-channel transceivers are a necessity if you want to receive full ATC services, particularly in busy terminal areas. If you have only 360-channel capability, you can still operate in most areas, but delays can be expected and some services may not be available. Occasionally, you may encounter transceivers with only 90-, 100-, or 180- channel communications capability. When you do, be sure your frequency capability will be adequate for the type of facilities you plan to contact.

When you need to change from one frequency to another, use the frequency selectors and check the display to verify that the correct frequency has been set in the transceiver. Because of varying noise levels inside the cockpit, you can adjust the volume of the receiver with the on/off/volume control. If you want to adjust the volume when no one is talking on the frequency, turn the squelch control until you hear background noise. Then, adjust the volume and turn the squelch down until you can't hear the background noise. Most of the time, you will keep the squelch turned down, although turning it up actually increases reception range. This can be important in situations where you want to hear a station that is almost out of range.

The range of VHF transmissions is limited to **line of sight**, meaning that obstructions such as buildings, terrain, or the curvature of the earth block the airwaves that carry radio signals. In areas where the terrain is not mountainous, reception is still limited to line of sight because the curvature of the earth eventually blocks the radio waves. [Figure 5-12]

Aircraft Altitude (ft.)	Range (n.m.)
500	28
1,000	39
1,500	48
2,000	55
3,000	69
5,000	87
10,000	122
15,000	152
20,000	174

Figure 5-12. Because VHF radio signals are limited to line of sight, aircraft flying at higher altitudes are able to transmit and receive at greater distances. For example, an aircraft at 1,000 feet AGL over flat terrain may receive transmissions from 39 miles. At 3,000 feet AGL, the distance may be 69 miles; an aircraft at 20,000 feet AGL may transmit and receive from as far away as 174 miles.

Figure 5-13. Normally, a VHF antenna is installed for each transceiver in the airplane. An airplane equipped with two transceivers usually has a microphone selector switch for the respective radios, so a second microphone is not required.

Your transceiver requires a VHF antenna for proper operation. You will notice several different antennas mounted on airplanes, but VHF antennas usually are the bent whip rods or plastic-encapsulated blade types that are mounted on top of the cabin. [Figure 5-13]

FEDERAL COMMUNICATIONS COMMISSION

Within the U.S., one of the functions of the **Federal Communications Commission** (FCC) is to regulate types of aircraft radios. When a radio is used for transmitting, it becomes a radio station. As a result, the FCC requires a **radio station license** for communications radios used for aviation purposes. Although this is not an FAA requirement, the FCC does require that this license be carried on board the aircraft.

The FCC also requires U.S. pilots who fly internationally to have a **restricted radiotelephone operator permit**. The only time that this permit is required within the U.S. is when long-range, high frequency (HF) radios are used. This permit can be obtained by completing an application form obtained from an FCC field office and returning it to the FCC. If you fly within the 48 mainland states, you typically use only VHF communications radios, so the permit normally is not required.

INTERNATIONAL CIVIL AVIATION ORGANIZATION

As you know, the FAA is the regulatory agency for U.S.-based aircraft flying within the country. Throughout the world, an agency of the United Nations, known as the **International Civil Aviation Organization** (ICAO), coordinates international flight activities.

Due to the nature of international travel, it would be difficult for pilots to speak all of the languages that could be involved. Therefore, the English language is recommended by ICAO for international air/ground communications. In countries where English is not the official language, ICAO member states have agreed to make English available upon request. ICAO also adopted a phonetic alphabet to be used in radio transmissions. [Figure 5-14]

You will learn to use the phonetic alphabet as a routine measure when you identify your aircraft during initial contact with ATC or other facilities. The phonetic equivalents for single letters should also be used to spell out difficult words or groups of letters when conditions are adverse to good communications.

USING NUMBERS ON THE RADIO

Sometimes, there may be confusion when you transmit or receive numbers over the radio. Use of proper procedures will eliminate most of these problems. Each number is spoken the same way you are used to saying it, with the exception of the number nine. It is spoken as *"niner"* to distinguish it from the German word *"nein,"* which means "no."

When talking to ATC, you can expect to receive numerous headings, altitudes, and frequencies, all of which contain numbers. To reduce confusion between the sets of numbers included in these instructions, they usually

Numbers above 9,900 are spoken by separating the digits preceding the word "thousand." For example, the number 10,000 is spoken as *"one zero thousand."*

ICAO Phonetic Alphabet							
A	Alfa	(**Al**-fah)	· —	**N**	November	(No-**vem**-ber)	— ·
B	Bravo	(**Brah**-voh)	— · · ·	**O**	Oscar	(**Oss**-cah)	— — —
C	Charlie	(**Char**-lee) or	— · — ·	**P**	Papa	(Pah-**pah**)	· — — ·
		(**Shar**-lee)		**Q**	Quebec	(Keh-**beck**)	— — · —
D	Delta	(**Dell**-tah)	— · ·	**R**	Romeo	(**Row**-me-oh)	· — ·
E	Echo	(**Eck**-oh)	·	**S**	Sierra	(See-**air**-rah)	· · ·
F	Foxtrot	(**Foks**-trot)	· · — ·	**T**	Tango	(**Tang**-oh)	—
G	Golf	(Golf)	— — ·	**U**	Uniform	(**You**-nee-form) or	· · —
H	Hotel	(Hoh-**tell**)	· · · ·			(**Oo**-nee-form)	
I	India	(**In**-dee-ah)	· ·	**V**	Victor	(**Vik**-tah)	· · · —
J	Juliett	(**Jew**-lee-ett)	· — — —	**W**	Whiskey	(**Wiss**-key)	· — —
K	Kilo	(**Key**-loh)	— · —	**X**	X-ray	(**Ecks**-ray)	— · · —
L	Lima	(**Lee**-mah)	· — · ·	**Y**	Yankee	(**Yang**-key)	— · — —
M	Mike	(Mike)	— —	**Z**	Zulu	(**Zoo**-loo)	— — · ·

Figure 5-14. Because letters such as "B," "C," "D," and "E" all have similar sounds, they can easily be mistaken for one another, especially during radio transmissions. The phonetic alphabet was developed to avoid misunderstandings of this type. The associated Morse code is also helpful when tuning and identifying navigation facilities, which typically use three-letter identifiers.

Numbers in Radio Communications	
Headings:	
087°	*"Zero eight seven"*
259°	*"Two five niner"*
Altitudes:	
8,500	*"Eight thousand five hundred"*
12,500	*"One two thousand five hundred"*
FL 330	*"Flight level three three zero"*
Frequencies:	
121.5	*"One two one point five"*
135.9	*"One three five point niner"*
Airways:	
V11	*"Victor eleven"*
J521	*"J five twenty-one"*
Altimeter Settings:	
29.92	*"Two niner niner two"*
30.14	*"Three zero one four"*

Figure 5-15. If you study these examples, you will become more familiar with correct pronunciation of numbers. Although you normally pronounce groups of numbers by their individual digits, notice that airways are an exception.

are referred to as individual numbers. When you state radio frequencies, the decimal is pronounced as *"point,"* but the decimal is dropped when you state an altimeter setting. [Figure 5-15]

COORDINATED UNIVERSAL TIME

Because a flight may cross several time zones, it would be very confusing to estimate your arrival time at the destination using only the local time at the departure airport. To overcome this problem, aviation uses the 24-hour clock system, along with an international standard called Coordinated Universal Time (UTC). The 24-hour clock eliminates the need for a.m. and p.m. designations, since the 24 hours of the day are numbered consecutively. For instance, 9 a.m. becomes 0900 hours; 1 p.m. becomes 1300 hours, and so on.

In the U.S., add hours when converting local time to Zulu; subtract hours when converting Zulu time to local.

Coordinated Universal Time, which is referred to as Zulu time in aviation, actually places the entire world on one time standard. When a given time is expressed in UTC or Zulu, it really is the time at the 0° line of longitude which passes through Greenwich, England. All of the 24 time zones around the world are based on this reference, so you will need to convert

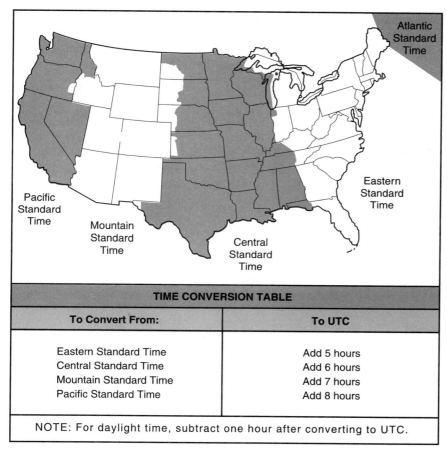

Figure 5-16. ATC operates on UTC or Zulu time regardless of which time zone the facility is located in. When you need to refer to a specific time, first convert it from your local time to the 24-hour clock and then to UTC.

local time to Zulu time and vice versa. In the United States, when you convert local time to Zulu time you add hours; when you convert Zulu time to local time you subtract hours. [Figure 5-16]

USING THE RADIO

Talking on the radio should be done in a professional manner, because slang, CB jargon, and incorrect radio procedures can compromise your safety and the safety of others. One of the most important items in radio communication is for you to speak in a manner that will ensure that others understand what you have said. Before you depress the microphone button to talk (key the mike), first think of what you will say. Radio transmissions usually can be quite brief. You should state who you are, where you are, and what type of service you are requesting. Any other information may be excessive, especially in busy terminal areas. Next, listen for a few moments before speaking to make sure that someone else is not already talking or waiting for a response.

When you are ready to talk, hold the microphone very close to your lips. Then, key the microphone and speak into it in a normal, conversational tone. It may take a few moments for the facility you have called to respond. If you do not get a response, try again. If there is a lack of sounds from your speaker, check your radio to see if it is working properly. Make sure the microphone is not stuck in the transmitting position. This can block other transmissions on the frequency in use and disrupt communications for an extended period of time.

RADIO PROCEDURES

On initial contact, state the name of the facility you are contacting and then state your aircraft type and full call sign.

Generally, you will be the one to initiate radio contact with ATC or other facilities. Therefore, it is important to make your initial contact correctly, so the important information will be received and understood the first time. On initial callups, you should state the name of the facility you are calling and then give your aircraft type, model, or manufacturer and registration number. If you state the manufacturer's name or model, you may drop the "N" prefix of the registration.

In the U.S., each aircraft is identified by a registration number which is painted on the outside of the airplane. Registration numbers are usually a combination of five letters and numbers. They are sometimes referred to as the "tail number," or "N-number," because all U.S.-registered aircraft have an "N" preceding the number.

An example of an initial callup is, *"Great Falls Tower, Cessna 8458 Romeo."* If your message is lengthy, it is better to wait until ATC asks you for it, because this means they are prepared to receive your information. If your request is short, you may also include the request and your position and altitude with the callup. An example of a short request to a control tower might be something like, *"Great Falls Tower, Cessna 8458 Romeo, 5 south, 5,500, landing, Information Charlie."* If there is not another aircraft nearby with a similar number, the controller may shorten your call sign to the last three numbers or letters. In this case, the controller may respond with, *"Cessna 58 Romeo, Great Falls Tower, report entering left downwind runway 21."* Shortening the call sign reduces the amount of air time needed for further transmissions. If there are other aircraft in the area with a similar number, the controller probably will not shorten the number. You are not allowed to shorten your call sign until the controller does so first.

An **air traffic control clearance** is defined as an authorization by ATC for an aircraft to proceed under specified traffic conditions within controlled airspace. Its purpose is to prevent collisions between known aircraft. If you receive an ATC clearance and do not hear all of it or do not understand it, ask the controller to *"say again"* and the controller will repeat the last message. If you are having a difficult time because the controller is talking too fast, ask the controller to *"speak slower"* and the controller will repeat the previous transmission more slowly. Sometimes either you or the controller may repeat what was said to verify that it was heard correctly. The response in these situations usually is, *"that is correct."* The use of the word *"over"* indicates that your transmission is complete and that you expect a response. On subsequent contacts, the ground station name and the word *"over"* may be omitted if the message requires an obvious reply and there is no danger of misunderstanding. An example of an abbreviated request to Great Falls Tower is, *"Cessna 58 Romeo, entering left downwind runway 21."*

When you are talking to controllers, they may answer you right away, or they may ask you to *"stand by,"* which means that they know you called and will get back to you as soon as they can. They may be talking to someone else on a different frequency.

If a controller contacts you with a request, you should acknowledge it and quickly restate any instructions given to you in order to reduce the possibility of a misunderstanding. For example, if asked to turn right to a heading of 210°, you should respond with, *"Cessna 58 Romeo, roger, turn right heading 210."*

There are occasions when controllers issue time-critical instructions such as, *"Cessna 58 Romeo, expedite your turnoff at the next available taxiway."* You may acknowledge these with *"wilco,"* *"affirmative,"* or *"negative,"* as appropriate, preceded by your call sign. You should respond immediately to time-critical requests. If, at any time, you are given an instruction that is beyond the capabilities of your airplane, is not safe to follow, or would cause you to violate an FAR, you must inform the controller that you are *"unable"* to comply with the directions. The controller should then give you an amended clearance with instructions that you can follow without compromise.

Time-critical instructions require that you respond immediately to the controller's request, which may include the word *"expedite."*

If you are asked to contact the same controller on a different frequency, the controller will state your aircraft call sign and say, *". . . change to my frequency, 123.4."* This means the controller wants you to change frequencies, not contact another controller. In these situations, you can abbreviate your callup by saying, *"Cessna 58 Romeo on 123.4."*

At times, such as when you are flying into Class B or C airspace, you may talk to a succession of controllers on different frequencies. Each controller will tell you when to change to the next frequency and what frequency to use. This is called a "handoff" from one controller to another. Before you change frequencies, you should ensure that you heard the new frequency correctly. You can do this with a readback such as, *"Cessna 145, roger, contact tower 118.3."* This informs the original controller that you received the instruction correctly. Since the two controllers have already coordinated the handoff, the tower will be expecting your call. Usually, the tower controller will acknowledge your call quickly and provide additional landing instructions.

As a student pilot, you can request additional assistance from ATC simply by identifying yourself as a student pilot. For example, assume you were approaching a controlled field with heavy traffic and you were unfamiliar with the airport. In this situation, you should make your initial callup as follows: *"Centennial Tower, this is Cessna 5289 Tango, student pilot."* This procedure is not mandatory, but it does alert controllers so they can give you extra assistance and consideration, if needed. Identifying yourself as a student may be advantageous in other situations, too. For example, you may want to do so when you self-announce your position over the CTAF at uncontrolled fields.

COMMON TRAFFIC ADVISORY FREQUENCY

Communications procedures at uncontrolled airports are significantly different from those at airports with an operating control tower. Without ATC, it is your responsibility as pilot-in-command to determine which runway to use and how to enter the pattern. You also must see and avoid other air traffic and maintain proper spacing in the pattern. In these situations, the **common traffic advisory frequency** (CTAF) is used by pilots in the area to receive advisories and to broadcast their intentions. When available, advisories usually include wind direction and speed, favored runway, and known traffic. To achieve the greatest degree of safety possible, it is essential that all aircraft equipped with radios use the same frequency. The designated CTAF varies with the type of airport and its facilities. [Figure 5-17]

Transmitting in the blind is a way for you to communicate your position to other pilots at uncontrolled fields.

At some airports, the control tower does not operate 24 hours a day. In this case, you should announce your intentions "in the blind" using the CTAF, which usually is the tower frequency. Transmitting in the blind is part of the **self-announce concept**, in which you broadcast your position and intentions to other traffic in the area.

If you use the self-announce concept when inbound, you should make your initial call when you are 10 miles from the airport. You should also report when entering your downwind, base, and final legs, and when leaving the runway. An example of a radio call for entering the pattern might be as follows: *"Alameda traffic, Cessna 5280 Quebec, entering downwind for runway 17, Alameda."* Because there may be other uncontrolled airports within reception range using the same frequency, it is helpful to repeat the name of the airport at the end of your transmission.

Communications/Broadcast Procedures	Facility at Airport	Frequency to Use
Inbound 10 miles out; entering downwind, base, and final; leaving the runway	Tower or FSS Not in Operation	Self-announce on CTAF.
	FSS Closed (No Tower)	Self-announce on CTAF.
	No Tower in Operation, FSS Open	Communicate with FSS on CTAF frequency.
Outbound Before taxiing and before taxiing on the runway for departure	No Tower, FSS, or UNICOM	Self-announce on MULTI-COM frequency 122.9.
	UNICOM (No tower or FSS)	Communicate with UNICOM station on published CTAF 122.7, 122.725, 122.8, 122.975, or 123.0.

Figure 5-17. The principal concept of a common traffic advisory frequency (CTAF) is to provide a method for pilots to communicate with each other at uncontrolled airports. By broadcasting their positions at specified locations, it is much easier for pilots to establish and maintain visual contact.

When departing an airport with a CTAF, you should announce your intentions before taxiing from the parking ramp and before taxiing onto the runway for departure. Here is a typical radio call that you might hear in this situation: *"Mid Valley traffic, Cessna 9668 Hotel, departing runway 35 to the northeast, climbing to 8,500, Mid Valley."* By announcing what you intend to do, you alert inbound aircraft to your departure.

While use of the CTAF is highly recommended, you will find certain situations when you can benefit from using other air/ground communications facilities at an uncontrolled airport, in addition to the CTAF. For example, if a part-time FSS or Tower is closed, airport advisory service is not available on the CTAF. However, you can often receive similar information about the airport from an aeronautical advisory station or **UNICOM**. In this case, the UNICOM frequency is not the CTAF and you must return to the designated CTAF to listen for other aircraft and self-announce your position and intentions.

At other airports, the UNICOM may be the designated CTAF and you do not have to change frequencies to get advisory information. Since UNICOMs are privately operated, you can also request other information or services through these facilities. A request for refueling service is an example. Announcing your position and intentions is also standard procedure at airports where the designated CTAF is the UNICOM frequency. There are a limited number of UNICOM frequencies available. If an airport

UNICOM stations handle a variety of information and service requests, including refueling, at many airports.

has pilot-controlled lighting, the frequency required to operate the lighting is usually the same as the CTAF. This eliminates the need for changing frequencies to activate the lighting and allows for continuous monitoring for other traffic.

If your flight takes you to an airport that does not have a tower, an FSS, or a UNICOM, the CTAF will be the **MULTICOM** frequency, 122.9 MHz. The purpose of MULTICOM is to provide a frequency for aircraft in the area to use for air-to-air communications. At airports where MULTICOM is the CTAF, pilots are responsible for determining the favored runway and self-announcing their position and intentions. For example, consider the following announcement: *"Coronado traffic, Cessna 7806 Lima, departing runway 17, remaining in the pattern, Coronado."* If you were departing or arriving, you would know that at least one other aircraft was in the traffic pattern. Common traffic advisory frequencies are listed in the *Airport/Facility Directory* and indicated on sectional and VFR terminal area charts. CTAFs also may be obtained from the nearest FSS.

At nontower airports without an FSS or UNICOM, MULTICOM is used by pilots to self-announce their position and intentions to other pilots.

FLIGHT SERVICE STATIONS

Aside from providing local airport advisories and issuing NOTAMs, flight service stations provide many other services, including search and rescue operations. FSSs are responsible for processing flight plans. When you file a **flight plan** with an FSS, a record is made which includes your destination, route of flight, arrival time, and number of people on board. Once airborne, you "open" your flight plan so the FSS can keep track of your airplane's estimated arrival time. If, 30 minutes after the estimated arrival time, you have not closed or cancelled the flight plan, the FSS initiates search and rescue procedures to find your aircraft. The FAA does not require pilots of VFR aircraft to file flight plans. However, if you file and open a VFR flight plan, you must close it after arriving at your destination. If you decide not to go to your original destination, or if you will be at least 15 minutes later than you had planned, inform the nearest FSS accordingly.

After you open your flight plan, you should give occasional position reports to FSSs along the way. In the event that an aircraft does not arrive at its destination, the FSS has an idea of the aircraft's last known position. Usually, the Civil Air Patrol (CAP), a civilian extension of the U.S. Air Force, assists in search and rescue operations.

If you get disoriented while on a cross-country trip, an FSS specialist may be able to locate you with a **VHF direction finder** (VHF/DF). Direction finding equipment requires two-way radio communications with the FSS. The FSS specialist will ask you to key your microphone while the direction finding equipment "homes" in on your radio signal. The specialist can determine your location from the FSS and then give you headings to guide you to an airport or provide other assistance. Unlike radar, DF determines only your direction from the FSS. It does not reveal how far away you are. Many air traffic control towers also have direction finding equipment. Towers and FSSs with DF service are listed in the *Airport/Facility Directory*.

At times, you will talk to an FSS on one frequency while listening for a response over the frequency used for a navigation aid in the area. Most often, this is done using a VOR station, which is a common type of navigation aid that we will discuss in detail later in Chapter 7. Whenever you initiate contact with an FSS, give the name of the facility followed by *"radio,"* such as *"Prescott Radio."* If you are listening for a response over a VOR frequency, tell the FSS which VOR you are listening to. Consider this example: *"Albuquerque Radio, Cessna 8852 Papa, receiving Corona VOR."* If contact is initiated in this manner, the FSS specialist, who can respond over several VOR frequencies, knows which frequency to use in answering your call.

CHECKLIST

After studying this section, you should have a basic understanding of:

✓ **Very high frequency** — What the characteristics of VHF radio waves are and what advantages they have for communications purposes.

✓ **Line of sight** — What it means with respect to radio communications and how range increases with altitude.

✓ **Coordinated universal time** — How to apply the 24-hour clock and how to convert local time to Zulu time.

✓ **Common traffic advisory frequency** — The purpose of CTAF and what types of airports use it.

✓ **UNICOM** — What the function of an aeronautical advisory station is, which airports have it, and which frequencies are used for this purpose.

✓ **MULTICOM** — How to communicate with other aircraft, what frequency to use, and why transmitting in the blind enhances safety.

✓ **Flight plan** — Where to file it, what information it contains, and when search and rescue is initiated.

✓ **Direction finding equipment** — What to do when you are lost, who to contact, and what is required to get the service.

RADAR AND ATC SERVICES

So far, we have discussed important safety-of-flight issues, described airports and airspace, and explained how to use the radio. In this section, we will discuss a variety of air traffic control services that are available when you operate under VFR. To use these services effectively, you must become proficient in radio communications and also acquire an understanding of the capabilities of radar and transponders.

Today, radar has a predominant role in the ATC system. Without radar, it would be virtually impossible for ATC to handle the current nationwide volume of traffic. ATC radar facilities provide both VFR and IFR aircraft with a wide range of services, including traffic advisories, vectoring, sequencing, and separation.

RADAR

Radar uses pulses of microwave energy to determine the azimuth and distance of your aircraft from the radar station. **Azimuth** is the direction or angle between the radar site and your aircraft. It is measured clockwise from north in a horizontal plane. There are two types of radar systems — primary and secondary.

Primary radar is a ground-based system with a rotating antenna that sends out pulses of radio energy. These are reflected back to the site, processed, and displayed. Primary radar works on the echo principle. When these pulses of radio energy reach your aircraft, some of the energy is reflected back to the radar antenna. The reflected energy, or echo, is then processed and displayed on a radarscope, which is really a cathode ray tube (CRT). Your distance from the site is determined by measuring the time lapse between the original radar pulse and its echo, or return. An electron beam (sweep) emanates from the center of the scope and moves in the same direction as the rotating radar antenna. The intensity of the sweep is too low to generate much light on the face of the tube until it reaches a point corresponding to the range and azimuth of your aircraft. At this point, the return echo is intensified to produce a "blip" of light that represents your aircraft. [Figure 5-18]

The ATC radar beacon system (ATCRBS) is the official name for **secondary surveillance radar** or, simply, secondary radar. Secondary radar is a separate system and is capable of operating independently from primary radar. However, in normal air traffic control, they are used together.

Secondary radar requires three components in addition to primary radar. These are a decoder, an interrogator, and a transponder. The decoder is attached to a radarscope console in ATC facilities. The interrogator is mounted on the radar antenna, and the transponder is located in the aircraft. The decoder has two ATC functions. It controls the interrogator, and it interprets the signals received from the transponder. In turn, the interrogator transmits radar pulses and receives replies from the transponder. Both primary and secondary radar returns are usually displayed on the same radarscope. Secondary returns from transponder-equipped aircraft have enhanced presentations. [Figure 5-19]

In spite of its capabilities, primary radar has some serious limitations. One of these is the bending of radar pulses, which can be caused by atmospheric temperature inversions. If the beam is bent toward the ground, extraneous returns, known as "ground clutter," may appear on the scope. If the beam is bent upward, detection range will be reduced.

Another problem with primary radar is that precipitation or heavy clouds can block radar returns, leaving some aircraft undetected. Areas of heavy precipitation are good reflectors of radar energy. Controllers can use a device to eliminate slow-moving objects such as clouds, but they are

Because heavy clouds and areas of precipitation can reflect radar energy, primary radar returns from distant aircraft may be completely blocked.

Figure 5-18. The "blips" of light on the screen are called raw radar returns, or skin paints. They are simply the reflected radio energy of the original radar pulse. The controller is then able to interpret both the range and azimuth of your aircraft.

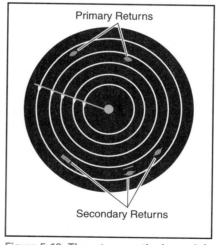

Primary Returns

Secondary Returns

Figure 5-19. The return on the lower left shows what the controller sees when you activate the IDENT feature of your transponder. The return in the lower center shows two control slashes, which result when the transponder and decoder are set to the same code. The return on the lower right represents an aircraft whose transponder code is different from the one the controller is interrogating.

unable to solve the problem altogether. This is a serious disadvantage for a controller who is trying to help a pilot avoid an area of bad weather such as a line of thunderstorms. A further drawback of primary radar is that the size of the radar return is determined by the reflective surface of the aircraft. Therefore, returns from small aircraft often are intermittent when compared to those of large aircraft, particularly at long range. However, one of the biggest problems with the primary radar system is its inability to easily identify an individual aircraft return. For example, the controller usually asks you for your position from a navaid to establish positive identification. With primary radar, the controller is also unable to determine the altitudes of various aircraft without contacting each pilot. In many situations, this can hamper the controller's ability to provide vertical separation of aircraft.

The strength of secondary radar returns is not dependent on the size of an aircraft's reflective surface.

Secondary radar overcomes most of the limitations of primary radar. Radar returns from secondary radar are much stronger than those from primary radar. This permits controllers to track your aircraft through most weather conditions and extends radar coverage farther than is possible with primary radar. Unlike primary radar, secondary radar returns are independent of an aircraft's reflective surface. Today, controllers depend almost exclusively on secondary radar.

TRANSPONDER

To operate a transponder in controlled airspace, it must be tested and inspected within the preceding 24 calendar months.

A transponder is the airborne portion of the secondary surveillance radar system. The coded signal transmitted by the interrogator causes the aircraft transponder to reply automatically with a specific coded signal. This produces a distinctive return on the controller's radarscope. Since transponder returns are the basis for radar separation, regulations require they be tested and inspected every 24 calendar months for operations in controlled airspace. Regulations further require that if your aircraft is transponder-equipped, you must operate the transponder when you are in controlled airspace, including the Mode C feature (if installed). There are only two exceptions to these transponder operating rules: when the controller instructs you to operate it differently or when your transponder equipment has not been tested and calibrated as required by regulation. If you fly at and above 10,000 feet MSL (except for the airspace at and below 2,500 feet AGL) or within 30 nautical miles of any designated Class B airspace primary airport from the surface to 10,000 feet MSL, you must have and operate a transponder with Mode C capability. Although transponders are relatively simple to use, there are a number of features you need to become familiar with for correct operation. [Figure 5-20]

The function selector of a typical transponder has several positions. They usually include OFF, STY (STANDBY), ON, ALT (ALTITUDE), and TST (TEST). In the **STANDBY** position, the transponder is warmed up and ready for operation but does not reply to interrogations. You usually set

Figure 5-20. A typical transponder has four windows which can be set to any number between zero and seven. This gives a total of 4,096 possible codes. The function selector turns the unit on or off and controls the mode of operation. The reply/monitor light illuminates when you select the test feature to show proper operation. It also flashes when the transponder is replying to interrogation signals or transmitting ident pulses.

your transponder to STANDBY during taxi operations prior to departure. Occasionally, during flight, the controller may direct you to *"squawk standby"* for operational reasons. The term **"squawk"** is used by the controller to tell you which transponder function you should select, as well as which four-digit code you should use. [Figure 5-21]

TRANSPONDER PHRASEOLOGY

"Squawk (Number)"
Operate your transponder on designated code in Mode A.

"Squawk Standby"
Switch your transponder to STANDBY position.

"Stop Altitude Squawk"
Turn altitude reporting switch OFF. If your equipment does not have this capability, turn Mode C OFF.

"Squawk Altitude"
Activate Mode C with automatic altitude reporting.

"Ident"
Press the IDENT feature of your transponder.

"Squawk (Number) and Ident"
Operate your transponder on specified code in Mode A and press the IDENT feature.

"Squawk Low/Normal"
Operate your transponder on LOW or NORMAL, as specified. Transponder is operated in NORMAL position unless ATC specifies LOW. ON is used instead of NORMAL on some types of transponders, and many do not have a LOW position.

"Stop Squawk"
Switch your transponder OFF.

"Squawk MAYDAY"
Operate your transponder in the emergency position, Mode A Code 7700/ Emergency, and Mode C altitude reporting.

"Squawk VFR"
Operate transponder on Code 1200.

Figure 5-21. Controllers use distinctive phraseology when referring to the operation of your transponder. You should become familiar with this phraseology so you can respond quickly to controller directions. Normally, you must comply with all ATC clearances and instructions, including operation of your transponder.

As a general rule, you should switch the transponder from STANDBY to ON as late as practical on takeoff. Switch to ALTITUDE if your transponder has Mode C automatic altitude reporting equipment. The ON position selects Mode A and is appropriate when your transponder doesn't have Mode C automatic altitude equipment. It is also appropriate when the controller specifies, *"stop altitude squawk."* This means you should turn off Mode C altitude reporting but continue to operate your transponder on Mode A. If the controller subsequently needs your Mode C information, the phrase *"squawk altitude"* will be used. When you land, you should switch your transponder to OFF or STANDBY as soon as practical.

Before using the Mode C information from your transponder for aircraft separation purposes, the controller must make sure your altitude readout is valid. In other words, are you at the altitude your Mode C equipment says you are? For VFR operations where you are in level flight, the controller typically will say, *"verify at 7,500,"* (or other appropriate altitude). If your response is *"affirmative,"* the altitude readout can be used for separation. You also can save the controller some time on your initial callups by stating your exact altitude to the nearest 100 feet.

In cases where your altitude readout differs significantly (300 feet or more) from your reported altitude, the controller will issue instructions such as, *"Stop altitude squawk, altitude differs by 350 feet."* This could mean your Mode C equipment is not calibrated properly or you have an incorrect altimeter setting. The wrong altimeter setting has no direct effect on your Mode C readout, since that equipment is preset to 29.92. However, it would cause your actual altitude to vary from the one assigned by the controller. Be sure to verify that your altimeter setting is correct whenever the controller indicates your Mode C readout is invalid.

The ident feature should not be used unless the controller specifically calls for it.

ATC may ask you to *"squawk ident."* If so, you should press the IDENT button momentarily and release it. This causes the transponder return to "blossom" on the radar screen for a few seconds. The IDENT presentation is the basis for the controller to establish positive radar contact.

Of course, your transponder must be set to the correct code for the IDENT feature to work. The knobs on the face of the transponder are used to select the four-digit numerical codes assigned by the controller. For example, a controller might tell you to *"squawk 1704, and ident."*

Code 1200 is assigned to all VFR aircraft not under radar control, regardless of altitude.

For VFR operations, you normally use code 1200 unless a different code is assigned by a controller. This might happen during an arrival or departure from an airport served by radar facilities. However, when not in a radar environment, you are responsible for correct transponder operation. You should be careful to avoid codes 7500, 7600, and 7700 when you are making routine code changes on your transponder. Inadvertent selection of these codes may cause momentary false alarms at radar facilities. Code 7500 alerts ATC that an aircraft has been hijacked; 7600 is used after the failure of two-way radio communications; and 7700 is used for emergencies. As an example, when switching from code 2700 to code 7200, switch first to 2200, then to 7200; do not switch to 7700 and then to 7200. This procedure also applies to code 7500 and all codes in the 7600 and 7700 series (7600-7677 and 7700-7777).

FAA RADAR SYSTEMS

The FAA operates two basic radar systems, referred to as airport surveillance radar and air route surveillance radar. Both of these surveillance systems use primary and secondary radar returns. Both systems also use sophisticated computers and software programs designed to give the controller additional information to help in maintaining aircraft identification and separation. For example, some of these programs provide a readout of aircraft speed and altitude, as well as other information on the radarscope.

AIRPORT SURVEILLANCE RADAR

The direction and coordination of IFR traffic within specific terminal areas is delegated to **airport surveillance radar** (ASR) facilities. These are commonly called approach and departure control. ASR is designed to provide relatively short-range coverage in the airport vicinity and to serve as an expeditious means of handling terminal area traffic. The ASR can also be used as an instrument approach aid.

AUTOMATED RADAR TERMINAL SYSTEM

Most ASR facilities throughout the country utilize the **automated radar terminal system** (ARTS) in one form or another. This system has several different configurations, depending on the computer equipment and software programs used. Usually the busiest terminals in the country have the most sophisticated computers and programs. The type of system installed is designated by a suffix of numbers and letters. For example, an ARTS-IIIA installation can detect, track, and predict primary, as well as secondary, radar returns.

ARTS equipment usually is computer controlled. On a controller's radar screen, it automatically provides a continuous display of an aircraft's actual altitude, groundspeed, position, and other pertinent information. This information is updated continuously as the aircraft progresses through the terminal area. To gain maximum benefit from the system, each aircraft in the area must be equipped with a Mode C transponder and its associated altitude encoding altimeter, although this is not an operational requirement. Direct altitude readouts eliminate the need for time consuming, verbal communications between controllers and pilots to verify altitude. This helps to increase the number of aircraft which may be handled by one controller at a given time.

Figure 5-22. The data block at the top shows a call sign of N3804P, an altitude of 14,300 feet, and a groundspeed of 170 knots. The "F" designates the control position handling the traffic, which is the final controller in this case. As shown in the lower portion, additional information is also displayed in the data block on a time-share basis. For example, the groundspeed alternates with aircraft type. An asterisk after the altitude is used when it is not a Mode C readout.

An ARTS-III radar display shows primary and secondary returns, as well as computer-generated alphanumerics. The alphanumeric data include the aircraft call sign, the altitude readout, and the groundspeed. [Figure 5-22]

AIR ROUTE SURVEILLANCE RADAR

ARSR is a long range radar system designed primarily to monitor IFR enroute traffic over a large area.

In controlled airspace, the long range radar system that displays traffic in the area is the **air route surveillance radar** (ARSR) system. There are approximately 100 ARSR facilities to relay traffic information to radar controllers throughout the country. Some of these facilities can detect only transponder-equipped aircraft and are referred to as beacon-only sites. Each air route surveillance radar site can monitor aircraft flying within a 200-mile radius of the antenna, although some stations can monitor aircraft as far away as 600 miles through the use of remote sites.

The direction and coordination of IFR traffic in the U.S. is assigned to **air route traffic control centers** (ARTCCs). Each center is responsible for IFR traffic within its assigned geographical area. [Figure 5-23]

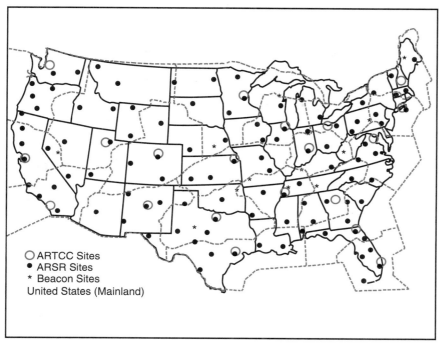

Figure 5-23. ARTCCs are the authority for issuing IFR clearances. There are 20 centers established within the conterminous U.S. Centers also provide services to VFR pilots. If controller workload permits, they will provide traffic advisories and course guidance, or vectors, if requested. Because of their extensive radar coverage, centers can be of assistance to lost and disoriented pilots.

VFR RADAR SERVICES

ATC radar facilities routinely provide traffic information to IFR aircraft. Pilots of VFR aircraft may also receive the same service on request. **Radar traffic information service**, also called VFR radar advisory service, is intended to alert you to air traffic that is relevant to your route of flight. When the controller calls out traffic, you should find it much easier to locate, and you will be in a better position to take evasive action, if necessary.

When controllers call out a possible conflict, they will reference the traffic's position relative to yours. For instance, if a controller says, *"traffic at 11 o'clock,"* it means the traffic appears to the controller to be about 30° left of your nose. You should look for the traffic anywhere between the nose (12 o'clock) and left wing (9 o'clock) of your airplane. After you locate the traffic, tell the controller that you have the traffic *"in sight."* You should maintain visual contact with the traffic until it is no longer a factor. If you do not see the traffic, acknowledge the advisory by telling the controller *"negative contact."* [Figure 5-24]

Radar traffic information service is usually available from any ATC radar facility. This includes air route traffic control centers, as well as radar approach and departure control facilities in terminal areas. However, keep in mind that many factors, such as limitations of radar, volume of traffic, controller workload, or frequency congestion, may prevent the controller from providing this service. Even when it is available, it is not intended to relieve you of your responsibility for collision avoidance. When ATC instructs you to follow a preceding aircraft, you are not authorized to comply with any instructions issued to the preceding aircraft.

When you are operating in the radar environment, you should remember that the altitude of the reported traffic may not be known if the aircraft isn't equipped with a Mode C transponder and the pilot is not in communication with ATC. Therefore, the traffic may be well above or below your flight path. In any case, the basic purpose of radar service is to alert you to possible conflicting traffic. VFR pilots must understand that this service is available only as controller workload permits. The controller's first responsibility is to serve the needs of aircraft flying on IFR flight plans.

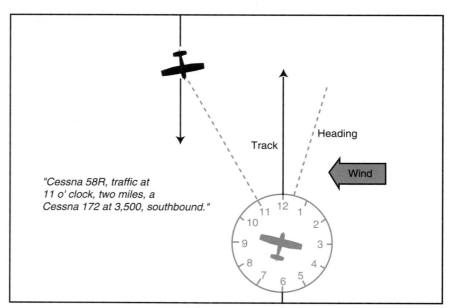

"Cessna 58R, traffic at 11 o' clock, two miles, a Cessna 172 at 3,500, southbound."

Track

Heading

Wind

Figure 5-24. When giving traffic alerts, controllers will reference traffic from your air-plane as if it were a clock. Since a radar screen can't account for the amount of wind correction you may be using to maintain your track over the ground, you need to take this into account. In this example, the controller thinks that the traffic is at your 11 o'clock position, but your wind correction angle places it at your 10 o'clock position.

TERMINAL VFR RADAR SERVICE

This is a national program which extends the terminal radar services for IFR aircraft to VFR aircraft. The program has four types of service — basic radar service, terminal radar service area (TRSA) service, Class C service and Class B service. The type of service provided at a given airport is published in the *Airport/Facility Directory*.

Basic radar service includes safety alerts, traffic advisories, limited radar vectoring when requested by the pilot, and sequencing at locations where procedures have been established for this purpose. The objective of this service is to adjust the flow of arriving IFR and VFR aircraft into the traffic pattern in a safe and orderly manner and to provide traffic advisories to departing VFR aircraft. Departing VFR pilots should request the service through ground control on initial contact.

Basic radar service includes traffic advisories and limited vectoring for VFR aircraft. It should be requested through ground control before departure.

TRSA service provides the basic service, as well as sequencing of all IFR and participating VFR aircraft to the primary airport and separation between all participating VFR aircraft. The purpose of this service is to provide separation between all participating VFR aircraft and all IFR aircraft operating within the area defined as a TRSA.

Besides the basic service, TRSA service includes sequencing and separation for participating VFR aircraft.

Class C service provides, in addition to basic radar service, approved separation between IFR and VFR aircraft, and sequencing of VFR aircraft, including sequencing of VFR arrivals to the primary airport.

Class B service provides, in addition to basic radar service, approved separation of aircraft based on IFR, VFR, and/or weight, and sequencing of VFR arrivals to the primary airport, or airports.

Pilots operating under V FR are required to participate in Class B and C services. However, participation in basic and TRSA service, although encouraged, is voluntary for VFR pilots.

ATC radar facilities also issue safety alerts to aircraft under their control when, in the controller's judgment, safety may be compromised. **Safety alerts** are issued when an aircraft is in unsafe proximity to terrain, obstructions, or other aircraft. If terrain or obstructions are involved, the controller will say, *". . . low altitude alert, check your altitude immediately."* If other traffic is involved, the controller may say, *". . . traffic alert, advise you turn right, heading 090 or climb to 8,000 immediately."* Safety alerts are contingent on the capability of the controller to recognize unsafe situations. These situations often involve uncontrolled aircraft. Safety alerts are not automatic, although an ARTS function called **minimum safe altitude warning** (MSAW) will alert the controller when an aircraft is in unsafe proximity to terrain or obstructions. Another limiting factor is that the primary method of detecting unsafe proximity is through Mode C altitude readouts. Pilots of VFR aircraft may request MSAW monitoring if their aircraft are Mode C equipped.

CLASS C AIRSPACE

All aircraft flying in Class C airspace must be equipped with and use a Mode C transponder and be in two-way radio contact with ATC, and their operations must be in compliance with ATC clearances and instructions.

It is mandatory for pilots of VFR aircraft to participate in ATC radar services within Class C airspace. Radar service includes sequencing of all aircraft arriving at the primary airport. Traffic advisories and conflict resolution are provided for IFR and VFR traffic operating in Class C airspace. This means that on the controller's screen, aircraft targets do not touch, and vertical separation is at least 500 feet. Between VFR aircraft, traffic advisories and safety alerts are provided. The same services are provided for aircraft operating within the outer area when two-way communications and radar contact are established.

ATC FACILITIES AT CONTROLLED AIRPORTS

Now that you have a basic understanding of transponders, radar, and associated VFR radar services, it's time to consider ATC facilities and services overall. To operate within a larger terminal area, you will need to be familiar with a number of ATC functions that are necessary to coordinate departures and arrivals at controlled airports.

In the following discussion, we will cover the various ATC functions in the normal order you would use them. Departure procedures for a large airport will be covered first. Following that, arrival procedures at the same airport will be described. The airport used in these examples is Phoenix Sky Harbor International Airport, which serves Phoenix, Arizona. This is the primary airport within the Phoenix Class B airspace.

DEPARTURE PROCEDURES

The departure procedures for all controlled airports have certain similarities, since you must always receive permission from a controller to taxi to the active runway and subsequently be cleared for takeoff. You can expect more complex departure procedures at larger airports, because they usually have heavier traffic and require more ATC services. Before contacting ground control, for example, you usually listen to a recording which includes current airport weather and other information, such as the altimeter setting and active runway. The recording may direct you to contact clearance delivery so you can inform them of your destination or direction of flight. Clearance delivery may provide detailed departure instructions and then tell you to contact ground control.

AUTOMATIC TERMINAL INFORMATION SERVICE

ATIS is a noncontrol information service provided by ATC at selected high-activity terminal areas.

At busy airports, it would be difficult and time consuming for controllers to give every aircraft a separate airport advisory. To improve controller effectiveness and to reduce frequency congestion, **automatic terminal information service** (ATIS) is available. ATIS is prerecorded and broadcast on its own frequency. It includes routine, noncontrol information usually available in an airport advisory. At the larger airports, there may be one ATIS frequency for departing aircraft and another one for arriving aircraft.

ATIS, which is broadcast continuously, is updated whenever any official weather is received, regardless of content change. It is also updated whenever airport conditions change. ATIS broadcasts are labeled with successive letters from the phonetic alphabet, such as "Information Alpha" or "Information Bravo." When a new ATIS is broadcast, it is changed to the next letter.

Following the phonetic letter on the broadcast, the ATIS information will state the Zulu time of the current weather report, ceiling, visibility, obstructions to visibility, temperature, dewpoint (if available), magnetic wind direction and velocity, altimeter setting, instrument approach, and runway in use. It will also contain any other pertinent remarks relating to operations on or near the airport, like closed runways or temporary obstructions. If the weather is above a ceiling/sky condition of 5,000 feet and the visibility is five statute miles or more, inclusion of the ceiling/ sky condition, visibility, and obstructions to vision in the ATIS message is optional. You may find it helpful to write down the information that is contained in the ATIS. You may also listen to it as many times as necessary. Here is an example of an ATIS departure broadcast.

> *"Phoenix Sky Harbor International, Departure Information Delta, 1745 Zulu weather, measured ceiling 5,000 overcast, visibility 10, haze. Temperature 95, wind 280 at 8. Altimeter 29.92. Runways 26 left and 26 right in use. Notice to Airmen, there are numerous construction cranes in the vicinity of Sky Harbor Airport. Before taxi, all departures contact clearance delivery 118.1. VFR aircraft state destination. All IFR departures contact ground prior to pushback and engine start. Advise on initial contact you have Departure Information Delta."*

CLEARANCE DELIVERY

After listening to ATIS, you will contact Phoenix Sky Harbor's **clearance delivery** on a frequency of 118.1 MHz. The clearance delivery facility is established at busy airports mainly for ATC to relay IFR clearances to departing IFR traffic. However, when the ATIS message so indicates, you should contact clearance delivery to inform them of your intentions. This allows departure controllers to improve traffic coordination.

There are several items that you should provide, including your N-number and aircraft type. You should also tell them you are VFR and have listened to the current ATIS. Most important, you should advise them of your destination or direction of flight. Your initial callup to clearance delivery should sound like this, *"Sky Harbor Clearance Delivery, Cessna 8458 Romeo, Information Delta, VFR to the southwest."*

The controller will respond and give you a departure clearance, which includes a heading and an altitude, along with a transponder code and the departure control frequency. Your clearance may sound something like this, *"Cessna 8458 Romeo, after departure, fly heading 250, climb and maintain 4,500 feet, squawk 3504, departure frequency will be 123.7, contact ground control 121.9 when ready to taxi."* You should write down the clearance, then read it back to the controller to ensure that you heard everything correctly.

GROUND CONTROL

After talking with clearance delivery, you will call ground control. **Ground control** is an ATC function for directing the movement of aircraft and other vehicles on the airport surface. Before leaving the parking area, you must receive a clearance from ground control to taxi to the active runway. When you call ground control, you should say, *"Phoenix Sky Harbor Ground, Cessna 8458 Romeo, at the general aviation ramp, ready to taxi to runway 26 right for departure."* The controller will probably respond with something like, *"Cessna 58 Romeo, taxi to runway 26 right."* When taxiing at unfamiliar airports, you can inform the controller that you are not familiar with the airport, and may request specific instructions.

A clearance to *"taxi to"* your assigned takeoff runway authorizes you to cross any runways (except the active runway) intersecting your taxi route, but not to taxi onto the departure runway. If you are asked to *"hold short"* of a runway, you must read back the "hold short" clearance to the controller, stop at the hold lines preceding the runway, check for traffic, and continue only after cleared to do so. At busy airports, you might be instructed to wait in a holding area near the runway. After taxiing to the departure runway switch to the control tower frequency. After completing the before takeoff checklist, you could say, *"Phoenix Tower, Cessna 8458 Romeo, ready for takeoff, runway 26 right."* If the final approach path is clear, the controller might say, *"Cessna 8458 Romeo, cleared for takeoff."* You should make a final check for traffic before you taxi onto the runway for takeoff. You might also be asked to *". . . taxi into position and hold."* This means that you may position yourself on the runway for takeoff while waiting for another aircraft to clear the runway. Usually, you can expect to be cleared to take off after the other aircraft is clear.

DEPARTURE CONTROL

The term *"radar contact"* is used by ATC to advise you that your aircraft has been identified and radar flight following will be provided until radar identification has been terminated.

Shortly after you take off, the tower controller will direct you to *". . . contact departure control, 123.7."* When you initiate contact with **departure control**, you can be very brief, since they are familiar with your departure clearance. *"Departure Control, Cessna 8458 Romeo, climbing through 2,100 for 4,500."* The controller may respond, *"Cessna 8458 Romeo, radar contact, report reaching 4,500."* The term **radar contact** means your aircraft has been radar identified and flight following will be provided. **Flight**

following means the controller is observing the progress of your aircraft while you provide your own navigation. Being in radar contact is no guarantee you have or will maintain separation from other aircraft. Radar service in the form of traffic advisories and other instructions normally is provided on a workload-permitting basis as you depart the area. If the controller's workload permits, this will continue until you are clear of the outer area as well. It is important to remember that the controller will not provide terrain and obstruction clearance just because your flight is in radar contact. During departure, terrain and obstruction clearance remains your responsibility until the controller begins to provide navigational guidance in the form of radar vectors. When you are clear of the Class B airspace, the departure controller will inform you that *". . . radar service is terminated, frequency change is approved, squawk 1200."*

When departing Class B or Class C airspace, and ATC advises you that radar service is terminated, your transponder should be set to 1200.

ARRIVAL PROCEDURES

When you return to Phoenix, listen to the current ATIS as soon as you can receive it. While you are still outside of the Class B airspace, contact approach control over a designated visual checkpoint or other prominent landmark. **Approach control** is the ATC function that provides separation and sequencing of inbound aircraft. It also provides traffic advisories or safety alerts when necessary.

When you contact approach control, let them know if you are planning other than a full-stop landing. This may determine how you are sequenced into the flow of traffic.

Approach control frequencies are published on sectional charts and broadcast over ATIS. At large terminals, expect different frequencies for approach control, depending on your arrival sector. A typical call to an approach facility might be: *"Phoenix Sky Harbor Approach, Cessna 8458 Romeo, over Avondale, with Sierra, at 4,500 feet, landing."* Usually, approach control will provide a transponder code and ask you to *". . . squawk ident."* After radar contact is established, the controller may say, *". . . radar contact, 15 miles west of Phoenix Sky Harbor Airport, cleared to operate in the Class B airspace, turn right, heading 080 for a left downwind to runway 26 left."* The controller will tell you to *". . . contact tower on 118.7"* at the appropriate time. After contacting the tower, continue your approach and follow any other instructions given to you by the tower controller. At tower-controlled airports, you cannot land without permission. On your approach, the tower controller will tell you when you are *". . . cleared to land runway 26 left."*

You can obtain approach control frequencies from sectional charts ATIS broadcasts, and the *Airport/Facility Directory.*

On initial contact, ATC will routinely provide you with wind, runway, and altimeter information unless you indicate you have received the ATIS or you use the phrase *"have numbers." **"Have numbers"*** means you have already received wind, runway, and altimeter information so the controller does not need to repeat it. The phrase does not indicate you have received ATIS and should not be used for that purpose. There may be

The controller will delete wind, runway, and altimeter information on initial contacts when you use the phrase *"have numbers."*

times when you want to stay in the traffic pattern to practice landings. You should advise approach control or the tower on initial contact that you will be *". . . remaining in the pattern."* The tower controller may ask you to *". . . make closed traffic . . . ."* This means you should remain in the traffic pattern unless you are otherwise instructed. It is helpful to the tower controllers if you report each time you are on the downwind leg. On your last time around the pattern, request a *"full-stop"* landing. During your roll-out, the tower should instruct you to *". . . turn left on the next available taxiway and contact ground, point niner."* Ground control, on 121.9 MHz, will provide a taxi clearance to the parking area. You should not switch to ground control before the tower instructs you to do so.

LOST COMMUNICATIONS PROCEDURES

You can indicate a loss of two-way radio capability by setting the transponder to Code 7600.

As you are aware, establishing two-way radio communications with the control tower is required before you enter Class D airspace. If your communications radios become inoperative, it is still possible to land at a tower-controlled airport by following the lost communication procedures. If you believe that your radio has failed, set your transponder to Code 7600. This will alert ATC if you are in an area of radar coverage.

It is possible for only the transmitter or the receiver to fail. For instance, if you are fairly sure that only the receiver is inoperative, you should remain outside or above the Class D airspace until you have determined the direction and flow of traffic. Then, advise the tower of your aircraft type, position, altitude, intention to land, and request to be controlled by light signals. When you are approximately three to five miles away from the airport, advise the tower of your position and join the traffic pattern. From this point on, watch the tower for light signals. And, if you fly a complete pattern, self-announce your position when you are on downwind and/or turning base. [Figure 5-25]

If only your transmitter is not working, follow the same procedure that you would when the receiver is inoperative, but do not self-announce your intentions. Monitor the airport frequency for landing or traffic information, and look for a light signal which may be addressed to your aircraft.

If neither your transmitter nor your receiver are working, you again need to remain outside or above the Class D airspace until you have determined the direction and flow of traffic. Then, join the airport traffic pattern and maintain visual contact with the tower to receive light signals.

If you receive light signals during the daytime, you should acknowledge tower transmission or light signals by rocking your wings. At night, acknowledge them by blinking your landing light or navigation lights to indicate that you understand the light signals and will comply with them.

COLOR AND TYPE OF SIGNAL	MEANING	
	On the Ground	In Flight
Steady Green	Cleared for takeoff	Cleared to land
Flashing Green	Cleared to taxi	Return for landing (to be followed by steady green at proper time)
Steady Red	Stop	Give way to other aircraft and continue circling
Flashing Red	Taxi clear of landing area (runway) in use	Airport unsafe— do not land
Flashing White	Return to starting point on airport	(No assigned meaning)
Alternating Red and Green	Exercise extreme caution	Exercise extreme caution

Figure 5-25. Control towers have a powerful light that controllers can use to direct light beams of various colors toward your aircraft. Each color or color combination has a specific meaning for an aircraft in flight, or on the airport surface.

If there is an uncontrolled airport nearby which may be more convenient to land at than a controlled airport, you may decide to land there instead. If so, you should also determine the landing direction by observing other traffic and the wind direction indicator prior to entering the pattern.

EMERGENCY PROCEDURES

An emergency can be either a distress or an urgency condition. The *Airman's Information Manual* defines **distress** as a condition of being threatened by serious and/or imminent danger and of requiring immediate assistance. An **urgency** situation is a condition of being concerned about safety and of requiring timely, but not immediate, assistance — a potential distress condition. If you become apprehensive about your safety for any reason, you should request assistance immediately.

The frequency of 121.5 MHz is used across the country for transmitting emergency messages. Although range is limited to line-of-sight, it is guarded by military towers, most civil towers, FSSs, and radar facilities. In a distress situation, use of the word "MAYDAY" commands radio silence on the frequency in use. When you hear the words "PAN-PAN," the urgency situation in progress has priority over all other communications and warns other stations not to interfere with these transmissions.

Radar-equipped ATC facilities can provide radar assistance and navigation service to you if you are within an area of radar coverage. Remember that an authorization to proceed in accordance with radar assistance does not constitute authorization for you to violate FARs. The pilot-in-command is still responsible for the airplane and for the safety of the flight.

Emergency Message	
Distress or Urgency	*"MAYDAY, MAYDAY, MAYDAY* *(or PAN-PAN, PAN-PAN, PAN-PAN),*
Name of station addressed	*Denver Radio,*
Identification and type of aircraft	*5674R Cessna 172,*
Nature of distress or urgency	*trapped above overcast,*
Weather	*MVFR,*
Your intentions and request	*request radar vectors to nearest* *VFR airport,*
Present position and heading	*Newberg VOR, heading 253°,*
Altitude	*6,500,*
Fuel remaining in hours and minutes	*estimate 30 minutes fuel remaining,*
Number of people aboard	*three people aboard,*
Any other useful information	*Squawking 7700."*

Figure 5-26. If you are in distress, your initial communication and any subsequent transmissions should begin with the word *"MAYDAY"* repeated three times. *"PAN-PAN"* should be used in the same manner for an urgency situation. Following this, you need to provide important information about your situation and the assistance you would like to have.

One of the ways you can be identified easily on radar is to change your transponder to code 7700. This code triggers an alarm, or special indicator, at all control positions in radar facilities. If you are not sure whether you are within radar coverage, go ahead and squawk 7700, anyway. When you are under radar control already, you usually are in radio contact with ATC. In this case, you should continue squawking the code assigned, unless instructed otherwise. [Figure 5-26]

A VHF transmitter/receiver is the only equipment required to use VHF/DF facilities

As we mentioned before, direction finding equipment has been used for many years to locate lost aircraft or to guide aircraft to areas of good weather. The only aircraft equipment required for VHF direction finding assistance is an operable VHF transmitter and receiver. At most DF-equipped airports, DF instrument approaches may be given to aircraft in a distress or urgency situation. Most emergencies requiring DF assistance involve pilots with a limited amount of flight experience. These approaches are for emergency use only and will not be issued in IFR conditions unless a distress or urgency situation has been declared. Practice DF approaches may be given in VFR weather conditions if they are requested.

If you are lost, there are some good, common sense lost procedures you can follow. Keep in mind, the **"Four C's"** — **Climb, Communicate, Confess,** and **Comply.** You climb for better radar and DF coverage.

Altitude also increases radio and navigation aid reception range. Communicate with any available facility using frequencies shown on your sectional chart in the *Airport/Facility Directory*. Confess means admit you are lost when contacting ATC or another ground facility. If your situation is threatening, clearly explain your problems, using the emergency frequency 121.5 MHz, if necessary. Then, comply with assistance instructions.

Another device that provides emergency aid is the **emergency locator transmitter** (ELT), which is required for most general aviation airplanes. Various types of ELTs have been developed as a means of locating downed aircraft. These electronic, battery-operated transmitters emit a distinctive audio tone on 121.5 MHz (VHF) and 243.0 MHz (UHF). If "armed" and subjected to crash-generated forces, they are designed to activate automatically. The transmitters should operate continuously for at least 48 hours, over a wide range of temperatures. A properly installed and maintained ELT can expedite search and rescue operations and save lives.

As with other equipment, ELTs must be tested and maintained according to the manufacturer's instructions. Required maintenance includes replacing or recharging the battery (for a rechargeable battery) after one-half of the battery's useful life. You should conduct ELT testing only during the first five minutes after the hour, and for no longer than three audible sweeps. Airborne tests of ELTs are not allowed.

An ELT battery must be replaced or recharged (if rechargeable) after one-half its useful life.

Be careful that you do not accidentally activate your ELT in the air or while you are handling it on the ground. Accidental or unauthorized activation generates the emergency signal, leading to expensive and frustrating searches. A false ELT signal can interfere with genuine emergency transmissions and hinder or prevent the timely location of crash sites. Many cases of activation have occurred unintentionally as a result of aerobatics, hard landings, movement by ground crews, and aircraft maintenance. ELT false alarms can be minimized by monitoring 121.5 MHz during flight, prior to engine shut down, and after maintenance.

You are also encouraged to monitor 121.5 MHz while you are flying to assist in identifying possible emergency ELT transmissions. If you do hear an ELT, report your position to the nearest ATC facility the first and last time you hear the signal. Also report your position and cruising altitude at maximum signal strength.

Search and rescue (SAR) is a lifesaving service provided through the combined efforts of federal and state agencies. ARTCCs and FSSs will alert the SAR system when information is received from any source that an aircraft is in difficulty, overdue, or missing. Flight plan information is invaluable to SAR forces for search planning and for executing search efforts. For more information on flight plans, SAR operations, or other emergency procedures refer to the *Aeronautical Information Manual*.

CHECKLIST _____

After reading this section, you should have a basic understanding of:

✓ **Primary radar** — How it works and what its limitations are.

✓ **Secondary surveillance radar** — What advantages it has, the additional components needed, and how they operate.

✓ **Transponders** — How they operate, how to select functions and codes, and what code is used for VFR operations.

✓ **Airport surveillance radar** — Where it is used and what type of services it provides.

✓ **ARTS-III** — What the advantages of this automated system are, what equipment is required, and what information it gives the controller.

✓ **Air route surveillance radar** — What the radar does and how it complements air route traffic control center operations.

✓ **Terminal radar service** — What radar programs are available for VFR aircraft and what types of service they provide.

✓ **Automatic terminal information service** — What ATIS is, what information it provides, and when you will use it.

✓ **Clearance delivery** — What type of service it is and why its use is important.

✓ **Ground control** — When you need clearance to taxi and the types of clearances you can obtain.

✓ **Departure control** — When you will need to contact them and what services they can provide.

✓ **Approach control** — When you should initiate contact and what services they can provide.

✓ **Lost communications procedures** — What procedures you should follow, the transponder codes to use, and what the light gun signals mean.

✓ **Emergency procedures** — Who to talk to on what frequency and what transponder code to use.

✓ **Lost procedures** — How best to obtain assistance and follow recommended practices.

✓ **Emergency locator transmitter** — What it is and how to effectively use it.

PREDICTING PERFORMANCE

Your ability to predict the performance of an airplane is extremely important. It allows you to determine how much runway you need for takeoff, if you can safely clear obstacles in the departure path, how long it will take you to reach a destination, how much fuel is required, and how much runway you'll need for landing.

In addition to predicting performance, you must also observe the airplane's **operating limitations**. These limits establish the boundaries within which the airplane must be flown. They are often referred to as the flight or performance envelope. Operating within the envelope is safe, while operating outside the envelope may cause structural damage or even failure. If you understand an airplane's operating limitations, you are unlikely to fly outside its performance envelope.

> Operating limitations define the performance envelope of the airplane.

According to FARs, operating limitations may be found in the approved airplane flight manual; approved manual materials, markings, and placards; or any combination of these. For most light airplanes manufactured in the U.S. after March 1, 1979, the pilot's operating handbook is the approved flight manual, and a page in the front of the handbook will contain a statement to that effect. This section emphasizes the performance data and limitations of typical training airplanes. Before you operate any airplane, be sure you consult the pilot's operating handbook or other approved documents for the specific operating limitations, systems information, and performance figures that apply to that airplane.

> Aircraft operating limitations may be found in the approved flight manual, markings, placards, or a combination of these.

PERFORMANCE SPEEDS

In determining performance speeds, airplane manufacturers must consider many factors. To compute maximum level flight speed, engine power is compared against total drag. For climbs, excess power and thrust are the important factors; for range and endurance, speeds that result in minimum drag or require minimum power are important.

MAXIMUM LEVEL FLIGHT SPEED

In level flight, the maximum speed of the airplane is limited by the amount of power produced by the engine and the total drag generated by the airplane. If thrust exceeds total drag when you apply full power, the airplane accelerates. This continues until the force of total drag equals the

Figure 5-27. The curved power-required line shows the amount of power necessary to maintain level flight at various speeds. The power-available line also is curved, since power available in the typical single-engine airplane is a function of airspeed. The speed at which these two curves cross is where the forces of thrust and drag are in balance and where maximum level flight speed occurs. Note that the power required to operate the airplane at point A is the same as that required at point B, even though the speeds are different. If you were flying at point A, you would be operating on the back side of the power curve, where any decrease in airspeed requires an increase in power. At point A, you are very close to minimum flying speed.

force of thrust. At this point, the airplane is flying at its maximum level flight speed. [Figure 5-27]

CLIMB SPEEDS

The pilot's operating handbook for the airplane you're flying will list airspeeds for a variety of climbing flight conditions. Two of the most important are the **best angle-of-climb airspeed** (V_X), and the **best rate-of-climb airspeed** (V_Y). [Figure 5-28]

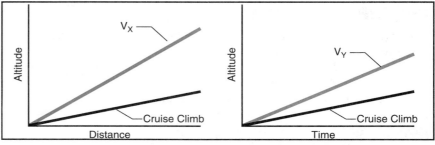

Figure 5-28. Climbing at V_X gives you the greatest gain in altitude for horizontal distance traveled. This airspeed is lower than other climb speeds and results in a fairly steep nose-high pitch attitude. Climbing at V_Y gives you the greatest gain in altitude over a period of time. Best rate-of-climb airspeed is higher than best angle-of-climb airspeed, and provides better forward visibility.

The best angle-of-climb airspeed is normally used immediately after take-off for obstacle clearance. Because of the increased pitch attitude at V_X, your forward visibility is limited. If you happen to lift off prematurely during takeoff, you should accelerate the airplane while you are still in ground effect to at least the best angle-of-climb airspeed before attempting to climb. This technique is often used by pilots when taking off from soft fields.

Normally, you use V_Y after you have cleared all obstacles during departure. In addition, you may use a **cruise climb** after traffic pattern departure when climbing to cruising altitude. You can also use it during the cruise portion of a flight to climb to a higher cruising altitude. Normally, the cruise-climb speed is higher than V_X or V_Y, and the rate of climb is slower. The advantages of higher indicated climb speed are better engine cooling and improved forward visibility.

Before an airplane can climb, it must have a reserve of power or thrust. At a given speed, more power is required for a sustained climb than for unaccelerated level flight. Since propeller-driven airplanes lose power and thrust with increasing altitude, both the best angle-of-climb and best rate-of-climb speeds change as you climb. When the airplane is unable to climb any further, it will have reached its **absolute ceiling**. Another important altitude, known as the **service ceiling**, refers to the altitude where a single-engine airplane is able to maintain a maximum climb of only 100 feet per minute. This altitude is more commonly used than absolute ceiling, since it represents the airplane's practical ceiling.

> Excess power or thrust must be available for the airplane to climb.

As altitude increases, the speed for best angle-of-climb increases, and the speed for best rate-of-climb decreases. The point at which these two speeds meet is the absolute ceiling of the airplane.

CRUISING SPEEDS

In selecting your cruising speed, you usually want to cover the distance to be traveled in the shortest period of time. However, just as an airplane can only fly so fast, it can only go so far and stay up only so long before it runs out of fuel. When range or endurance are important factors, you must select the proper speed for the flight.

Maximum endurance speed is the speed which allows the airplane to remain aloft while using the least amount of power necessary to sustain level flight. The minimum power setting provides the lowest rate of fuel consumption. In contrast, the **maximum range speed** provides the greatest distance for a given amount of fuel. You can think of it as getting the most miles per gallon out of the airplane. To determine this speed, you must consider the speed and rate of fuel consumption for any given power setting. The setting which yields the greatest distance traveled per gallon of fuel burned is the power setting which provides maximum range speed.

As you may recall from the discussion of drag in Flight Prep 1, this speed produces the minimum total drag. It is where the lift-to-drag ratio is greatest, and it is referred to as L/D max. [Figure 5-29]

FACTORS AFFECTING PERFORMANCE

Anything that affects an engine's operating efficiency affects performance. Full power for a normally aspirated engine is based on conditions at sea level in a standard atmosphere. In fact, standard atmospheric conditions are the basis for estimating airplane performance. However, airplanes are rarely flown at sea level and they are almost never operated in weather conditions that exactly duplicate a model of the standard atmosphere. Temperature, pressure, humidity, and wind conditions constantly vary. In addition, the airport elevation, runway slope, and the condition of the runway surface also affect takeoff performance.

DENSITY ALTITUDE

With normally aspirated engines, any increase in density altitude results in a decrease in engine power.

Earlier, you learned that density altitude is pressure altitude corrected for nonstandard temperature. In other words, density altitude at a given level is equal to the pressure altitude only when standard atmospheric conditions exist at that level. You should be concerned about density altitude, because the density of the air directly affects the performance of your airplane. In fact, the primary reason for computing density altitude is to determine aircraft performance. Low density altitude (dense air) is favorable and high density altitude (thin air) is unfavorable. As density altitude

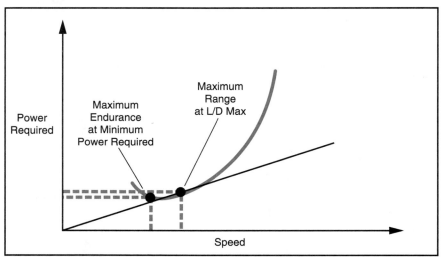

Figure 5-29. Maximum endurance speed occurs at the lowest point on the power-required curve. This is the speed where the lowest power setting will sustain an airplane in steady, level flight. Maximum range speed is a higher indicated airspeed that minimizes total drag.

increases, engine power output, propeller efficiency, and aerodynamic lift decrease. The performance degradation occurs throughout the airplane's operating envelope, but it is especially noticeable in takeoff and climb performance.

One of the ways you can determine density altitude is through the use of charts designed for that purpose. For example, assume you are planning to depart an airport where the field elevation is 1,165 feet MSL, the altimeter setting is 30.10, and the temperature is 70°F. What is the density altitude? [Figure 5-30]

Most modern performance charts do not require you to compute density altitude. Instead, the computation is built into the performance chart itself. All

Engine power output, propeller efficiency, and aerodynamic lift decrease as density altitude increases.

Altimeter Setting	Pressure Altitude Conversion Factor
28.0	1,824
28.1	1,727
28.2	1,630
28.3	1,533
28.4	1,436
28.5	1,340
28.6	1,244
28.7	1,148
28.8	1,053
28.9	957
29.0	863
29.1	768
29.2	673
29.3	579
29.4	485
29.5	392
29.6	298
29.7	205
29.8	112
29.9	20
29.92	0
30.0	-73
30.1	-165
30.2	-257
30.3	-348
30.4	-440
30.5	-531
30.6	-622
30.7	-712
30.8	-803
30.9	-893
31.0	-983

Figure 5-30. First, correct for nonstandard pressure by subtracting 165 feet from the field elevation to obtain the pressure altitude of 1,000 feet. Then, enter the chart at the bottom, just above the temperature of 70°F (21°C). Proceed up the chart vertically until you intercept the diagonal 1,000-foot pressure altitude line, then move horizontally to the left and read the density altitude of approximately 2,000 feet. This means your airplane will perform as if it were at 2,000 feet MSL on a standard day.

you have to do is enter the chart with the correct pressure altitude and the temperature. Older charts, however, may require you to compute density altitude before entering them. Another way to compute density altitude is with a flight computer, which is covered later in Flight Prep 8.

HUMIDITY

Humidity refers to the amount of water vapor contained in the atmosphere, and it is expressed as a percentage of the maximum amount of vapor the air can hold. This amount varies with air temperature. As air temperature increases, the maximum amount of water vapor the air can hold increases. At a given temperature, perfectly dry air has a humidity of 0%. When the same air is saturated, it cannot hold any more water vapor at the same temperature, and its humidity is 100%.

You should consider possible effects of high humidity, even though it causes only a small loss of power.

Although humidity alone is usually not considered an important factor in reducing airplane performance, it does contribute. It affects performance by taking up airspace that is normally available for vaporized fuel. As humidity increases, less air enters the engine. This has the effect of causing a small increase in density altitude. The moist air also tends to retard even fuel burning in the cylinder. When the relative humidity is very high, the engine power loss may be as high as seven percent, and the airplane's total takeoff and climb performance may be reduced by as much as 10%. Under conditions of high humidity, you should take extra time in setting the mixture control to the manufacturer's specifications to provide the maximum available power.

High humidity causes decreased takeoff and climb performance and a higher landing speed.

Anytime the humidity or other conditions are apt to increase the density altitude, you should provide yourself with an extra margin of safety by using longer runways and by expecting a decrease in takeoff and climb performance. You also can expect a higher landing speed and a longer landing roll in less dense, humid air. Remember, conditions that cause high density altitude are "high, hot, and humid."

SURFACE WINDS

Winds also can have a significant impact on airplane operations. When they are used to your advantage, they reduce takeoff and landing distances. Since surface winds are rarely aligned with the runway in use, you need a method of determining what portion of the wind is acting along the runway and what portion is acting across it. **Headwind** or **headwind component** refers to that portion of the wind which acts straight down the runway toward the airplane. **Tailwind** or **tailwind component** describes that portion of the wind which acts directly on the tail of the airplane. A wind can be either a headwind or a tailwind, but not both. A headwind is desirable for takeoffs and landings, since it decreases takeoff distance and runway length requirements.

A **crosswind** or **crosswind component** refers to that portion of the wind which acts perpendicular to the runway. Most airplanes have a maximum demonstrated crosswind component listed in the POH. Of course, your personal crosswind limit is based on your skill level, as well as any limitations set forth by your instructor during training.

Since headwinds are better for takeoffs and landings, the runway in use normally is a runway that provides some headwind. You can easily compute headwind, as well as crosswind, components by use of a wind component chart. When you use a wind component chart, remember that both the runway number and surface winds are given in magnetic direction.

To use a sample wind component chart, you first need to know the wind direction and the velocity. Next, you find the angle between the runway in use and the wind. For example, assume you are departing on runway 03 and the wind is from 060° at 20 knots. The angle between the runway and the wind is 30° (060 – 030 = 030). In this case, you have a headwind 30° off the runway heading. Since the headwind is from the right, you also have a crosswind component. [Figure 5-31]

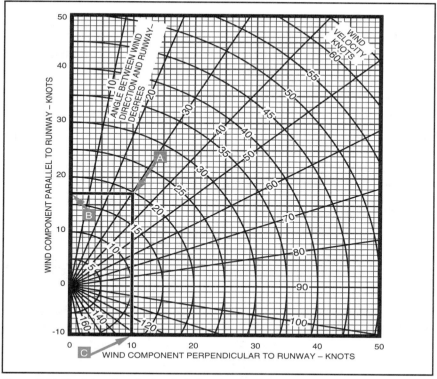

Figure 5-31. To determine the headwind and crosswind components, enter the sample chart at the point where the wind angle and the wind velocity arc meet (point A). Proceed horizontally to the left to find the headwind component of 17 knots (point B). Find the crosswind component by following the vertical lines down from point A to the bottom of the chart. The crosswind component is 10 knots (point C).

WEIGHT

As the weight of the airplane increases, performance decreases. Conversely, as weight decreases, performance increases.

As discussed earlier, the amount of lift required to maintain altitude during flight is directly related to the weight of the airplane. With a constant angle of attack, the airspeed necessary to provide sufficient lift to maintain level fight increases as weight increases. An overloaded airplane must accelerate to a higher-than-normal speed to generate sufficient lift for flight. This means the airplane requires more runway for takeoff, since it must attain a higher speed. The additional weight also reduces acceleration during the takeoff roll, and this adds to the total takeoff distance.

Problems do not end once the airplane is airborne. An overloaded airplane suffers a reduction in climb performance, and its service ceiling is decreased. This is because excess power and thrust are limited. In addition, exceeding the maximum allowable weight may cause the airplane to become unstable and difficult to fly.

For an airplane to be safe, it must be operated within weight limitations. In addition, the weight must be distributed, or balanced, properly. When you operate within weight and balance limitations, you can expect reduced takeoff distances, improved climb performance, and a higher ceiling. If you find you will be unable to safely take off or land at a particular airport at the airplane's maximum allowable weight, you should refer to the pilot's operating handbook. Most performance charts include weight as one variable. By reducing the weight of the airplane, usually by carrying less fuel, you may find that you are able to safely take off or land at that airport. If you are in doubt, a better procedure would be to delay your takeoff for more favorable density altitude conditions and, if airborne, land at a nearby airport with a more suitable runway.

RUNWAY CONDITIONS

Runway conditions relating to aircraft performance data generally specify a paved and level runway with a smooth dry surface. If any one of these conditions does not exist for the runway you use, the takeoff and landing distances will not agree with the values listed in the performance charts.

A positive runway gradient adversely affects takeoff performance, but it is beneficial during landing. A negative gradient shortens the takeoff roll, but lengthens the landing distance.

Completely level runways are rare. The **gradient**, or **slope**, of the runway refers to the amount of change in runway height over its length. Gradient is usually expressed as a percentage. For example, a gradient of two percent means the runway height changes two feet for each 100 feet of runway length ($100 \times 2\% = 2$). A positive gradient indicates the height of the runway increases, while a negative value means it decreases. A positive gradient is unfavorable for takeoff, because the airplane must take off uphill. However, it is desirable for landings, since landing uphill reduces the landing roll. A negative gradient has the opposite effects on both takeoffs and landings. Runway gradient is listed in the *Airport/Facility Directory* when it is three-tenths of one percent or more.

Runway surface refers to what the runway is made of and what, if anything, is covering it. Generally, any surface that is not hard, smooth, and dry will increase the takeoff roll. This is due to the inability of the tires to roll smoothly along the runway. For example, on soft runways, the tires may sink into the ground and must constantly climb out of small ruts or holes. If a runway is muddy, wet, or covered with grass or snow, the tires must push obstructions out of the way. This reduces the airplane's acceleration. Sometimes, the reduction in acceleration is so great that it may be impossible to accelerate to takeoff speed.

Mud, water, snow, or grass usually increase takeoff distances.

The condition of the runway surface also affects the landing roll. A major concern is braking. **Braking effectiveness** refers to how much braking power you can apply to the runway. It depends, to a large extent, on the amount of friction between the tires and the runway. A great deal of friction and, therefore, braking power is normal on a dry runway. If the runway is wet, however, less friction is available and your landing roll-out will increase. In some cases, you may lose braking effectiveness because of hydroplaning or standing water or slush. **Hydroplaning** is caused by a thin layer of water that separates the tires from the runway. Braking effectiveness also may be completely lost on ice-covered runways. If you must operate in conditions where braking effectiveness is poor or nil, be sure the runway length is adequate and surface wind is favorable.

Although other runway surface conditions, such as mud, grass, and snow reduce the level of friction between tires and runway, in some circumstances they may provide a significant decrease in the landing roll. This occurs because they act as an obstruction to the tires. In extreme cases, this retarding force alone may be strong enough to bring the airplane to a complete stop without use of the brakes.

THE PILOT'S OPERATING HANDBOOK

Originally, airplane manuals did not follow a standardized format, and they often contained minimal information. In an effort to standardize style, format, and content, the pilot's operating handbook (POH) was developed, which includes standardized information. The format divides the POH into several sections and defines the kind of information included in each section. Most light airplanes built after 1975 use this new format. As mentioned earlier, the POHs for most light airplanes built after

March 1, 1979, are also designated as the FAA approved flight manual. The typical POH includes the following types of information:

General — Presents basic information of general interest. The information is useful in loading, sheltering, handling, and preflight inspection. Definitions, explanations of symbols, abbreviations, and terminology also are included. In addition, this section contains descriptive data such as principal dimensions, engine type, horsepower rating, propeller type, and fuel specifications.

Limitations — Contains only those limitations required by regulation or necessary for the safe operation of the airplane, powerplant, systems, and equipment. It includes the operating limitations, instrument markings (including color coding), and placards.

Emergency Procedures — Clearly describes the recommended procedures for dealing with various types of emergencies or hazardous situations. Other system malfunctions or situations which, by their nature, are not emergencies may be included in this section or in a separate **Abnormal Procedures** section. Information typically found in the emergency procedures section includes such items as landing with a flat tire, flap and gear malfunctions, and engine and electrical fires. Since procedures contained in this section vary widely from airplane to airplane, you should be certain to become familiar with the procedures listed for the airplane you fly.

Normal Procedures — Presents recommended procedures for the normal operation of the airplane. It also includes airplane checklists and normal procedures to be used with optional equipment or systems. Checklists are guides intended to help you make sure you check all necessary items in a logical sequence. The use of an appropriate written checklist for preflight inspection, engine starting, and other ground procedures is highly recommended.

Performance — Contains all performance information required by the FAA, including performance charts or tables. Additional information, such as a flight planning example, may be included to help you interpret the various performance charts.

Weight and Balance — Presents all information required by the FAA that is necessary to calculate weight and balance.

Airplane Systems — Describes airplane systems in a manner appropriate to the kind of pilot considered most likely to operate the airplane. For advanced airplanes, the manufacturer may assume the pilot has a high degree of knowledge about airplanes in general.

Handling, Servicing, and Maintenance — Presents information to ensure that necessary handling, servicing, and maintenance can be accomplished. It is assumed that the person reading the POH is not a mechanic or technician.

Supplements — Contains operating information for various optional equipment and systems not included on the standard airplane.

In addition to these sections, manufacturers may, at their option, include additional sections. For example, a **Safety and Operational Tips** section or a comprehensive **Alphabetical Index** may be included.

PERFORMANCE CHARTS

In developing performance charts, airplane manufacturers must make assumptions about the condition of the airplane and ability of the pilot. They assume the airplane to be in good condition, and that the engine has been properly tuned and is developing its rated power. Also, the brakes are considered to be in good condition. The pilot of the airplane is expected to follow normal checklist procedures and to have average flying abilities. "Average" means the person is not a highly trained test pilot with exceptional reaction time. At the same time, a student pilot or a person who has not flown for a long time is not considered average. In this context, average means a pilot capable of doing each of the required tasks correctly and at the appropriate times.

Performance charts assume a properly tuned airplane in good condition with good brakes, and the data is based on average piloting abilities.

With the aid of these assumptions, the manufacturer develops performance data for the airplane based on actual flight tests. Manufacturers, however, do not test airplanes under each and every condition shown on a performance chart. Instead, they evaluate specific flight data and, based on that data, mathematically derive the remaining data. As a practical consideration, you should remember that the original flight tests were conducted by test pilots flying a new airplane. With this in mind, you should look at performance data with a skeptical eye to ensure yourself a margin of safety. For example, departing on a 2,000-foot runway when performance charts indicate 1,900 feet are required for takeoff is very dangerous and reflects poor judgment.

Performance charts are developed by deriving the data from actual flight tests.

TYPICAL CHARTS

Keep in mind that all performance charts in this presentation are samples only. They must never be used with any specific airplane you may be flying.

When determining performance data for a given airplane, refer only to the POH for that particular airplane. Performance data can vary significantly between similar models or even from one model year to the next. The POH presents numerous charts which allow you to predict the airplane's performance accurately. They pertain to the takeoff, climb, cruise, descent, and landing phases of flight. Some of the typical charts found in the POH include:

Takeoff Distance Chart — Provides the distance required for the airplane to accelerate to takeoff speed and become airborne. These charts usually allow you to determine the actual ground roll distance of the airplane, as well as the total distance required to take off and climb to an altitude of 50 feet.

Maximum Rate of Climb Chart — Helps determine the maximum rate of climb for the airplane under a given set of conditions. This chart is of particular importance when obstructions, such as high terrain, are in the departure path immediately after takeoff.

Time, Fuel, and Distance to Climb — Primarily used as a flight planning tool, this chart allows you to calculate how long it will take the airplane to climb to a selected cruise altitude. You may also determine the fuel required and distance traveled to reach the desired altitude.

Cruise Performance — Provides the speed of the airplane, as well as fuel consumption rate at various altitudes and power settings.

Range Profile — Allows you to determine the maximum distance the airplane can fly at a given power setting. Since this chart typically assumes no wind, be sure to consider its effect.

Endurance Profile — Indicates the maximum length of time the airplane can remain aloft based on the power setting you select. This chart is similar to the range profile chart.

Landing Distance — Allows you to determine how much runway is required to land the airplane safely. This chart, like the takeoff distance chart, usually provides you with the ground roll distance, as well as the distance required to descend over a 50-foot obstacle, land, and bring the airplane to a full stop.

ADDITIONAL CHARTS

The style and content of performance charts vary from one manufacturer to another. You should be familiar with all performance charts in the POH for the airplane you fly. The following additional charts usually are included in the performance section of the POH:

Airspeed Calibration — The airspeed indicator is not a perfect instrument. It cannot accurately display correct readings throughout its entire range, and certain corrections are necessary. You use this chart to correct indicated airspeed (IAS). The result is called calibrated airspeed (CAS).

Fahrenheit/Celsius Conversion — This chart allows you to convert back and forth quickly between degrees Fahrenheit and Celsius.

Stall Speeds — Earlier you learned that the stall speed of an airplane varies with the airplane's weight, angle of bank, and flap setting. The stall speed chart indicates predicted stall speeds at various combinations of weight, bank angle, and flap settings.

Wind Component Chart — You use this chart to determine the headwind (or tailwind) and crosswind components based on current conditions.

Glide Distance Chart — In the event of an engine failure, the airplane will continue to travel in a forward direction as it loses altitude. The glide distance chart tells you how far the airplane can be flown based on the airplane's AGL altitude at the time the engine fails. Some manufacturers include this chart in the emergency section of the POH instead of the performance section.

CHART PRESENTATIONS

Performance charts generally present their information in either a table or a graph format. The table format usually contains several notes which require you to make adjustments for various conditions which are not accounted for in the body of the chart. Graph presentations, though somewhat harder to use, usually incorporate more variables and adjustments may not be required. Almost every chart, whether a table or a graph, will specify a set of conditions under which the chart is valid. For example, a takeoff chart may only be valid for a particular weight and flap setting. Therefore, you should always check the chart conditions before using it.

TAKEOFF CHARTS

For this first sample chart, assume you are planning to depart an airport under the following conditions, and want to determine the ground roll and total distance required to clear a 50-foot obstacle. [Figure 5-32]

Pressure altitude	2,000 ft.
Temperature	30°C
Flaps	10°
Runway	Paved, level, and dry
Wind	Calm
Weight	1,670 lbs.

In the example, the wind condition was calm, but how would the problem change with a headwind? You can find the answer in the notes listed for the chart. According to note number 3, the distances decrease by 10% for each nine knots of headwind. For example, with an 18-knot headwind, the ground roll is reduced by 20%, to 784 feet (980 − 196 = 784), and total distance is reduced by 20% to 1,456 feet (1,820 − 364 = 1,456). With a dry grass runway surface, note number 4 is applicable. In this case, both distances are increased by 15% of the ground roll figure. This means the actual ground roll increases to 1,127 feet (980 × 15% = 147 + 980 = 1,127). The total distance to clear a 50-foot obstacle also increases to 1,967 feet (1,820 + 147 = 1,967).

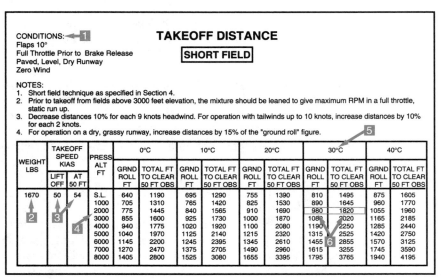

Figure 5-32. A quick check of the conditions (item 1) and the takeoff weight (item 2) indicate you are using the correct chart. Note the takeoff speed of 50 knots and the speed of 54 knots shortly after takeoff at 50 feet (item 3). Enter the tabular data at the pressure altitude of 2,000 feet (item 4) and proceed horizontally to the column for 30°C (item 5). The ground roll distance is 980 feet, and the total distance to clear a 50-foot obstacle is 1,820 feet (item 6).

For this sample chart, assume you are planning to depart under the following conditions. This time you are only concerned with the distance required to clear a 50-foot obstacle. [Figure 5-33]

Pressure altitude...1,500 ft.
Temperature ....27°C
Flaps...Up
Runway ....Paved, level, and dry
Wind ....15 kts. headwind
Weight ....2,316 lbs.

Since a graphic chart often includes more variables in a single chart, you must use extra care when using it. For example, you generally estimate where two lines meet on the chart. There is also a tendency to "eyeball" the chart. This means that instead of drawing out your lines carefully, you simply select line positions and intersections visually. This can lead to substantial errors.

Figure 5-33. After checking the associated conditions (item 1), you can see that this chart is appropriate. Enter the graph at a temperature of 27°C (item 2) and proceed vertically to the pressure altitude of 1,500 feet (item 3). Next, proceed horizontally to the first reference line (item 4), then diagonally down until you intercept the takeoff weight of 2,316 pounds (item 5). Continue across to the second reference line (item 6), and correct for the headwind by paralleling the diagonal line downward until you intercept the 15-knot mark (item 7). You find the takeoff distance of 2,100 feet on the right side of the graph (item 8). To determine the appropriate takeoff and 50-foot barrier speeds, proceed vertically up from the takeoff weight (item 5) to the speeds listed at the top of the chart (item 9). The takeoff speed is 50 knots and the barrier (50-foot obstacle) speed is 55 knots. Note, these speeds are not directly indicated. You have to check the available information carefully and extract the speeds that correspond to the takeoff weight.

TIME, FUEL, AND DISTANCE TO CLIMB CHART

This sample chart is a little different from the others. First, you determine the time, fuel, and distance to climb to your cruise altitude, then you apply a credit for departing any airport above sea level. For this example, assume the following conditions, and determine the time, fuel, and distance required to climb from the airport elevation of 2,000 feet to 8,000 feet. [Figure 5-34]

Cruise altitude ....8,000 ft.
Airport elevation ....2,000 ft.
Flaps ....Up
Power ....Full throttle
Temperature ....Standard
Weight ....1,670 lbs.

TIME, FUEL, AND DISTANCE TO CLIMB

CONDITIONS: ◄—■1   MAXIMUM RATE OF CLIMB
Flaps Up
Full Throttle
Standard Temperature

NOTES: ◄—4
1. Add 0.8 of a gallon of fuel for engine start, taxi and takeoff allowance.
2. Mixture leaned above 3000 feet for maximum RPM.
3. Increase time, fuel and distance by 10% for each 10°C above standard temperature.
4. Distances shown are based on zero wind.

WEIGHT LBS	PRESSURE ALTITUDE FT	TEMP °C	CLIMB SPEED KIAS	RATE OF CLIMB FPM	FROM SEA LEVEL		
					TIME MIN	FUEL USED GALLONS	DISTANCE NM
1670	S.L.	15	67	715	0	0	0
	1000	13	66	675	1	0.2	2
	2000	11	66	630	3	0.4	3
	3000	9	65	590	5	0.7	5
	4000	7	65	550	6	0.9	7
	5000	5	64	505	8	1.2	9
	6000	3	63	465	10	1.4	12
	7000	1	63	425	13	1.7	14
	8000	-1	62	380	15	2.0	

Figure 5-34. First, check the conditions (item 1). Then, read the time, fuel, and distance to climb to 8,000 feet of 15 minutes, 2.0 gallons, and 17 miles, respectively (item 2). Next, determine the time, fuel, and distance credits to be applied for departing an airport at 2,000 feet. These values are 3 minutes, 0.4 gallons, and 3 miles (item 3). After you subtract the credits, the net values are 12 minutes, 1.6 gallons, and 14 miles. A check of the notes, however, indicates that you must add an additional 0.8 gallons of fuel for the engine start, taxi, and takeoff allowances (item 4). The final values of time, fuel, and distance to climb from 2,000 feet to 8,000 feet are 12 minutes, 2.4 gallons (1.6 + .8), and 14 miles.

CRUISE PERFORMANCE CHART

These charts vary considerably. Before you use a particular chart, make sure you understand how the information is portrayed. Temperatures for cruise may include International Standard Atmosphere (ISA) values, as well as colder and warmer temperatures. For instance, temperature categories may specify ISA –20°C, standard day ISA, and ISA +20°C. Both Celsius and Fahrenheit temperatures may be included. In addition, the temperature figures for some manufacturers may be adjusted for frictional heating of the temperature probe. Assume you are planning a flight under the following conditions, and wish to determine the manifold pressure setting, fuel flow, and cruise true airspeed. [Figure 5-35]

Pressure altitude...8,000 ft.
Temperature ....ISA –20°C
Power...2,400 r.p.m.
Weight ....2,600 lbs.

CRUISE POWER SETTINGS – 2400 RPM

65% MCP (or FULL THROTTLE) – 2600 POUNDS

PRESS ALT.	ISA – 36°F (-20°C)							STANDARD DAY (ISA)							ISA + 36°F (+20°C)						
	IOAT		MAN. PRESS	FUEL FLOW		TAS		IOAT		MAN. PRESS	FUEL FLOW		TAS		IOAT		MAN. PRESS	FUEL FLOW		TAS	
FEET	°F	°C	IN HG	PPH	GPH	KTS	MPH	°F	°C	IN HG	PPH	GPH	KTS	MPH	°F	°C	IN HG	PPH	GPH	KTS	MPH
SL	25	-4	22.3	54	9.0	116	134	61	16	22.9	54	9.0	118	136	97	36	23.5	54	9.0	120	138
1000	21	-6	22.0	54	9.0	117	135	57	14	22.6	54	9.0	119	137	93	34	23.2	54	9.0	121	139
2000	18	-8	21.7	54	9.0	118	136	54	12	22.3	54	9.0	120	138	90	32	23.0	54	9.0	122	140
3000	14	-10	21.5	54	9.0	118	136	50	10	22.1	54	9.0	121	139	86	30	22.7	54	9.0	123	142
4000	10	-12	21.2	54	9.0	119	137	46	8	21.8	54	9.0	122	140	84	29	22.4	54	9.0	124	143
5000	7	-14	20.9	54	9.0	120	138	43	6	21.5	54	9.0	123	142	81	27	22.2	54	9.0	125	144
6000	3	-16	20.7	54	9.0	121	139	41	5	21.3	54	9.0	124	143	77	25	22.0	54	9.0	126	145
7000	1	-17	20.5	54	9.0	122	140	37	3	21.1	54	9.0	125	144	73	23	21.7	54	9.0	126	145
8000	-2	-19	20.3	54	9.0	123	142	34	1	20.9	54	9.0	125	144	70	21	21.5	54	9.0	127	146
9000	-6	-21	20.1	54	9.0	124	143	30	-1	20.7	54	9.0	126	145	66	19	21.3	54	9.0	127	146
10000	-9	-23	19.9	54	9.0	125	144	27	-3	20.5	54	9.0	127	146	63	17	20.8	53	8.8	127	146
11000	-13	-25	19.8	54	9.0	125	144	23	-5	20.1	53	8.8	126	145	59	15	20.1	52	8.7	126	145
12000	-17	-27	19.3	54	9.0	125	144	19	-7	19.3	52	8.7	125	144	55	13	19.3	51	8.5	123	142
13000	-20	-29	18.6	52	8.7	124	143	16	-9	18.6	51	8.5	123	142	52	11	18.6	49	8.2	120	138
14000	-24	-31	17.9	51	8.5	121	139	12	-11	17.9	49	8.2	120	138	48	9	17.9	48	8.0	117	135

NOTES: 1. Shaded area represents operation with full throttle.
2. Full throttle manifold settings are approximate.

Figure 5-35. This sample chart includes data for three sets of temperature conditions: ISA –20°, ISA, and ISA +20°. In this example, the appropriate temperature conditions are ISA –20°C (item 1). Below this subheading proceed down to the line for the cruise pressure altitude of 8,000 feet (item 2). With a temperature 20°C below standard, the indicated outside air temperature (IOAT) at 8,000 feet is –2°F or –19°C (item 3). In this case, the figures do include adjustments for frictional heating of the OAT gauge. The significant values are the manifold pressure of 20.3 in. Hg (item 4), fuel flow of 54 pounds per hour or 9.0 gallons per hour (item 5), and a cruise speed of 123 knots or 142 miles per hour (item 6).

LANDING DISTANCE CHART

Landing distance charts are similar to takeoff distance charts. For this sample of a graph-style performance chart, use the following conditions to determine the distance to land over a 50-foot obstacle and bring the airplane to a complete stop. [Figure 5-36]

Pressure altitude...2,500 ft.
Temperature ....24°C
Flaps ....40°
Runway ....Paved, level, and dry
Wind ....Calm
Weight ....2,179 lbs.
Braking ....Maximum

Figure 5-36. First, check the associated conditions listed on the sample chart (item 1). Next, enter the chart at the given temperature of 24°C (item 2) and proceed vertically up to the pressure altitude of 2,500 feet (item 3). Proceed horizontally to the first reference line, which is labeled REF. LINE-2400 LBS., then diagonally down to a weight of 2,179 pounds (item 4). Continue horizontally to the right to the second reference line. Note that since the reported wind is calm, no correction is required here for headwind or tailwind. Read the distance required of 1,135 feet on the right side of the chart (item 5). The approach and touchdown speeds are indicated straight up from the landing weight near the top of the chart (item 6). The approximate approach and touchdown speeds are 63 knots and 42 knots, respectively.

WEIGHT LBS	TAKEOFF SPEED KIAS		PRESS ALT FT	0°C		10°C		20°C		30°C		40°C	
	LIFT OFF	AT 50 FT		GRND ROLL FT	TOTAL TO CLEAR 50 FT OBS	GRND ROLL FT	TOTAL TO CLEAR 50 FT OBS	GRND ROLL FT	TOTAL TO CLEAR 50 FT OBS	GRND ROLL FT	TOTAL TO CLEAR 50 FT OBS	GRND ROLL FT	TOTAL TO CLEAR 50 FT OBS
1670	50	54	S.L.	640	1190	695	1290	755	1390	810	1495	875	1605
			1000	705	1310	765	1420	825	1530	890	1645	960	1770
			2000	775	1445	840	1565	910	1690	980	1820	1055	1960
			3000	855	1600	925	1730	1000	1870	1080	2020	1165	2185

Figure 5-37. Looking at the sample takeoff chart excerpt, you can see that the given pressure altitude of 1,500 feet falls between the 1,000- and 2,000-foot pressure altitude values. This means your ground roll distance will fall between 890 and 980 feet. Interpolation is required.

INTERPOLATION

The sample problems you have looked at so far used convenient altitudes and temperatures which permitted you to extract your answers directly. To see how to solve a problem when this is not the case, work another takeoff performance problem. In this example, assume you need to know the ground roll requirement under the given conditions. [Figure 5-37]

Pressure altitude..1,500 ft.
Temperature ....30°C
Flaps ....10°
Runway ....Paved, level, and dry
Wind ....Calm
Weight ....1,670 lbs.

Interpolation refers to the process of finding an unknown value between two known values. Often this is necessary when you use charts with tabular information. In this case, you know the ground roll figures for 1,000 and 2,000 feet and want to determine the ground roll for 1,500 feet. The first step in interpolation is to compute the differences between known values.

	Pressure Altitude	**Ground Roll**
	2,000 ft.	980 ft.
	1,000 ft.	890 ft.
Difference	1,000 ft.	90 ft.

The 1,500-foot airport pressure altitude is 50% of the way between 1,000 and 2,000 feet. Therefore, the ground roll also is 50% of the way between 890 and 980 feet. The answer then, is 935 feet (90-foot difference X .5 + 890 feet = 935 feet).

In practice, pilots often round off values derived from table charts to the more conservative figure. This practice gives you a good estimate of performance data, and it also provides a margin of safety.

CHECKLIST _____

After studying this section, you should have a basic understanding of:

✓   **Performance speeds** — How maximum level speed, best angle-of-climb, and best rate-of-climb speeds are determined.

✓   **Service and absolute ceilings** — What they are and how they are determined.

✓   **Cruising airspeeds** — How maximum range and maximum endurance airspeeds are determined.

✓   **Factors affecting performance** — How density altitude, humidity, winds, and runway conditions affect airplane performance.

✓   **The pilot's operating handbook (POH)** — How this publication is organized and the type of information included in each section.

✓   **Performance charts** — What some of the more common performance charts are and how they are used.

WEIGHT AND BALANCE

In previous sections, you learned about airplane design and how the location of the airplane's center of gravity (CG) directly affects stability. This section expands the center of gravity concept by providing you with some of the terminology and techniques you use in determining weight and balance. Keep in mind that the weight and balance charts, graphs, and tables in this presentation are samples only. They must never be used with any specific airplane you may be flying. When determining the weight and balance condition for a given airplane, refer only to the POH for that airplane.

AIRPLANE WEIGHT

You are already aware that weight is caused by the downward pull of gravity and varies with several factors. These factors include the weight of the basic airplane, installed equipment, passengers, cargo, and fuel. You also know that the effective weight varies when you maneuver the airplane in flight. This is called load factor. In this section, however, we are concerned primarily with the weight of the airplane and its contents when at rest. The starting point for weight computation is the weight of the airplane before passengers, cargo, and fuel are added. The term **basic empty weight** includes the weight of the standard airplane, optional equipment, unusable fuel, and full operating fluids including full engine oil. Older airplanes might use the term **licensed empty weight**, which is similar to basic empty weight except that it does not include full engine oil. Instead, it includes only the weight of undrainable oil. If you fly an airplane that lists a licensed empty weight, be sure to add the weight of oil to your computations.

The empty weight of an aircraft always includes unusable fuel and optional equipment.

Standard weights are used for computing the weight of aviation gasoline (avgas) and engine oil. Avgas weighs 6 pounds per gallon, while oil weighs 7.5 pounds per gallon. Remember that engine oil capacity is usually given in quarts; therefore, you must convert it to gallons before determining its weight.

One gallon of avgas equals 6 pounds; one gallon of oil equals 7.5 pounds.

Another term, **payload**, refers to the weight of the flight crew, passengers, and any cargo or baggage; **useful load** is the difference between maximum takeoff weight and basic empty weight. Useful load includes payload and usable fuel. **Usable fuel** is the fuel available for the flight. It does not include **unusable fuel**, which is the quantity of fuel that cannot be safely used during flight. The following summary should help you understand how various weights are calculated:

Basic Empty Weight
+ <u>Payload</u>
= Zero Fuel Weight
+ <u>Usable Fuel</u>
= Ramp Weight
− <u>Fuel Used for Start, Taxi, and Engine Runup</u>
= Takeoff Weight
− <u>Fuel Used During Flight</u>
= Landing Weight

WEIGHT LIMITATIONS

Operating above the maximum weight limitation compromises the structural integrity of the airplane and adversly affects performance.

Some weight and balance terms may be preceded by the word **maximum**. When this word is used, it indicates a limitation which must not be exceeded. For example, the **maximum ramp weight** is the maximum weight approved for ground operations, while **maximum takeoff weight** is the maximum weight approved for the start of the takeoff roll. Weight limitations are necessary to guarantee the structural integrity of the airplane, as well as enable you to predict airplane performance accurately. For example, airplanes certified in the normal category usually are capable of withstanding a positive load factor of 3.8 G's and have an additional safety factor built in. Regardless of the safety factor, you should never intentionally exceed the limit loads for which an airplane is certificated. These structural limitations are based on an airplane operated at or below the maximum weight. Operating the airplane above this weight could result in structural deformation or failure during flight if you encounter excessive load factors, strong wind gusts, or turbulence. Operating in excess of the maximum weight also affects performance. It results in a longer takeoff roll, reduced climb performance, reduced cruising speed, an increase in fuel consumption, an increase in stall speed, and an increase in the landing roll.

DETERMINING EMPTY WEIGHT

Weight and balance information for each airplane can be found in the airplane's weight and balance records.

The airplane's weight and balance records contain essential data for the airplane, including a complete list of all optional equipment that has been installed. You use these records to determine the weight and balance condition of the empty airplane. From time to time, the owner or operator of an airplane may have equipment removed, replaced, or additional equipment installed. These changes must be made to the weight and balance records. In addition, major repairs or alterations to the airplane itself also must be recorded by a certificated mechanic. When the revised weight and moment are recorded on a new form, the old record is marked with the word "superseded" and dated with the effective date of the new record. In this way, you can easily determine which is the latest version.

AIRPLANE BALANCE

The center of gravity of an airplane is defined as the theoretical point where all of the airplane's weight is considered to be concentrated. As you learned in Chapter 1, the location of this point is critical to an airplane's stability and stabilator (or elevator) effectiveness. Improper balance of the airplane's load can result in serious control problems. Fortunately, you can avoid these problems by taking the time to determine the location of the CG prior to flight and then comparing the computed location to the acceptable limits prescribed by the manufacturer. If the CG is located within these limits, the airplane can be flown safely. However, if it is located outside of these limits, you will have to relocate fuel, passengers, or cargo in order to move the CG within acceptable limits. It is equally important to maintain this distribution of weight during flight, since any movement of passengers or cargo will change the location of the CG.

Airplanes must be loaded within acceptable CG limits before flight and the distribution of the load must be maintained during flight.

WEIGHT AND BALANCE CONTROL

There are three different methods commonly used in determining weight and balance. They include the computational, graph, and table methods. It is important to note that each method is only as accurate as the information you provide. Therefore, you should ask passengers what they weigh and add a few pounds to cover the additional weight of clothing, especially during the winter months. The weight of baggage should be determined by the use of a scale, if practical. If a scale is not available, be conservative and overestimate the weight. When estimating weights, you can use certain standard weights designated by the FAA. A person of average stature is considered to weigh 170 pounds, and a child between 2 and 12 years of age is considered to weigh 80 pounds. However, if the aircraft is loaded near a weight and balance limit, or a passenger's weight is obviously different from these standard weights, you should use actual weights.

Whenever practical, ask your passengers for their actual weights and use a scale to weigh baggage.

Balance is determined by the location of the CG, which is usually described as a given number of inches aft of the reference datum. The **reference datum** is an imaginary vertical plane, arbitrarily fixed somewhere along the longitudinal axis of the airplane, from which all horizontal distances are measured for weight and balance purposes. There is no fixed rule for its location. It may be located on the nose of the airplane, the firewall, the leading edge of the wing, or even at a point in space ahead of the airplane. The location of the datum is established by the manufacturer and is defined in the POH or in the airplane's weight and balance papers. The horizontal distance from the datum to any component of the airplane or to any object located within the airplane is called the **arm**. Another term which can be used interchangeably with arm is **station**. If the component or object is located to the rear of the datum, it is measured as a positive number and usually is referred to as inches aft of the datum. Conversely,

The reference datum is an arbitrarily fixed vertical plane.

Figure 5-38. For this airplane, the manufacturer has arbitrarily fixed the datum at the front face of the firewall. The arm of the propeller spinner is -36.2 inches (36.2 inches ahead of the datum plane). The rotating beacon, located on the tail, has an arm of 217.2 inches aft of the datum plane.

if the component or object is located forward of the datum, it is indicated as a negative number and is usually referred to as inches forward of the datum. [Figure 5-38]

Moment = Weight × Arm

If the weight of an object is multiplied by its arm, the result is known as its **moment.** You may think of moment as a force which results from an object's weight acting at a distance. Moment is also referred to as the tendency of an object to rotate or pivot about a point. The farther an object is from a pivotal point, the greater its force. The concept of weight, arm, and moment can be shown with a teeter-totter. [Figure 5-39]

Just like the children on the teeter-totter, each component of an airplane, as well as each object it carries, exerts a moment proportional to its weight and distance from the designated reference datum. By totaling the weights and moments of all components and objects carried, you can determine the point where a loaded airplane would balance on an imaginary fulcrum. This is the airplane's CG.

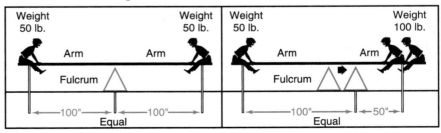

Figure 5-39. The teeter-totter on the left shows that each child is exerting a moment of 5,000 lb.-in. (50-pound weight times 100-inch arm). As long as each child maintains the same distance from the fulcrum, their moments are balanced. The teeter-totter on the right shows that unequal weights also can be balanced if the distance from the fulcrum is adjusted. In this case, 100 pounds at 50 inches exerts the same moment as 50 pounds at 100 inches.

COMPUTATIONAL METHOD

With the computational method, you use simple mathematics to solve weight and balance problems. The first step is to look up the basic empty weight and total moment for the particular airplane you fly. If the center of gravity is given, it should also be noted. The empty weight CG can be considered the "arm" of the empty airplane. As mentioned earlier, this information is contained in the airplane's weight and balance records. You should record it as the first item on the weight and balance form. [Figure 5-40]

Next, the weights of the fuel, pilot and passengers, and baggage are recorded. Since avgas weighs six pounds per gallon, multiply the gallons of usable fuel by six to get the total fuel weight. For example, 38 gallons of avgas weighs 228 pounds. Use care in recording the weight of each item, since some airplanes have several rows of seats and baggage compartments. Recording each weight in its proper location is extremely important to the accurate calculation of a CG. Once you have recorded all of the weights, add them together to determine the total weight of the loaded airplane.

Now, check to see that the total weight does not exceed the maximum allowable weight under existing conditions. If it does, you will usually

$$CG = \frac{\text{Total Moment}}{\text{Total Weight}}$$

WEIGHT and BALANCE FORM			
ITEM	WEIGHT (pounds)	ARM (inches)	MOMENT (pound-inches)
BASIC EMPTY WT.	*1,437*	*38.75*	*55,684*
FUEL		48.0	
PILOT & PASSENGER		37.0	
REAR PASSENGERS		73.0	
BAGGAGE		95.0	
TOTAL			
CG = _____ INCHES			

Figure 5-40. In this example, the airplane's weight of 1,437 pounds is recorded in the first column, its CG or arm of 38.75 inches in the second, and its moment of 55,684 pound-inches in the last. Notice that the weight of the airplane multiplied by its CG equals its moment. Also, note the arm for each of the other items has already been recorded by the manufacturer. However, some manufacturers require you to look up and record this information yourself.

WEIGHT and BALANCE FORM			
ITEM	WEIGHT (pounds)	ARM (inches)	MOMENT (pound-inches)
BASIC EMPTY WT.	1,437	38.75	55,684
FUEL (38 gal.)	228	48.0	10,944
PILOT & PASSENGER	340	37.0	12,580
REAR PASSENGERS	280	73.0	20,440
BAGGAGE	15	95.0	1,425
TOTAL	2,300	/////	101,073
CG = ___43.9___ INCHES			

Figure 5-41. Here is an example of a completed weight and balance form. The appropriate weight is recorded next to each item. Notice that the amount of fuel in gallons also has been recorded on the fuel line. The CG, filled in at the bottom of the form, is determined by dividing the total moment of the airplane by its total weight.

reduce the amount of fuel you are carrying and plan an extra fuel stop. Once you are satisfied that the total weight is within prescribed limits, multiply each individual weight by its associated arm to determine its moment. Then, add the moments together to arrive at the total moment for the airplane. Your final computation is to find the center of gravity of the loaded airplane by dividing the total moment by the total weight. [Figure 5-41]

After determining the airplane's weight and center of gravity location, you need to determine if the CG is within acceptable limits. This is usually done by consulting the airplane's center of gravity limits graph. If the CG falls outside of acceptable limits, you will have to adjust the loading of the airplane. To determine if the center of gravity is within limits, plot the point at which the airplane's total weight and CG meet. If this point is within the approved limits on the graph, the airplane is considered to be properly loaded. [Figure 5-42]

GRAPH METHOD

The graph method is a simplification of the computational method. Instead of multiplying weight times arm to determine moment, you simply use a graph supplied by the manufacturer. In addition, when a manufacturer uses this method, the center of gravity limits graph usually reflects weight and moment instead of weight and CG.

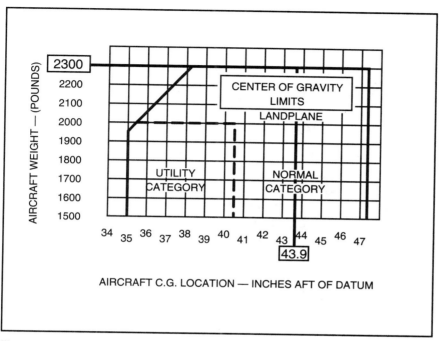

Figure 5-42. In this example, notice that a weight of 2,300 pounds and a CG location of 43.9 inches are within acceptable limits for operations in the normal category. However, the airplane is too heavy and is loaded with the CG too far aft for operations in the utility category.

The graph method uses the same first step as the computational method. Record the basic empty weight of the airplane, along with its total moment. (The CG, if provided, is not required.) Remember to use the actual weight and moment of the airplane you will be flying. Next, record the weights of the fuel, pilot, passengers and baggage on the weight and balance worksheet. Then, determine the total weight of the airplane.

If this weight exceeds the maxim um allowable weight, you will have to make some adjustments to fuel, baggage, or passengers. For example, assume the maximum allowable weight for the airplane is 2,400 pounds and the total weight of the loaded airplane comes to 2,550 pounds. In this situation, the airplane is 150 pounds over its maximum allowable weight. To make this flight, you will need to carry 25 gallons less fuel (25 gal. × 6 lb./gal. = 150 lb.) or leave 150 pounds of baggage behind. Another option is to leave behind a passenger who weighs 150 pounds or more. Once you have determined the weight to be within prescribed limits, compute the moment for each weight and for the loaded airplane. You do this using a loading graph provided by the manufacturer. For example, let's assume

If the airplane is too heavy for the flight, you must leave some fuel, baggage, or a passenger behind.

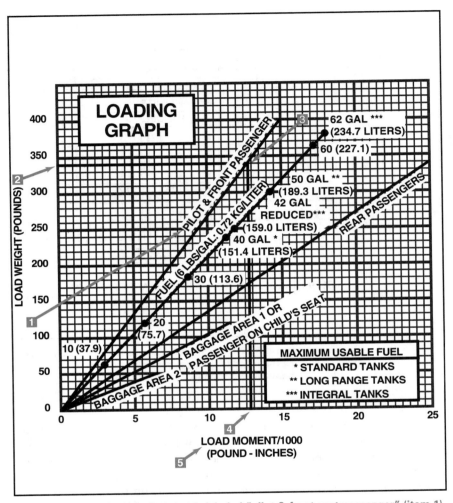

Figure 5-43. First, find the line that is labeled "pilot & front seat passenger" (item 1). Now, enter the graph from the left side at a weight of 340 pounds (item 2), and proceed horizontally to the appropriate line (item 3). Next, drop straight down and read the moment of 12.6 (item 4). Notice that numbers on this scale represent the load moment/1,000 (item 5). This is referred to as a reduction factor. In this case, the moment of 12.6 actually represents a moment of 12,600 pound-inches.

the pilot and front seat passenger have a combined weight of 340 pounds. [Figure 5-43]

Reduction factors are commonly used to reduce the size of large numbers to manageable levels. In most cases, you need not be concerned with a reduction factor. This is because the CG moment envelope chart normally uses the same reduction factor. [Figure 5-44]

SAMPLE LOADING PROBLEM	SAMPLE AIRPLANE		YOUR AIRPLANE	
	Weight (lbs.)	Moment (lb.-ins. /1000)	Weight (lbs.)	Moment (lb.-ins. /1000)
1. Basic Empty Weight..............................	1467	57.3	1,522	56.2
2. Usable Fuel (At 6 Lbs./Gal.) Standard Tanks (40 Gal. Maximum).................	240	11.5	240	11.5
3. Pilot and Front Passenger (Station 34 to 46)......................................	340	12.6	340	12.6
4. Rear Passengers....................................	340	24.8		
5. *Baggage Area 1 or Passenger on Child's Seat (Station 82 to 108, 120 Lbs. Max).....................	20	1.9		
6. *Baggage Area 2 (Station 108 to 142, 50 Lbs. Max.).....................				
7. RAMP WEIGHT AND MOMENT	2407	108.1	2,102	80.3
8. Fuel allowance for engine start, taxi, and runup	-7	-.3	-7	-.3
9. TAKEOFF WEIGHT AND MOMENT (Subtract Step 8 from Step 7)	2400	107.8	2,095	80.0

Figure 5-44. After recording the basic empty weight and moment of the airplane, and the weight and moment for each item, total and record all weights and moments. Notice that you apply a weight and moment credit for fuel used during engine start, taxi, and runup. Next, plot the listed takeoff weight and moment on the sample moment envelope graph. Based on a weight of 2,095 pounds and a moment/1,000 of 80 pound-inches, the airplane is properly loaded for flight in the utility category.

	FRONT SEATS			3RD AND 4TH SEATS	
	FWD POS.		AFT POS.	BENCH SEAT	SPLIT SEAT
	ARM 104	ARM 105	ARM 112	ARM 142	ARM 144
WEIGHT	MOM/100	MOM/100	MOM/100	MOM/100	MOM/100
120	125	126	134	170	173
130	135	137	146	185	187
140	146	147	157	199	202
150	156	158	168	213	216
160	166	168	179	227	230
170	177	179	190	241	245
180	187	189	202	256	259
190	198	200	213	270	274
200	208	210	224	284	288

Figure 5-45. Note that this table uses a reduction factor of 100 and the highest weight given is 200 pounds. To determine the moment/100 for 340 pounds, look up the moments for 200 pounds and 140 pounds (200 lb. + 140 lb. = 340 lb.). In this case, the moment/100 is 483 pound-inches (284 lb.-in. + 199 lb.-in.).

TABLE METHOD

The table method is a further refinement of the computational and graph methods. Using this method, you locate a given weight on the appropriate table, then look up its corresponding moment. Often, however, the exact weight you are looking for is not found on the table. In these situations, look up two smaller weights which add up to the total weight you want, and add their corresponding moments. Assume you need to determine the moment for the third and fourth seat occupants whose combined weight is 340 pounds. Also, assume this airplane has a bench seat. [Figure 5-45]

After the weight and balance worksheet is complete, you must check to see if the airplane is loaded within acceptable limits for flight. You have already seen one method of doing this — consulting a center of gravity moment envelope. Another method is to check a "moment limit versus weight table" provided by some manufacturers. To use this table, first find the loaded weight of the airplane. Then, check to see if the loaded moment falls within the minimum and maximum values given for that weight. [Figure 5-46]

WEIGHT SHIFT

Often during weight and balance computations, you will find that either the weight of the airplane or its CG location is beyond acceptable limits.

ITEM		WEIGHT	MOM/100
1.	BASIC EMPTY CONDITION	1,728	1,912
2.	FRONT SEAT OCCUPANTS	340	357
3.	3rd & 4th SEAT OCCUPANTS	340	483
4.	5th & 6th SEAT OCCUPANTS		
5.	BAGGAGE	100	167
6.	CARGO		
7.	**SUB TOTAL**	2,508	2,919
8.	FUEL LOADING (40 gal.)	240	281
9.	**SUB TOTAL** RAMP CONDITION	2,748	3,200
10.	*LESS FUEL FOR START, TAXI AND TAKE-OFF	-8	-9
11.	**SUB TOTAL** TAKE-OFF CONDITION	2,740	3,191
12.	LESS FUEL TO DESTINATION	162	189
13.	**LANDING CONDITION**	2,578	3,002

*Fuel for start, taxi and take-off is normally 8 lbs at an average mom/100 of 9.

MOMENT LIMITS vs WEIGHT

Weight	Minimum Moment 100	Maximum Moment 100
2500	2775	2958
2510	2788	2969
2520	2801	2981
2530	2814	2993
2540	2828	3005
2550	2841	3017
2560	2854	3028
2570	2867	3040
2580	2880	3052
2590	2894	3064
2600	2907	3076
2610	2920	3088
2620	2933	3099
2630	2947	3111
2640	2960	3123
2650	2973	3135
2660	2987	3147
2670	3000	3159
2680	3013	3170
2690	3027	3182
2700	3040	3194
2710	3054	3206
2720	3067	3218
2730	3081	3230
2740	3094	3241
2750	3108	3253

Figure 5-46. On the left is a completed weight and balance worksheet using given values for a sample flight. Note the takeoff weight of 2,740 pounds and moment/100 of 3,191 pound-inches. Using the table on the right, for a weight of 2,740 pounds, the minimum acceptable moment/100 is 3,094 pound-inches and the maximum is 3,241 pound-inches. Since our moment is well within these limits, the airplane is safely loaded for flight.

Usually, decreasing weight is a fairly simple matter, especially if you accomplish it before the airplane's CG is calculated. However, if you change the load in order to adjust the CG, the computations are somewhat more complex. [Figure 5-47]

Weight Shift Formula

$$\frac{\text{Weight of Cargo Moved}}{\text{Weight of Airplane}} = \frac{\text{Distance CG Moves}}{\text{Distance Between Arm Locations}}$$

Figure 5-47. Use this formula to determine changes in CG when weight must be shifted. An easy way to remember this formula is to note that the small values are on top of the formula and the large values are on the bottom.

Figure 5-48. As shown in this illustration, the first step is to determine the known values. For example, the distance between cargo areas "A" and "B" is 29 inches. Next, insert the other known values into the formula and solve for the unknown. In this case, the unknown value is the distance the CG moves forward when the weight is shifted. Solving this equation results in the answer of 1.1 inches.

Perhaps the easiest way to see how to apply this formula is to work two different weight shift problems. In the first, assume a loaded airplane weight of 3,200 pounds and a CG of 45.6 inches. A box weighing 120 pounds is moved from cargo area "B" which has an arm of 99 inches, to cargo area "A," whose arm is 70 inches. How many inches will the CG move when this weight is shifted? [Figure 5-48]

For the next example, assume the CG is located aft of acceptable limits and you need to determine the amount of weight to be shifted from the aft cargo area to the forward one. Again, the same formula is used; the only difference is which value is unknown. [Figure 5-49]

Figure 5-49. As with the previous problem, insert the known values into the formula. In this case, you are solving for the weight of the cargo to be moved. Solving this equation results in an answer of 99.4 pounds.

CHECKLIST _____

After studying this section, you should have a basic understanding of:

✓　**Airplane weight** — What terms are used to describe various weights and what the hazards of overloading an airplane are.

✓　**Empty weight** — What the difference is between basic empty weight and licensed empty weight.

✓　**Airplane balance** — What the terms arm, moment, and CG mean; how they are determined; and what the effects of operating an airplane outside prescribed CG limits are.

✓　**Determining weight and balance** — How the weight and balance condition of an airplane can be determined and what three methods are used.

✓　**Weight shift** — What the weight shift formula is and how to use it.

flight prep 6

BASIC WEATHER THEORY

Weather conditions take on new meaning when you soar above the earth. There's more at stake now than deciding whether to take your umbrella. When you fly, you are literally inside the environment that ruled you on the ground. You move with it in much the same way that a balloon does as it drifts through the air. To fully appreciate weather, you will need to evaluate day-to-day elements like clouds, wind, and rain, so you can determine their impact on your flying. This isn't a difficult task if you start with a solid understanding of weather and its causes. This section provides a basic framework for that understanding.

THE ATMOSPHERE

The earth's atmosphere is a mixture of gases that is in constant motion. If you could see it, it might look like the ocean, with swirls, eddies, rising and falling air, and waves that travel for great distances.

COMPOSITION OF THE ATMOSPHERE

Water is constantly being absorbed and released in the atmosphere. This action is responsible for major changes in the weather.

If you could capture a cubic foot of typical atmosphere and analyze it, you would find it is composed of about 78% nitrogen and 21% oxygen. The remaining 1% is made up of several other gases, primarily argon and carbon dioxide. This cubic foot of atmosphere also contains some water vapor, but the amount can vary from almost zero to about five percent by volume. This relatively small amount of water vapor is responsible for major changes in the weather. [Figure 6-1]

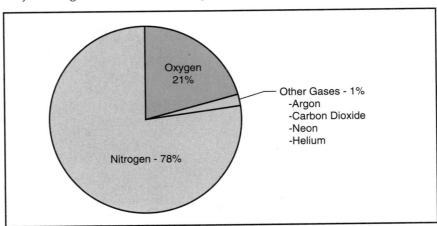

Figure 6-1. The atmosphere is a mixture of gases that exists in fairly uniform proportions up to approximately 30 miles above the earth.

ATMOSPHERIC LEVELS

The atmosphere is divided into layers, or spheres, according to the characteristics of each layer. The **troposphere** is the one closest to the earth, extending from the surface to an average altitude of about six or seven miles.

The **tropopause** is a thin layer of the atmosphere at the top of the troposphere. It acts as a lid to confine most of the water vapor. This, in turn, keeps most of the weather below the tropopause.

Above the tropopause are three more atmospheric layers. The first is the **stratosphere**, which extends to a height of approximately 19 to 22 miles. It has much the same composition as the troposphere and is important to you because certain types of clouds occasionally extend into it. Above the stratosphere are the **mesosphere** and the **thermosphere**, which have little practical influence over weather. [Figure 6-2]

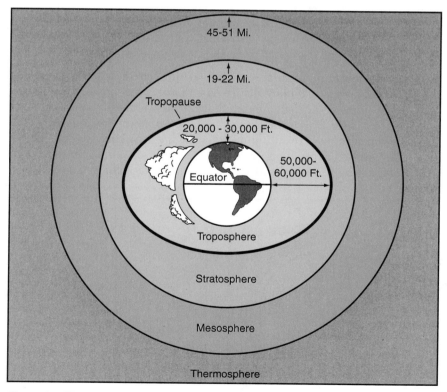

Figure 6-2. The height of the troposphere varies. It slopes upward from about 20,000 feet at the poles to 60,000 feet at the equator. It is also higher in the summer than it is in the winter. Of the various atmospheric layers, the troposphere has the greatest impact on weather.

ATMOSPHERIC CIRCULATION

Now that you've looked at the basic features of the atmosphere, let's consider the factors that set it in motion. This information will provide you with an understanding of the phenomenon we call wind, including the reasons for its speed and direction.

CONVECTION

Uneven heating of the earth's surface causes variations in air temperature and density.

The uneven heating of the earth's surface is the major force that sets the atmosphere in motion. This movement is generally referred to as **circulation**. It occurs through a process known as **convection**, which is defined as the circulating motion that results when warm air rises and is replaced by cooler air.

To understand the convection process, it helps to know what happens to air when it warms up and cools off. When air is heated, its molecules spread apart. As the air expands, it becomes less dense and lighter than the surrounding air. As air cools, the molecules become packed more closely together, making it denser and heavier than warm air. As a result, the cool, heavy air tends to sink and replace warmer, rising air. You may have noticed the effect of this convection process when you've felt a cold draft along the floor, or encountered warmer air near the ceiling while working on a ladder.

Although atmospheric circulation is the result of several factors, it will be easier to understand if we initially assume that it is caused only by convection. In this convection-only model, the earth is warmed by energy radiating from the sun. This solar energy strikes equatorial regions in much greater concentrations, resulting in much higher temperatures than at the poles. As a result, cold, dense air from the poles sinks and flows toward the equator, where it displaces rising air that is warmer and less dense. [Figure 6-3]

Figure 6-3. If the earth did not rotate, a huge **convective** circulation pattern would develop as air flowed from the poles to the equator and back again.

ATMOSPHERIC PRESSURE

As we have seen, the unequal heating of the surface modifies air density and creates circulation patterns. It also causes changes in pressure. This is one of the main reasons for differences in altimeter settings between weather reporting stations. Meteorologists plot these pressure readings on weather maps and connect points of equal pressure with lines called **isobars**. Isobars are measured in millibars and are usually drawn at four-millibar intervals. The resulting pattern reveals the **pressure gradient**, or change in pressure over distance. When isobars are spread widely apart, the gradient is considered to be weak, while closely spaced isobars indicate a strong gradient. Isobars also help to identify pressure systems, which are classified as highs, lows, ridges, troughs, and cols. A **high** is a center of high pressure surrounded on all sides by lower pressure. Conversely, a **low** is an area of low pressure surrounded by higher pressure. A **ridge** is an elongated area of high pressure, while a **trough** is an elongated area of low pressure. A **col** can designate either a neutral area between two highs and two lows, or the intersection of a ridge and a trough. [Figure 6-4]

Air flows from the cool, dense air of highs into the warm, less dense air of lows. The speed of the resulting wind depends on the strength of the pressure gradient. A strong gradient tends to produce strong wind, while a weak gradient results in lighter winds. The force behind this movement is caused by the pressure gradient and is referred to as **pressure gradient force**.

Variations in altimeter settings between weather reporting points are primarily caused by the unequal heating of the earth's surface.

Figure 6-4. High pressure systems generally provide favorable flying weather, with good visibility, calm or light winds, and few clouds. Ridges also normally present good weather. In the area of a low, on the other hand, you can anticipate generally poor weather with possible low clouds, poor visibility, precipitation, gusty winds, and turbulence. Weather may be very violent in the area of a trough.

CORIOLIS FORCE

If the earth did not rotate, pressure gradient force would propel wind directly from highs to lows. Instead, the earth's rotation introduces another force, called Coriolis, that affects air circulation.

Coriolis is a deflective force that is created by the difference in rotational velocity between the equator and the poles. To complete one revolution, a point on the equator must travel faster than a point near the poles. In fact, the velocity of the earth's surface varies from about 900 knots at the equator to zero at the poles. As long as air remains stationary over one position on the surface of the earth, gravity tends to hold it in place. However, once air begins to migrate in its normal circulation patterns, it moves into areas of different surface velocity. Coriolis force deflects this air to the right in the northern hemisphere and to the left in the southern hemisphere. This principle can be shown using the turntable of a record player. [Figure 6-5]

Now let's apply this principle to the rotating earth, concentrating on the northern hemisphere. As the earth rotates from west to east, air migrating toward the north passes over surface areas that are moving slower than the source region. Similarly, air moving toward the south passes over surface areas that are moving faster. [Figure 6-6]

Apparent Path
Path Drawn on Turntable

Figure 6-5. The rotating turntable causes the same type of deflection as the earth's rotation. You can demonstrate this phenomenon by using a piece of chalk and a ruler. First, visualize the nearly stationary center of the turntable as the north pole, and the fast-moving outer edge as the equator. Next, draw a straight line from the center of the rotating turntable to the outer edge. When you stop the turntable you will see that your "straight" line is really curved.

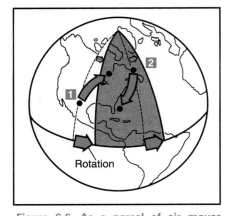

Rotation

Figure 6-6. As a parcel of air moves northward (item 1), the surface speed of the earth below it is progressively slower. Because of this, the movement of air seems to be directed to the east. When air moves south (item 2), it passes over a faster-moving surface and is deflected westward. No matter which direction air moves, Coriolis force always deflects it to the right in the northern hemisphere and to the left in the southern hemisphere.

The amount of deflection produced by Coriolis force varies with latitude. It is zero at the equator and increases toward the poles. It also is proportional to the speed of the airmass. The faster the air moves, the greater the deflection.

WIND

Pressure gradient and Coriolis forces work in combination to create wind. Pressure gradient force causes air to move from high pressure areas to low pressure areas. As the air begins to move, Coriolis force deflects it to the right in the northern hemisphere. This results in a clockwise flow around the high. The deflection continues until pressure gradient force and Coriolis force are in balance, and the wind flows roughly parallel to the isobars. As the air flows into the low pressure area, it moves counterclockwise around the low. The speed of the resulting wind is proportional to the pressure change — the stronger the pressure gradient, the stronger the wind.

Winds in the northern hemisphere flow clockwise around highs and counterclockwise around lows.

Within about 2,000 feet of the ground, friction caused by the earth's surface slows the moving air. This diverts the wind from its path along the isobars. [Figure 6-7]

Friction causes a wind shift near the earth's surface.

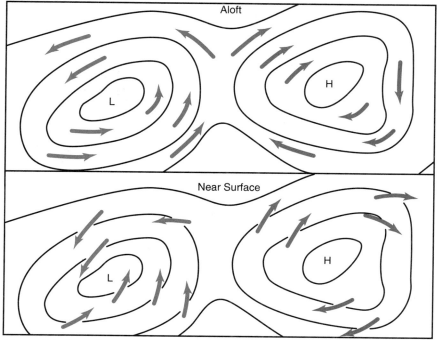

Figure 6-7. As surface friction retards the airflow, Coriolis force is weakened. This allows pressure gradient force to shift the airflow toward areas of lower pressure, causing the wind to blow at an angle across the isobars.

GLOBAL WIND PATTERNS

When Coriolis force is applied to the global circulation pattern, the simple, convection-only model is modified. As tropical air rises and flows northward, it is deflected to the right by Coriolis. Around 30° north, the flow is eastward, causing air to pile up at this latitude. This creates a semipermanent high pressure area. At the surface, air flows back toward the equator. This low-level southerly flow is deflected to the right again and creates the northeast trade winds common to areas like the Caribbean. [Figure 6-8]

The low-level air flowing northward from the high pressure at 30° also is deflected to the right by Coriolis. This creates the prevailing westerlies common to the mid section of North America.

The cold polar air that flows southward is deflected to the right to create the polar easterlies. As this cold air meets the relatively warmer air from the prevailing westerlies, a semipermanent low pressure area is formed around 60° north latitude. The line separating the airmasses in this region is called the polar front.

LOCAL WIND PATTERNS

Our discussion so far has centered on the circulation of winds on a global scale. Of greater practical importance to you as a pilot are the winds in the area where you will be flying. These localized wind patterns are caused by

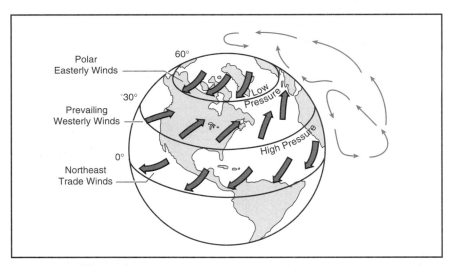

Figure 6-8. In the northern hemisphere, Coriolis force produces a three-cell circulation pattern around a semipermanent high pressure area at 30° north latitude and a semipermanent low pressure area near 60° north latitude. The deflection of air within each cell creates prevailing surface wind patterns.

terrain variations such as mountains, valleys, and water. The force behind these winds — cool air replacing warm air — is the same as it is for global wind patterns, but on a much smaller scale.

SEA AND LAND BREEZES

If you have ever wondered why waves striking a beach increase in size throughout the day, the sea breeze provides the answer. Land surfaces warm or cool more rapidly than water surfaces; therefore, land is warmer than water during the day. This creates the **sea breeze**, a wind that blows from the cool water to the warmer land. As afternoon heating increases, so does the sea breeze. At night, land cools faster than water, and a **land breeze** blows from the cooler land to the warmer water.

VALLEY AND MOUNTAIN WINDS

Local wind patterns also develop near hilly or mountainous terrain. In the daytime, as mountain slopes are warmed by the sun, air adjacent to them also is heated. A **valley wind** is created as the cooler air over the valley sinks and air close to the mountain flows upward. At night, the surface of the slope cools rapidly, lowering the temperature of the air close to the surface. The cooler air flows down the slope and displaces the air in the valley. This is called a **mountain wind**.

KATABATIC WINDS

A katabatic wind is the name given to any wind blowing down an incline. As you can see from the preceding discussion, a mountain wind is one type of katabatic wind. Depending upon local conditions, katabatic winds may have a dramatic effect on temperature. They occur when cold, dense air spills over a mountain and flows down the slope, displacing the air ahead of it. If this continues over sufficient altitude, the descending air is warmed by compression until it is warmer than the air it is displacing. A warm descending wind is called a **foehn wind**, but may also be referred to locally by other names, such as the **Santa Ana** in California and the **chinook** in the Rockies.

Occasionally, a descending airmass will be so cold that, even though it is warmed during the descent, it is still colder than the air it displaces. This is known as a **fall**, or **gravity**, **wind**.

MOISTURE

Weather is very dependent upon the moisture content of the air. If the air is dry, the weather usually will be good. If the air is very moist, poor or even severe weather can occur. This section looks at the basic properties and characteristics of moisture, and provides you with information that is important in the safe operation of your aircraft.

CHANGE OF STATE

Every physical process of weather is accompanied by a heat exchange.

Water is present in the atmosphere in three states: solid, liquid, and gas. All three states are found within the temperature ranges normally encountered in the atmosphere, and the change from one to another happens readily. Changes in state occur through the processes of evaporation, condensation, sublimation, melting, and freezing. As water changes from one physical state to another, an exchange of heat takes place.

Water vapor is added to the atmosphere by evaporation and sublimation.

Evaporation is the changing of liquid water to invisible water vapor. As water vapor forms, heat is absorbed from the nearest available source. For example, as perspiration evaporates from your body, you feel cooler because some of your body heat has been absorbed by the water vapor. This heat exchange is known as the **latent heat of evaporation**. The reverse of evaporation is **condensation**. It occurs when water vapor changes to a liquid, as when water drops form on a cool glass on a warm day. When condensation takes place, the heat absorbed by water vapor during evaporation is released. The heat released is referred to as the **latent heat of condensation**. It is an important factor in cloud development.

Sublimation is the changing of ice directly to water vapor, or of water vapor to ice. In sublimation, the liquid state is bypassed. Melting and freezing are well known to you. **Melting** is the change of ice to water. **Freezing** is the reverse process. The heat exchange in each of these processes is small and has relatively little effect on weather.

HUMIDITY

The amount of moisture in the air depends on air temperature. Dewpoint is the temperature at which air becomes saturated.

Since the amount of water vapor in the air is of such importance, scientists have developed several ways to measure and describe it. **Humidity** simply refers to moisture in the air; for example, on warm, muggy days when you perspire freely, the air is said to be humid. **Relative humidity** is the actual amount of moisture in the air compared to the total amount that could be present at that temperature. **Dewpoint** is the temperature at which air reaches a state where it can hold no more water. When the dewpoint is reached, the air contains 100% of the moisture it can hold at that temperature, and it is said to be **saturated**. Note that each of these terms relates moisture to temperature, two inseparable features of our weather. [Figure 6-9]

VISIBLE MOISTURE

Clouds, fog, or dew always form when water vapor condenses.

As air cools to its saturation point, the processes of condensation and sublimation change invisible water vapor into states that are readily seen. Most commonly, this visible moisture takes the form of clouds or fog. [Figure 6-10]

Figure 6-9. Three parcels of air can be used to show the relationship between relative humidity, temperature, and dewpoint. The parcel of air on the left at 55°F (13°C) contains only half the water vapor it could hold, so its relative humidity is 50%. If the temperature of the same parcel drops to 44°F (7°C), it can hold less water vapor than at 55°F, increasing its relative humidity to 75%. The parcel on the right shows the air at 37°F (3°C) to be completely saturated with a relative humidity of 100%.

Figure 6-10. Air can be cooled by lifting it, by moving it over a cooler surface, or by cooling the underlying surface. Depending upon the temperature of the air, water vapor may condense into visible water droplets or sublimate into snow.

CLOUDS AND FOG

A small and decreasing temperature/dewpoint spread indicates conditions are favorable for the formation of fog.

Clouds are one of the most fascinating forms of visible moisture. They are composed of very small droplets of water or, if temperature is low enough, ice crystals. The droplets condense or sublimate on very small particles of solid matter in the air. These particles, called **condensation nuclei**, can be dust, salt from evaporating sea spray, or products of combustion. When clouds form near the surface, they are referred to as fog.

Clouds and fog usually form as soon as the air becomes saturated. You can anticipate the formation of fog or very low clouds by monitoring the difference between surface temperature and dewpoint, usually referred to as the **temperature/dewpoint spread**. When the spread reaches 4°F (2°C) and continues to decrease, the air is nearing the saturation point and the probability of fog and low clouds forming increases.

PRECIPITATION

Drizzle, rain, snow, hail, ice pellets, and ice crystals are all forms of **precipitation**. They occur when the particles of moisture in a cloud grow to a size where the atmosphere can no longer support their weight and they fall from the atmosphere.

Ice pellets at the surface are an indication of a temperature inversion and freezing rain at a higher altitude.

Water droplets that remain liquid fall as drizzle or rain. Precipitation that forms by sublimation falls as snow, provided the temperature of the air remains below freezing. As precipitation falls, it may change its state due to the temperature it encounters. For example, falling snow may melt to form rain. Rain that remains liquid even though its temperature is below freezing is considered to be **supercooled**, and is referred to as **freezing rain**. When a temperature inversion exists, rain falls through warm air aloft and freezes as it passes through colder air, striking the ground as **ice pellets**. In clouds with strong upward currents and cold temperatures, water droplets may freeze. As they rise and fall, they increase in size from collisions with other freezing water droplets. Eventually they become too large for air currents to support, and they fall as **hail**.

DEW AND FROST

Frost forms on aircraft surfaces when the surface temperature is at or below the dewpoint of the surrounding air and the dewpoint is below freezing.

On cool, still nights, surface features and objects may cool to a temperature below the dewpoint of the surrounding air. Moisture then condenses out of the air in the form of dew, which explains why grass is often moist in the early morning. If the temperature of the surrounding air is below freezing, moisture sublimates out of the air and forms frost. From late fall through early spring, you may frequently encounter frost on your airplane on early morning flights.

CHECKLIST

After studying this section, you should have a basic understanding of:

✓ **Characteristics of the atmosphere** — What its composition is and the names and features of its layers.

✓ **Hemispherical convection currents** — What causes convection currents and how they affect global circulation.

✓ **Atmospheric pressure** — What atmospheric pressure is, why it varies from one location to another, and how it affects wind.

✓ **Coriolis force** — What it is and how it affects wind direction.

✓ **Local wind patterns** — What causes them and how they influence local weather.

✓ **Moisture in the atmosphere** — How it is measured, under what conditions moisture in the atmosphere will increase, and how it affects weather.

✓ **Change of state** — What the physical states of moisture are in the atmosphere and the processes involved in change of state.

✓ **Clouds and fog** — How clouds and fog are formed, what their relationship is to condensation nuclei, and how temperature/dewpoint spread can be used to predict cloud formation.

✓ **Dew and frost** — What conditions are favorable for the formation of dew and frost. At what time of day their formation would usually occur.

WEATHER PATTERNS

In the previous section, we looked at the basic weather principles and the influence of temperature, pressure, and moisture. This section begins with a discussion of how these conditions combine to cause stable or unstable weather. It then examines the cause, development, and interaction of large airmasses. As we proceed, you will begin to broaden your view of what is happening in the atmosphere, based on your own observations and those you receive from a weather briefer.

ATMOSPHERIC STABILITY

In order to have a good understanding of weather, you must have a thorough knowledge of atmospheric stability. If you understand stability, including the properties of stable and unstable air, you will be much better prepared to evaluate weather conditions and to make intelligent decisions about the operation of your airplane.

Stability is the atmosphere's resistance to vertical motion. Put another way, the stability of air determines whether it will rise or descend in relation to the air around it. This is very important, because stable air resists vertical motion and tends to inhibit cloud formation, precipitation, and severe weather. Unstable air has a tendency to move vertically. This can lead to significant cloud development, turbulence, and hazardous weather. To determine whether a parcel of air is stable or unstable, you need to know about its temperature and moisture content.

TEMPERATURE AND MOISTURE

Stability of an airmass is decreased by warming from below.

A major factor affecting the stability of air is its temperature. As we learned in Section A, the uneven heating of the earth's surface creates variations in the density of the overlying air. These variations produce convective currents in which warm air rises and is replaced by cooler, denser air. Stability of the air is decreased by heating from below, which causes the air to rise. Moisture is another factor affecting stability. Water vapor is lighter than air. Therefore, as moisture is added to air, its density decreases and it tends to rise. Conversely, as moisture decreases, air becomes denser and it tends to sink. [Figure 6-11]

The combined effects of temperature and moisture determine the stability of the air and, to a large extent, the type of weather produced. You can see that the greatest instability occurs when the air is both warm and moist. Tropical weather, with its almost daily thunderstorm activity, is a perfect example of weather that occurs in very unstable air. Air that is both cool and dry resists vertical movement and is very stable. A good example of

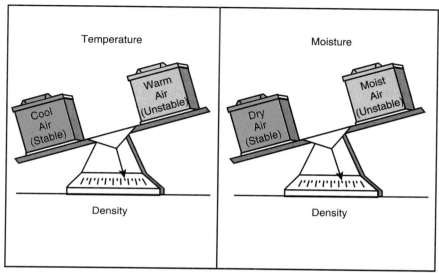

Figure 6-11. The stability of a parcel of air is determined by its density. Air that is warm or moist is unstable; air that is cool or dry is stable.

this can be found in arctic regions in winter, where stable conditions often result in very cold, generally clear weather. Now that you understand why air rises and falls, let's see what takes place within a parcel of ascending or descending air.

RISING AND DESCENDING AIR

Air that moves upward expands due to lower atmospheric pressure. When air moves downward, it is compressed by the increased pressure at lower altitudes. As the pressure of a given portion of air changes, so does its temperature. The temperature change is caused by a process known as **adiabatic heating** or **cooling,** which is a change in the temperature during expansion or compression when no heat is added to or removed from the air.

The adiabatic process takes place in all upward and downward moving air. When air rises into an area of lower pressure, it expands to a larger volume. As the molecules of air expand, the temperature of the air lowers. As a result, when a parcel of air rises, pressure decreases, volume increases, and temperature decreases. When air descends, the opposite is true.

The rate at which temperature decreases with an increase in altitude is referred to as its **lapse rate.** As you ascend through the atmosphere, the average rate of temperature change is 2°C (3.5°F) per 1,000 feet. The adiabatic lapse rate of a parcel of air that is lifted depends on the amount of

You can use the actual lapse rate to determine the stability of the atmosphere.

moisture present in the air. The dry adiabatic lapse rate (unsaturated air) is 3°C (5.4°F) per 1,000 feet. The moist adiabatic lapse rate varies from 1.1°C to 2.8°C (2°F to 5°F) per 1,000 feet. However, it is always less than the rate for dry air.

When you compare the adiabatic lapse rates, you can see that they can be used to indicate the stability of the air. For example, moist air is less stable than dry air, because it cools at a slower rate. This means that moist air must rise higher before its temperature cools to that of the air around it.

When warm, moist air begins to rise in a convective current, cumulus clouds often form at the altitude where its temperature and dewpoint reach the same value. When lifted, unsaturated air cools at about 5.4°F per 1,000 feet, and the dewpoint temperature decreases at about 1°F. Therefore, the temperature and dewpoint converge at about 4.5°F per 1,000 feet.

The lapse rate and the temperature/dewpoint spread can be used to calculate cloud bases.

You can use these values to estimate cloud bases. For example, if the surface temperature is 80°F and the surface dewpoint is 62°F, the spread is 18°F. This difference, divided by the rate that the temperature approaches the dewpoint (4.5°F), will help you judge the approximate height of the base of the clouds in thousands of feet (18 ÷ 4.5 = 4 or 4,000 feet AGL).

TEMPERATURE INVERSIONS

A stable layer of air and a temperature increase with altitude are features of a temperature inversion.

Although temperature usually decreases with an increase in altitude, the reverse is sometimes true. When temperature increases with altitude, a **temperature inversion** exists. Inversions are usually confined to fairly shallow layers and may occur near the surface or at higher altitudes. They act as a lid for weather and pollutants. Visibility is often restricted by fog, haze, smoke, and low clouds. Temperature inversions occur in stable air with little or no wind and turbulence.

A surface-based temperature inversion is often produced by terrestrial radiation on clear, cool nights when the air is relatively calm.

One of the most familiar types of inversion is the one that forms near the ground on cool, clear nights when the wind is calm. As the ground cools, it lowers the temperature of the adjacent air. If this process of terrestrial radiation continues, the air within a few hundred feet of the surface may become cooler than the air above it. An inversion can also occur when cool air is forced under warm air, or when warm air spreads over cold. Both of these are called frontal inversions.

OBSERVING STABLE AND UNSTABLE AIR

Moist, unstable air causes the formation of cumuliform clouds and showers.

With a little practice, you can easily tell the difference between areas of stable and unstable air. By observing features such as cloud types, precipitation, and visibility, you should be able to distinguish between stable and unstable air and predict other weather conditions, such as turbulence and icing. Turbulence and aircraft icing will be discussed in detail in the next section. [Figure 6-12]

CLOUDS

Clouds are your weather signposts in the sky. They provide a visible indication of the processes occurring in the atmosphere. To the astute observer, they give valuable information about current and future conditions. Your understanding of how weather affects your flight will be greatly improved if you are able to read and interpret these signposts.

TYPES OF CLOUDS

Clouds are visible moisture that has condensed or sublimated onto condensation nuclei such as dust, salt, or combustion particles. Individual condensation nuclei are extremely small, as are the water or ice particles that adhere to them. Before precipitation can occur, these particles must grow in size. They do this by constantly colliding and merging with other particles, a process most apparent in the strong updrafts of cumulus

CHARACTERISTICS OF STABLE AND UNSTABLE AIR		
	Stable Air	**Unstable Air**
Clouds	Wide areas of layered clouds or fog; gray at low altitude, thin white at high altitude	Extensive vertical development; bright white to black; billowy
Precipitation	Small droplets in fog and low-level clouds; large droplets in thick stratified clouds; widespread and lengthy periods of rain or snow	Large drops in heavy rain showers; showers usually brief; hail possible
Visibility	Restricted for long periods	Poor in showers or thundershowers, good otherwise
Turbulence	Usually light or nonexistent	Moderate to heavy
Icing	Moderate in mid-altitudes; freezing rain, rime, or clear ice	Moderate to heavy clear ice
Other	Frost, dew, temperature inversions	High or gusty surface winds, lightning, tornadoes

Figure 6-12. Stable air is generally smooth, with layered or stratiform clouds. Visibility is usually restricted, with widespread areas of clouds and steady rain or drizzle. Unstable air is usually bumpy, with good surface visibility outside of scattered rain showers.

Family	Altitude (Middle Latitude)	Cloud Type
Low	Bases range from the surface to 6,500 ft. AGL	Cumulus Stratocumulus Stratus
Middle	Bases range from 6,500 ft. AGL to 23,000 ft. AGL	Altocumulus Altostratus Nimbostratus
High	Bases usually range from 16,500 ft. AGL to 45,000 ft. AGL	Cirrus Cirrocumulus Cirrostratus
Clouds with Extensive Vertical Development	Bases range from 1,000 ft. AGL or less to 10,000 ft. AGL or more; tops sometimes exceed 60,000 ft. MSL	Towering Cumulus Cumulonimbus

Figure 6-13. Cumulus clouds form in unstable air, while stratus clouds form in stable air. The term "nimbus" describes clouds that produce rain.

clouds. Clouds are divided into four basic groups, depending upon their characteristics and the altitudes where they occur. [Figure 6-13]

LOW CLOUDS

Low clouds extend from near the surface to about 6,500 feet AGL. A surface-based cloud most people are familiar with is **fog**. Low clouds usually consist almost entirely of water but sometimes may contain supercooled water which can create an icing hazard for aircraft.

Stratus clouds form when moist, stable air flows upslope.

Stratus clouds are layered clouds that form in stable air near the surface due to cooling from below. Although turbulence in these clouds is low, they usually restrict visual flying due to low ceilings and visibility. Icing conditions are possible if temperatures are at or near freezing. Stratus clouds may form when moist stable air is lifted up sloping terrain, or when warm rain evaporates as it falls through cool air. [Figure 6-14]

Stratocumulus clouds are white, puffy clouds that form as stable air is lifted. They often form as a stratus layer breaks up or as cumulus clouds spread out. [Figure 6-15]

Cumulus clouds form in convective currents resulting from the heating of the earth's surface. They usually have flat bottoms and dome-shaped tops. Widely spaced cumulus clouds that form in fairly clear skies are called fair weather cumulus and indicate a shallow layer of instability. You can expect turbulence, but little icing and precipitation.

Figure 6-14. Stratus clouds have a gray, uniform appearance and generally cover a wide area.

Figure 6-15. These are mainly stratocumulus clouds. A few cumulus clouds indicate an area with slightly more convective currents than the surrounding areas.

MIDDLE CLOUDS

Middle clouds have bases that range from about 6,500 to 23,000 feet AGL. They are composed of water, ice crystals, or supercooled water. They may contain moderate turbulence and potentially severe icing.

Altostratus clouds are flat, dense clouds that cover a wide area. They are a uniform gray or gray-white in color. Although they produce minimal turbulence, they may contain moderate icing. **Altocumulus clouds** are gray or white, patchy clouds of uniform appearance that often form when altostratus clouds start to break up. They may produce light turbulence and icing. [Figure 6-16]

Nimbostratus clouds are gray or black clouds that can be more than several thousand feet thick and contain large quantities of moisture. If temperatures are near or below freezing, they may create heavy icing. [Figure 6-17]

HIGH CLOUDS

These clouds have bases that range from about 16,500 to 45,000 feet AGL. They are generally white to light gray in color and form in stable air. They

Figure 6-16. Altocumulus clouds extend over a wide area and may contain highly supercooled water droplets.

Figure 6-17. Nimbostratus clouds produce widespread areas of rain or snow. Although they are classified as middle clouds, they may merge into low stratus or stratocumulus.

are composed mainly of ice crystals and seldom pose a serious turbulence or icing hazard.

Cirrus clouds are thin, wispy clouds that usually form above 30,000 feet. White or light gray in color, they often exist in patches or narrow bands that cross the sky. They are sometimes blown from the tops of thunderstorms or towering cumulus clouds. [Figure 6-18]

Cirrostratus clouds also are thin, white clouds that often form in long bands or sheets against a deep blue background. Although they may be several thousand feet thick, moisture content is low and they pose no icing hazard. In contrast, **cirrocumulus clouds** are white patchy clouds that look like cotton. They form as a result of shallow convective currents at high altitude and may produce light turbulence.

CLOUDS WITH EXTENSIVE VERTICAL DEVELOPMENT

The bases of vertically developed clouds are found in altitudes associated with low to middle clouds, and their tops extend into the altitudes associated with high clouds. Frequently, these cloud types are obscured by other cloud formations. When this happens, they are said to be **embedded**.

Vertical cloud development and turbulence result from the lifting of unstable air.

Towering cumulus clouds are similar to cumulus clouds, except they have more vertical development. They look like large mounds of cotton with billowing cauliflower tops. Their color may vary from brilliant white at the top

Figure 6-18. Cirrus clouds form in stable air at high altitudes. In some cases, they are an advance warning of approaching bad weather.

to gray near the bottom. Towering cumulus clouds indicate a fairly deep layer of unstable air. They contain moderate to heavy turbulence with icing and often develop into thunderstorms. [Figure 6-19]

Cumulonimbus clouds, which are more commonly called thunderstorms, are large, vertically developed clouds that form in very unstable air. They are gray-white to black in color and contain large amounts of moisture. Many flying hazards are linked with cumulonimbus clouds. These hazards are discussed in Section C.

Cumulonimbus clouds form when moist, unstable air is lifted.

AIRMASSES

Now that you have a good understanding of atmospheric stability and the types of clouds that are produced, let's look at airmasses and the way they influence weather. An **airmass** is a large body of air with fairly uniform temperature and moisture content. It may be several hundred miles across and usually forms where air remains stationary or nearly stationary for at least several days. During this time, the airmass takes on the temperature and moisture properties of the underlying surface.

SOURCE REGIONS

The area where an airmass acquires the properties of temperature and moisture that determine its stability is called its **source region**. An ideal source region is a large area with fairly uniform geography and temperature. A source region is usually located where air tends to stagnate. The best areas for airmass development are in the regions where atmospheric circulation has caused the buildup of semipermanent areas of high pressure. Some excellent areas are snow and ice covered polar regions, tropical oceans, and large deserts. The middle latitudes are poor source regions

Figure 6-19. Towering cumulus clouds develop in unstable air and often contain strong vertical currents.

because of the strong westerly winds and the continual mixing of tropical and polar airmasses.

CLASSIFICATIONS

Airmasses are classified according to the regions where they originate. They are generally divided into polar or tropical to identify their temperature characteristics and continental or maritime to identify their moisture content. A continental polar airmass, for example, originates over a polar land mass and contains cold, dry, and stable air. A maritime tropical airmass originates over water and contains warm, moist, and unstable air. [Figure 6-20]

MODIFICATION

As an airmass moves out of its source region, it is modified by the temperature and moisture of the area over which it moves. The degree to which an airmass is changed depends on several factors:

1. Its speed
2. Nature of the region it moves over
3. Temperature difference between the airmass and the new surface
4. Depth of the airmass

WARMING FROM BELOW

Warming from below decreases airmass stability.

As an airmass moves over a warmer surface, its lower layers are heated and vertical movement of the air develops. Depending on temperature and moisture levels, this can result in extreme instability. [Figure 6-21]

Figure 6-20. Airmass source regions surround North America. As airmasses move out of their source regions, they often converge and give birth to the continent's major weather systems.

Figure 6-21. The Great Lakes do much to modify continental polar airmasses moving out of Canada. In early winter, the lakes heat and moisten air near the surface, creating very unstable air. This often results in large quantities of snow over the Great Lakes and downwind of them.

COOLING FROM BELOW

When an airmass flows over a cooler surface, its lower layers are cooled and vertical movement is inhibited. As a result, the stability of the air is increased. If the air is cooled to its dewpoint, low clouds or fog may form. This cooling from below creates a temperature inversion and may result in low ceilings and visibility for long periods of time. [Figure 6-22]

Cooling from below may cause smooth air and poor visibility.

Figure 6-22. In winter months, warm, moist Pacific air flows into the Sacramento Valley of California and is cooled from below. As its temperature drops, its stability increases. Prolonged cooling causes the air to cool to its dewpoint, often resulting in widespread stratus clouds or fog that may persist for weeks.

FRONTS

When an airmass moves out of its source region, it comes in contact with other airmasses that have different moisture and temperature characteristics. The boundary between airmasses is called a **front**. Since the weather along a front often presents a serious hazard to flying, you need to have a thorough understanding of this weather.

TYPES OF FRONTS

Fronts are named according to the temperature of the advancing air relative to the temperature of the air it is replacing. A **cold front** is one where cold air is moving to displace warmer air. In a **warm front**, warm air is replacing cold air. A **stationary front** has no movement. Cold fronts are usually fast moving and often catch up to and merge with a slower moving warm front. When cold and warm fronts merge, they create an **occluded front**.

FRONTAL DISCONTINUITIES

In weather terminology, frontal discontinuities refer to the comparatively rapid changes in the meteorological characteristics of an airmass. When you cross a front, you move from one airmass into another airmass with different properties. The changes between the two may be very abrupt, indicating a narrow frontal zone. On the other hand, the changes may occur gradually, indicating a wide and, perhaps, diffused frontal zone. These changes can give you important cues to the location and intensity of the front.

TEMPERATURE

One of the most easily recognized discontinuities across a front is the change in temperature.

Temperature is one of the most easily recognized discontinuities across a front. At the surface, the temperature change is usually very noticeable and may be quite abrupt in a fast-moving front. With a slow-moving front, it usually is less pronounced. When you are flying through a front, you can observe the temperature change on the outside air temperature gauge. However, the change may be less abrupt at middle and high altitudes than it is at the surface.

WIND

When you are flying across a front, you will notice a change in wind direction. Wind speed also may change.

The most reliable indications that you are crossing a front are a change in wind direction and, less frequently, wind speed. Although the exact new direction of the wind is difficult to predict, the wind always shifts to the right in the northern hemisphere. When you are flying through a front at low to middle altitudes, you will always need to correct to the right in order to maintain your original ground track.

PRESSURE

As a front approaches, atmospheric pressure usually decreases, with the area of lowest pressure lying directly over the front. Pressure changes on the warm side of the front generally occur more slowly than on the cold side. When you approach a front toward the cool air, pressure drops slowly until you cross the front, then rises quickly. When you are crossing toward the warm air, pressure drops abruptly over the front and then rises slowly. The important thing to remember is that you should update your altimeter setting as soon as possible after crossing a front.

FRONTAL WEATHER

The type and intensity of frontal weather depend on several factors. Some of these factors are the availability of moisture, the stability of the air being lifted, and the speed of the frontal movement. Other factors include the slope of the front and the moisture and temperature variations between the two fronts. Although some frontal weather can be very severe and hazardous, other fronts produce relatively calm weather. Before beginning a flight that will penetrate a front, you should obtain a complete weather briefing on the conditions you might encounter.

COLD FRONTS

A cold front separates an advancing mass of cold, dense air from an area of warm, lighter air. Because of its greater density, the cold air moves along the surface and forces the less dense, warm air upward. In the northern hemisphere, cold fronts are usually oriented in a northeast to southwest line and may be several hundred miles long. Movement is usually in an easterly direction. The speed of a cold front usually dictates the type of weather associated with the front. However, there are some general weather characteristics that are found in most cold fronts. These include:

1. Cumulus clouds
2. Turbulence
3. Showery precipitation
4. Strong, gusty winds
5. Clearing skies and good visibility after the front passes

FAST-MOVING COLD FRONTS

Fast-moving cold fronts are pushed along by intense high pressure systems located well behind the front. Surface friction acts to slow the movement of the front, causing the leading edge of the front to bulge out and to steepen the front's slope. These fronts are particularly hazardous

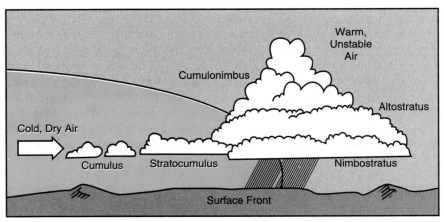

Figure 6-23. Fast-moving cold fronts force warmer air to rise. This causes widespread vertical cloud development along a narrow frontal zone if sufficient moisture is present. An area of severe weather often forms well ahead of the front.

because of the steep slope and wide differences in moisture and temperature between the two airmasses. [Figure 6-23]

When a cold front pushes into extremely moist, unstable air, a **squall line** often forms ahead of the front itself. The squall line is an area of severe weather characterized by extensive vertical cloud development and turbulence. It often develops 50 to 300 miles ahead of the front and frequently contains weather more severe than that found along the front.

The weather usually clears quickly behind a cold front. You will often notice reduced cloud cover, improved visibility, lower temperatures, and gusty surface winds following the passage of a fast-moving cold front.

SLOW-MOVING COLD FRONTS

The leading edge of a slow-moving cold front is much shallower than that of a fast-moving front. This produces clouds which extend far behind the surface front. A slow-moving cold front meeting stable air usually causes a broad area of stratus clouds to form behind the front. When a slow-moving cold front meets unstable air, large numbers of vertical clouds often form at and just behind the front. Fair weather cumulus clouds are often present in the cold air, well behind the surface front. [Figure 6-24]

WARM FRONTS

Steady precipitation with little turbulence usually precedes a warm front.

Warm fronts occur when warm air overtakes and replaces cooler air. They usually move at much slower speeds than cold fronts. The slope of a warm front is very gradual, and the warm air may extend up over the cool air for

Figure 6-24. As a slow-moving cold front meets unstable air, cumulonimbus and nimbostratus clouds may develop near the surface front, creating hazards from icing and turbulence.

several hundred miles ahead of the front. Some of the common weather patterns found in a typical warm front include:

1.   Stratus clouds, if the air is moist and stable
2.   Little turbulence, except in an unstable airmass
3.   Precipitation ahead of the front
4.   Poor visibility with haze or fog
5.   Wide area of precipitation

The stability and moisture content of the air in a warm front determines what type of clouds will form. If the air is warm, moist, and stable, stratus clouds will develop. If the air is warm, moist, and unstable, cumulus clouds will develop. [Figure 6-25]

Figure 6-25. Stratus clouds usually extend out ahead of a slow-moving warm front. Vertical clouds sometimes develop along and ahead of the surface front, depending on the stability and moisture content of the warm air. When ice pellets are reported at the surface, you can expect freezing rain at a higher altitude.

Figure 6-26. When the air being lifted by a cold front occlusion is moist and stable, the weather will be a mixture of that found in both a warm and cold front.

STATIONARY FRONTS

Stationary fronts have qualities of both warm and cold fronts.

When the opposing forces of two airmasses are relatively balanced, the front that separates them may remain stationary and influence local flying conditions for several days. The weather in a stationary front is usually a mixture of that found in both warm and cold fronts.

FRONTAL OCCLUSIONS

A frontal occlusion occurs when a fast-moving cold front catches up to a slow-moving warm front. The difference in temperature within each frontal system is a major factor that influences which type of front and weather are created. A **cold front occlusion** develops when the fast-moving cold front is colder than the air ahead of the slow-moving warm front. In this case, the cold air replaces the cool air at the surface and forces the warm front aloft. [Figure 6-26]

A **warm front occlusion** takes place when the air ahead of the slow-moving warm front is colder than the air within the fast-moving cold front. In this case, the cold front rides up over the warm front, forcing the cold front aloft. [Figure 6-27]

Figure 6-27. When the air being lifted by a warm front occlusion is moist and unstable, the weather will be more severe than that found in a cold front occlusion.

CHECKLIST _____

After studying this section, you should have a basic understanding of:

✓   **Stability** — What it is and what determines whether air is stable or unstable.

✓   **Effect of moisture and temperature** — How they influence stability.

✓   **Lapse rates** — What they represent and their relationship to stability.

✓   **Temperature inversions** — What they are and what kind of weather is associated with them.

✓   **Characteristics of stable and unstable air** — What cloud types, precipitation, visibility, and turbulence you can expect to encounter in stable and unstable air.

✓   **Clouds** — How clouds are classified and the characteristics associated with each class.

✓   **Airmasses** — What they are, where they come from, and how they influence weather.

✓   **Fronts** — What the types of fronts are and their associated weather.

WEATHER HAZARDS

Weather hazards come in many forms. Often, they are plainly visible, but serious hazards can also exist in clear skies and at times when you least expect them. It is important to understand these hazards and to know how to avoid them. We will begin our discussion with thunderstorms, since they produce a number of dangerous weather elements.

THUNDERSTORMS

Thunderstorm formation requires unstable conditions, a lifting force, and high moisture levels.

Three conditions are necessary to create a thunderstorm — air that has a tendency toward instability, some type of lifting action, and relatively high moisture content. The lifting action may be provided by several factors, such as rising terrain (orographic lifting), fronts, or heating of the earth's surface (convection).

LIFE CYCLE

The three stages of a thunderstorm are cumulus, mature, and dissipating.

Thunderstorms progress through three definite stages — cumulus, mature, and dissipating. You can anticipate the development of thunderstorms and the associated hazards by becoming familiar with the characteristics of each of these. [Figure 6-28]

The cumulus stage is characterized by continuous updrafts.

In the **cumulus stage**, a lifting action initiates the vertical movement of air. As the air rises and cools to its dewpoint, water vapor condenses into small water droplets or ice crystals. If sufficient moisture is present, heat

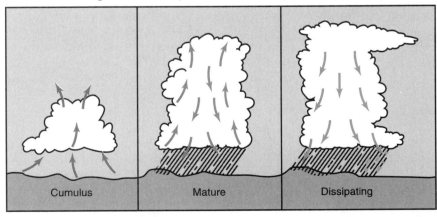

Cumulus   Mature   Dissipating

Figure 6-28. These distinctive cloud shapes signal the stages of a thunderstorm. Although not every cumulus cloud develops into a thunderstorm, all storms do begin at the cumulus stage. You should be aware that other weather phenomena may prevent you from seeing these characteristic shapes. For example, a cumulonimbus cloud may be embedded, or obscured, by massive cloud layers. There may also be a number of thunderstorms in an area, all in different stages of development.

released by the condensing vapor provides energy for continued vertical growth of the cloud. Because of strong updrafts, precipitation usually does not fall. Instead, the water drops or ice crystals rise and fall within the cloud, growing larger with each cycle. Updrafts as great as 3,000 feet per minute (f.p.m.) may begin near the surface and extend well above the cloud top.

As the drops in the cloud grow too large to be supported by the updrafts, precipitation begins to fall. This creates a downward motion in the surrounding air and signals the beginning of the **mature stage**. The resulting downdraft may reach a velocity of 2,500 f.p.m. The down-rushing air spreads outward at the surface, producing a sharp drop in temperature, a rise in pressure, and strong, gusty surface winds. The leading edge of this wind is referred to as a **gust front**, or the **first gust**. As the thunderstorm advances, a rolling, turbulent, circular-shaped cloud may form at the lower leading edge of the cloud. This is called the **roll cloud**. Early in the mature stage, the updrafts continue to increase up to speeds of 6,000 f.p.m. The adjacent updrafts and downdrafts cause severe turbulence. The most violent weather occurs during this phase of the life cycle.

Thunderstorms reach the greatest intensity during the mature stage, which is signaled by the beginning of precipitation.

As the mature stage progresses, more and more air aloft is disturbed by the falling drops. Eventually, the downdrafts begin to spread out within the cell, taking the place of the weakening updrafts. Because upward movement is necessary for condensation and the release of the latent energy, the entire thunderstorm begins to weaken. When the cell becomes an area of predominant downdrafts, it is considered to be in the **dissipating stage**. During this stage, the upper level winds often blow the top of the cloud downwind, creating the familiar anvil shape. The anvil, however, does not necessarily signal the storm's dissipation; severe weather can still occur well after its appearance.

A dissipating thunderstorm is characterized by downdrafts.

Occasionally, a thunderstorm doesn't dissipate in the typical manner. If winds become markedly stronger with altitude, the upper portion of the cloud may be "tilted," or blown downwind. In this case, precipitation falls through only a small portion of the rising air, or it may fall completely outside the cloud. As a result, the mature stage can be prolonged as the updrafts continue, until their source of energy is exhausted. This is commonly referred to as a **steady-state** thunderstorm, which can produce very severe weather.

TYPES OF THUNDERSTORMS

Thunderstorms usually have similar physical features, but their intensity, degree of development, and associated weather do differ. They are generally classified as airmass or frontal storms. **Airmass thunderstorms**

Airmass storms are usually caused by convection or orographic lifting.

generally form in a warm, moist airmass and are isolated or scattered over a large area. They are usually caused by solar heating of the land, which results in convection currents that lift unstable air, and are most common during summer afternoons or in coastal areas at night. Airmass storms can also be caused by orographic lifting. Although they are usually scattered along individual mountain peaks, they may cover large areas. They may be embedded in other clouds, making them difficult to identify when approached from the windward side of a mountain. Nocturnal thunderstorms can occur in late spring and summer during the late night or early morning hours when relatively moist air exists aloft. They are usually found from the Mississippi Valley westward. Nocturnal storms cover many square miles, and their effects may continue for hours at a given location.

Frontal thunderstorms can be associated with any type of front. Those which occur with a warm front are often obscured by stratiform clouds. You should expect thunderstorms when there is showery precipitation near a warm front. In a cold front, the cumulonimbus clouds are often visible in a continuous line parallel to the frontal surface. Occlusions can also spawn storms.

A squall line is a non-frontal band of thunder-storms that contains the most severe types of weather-related hazards.

A **squall line** is a narrow band of active thunderstorms which normally contains very severe weather. While it often forms 50 to 300 miles ahead of a fast-moving cold front, the existence of a front is not necessary for a squall line to form.

THUNDERSTORM HAZARDS

Thunderstorms typically contain many severe weather hazards. In addition to lightning, they may include, hail, turbulence, gusty surface winds, or even tornadoes. These hazards are not confined to the cloud itself. For example, you can encounter turbulence in VFR conditions as far as 20 miles from the storm. It might help to think of a cumulonimbus cloud as the visible part of a widespread system of turbulence and other weather hazards. In fact, the cumulonimbus cloud is the most turbulent of all clouds. Now, let's look at some of the associated weather elements separately.

The cumulonimbus is the type of cloud that produces the most severe turbulence.

Lightning is always associated with thunderstorms.

Lightning is one of the hazards which is always associated with thunderstorms. While it rarely causes crew injury or substantial damage to the aircraft structure, it can cause temporary loss of vision and puncture the aircraft skin or damage electronic navigation and communications equipment.

Hail can occur at all altitudes within or outside a storm. You can encounter it in flight, even when no hail is reaching the surface. In addition, large hailstones have been encountered in clear air several miles downwind from a thunderstorm.

Thunderstorm turbulence develops when air currents change direction or velocity rapidly over a short distance. The magnitude of the turbulence depends on the differences between the two air currents. Within the thunderstorm cloud, the strongest turbulence occurs in the shear between the updrafts and downdrafts. Near the surface, there is a low-level area of turbulence which develops as the downdrafts spread out at the surface. These create a **shear zone** between the surrounding air and the cooler air of the downdraft. The resulting area of gusty winds and turbulence can extend outward for many miles from the center of the storm.

Funnel clouds are violent, spinning columns of air which descend from the base of a cloud. Wind speeds within them may exceed 200 knots. If a funnel cloud reaches the earth's surface, it is referred to as a **tornado**. If it touches down over water, it is called a **waterspout**.

> Severe turbulence often exists in a thunderstorm.

TURBULENCE

We discussed turbulence briefly with relation to thunderstorms. Now, let's take a closer look at this dangerous weather phenomenon. There are many causes of turbulence, including wind shear, convective currents, obstructions to wind flow, clear air turbulence, and wake turbulence. Its effect can vary from occasional light bumps to severe jolts which can cause personal injury to occupants and/or structural damage to the airplane. To avoid or minimize the effects of turbulence, you must understand its causes and know where it is likely to be found. If you enter turbulence or expect that you will encounter it during flight, slow the airplane to maneuvering speed or less, maintain attitude, and accept variations in airspeed and altitude. If you encounter turbulent or gusty conditions during an approach to a landing, the recommended procedure is to fly a power-on approach at an airspeed slightly above the normal approach speed.

> If you encounter turbulence during flight, establish maneuvering speed and try to maintain a level flight attitude.

WIND SHEAR

Wind shear is a sudden, drastic shift in wind speed and/or direction that may occur at any altitude in a vertical or horizontal plane. It can subject your aircraft to sudden updrafts, downdrafts, or extreme horizontal wind components, causing loss of lift or violent changes in vertical speeds or altitudes.

> Wind shear can exist at any altitude and may occur in a vertical or horizontal direction.

You should anticipate wind shear when frontal systems and thunderstorms are in the area. It also may occur during a low-level temperature inversion when cold, still surface air is covered by warmer air which contains winds of 25 knots or more at 2,000 to 4,000 feet above the surface. A low-level wind shear alert system (LLWAS) is installed at some airports. If the system indicates a significant difference between the surface wind at center field and peripheral sensors, tower controllers will alert you by advising you of the wind velocities at two or more of the sensors.

> Wind shear often exists near the surface when there is a frontal system, thunderstorm, or temperature inversion with strong upper winds in the area.

Figure 6-29. As this aircraft inadvertently takes off into a microburst, it first experiences a headwind which increases performance (position 1). This is followed rapidly by decreased performance as the downdraft is encountered (position 2) and the wind shears to a tailwind (position 3). This may result in terrain impact or operation dangerously close to the ground (position 4).

MICROBURSTS AND DOWNBURSTS

A microburst is an intense downburst which covers only a small area and has a very short life cycle. However, a downburst covers a larger area and may last up to 30 minutes.

A **microburst** is an intense, localized downdraft which spreads out in all directions when it reaches the surface. This creates severe horizontal and vertical wind shears which pose serious hazards to aircraft, particularly those near the surface. A microburst typically covers less than two and a half miles at the surface, with peak winds as high as 150 knots and lasting only two to five minutes. Any convective cloud can produce this phenomenon. Although microbursts commonly occur during heavy precipitation in thunderstorms, they often are associated with **virga**, or streamers of precipitation that trail beneath a cloud but evaporate before they reach the ground. If there is no precipitation, your only cue may be a ring of dust at the surface. If you suspect the presence of microbursts in your local area, don't fly. A related phenomenon is the **downburst** which can cover an area up to 10 miles in diameter and last up to 30 minutes. [Figure 6-29]

CONVECTIVE CURRENTS

When sufficient moisture is present, cumulus clouds indicate the presence of convective turbulence.

Convective turbulence is caused by currents which develop in air heated by contact with the warm surface below. This heating can occur when cold air is moved horizontally over a warmer surface or when the ground is heated by the sun. The strength of the convective currents depends on the type of substance being heated and the intensity of the heat. For example, rocky or barren land heats more quickly than areas covered by heavy vegetation. In addition, the strongest convective currents are found on hot summer afternoons. Generally, the effect of these currents decreases with altitude. When the air is moist, the currents are marked by the cumulus clouds which form near their tops. Some of these clouds may grow into towering cumulus clouds and develop into thunderstorms.

OBSTRUCTIONS TO WIND FLOW

When obstacles like buildings or rough terrain interfere with the normal wind flow, turbulence develops. This phenomenon, referred to as **mechanical turbulence**, is often experienced in the traffic pattern when the wind blows around or over hangars and causes eddies to form.

Mechanical turbulence also occurs when strong winds flow nearly perpendicular to mountain ridges. If the air is unstable, expect turbulence on the windward side of the mountain. If the air is both moist and unstable, orographic thunderstorms may develop. As the unstable air spills down the leeward side, violent downdrafts may develop. These downdrafts can exceed the climb capability of an aircraft.

In contrast, when stable air crosses a mountain barrier, the airflow is smooth on the windward side. Wind flow across the barrier is laminar — that is, it tends to flow in layers. The barrier may set up waves, called **mountain waves**. Mountain wave turbulence is possible as the stable air moves across a ridge and the wind is 40 knots or greater. The wave pattern may extend 100 miles or more downwind, and the crests may extend well above the highest peaks. Below the crest of each wave is an area of rotary circulation, or a **rotor**, which forms below the mountain peaks. Both the rotor and the waves can create violent turbulence. If sufficient moisture is present, characteristic clouds will warn you of the mountain wave. [Figure 6-30]

Mountain wave turbulence can be anticipated when the winds across a ridge are 40 knots or more, and the air is stable.

The following discussion presents only general information about flying near mountains. It does not preclude the need for a thorough mountain checkout by a qualified flight instructor. You should anticipate some mountain wave activity whenever the wind is in excess of 25 knots and is blowing roughly perpendicular to mountain ridges. As wind speed increases, so does the associated turbulence. When conditions indicate a possible mountain wave, recommended cruising altitudes are at least 3,000 to 5,000 feet above the peaks. You should climb to the selected

Figure 6-30. The crests of the waves may be marked by lens-shaped, or lenticular, clouds. These clouds form in the updrafts and dissipate in the downdrafts so they appear stationary, although they may contain winds of 50 knots or more. Because of this, they are sometimes referred to as standing lenticulars. Rotor clouds may also form in the rotors, and cap clouds may obscure the mountain peaks.

altitude while approximately 100 miles from the range, depending on wind and aircraft performance. Approach the ridge from a 45° angle to permit a safer retreat if turbulence becomes too severe. If winds at the planned flight altitude exceed 30 knots, the FAA recommends against flight over mountainous areas in small aircraft.

CLEAR AIR TURBULENCE

Clear air turbulence (CAT) is commonly thought of as a high altitude phenomenon; however, it can take place at any altitude and is often present with no visual warning. Clear air turbulence may be caused by wind shear, convective currents, or obstructions to normal wind flow. It often develops in or near the **jet stream**, which is a narrow band of high altitude winds near the tropopause.

WAKE TURBULENCE

Wingtip vortices are created when an airplane generates lift.

Whenever an airplane generates lift, air spills over the wingtips from the high pressure areas below the wings to the low pressure areas above them. This flow causes rapidly rotating whirlpools of air called **wingtip vortices**, or **wake turbulence**. The intensity of the turbulence depends on aircraft weight, speed, and configuration.

The greatest vortex strength occurs when the generating aircraft is heavy, slow, and in a clean configuration. Wingtip vortices tend to sink below the flight path of the aircraft which generated them and are most hazardous during light, quartering tailwind conditions.

The greatest wake turbulence danger is produced by large, heavy aircraft operating at low speeds, high angles of attack, and in a clean configuration. Since these conditions usually exist on takeoff and landing, be alert for wake turbulence near airports used by large airplanes. In fact, wingtip vortices from commercial jets can induce uncontrollable roll rates in smaller aircraft. Although wake turbulence settles, it persists in the air for several minutes, depending on wind conditions. In light winds of three to seven knots, the vortices may stay in the touchdown area, sink into your takeoff or landing path, or drift over a parallel runway. The most dangerous condition for landing is a light, quartering tailwind. It can move the upwind vortex of a landing aircraft over the runway and forward into the touchdown zone. [Figure 6-31]

Wake turbulence can be extremely hazardous, particularly to pilots of small aircraft taking off or landing behind large aircraft.

If you are in a small aircraft approaching to land behind a large aircraft, controllers must ensure a separation of four miles (six miles behind a heavy jet). However, if you accept a clearance to follow an aircraft you have in sight, the responsibility for wake turbulence avoidance is transferred from the controller to you. On takeoff, controllers provide a two-minute interval behind departing heavy jets (three minutes for intersection takeoffs or takeoffs in the opposite direction on the same runway). You may waive these time intervals if you wish, but this is not a wise procedure.

Jet engine blast is a related hazard. It can damage or even overturn a small airplane if it is encountered at close range. To avoid exhaust velocities in excess of 20 knots, you must stay several hundred feet behind a jet with its engines operating, even when it is at idle thrust.

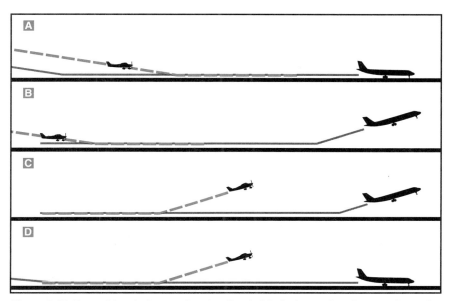

Figure 6-31. To avoid turbulence when landing behind a large aircraft, stay above the large airplane's glide path and touch down beyond its touchdown point (part A). If a large airplane has just taken off as you approach to land, touch down well before the large aircraft's liftoff point (part B). When taking off behind a large aircraft, lift off before the large airplane's rotation point and climb out above or upwind of its flight path (part C). When departing after a large aircraft has landed, lift off beyond its touchdown point (part D).

REPORTING TURBULENCE

You are encouraged to report encounters with turbulence, including the frequency and intensity. Turbulence is considered to be "occasional" when it occurs less then one-third of a given time span, "moderate" when it covers one-third to two-thirds of the time, and "continuous" when it occurs more than two-thirds of the time. You can classify the intensity using the following guidelines:

Light — Slight erratic changes in altitude or attitude; slight strain against seat belts. **Light chop** is slight, rapid bumpiness without appreciable changes in altitude or attitude.

Moderate — Changes in altitude or attitude occur, but aircraft remains in positive control at all times; usually changes in indicated airspeed; definite strains against seat belts. **Moderate chop** is rapid bumps or jolts without appreciable changes in altitude or attitude.

Severe — Abrupt changes in altitude or attitude; usually large variations in indicated airspeed; aircraft may be momentarily out of control; occupants forced violently against seat belts.

Extreme — Aircraft practically impossible to control; may cause structural damage.

ICING

Structural icing can occur during flights in areas of visible moisture, when the temperature of the aircraft surface is 0°C or colder. Ice can build up on any exposed surface of an aircraft, causing a loss of lift, an increase in weight, and control problems. There are two general types of ice — rime and clear. Mixed icing is a combination of the two. **Rime ice** normally is encountered in stratus clouds and results from instantaneous freezing of tiny water droplets striking the aircraft surface. It has an opaque appearance caused by air being trapped in the water droplets as they freeze instantly. A major hazard is its ability to change the shape of an airfoil and destroy its lift. Since rime ice freezes instantly, it builds up on the leading edge of airfoils, but it does not flow back following the basic curvature of the wing and tail surfaces. **Clear ice** may develop in areas of large water droplets which are in cumulus clouds or in freezing rain beneath a warm front inversion. The highest accumulation rate generally occurs in freezing rain. When the droplets flow over the aircraft structure and slowly freeze, they can glaze the aircraft's surfaces. Clear ice is the most serious form of ice because it adheres tenaciously to the aircraft and is difficult to remove.

Frost is a related element which poses a serious hazard during takeoffs. It interferes with smooth airflow over the wings and can cause early airflow separation, resulting in a loss of lift. It also increases drag and, when combined with the loss of lift, may prevent the aircraft from becoming airborne. Always remove all frost from the aircraft surfaces before flight.

RESTRICTIONS TO VISIBILITY

Up to this point, most of the hazards we have discussed occur at altitude. Let's complete our discussion with a look at some ground-based weather hazards which can restrict visibility.

Fog is classified according to the way it forms. **Radiation fog**, also known as **ground fog**, is very common. It forms over low-lying fairly level surfaces on clear, calm, humid nights. As the surface cools by radiation, the adjacent air is also cooled to its dewpoint. Radiation fog usually occurs in stable air associated with a high pressure system. As early morning temperatures increase, the fog begins to lift and usually "burns off" by mid-morning. If higher cloud layers form over the fog, visibility will improve more slowly.

Advection fog is caused when a low layer of warm, moist air moves over a cooler surface. It is most common under cloudy skies along coastlines where sea breezes transport air from the warm water to the cooler land. Winds up to about 15 knots will intensify the fog. Above 15 knots, turbulence creates a mixing of the air, and it usually lifts sufficiently to form low stratus clouds. **Upslope fog** forms when moist, stable air is forced up a sloping land mass. Like advection fog, upslope fog can form in moderate to strong winds and under cloudy skies.

Precipitation-induced fog may form when warm rain or drizzle falls through a layer of cooler air near the surface. Evaporation from the falling precipitation saturates the cool air, causing fog to form. This fog can be very dense, and usually it does not clear until the rain moves out of the area. **Steam fog**, which is often called sea smoke, occurs as cold, dry air moves over comparatively warmer water. It rises upward from the water's surface and resembles rising smoke. It is composed entirely of water droplets that often freeze quickly and fall back into the water as ice particles. Low-level turbulence can occur and icing can become hazardous in steam fog.

Low-level turbulence and icing are associated with steam fog.

Haze, smoke, smog, and blowing dust or snow can also restrict your visibility. **Haze** is caused by a concentration of very fine salt or dust particles suspended in the air. It occurs in stable atmospheric conditions with relatively light winds. Haze is usually no more than a few thousand feet thick, but it may occasionally extend to 15,000 feet. Visibility above the haze layer is usually good; however, visibility through the haze can be very poor. Smoke is usually much more localized; it is generally found in industrial areas and is a hazard only when it drifts across your intended landing field. On the other hand, **smog**, which is a combination of fog and smoke, can spread very poor visibility over a large area. Blowing dust and blowing snow present similar problems. They occur in moderate to high winds and can extend to an altitude of several thousand feet.

VOLCANIC ASH

Smoke and ash from volcanoes can also create reduced visibility. In addition, flying into volcanic ash can be extremely hazardous, causing engine failure in jets and severe damage to piston-powered aircraft. Depending on weather conditions, ash clouds may not be visible, and are not displayed on radar screens. You must rely on reports from ATC and other pilots regarding the location of an ash cloud, and you should take the necessary action to avoid the cloud and remain upwind of the volcano.

If you do encounter a volcanic ash cloud, you should reduce power to a minimum, altitude permitting, and reverse course to escape the cloud. An ash cloud may extend a great distance. You should not attempt to fly through or climb above the cloud.

In the event that you observe a volcanic eruption or ash cloud which has not been previously reported, immediately notify ATC. If possible, provide the location of the cloud, altitude, wind direction, and description of the ash cloud and eruption.

Takeoffs and landings where ash has fallen should be avoided, if possible. Ash on the runway can reduce braking action, and flowing ash reduces visibility while increasing the hazard to aircraft engines. Before departing, you should allow the ash to settle. It is recommended that you delay flap extension until the before-takeoff checklist, and use a rolling takeoff to minimize blowing ash back into the air.

CHECKLIST _____

After studying this section, you should have a basic understanding of:

✓ **Thunderstorms** — What the conditions are for their formation, and what the types, characteristics, and hazards of thunderstorms are.

✓ **Turbulence** — What the various types are and the hazards associated with them.

✓ **Structural icing** — What the types of structural icing are, how each type forms, and the hazards associated with each.

✓ **Restrictions to visibility** — What they are, what causes their formation, and what their associated hazards are.

✓ **Volcanic ash hazards** — What the hazards are and what pilot actions are recommended to minimize exposure.

ATTITUDE INSTRUMENT FLYING

Attitude instrument flying is a fundamental method for controlling an airplane by reference to instruments. It is based on an understanding of the flight instruments and systems. This knowledge will help you develop the skills required to interpret and translate the information presented by the instruments into precise airplane control. Instrument scanning (or cross-check), instrument interpretation, and airplane control are the three fundamental skills involved in all instrument flight maneuvers. You develop these skills individually, then integrate them into coordinated, positive control responses.

Instrument training is required for private pilot certification. The purpose of this is not to qualify you to fly in instrument weather conditions. Rather, this training will allow you to get out of instrument conditions quickly and safely in case of an unintentional encounter. Even after you have attained reasonable skill in performing the basic attitude instrument maneuvers and recoveries from critical or unusual flight attitudes, you should never undertake flight in instrument conditions until you are appropriately rated. However, these newly acquired skills will serve as a good foundation for further instrument training and the eventual addition of an instrument rating.

FLIGHT INSTRUMENTS

In visual flight, airplane attitude is usually determined by reference to the earth's horizon. For example, pitch attitude normally is determined by the position of the airplane's nose in relation to the natural horizon, while the wingtips provide information concerning bank. However, when you are flying in visual conditions, you do not determine the airplane's altitude by looking down at the ground and estimating the height, but by reference to the altimeter. You approximate the speed of the airplane by the sound of the slipstream, but you determine it more precisely through use of the airspeed indicator. You can estimate the direction of flight in relation to the sun's position, but it is easier to use the heading indicator. During flight by instrument references, the natural horizon is replaced by the attitude indicator, and the remaining instruments have the same function as during visual flight. The general information provided by the attitude indicator is correlated with the specific information gained from the altimeter, vertical speed indicator, heading indicator, turn coordinator, and airspeed indicator.

During flight by instrument references, use the attitude indicator as a substitute for the natural horizon.

SCANNING

Scanning is the term applied to the continuous systematic cross-check of flight instruments. The actual technique may vary somewhat, depending on individual differences, various maneuvers, and variations in airplane equipment, as well as your experience and proficiency level. [Figure 6-32]

At first, you may have a tendency to scan rapidly, looking directly at the instruments without knowing exactly what information you are seeking. However, with familiarity and practice, the instrument scan reveals definite trends during specific flight conditions. These trends will help you control the airplane as it makes a transition from one flight condition to another. You also learn that, during some phases of flight, the instrument scan must be more rapid than at other times.

Throughout our lifetimes, most of us have learned to apply full concentration to a single task to perform it well. However, this tendency causes several errors that you can eliminate through awareness.

If you apply your full concentration to a single instrument, you will encounter a problem called **fixation**. This results from a natural human inclination to observe a specific instrument carefully and accurately, often to the exclusion of other instruments. Fixation on a single instrument usually results in poor control. For example, while performing a turn, you

Figure 6-32. In most situations, the scan pattern includes the attitude indicator between the scan of each of the other instruments. A typical scan might progress as follows: attitude indicator — altimeter — attitude indicator — VSI — attitude indicator — heading indicator — attitude indicator, and so on.

may have a tendency to watch only the turn coordinator instead of including other instruments in your cross-check. This fixation on the turn coordinator often leads to a loss of altitude through poor pitch and bank control. You should look at each instrument only long enough to understand the information it presents, then continue on to the next one.

Similarly, you may find yourself placing too much **emphasis** on a single instrument, instead of relying on a combination of instruments necessary for airplane performance information. This differs from fixation in that you are using other instruments, but are giving too much attention to a particular one.

During performance of a maneuver, you may sometimes fail to anticipate significant instrument indications following attitude changes. For example, during leveloff from a climb or descent, you may concentrate on pitch control, while forgetting about heading or roll information. This error, called **omission**, results in erratic control of heading and bank.

In spite of these common errors, most pilots can adapt well to flight by instrument reference after instruction and practice. You may find that you can control the airplane more easily and precisely by instruments. In fact, during visual flight, beginning pilots sometimes rely too heavily on instrument references when they should rely more on outside visual references and watch for other air traffic.

INSTRUMENT INTERPRETATION

To fly effectively by instrument reference, you should understand each instrument's operating principles and limitations. In addition, you need to know what each instrument reveals about the airplane's performance. Each flight maneuver involves the use of combinations of instruments that you must read and interpret in order to control the airplane. For example, if you want to control pitch attitude, use the attitude indicator, airspeed indicator, altimeter, and vertical speed indicator. To control bank attitude, use the attitude indicator, turn coordinator, and heading indicator. To determine both pitch and bank attitude by instrument reference, you must include all of the flight instruments in your scan.

To control an airplane by reference to instruments, you must continue perfecting the techniques of proper pitch, bank, and power control that you practiced during flight by visual reference. Maintain a light touch on the controls and trim off any control pressures once the airplane has stabilized in a particular attitude. Abrupt and erratic airplane movement and pilot fatigue result when light control pressures and correct use of trim are not used.

SENSORY PERCEPTIONS

During instrument flight, you must disregard your sense of balance in favor of what your flight instruments indicate.

A human being's ability to maintain equilibrium depends primarily on three senses — the sense of sight, the sense of changing position which originates in the balance organs of the inner ear, and the postural sense (kinesthesia) which includes sensations of touch, pressure, and tension on muscles, joints, and tendons. When flying under visual conditions, your orientation is maintained by using these senses. The primary sense is sight, which uses the natural horizon of the earth as a reference. However, during instrument flight, you must use the indications of your flight instruments to maintain your orientation with the earth.

During instrument flight, some of the sensations from the inner ear and postural sense tend to send conflicting information to the brain. Confusion results when the brain is unable to interpret whether the pressure and tension of the muscles is a result of gravity or of load factors induced during maneuvering. Therefore, you must learn to trust your instruments and react accordingly.

STRAIGHT-AND-LEVEL FLIGHT

To maintain accurate straight-and-level flight by instrument reference, you must learn to control the pitch and bank of the airplane through interpretation of the flight instruments. The following discussion of airplane control and flight instruments outlines the proper use and interpretation of the instrument indications as they relate to straight-and-level flight.

PITCH CONTROL

When airspeed and power are held constant, pitch is used to maintain altitude.

At a constant airspeed and power setting, there is only one specific pitch attitude which will maintain level flight. The instruments used to maintain pitch control are the attitude indicator, airspeed indicator, altimeter, and vertical speed indicator. Any change in the pitching motion of the airplane registers a change on these instruments in direct proportion to the magnitude of the change. [Figure 6-33]

A pitch change to a nose-down attitude causes the miniature airplane on the attitude indicator to move below the horizon bar. In addition, an increase in airspeed, a decrease in altitude, and an indication of a descent on the vertical speed indicator are displayed on the flight instruments. Now let's take a closer look at the individual flight instruments.

ATTITUDE INDICATOR

The attitude indicator is the only instrument which indicates both pitch and bank attitude.

The attitude indicator is the only instrument which provides a pictorial display of the airplane's overall attitude. During instrument flight, all changes in pitch and bank are made by reference to this instrument. The other instruments are used to indicate when a change in attitude is required. [Figure 6-34]

Figure 6-33. As you enter a climb, the nose of the miniature airplane rises above the horizon bar of the attitude indicator. This causes a decrease in airspeed, an increase in altitude, and a positive rate-of-climb indication.

During instrument flight, your instructor will demonstrate the relationship between the miniature airplane and the horizon bar during pitch changes. The displacement between the miniature airplane and the horizon bar on the attitude indicator appears to be much smaller than displacement of the actual airplane's nose in relation to the natural horizon. Therefore, you should use light control pressures and make the required attitude changes slowly and smoothly.

Figure 6-34. The attitude indicator shown here represents an airplane in straight-and-level flight. You determine pitch attitude by comparing the nose of the miniature airplane to the horizon bar or to the pitch indexes located on the face of the instrument. You can also determine bank by comparing the wings of the miniature airplane to the horizon bar or by comparing the bank pointer to the indexes located to each side.

When practicing pitch control using the attitude indicator, you should initially restrict the displacement of the horizon bar to a one-half bar width up or down, progressing later to a full bar width. Use greater displacement only when large attitude changes are required. The control pressures necessary to make pitch changes vary in different airplanes. However, you cannot feel control pressure changes if you have a tight grip on the control wheel. If you maintain light pressures and retrim the airplane after it is stabilized in a new attitude, the result will be smooth and precise attitude control.

ALTIMETER

At a constant airspeed and power setting, altitude is controlled by pitch. The altimeter provides an indication of pitch attitude. Since the altitude should remain constant when the airplane is in level flight, any deviation from the desired altitude indicates the need for a pitch change. Obviously, if the altitude is increasing, the nose must be lowered. The rate of movement of the altimeter needle is as important as its direction of movement in maintaining level flight. Large pitch attitude deviations from level flight result in rapid altitude changes; slight pitch deviations produce much slower changes in the altimeter needle movement. Remember to make all adjustments to pitch by using the attitude indicator.

Altitude Correction Rules

A common rule for altitude corrections of less than 100 feet is to use a one-half bar width adjustment on the attitude indicator. For corrections in excess of 100 feet, use a full bar width correction. As you establish these corrections, observe the rate of altitude change on the vertical speed indicator and the altimeter.

If the deviation from the desired altitude is less than 100 feet, you can make the attitude adjustment you need to return to the correct altitude without changing the power setting. However, if the deviation from the desired altitude is greater than 100 feet, you should make a change in power setting and an appropriate trim adjustment.

VERTICAL SPEED INDICATOR

The normal function of the vertical speed indicator is to help you establish and maintain a desired rate of climb or descent. Due to the design of the instrument, there is a lag of approximately six to nine seconds before the correct rate of change is registered. Even though this lag exists, you may use the vertical speed indicator as a trend instrument for maintaining a desired pitch attitude. As a trend instrument, it indicates the direction of pitch change almost instantaneously.

If the needle deviates from the zero position, the instrument is indicating that the pitch is changing. Apply corrective pressures while referring to the attitude indicator. This pressure will stop the needle movement and place the airplane in a level attitude again. However, you should not try to return the needle to zero, since the lag in the vertical speed indicator will cause a tendency to overcontrol. Instead, after you have made a pitch correction to return to level flight, you should make an additional slight pitch correction to return to the desired altitude. Your judgment and experience in a particular airplane dictate the rate of altitude correction. As a guide, adjust the miniature airplane on the attitude indicator to produce a rate of change which is double the amount of altitude deviation, and use power as necessary. For example, if an airplane is 100 feet below the desired altitude, select a climb rate of 200 f.p.m. Estimate the initial amount of pitch change required to stop the descent and climb at 200 f.p.m. Hold it constant until the vertical speed indicator displays an accurate rate, then adjust it as necessary.

For small adjustments in altitude, use a vertical speed equal to approximately twice the desired altitude change.

AIRSPEED INDICATOR

The airspeed indicator will also indicate pitch attitude. If you establish a constant pitch attitude and power setting and permit the airplane to stabilize, the airspeed remains constant. As you raise the pitch attitude, the airspeed decreases slightly. On the other hand, as you lower the pitch attitude, the airspeed increases somewhat.

A rapid change in airspeed indicates that a large pitch change has occurred; you should apply smooth control pressure in the opposite direction. Again, however, look at the attitude indicator to note the amount of pitch change caused by control pressure. This will help you avoid overcontrolling the airplane. You will know the airplane is passing through approximately level flight when the needle stops its movement in one direction and begins to move in the opposite direction. Therefore, when you include the airspeed indicator in the scan with the attitude indicator, altimeter, and vertical speed indicator, it gives you positive pitch control information.

BANK CONTROL INSTRUMENTS

Banking the wings of an airplane normally results in a turn. Therefore, in order to fly a given heading, you should attempt to keep the wings of the airplane level with the horizon while maintaining coordinated flight.

ATTITUDE INDICATOR

The principal instrument used for bank control is the attitude indicator. The heading indicator and turn coordinator are used to indicate when a change in bank is required.

HEADING INDICATOR

In coordinated flight, bank attitude also is indicated on the heading indicator. Generally, if the heading displayed on the indicator is not changing, the wings are level. On the other hand, a slow heading change indicates a shallow bank angle, while a rapid change in heading indicates a steep bank.

TURN COORDINATOR

When the miniature airplane in the turn coordinator is in a wings-level position, the airplane is maintaining a constant heading. If the wings of the miniature airplane are displaced from the level flight position, the airplane is turning in the direction that the miniature airplane is banking. [Figure 6-35]

Remember that the ball in the inclinometer indicates whether you are maintaining coordinated flight. If the ball is off center, the airplane is slipping or skidding. When this occurs, make corrections with appropriate coordinated rudder and aileron pressure. [Figure 6-36]

To correct a heading deviation, use a bank angle equal to one-half the deviation, but do not exceed the bank required for a standard-rate turn.

The principal reference for making bank corrections is the attitude indicator. To make a heading change, use a bank angle equal to one-half of the difference between the present heading and the desired heading. However, the angle you use should not exceed that necessary for a standard-rate

Figure 6-35. The turn coordinator indicates the rate of turn. When a wingtip of the miniature airplane is aligned with one of the white marks at the side of the instrument, the airplane is turning at three degrees per second. This is a standard-rate turn.

Figure 6-36. This instrument indicates a slip, since the ball of the inclinometer is off-center in the same direction the miniature airplane is banked. To correct this problem, apply right rudder pressure to center the ball and coordinated aileron pressure to maintain the desired rate of turn.

turn. For example, if your desired heading is 300° and your present heading is 290°, you need to change your heading by 10°. Therefore, you should use a bank angle no greater than one-half of 10° or, in this example, 5° of bank.

CLIMBS

You enter a climb by applying back pressure to the control wheel and using the attitude indicator to establish climb attitude. Once airspeed has stabilized, use the attitude indicator to further adjust pitch attitude to achieve a desired airspeed. [Figure 6-37]

Use light control pressures to initiate and maintain the climb, since pressures change as the airplane decelerates. You may advance power to the climb power setting at the same time you change pitch, provided you do not exceed maximum r.p.m. limits.

If you have made the transition smoothly, the vertical speed indicator will show an immediate upward trend and will stabilize at a rate appropriate to the stabilized airspeed and pitch attitude. As you make the transition from cruise to climb, use additional right rudder pressure in order to compensate for P-factor and to maintain the desired heading.

During climb entry, maintain directional control by referring to the attitude indicator, heading indicator, and turn coordinator. Once you have established and stabilized the climb, trim away control pressures. If the instrument scan reveals any deviation from the desired heading or

Figure 6-37. To establish a climb from cruising airspeed, raise the nose to about a two-bar width, nose-high pitch attitude. This adjustment is a general guideline and varies with the airplane you use, as well as the rate of climb and the climb airspeed you desire.

Figure 6-38. Here are the typical instrument indications of a training airplane in a stabilized, straight climb. The only instrument which changes is the altimeter. All others should remain steady.

pitch attitude, make the required correction by referring to the attitude indicator while continuing the scan. [Figure 6-38]

LEVELOFF FROM CLIMBS

Lead the leveloff by 10% of the vertical speed.

You should initiate the leveloff from a climb before reaching the desired altitude because the airplane continues to climb at a decreasing rate throughout the transition to level flight. An effective guideline is to lead the altitude by 10% of the vertical speed indication. For example, if the airplane is climbing at 500 feet per minute, you should begin the leveloff 50 feet prior to reaching the desired altitude. To level off and accelerate to cruise speed, apply smooth, steady, forward elevator pressure. During the transition from climb to cruise, relax right rudder pressure and check the heading indicator to ensure that you maintain the desired heading. As you establish level flight using the attitude indicator, the airspeed increases to cruise speed and the vertical speed needle moves slowly toward zero. At this time, you may make rough trim adjustments. Then, as you reach cruise speed, reduce power to the recommended cruise setting and make final trim adjustments.

DESCENTS

To enter a descent, use the attitude indicator to establish the descent attitude, then reduce the power as required. As the pitch attitude and descent rate stabilize, trim the airplane. For a constant-rate descent, use the vertical speed indicator to tell you when to change pitch. During a constant airspeed descent, you will need to adjust the pitch anytime you deviate from the desired airspeed. You perform constant airspeed descents by using the pitch attitude of the airplane to control airspeed and engine power to control rate of descent. To enter a descent from cruise without a change in airspeed, smoothly reduce the power to the desired setting and reduce the pitch attitude slightly so the airspeed remains constant. The degree of pitch change and power reduction will vary according to the particular airplane used for training. Once the pitch attitude and power are established, you should cross-check the airspeed indicator with the attitude indicator.

When the airplane is descending at cruise airspeed, you control the rate of descent with small power adjustments. However, when a power change is made, you must cross-check the airspeed and attitude indicator to ensure the airspeed remains constant. This is important, because any change you make in power also requires a corresponding change in pitch attitude to maintain a constant airspeed.

LEVELOFF FROM DESCENTS

As in other leveloff procedures, begin leveloff from a descent before you reach the desired altitude; the amount of lead depends on the rate of descent. In a standard 500 f.p.m. rate of descent, the leveloff normally is led by 10% of the descent rate (50 feet). As you reach the lead-point, slowly add power to the appropriate level flight cruise setting, and smoothly adjust the pitch to a level flight attitude. Frequently, include the attitude indicator in your scan as you level off. After you have stabilized the pitch attitude and airspeed in straight-and-level flight, remove control pressures by trimming.

TURNS

To enter a turn, apply coordinated aileron and rudder pressure in the direction of the turn. Use the attitude indicator to establish the approximate angle of bank required for a standard-rate turn. Additional lift is needed to offset that portion of the vertical component of lift which is diverted in the turn. Therefore, raise the pitch attitude slightly to maintain altitude. As you establish the turn, adjust the nose of the miniature airplane so it is slightly above the level flight position on the horizon bar.

As the turn progresses, check the turn coordinator to determine if you are maintaining a standard-rate turn. If you are not, make a bank adjustment on the attitude indicator. Include the heading indicator in your scan to determine progress toward the desired heading.

Figure 6-39. These instruments show a level, standard-rate turn to the right. The bank index at the top of the attitude indicator displays the bank angle as 15°. Notice, too, how the nose of the miniature airplane is slightly above the horizon bar.

Furthermore, check the altimeter to determine that a constant altitude is being maintained throughout the turn. [Figure 6-39]

The principal instrument reference for the roll-out is the attitude indicator. Since you have held a slightly nose-high attitude throughout the turn, relax control wheel back pressure to prevent an altitude gain as you return the airplane to straight-and-level flight. As you attain the wings-level position, continue your instrument scan.

A guideline for determining the amount of lead required for roll-out from a turn is to use approximately one-half the angle of bank. For example, if you are making a standard-rate turn at a bank angle of 15°, begin the roll-out approximately eight degrees before you reach the desired heading.

CLIMBING AND DESCENDING TURNS

To make climbing and descending turns properly, you will need to combine the techniques used in straight climbs and descents with turning techniques. Initially, establish the climb or descent first, then roll into the turn as the pitch attitude stabilizes. However, as proficiency increases, you should establish the climb or descent simultaneously with the turn.

UNUSUAL ATTITUDES AND RECOVERIES

Any airplane attitude you do not normally use is considered to be an unusual or critical attitude. Such an attitude may result from any number of conditions such as turbulence, disorientation, confusion, preoccupation with cabin duties, carelessness in scanning, errors in instrument interpretation, or lack of proficiency in basic airplane control. By the time you realize the need to concentrate on the instruments, the attitude of your airplane may require immediate attention and recovery.

During the more advanced phases of private pilot training, you may be instructed to take your hands and feet off the controls and close your eyes while your instructor puts the airplane in a unusual attitude. As soon as control of the airplane is returned to you, check the attitude indicator to determine pitch and bank. Then, make immediate corrections to return the airplane to straight-and-level flight.

NOSE-HIGH UNUSUAL ATTITUDE

An unusually high attitude displayed on the attitude indicator may be evidence of a nose-high unusual attitude. Before you initiate recovery, check the other instruments to confirm the reliability of the attitude indicator, since it is possible for the airplane to be in a normal flight attitude with an inoperative attitude indicator. The indications of a nose-high unusual attitude are: a nose-high pitch attitude, decreasing airspeed, and a gain in altitude. [Figure 6-40]

Figure 6-40. Here are the instrument indications of a typical nose-high unusual attitude. The primary objective for recovery from this situation is to prevent a stall. Therefore, you should simultaneously decrease pitch to reduce the angle of attack, increase power, and roll the wings level.

Figure 6-41. This airplane is in a nose-low unusual attitude. In this case, you should simultaneously reduce power and roll the wings level. Then, gently raise the nose to the level flight attitude. If you attempt to raise the nose before you roll the wings level, the increased load factor can result in an accelerated stall, a spin, or a force exceeding the airplane design load factor.

NOSE-LOW UNUSUAL ATTITUDE

The indications of a nose-low unusual attitude are: a nose-low pitch attitude, increasing airspeed, rapid loss of altitude, and a high rate of descent. Your primary objective in a nose-low unusual attitude recovery is to avoid an excessively high airspeed or load factor. [Figure 6-41]

Pilots without instrument ratings who continue flight into adverse weather conditions almost always encounter well-developed, power-on spirals resulting from nose-low unusual attitudes. In this situation, they sense the increased speed of the airplane due to the increased slipstream noise and obviously high engine r.p.m. The normal reaction to a nose-down attitude is to apply control wheel back pressure. However, in this instance, back pressure will result in a continually tightening spiral.

CHECKLIST

After studying this section, you should have a basic understanding of:

✓ **Flight instruments** — How to use each of the flight instruments during instrument flight.

✓ **Scanning** — What scanning is, how to use it correctly, and what some of the common scanning problems are.

✓ **Straight-and-level flight** — How straight-and-level flight is maintained solely by reference to instruments, which instruments show deviations in heading and altitude, and how to correct these deviations.

✓ **Climbs and descents** — How to enter, maintain, and level off from climbs and descents by instrument references.

✓ **Turns** — What a standard-rate turn is and how to make a turn at a standard rate to a preselected heading.

✓ **Unusual attitude recoveries** — How to recognize and recover from nose-high and nose-low unusual attitudes.

flight prep

7

PRINTED REPORTS AND FORECASTS

Before beginning any flight as pilot-in-command of an aircraft, you are required to familiarize yourself with all available information concerning that flight. For a flight not in the vicinity of an airport, that information must include the latest or most current weather reports and forecasts. Aviation weather services are designed to provide you with the necessary information. To take advantage of these services, you need to know enough about them to ask the right questions. For short, local flights, you may need to know only the general weather conditions. For extended cross-country flights, you need more detailed information.

AVIATION ROUTINE WEATHER REPORT

An observation of surface weather which is reported and transmitted is called an **aviation routine weather report (METAR)**. Learning the common weather abbreviations, symbols, and word contractions will help you understand this type of report, as well as others that are important for flight planning. Content may vary somewhat, depending on who, or what type of facility, issues the report. A typical METAR may contain 10 or more separate elements, which are discussed in the following paragraphs. [Figure 7-1]

TYPE OF REPORT

The two types of weather reports are the scheduled **METAR**, which is taken every hour, and the **aviation selected special weather report (SPECI)**. The special METAR weather observation is an unscheduled report indicating a significant change in one or more elements.

STATION DESIGNATOR AND DATE/TIME OF REPORT

Each reporting station is listed by its four-letter International Civil Aviation Organization (ICAO) identifier. In the contiguous 48 states, the letter "K" prefixes the three-letter domestic location identifier. For example, the domestic identifier for Denver is DEN, and the ICAO identifier is KDEN. In other areas of the world, the first two letters indicate the region, country, or state. Identifiers for Alaska begin with "PA," for Hawaii, they begin with "PH," and for Canada, the prefixes are "CU," "CW," "CY," and "CZ." A list of station designators is usually available at an FSS or NWS office. You can also use the *Airport/Facility Directory* to decode the identifiers.

Following the station identifier is the date (day of the month) and time of the observation. The time is given in UTC or Zulu, as indicated by the Z following the time.

1 Type of Report

METAR Hourly Observation
SPECI Special, unscheduled report

2 Station Designator and Date/Time

Four-letter ICAO location identifier
Date and Time of report in Zulu (UTC)

3 Modifier

Auto = Automated
COR = Corrected

4 Wind Information

First three digits = Direction, or VRB = Variable
Next two digits = Speed in knots (KT), or three digits if speed
>99KT. G = highest gust, followed by speed. 00000KT = calm

5 Visibility

Prevailing visibility, statute miles (SM). Runway visual range:
R, runway number, / , visual range in feet (FT).

6 Present Weather

Intensity: -light, +heavy, no sign for moderate.

Proximity: VC = weather 5 to 10 miles from airport center

Descriptor: for precipitation or obstructions to visibility:
TS Thunderstorm	DR low drifting
SH Shower(s)	MI Shallow
FZ Freezing	BC Patches
BL Blowing	PR Partial

Precipitation types:
RA Rain	GR Hail (1/4" increments)
DZ Drizzle	GS Small hail/snow pellets
SN Snow	PE Ice Pellets
SG Snow grains	IC Ice Crystals
	UP Unknown Precipitation (Auto-mated stations only)

Obscurations to visibility:
FG Fog (vsby<5/8SM)	PY Spray
BR Mist (vsby 5/8 to 6SM)	SA Sand
FU Smoke	DU Widespread Dust
HZ Haze	VA Volcanic Ash

Other Phenomena:
SQ Squalls	SS Sandstorm
DS Duststorm	PO Dust/Sand swirls
FC Funnel cloud	+FC Tornado or Waterspout

7 Sky Condition

Amount of sky cover:
SKC Clear (no clouds)
FEW (Less than 1/8 to 2/8 sky cover)
SCT Scattered (3/8 to 4/8 sky cover)
BKN Broken (5/8 to 7/8 sky cover)
OVC Overcast (8/8 sky cover)

Height: three digits in hundreds of feet AGL

Type: towering cumulus (TCU) or cumulonimbus (CB) clouds
reported after the height of their base.
Vertical visibility (VV): height into a total obscuration in
hundreds of feet.

8 Temperature/Dew Point

Degrees Celsius, two-digit form. Prefixed "M" = minus (below
zero)

9 Altimeter

Inches of mercury, prefixed by "A".

10 Remarks

Prefixed by "RMK"
A01 or A02 = Station type (automated)
PK WND 28045/30 = Peak wind from 280°, 45 knots, at 30 minutes
past the hour.
WSHFT 30 FROPA = Wind shift accompanied by frontal passage
beginning at 30 minutes after the hour.
B (Began) or E (Ended) followed by time (minutes after the hour).
TS SE MOV NE = Thunderstorms southeast moving northeast
SLP134 = Sea level pressure in hectoPascals (1013.4 hPa)

DECODED REPORT: Routine observation for Tampa, FL, on the 12th day of the month at 2150 UTC. Automated Station. Wind from 080° at 20 knots with gusts to 38 knots. Prevailing visibility 1/2 statute mile, runway 36 Left visual range 2,400 feet. Thunderstorm with heavy rain. Scattered clouds at 800 feet AGL, overcast cumulonimbus clouds with bases of 1,200 feet AGL. Temperature 20°C, dewpoint 18°C. Altimeter setting 29.95 inches of mercury. Remarks: Automated station, precipitation discriminator indicated by A02, thunderstorm began 24 minutes past the hour, rain began 24 minutes past the hour, sea level pressure 1013.4 hectoPascals (Note: 1 hPa = 1 millibar).

Figure 7-1. A METAR usually contains most of these elements. If an element cannot be observed at the time of the report, it will be omitted. An item also may be omitted if it is not occurring at the observation time. It may be helpful to refer back to this example as you read the description of each element.

If the wind direction varies 60° or more, the variability follows the wind group, with the extremes in direction separated by a "V." For example, 190V260 indicates the wind direction varies from 190° to 260°.

Some typical examples of weather and descriptors are: +SN for heavy snow, -RA FG for light rain and fog, BR HZ for mist and haze (visibility >5/8 SM), FZDZ for freezing drizzle, BLDU for blowing dust, and VCSHRA for a rain shower in the vicinity.

Sky cover reported as SCT025TCU BKN080 is interpreted as scattered towering cumulus clouds with bases at 2,500 feet AGL, and broken clouds at 8,000 feet.

Fog obscuring the sky might be reported as 1/8SM FG VV006. The horizontal visibility is one eighth mile in fog, and vertical visibility is 600 feet. On automated reports, visibility less than 1/4 statute mile is reported as M1/4.

A temperature of eight degrees below zero Celsius is reported as M08.

A METAR containing the RMK RAE42SNB42 means that rain ended at 42 minutes past the hour and snow began at that time.

MODIFIER

When a METAR is created by a totally automated weather observation station, the modifier **AUTO** will follow the date/time element. These stations are grouped by the type of sensor equipment used to make the observations, and A01 or A02 will be noted in the remarks section of the report. **RMK A02** indicates the weather observing equipment used has the capability of distinguishing precipitation type. The modifier **COR** is used to indicate a corrected METAR which replaces a previously disseminated report. When the abbreviation COR is used, the station type designator, A01 or A02, is removed from the remarks section. No modifier indicates a manual station or manual input at an automated station.

WIND INFORMATION

The wind direction and speed are reported in a five digit group, or six digits if the speed is over 99 knots. The first three digits represent the direction from which the wind is blowing, in reference to true north. If the direction is variable, the letters "VRB" are used. The next two (or three) digits show the speed in knots (KT). Calm winds are reported as "00000KT."

If the wind direction varies 60° or more and the speed is above six knots, a variable group follows the wind group. The extremes of wind direction are shown, separated by a "V." For example, if the wind is blowing from 020°, varying to 090°, it is reported as "020V090."

In addition to direction and speed, the character, or type, of wind may be reported. Gusty winds are reported with a "G," followed by the highest gust. For example, wind from 080° at 32 knots with gusts to 45 is reported as 08032G45. [Figure 7-2]

VISIBILITY

Prevailing visibility is the greatest distance an observer can see and identify objects through at least half of the horizon. Visibility is reported in statute miles with "SM" appended to it. Examples are 1/2SM for one half statute mile

Coded Data	Explanations
00000KT	Calm
20014KT	Wind from 200° at 14 knots
15010G25	Wind from 150° at 10 knots, gusts to 25 knots
VRB04KT	Wind variable in direction at 4 knots
210103G130KT	Wind from 210° at 103 knots with gusts to 130 knots

Figure 7-2. This figure shows several examples of wind information as it appears on the METAR. The decoded wind direction, speed, and character are shown to the right.

and 7SM for seven statute miles. When **runway visual range** (RVR) is reported, it follows prevailing visibility. It is designated with an "R," followed by the runway number, a "/," and the visual range in feet (FT). For example, R32L/1200FT means runway 32 left visual range is 1,200 feet. Variable RVR is shown as the lowest and highest visual range values separated by a "V." Outside the United States, RVR is normally reported in meters.

In a METAR, visibility is reported in statute miles and fractions with a space between the whole number and the fraction. If RVR is reported, it is in feet.

PRESENT WEATHER

When weather or obscurations to vision are present at the time of the observation, you will find them immediately after the visibility. The type of precipitation or obscuration is shown in codes, preceded by intensity symbols, proximity, and descriptor. Intensity levels are shown as light (-), moderate (no sign), or heavy (+). Weather obscurations occurring between 5 and 10 statute miles of the airport are shown by the letters "VC." For precipitation, VC applies within 10 statute miles of the observation point. Next is a descriptor of the precipitation or obscurations to visibility. For example, blowing snow is reported as BLSN, freezing drizzle as FZDZ, and a thunderstorm in the vicinity of the airport with moderate rain is reported as VCTSRA. Some typical obscurations to visibility are smoke (FU), haze (HZ), and dust (DU). Fog (FG) is listed when the visibility is less than 5/8 mile, and when it is between 5/8 and 6 miles, the code for mist (BR) is used. For instance, when fog causes a visibility of 1/4 mile, it is reported as 1/4SM FG. If mist and haze reduce visibility to 1-1/2 miles, it is shown as 1 1/2SM BR HZ. Following the obscurations, other weather phenomena may be listed, such as sandstorm (SS), duststorm (DS), or a funnel cloud (FC).

Fog (FG) is reported only when the visibility is less than 5/8 of a mile. Mist (BR) indicates the visibility is between 5/8 of a mile and 6 miles. Note, 5/8 of a mile is approximately 1,000 meters.

SKY CONDITION

The amount of clouds covering the sky is reported in eighths of sky cover. A clear sky is designated by SKC in a manual report and CLR in an automated report. FEW is used when cloud coverage is 1/8 to 2/8. However, any amount less than 1/8 can also be reported as FEW. Scattered clouds, which cover 3/8 to 4/8 of the sky, are shown by SCT. Broken clouds, covering 5/8 to 7/8 of the sky, are designated by BKN, while an overcast sky is reported as OVC.

The height of clouds or the vertical visibility into obscuring phenomena is reported with three digits in hundreds of feet above ground level (AGL). To determine the cloud height, add two zeros to the number given in the report. When more than one layer is present, the layers are reported in ascending order. However, the sky cover condition for any higher layers represents total sky coverage, which includes any lower layer. For example, a scattered layer at 900 feet and a broken layer at 3,000 feet AGL would be reported as SCT009 BKN030. In addition, if towering cumulus clouds (TCU) or cumulonimbus clouds (CB) are present, their code is shown following the height of their base, such as BKN040TCU or OVC050CB.

Figure 7-3. Note that the upper layer is reported as broken, even though that layer by itself covers less than 5/8 of the horizon. If the total coverage did not exceed 4/8, the upper layer would be reported as scattered.

For a layer of clouds to be classified as a ceiling, it must be reported as either broken, overcast, or as an obscuration.

Although not designated by a METAR code, a **ceiling** is the AGL height of the lowest layer of clouds aloft that is reported as broken or overcast, or the vertical visibility into an obscuration, such as fog or haze. In general terms, a ceiling exists when more than half of the sky is covered. [Figure 7-3]

A ceiling is usually determined with an electronic device called a rotating beam ceilometer. Other means may also be used, such as a ceiling light, cloud detection radar, or by the unobscured portion of a landmark that rises into the ceiling layer. Ceiling heights may also be estimated by the use of pilot reports, balloons, or other measurements. When a ceiling is estimated from a pilot report, the MSL altitude reported by the pilot is converted to an AGL height. Balloon-estimated ceilings are based on the time it takes for the balloon to ascend, and they may be inaccurate because of convective air currents. Other measurements include estimates by meteorologists who must rely on experience and knowledge of cloud formations.

TEMPERATURE AND DEWPOINT

The current air temperature and dewpoint are reported in two-digit form in degrees Celsius and are separated by a slash. For example, "18/09" indicates a surface temperature of 18°C and a dewpoint of 9°C. Temperatures below 0° Celsius are prefixed with an "M" to indicate minus. For instance 10° below zero would be shown as M10. Temperature and dewpoint also may be added to remarks in an eight-digit format showing tenths of °C.

ALTIMETER

The altimeter setting is reported in inches of mercury in a four digit group without the decimal point, and is prefixed by an "A." An example is A3012, indicating an altimeter setting of three zero point one two inches. Altimeter settings reflect local station pressure.

Coded Data	Explanations
A02	Automated station with precipitation discriminator
PK WND 20032/25	Peak wind from 200° at 32 knots, 25 minutes past the hour
VIS 3/4V1 1/2	Prevailing visibility variable 3/4 to 1 and 1/2 miles
FRQ LTG NE	Frequent lightning to the northeast
FZDZB45	Freezing drizzle began at 45 past the hour
RAE42SNB42	Rain ended and snow began at 42 past the hour
PRESFR	Pressure falling rapidly
SLP045	Sea level pressure in hectoPascals and tenths, 1004.5 hPa
T00081016	Temperature/dewpoint in tenths °C, .8 °C/–1.6 °C

Figure 7-4. Examples of coded remarks are shown in the left column, with the corresponding explanations on the right.

The remark, T00081016, is temperature and dewpoint in tenths °C. The first zero indicates a plus value for temperature (+.8 °C) and the first one indicates a minus value for dewpoint (–1.6 °C).

REMARKS

Certain remarks are included to report weather considered significant to aircraft operations. The types of information that may be included are wind data, variable visibility, beginning and ending times of a particular weather phenomena, pressure information, and temperature/dewpoint in tenths °C. In most cases, you will notice more remarks when the weather is bad and the airport is approved for IFR operations. The remarks section begins with "RMK." The beginning of an event is shown by a "B," followed by the time in minutes after the hour. The ending time is noted by an "E" and the time in minutes. [Figure 7-4]

ADDITIONAL REPORTS

For a more complete picture, you may also refer to separate reports or messages that provide specific information for pilots. These include freezing level reports, notices to airmen, pilot weather reports, and radar weather reports.

Freezing level data is available at airports where upper air observations are taken. You can identify this information by the letters RADAT, followed by a coded group of numbers. RADATs contain information on the relative humidity at the freezing level or levels. Up to three freezing levels (low, medium, and high) may be reported. "RADAT 87045," for instance, means the relative humidity is 87 percent and the freezing level is at 4,500 feet MSL. Later, you will see that freezing level information is also indicated on some weather forecasts and charts.

Notices to Airmen (NOTAMs) are transmitted as separate lines of information. NOTAMs report changes in the status of airports or airway facilities that could affect your decision to make a flight. They include such information as runway closures, obstructions in the approach and

PIREP Elements	Explanations
UA or UUA	Type of report – UA is routine PIREP; UUA is urgent PIREP
/OV	Location – In relation to VOR or route segment (station identifier, radial, DME)
/TM	Time – Coordinated Universal Time (UTC)
/FL	Altitude – Above mean sea level (MSL)
/TP	Type of aircraft – Example, C172
/SK	Sky cover – Cloud bases and tops (both MSL), amount of coverage (scattered, broken, overcast)
/WX	Weather – Precipitation, visiblity, restrictions to vision
/TA	Temperature – Degrees Celsius
/WV	Wind – Direction in degrees, speed in knots
/TB	Turbulence – Light, moderate, severe, as appropriate
/IC	Icing – Trace, light, moderate, severe, as appropriate
/RM	Remarks – To clarify the report or for additional information

Coded PIREP: UA/OV OKC 063064/TM 1522/FL 080/TP C172/TA -04/WV 245040/TB LGT/RM IN CLR

Decoded PIREP: Routine pilot report . . . 64 n.m. on the 063° radial from Oklahoma City VOR . . . at 1522 UTC . . . flight altitude 8,000 ft . . . type of aircraft is a Cessna 172 . . . outside air temperature is minus four degrees Celsius . . . wind is from 245° at 40 knots . . . light turbulence and clear skies.

Figure 7-5. PIREPs are made up of several elements, as indicated in the upper portion of this figure. The lower part provides a sample PIREP and its plain-language interpretation. Notice that MSL altitudes are used. Although PIREPs should be complete and concise, you should not be overly concerned with strict format or terminology. The important thing is to forward the report so other pilots can benefit from it.

departure paths to airports, and outages or curtailed operation hours of navaids and ATC facilities.

Pilot weather reports (PIREPs) of current weather conditions often confirm such information as the height of bases and tops of cloud layers, inflight visibility, icing conditions, wind shear, and turbulence, which are not routinely available from other observation sources. When you encounter unexpected weather conditions, you are encouraged to make a pilot report. If the ceiling is at or below 5,000 feet, or visibility is at or below five miles, ATC facilities are required to solicit PIREPs. If you make a PIREP, the ATC facility or the FSS can add your report to the distribution system, and it can be used to brief other pilots or to provide in-flight advisories. [Figure 7-5]

General areas of precipitation, especially thunderstorms, are observed by radar on a routine basis. Most radar stations issue **radar weather reports** (SDs) each hour, with intervening special reports as required. These reports are routinely transmitted on weather service circuits and some are included in FSS weather broadcasts.

SDs not only define the areas of precipitation, they also provide information on the type, intensity, and trend. In addition, these reports normally include movement (direction and speed) of the precipitation areas, as well as maximum height. When the clouds extend to high levels, thunderstorms are likely. This means you can expect turbulence and the possibility of hail.

TERMINAL AERODROME FORECAST

A prediction of surface weather expected at an airport is a **terminal aerodrome forecast** (TAF). It is one of your best sources for an estimate of what the weather will be in the future at a specific terminal. TAFs normally are scheduled four times a day at 0000Z, 0600Z, 1200Z, and 1800Z, each for a 24-hour period. Each TAF contains these elements: type, location, issuance date and time, valid date and time, and the forecast. With few exceptions, the codes used in the TAF are the same as those used for METAR.

TYPE OF REPORT

The terminal forecast will either be a routine TAF, or an amended forecast (TAF AMD). An amended TAF is issued when the current TAF no longer represents the expected weather. TAF or TAF AMD appears in a header line prior to the text of the forecast. If a TAF is corrected (COR) or delayed (RTD), it will be noted only in the header which precedes the actual forecast. [Figure 7-6]

LOCATION IDENTIFIER AND ISSUANCE DATE/TIME

The four letter ICAO location identifier is the same as that used for METAR. The first two numbers of the date/time group represent the day of the month, and the next four digits are the Zulu time that the forecast was issued.

VALID PERIOD

Normally, the forecast is valid for 24 hours. The first two digits represent the valid date. Next is the beginning hour of the valid time in Zulu, and the last two digits are the ending hour. For example, a valid period of 161212 means the forecast is valid for 24 hours, from 1200Z on the 16th to 1200Z the next day. The valid time may be less than 24 hours for an amended, corrected, or delayed TAF. At an airport that is open part time, amendments are not issued after closing time. If an airport closes at 0500Z,

1 **Type of Report** – Routine terminal aerodrome forecast (TAF)

2 **Location Identifier** – ICAO four-letter identifier

3 **Issuance Data and Time** – Two-digit day of the month and the time in Zulu (Z)

4 **Valid Period** – TAF valid time, two-digit date followed by the beginning and ending hours in Zulu

Forecast Elements: Wind/Visibility/Weather/Sky Condition

5 **Wind** – Three-digit direction, two-or three-digit speed in knots (KT)

6 **Visibility** – Expected prevailing visibility in statute miles. Forecast visibility greater than 6 miles is coded as P6SM (plus 6 SM).

7 **Weather** – Significant weather and obstructions to visibility

8 **Sky Condition** – Amount, height (CB) or vertical visibility
Cumulonimbus (CB) is the only type of cloud included in the TAF
North America TAFs will also include nonconvective low-level wind shear (WS), up to 2000 feet. When forecast, WS will appear after the cloud forecast group

9 **Temporary Conditions** – (TEMPO) Fluctuations expected to last less than an hour in each instance and, in aggregate, to cover less than half of the period, two-digit beginning time, in hours, and two-digit ending time, also in hours

10 **Forecast Change Group** – Significant, permanent changes in conditions; from (FM), four-digit hour and minute time the change is expected to begin; or becoming (BECMG) with a four-digit time group to indicate beginning hour and ending hour times

11 **Probability Forecast** – Probability of thunderstorms or precipitation (in percent), along with associated weather conditions (wind, visibility, and sky condition); the four-digit beginning hour and ending hour follows the abbreviation PROB40

12 **End of Report Separator** – (=)

DECODED REPORT:
Routine TAF for Oklahoma City, OK...on the 5th day of the month, at 1130Z...valid for 24 hours from 1200Z on the 5th to 1200Z on the 6th...Wind from 140° at 8 knots...visibility 5 statute miles in mist...broken clouds at 3,000 feet...Temporary condition, between 1300Z and 1600Z, 1 1/2 statue miles visibility in mist...From 1600Z, wind from 160° at 10 knots...visibility greater than 6 miles and sky clear...Becoming, between 2200Z and 2400Z, wind from 200° at 13 knots, gusting to 20 knots, visibility 4 miles with moderate rain showers, sky overcast at 2000 feet...Between midnight (0000Z) and 0600Z, a 40% probability of 2 statute miles visibility with thunderstorms and moderate rain, sky overcast with the bases of cumulonimbus clouds at 800 feet AGL...Becoming, 0600Z to 0800Z, wind 210° at 15 knots, visibility greater than 6 statute miles and no significant weather.

Figure 7-6. TAF codes are similar to those used in the METAR. This example shows the National Weather Service TAF format. The format for TAFs transmitted by FAA weather briefers may be slightly different.

for instance, the TAF may include a statement such as, "NIL AMD NOT SKED AFT 0500Z." While part-time airports are closed, the word "NIL" appears in place of the forecast for those locations.

FORECAST

The body of the TAF contains codes for forecast wind, visibility, weather, and sky condition in much the same format as METAR. Weather, including obstructions to visibility, is added to the forecast only when it is significant to aviation. One difference between TAF and METAR is that forecast visibility greater than six miles is reported as P6SM, or plus six statute miles, in the TAF. In addition, TAFs may include the probability of thunderstorms or precipitation events and associated conditions. A PROB group is used when the probability of occurrence is between 30% and 49%, and is followed by a beginning and ending time. For example, PROB40 1923 TSRA forecasts a 40% chance of a thunderstorm with moderate rain between 1900Z and 2300Z.

When a significant permanent change to the weather conditions is expected during the valid time, a change group is used. If a rapid change, usually within one hour, is expected, the code for from (FM) is used with the time of change. A forecast of FM0600 16010KT indicates that around 0600Z, the wind will be from 160 degrees at 10 knots. This wind condition will continue until the next change group or the end of the valid time of the TAF.

The from group is used when a fairly rapid change is expected. FM is followed by the four-digit beginning time coded in hours and minutes.

A more gradual change in the weather, taking about two hours, is coded as BECMG, followed by beginning and ending times. For instance, the code BECMG 0608 21015KT P6SM NSW SCT040 means that between 0600Z and 0800Z the weather will gradually change, wind becoming 210 degrees at 15 knots, visibility greater than 6 statute miles, no significant weather, sky scattered at 4,000 feet.

The becoming group (BECMG) shows a gradual change, usually over a period of two hours.

Conditions that are expected to last less than an hour at a time are described in a temporary (TEMPO) group, followed by beginning and ending times. An example would be 5 miles of visibility in mist, but between 0100Z and 0500Z visibility of 1 mile in low drifting snow. These conditions would appear in the TAF as: 5SM BR TEMPO 0105 1SM DRSN.

AREA FORECASTS

An area forecast (FA) covers general weather conditions over a wide area and is a good source of information for enroute weather. It also helps you determine the conditions at airports that do not have terminal forecasts. FAs are issued three times a day in the 48 mainland states. Weather Service Forecast Offices issue FAs for Hawaii and Alaska; however, the Alaska FA utilizes a different format. An additional specialized FA is

To determine forecast weather conditions between reporting stations, refer to the area forecast.

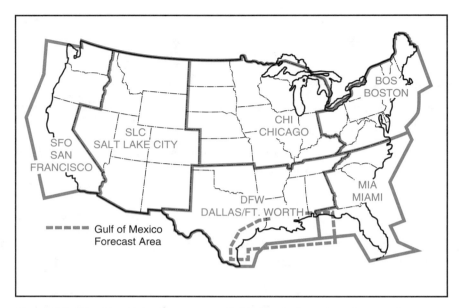

Figure 7-7. The 48 mainland states are divided into six regions for area forecasts. FAs are issued by the National Aviation Weather Advisory Unit in Kansas City, MO. A specialized Gulf of Mexico FA is issued by the National Hurricane Center in Miami, Florida..

issued for the Gulf of Mexico by the National Hurricane Center in Miami, FL. [Figure 7-7]

COMMUNICATIONS AND PRODUCT HEADERS

The FA is comprised of four sections: a communications and product header section, a precautionary statement section, and two weather sections; a SYNOPSIS section and a VFR CLOUDS/WX section. Each area forecast covers an 18 hour period. [Figure 7-8]

In the heading "SLCC FA 141045," the "SLC" identifies the Salt Lake City forecast area, "C" indicates the product contains a Clouds and Weather forecast, "FA" means area forecast, and "141045" tells you this forecast was issued on the 14th day of the month at 1045 Zulu. Since these forecasts are rounded to the nearest full hour, the valid time for the report begins at 1100Z. The synopsis is valid until 18 hours later, which is shown as the 15th at 0500Z. The Clouds and Weather section forecast is valid for a 12-hour period, until 2300Z on the 14th. The outlook portion is valid for six hours following the forecast, from 2300Z on the 14th to 0500 on the 15th. The last line of the header lists the states that are included in the Salt Lake City forecast area.

1 SLCC FA 141045
SYNOPSIS AND VFR CLDS/WX
SYNOPSIS VALID UNTIL 150500
CLDS/WX VALID UNTIL 142300...OTLK VALID 142300-150500
ID MT NV UT WY CO AZ NM

2 SEE AIRMET SIERRA FOR IFR CONDS AND MTN OBSCN.
TSTMS IMPLY PSBL SVR OR GTR TURBC SVR ICG LLWS
AND IFR CONDS.

NON MSL HGTS ARE DENOTED BY AGL OR CIG.

3 SYNOPSIS...HIGH PRES OVER NERN MT CONTG EWD
GRDLY. LOW PRES OVR AZ NM AND WRN TX RMNG
GENLY STNRY. ALF...TROF EXTDS FROM WRN MT INTO
SRN AZ RMNG STNRY..

4 .
ID MT
FROM YXH TO SHR TO 30SE BZN TO 60SE PIH TO LKT TO
YXC TO YXH.
70-90 SCT-BKN 120-150. WDLY SCT RW-. TOPS SHWRS 180.
OTLK...VFR
RMNDR AREA...100-120. ISOLD RW- MNLY ERN PTNS AREA.
OTLK...VFR

.
UT NV NM AZ
80 SCT-BKN 150-200. WDLY SCT RW-/TRW-. CB TOPS 450.
OTLK...VFR

.
WY CO
FROM BZN TO GCC TO LBL TO DVC TO RKS TO BZN.
70-90 BKN-OVC 200. OCNL VSBY 3R-F. AFT 20Z WDLY SCT
TRW-. CB TOPS 450. OTLK...MVFR CIG RW.

1 Heading Section   3 Synopsis

2 Precautionary Statements   4 VFR Clouds and Weather

Figure 7-8. The area forecast has four sections, beginning with a communications and product header, which identifies the area and provides the valid times. Area forecasts contain standard abbreviations and word contractions. The information in this sample forecast is interpreted in the accompanying paragraphs.

PRECAUTIONARY STATEMENTS

Following the headers are three precautionary statements which are part of all FAs. The first alerts you to check the latest AIRMET Sierra, which describes areas of mountain obscuration which may be forecast for the area. The next statement is a reminder that thunderstorms imply possible severe or greater turbulence, severe icing, low-level wind shear, and instrument conditions. Therefore, when thunderstorms are forecast, these hazards are not included in the body of the FA. The third statement points out that heights which are not MSL are noted by the letters AGL (above ground level) or CIG (ceiling). All heights are expressed in hundreds of feet.

SYNOPSIS

The location and movement of fronts and pressure systems is described in the synopsis.

The synopsis is a brief description of the location and movement of fronts, pressure systems, and circulation patterns in the FA area over an 18-hour period. When appropriate, forecasters may use terms describing ceilings and visibilities, strong winds, or other phenomena. In the example, high pressure over northeastern Montana will continue moving gradually eastward. A low pressure system over Arizona, New Mexico, and western Texas will remain generally stationary. Aloft (ALF), a trough of low pressure extending from western Montana into southern Arizona is expected to remain stationary.

VFR CLOUDS AND WEATHER

The VFR Clouds and Weather (VFR CLDS/WX) portion is usually broken down into several paragraphs, and by states or geographical regions. It describes clouds and weather which cover an area of 3,000 square miles or more, and which could affect VFR operations. The forecast is valid for 12 hours, and is followed by a 6-hour categorical outlook (18 hours in Alaska).

When the surface visibility is expected to be six statute miles or less, the visibility and obstructions to vision are included in the forecast. When precipitation, thunderstorms, and sustained winds of 20 knots or greater are forecast, they will be included in this section. The term OCNL (occasional) is used when there is a 50% or greater probability of cloud or visibility conditions which could affect VFR flight. The percentage of an area covered by showers or thunderstorms is indicated by the terms ISOLD (isolated, meaning single cells), WDLY CST (widely scattered, less than 25% of the area), CST or AREAS (25 to 54% of the area), and NMRS or WDSPRD (numerous or widespread, 55% or more of the area).

In addition, the term ISOLD is sometimes used to describe areas of ceilings or visibilities which are expected to affect areas of less than 3,000 square miles.

The outlook follows the main body of the forecast, and gives a general description of the expected weather, using the terms VFR, IFR, or MVFR (marginal VFR). Ceilings less than 1,000 feet and/or visibility less than 3 miles is considered IFR. Marginal VFR areas are those with ceilings from 1,000 to 3,000 feet and/or visibility between 3 and 5 miles. Abbreviations are used to describe causes of IFR or MVFR weather. Ceilings are noted by CIG, and restrictions to visibility are described by codes such as TRW, F, L, or BD.

Let's take a look at a portion of the VFR CLDS/WX section in our example. For Wyoming and Colorado, three-letter identifiers outline an area of coverage for the specific forecast. This area extends from Bozeman, MT, to Gillette, WY, to Liberal, KS, to Dove Creek, WY, to Rock Springs, WY, and back to Bozeman. As mentioned previously under the header, the valid time begins on the 14th day of the month at 1100Z for a 12-hour period. A broken to overcast cloud layer begins between 7,000 to 9,000 feet MSL, with tops extending to 20,000 feet. Since visibility and wind information is omitted, the visibility is expected to be greater than six statute miles, and the wind less than 20 knots. However, the visibility is forecast to be occasionally 3 miles in light rain and fog. After 2000Z, widely scattered thunderstorms with light rain showers are expected, with cumulonimbus (CB) cloud tops to 45,000 feet. The 6-hour categorical outlook covers the period from 2300Z on the 14th to 0500 on the 15th. The forecast is for marginal VFR weather due to ceilings (CIG) and rain showers.

AMENDMENTS

Amendments to FAs are issued whenever the weather significantly improves or deteriorates based on the judgment of the forecaster. An amended FA is identified by the contraction "AMD" in the header along with the time of the amended forecast. When an FA is corrected, the contraction "COR" appears in the heading, also with the time of the correction.

WINDS AND TEMPERATURES ALOFT FORECASTS

Winds and temperatures aloft forecasts provide an estimate of wind direction in relation to true north, wind speed in knots, and the temperature in degrees Celsius for selected altitudes. Depending on the station elevation,

Winds aloft are forecast in true direction and knots.

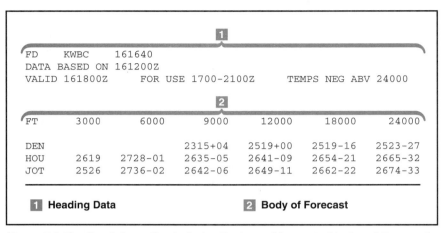

Figure 7-9. Heading information includes the type of forecast, the day of the month, and time of transmission. The second line tells you the forecast is based on observations at 1200Z and is valid at 1800Z on the 16th. It is intended for use between 1700Z and 2100Z on the same day. Since temperatures above 24,000 feet are always negative, a note indicates that the minus sign is omitted for 30,000 feet and above. The column on the left lists the FD location identifiers. The columns to the right show forecast information for each level appropriate to that location. This excerpt shows winds only to the 24,000 foot level.

winds and temperatures are usually forecast for nine levels between 3,000 and 39,000 feet. [Figure 7-9]

The FD does not include levels within 1,500 feet of the station elevation, and temperatures are not forecast for the 3,000-foot level or for a level within 2,500 feet of the station elevation. At Denver (DEN), for example, the forecast for the lower two levels is omitted, since the station elevation at Denver is over 5,000 feet.

The wind information included in the body of the FD is presented almost like it is on other reports and forecasts. The first two numbers indicate the true direction from which the wind is blowing. For example, "2736-02" indicates the wind is from 270° at 36 knots and the temperature is –2°C. Quite often you must interpolate between the two levels. For instance, if you plan to fly near Joliet (JOT) at 7,500 feet, you must interpolate between 6,000 and 9,000 feet. In this case, your planned flight altitude is midway between them. A good estimate of the wind is 265° at 39 knots with a temperature of –04°C.

Wind speeds between 100 and 199 knots are encoded so direction and speed can be represented by four digits. This is done by adding 50 to the two-digit wind direction and subtracting 100 from the velocity. For example, a wind of

270° at 101 knots is encoded as "7701" (27 + 50 = 77 for wind direction, and 101 − 100 = 01 for wind speed). A code of 9900 indicates light and variable winds (less than five knots).

When wind speeds are 100 to 199 knots, decode by subtracting 50 from the first two digits and adding 100 to the next two digits. The code 9900 means light and variable.

SEVERE WEATHER REPORTS AND FORECASTS

Although most weather gathering activity is concerned with routine reports and forecasts, considerable effort is devoted to monitoring and reporting severe weather conditions. The National Hurricane Center in Miami, Florida issues hurricane advisories; the National Severe Storms Forecast Center in Kansas City, Missouri also issues special forecasts and reports for severe weather conditions. These include convective outlook forecasts and severe weather watch bulletins.

The **convective outlook** (AC) forecasts general thunderstorm activity for the next 24-hour period. ACs are used by meteorologists to prepare graphic charts. You may use the data for planning flights within the forecast period. A **severe weather watch bulletin** (WW) is a weather report that defines areas of possible severe thunderstorms or tornadoes. WWs are issued on an unscheduled basis and are updated as required. Satellite photos have improved the accuracy of forecasting severe weather phenomena. Normally, you will know about severe weather conditions well in advance of the actual occurrence. Since severe weather forecasts and reports may affect the general public, as well as pilots, they are widely disseminated through all available media.

CHECKLIST

After studying this section, you should have a basic understanding of:

✓ **Aviation routine weather reports (METARs)** — What the basic types are, the main information elements they provide, and how they are interpreted.

✓ **METAR remarks** — How remarks pertain to the basic report and the type of information that may be included.

✓ **Pilot Reports (PIREPs)** — What they are and the type of information typically included.

✓ **Radar weather reports (SDs)** — What information they provide.

✓ **Terminal aerodrome forecasts (TAFs)** — What they are, where they apply, and what information they contain.

✓   **Area forecast (FA)** — What information the various sections contain and how to interpret the information.

✓   **Winds and temperatures aloft forecasts (FDs)** — What the basic format is and how to interpret it.

✓   **Severe weather reports and forecasts** — What their significance is and what types are available.

GRAPHIC WEATHER PRODUCTS

Besides printed weather reports and forecasts, the National Weather Service also produces a variety of graphic weather charts which are available at flight service stations and weather service offices. These charts give you a pictorial view of large-scale weather patterns and trends.

SURFACE ANALYSIS CHART

The surface analysis chart, also referred to as a surface weather analysis chart, shows weather conditions as they existed a few hours ago. By reviewing this chart, you can get a picture of atmospheric pressure patterns at the earth's surface. More importantly, you also can see the locations of high and low pressure systems and associated fronts. This chart is transmitted every three hours. [Figure 7-10]

The surface analysis chart shows pressure patterns, high and low pressure areas, fronts, and station models.

Figure 7-10. The box at the lower left of this excerpt reflects the date and time of the plotted observations. In this case, they were made at 1800Z on December 20. An inset at the lower right shows the symbols that represent various types of fronts, as well as squall lines. The symbols for cold, warm, and occluded fronts point in the direction of frontal movement.

Weather briefers often color code fronts and squall lines.

Weather briefers often color code fronts and squall lines for quick identification. The cold front is blue; the warm front is red. Stationary fronts are both blue and red, since they represent both warm and cold fronts. Occluded fronts and squall lines are purple.

A station model reflects the weather at a given reporting point.

The surface analysis chart also provides surface weather observations for a large number of reporting points throughout the United States. Each of these points is illustrated by a **station model**. To interpret these models, you first need to become familiar with the symbols that are used. Round station symbols depict stations where observations are taken by observers. Square station symbols indicate automated sites. [Figure 7-11]

Wind direction is shown relative to true north, and wind velocity is given in knots.

Symbols extending out from the station circle give wind information. The symbol shows the general true direction the surface wind is blowing from and gives the velocity in knots. The absence of a wind symbol and a double circle around the station means calm wind. True wind direction is shown by the orientation of the wind pointer. Velocity is indicated by barbs and/or pennants attached to the wind pointer. One short barb is five knots, a longer barb is 10 knots, and a pennant is 50 knots. For example, the wind pointer in the sample station model shows the wind is from the northwest at 15 knots.

Low cloud symbols are placed below the station model, while middle and high cloud symbols are placed immediately above it. A typical station model may include only one cloud type; seldom are more than two included. Decoding information for these symbols is available in various FAA publications and at flight service stations.

Temperature is given in degrees Fahrenheit, while pressure is given in millibars.

Temperatures are shown in degrees Fahrenheit; pressure is given in millibars. For example, the temperature at the sample station is 34°F, and the atmospheric pressure is 1014.7 millibars/hPa. Just below the station pressure, the number "28" indicates the pressure at this station has increased 2.8 millibars in the past three hours and is now steady. The ".45" below the pressure change tells that 45-hundredths of an inch of precipitation fell within the past six hours.

WEATHER DEPICTION CHART

The weather depiction chart may be thought of as a simplified version of the surface weather chart. It is an excellent source to help you determine general weather conditions during flight planning. Information plotted on this chart is derived from aviation routine weather reports (METARs).

Figure 7-11. A sample station model is shown at the top of the illustration. The table at the lower left presents some common weather symbols used for current weather. According to the sample station model, continuous snowfall is in progress. The table at the lower right explains the symbols used for sky cover. The sample station indicates a broken sky cover.

For flight planning, the weather depiction chart is most useful for determining general weather conditions and quickly locating areas of adverse weather.

Like the surface chart, the weather depiction chart is also prepared and transmitted by computer every three hours. Unlike the surface chart, pressure patterns and wind information are not provided. However, frontal activity and abbreviated station models are included. Symbols for fronts are the same as those used with surface charts. The most distinctive and useful feature of the weather depiction chart is that you can immediately locate areas of adverse weather simply by scanning it. [Figure 7-12]

The station model used for the weather depiction chart is a simplified version of the one used for the surface weather chart.

Weather depiction charts also feature simplified station models, with one primary difference from surface analysis charts. All station models are

Figure 7-12. This excerpt of a weather depiction chart covers the eastern United States. The legend at the lower right gives the definitions and symbols for IFR, marginal VFR, and VFR weather areas shown on the chart. The inset at the upper left shows a sample of the station model. You may wish to refer back to this illustration during the following discussion.

depicted as circles, and automated stations are shown with a bracket symbol to the right of the station. Sky cover symbols are the same as those used for the surface analysis chart. The number directly below the station is the height of the cloud layer in hundreds of feet. In the sample station model, the ceiling is 500 feet overcast. To the left of the station, the visibility is provided in statute miles or fractions of a mile if it is six miles or less. The reason for the obstruction to vision also may be given. In this case, the reported visibility is one-quarter mile in intermittent snow.

IFR, represented by enclosed shaded areas, means the ceiling is less than 1,000 feet AGL and/or the visibility is less than three statute miles. Marginal VFR is indicated by enclosed areas without shading. Marginal means the ceiling is 1,000 to 3,000 feet AGL inclusive and/or the visibility is three to five miles. In VFR conditions which are located outside enclosed areas, there is no ceiling, or the ceiling is greater than 3,000 feet AGL, and the visibility is greater than five miles.

RADAR SUMMARY CHART

The radar summary chart provides a graphic illustration of certain types of weather phenomena that special weather radar systems can detect. Pulses of radar energy are transmitted in a specific direction by a rotating antenna. When the signals encounter precipitation, they are reflected back to the antenna. The reflected signals, also called echoes, are then presented on a radar display which shows the strength and location of the radar return.

Computers prepare radar summary charts from these radar observations. The charts show lines and cells of hazardous thunderstorms. They depict the location, size, shape, and intensity of returns, as well as the intensity trend and direction of movement. As you examine the chart, keep in mind that the intensity of the radar returns increases as storms become more severe. In addition, the chart provides echo heights of the tops and bases of associated precipitation areas. However, the absence of echoes does not guarantee clear weather. Radar only detects precipitation, either in frozen or liquid form; it does not detect all cloud formations. For instance, fog is not displayed, and actual cloud tops may be higher or lower than the precipitation returns indicate.

Radar summary charts display only precipitation that can be detected by weather radar. Lines and cells of hazardous thunderstorms are depicted on these charts.

While the radar summary chart is a valuable preflight briefing aid, it has certain limitations. Keep in mind that it is an observation of conditions that existed at the valid time. Since thunderstorms develop rapidly, you should examine other weather sources for current and forecast conditions that may affect your flight.

Thunderstorms develop rapidly, so be sure to check other reports and forecasts for the latest weather conditions.

Figure 7-13. This excerpt of a radar summary chart covers the southeastern United States. The highlighted section represents one area of precipitation. Within the second contour, the radar returns correspond to level three or four (heavy to very heavy precipitation). The number "220" to the lower left indicates the top of a single cell within this area to be 22,000 feet MSL. The line from the number into the return area marks the location of the cell. You may wish to refer back to this illustration during the following discussion.

The radar summary chart displays precipitation in one of three contour levels representing precipitation intensity.

Intensity is shown on the chart by **contours**. The six levels displayed on a radar display are combined into three contours which are printed on the radar summary chart. The first contour represents levels one and two (light to moderate precipitation), the second shows levels three and four (heavy to very heavy precipitation), and the third outlines levels five and six (intense to extreme precipitation). [Figure 7-13]

There are several other symbols you need to be familiar with when interpreting a radar summary chart. For example, the arrow pointing to the right indicates an area of precipitation is moving to the east at 15 knots. The letters "TRW+" tell you that a new thunderstorm, or one that is in progress, is building in intensity. A rectangular dashed-line box denotes a severe

Symbol	Meaning	Symbol	Meaning
(echo symbol)	Intensity level 1-2 Weak and moderate	$\frac{240}{80}$	Echo top 24,000' MSL Echo base 8,000' MSL
(echo symbol)	Intensity level 3-4 (second contour) Strong and very strong	+	Intensity increasing or new echo
(echo symbol)	Intensity level 5-6 (third contour) Intense and extreme	–	Intensity decreasing
(dashed box)	Dashed lines define areas of severe weather	SLD	Solid, over 8/10 coverage
(box)	Area of echoes	LEWP	Line echo wave pattern
		HOOK	Hook echo
		HAIL	Hail
(curved line)	Line of echoes	WS999	Severe thunderstorm watch
		WT999	Tornado watch
→20	Cell moving east at 20 knots	NE	No echoes
		NA	Observation not available
(barb line)	Line or area is moving east at 20 knots (10 knot barbs)	OM	Equipment out for maintenance
		STC	STC on - all precipitation may not be seen

Figure 7-14. Here are some of the symbols which may appear on the radar summary chart, along with brief explanations of their meanings.

weather watch area. In this case, the notation "WS473" appears above the upper right corner of the box. The letters "WS" identify this as a severe thunderstorm watch area. The numbers "473" mean this is the 473rd severe weather watch to be issued during the year. According to the notation at the lower left margin of the chart, this watch began at 1903Z and continues until 0100Z. [Figure 7-14]

A line of echoes is often shown on the chart. If there is at least 8/10 coverage, the line is labeled "SLD" at both ends. A **hook-shaped echo** (HOOK) may be associated with a tornado. In a **line echo wave pattern** (LEWP), one portion of a squall line bulges out ahead of the rest producing strong, gusty winds. **Sensitivity time control** (STC) is a radar feature which diminishes nearby echoes to enhance reception of more distant returns. This may mask some echoes or distort their relative intensities.

LOW-LEVEL SIGNIFICANT WEATHER PROG

The three charts we have discussed so far — the surface analysis, weather depiction, and radar summary charts — are all based on weather observations of the conditions that existed at a particular time. The next chart is a forecast chart instead of an observation chart. The U.S. low-level significant weather prognostic chart is valid from the surface up to the 400-millibar pressure level (24,000 feet). It is, therefore, designed for use in planning flights below this altitude. A prognostic chart is usually referred to as a "prog" chart. [Figure 7-15]

Low-level prog charts are issued four times each day. The valid time is printed on the lower margin of each panel. Since the two panels on the left forecast the weather 12 hours from the issue time and the two panels on the right forecast 24 hours, you can compare the two sets of panels and note expected changes between the two time frames.

SIGNIFICANT WEATHER PANELS

The upper panels show areas of IFR and marginal VFR weather, turbulence, and freezing levels. These panels of the prognostic chart help you determine areas to be avoided. Smooth lines enclose areas of forecast IFR weather; scalloped lines represent marginal VFR. As shown by the legend information, IFR areas have ceilings less than 1,000 feet and/or visibility less than three statute miles. Scalloped lines enclose marginal VFR (MVFR) ceilings from 1,000 to 3,000 feet and/or visibilities of three to five miles inclusive. Although the definitions of IFR and MVFR for this chart are the same as the weather depiction chart, the symbols for portraying the areas are different.

Low-level progs provide nonconvective turbulence and icing forecasts. Dashed lines enclose areas of moderate or greater turbulence. Numbers within these areas give the height of the turbulence in hundreds of feet MSL. Figures below a line show the expected base, while figures above a line represent the top of the turbulence. For example, 180 indicates turbulence from the surface to 18,000 feet MSL. Since thunderstorms always imply moderate or greater turbulence, areas of possible thunderstorm turbulence are not outlined. **Freezing level height contours** for the highest freezing level are drawn at 4,000-foot intervals with dashed lines. These contours are labeled in hundreds of feet MSL. A zig-zag line labeled "SFC" shows the surface location of the freezing level.

Since graphic weather charts cover large areas of the United States, they are most useful as aids during the planning phase of a cross-country flight. They should also be used as a starting point when you obtain a preflight weather briefing, since they allow you to get the "big picture" of the weather likely to affect your flight.

SURFACE PROG PANELS

The two lower panels are the surface prog panels. They contain standard symbols for fronts and pressure centers. Direction of pressure center

Figure 7-15. A low-level prog chart consists of four panels. The two lower panels are 12- and 24-hour forecasts of surface weather conditions, while the two upper panels are 12- and 24-hour forecasts of weather between the surface and 24,000 feet. Legend information is included between the two upper panels.

Symbol	Meaning	Symbol	Meaning	Symbol	Meaning
	Showery precipitation (thunderstorms/rain showers) covering half or more of the area		Rain shower	⌒	Moderate turbulence
	Continuous precipitation (rain) covering half or more of the area		Snow shower	⌃	Severe turbulence
	Showery precipitation (snow showers) covering less than half of the area	Ƙ	Thunderstorms	Ψ	Moderate icing
		∿	Freezing rain	Ψ	Severe icing
	Intermittent precipitation (drizzle) covering less than half of the area	Ϭ	Tropical storm	●	Rain
		Ϭ	Hurricane (typhoon)	✳	Snow
				͵	Drizzle

NOTE: **Character of stable precipitation is the manner in which it occurs. It may be intermittent or continuous. A single symbol means intermittent, and a pair of symbols means continuous.**

Figure 7-16. An area which is expected to have continuous or intermittent (stable) precipitation is enclosed by a solid circle. If only showers are expected, the area is enclosed with a dot-dash pattern. When precipitation covers one-half or more of the area, it is shaded.

movement is shown by an arrow; the speed is listed in knots. Areas of forecast precipitation, as well as thunderstorms, are outlined. Prog charts also have several unique symbols that are used to forecast weather conditions. [Figure 7-16]

CHECKLIST

After studying this section, you should have a basic understanding of:

✓ **Surface analysis charts** — How they represent atmospheric pressure patterns and weather at reporting stations across the country.

✓ **Weather depiction charts** — How you can use these charts to determine areas of IFR and marginal VFR weather.

✓ **Radar summary charts** — How these charts show thunderstorm activity based on radar returns from precipitation.

✓ **Low level significant weather progs** — How you can use these charts to forecast weather conditions 12 to 24 hours in the future.

Now that you are able to interpret printed reports and forecasts and weather charts, you also need to become familiar with sources of weather information. Aside from your primary contacts with FSS and NWS telephone briefers, there are several other sources of supplemental weather information. This section will explain how to obtain a formal weather briefing from FSS or NWS personnel, as well as how to use supplemental weather sources effectively.

PREFLIGHT WEATHER BRIEFINGS

Flight service stations are your primary source for preflight and in-flight weather information. In areas not served by an FSS or a newer automated FSS (AFSS), Weather Service Offices (WSOs) may provide pilot weather briefings and also supply backup service to the FSS network. Telephone numbers for these outlets are available in the *Airport/Facility Directory* (A/FD). You also may find them in the telephone directory within the U.S. Government listings. Look under the Department of Transportation for the FAA or the Department of Commerce for the NWS.

When you request a briefing, you need to identify yourself as a pilot and supply the briefer with the following background information: type of flight planned (VFR or IFR), aircraft number or pilot's name, aircraft type, departure airport, route of flight, destination, flight altitude(s), ETD, and ETE.

When you contact a weather briefer, identify yourself as a pilot flying VFR and provide relevant background data for the flight.

The briefer can then proceed directly with the briefing and concentrate on weather affecting your flight. FSS personnel are certified by the NWS as pilot weather briefers. While they do not make original forecasts, they do translate and interpret reports and forecasts into terms that describe the weather conditions you can expect along your route of flight and at your destination. Generally, there are three types of preflight weather briefings, and you should request the appropriate one when you contact the briefer. These include the standard, abbreviated, and outlook briefings.

STANDARD BRIEFING

Whenever you are planning a trip and have not had the opportunity to obtain preliminary weather or a previous briefing, you should request the **standard briefing**. This is the most complete weather briefing, since it assumes you have no basic familiarity with the overall weather picture. When you request the standard briefing, the briefer automatically provides certain types of information in sequence, if applicable to your proposed flight. The first three items may be combined in any order when, in the briefer's opinion, it will help to describe conditions more clearly to you.

The standard briefing provides the most information concerning weather for your flight.

The following items are included in the standard briefing:

1. **Adverse Conditions** — This includes the type of information that might influence you to alter your proposed route or cancel the flight altogether. Examples include such things as hazardous weather, closed runways, or navigation aids out of service.

2. **VFR Flight Not Recommended** — This statement, if made by a flight service briefer, means that, in the briefer's judgment, it is doubtful that you can complete the flight under VFR. Although the final decision to conduct the flight rests with you, this advisory should be taken very seriously.

3. **Synopsis** — The briefer will provide you with a broad overview of the major weather systems or airmasses that affect the proposed flight.

4. **Current Conditions** — This information is a rundown of existing conditions, including pertinent hourly, pilot, and radar reports. If your proposed departure time is beyond two hours, this item is omitted unless you specifically request it.

5. **Enroute Forecast** — This is a summary of forecast conditions in a logical order along the proposed route.

6. **Destination Forecast** — The briefer will provide the forecast for your destination at the ETA and also include any significant changes within ± one hour.

7. **Winds and Temperatures Aloft** — The briefer will provide you with a summary of forecast winds and temperatures for your route and interpolate wind direction and speed between levels and stations for your planned cruising altitude(s).

8. **Notices to Airmen** — You will receive pertinent NOTAM information from the briefer. However, information which has already been published in the *Notices to Airmen* publication will not be included unless you specifically request it.

9. **ATC Delays** — You will be advised of any known air traffic control delays that might affect your proposed flight.

10. **Request for PIREPs** — Briefers may ask you to make pilot weather reports, especially regarding cloud bases or tops, icing, turbulence, or any other significant weather.

The briefer will provide you with other information upon request. Examples include MOA and MTR activity within 100 n.m. of the FSS, a review of the *Notices to Airmen* publication, and approximate density altitude. Other "on-request" items include information concerning ATC services and rules, as well as customs and immigration procedures.

ABBREVIATED BRIEFING

When you need to update weather information that you obtained from mass dissemination sources, a previous briefing, or when you need only one or two specific items, you should request an **abbreviated briefing**. Tell the briefer the source of the prior information and the time you received it, plus any other pertinent background information. This allows the briefer to limit the conversation to information you did not receive, plus any significant changes in weather conditions. Usually, the sequence of information will follow that of the standard briefing. If you request only one or two items, you still will be advised if adverse conditions are present or forecast. If they are, you should request clarifying details.

> Request an abbreviated briefing to update weather information you receive from mass dissemination sources, or an earlier briefing.

OUTLOOK BRIEFING

Whenever your proposed departure time is six or more hours away, it is appropriate to request an **outlook briefing**. The briefer will provide forecast information appropriate to the proposed flight, which will help you make an initial judgment about the feasibility of the trip. As your departure time draws near, you will need to request either a standard or abbreviated briefing to receive current conditions and the latest forecasts.

> You should request an outlook briefing when your proposed departure is six or more hours away.

Following the briefing, feel free to ask for any information you or the briefer may have missed. It helps to save your questions until the briefing has been completed. This allows the briefer to present the information logically and lessens the chance that items will be overlooked.

SUPPLEMENTAL WEATHER SOURCES

As you might expect, the high volume of flight operations generates a tremendous demand for weather information. Because of this, many FSSs provide recorded data. By listening to the recordings, you can obtain preliminary weather and decide whether you need to talk to a briefer for more detailed information. In many instances, recorded weather briefings may be sufficient for local flights. In other cases, you can use them to help develop an overall picture of the weather for a proposed trip. You may use this preliminary information to make an initial decision on the feasibility of the trip, much as you would do with an outlook briefing.

Another type of recorded weather information is the **transcribed weather broadcast** (TWEB), which is broadcast continuously over selected low frequency NDBs (190-535 kHz) and/or VORs. Frequencies are published on aeronautical charts. The broadcasts are made from a series of individual tape recordings, and changes are transcribed into the tapes as they occur. At some locations, telephone access to the recording is provided (TEL-

> TWEB recordings are broadcast over selected VORs and NDBs. Usually they include specific route forecasts, as well as winds aloft information.

TWEB). The information in a TWEB varies with the type of recording equipment that is available. Generally, the broadcast includes route-oriented data with specially prepared National Weather Service forecasts, in-flight advisories, winds aloft, and preselected information such as weather reports, NOTAMs and special notices.

At some locations, the information is broadcast over the local VOR only and is limited to items such as the hourly weather for the parent station and up to five adjacent stations, local NOTAM information, terminal forecast for the parent station, adverse weather conditions, and other potentially hazardous conditions.

TWEBs are designed primarily for preflight and inflight planning. As a general rule, a TWEB should not be considered as a substitute for a formal weather briefing. Phone numbers for transcribed weather broadcasts are listed in the *Airport/Facility Directory*.

In addition to these automated weather information sources, you can also use TOUCH-TONE® phones to access a complete menu of recorded weather information from an **automated flight service station** (AFSS). When you reach the FSS, you will hear an informational recording telling you how to access further information or how to go directly to a weather briefer. **Telephone information briefing service** (TIBS), for example, provides a continuous recording of meteorological and/or aeronautical information. These automated systems are easy to use and they provide local and route-oriented information. After you have selected the recordings you need, you can transfer directly to a briefer if you need more detailed information.

Because of FSS consolidation, you may often find yourself at airports which are beyond local calling distance. To counter this problem, many FSSs have toll-free telephone numbers. To use these numbers, dial "1 + 800" and the number. Check the *Airport/Facility Directory* for further details. Another method of calling an FSS is through a "direct line," which is often available at a local airport or FBO.

At selected FSSs, you can also use the **fast-file flight plan system** to file your VFR flight plan. This is appropriate when you have already received your weather briefing and just want to file. After reaching the special telephone number, you file your flight plan using recorded instructions. VFR flight plans are transcribed and retained at the FSS for activation by the pilot. When you use this system, remember to speak at a normal rate and avoid lengthy pauses between items, since the system will automatically disconnect eight seconds after you stop speaking. Also, remember to file at least 30 minutes in advance of your proposed departure time.

Since weather briefing and flight plan filing procedures are subject to new technology, make sure you check the *Airman's Information Manual* or the *Airport/Facility Directory* for the latest systems descriptions. For example, with the **direct user access terminal system** (DUATS), you can file flight plans and receive weather briefings directly. You access DUATS through toll-free numbers and a personal computer. Finally, don't overlook your local TV weather programs or, if available, the cable weather channel. They can help you size up the general weather picture a day or two before a flight.

IN-FLIGHT WEATHER SERVICES

As you already know, forecasting is still an inexact science, and weather conditions can change rapidly in the course of a few hours. During flight, you need to update your weather information on a continual basis. You may do this by contacting an FSS. In other situations, you can receive in-flight weather broadcasts by monitoring appropriate FSS radio frequencies. TWEBs are also available from selected NDBs and VORs.

ENROUTE FLIGHT ADVISORY SERVICE

An FSS service specifically designed to provide timely enroute weather information upon pilot request is referred to as **enroute flight advisory service** (EFAS), or Flight Watch. You can usually contact an EFAS specialist from 6 A.M. to 10 P.M. anywhere in the conterminous U.S. The discrete EFAS frequency, 122.0 mHz, is established for pilots of aircraft flying between 5,000 feet AGL and 17,500 feet MSL. Different frequencies are allocated for each ARTCC area for operations above 18,000 feet MSL.

The frequency for EFAS (Flight Watch) below FL180 is 122.0 mHz.

The weather advisories you receive are tailored to the type of flight you are conducting and are appropriate to your route and cruising altitude. In addition, EFAS is a central collection and distribution point for pilot weather reports (PIREPs), so you normally receive very current or real-time weather information. This includes any thunderstorm activity along your route.

EFAS facilities provide actual weather, including any thunderstorm activity that might affect your route.

When you wish to contact EFAS, use the words *"Flight Watch."* A flight watch facility usually serves a large geographic area through remote communications outlets (RCOs). Because of this, you should make your initial callup using the name of the air route traffic control center (ARTCC) serving the area. Then give your aircraft identification and the name of the VOR nearest your position. For example, *"Denver Flight Watch, Cessna 141 Foxtrot Sierra, Casper VOR."* This way, the briefer will know which RCO to use for the reply. Since sectional charts do not show flight watch outlets or parent facilities, there may be times when you won't know your flight watch area. In these situations, you can make your initial callup as follows: *"Flight Watch, Cessna 141 Foxtrot Sierra, Casper VOR."* The flight watch briefer then responds with the name of the controlling facility. The A/FD contains a chart depicting the locations of flight watch control stations and the outlets they use.

All EFAS facilities and many FSSs have equipment to directly access weather radar displays. This system is designed to provide real-time radar weather information from a national network of radar sites. The radar units use color to display weather returns, which makes them easier to interpret. This information is available for preflight as well as in-flight briefings.

Keep in mind that flight watch is not intended for matters relating to flight plans, position reports, preflight briefings, or to obtain weather reports or forecasts unrelated to your flight. For these items, you should contact an FSS on other published frequencies. On the other hand, pilot participation is essential to the success of flight watch, and you are encouraged to make pilot reports of the flight conditions you encounter, whether favorable or unfavorable.

IN-FLIGHT AVIATION WEATHER ADVISORIES

The purpose of in-flight advisories is to notify pilots of the possibility of encountering hazardous flying conditions which may not have been forecast at the time of the preflight briefing. Whether or not the conditions may be hazardous to a flight is something that you, as the pilot, must evaluate on the basis of experience and the operational limits of the airplane. The first advisories to be discussed are called AIRMETs and SIGMETs. **AIRMET** is an acronym for "airman's meteorological information," and **SIGMET** means "significant meteorological information."

AIRMETs and SIGMETs

AIRMETs warn of weather hazards which mainly concern light aircraft.

AIRMETs (WAs) are issued every six hours with amendments issued, as necessary, for weather phenomena which are of operational interest to all aircraft. These weather conditions are potentially hazardous to aircraft having limited capability because of lack of equipment, instrumentation, or pilot qualifications. AIRMETs concern weather of less severity than that covered by SIGMETs. They are of particular concern to pilots of light aircraft. AIRMETs are issued for moderate icing, moderate turbulence, sustained winds of 30 knots or more at the surface, ceilings less than 1,000 feet and/or visibility less than three miles affecting over 50 percent of an area at any one time, and extensive mountain obscurement.

Nonconvective SIGMETs (WSs) are issued for hazardous weather (other than convective activity) which is considered significant to all aircraft. SIGMET criteria include severe icing, severe and extreme turbulence, volcanic eruptions and duststorms, sandstorms, or volcanic ash lowering visibility to less than three miles.

SIGMETs warn of weather hazards which concern all aircraft.

WSs are issued whether or not the conditions were included in the area forecast. Both SIGMETs and AIRMETs are identified by an alphanumeric designator. AIRMETs use Zulu for icing and freezing levels, Tango for turbulence, strong surface winds, and low level wind shear, and Sierra for IFR and mountain obscuration. Nonconvective SIGMETs use consecutive alphanumeric designators November through Yankee excluding those designators reserved for scheduled AIRMETs. [Figure 7-17]

Convective SIGMETs (WSTs) are issued for hazardous convective weather (existing or forecast) which is significant to the safety of all aircraft. They always imply severe or greater turbulence, severe icing, and low-level wind shear, so these items are not specified in the advisory. WSTs are unscheduled and may be issued for any convective situation which the forecaster considers hazardous to all categories of aircraft. They include any of the following phenomena: tornadoes, lines of thunderstorms, thunderstorms over a wide area, embedded thunderstorms, hail greater than or equal to three-fourths of an inch in diameter, and/or wind gusts to 50 knots or greater.

Convective SIGMETs include tornadoes, thunderstorms, and hail.

```
DFWP UWS 051710                    MIAT WA 151900 AMD
SIGMET PAPA 1 VALID UNTIL          AIRMET TANGO UPDT 2 FOR TURBC
052110                             VALID UNTIL 160100
AR LA MS                           AIRMET TURBC...GA FL
FROM MEM TO 30N MEI TO BTR         FROM SAV TO JAX TO CTY TO TLH
TO MLU TO MEM                      TO SAV
OCNL SVR ICING ABV FRZLVL          MDT TURBC BLO 100 EXPCD
EXPCD.                             CONDS IPVG
FRZLVL 080 E TO 120 W.             AFT 160000Z
CONDS CONTG BYD 2100Z.
```

Figure 7-17. The first issuance of a SIGMET, as shown on the left, is labeled UWS (Urgent Weather SIGMET). PAPA 1 means it is the first issuance for a SIGMET phenomenon; PAPA 2 would be the second issuance for the same phenomenon. In the example on the right, AMD means this is an amended AIRMET of the phenomenon (moderate turbulence) identified as TANGO. The alphanumeric designator stays with the phenomenon even when it moves across the country.

```
MKCC WST 221655              MKCC WST 221655
CONVECTIVE SIGMET 17C        CONVECTIVE SIGMET 18C
VALID UNTIL 1855Z            VALID UNTIL 1855Z
KS OK TX                     SD NE IA
VCNTY GLD-CDS LINE           FROM FSD TO DSM TO GRI TO BFF
NO SGFNT TSTMS RPRTD         TO FSD
LINE TSTMS DVLPG BY 1755Z WILL   AREA TSTMS WITH FEW EMBDD
MOV EWD 30-35 KT THRU 1855Z  CELLS MOVG FROM 2725 TOPS 300
HAIL TO 1 1/2 IN PSBL.       FCST TO 1855Z DSPTG AREA WILL
                             MOV EWD 25 KT.
```

Figure 7-18. WST in the header identifies these reports as convective SIGMETs. The designators 17C and 18C indicate they are consecutive issuances for the Central U.S. One forecasts a line of thunderstorms with possible hail, while the other forecasts embedded thunderstorms over a large area.

Convective SIGMETs are issued for the Eastern (E), Central (C), and Western (W) United States. Individual convective SIGMETs are numbered sequentially for each area (01-99) each day. [Figure 7-18]

SEVERE WEATHER FORECAST ALERTS

An unscheduled message which is issued to alert forecasters, briefers, and pilots that a severe weather watch bulletin is being issued is called a **severe weather forecast alert** (AWW). These preliminary messages define areas of possible severe thunderstorms or tornado activity. Beginning with the first January every year, each AWW is numbered sequentially. [Figure 7-19]

CENTER WEATHER ADVISORIES

An unscheduled weather advisory issued by an ARTCC to alert pilots of existing or anticipated adverse weather conditions within the next two hours is called a **center weather advisory** (CWA). A CWA may supplement an existing in-flight advisory and is intended primarily for IFR traffic. It may also alert pilots when a SIGMET has not been issued, but conditions meet those criteria based on current pilot reports. CWAs are one of the most current sources for existing or forecast hazardous weather.

```
MKC AWW 241817
WW 256 TORNADO NE 241900Z - 250000Z
AXIS..70 STATUTE MILES EAST AND WEST OF LINE..
55SSW EAR/KEARNEY NE/ - 65NNW OFK/NORFOLK NE/
HAIL SURFACE AND ALOFT. . 2 1/2 INCHES. WIND GUSTS..70KT.
MAX TOPS TO 550. MEAN WIND VECTOR 260/35.
```

Figure 7-19. "AWW" in the header identifies this report as a severe weather forecast alert. This message warns of possible tornado activity in Nebraska and defines the watch area. Hail and high winds also are possible. A detailed severe weather watch bulletin (WW) immediately follows the alert message.

Air Route Traffic Control Centers broadcast AIRMETs, SIGMETs, Convective SIGMETs, AWWs, and CWAs once on all frequencies, except emergency, when any part of the area described is within 150 miles of the airspace under their jurisdiction. These broadcasts contain SIGMET or CWA identification and a brief description of the weather activity and general area affected.

Beginning with the second hour, a summarized alert notice is broadcast. It simply states that the particular advisory is current and briefly describes the weather phenomenon and the area affected. If you hear an alert notice and have not received the advisory, you should contact the nearest FSS for more detailed information, since it might be pertinent to your flight. Affected ARTCCs and terminal control facilities also make a single broadcast on all normal frequencies when a SIGMET, AWW, or CWA is issued. In terminal areas, local control and approach control may limit these broadcasts to weather occurring within 50 n.m. of the airspace under their jurisdiction.

HAZARDOUS IN-FLIGHT WEATHER ADVISORY SERVICE

A program for broadcasting hazardous weather information on a continuous basis over selected VORs is called **hazardous in-flight weather advisory service** (HIWAS). The broadcasts include summarized AIRMETs, SIGMETs, convective SIGMETs, AWWs, CWAs and urgent PIREPs. In areas where HIWAS is implemented, you should be aware that ARTCC, terminal ATC, and FSS facilities have discontinued their normal broadcasts of in-flight advisories. However, FSSs and ARTCCs announce updates to HIWAS information on all normal frequencies. While HIWAS is an additional source of hazardous weather information, it is not a replacement for preflight or in-flight briefings or real-time weather updates from flight watch. VORs used for HIWAS broadcasts can be found in the A/FD. Since HIWAS is a developing program, check the *Airman's Information Manual* and NOTAMs publication for the latest information.

HIWAS continuously broadcasts summaries of in-flight advisories and PIREPs.

AUTOMATED WEATHER OBSERVING SYSTEM

Another source of weather is an automated unit which can make surface weather observations and transmit them directly to you during flight. This unit is the **automated weather observing system** (AWOS), which uses various sensors, a voice synthesizer, and a radio transmitter to provide real-time weather data. AWOS transmissions can usually be received within 25 n.m. of the site, at or above 3,000 feet AGL. Most units transmit a 20- to 30-second weather message updated each minute. These minute-by-minute weather messages can be accessed via telephone at most AWOS sites. Locations where AWOS is installed are published in the A/FD.

You should be aware that AWOS sensors have some limitations which are related to the configuration of individual systems. Refer to the *Aeronautical Information Manual* for a description of specific limitations.

AUTOMATED SURFACE OBSERVATION SYSTEM

The primary surface weather observing system in the United States is the **automated surface observation system** (ASOS). It is designed to support aviation operations and weather forecast activities. Using an array of sensors, computers, and digitized voice communications, ASOS provides continuous minute-by-minute observations. These weather reports are broadcast over VHF frequencies, VORs, and/or telephone lines, as indicated in the A/FD. An ASOS report which has not been modified by a weather observer is noted by the word "AUTO." In this case, the report only contains information that can be reported automatically, such as cloud height, visibility, precipitation identification, pressure sensors, temperature/dewpoint, wind direction and speed, and rainfall accumulation. In addition, some automatic ASOS stations can determine the difference between liquid precipitation and frozen or freezing precipitation. The stations where this distinction can be made are identified with an "A02." An "A01" station does not have this capability.

CHECKLIST _____

After studying this section, you should have a basic understanding of:

✓   **Preflight weather briefings** — What the three types are and which type you should request.

✓   **Supplemental weather sources** — What the various sources are, including PATWAS, TWEB, TIBS, and DUATS, and how to access them.

✓   **In-flight weather services** — What the various sources of in-flight weather services are, including EFAS, and how to contact them.

✓   **In-flight advisories** — What the criteria for issuance of AIRMETs, SIGMETs, convective SIGMETs, AWWs, and CWAs are and how to receive them in flight.

✓   **HIWAS** — What it is and how you can benefit from it during flight.

✓   **AWOS and ASOS** — What these systems are and how to access them.

flight prep   8

AERONAUTICAL CHARTS

Whenever you fly away from your home base airport, you will need aeronautical charts to help you navigate accurately. The charts you will be using provide a detailed portrayal of the topography of the covered area and also include aeronautical information. Because you will navigate initially with visual reference to objects or landmarks on the surface, topographical information will be very useful. The National Ocean Service (NOS) publishes several charts which supply an abundance of information for pilots operating under visual flight rules.

SECTIONAL CHARTS

The charts most commonly used for VFR flight are **sectional charts**. They cover all of the 48 mainland states, plus Alaska, Hawaii, Puerto Rico, and the Virgin Islands. To allow for greater detail, each chart shows a section of the country and is given the name of a primary city within its coverage.

Sectional aeronautical charts use a scale of 1:500,000.

Topographical information includes relief features (such as terrain contours), cities, towns, rivers, highways, railroads, and other distinctive landmarks which you can use as visual checkpoints. Along with airport depictions, sectionals also contain aeronautical information pertaining to navigation and communication facilities, as well as airspace and obstructions. The scale of a sectional chart is 1:500,000. This means that each inch on the sectional chart represents 500,000 actual inches. This translates to one inch on the sectional equaling approximately seven nautical or eight statute miles on the earth's surface. Most sectionals are revised every six months, but some outside the 48 mainland states are on an annual revision schedule. [Figure 8-1]

The chart index on the front panel of a sectional tells you the names of the adjoining charts. If your route of flight is near the edge of a chart, you should always take along appropriate adjoining charts. The back panel contains detailed legend information which will receive special coverage later in this section.

Aeronautical charts are folded for easy handling, storage, and identification during flight. Most are printed on both sides in order to reduce the total number of charts required. When you look at the front panel of a sectional, you will notice arrows labeled "North" and "South." When you unfold the chart, these arrows direct you to the northern and southern portions of the covered area.

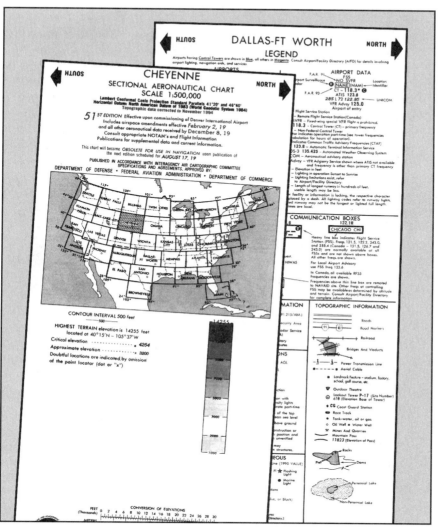

Figure 8-1. You can easily identify a sectional chart by the name or title printed on the front and back panels. Below the title, dates are provided to tell you when the chart is effective, and when it is scheduled to become obsolete for navigation.

Important terrain information is shown on the front of each chart. The colors, or gradient tints, assigned to each thousand feet of elevation are shown by a graph. Colors range from green at sea level to brown for elevations above 12,000 feet MSL. The contour intervals appearing on the sectional are also shown on the front. These contour lines connect areas of equal elevation, and are a good reference for determining the mean sea level elevations of the terrain you're flying over. The front panel also contains information concerning the highest terrain and other known features

Contour lines connect points of equal elevation.

CONTOUR INTERVAL 500 feet

— 500 —

HIGHEST TERRAIN elevation is 8720 feet
located at 36°42'N – 103°53'W

Critical elevation .... • *4254*

Approximate elevation .... x *3200*

Doubtful locations are indicated by omission
of the point locator (dot or "x")

— ATTENTION —
THIS CHART CONTAINS MAXIMUM
ELEVATION FIGURES (MEF). The
Maximum Elevation Figures shown in
quadrangles bounded by ticked lines of
latitude and longitude are represented in
THOUSANDS and HUNDREDS of feet
above mean sea level. The MEF is based
on information availiable concerning the
highest known feature in each quadrangle,
including terrain and obstructions (trees,
towers, antennas, etc.).

Example: 12,500 feet **12⁵**

Figure 8-2. In this example, a chart inset has been placed over the front panel. The
inset shows the location of the highest elevation for this sectional, which is 8,720 feet
MSL. Near the center of the inset, the maximum elevation figure (MEF) is shown by
"91" (9,100 feet MSL).

for the entire area of the chart, including **maximum elevation figures
(MEFs)**. MEFs are rounded to the next 100-foot level and adjusted upward
approximately 100 to 300 feet, depending on the nature of the terrain
and/or obstacles. [Figure 8-2]

VFR TERMINAL AREA CHARTS

VFR terminal area charts
use a scale of 1:250,000.

Whenever you're flying VFR in or around Class B airspace, **VFR terminal
area charts** will help significantly with orientation and navigation. These
charts have a large scale (1:250,000) and give you a more detailed display
of topographical features than sectional charts. VFR terminal charts are
revised every six months. [Figure 8-3]

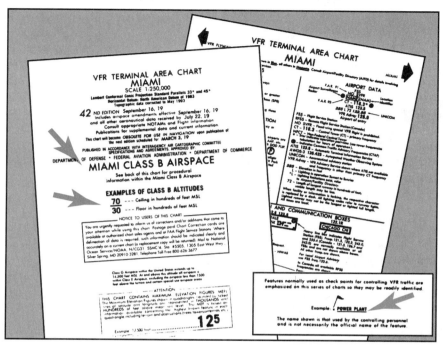

Figure 8-3. The title block of the terminal area chart clearly identifies its location. The symbology used to designate ceilings and floors within the Class B airspace is also shown on the front panel. Legend information on the back panel is the same as you will find on sectional charts. VFR checkpoints used to identify your position upon initial callup to approach control are shown by a magenta flag.

Terminal area charts show the lateral limits of the various sections of the Class B area. The lateral boundaries are marked by a heavy blue line which encircles the Class B area. Ceilings and floors are designated in hundreds of feet MSL. On sectional charts, the availability of a terminal area chart is indicated by a wide, blue band which encloses the Class B airspace and reflects the boundaries of the terminal area chart.

> Bold numbers above and below a horizontal line indicate the ceilings and floors of Class B areas.

The most efficient means of avoiding conflict with major traffic flows in and out of a Class B area is to refer to the VFR flyways shown on the reverse side of some terminal area charts. **VFR flyway planning charts** depict multiple routes for use by VFR pilots as alternatives to flight within Class B airspace. They are not intended to discourage requests for VFR operations, but are designed to aid pilots planning to avoid heavily congested areas, such as IFR arrival and departure routes. Flyway charts omit most of the terrain features and geographic information found on terminal area charts because they are for planning, not navigating. However, major landmarks are shown as visual aids to orientation. Although these routes go through areas of reduced air traffic congestion,

Figure 8-4. Flyways are marked by wide blue arrows and show the recommended VFR altitudes to fly. Although you are not required to use the flyways when operating VFR, you will find they usually are convenient routes between frequently traveled areas.

you should be aware that flying through them does not mean you have separation from other aircraft. [Figure 8-4]

WORLD AERONAUTICAL CHARTS

WAC charts use a scale of 1:1,000,000.

A **world aeronautical chart** (WAC) is similar to a sectional, but it uses a scale of 1:1,000,000. At this scale, approximately 14 nautical miles, or 16 statute miles, are represented by one inch on the map. The symbols are basically the same as those found on sectionals, but some of the detail is omitted due to the smaller scale. [Figure 8-5]

Figure 8-5. WAC charts are often used by pilots of high-performance airplanes, since they fly at higher altitudes and airspeeds. WAC charts not only reduce the total number of charts needed, but also reduce the need to change charts frequently.

In addition to the contour intervals and elevation information, the front shows a map index of the charts which can be placed together to incorporate the total network. The date at which the chart becomes effective is shown, as well as the date it is expected to become obsolete for navigation. Usually, this date is keyed to the publication schedule of the next edition. Most WAC charts are revised on a yearly basis.

LATITUDE AND LONGITUDE

Because the key to navigation is knowing where you are at a given a system was established to reference the exact location of any point on the earth. This system is based on latitude and longitude.

The equator is the imaginary line which circles the earth midway between the north and south poles. To aid in determining locations on a map, a system of lines parallel to the equator was established. These lines are called **lines of latitude**. As a reference point, the equator is labeled as 0° of latitude. The parallel lines north of the equator are numbered from 0° to 90°, with 90° north latitude positioned at the north pole. Parallels in the southern hemisphere are also numbered from 0° to 90°, with 90° south latitude representing the south pole. You can locate a position north or south of the equator by using lines of latitude.

The location of an airport can be determined by the intersection of lines of latitude and longitude.

Meridians, or **lines of longitude**, are imaginary lines which extend from the north to the south pole. Because they connect the poles, lines of longitude are always given in a direction of true north and south. Just as the equator is designated 0° of latitude, the **Prime Meridian**, which passes through Greenwich, England, is labeled 0° of longitude. [Figure 8-6]

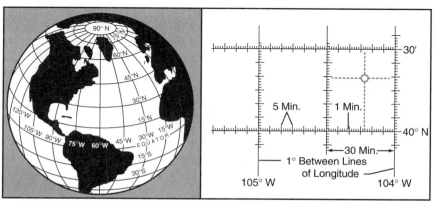

Figure 8-6. The lines of latitude and longitude are printed on aeronautical charts, with each degree subdivided into 60 equal segments called minutes. By knowing the geographic coordinates (or the intersection of the lines of latitude and longitude), you can locate any position on the earth. In this example, the airport is located at 40°20'N, 104°13'W.

There are a total of 360° of longitude encompassing the earth, with 180° on the east and 180° on the west side of the Prime Meridian. The line of 180° of longitude is on the opposite side of the earth from the Prime Meridian. The International Date Line approximately corresponds with the 180° line of longitude, although segments of the Date Line actually vary as much as 20°. When you locate a position east or west of the Prime Meridian, you will be determining a position in reference to a line of longitude.

PROJECTIONS

Navigating with reference to latitude and longitude could be done by using a globe. However, this procedure would be very impractical, since you would have to use an extremely large globe to show the required detail. For convenience, the spherical surface of the earth is "flattened" on aeronautical charts. Since this is like pressing a section of orange peel on a flat surface, some distortion ultimately occurs in this process.

Projections are used for transferring a section of the earth's surface onto a flat chart. Two of the most common types of projections are the Mercator and the Lambert Conformal Conic. The **Lambert Conformal Conic** is frequently used on aeronautical charts because it minimizes distortion. **Mercator** charts are usually used as wall maps. Their distortion increases with distance from the equator. [Figure 8-7]

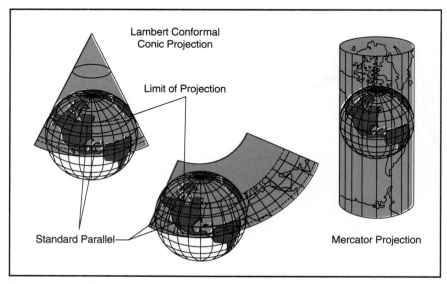

Figure 8-7. Sectional, VFR terminal, and world aeronautical charts are all Lambert projections. The overall scale inaccuracies which you obtain when comparing nautical miles on a Lambert chart to actual miles on earth are small enough that you can consider them negligible on a single chart.

LEGEND

Besides the topographical elevation information given on the front of the chart, the **legend** supplies an abundance of information to help you understand chart symbols. Symbols used in the legend include: airports, airport data, radio aids to navigation and communication, airspace information, topographical information, obstructions to flight, and other miscellaneous symbols.

AIRPORT SYMBOLOGY

As you study a sectional chart, you will notice several types of airport diagrams. Information provided in the legend will help answer questions you might have concerning a specific airport. There are thousands of airports identified by symbols on sectional charts. Because of the variety of airport types, shapes, and sizes, these symbols help you picture the actual airport being illustrated. [Figure 8-8]

> Tick marks extending from airport symbols show that fuel is available, and that the airport is attended during normal working hours.

Airports having control towers are shown in blue, while all others are identified by a magenta color. Although the color blue signifies an airport with a control tower, it does not mean that the control tower operates

> Airports with control towers are shown in blue; uncontrolled airports are shown in magenta.

Figure 8-8. The airport portion of the legend helps you to understand and interpret the symbols used. The star that appears above the diagram for Mamou Airport marks an airport beacon which normally operates from sunset to sunrise. The tick marks extending from the airport diagram at Eunice indicate that fuel is available and that the field is attended, at least during normal working hours.

continuously. The chart margin on an inside panel of the sectional will give you information about the hours of operation of a particular control tower.

Circular symbols are used to represent most airports. If an airport has at least one hard-surfaced runway 1,500 to 8,069 feet long, the runway will be shown inside the circle. It also will be oriented to reflect its approximate magnetic direction.

Runways are not enclosed in a circle at larger airports where at least one runway is longer than 8,069 feet. However, the outline of the runways will still be shown to reveal the general layout. If you were flying over the airport, you could recognize all hard-surfaced runways, since they would show the same pattern as the chart. Even hard-surfaced runways that are closed will be shown to aid in identification.

Private airports have landmark value and practical use in an emergency.

When an open circle is used and no runway pattern is shown, the airport does not have a hard-surfaced runway. Private airports appear as the letter "R" enclosed in an open circle. Although landing at a private airport requires the owner's permission, you could use one in an emergency, and they also have landmark value in navigation.

Military airports have the same appearance as civilian airports and are identified by abbreviations such as AFB, NAS, and AAF. Military airports with other than hard-surfaced runways are shown as one circle inside another. Other miscellaneous types of aerodromes, such as seaplane bases, heliports, ultralight flight parks, and unverified airports, are shown by additional symbols. A circle with an "X" superimposed over it represents a closed or abandoned airport.

AIRPORT DATA

The MSL elevation is shown underneath the name of the airport.

A second portion of the sectional legend explains the data printed near each individual airport. While the amount of information available is limited at some of the smaller, remote airports, you can obtain an abundance of facts from the airport data at larger airports. [Figure 8-9]

When applicable, the control tower frequency will be listed, following the letters "CT," as part of the airport data. Any time the tower is not in operation continuously, a star is placed after the frequency. Non-Federal control towers are marked by the abbreviation NFCT.

If automatic terminal information service is available at the airport, the designation "ATIS" is printed in this section, along with the frequency used to obtain it. If UNICOM is available, the frequency will be shown at the end of the airport data.

Figure 8-9. The airport data portion of the legend helps you to interpret information about a particular airport. The letters "FSS" tell you there is a flight service station on the field at the Eagle County Regional Airport, 122.95 MHz is the UNICOM frequency, and the letter "C" following the frequency 123.6 MHz indicates the CTAF. The number "6535" shows the airport elevation above sea level, and the "L 80" to the right of the elevation indicates lighting and the length of the longest runway in hundreds of feet (8,000).

The common traffic advisory frequency (CTAF) at uncontrolled airports is indicated on sectional charts in the airport data. For example, if the data for an airport doesn't list a frequency, the CTAF should be the MULTICOM frequency of 122.9 MHz. If only a UNICOM frequency is shown, that will be the designated CTAF unless there is an FSS on the field. When an FSS is located on the field, 123.6 MHz is usually the CTAF. At controlled fields where the tower operates part time, the tower frequency normally is used as the CTAF after the tower closes.

Airport data also tells you if lighting is available at an airport. A capital "L" designates lighting that is in operation at the airport from sunset to sunrise. Lighting available on request, part-time lighting, or pilot-controlled lighting is shown by an "L" with an asterisk next to it.

> When a part-time tower is closed, the CTAF is normally the tower frequency.

NAVIGATION AIDS

For cross-country planning and flight, you will find a significant amount of sectional chart information concerning navigation and communication facilities. An area of the legend has been set aside to help you interpret information in these navaids. [Figure 8-10]

Rectangular boxes printed on charts provide data on navaids and communication frequencies. These boxes are placed near the appropriate navaid, and include the name, frequency, and Morse code identifier of the navaid. VHF radio frequencies are colored blue, while low-and medium-frequency facilities are printed in magenta. [Figure 8-11]

The frequencies for an FSS are printed on the top of the communications box. Usually, you can transmit and receive on the same frequency when you are communicating with an FSS. In some cases, though, the navigation facility may be located a long way from the flight service station. In this situation, you may need to transmit to the FSS on 122.1 MHz and receive a reply on the navaid frequency. When the FSS can receive only on a given frequency, the letter "R" follows the frequency listing.

Figure 8-10. The triangular symbol marks a **VORTAC** facility located south of the Cherry Capital Airport. The circular dot pattern east of the airport represents a nondirectional radio beacon (NDB). The insert shows the symbols for these and other navaids that you will become familiar with in Flight Prep 9.

Figure 8-11. Information about the Forsyth NDB is printed in a magenta box. The underlined frequency indicates there is no voice capability on the frequency, and only the Morse code identifier is audibly transmitted.

At some airports, an FSS may be available for local airport advisory (LAA) service on the two-way frequency of 123.6 MHz. These FSSs are physically located on an airport which does not have a control tower or where the tower is operated on a part-time basis. The FSS uses this frequency to provide you with advisories concerning known traffic, wind, altimeter setting, and recommended runway. The emergency frequency, 121.5 MHz, and the two-way frequency, 122.2 MHz, are normally available at all FSSs and are not listed on the chart.

The common FSS frequency for airport advisory service is 123.6 MHz.

Enroute navigation facilities can provide you with a wide variety of in-flight weather updates. Whenever a square is located in the bottom right-hand corner of a communications box, HIWAS is available at the navaid. A circled "T" in the communications box indicates a TWEB is broadcast over the navaid. Enroute flight advisory service (EFAS) can be obtained by contacting Flight Watch on 122.0 MHz.

A "T" in the upper right corner of a communications box shows the availability of a TWEB. Flight Watch is available on 122.0 MHz.

AIRSPACE

Special-use airspace and some types of controlled airspace are shown by distinctive symbols on aeronautical charts. Because of the regulatory requirements for flying through the various classifications of airspace, you must be able to identify them and apply the appropriate flight rules.

A flag symbol marks a recommended visual checkpoint for identifying your position on initial callup.

Some symbols simply alert you to special information, such as the flag which is used to designate recommended checkpoints for initial callup. [Figure 8-12]

If requested, FSS specialists will provide information on military training activity within 100 nautical miles of your flight plan area.

Although permission is not required to fly through a military operations area, you should exercise extreme caution if military aircraft are using it. You can determine military activity within an MOA by contacting the nearest FSS. To help you locate this type of special-use airspace, a solid magenta line is printed on sectionals, with crosshatched lines extending into the MOA. [Figure 8-13]

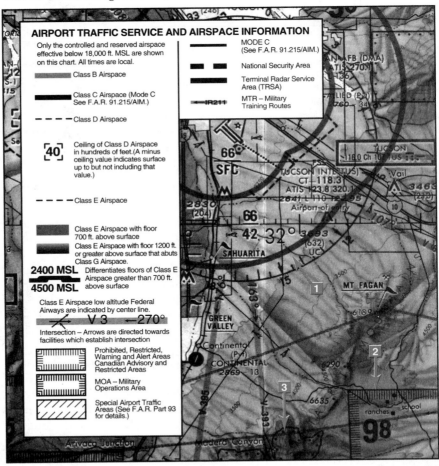

Figure 8-12. The boundary of the Tucson Class C airspace appears as a heavy solid magenta line (item 1). Prohibited, restricted, alert, or warning areas are marked by a blue crosshatched line (item 2). Areas regulated by the National Park Service, U.S. Fish and Wildlife Service, and the U.S. Forest Service are identified by a line and dot pattern (item 3). You are requested to maintain an altitude of at least 2,000 feet above these areas. Other designations are shown on the legend excerpt.

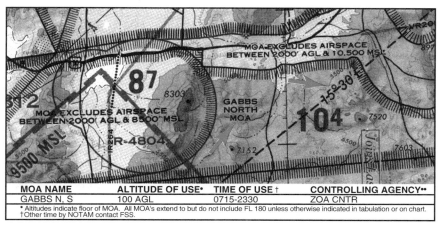

MOA NAME	ALTITUDE OF USE*	TIME OF USE †	CONTROLLING AGENCY**
GABBS N, S	100 AGL	0715-2330	ZOA CNTR

* Altitudes indicate floor of MOA. All MOA's extend to but do not include FL 180 unless otherwise indicated in tabulation or on chart.
† Other time by NOTAM contact FSS.

Figure 8-13. The name of the MOA, such as the "Gabbs North MOA," is printed within the boundaries. The margin of the sectional provides a table listing the name, applicable altitudes, times, and controlling agency for all MOAs shown on the chart. The dashed line and notation "15° 30'E" represent an isogonic line used to indicate the magnetic variation for this area of the chart.

Military training routes, or MTRs, also are shown on sectional charts by gray lines labeled with identifiers, such as "VR1218" or "IR252." VR or IR followed by a three-digit number means the route includes one or more segments above 1,500 feet AGL. Four digits mean the VR or IR route is flown at or below 1,500 feet. Regardless of your cruising altitude, you should always remain alert when crossing an MTR.

MTRs with operations above 1,500 feet AGL are given three-digit identifiers, while those at or below 1,500 feet AGL are designated with four digits.

The limits of controlled airspace are shown by tint bands which are color coded. The 700-foot floor of Class E airspace is enclosed by a magenta tint, while the area outside of this enclosed area has a floor 1,200 feet above the surface. The outer limits of controlled airspace are shown by a dark edge, and the color dissolves into the controlled portion. [Figure 8-14]

Figure 8-14. Although Federal airways normally begin at 1,200 feet AGL and extend up to 18,000 feet MSL, the floor of the V-19-257, in this example, is 5,600 feet MSL (item 1). Big Sandy Airport (item 2) lies in Class G airspace extending from the surface up to 14,500 feet MSL.

Many of the nation's busiest airports have unique operational requirements that impose certain regulatory limitations. Included are controlled airports within Class B and Class C airspace. On sectional charts, "NO SVFR" appears above the airport name, meaning no special VFR is permitted. Sectional charts also display the floor and ceiling of each segment of Class B and Class C airspace, shown in hundreds of feet MSL. [Figure 8-15]

Wherever an ADIZ is located, it will be marked by a blue line with dotted shading. The name of the zone, such as "Atlantic Coastal Air Defense Identification Zone," will appear in bold letters. In the interest of national security, you should pay close attention to these areas on sectionals and follow the procedures outlined in the *Airman's Information Manual* when you are penetrating them.

Figure 8-15. The Class B or C airspace area within which fixed-wing special VFR flight is prohibited is identified by the letters "NO SVFR" above the airport name (item 1). Victor airways are displayed as light blue lines connecting VOR, VOR/DME, or VORTAC facilities. The radial, or magnetic course, of the airway is shown (item 2), as well as the airway number, such as V-306 (item 3). The floor of the Class B airspace segment shown here (item 4) is 3,000 feet MSL, and the ceiling is 10,000 feet MSL.

OBSTRUCTIONS

Besides being concerned with the terrain elevations, you must also be aware of man-made obstructions to flight. While some structures may extend only several feet above the ground, others may rise more than 1,000 feet and impose a hazard to aircraft in flight. Sectional charts provide information about the locations and heights of obstructions. [Figure 8-16]

Groups of obstructions are marked by two symbols placed side by side. Two elevation figures may be located next to the symbol and represent the MSL and AGL heights of the obstacle. While obstructions impose hazards to flight, they can also be good references in identifying your position.

When two elevation figures are used to specify an obstacle's height, the bold number indicates MSL height and the figure in parentheses denotes AGL height.

TOPOGRAPHICAL INFORMATION

With the help of contour lines, spot elevations, and the elevations of obstructions, you can choose a safe cruising altitude. You can also determine whether or not you will be more than 3,000 feet AGL and will need to use the required VFR cruising altitudes.

You can choose a safe and appropriate VFR cruising altitude by referring to topographical information.

Figure 8-16. Item 1 represents an obstruction that is less than 1,000 feet AGL. Item 2 marks an obstruction that stands 1,000 feet or more above the ground. The symbol atop the figure indicates that high intensity lighting is used for collision avoidance. The dot below each symbol shows the actual location of the structure. Item 3 is a caution box which alerts pilots to unusual hazards, such as tethered balloons or guy wires.

The locations of natural and man-made features are shown as reference points for navigation. Features such as lakes, rivers, railroads, roads and highways are clearly represented. Miscellaneous symbols also help you locate areas of parachuting and heavy glider and ultralight activity. [Figure 8-17]

Finally, changes in aeronautical data that could affect your flight might occur between chart revisions. For this reason, you should consult the *Airport/Facility Directory* prior to flight and review the "Aeronautical Chart Bulletin" contained in the *Notices to Airmen*. A discussion of these sources of flight information will follow later in this flight prep.

Figure 8-17. Another topographical symbol is the one for a lookout tower (item 1). The site number, such as "W-14," is painted on the tower and can be seen from the air. The elevation at the base of the tower is 5,867 feet MSL. Power transmission lines are shown by thin black lines connecting symbols for their supporting towers (item 2).

CHECKLIST

After studying this section, you should have a basic understanding of:

✓   **Aeronautical charts** — The differences between sectional charts, world aeronautical charts, and VFR terminal area charts.

✓   **Terrain information** — How contour lines, gradient tints, and elevation figures help you determine your altitude above the ground.

✓   **Latitude and longitude** — How the location of an airport can be determined from its geographic coordinates.

✓   **Airport data** — How to interpret printed information about each airport, including symbols, frequencies, length of the longest runway, airport elevation, and the availability of lighting.

✓   **Radio aids to navigation and communication** — The symbols used for various navigational facilities, as well as information concerning communications with flight service stations.

✓   **Airspace symbology** — How symbols on aeronautical charts alert you to various types of airspace along your route.

✓   **Obstructions** — How to interpret the symbols used to mark the locations and heights of hazardous obstructions.

✓   **Topographical information** — How natural and man-made features are shown on charts as reference points for navigating.

FLIGHT COMPUTERS

This section introduces you to mechanical and electronic flight computers. Both of these computers allow you to solve most of the navigation problems you will encounter during flight planning and in-flight operations. The first part of this section discusses the theory behind some of these calculations. Next, depending on what calculator you are using, you should review the appropriate set of problems and solutions. One set is based on the mechanical slide graphic computer (CSG) and one is for the TechStar electronic flight computer. Although this section offers theory and practice on the use of both types of computers, it is intended only as an introduction. For complete information on the features and operation of your unit, be sure to study the computer manual carefully.

NAVIGATION THEORY

Perhaps the best way to understand the problem-solving capabilities of a flight computer is to analyze some of the computations required to plan a typical cross-country flight. Some of your objectives are to determine the heading which will compensate for the effects of wind, and to estimate groundspeed, time enroute, and fuel requirements.

COMPENSATING FOR WIND

Whenever you fly in wind, your aircraft's performance is affected. The wind direction and speed have a direct impact on your aircraft's direction of flight and groundspeed. This may be easier to visualize if you first think of a balloon as it drifts freely in the wind. [Figure 8-18]

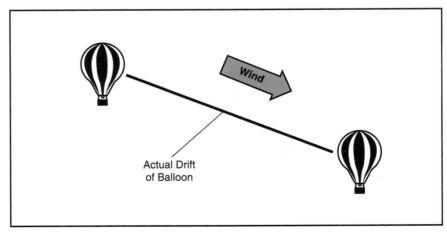

Figure 8-18. A balloon simply moves with the wind and drifts above the terrain in the same direction and at the same speed as the wind.

The effect of wind on a moving object, such as an airplane, is somewhat different. It deflects the object from its intended path (course) and alters its speed over the ground. That portion of the wind which causes the airplane to drift off course is called the **crosswind component**, while the **headwind** or **tailwind component** decreases or increases the airplane's forward speed. [Figure 8-19]

In order to compensate for the effects of wind, it is important to understand the terms course, heading, and wind correction angle. **Course** is the intended flight path, or direction of travel, over the surface of the earth with respect to north. **Heading** is the direction in which the longitudinal axis of the airplane is pointing in relation to north. In a no-wind situation (or with a direct headwind or tailwind), course and heading are the same. **Wind correction angle** (WCA) is the difference between the heading of an airplane and the desired course. It tells you how much you need to adjust your heading to maintain the desired course. [Figure 8-20]

Wind correction angle is applied to course to determine heading.

With the mechanical slide graphic computer, you solve for wind correction angle first; then you apply the correction to your course. The electronic flight computer eliminates a step in the wind problems by automatically applying the WCA to the course. It solves directly for the heading necessary to maintain course.

Another way you look at the wind problem is that your course, corrected for wind, equals your heading. When the wind is blowing from the left, you subtract the WCA from your desired course. When it is blowing from the right, you add the WCA to your course.

The WCA is subtracted from the course for a left crosswind and added to the course for a right crosswind.

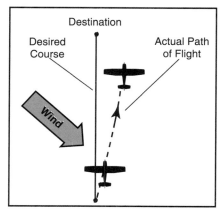

Figure 8-19. In this example, the wind pushes the airplane off course to the right and retards the airplane's forward motion.

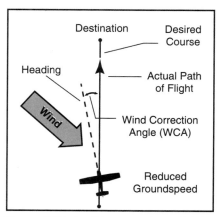

Figure 8-20. In this case, to maintain your desired course, you must adjust your heading to the left, into the wind.

Let's take a moment and review the information you need to solve wind problems. First, you need the direction you intend to fly. This is your course which is usually obtained by direct measurement from your aeronautical chart. You also must know how fast you intend to fly. This is the actual speed of the airplane through the air, or true airspeed, as found in the pilot's operating handbook. Next, you need the predicted wind direction and speed. As you learned earlier, this information is obtained from the winds and temperatures aloft forecast.

With these four variables — course, true airspeed, wind direction, and wind speed — you can use a slide graphic flight computer to determine the wind correction angle and resultant groundspeed. By applying the wind correction angle to the course, you will find the appropriate heading that compensates for the wind. An electronic computer uses the same four variables to solve the problem. However, the electronic computer applies the wind correction angle and solves directly for heading and groundspeed.

TIME AND FUEL REQUIRED

Based on the computed groundspeed and the distance to the destination, you can use the flight computer to determine how long the flight will take. Next, you will want to calculate the amount of fuel required. You will also need to consult the pilot's operating handbook to determine the fuel consumption rate. With this figure and the estimated time enroute, you can use the flight computer to determine fuel requirements for the trip. After adding required reserves, you can tell if the airplane carries sufficient fuel to make the flight nonstop.

IN-FLIGHT CALCULATIONS

The flight computer also provides several important in-flight calculations, such as true airspeed and actual winds aloft. You can then compare these values to the estimated true airspeed and the winds aloft forecast used to plan the flight. For example, if the actual true airspeed is slower than the speed used in planning, it will take longer to reach your destination and will require additional fuel. This may necessitate a fuel stop at some intermediate airport.

TRUE AIRSPEED

To compute true airspeed during flight, you need to know your pressure altitude, outside air temperature, and calibrated airspeed. You determine pressure altitude by temporarily resetting the altimeter to 29.92 and reading pressure altitude directly off the altimeter. Remember to note the original setting, so you can reset the altimeter after you have read the pressure altitude.

You can read the air temperature directly off the outside air temperature gauge found in most airplanes. The temperature read off this gauge is called **indicated air temperature**. Due to the friction of the air passing over the temperature probe, the indicated temperature is slightly higher than the actual, or static, air temperature. At speeds below 200 knots, however, this error is negligible and may be disregarded.

To determine calibrated airspeed, read the indicated airspeed off the airspeed indicator, then correct it using the airspeed correction table found in the pilot's operating handbook. With pressure altitude, temperature, and calibrated airspeed established, you then use the flight computer to determine actual true airspeed.

ACTUAL WINDS ALOFT

Another in-flight computation you will find useful is to determine the actual winds aloft and compare them to the forecast winds used during flight planning. To do this, you will need to know the planned course (from flight planning calculations), the actual heading being used to maintain the planned course (read off the heading indicator), actual true airspeed (determined by your flight computer), and actual groundspeed (determined from groundspeed checks). The flight computer uses these variables to calculate the actual wind direction and speed.

During cross-country flights, you will soon realize that actual winds are seldom the same as forecast. As a result, you can usually expect your actual groundspeed to vary somewhat from that estimated. If your groundspeed is faster than planned, you will use less fuel, so your reserve will be more than adequate. It is when your groundspeed is significantly slower than planned that you can have fuel problems. The additional time needed to complete the flight will translate directly into fuel consumed.

MECHANICAL FLIGHT COMPUTERS

In this segment, we will work through several typical computations you normally perform before and during cross-country flights. The mechanical flight computer used in this discussion is referred to as a slide graphic computer (CSG). The operations presented here apply to many of the more common mechanical computers available on the market. However, since we are providing only introductory material, be sure to consult your computer manual for any differences in operation or additional features.

CSG computers have two sides which are referred to as the calculator side and the wind side. The calculator side uses two circular discs which are fastened together in the center. The top disc usually has windows or cutouts. The two discs are mounted so you can rotate the top disc, using the windows to align various values on the three scales which are printed on the two discs. Since the top disc is smaller than the bottom disc, you can align an "index pointer" on one scale to a value or pointer on the

Figure 8-21. The main portion of the calculator side of the flight computer consists of two discs, three windows, and three separate scales. The outer "A" scale, printed on the bottom disc, is fixed. Scales "B" and "C" are printed on the top disc, which is free to pivot over the bottom disc.

other. The **"A" scale** may be used to represent speed, distance, fuel, or other units, depending on the problem being worked. The **"B" scale** also may represent speed, distance, or fuel, as well as time. The **"C" scale** is used almost exclusively to represent time. [Figure 8-21]

A single number on the "A" or "B" scale can represent that number to any power of ten. For example, the number "40" can stand for .04, .4, 4, 40, 400, etc. For any given problem, you must use common sense to determine which value is correct. If a short distance is involved, 25 on the "A" scale might be read as 2.5 miles. If a long distance is involved, zeros are added to the 25 to get the proper answer. For instance, 25 might be 250 or 2,500 miles.

A number on the computer scales can represent that number to any power of ten.

Notice also that the graduations between all the values are not equal. On the "A" and "B" scales, for example, there are 10 graduations between 14 and 15, and 5 between 15 and 16. Graduations on the "C" scale can reflect increments of 5 or 10 minutes. Therefore, you should always use care to determine the value of each graduation.

TIME-SPEED-DISTANCE

This type of problem involves three variables: elapsed time, speed (usually groundspeed), and distance. When any two of the three variables are known, you can use your flight computer to determine the third. For example, when speed and distance are known, rotate the disc until the **speed index** pointer is on the specified speed. Then, locate the distance on the "A" scale and read the required time in hours and minutes on the "C" scale. You can also read time in minutes on the "B" scale. [Figure 8-22]

Speed × Time = Distance

Figure 8-22. In this example, you want to know how long it will take to fly 150 n.m. at 90 knots. First, place the speed of 90 knots opposite the speed index pointer (item 1). Next, find the distance of 150 n.m. on the "A" scale (item 2) and directly opposite it read the time required of 100 minutes on the "B" scale (item 3). You also can read the time of 1 hour, 40 minutes (1:40) on the "C" scale.

FUEL CONSUMPTION

Fuel consumption and time-speed-distance problems are very similar. Both types of problems have the same mathematical relationships. However, when solving fuel problems, "gallons per hour" is used instead of knots, and "gallons of fuel consumed" is used instead of distance traveled.

Fuel Flow × Time = Fuel Consumed

FUEL REQUIRED

Suppose you want to determine how much fuel you will need, based on a known fuel consumption rate and flight time. To accomplish this, place the fuel consumption rate opposite the speed index and read the fuel required ("A" scale) opposite the flight time ("B" or "C" scales). [Figure 8-23]

Remember to consider required reserves whenever you are determining the amount of fuel needed.

Figure 8-23. Assume a fuel consumption rate of 8.5 g.p.h. and a flight time of 1:40. First, place the consumption rate opposite the speed index pointer (item 1). Next, find the flight time on the "C" scale (item 2) and read the fuel requirement of 14.2 gallons on the "A" scale. (item 3).

Figure 8-24. Assume a fuel quantity of 31.5 gallons and a consumption rate of 9 g.p.h. To solve this problem, place the fuel consumption rate of 9 g.p.h. opposite the speed index (item 1). Now locate the fuel quantity of 31.5 gallons on the "A" scale (item 2) and read the endurance of 210 minutes on the "B" scale or 3:30 on the "C" scale (item 3).

ENDURANCE

Endurance refers to the amount of time you can remain aloft, based on a known fuel quantity and consumption rate. Since a fuel consumption rate is rarely constant for an entire flight, think of endurance as an approximation and not as an absolute value. [Figure 8-24]

ACTUAL CONSUMPTION RATE

After completing a flight, you may wish to determine the actual fuel consumption rate, based on the total amount of fuel used. You can then compare this figure against the original fuel consumption rate and take it into consideration for future flight planning. [Figure 8-25]

DENSITY ALTITUDE

Solving for density altitude requires you know the pressure altitude and outside air temperature. You may read the pressure altitude directly off the altimeter when it is set to 29.92. Temperature is usually determined by reading the outside air temperature gauge or by using reported surface temperature for the airport. Since most computers use temperature in

Figure 8-25. For this example, assume that 18 gallons of fuel were consumed over a 2:15 flight. To solve this problem, place the fuel consumed on the "A" scale (item 1) over the elapsed time on the "C" scale (item 2). You can then read the fuel consumption rate of 8.0 g.p.h. opposite the speed index pointer (item 3).

Figure 8-26. Assume the pressure altitude is 3,000 feet and the temperature is 77°F. First, use the scale at the bottom of the computer to determine that 77°F is equal to 25°C (item 1). Next, use the window for true airspeed and density altitude computations (item 2), and set the pressure altitude opposite the temperature (item 3). Read the density altitude of approximately 4,800 feet in the density altitude window (item 4).

degrees Celsius for this computation, you must convert Fahrenheit values to Celsius. [Figure 8-26]

AIRSPEED CALCULATIONS

You can use the flight computer to determine true airspeed (TAS), based on calibrated airspeed (CAS), or you can determine calibrated airspeed if you know true airspeed. To solve either of these problems, you must know the pressure altitude and outside air temperature. [Figure 8-27]

Using your CSG, you can solve for TAS if CAS is known, or vice versa.

Figure 8-27. Assume you wish to determine your true airspeed using a pressure altitude of 5,000 feet, an outside air temperature of 10°C, and a calibrated airspeed of 90 knots. Use the true airspeed and density altitude window for this problem and place the pressure altitude opposite the outside air temperature (item 1). Read the true airspeed of 98 knots on the "A" scale opposite the calibrated airspeed of 90 knots on the "B" scale (item 2). You can also use true airspeed and pressure altitude to solve for calibrated airspeed. Using the same settings, 98 knots true airspeed equals 90 knots calibrated airspeed.

Figure 8-28. The components of the wind side include the rotating azimuth and the sliding grid. The sliding grid is a section of a graduated circle. The straight lines represent degrees right or left of the centerline and the curved lines represent speed. The sliding grid of this computer has two sides, a high speed side and a low speed side. The azimuth circle rotates freely and is graduated into 360°. The transparent portion is frosted so you can write on it with a pencil. In the center is a small circle called the grommet, which moves directly over the centerline of the grid.

WIND PROBLEMS

As discussed in navigation theory, wind problems involve six variables: course, true airspeed, wind direction, wind speed, heading, and ground-speed. During the flight planning process, you typically want to determine the wind correction angle and apply it to the course. This gives you the heading needed to compensate for the predicted winds. You also need to know your groundspeed to compute the estimated time enroute and fuel requirements. Wind problems are calculated using the wind side of the flight computer. [Figure 8-28]

Wind problems involve solving for heading and groundspeed based on course, true airspeed, wind direction, and wind speed.

HEADING AND GROUNDSPEED

For this example, assume a planned course of 239° and a true airspeed of 98 knots. According to the winds and temperatures aloft forecast, the winds at your cruising altitude are 100° true at 15 knots. The first step in this type of wind problem is to plot the predicted wind. Once the wind has been plotted, your next step is to place the planned course under the true index and position the wind dot based on the predicted true airspeed. Then read the wind correction angle and groundspeed. Finally, you must apply the WCA to the course to determine heading. [Figure 8-29]

Figure 8-29. The left illustration shows the first step, which is to set the wind direction of 100° under the true index located at the top of the computer (item 1). Next, place the center grommet over a convenient point, such as 100 knots (item 2), and plot the wind speed up from this point. In this case, the wind speed is 15 knots, so the wind dot is placed a distance equal to 15 knots above the grommet (item 3). The right illustration shows the second step, which is to rotate the azimuth until the course of 239° is set under the true index (item 4). Next, slide the scale to place the wind dot on the true airspeed line of 98 knots (item 5). The wind correction angle of 6° is indicated by the distance between the wind dot and centerline (item 6). Since the wind dot is to the left of center, the WCA should be subtracted from the course to determine the heading of 233°. The groundspeed of 109 knots is read directly under the grommet (item 7).

Figure 8-30. The left illustration shows how this problem is set up. The course of 320° is placed at the top of the flight computer under the true index (item 1). Next, slide the grid until the grommet is directly over the groundspeed of 100 knots (item 2). Now place a dot at the point where the true airspeed of 90 knots meets a right wind correction angle of 10° (item 3). Then, rotate the azimuth until the wind dot is above the grommet and directly on the centerline, as shown in the right illustration (item 4). The wind direction of 86° is read under the true index (item 5) and wind speed is equal to the distance between the grommet and the wind dot. In this case, the wind speed is 19 knots (item 6).

UNKNOWN WIND

To determine the actual winds aloft, you need to know true airspeed, groundspeed, course, and heading. Remember, the wind correction angle is the difference between the course and the heading being used to maintain that course. For this example, assume a true airspeed of 90 knots, a groundspeed of 100 knots, a course of 320°, and a heading of 330°. In this case, the wind correction angle is determined to be +10° (330 − 320 = 10). Once you have determined these values, enter them in the appropriate positions on the wind side of the flight computer. [Figure 8-30]

MOST FAVORABLE WINDS

Wind speed and direction typically change as altitude changes. This causes a change in groundspeed.

One of the factors you consider in selecting an altitude is the effect of wind on groundspeed. However, wind direction and speed usually change with altitude, so it is difficult to tell which altitude will result in the best groundspeed. The flight computer offers a fairly simple method of determining which altitude offers the most favorable winds for a given course. The first step is to plot the forecast wind direction and speed for each altitude. [Figure 8-31]

The next step is to rotate the azimuth until the course to be flown is directly under the true index. By measuring the distance between the grommet and each wind dot, you can select the best wind. For this example, assume you intend to fly a course of 250°. [Figure 8-32]

Based solely on the forecast winds aloft, the winds at 3,000 feet are most advantageous to the flight. Of course, other considerations, such as terrain or weather conditions, may affect your final choice of cruising altitudes.

CONVERSIONS

Flight computers incorporate many different conversion scales. In fact, you have already used one of these — the temperature conversion scale located at the bottom of the CSG. Other conversion scales are located directly on the "A" and "B" scales of the flight computer.

STATUTE TO NAUTICAL

Converting between statute and nautical miles is relatively easy. To see how this works, let's complete two conversions — one from nautical miles

Figure 8-31. The winds plotted here are 130° at 5 knots for 3,000 feet, 150° at 12 knots for 6,000 feet, and 170° at 20 knots for 9,000 feet.

Figure 8-32. On this course, the winds at 3,000 feet provide a 2-knot tailwind; the winds at 6,000 feet have almost no effect on groundspeed; and the winds at 9,000 feet produce a 6-knot headwind.

Figure 8-33. To convert 120 nautical miles to statute, place the 12 on the "B" scale directly under the "NAUT." arrow on the "A" scale (left illustration). Read the distance of 138 statute miles on the "B" scale directly under the "STAT." arrow. Next, convert 200 statute miles to nautical. This time, place the 20 on the "B" scale directly under the "STAT." arrow (right illustration), and read the answer of 174 nautical miles under the "NAUT." arrow.

to statute and the other from statute to nautical. Both conversions use the "NAUT. STAT." arc found on the "A" scale of the flight computer. [Figure 8-33]

OTHER CONVERSIONS

In weight and balance you learned that one gallon of aviation gasoline (avgas) weighs six pounds. Most flight computers allow you to directly convert avgas between gallons and pounds. [Figure 8-34]

Figure 8-34. For this conversion, align the "FUEL LBS." index pointer on the "A" scale with the "U.S. GAL." index pointer on the "B" scale (item 1). You can then read pounds on the "A" scale opposite gallons on the "B" scale. For example, 25 gallons of avgas weigh 150 pounds (item 2). See your computer manual for other useful conversions.

ELECTRONIC FLIGHT COMPUTERS

This section provides examples of typical aviation computations using the TechStar electronic flight computer. TechStar is a multi-function computer with memory, which has been especially designed by pilots, for use by pilots. Its ease of operation and extreme accuracy greatly simplify solving flight planning and in-flight problems. Since this segment provides only introductory material on TechStar's operation, be sure to consult your operator's manual for additional features and computations. [Figure 8-35]

AVIATION MODES

To solve a particular problem with TechStar, you must first access the applicable mode and select the unknown value you wish to determine from the menu screen. The computer then "prompts" the entry of all variables needed to solve the problem. To view the various modes, turn the computer on and press the Mode key.

The five modes are:
TSD–Time-Speed-Distance
ALT–Altitude/Airspeed
WND–Wind
W/B–Weight and Balance
TMR–Timer

TIME-SPEED-DISTANCE

To enter the time-speed-distance mode, access the mode screen and press the (TSD) parameter line key. Next, indicate the variable you want to find. For example, assume it took 1 hour, 30 minutes (1:30:00) to cover 210 n.m., and you want to know your groundspeed. When you enter data into the computer, the values will first appear in the scratchpad at the bottom of the screen. You assign these values to the appropriate parameters by pressing a parameter line key, shown in parentheses in the following

In the following examples, line keys to the right of the display will be shown in parentheses ( ).

1 Display

2 Parameter Line Keys

3 Compute Key

4 Clear Key

5 On/Off Key

6 Arithmetic Function Keys

7 Scroll Up/Down Keys

8 Mode Select Key

9 Conversion Select Keys

10 Time Colon Key

11 Store/Recall Keys

12 Backspace Key

Figure 8-35. The keyboard of the TechStar flight computer is shown here. Study the manual to familiarize yourself with the locations and functions of the various keys.

examples. To solve for groundspeed, press the (SPD) parameter line key and proceed as follows:

The abbreviations "In" and "C" appear next to "Input" and "Computed" values, respectively.

Press	Display	Comments
1 $\boxed{:}$	1:00	
30 (TIM)	1:30:00 In	Enter time
210 (DST)	210.In	Enter the distance flown
$\boxed{\text{CMP}}$	140.C	Groundspeed = 140 knots

FUEL REQUIRED

Since fuel consumption and time-speed-distance problems use the same mathematical relationships, you will need to be in the (TSD) mode.

For this example, assume a flight time of 2:32:15 and a fuel consumption rate of 8.5 g.p.h. To determine the fuel required for this flight, access the (TSD) mode, press the (F) "Fuel" parameter key, and proceed as follows:

Press	Display	Comments
2 $\boxed{:}$	2:00	
32 $\boxed{:}$	2:32:00	
15 (TIM)	2:32:15 In	Enter time
8.5 (FLO)	8.5 In	Enter fuel consumption rate
$\boxed{\text{CMP}}$	21.6 C	Fuel required = 21.6 gallons.

ENDURANCE

The airplane you are using carries 45 gallons of fuel. You intend to operate at a power setting which will cause fuel to be consumed at the rate of 9 g.p.h. To calculate how long you can remain aloft, access the (TSD) mode, press the (TIM) "Time" parameter key and solve as follows:

Press	Display	Comments
45 (F)	45.In	Enter fuel quantity available
9 (FLO)	9.In	Enter fuel consumption rate
$\boxed{\text{CMP}}$	5:00:00 C	Time = 5 hours

ACTUAL CONSUMPTION RATE

For this example, you determine that 80 gallons of fuel has been consumed over a 2:30:00 time period. To compute the actual fuel consumption rate, enter the (TSD) mode, press the (FLO) "Fuel flow" parameter key, and proceed as follows:

Press	Display	Comments
2 $\boxed{:}$	2:00	
30 (TIM)	2:30:00 In	Enter time
80 (F)	80.In	Fuel consumed
$\boxed{\text{CMP}}$	32.0 C	Actual fuel consumption rate 32 g.p.h

DENSITY ALTITUDE

You are departing from an airport with a pressure altitude of 2,000 feet and a true temperature of 25°C. To calculate the density altitude for this airport, access the (ALT) "Altitude/Airspeed" mode, press the (DA) "Density altitude" parameter key, and follow these steps:

Press	Display	Comments
2000 (PA)	2000.In	Enter pressure altitude
25 (T°C)	25.In	Enter true temperature in °C
CMP	3607.C	Density altitude = 3,607 feet

Altitude, airspeed, standard temperature, and mach computations are made in the in the (ALT) "Altitude/Airspeed" mode.

STANDARD TEMPERATURE

While planning a flight, you need to determine the standard temperature at a pressure altitude of 4,000 feet. Standard temperature is determined by entering the (ALT) mode, pressing the (ST°) "Standard temperature" key and continuing as follows:

Press	Display	Comments
4000 (PA)	4000.In	Enter the pressure altitude
CMP	7.1 C	Standard temperature = 7°C

TRUE AIRSPEED

You are flying at a pressure altitude of 12,000 feet, with a calibrated airspeed of 121 knots. The outside air temperature gauge reads –6°C. To determine the true airspeed of the airplane, access the (ALT) mode, press the (TAS) "True airspeed" key and use the following steps:

Press	Display	Comments
12000 (PA)	12000.In	Enter the pressure altitude
6 +/– (I°C)	–6.In	Change 6°C to –6°C
121 (CAS)	121.In	Enter CAS
CMP	145.C	TAS = 145 knots

In the preceding example, notice the temperature was entered as an indicated air temperature. This allows TechStar to adjust the temperature automatically to compensate for the effects of friction. As noted earlier, friction causes the indicated air temperature to read slightly warmer than its actual value. Although this small rise in temperature can normally be disregarded at speeds under 200 knots, entering it here allows TechStar to provide you with a more precise answer.

For in-flight calculations, enter the outside air temperature as indicated air temperature, not as true air temperature.

HEADING AND GROUNDSPEED

During flight planning, you determine that the forecast winds aloft at your cruising altitude are 080° at 20 knots. Your course and true airspeed will be 030° and 170 knots, respectively. Using TechStar, you compute the true heading and groundspeed in the (WND) "Wind" mode by pressing the (HDG) parameter key, and proceed as follows:

Press	Display	Comments
80 (WDR)	080.In	Enter wind direction
20 (WSP)	20.In	Enter wind speed
30 (CRS)	030.In	Course
170 (TAS)	170.In	True airspeed (knots)
CMP	035.C	True heading = 035°
	156.C	Groundspeed = 156 knots

UNKNOWN WIND

For this example, you want to calculate the actual winds aloft using a course of 175°, actual heading of 160°, true airspeed of 180 knots, and actual groundspeed of 144 knots. Now, enter the (WND) mode, press the (WDR) "Wind direction" parameter key and apply these factors to solve for wind direction and wind speed:

Press	Display	Comments
175 (CRS)	175.In	Enter the course
160 (HDG)	160.In	Enter the heading
180 (TAS)	180.In	True airspeed (knots)
144 (GS)	144.In	Groundspeed in knots
CMP	118.C	Wind direction = 118°
	55.C	Wind speed = 55 knots

CONVERSIONS

The TechStar is designed so you can access conversion functions at any point during an arithmetic or aviation mode operation. You can convert most commonly used values for distance, volume, weight, or barometric pressure and temperature by pressing the [Dist], [Vol], [Wt], or [Wx] key, as appropriate. Let's look at an example.

A distance of 124 statute miles is converted to nautical miles as follows:

Press	Display	Comments
[Dist]		Displays distance conversions
124 (SM)	124.In	Enter 124 s.m.
[CMP] (NM)	107.753 C	124 s.m. = 108 n.m.

A temperature of 81°F is converted to Celsius as follows:

Press	Display	Comments
[Wx]		Displays temperature conversion
81 (°F)	81.In	Enter 81°F
[CMP] (°C)	27.2222 C	81°F = 27°C

MULTI-PART PROBLEMS

Often a series of interrelated problems is required for a final solution. This is known as a multi-part problem. A good example of this is the following problem, which allows you to find the fuel required for an anticipated flight. The true airspeed is determined first, followed by the groundspeed and time enroute and, finally, the fuel required.

Given:

Pressure altitude. . . . . 7,500 ft.
Temperature . . . . 15°C (True)
Calibrated airspeed . . . . 105 kts.
Wind direction . . . . 035° at 12 kts.
Course . . . . 270°
Distance. . . . . 256 n.m.
Fuel consumption rate . . . . 11.5 g.p.h.

Press	**Display**	**Comments**
Mode (ALT)		Select altitude/airspeed mode
(TAS)		Select unknown variable
7500 (PA)	7500.In	Enter pressure altitude
15 (T°C)	15.In	Enter true air temperature °C
105 (CAS)	105.In	Enter CAS
CMP	121.C	TAS = 121 knots
Rcl (TAS)	120.553	Move TAS to scratch pad
Mode (WND)		Select wind mode
(GS)		Select unknown variable
(TAS)	120.553 In	TAS entered from scratch pad
35 (WDR)	035.In	Enter wind direction
12 (WSP)	12.In	Enter wind speed
270 (CRS)	270.In	Enter course
	275.C	Heading = 275
CMP	127.C	Groundspeed = 127 knots
Rcl (GS)	127.034	Move GS to scratch pad
Mode (TSD)		Select time-speed-distance mode
(TIM)		Select unknown variable
(SPD)	127.034 In	GS entered from scratch pad
256 (DST)	256.In	Enter distance
CMP	2:00:55 C	Time enroute = 2:00:55
CMP		Allows further computation
11.5 (FLO)	11.5 In	Enter fuel consumption rate
CMP (F)	23.2 C	Fuel consumed = 23.2 gallons

CALIBRATED AIRSPEED

Occasionally you will need to compute the CAS needed to maintain a given TAS. To solve this problem, use the altitude/airspeed mode, press the (CAS) parameter key, and enter the known values of pressure altitude, temperature, and TAS. For example, to maintain a TAS of 200 knots with a pressure altitude of 7,000 feet and a temperature of 5°C, what is the CAS?

Press	Display	Comments
Mode (ALT)		Select altitude/airspeed mode
(CAS)		Select unknown variable
7000 (PA)	7000.In	Enter pressure altitude
200 (TAS)	200.In	Enter true airspeed
5 (T°C)	5.In	Enter true air temperature °C
CMP	179.C	CAS = 179

CHECKLIST

After studying this section, you should have a basic understanding of:

✓ **Time-speed-distance problems** — How to determine any one of the three values if the other two are given.

✓ **Fuel problems** — Why fuel problems have the same relationships as time-speed-distance problems.

✓ **Density altitude problems** — How to compute density altitude when you know pressure altitude and temperature.

✓ **Standard temperature** — How to solve for standard temperature from pressure altitude.

✓ **Airspeed calculations** — How to compute true airspeed and what values are required.

✓ **Wind problems** — How to determine most favorable winds, as well as heading and groundspeed, during flight planning. What values are required for computation of actual wind speed and wind direction during flight.

✓ **Conversions** — How to perform conversions, including Fahrenheit to Celsius temperatures and nautical to statute distances.

PILOTAGE AND DEAD RECKONING

There are several methods of navigating from one point to another. In this section we will discuss two of the most common ones — pilotage and dead reckoning. Although pilotage and dead reckoning usually are presented as two different means of VFR navigation, you will find that they are normally used together.

PILOTAGE

In the early days of flight, pilots would find their way by following landmarks such as rivers, streams, or railroads. They also flew from one town to the next, using any prominent objects or structures in the area for guidance. This method, called **pilotage**, is a form of navigation by visual reference to landmarks. Today, flying by pilotage is accomplished by comparing symbols on aeronautical charts with their corresponding features on the earth's surface. Sectional charts are recommended for pilotage because of their detailed portrayal of terrain and man-made features.

Pilotage is navigation by reference to checkpoints.

Flying by pilotage requires that you select an altitude that allows you to identify the chosen landmarks, or checkpoints, on your route of flight. Obviously, if you fly at too high an altitude, the selected references may be so small that you can't identify them. On the other hand, flying too low also presents problems. Aside from the dangers of tall obstructions, flying too low gives you a poor perspective for identifying landmarks. Selection of a cruising altitude depends on the terrain you are flying over, as well as the types of checkpoints available. Of course, above 3,000 feet AGL, you also must comply with the east/west cruising altitude rules.

One of the advantages of pilotage is that, once you have received training and acquired experience, it is relatively easy to perform and does not require special instruments. The most basic airplane will enable you to navigate by pilotage. On the other hand, pilotage has a number of disadvantages. In areas where few prominent landmarks are present, pilotage can be difficult. A direct course may be impractical if there are few good landmarks. You are also limited by visibility. If your visibility is reduced by haze, smoke, or fog, your ability to navigate by pilotage diminishes.

SELECTING CHECKPOINTS

You should select check-points which are easy to identify from the air.

The checkpoints used to determine your position along a route of flight are useful only if they can be positively identified. When selecting checkpoints, you must attempt to pick those with distinctive features which will be easily recognizable from the air. Training and experience will help you evaluate chart symbology and select checkpoints that are useful in navigating.

There are no specific rules to follow when selecting checkpoints, since each route you travel is different. However, one general guideline is to avoid using any single landmark as a sole reference, if possible. For example, you should not rely solely on a water tower to identify a small town, since other small towns in the area may have water towers, too. When flying by pilotage, it is important to take a look at the "whole picture." Whenever possible, compare your selected checkpoint against a combination of ground features so you can identify your position positively. Another guideline is to fly with current aeronautical charts, even when flying over familiar territory. Man-made structures are always changing, and an out-of-date chart could be a deceptive tool when you are trying to identify your position.

Intersecting lines, such as highways, railroad tracks, powerlines, or rivers normally provide good references for position identification. However, it is important to compare them with the surrounding terrain and landmarks. [Figure 8-36]

Although primary roads are usually good checkpoints, secondary roads can be deceiving. Aeronautical charts do not print every road, although those shown are generally obvious when viewed from the air. You should also remember that new roads and highways are continuously under construction. This brings up an important point regarding aeronautical charts — they do not portray all of the surface details on the earth.

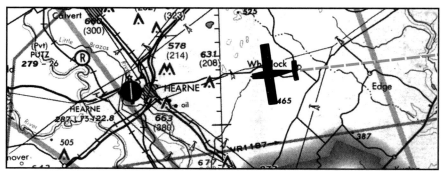

Figure 8-36. When you are flying toward Hearne Airport from the east, several check-points are available, including primary roads, railroad tracks, and powerlines that merge into the city. The position of the airport, on the west side of the city, also makes an excellent visual checkpoint.

Rivers often provide excellent landmarks, especially when they have significant bends or curves. However, they may be somewhat deceptive. Some rivers have numerous tributaries, and the main body may be difficult to follow. During a flood stage, the appearance from the air may be significantly different from the chart pattern. During a drought, on the other hand, the body of water shown on a sectional may actually be a dried-up river bed. Lakes usually provide good references for determining your position. As with rivers, certain cautions must be exercised. In many parts of the country, hundreds of small lakes exist within close proximity, and identifying a particular one can be extremely difficult. What appears to be a small lake on a chart may actually be a pond that has dried up.

Cities can have excellent landmark value. The yellow pattern printed on charts provides you with a good representation of the actual shape of the city when viewed from the air. You should be careful when using small towns and villages as checkpoints, though, because they often resemble one another from aloft.

Small towns and villages may not be good checkpoints, because they tend to look similar from the air.

FOLLOWING A ROUTE

There are two basic approaches to flying by pilotage. The first is to follow a major topographical feature, such as a river or highway. As the direction of the landmark changes, you simply alter your course to fly along its route. Although this is an easy means of navigating, a primary disadvantage is that a direct flight is usually impossible, so the length of your flight is increased. An alternative to meandering along an indirect route is to draw a straight line on your chart between the departure and destination airports. Instead of following a major topographical feature or flying from one particular landmark to another, you select checkpoints along a direct route of flight. A straight-line course not only decreases your time enroute, but also allows you to perform more accurate time, speed, and distance calculations.

ORIENTATION

Because pilotage is a visual means of navigation, maintaining an accurate orientation between your intended and actual routes of flight is fundamental. If you become disoriented over unfamiliar or featureless terrain, determining your position can be difficult. The key to preventing disorientation is in taking the time to plan your flight adequately.

Preparation for a cross-country flight by pilotage begins by studying the charts for the area you will be flying over. Use a straightedge to lay out a direct course between your departure and destination airports. With the course line drawn, you can select suitable checkpoints along your route. As you select them, mark them on the chart so you will remember them when airborne. This is important even for short routes. As you acquire

Figure 8-37. The outdoor theater northeast of Galion Airport between the two primary roads is a good selection for the first checkpoint. The Mansfield Lahm Airport is also a good checkpoint. The airport symbology alerts you to the fact that Class D airspace exists when the tower is in operation. The city of Ashland makes a final checkpoint before you land.

cross-country experience, you will be able to use fewer checkpoints and still maintain orientation to your route. [Figure 8-37]

You should always make a detailed study of your planned route of flight.

After laying out your course and marking your checkpoints, carefully study the entire route. One of the most significant items in the example is the Class D airspace at Mansfield Lahm Airport. You should overfly the airport above 3,800 feet MSL, the charted vertical limit of this airspace. This is because you normally should avoid Class D airspace except for the purpose of taking off or landing. Also, you should not overfly the airport any higher than 4,297 feet MSL unless you are able to comply with the east/west cruising altitude rules. If you wish to fly higher than 3,000 feet AGL, 5,500 feet MSL is the lowest appropriate altitude for your easterly course. This means you must climb more than 4,000 feet for this relatively short route. This may be reason enough to alter your planned course, depending on the performance capability of your airplane. For example, you could fly north beyond the city of Shelby, then turn east to avoid passing through the Class D airspace. Of course, you also could contact the tower and request permission to transit the area. If you do this, consider the operational requirements associated with the controlled airspace which is outlined by the dashed line on the chart. These are some of the things you should analyze when you study your planned route of flight.

DEAD RECKONING

Dead reckoning allows you to predict the movement of your aircraft along the planned route.

A second means of navigating cross-country stems from mathematical computations. **Dead reckoning** is a technique of navigation based on calculations of time, speed, distance, and direction. From the previous section on flight computers, you know the four variables required to solve for heading and groundspeed. They are TAS, course, wind direction, and wind speed. These values allow you to predict the movement of your airplane along your intended route of flight. However, before you can use the flight computer to solve for heading and groundspeed, you need to determine your course with a navigation plotter.

NAVIGATION PLOTTER

A navigation plotter is usually made of clear plastic, so that chart details can be seen through it. The **plotter** is a simple instrument which features a straightedge for drawing a course line, a protractor for measuring the direction of flight, and scales for measuring distance. Normally, the distance scales allow you to measure in either nautical or statute miles. In addition, most plotters provide scales for sectional, WAC, and VFR terminal area charts.

The plotter functions as a straightedge, protractor, and distance measuring device.

FLIGHT PLANNING

The first step in dead reckoning is to draw a line on the chart between your departure and destination airports. Then, use a plotter to determine the distance between them. It is important to make sure that you're using the correct scale on the plotter for this measurement. Your next step is to measure the true course. Actually, there are several ways to do this. The most common way is to place the small hole in the center of the plotter directly over one of the longitude lines printed on the chart. It is most accurate to select a line of longitude which is near the midpoint of the route. Then align the upper or lower edge of the plotter with the course line, and read your course where the line of longitude intersects the plotter azimuth. [Figure 8-38]

Figure 8-38. A course line has been drawn between airport "A" and airport "B." The distance between them is 50 n.m. (item 1). Notice that the grommet in the center of the protractor (item 2) is directly over the line of longitude, and the course line is aligned with the lower edge of the plotter. The true course between airports "A" and "B" is 70° (item 3). The inner scale provides the true course between "B" and "A," which is 250°. The directional arrows (item 4) signify that easterly courses are measured on the outside scale and westerly courses use the inside scale.

Sometimes, you will draw a course line that does not cross a meridian. Instead of extending the line until it finally crosses a line of longitude, you can use a parallel of latitude instead. The small north/south scale printed on the protractor allows you to do this. Now, let's look at an example of this, using an actual chart excerpt. [Figure 8-39]

Another problem you may encounter occurs when your departure and destination airports are on opposite sides of the same chart. Since the north and south sides of a chart depict adjacent areas, occasionally you will have to draw your course line from one side to the other. In order to

Figure 8-39. In determining your true course on a flight from Ogallala Airport to Grant Airport, the small hole on the plotter is placed directly over an intersection of the true course and a line of latitude. Your true course of 174° is read off the inner scale, which provides for northerly and southerly courses. You can see that the special north/south scale has two sets of numbers. The inner set of numbers, 210° decreasing to 150°, is for plotting courses to the south. The second set of numbers is for plotting courses to the north. For example, the northerly true course in the opposite direction from Grant Airport to Ogallala Airport is 354°. This is indicated on the outer portion of the special north/south scale.

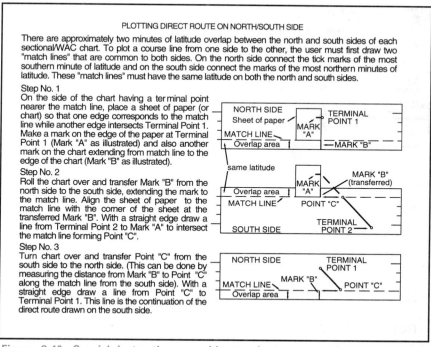

PLOTTING DIRECT ROUTE ON NORTH/SOUTH SIDE

There are approximately two minutes of latitude overlap between the north and south sides of each sectional/WAC chart. To plot a course line from one side to the other, the user must first draw two "match lines" that are common to both sides. On the north side connect the tick marks of the most southern minute of latitude and on the south side connect the marks of the most northern minutes of latitude. These "match lines" must have the same latitude on both the north and south sides.

Step No. 1
On the side of the chart having a terminal point nearer the match line, place a sheet of paper (or chart) so that one edge corresponds to the match line while another edge intersects Terminal Point 1. Make a mark on the edge of the paper at Terminal Point 1 (Mark "A" as illustrated) and also another mark on the chart extending from match line to the edge of the chart (Mark "B" as illustrated).

Step No. 2
Roll the chart over and transfer Mark "B" from the north side to the south side, extending the mark to the match line. Align the sheet of paper to the match line with the corner of the sheet at the transferred Mark "B". With a straight edge draw a line from Terminal Point 2 to Mark "A" to intersect the match line forming Point "C".

Step No. 3
Turn chart over and transfer Point "C" from the south side to the north side. (This can be done by measuring the distance from Mark "B" to Point "C" along the match line from the south side). With a straight edge draw a line from Point "C" to Terminal Point 1. This line is the continuation of the direct route drawn on the south side.

Figure 8-40. Special instructions provide step-by-step procedures for plotting north/south routes that start on one side of a chart and end on the other.

help you extend this line accurately, an instruction guide is printed in the chart margin. [Figure 8-40]

After plotting your true course, the next step in flight planning is to determine the effects of wind on your airplane at your planned flight altitude. Use forecast winds to determine your true heading and groundspeed. During the weather briefing prior to your flight, obtaining the winds aloft forecast will enable you to perform this calculation. As an example, assume you are making a flight between Kimball Airport and Sidney Airport. Use the following values for calculating your true heading and groundspeed:

True airspeed . . . . 105 kts.

True course . . . . 099°

True wind direction. . . . . 310°

Wind speed . . . . 15 kts.

Solving the wind problem with a flight computer results in a true heading of 095° for your trip. This is the true course minus the wind correction angle. Your groundspeed is 118 knots.

Pilotage and Dead Reckoning

Figure 8-41. The navigation log enables you to record the known values and compute the unknown values. Recording the winds aloft, true airspeed, and true course enables you to solve the wind problem and determine a wind correction angle (item 1). In this example, the WCA is subtracted from the true course to determine a true heading of 095° (item 2).

NAVIGATION LOG

To help with your flight planning and enroute calculations, use a navigation log to record data pertaining to your trip. The **navigation log** allows you to list information in a systematic fashion and also helps you to keep track of the progress of your flight. [Figure 8-41]

TRUE AND MAGNETIC VALUES

True values corrected for magnetic variation equal magnetic values.

Because the course line drawn on a chart is in relation to true north and you normally fly by magnetic reference, you will need to correct for the variation between the two. You can do this by adjusting true course for variation to get magnetic course, or by adjusting true heading for variation to get magnetic heading. Typically, you solve for true heading first, since winds aloft forecasts are given in true direction and you know the true course. Then, you apply variation to true heading to get magnetic heading.

The isogonic line of variation printed next to the true course from Kimball to Sidney is 11° east. The memory aid "east is least and west is best," tells you whether to add or subtract the variation. [Figure 8-42]

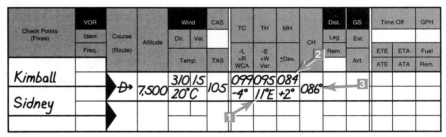

Figure 8-42. Subtracting the 11° easterly variation (item 1) from the true heading gives you a magnetic heading of 084° (item 2). The magnetic deviation noted from the compass correction card for this magnetic heading is added, and a compass heading of 086° will be flown between the two checkpoints on the first leg.

Check Points (Fixes)	VOR		Course (Route)	Altitude	Wind		CAS		TC	TH	MH		CH	Dist.		GS		Time Off		GPH
	Ident				Dir.	Vel.								Leg		Est.		7:45		8.0
	Freq.				Temp.		TAS		-L +R WCA	-E +W Var.	±Dev.			Rem. 136		Act.		ETE ATE	ETA ATA	Fuel Rem.
Kimball			↳ 7,500		310 20°C	15	105		099 -4°	095 11°E	084 +2°	086°		32	118	16		8:01	2.1
Sidney														104	113	17		8:02	37.9

Figure 8-43. By noting your departure time (item 1), you can determine differences in the estimated time of arrival (ETA) and your actual time of arrival (ATA) (item 2).

The navigation log is an excellent tool for determining your time enroute. By knowing the distance between checkpoints, along with your anticipated groundspeed, you can calculate the estimated time enroute (ETE) between them. While airborne, you can calculate your actual time enroute (ATE) and compare it to your estimated time to keep track of your flight's progress. If the actual winds aloft are substantially different than forecast, you can use your flight computer to recalculate your estimated time enroute and the fuel needed to reach your destination. [Figure 8-43]

During flight, the navigation log permits you to compare your estimates with the actual time enroute.

The key to computing ETE and fuel required during flight is an accurate groundspeed check. You can do this anywhere along a direct route. All you have to do is accurately record how long it takes to fly a known distance. For instance, if you fly 10 nautical miles in six minutes while maintaining a constant heading and indicated airspeed, your groundspeed is 100 knots.

Because of high terrain or weather conditions, you may find that a direct route to your destination is impractical. In these situations, you can plan your flight to include additional "legs." A leg may be any segment of a cross-country flight, such as the distance between checkpoints, intermediate stops, or course changes. In flight planning, legs often refer to any straight-line segment of a flight. Navigation logs are designed to accommodate multiple-leg flights, as well as direct flights. Depending on the total length of your trip, you may designate any number of checkpoints. Each checkpoint may be an entry on the navigation log. If your trip is not direct, you will need to solve a wind problem for each separate leg. The "Totals" line at the bottom of the navigation log allows you to add distances, times, and fuel consumption for multiple-leg flights. [Figure 8-44]

FUEL REQUIREMENTS

The total fuel requirement of 16.3 gallons includes an allowance for the time to climb to 2,500 feet MSL and time to enter the traffic pattern at the destination. FARs also require that day VFR flights carry enough fuel to fly to the first point of intended landing at normal cruise speed, and to fly after that for an additional 30 minutes. A reserve of 45 minutes is required for night flights.

FARs require a minimum of 30 minutes reserve fuel for day VFR flights.

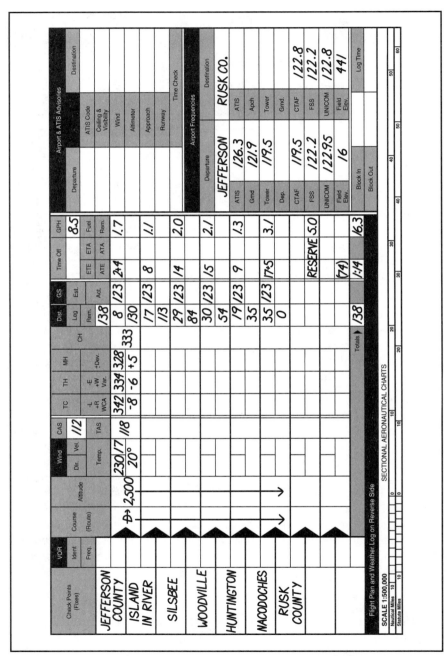

Figure 8-44. This is a completed navigation log for a direct flight. Notice the trip distance of 138 n.m. will require 1 hour, 14 minutes, at a groundspeed of 123 knots. Also note that the frequency box has been completed to provide easy access to this information during the flight.

FLIGHT PLAN

Aside from its value for preflight planning and its obvious use during flight, the navigation log also permits you to extract pertinent information you will need to complete an FAA flight plan. For convenience, the flight plan form is included on the reverse side of some navigation logs. [Figure 8-45]

Flight plan forms have several blocks for recording data pertinent to your flight. The information which follows describes the data appropriate to each numbered block on the flight plan form.

1. **Type of Flight Plan** — Mark "VFR" in this block, since you will be flying under visual flight rules. Only instrument-rated pilots can file "IFR" flight plans. Use "DVFR" when your flight will transit an ADIZ area. You can find more information on DVFR flight plans in the *Aeronautical Information Manual.*

2. **Aircraft Identification** — Use the full identification number of the aircraft, such as N5246R.

3. **Aircraft Type and Special Equipment** — Enter the designator for the aircraft, followed by a slash (/) and the transponder and DME code letter; for example, C-172/A. If the designator is unknown, call the FSS briefer for the proper code. You can find the equipment code letters in the *Aeronautical Information Manual* and at the bottom of the Cessna flight plan form.

Figure 8-45. After completing your navigation log, you should fill out a flight plan and file it with the nearest FSS.

4. **True Airspeed** — Give this figure in knots, based on the estimated TAS at the planned flight altitude.

5. **Departure Point** — Enter the departure point/airport identifier code or the name, if the identifier is unknown. Identifier codes are listed in the *Airport/Facility Directory*.

6. **Departure Time** — This is the proposed departure time stated in Coordinated Universal Time (UTC), or Zulu time. The use of Zulu time eliminates confusion when you cross time zone boundaries during a flight.

7. **Cruising Altitude** — On a VFR flight plan, enter only the initial VFR cruising altitude to assist briefers in providing weather and wind information.

8. **Route of Flight** — Define your proposed route using identifiable points of reference, particularly those which will mark a change in direction. This will assist search and rescue in retracing your route in the event of an emergency. These points may be navaids, airways, or prominent geographic features. When you are not flying on published airways, use the term "direct" to describe a straight-line course between two points.

9. **Destination** — Enter the destination airport identifier code or the name, if the identifier code is unknown. Include the city and state, if the airport name alone might be confused with another.

10. **Estimated Time Enroute** — Enter the total estimated time from takeoff to landing in hours and minutes, based on the latest forecast winds.

11. **Remarks** — Use this block to enter remarks pertinent to ATC or to clarify other flight plan information. This information could include a stopover at an intermediate airport to pick up a passenger or to refuel. You can also use this block to request customs service at an airport of entry.

12. **Fuel on Board** — Enter the total usable fuel on board the aircraft in hours and minutes.

13. **Alternate Airport(s)** — If you desire, specify an alternate airport.

14. **Pilot's Name, Address, Telephone Number, and Aircraft Home Base** — Specify a telephone number where someone will answer who is knowledgeable about your flight. For aircraft home base, include the name of the FBO (if appropriate), as well as the airport name.

15. **Number of Persons Aboard** — Enter the total number of persons on board, including yourself and any other crewmembers.

16. **Color of Aircraft** — List the major color or colors.

17. **Destination Contact/Telephone (Optional)** — Specify the telephone number for the place where you can be reached at the destination to assist search and rescue should you fail to report or cancel your flight plan within one-half hour after your ETA. Use the last line at the bottom of the flight plan to record the name of the FSS that serves your destination airport.

Whether you file the flight plan in person or by telephone, it gives you the opportunity to make a final check of the weather. In cases where no telephone is available, you can still file it over the radio after departure. However, this practice is discouraged unless it is absolutely necessary, because of frequency congestion.

After the flight plan has been filed, you should activate it once you are airborne by calling the FSS and informing them of your actual time of departure. If your flight plan has not been activated, it will be kept on file by the FSS for one hour after your proposed departure time, after which you must refile. When you know your departure will be delayed beyond one hour, you should advise the FSS by phone. When a stopover flight is anticipated, the FAA recommends that you file a separate flight plan for each "leg" if the stop is expected to be more than one hour.

After the flight plan is activated, the flight service station sends a flight notification message to the FSS nearest the destination. Normally, you close the flight plan after you arrive at the destination. You may elect to close the flight plan with a flight service station other than the one serving your destination. However, you should inform the departure FSS of this decision when the flight plan is filed. If you land at an alternate airport, or any airport that is not your filed destination, you should inform the FSS of your original destination when you close.

When the estimated time of arrival has changed significantly, it is important for you to extend the flight plan through any flight service station within radio range. You can see that it is extremely important to close the flight plan by contacting the destination flight service station when the flight is complete. You can do this by radio, if necessary, or by telephone after you have landed. In situations where an FSS is not available, you may request any ATC facility to relay your cancellation to an FSS. Remember that VFR flight plans are never opened or closed automatically by control towers or FSSs.

Control towers do not automatically close your flight plan. You must ask an ATC facility or FSS to close it for you.

If you fail to report or to cancel your flight plan within 30 minutes after your ETA, your aircraft is considered overdue. If your flight plan is not closed, the FSS will begin a telephone search to locate your overdue aircraft. If the FSS is unable to locate your aircraft, costly search-and-rescue procedures will be started.

If you forget to close your flight plan, a search for your aircraft will be initiated.

POSITION REPORTS

During the flight, you should make periodic position reports to flight service stations (or other ATC facilities) along the route. Although position reports are not required on VFR flight plans, they permit significant information to be passed to you by the FSS. They also mark the progress of your flight if, for some reason, you do not reach your destination. When you

Making position reports on VFR flight plans is a good operating practice.

make a position report, it should sound like this: *"Lufkin Radio, Cessna 5246R, over Lufkin at 1650 Zulu, VFR flight plan, 2,500, Beaumont to Henderson."*

FLYING OVER HAZARDOUS TERRAIN

In some parts of the country, regularly traveled VFR routes often cross large bodies of water, swamps, and mountains. Selected FSSs provide Hazardous Area Reporting Service. The locations where this service is available are indicated in the *Aeronautical Information Manual*. These areas are mainly in the northeastern section of the country (including the Great Lakes), while some are located in the swamplands of Florida. When you request this service, you are expected to make frequent radio contacts with the FSS. Refer to the AIM for specific information on each location where the service is available.

Mountain flying and flight over open water are potentially hazardous operations from several standpoints. To be conducted safely, they require specialized training from experienced instructors who are familiar with the area over which the flights will be conducted. Appropriate survival gear is an absolute necessity. Mountain flying and flight over open water are usually beyond the scope of private pilot training depending on where you learn to fly. Before undertaking these types of operations, be sure to obtain a local checkout. Mountain flying, in particular, carries numerous hazards for the inexperienced. High density altitude, turbulence, rapidly changing weather, and difficulty in identifying landmarks are just a few of the challenges facing you on a mountain flight.

You can see that pilotage and dead reckoning complement each other in VFR navigation. You use pilotage to maintain your orientation to the planned route of flight and to identify the landmarks you have selected for checkpoints. The use of dead reckoning computations during flight planning provides an estimate of the heading necessary to maintain course. You also know what groundspeed to expect and can calculate your estimated time enroute, as well as fuel requirements. By recording this information on a navigation log, you can compare your estimated time between checkpoints with your actual time during flight. The navigation log also provides information needed to fill out your FAA flight plan.

CHECKLIST _____

After studying this section, you should have an understanding of:

✓   **Pilotage** — How it is performed and what the advantages and disadvantages of this form of navigation are.

✓ **Orientation** — The importance of maintaining an orientation between your intended and actual routes of flight and how adequate flight planning will help to prevent disorientation.

✓ **Dead reckoning** — How performing calculations of time, speed, distance, and direction will help you to predict movement of your airplane along your intended route of flight.

✓ **Navigation plotter** — How its scales are used for measuring distance, and how its protractor is used to determine a true course.

✓ **Navigation log** — How it is used for flight planning and for in-flight calculations concerning the progress of your flight.

✓ **Flight plan** — How to fill one out and how to open and close it.

SOURCES OF FLIGHT INFORMATION

D

The need for current flight information has been a concern of cross-country pilots since the earliest days of aviation. As a pilot, you need to know when airports or runways are temporarily closed or when navigation aids are shut down for maintenance. You also need to be aware of new procedures and factors affecting flight safety as they are developed. While you study this section, you will find that aeronautical charts do not always provide the most current flight information. Updating and disseminating flight information on a timely basis is essential to safe flight operations. In this section, we will briefly summarize several important sources of flight information. These include the *Airport/Facility Directory* (A/FD), *Aeronautical Information Manual* (AIM), *Notices to Airmen* (NOTAMs), *Advisory Circulars* (ACs), and the *Jeppesen Pilot Resource Services*.

AIRPORT/FACILITY DIRECTORY

The *Airport/Facility Directory* contains all airports, seaplane bases, and heliports open to the public.

During your training, you will soon become familiar with one of the most comprehensive sources of flight information — the *Airport/Facility Directory*. Published by the National Ocean Service, it contains a descriptive listing of all airports, heliports, and seaplane bases which are open to the public. [Figure 8-46]

Figure 8-46. The *Airport/Facility Directory* consists of several volumes which are divided for regional coverage. The entire directory is reissued several times a year and is designed to be used in conjunction with aeronautical charts. The effective dates are shown on the cover of each volume, so you will know if you have the most recent issue.

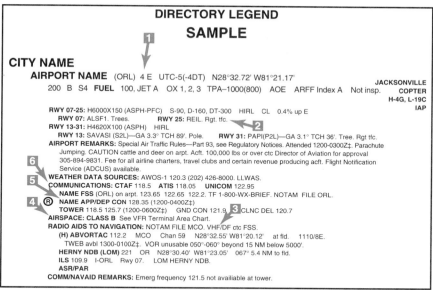

DIRECTORY LEGEND
SAMPLE

CITY NAME
AIRPORT NAME (ORL) 4 E UTC-5(-4DT) N28°32.72' W81°21.17' JACKSONVILLE **COPTER**
200 B S4 **FUEL** 100, JET A OX 1, 2, 3 TPA–1000(800) AOE ARFF Index A Not insp. **H-4G, L-19C** **IAP**

RWY 07-25: H6000X150 (ASPH-PFC) S-90, D-160, DT-300 HIRL CL 0.4% up E
RWY 07: ALSF1. Trees. RWY 25: REIL. Rgt. tfc.
RWY 13-31: H4620X100 (ASPH) HIRL
RWY 13: SAVASI (S2L)—GA 3.3° TCH 89'. Pole. RWY 31: PAPI(P2L)—GA 3.1° TCH 36'. Tree. Rgt tfc.
AIRPORT REMARKS: Special Air Traffic Rules—Part 93, see Regulatory Notices. Attended 1200-0300Z‡. Parachute
  Jumping. CAUTION cattle and deer on arpt. Acft. 100,000 lbs or over ctc Director of Aviation for approval
  305-894-9831. Fee for all airline charters, travel clubs and certain revenue producing acft. Flight Notification
  Service (ADCUS) available.
WEATHER DATA SOURCES: AWOS-1 120.3 (202) 426-8000. LLWAS.
COMMUNICATIONS: CTAF 118.5 ATIS 118.05 UNICOM 122.95
  NAME FSS (ORL) on arpt. 123.65 122.65 122.2. TF 1-800-WX-BRIEF. NOTAM FILE ORL.
Ⓡ NAME APP/DEP CON 128.35 (1200-0400Z‡)
  TOWER 118.5 125.7 (1200-0600Z‡) GND CON 121.9, CLNC DEL 120.7
AIRSPACE: CLASS B See VFR Terminal Area Chart.
RADIO AIDS TO NAVIGATION: NOTAM FILE MCO. VHF/DF ctc FSS.
  (H) ABVORTAC 112.2 MCO Chan 59 N28°32.55' W81°20.12' at fld. 1110/8E.
    TWEB avbl 1300-0100Z‡. VOR unusable 050°-060° beyond 15 NM below 5000'.
  HERNY NDB (LOM) 221 OR N28°30.40' W81°23.05' 067° 5.4 NM to fld.
  ILS 109.9 I-ORL Rwy 07. LOM HERNY NDB.
  ASR/PAR
COMM/NAVAID REMARKS: Emerg frequency 121.5 not availiable at tower.

Figure 8-47. The information provided in the A/FD includes the location of the airport, four miles east of the city (item 1). "Rgt. tfc." means you should fly a right-hand traffic pattern when landing on runway 25 (item 2). "VHF/DF" indicates the FSS has direction finding equipment (item 3). The Class B airspace designation notifies you of mandatory radar sequencing and separation for aircraft in Class B airspace (item 4). The approach and departure control frequency is 128.35 MHz (item 5). When the tower is closed, you should communicate on the CTAF frequency 118.5 (item 6).

DIRECTORY LEGEND

The airports presented in the *Airport/Facility Directory* are listed alphabetically by state, and then by the city associated with the airport. In order to help you interpret the abundance of information, there is a directory legend in the front of each regional volume. This sample gives you a thorough breakdown of all of the information in the booklet, including data pertaining to the airport's location, runways, lighting, ground services, communications facilities, and navigation aids. As well as showing the general sequence of the data, the legend also provides a detailed explanation of how to interpret each of the items. [Figure 8-47]

The directory legend gives a detailed description of each item in an airport listing.

OTHER FLIGHT PLANNING INFORMATION

Although airport listings make up the bulk of the directory, there are several other sections that contain essential information. Many of these pertain to VFR flight operations.

In the Special Notices section, you will find information concerning changes that affect the airspace system, as well as important miscellaneous items. Another section provides telephone numbers for the flight service stations and National Weather Service outlets located in the

1 **SPECIAL NOTICES**

NATIONAL PARK AREAS
VOLUNTARY OVERFLIGHT PRACTICES

As expressly encouraged by FAA Advisory Circular (AC) 91-36C, Visual Flight Rules (VFR) Near Noise-Sensitive Areas, *2,000 feet above the surface* of National Park areas (including Parks, Forests, Primitive Areas, Wilderness Areas, Recreational Areas, National Seashores, and National Wildlife Refuge and Range Areas).

NOTE: — AC 91-36C defines the *surface* of a National Park Area as: the highest terrain within 2,000 feet laterally of the route flight, **or** the upper-most rim of a canyon or valley.

2 ## FAA AND NWS

TELEPHONE NUMBERS

★ PATWAS
■ TWEB
◆ Restricted number for Aviation Weather Information
§§ Fast File (Flight Plan Filing Only)

Location and Identifier		Area Code	Telephone
Cedar Rapids CID . . . . .FSS		(319)	364-7127
Davenport (via Moline, Ill.) . . . . .WS		(309)	762-8347
Dubuque . . . . .WS		(319)	582-3171
Fort Dodge . . . . .FSS		(800)	WX-BRIEF ★§§

3 ## VOR RECEIVER CHECK POINTS

	111.6/FHU	G	210		On runup area rwy 02.
Prescott (Ernest A. Love Fld)	114.1/DRK	A/7000	124	5.0	Over apch end rwy 29.
Scottsdale Muni	115.6/SRP	A/7500	343	12.0	Over rwy 21 thld.
Tucson (Tucson Intl)	116.0/TUS	G	305	2.4	On int Twy A and 02 on apron.
		G	298	2.7	On west ramp at Twy B.

VOR TEST FACILITIES (VOT)

Facility Name (Airport Name)	Freq.	Type VOT Facility	Remarks
Pheonix Sky Harbor Intl.	109.0	G	

4 ## PARACHUTE JUMPING AREAS

LOCATION	DISTANCE AND RADIAL FROM NEAREST VOR/VORTAC	MAXIMUM ALTITUDE	REMARKS
Cedar Rapids	14 NM; 047° Cedar Rapids	15,000 AGL	3 NM Radius. Continuous
(c) Dallas Center, Husband Field . .	25 NM; 305° Des Moines	12,800	3 NM radius. Weekends and holi-days
Davenport	13 NM; 258° Davenport	12,500	2 NM radius. Daily
Decorah Arpt	15 NM; 264° Waukon	7,000 AGL	Summer. Tue-Thu 1700-SS, Sat-Sun 1000-SS. Winter. 1000-SS Sat, Sun.

5 ## AERONAUTICAL CHART BULLETIN

WICHITA SECTIONAL
37th Edition, November 20, 19___

Add obst 4275'MSL (315'AGL)UC 36°01'55"N 102°27'32"W   Add obst 3403'MSL (448'AGL)UC 36°03'12"N 100°48'07"W   Add obst 1649'MSL (499'AGL)UC 37°03'33"N 97°05'41"W   Add obst 1615'MSL (272'AGL) 37°34'35"N 97°29'44"W

Delete arpt SCHULZ FIELD 38°02'37"N, 98°46'36"W Add UNICOM 122.95 to SALINA MUNI 38°47'30"N 97°38'59"W

Figure 8-48. Other information contained in the *Airport/Facility Directory* includes Special Notices (item 1), FAA and NWS Telephone Numbers (item 2), VOR Receiver Check Points (item 3), Parachute Jumping Areas (item 4), and the Aeronautical Chart Bulletin (item 5).

region. In addition, numbers for PATWAS and TWEB are listed to provide you with recorded information. [Figure 8-48]

If you are planning to use VOR navigation, you may wish to consult the lists of ground and airborne checkpoints you can use to test the accuracy of your VOR receiver. If a symbol printed on the aeronautical chart alerts you to a parachute jumping area along your route of flight, you can check the A/FD for the location, maximum altitude, and pertinent remarks about those activities. When a glider symbol is printed near an airport, you may find further information listed in the remarks for that airport.

The A/FD provides information concerning parachute jumping areas and glider operations.

The Aeronautical Chart Bulletin provides you with major changes in aeronautical information that have occurred since the last publication date of each sectional, VFR terminal area, and WAC chart. It includes changes affecting airports, obstructions, and communications and navigation facilities. By consulting this listing, you can obtain current information that could affect your flight.

Consult the Aeronautical Chart Bulletin before your flight for changes to aeronautical charts.

A variety of miscellaneous information is also provided in the *Airport/Facility Directory*, which includes the address and phone number for each Flight Standards District Office (FSDO) in the region. A map showing stations that provide enroute flight advisory service is also furnished. Additional information of special interest to IFR pilots includes a regional list of sector frequencies for ARTCCs, as well as preferred IFR routes. Some A/FDs also include information on tower enroute control service between adjacent approach control facilities.

AERONAUTICAL INFORMATION MANUAL

Your official guide to basic flight information and ATC procedures is the *Aeronautical Information Manual.* It is revised several times a year, and it furnishes a detailed description of the national airspace system, including the procedures necessary to conduct flight operations in the United States. The AIM also includes items of special interest to pilots, such as medical facts and other flight safety information. [Figure 8-49]

The AIM contains information necessary for flight in the U.S.

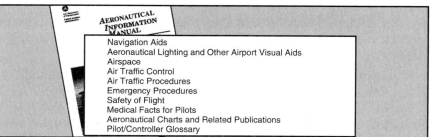

Figure 8-49. The AIM covers the general topics shown here. A comprehensive table of contents and an alphabetical index help you locate specific subjects. In addition, each new issue provides an explanation of major changes.

The AIM describes the various air navigation aids available to both VFR and IFR pilots. This information includes the capabilities, components, and procedures required for the use of each type of navaid. It also contains a discussion of radar services and procedures available to pilots, as well as information about the capabilities and limitations of radar. In addition, the AIM provides a comprehensive description of the many types of airport lighting and marking aids available.

It is a good idea to review airspace requirements and ATC procedures periodically. The AIM provides a means of doing this. It covers the various forms of controlled, uncontrolled, and special use airspace, as well as weather minimums and VFR cruising altitudes. A thorough discussion of the air traffic control system is also provided. This includes a description of the facilities and services available to pilots, such as air route traffic control centers, control towers, flight service stations, and aeronautical advisory stations. Because of the importance of the link between the pilot and controller in the ATC system, a discussion is devoted to radio communications phraseology and techniques. A related area, the Pilot/Controller Glossary, is intended to promote a common understanding of the terms used in the air traffic control system. International terms that differ from the FAA definitions are listed after their U.S. equivalents.

You can also find important information on emergency services available to you, such as radar, transponder operation, and VHF/DF instrument approach procedures. In addition, the AIM covers distress and urgency messages, as well as procedures for two-way radio communications failure. Numerous weather services available for your preflight and enroute operations are detailed in the Safety of Flight section. It discusses altimeter settings, wake turbulence avoidance, and potential flight hazards, as well as safety, accident, and hazard reporting procedures. Other areas outline pertinent medical factors and list the various aeronautical charts and publications available from the government.

NOTICES TO AIRMEN

NOTAMs supply time-critical changes in aeronautical information to pilots.

Often, changes in aeronautical information are not known far enough in advance to be included in the most recent aeronautical chart or *Airport/Facility Directory* (A/FD). The National Notices to Airmen System provides you with time-critical flight planning information. Each notice is categorized as a NOTAM(D), a NOTAM(L), or an FDC NOTAM.

NOTAM(D) information is disseminated for all navigational facilities that are part of the U. S. National Airspace System (NAS), all public use airports, seaplane bases, and heliports listed in the A/FD. The complete NOTAM(D) file is maintained in a computer database at the National Communications Center (NATCOM), located in Kansas City. This category of information is distributed automatically, appended to the hourly weather reports, via the Service A telecommunications system. Air traffic facilities, primarily FSSs, with

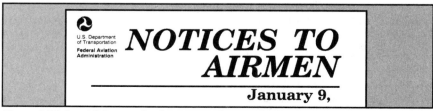

FORT SMITH LANDING STRIP (5U7) 1 N UTC-7(-6DT) N45°19'15" W107°55'50" **BILLINGS L-9C**
3242
RWY 07-25: H3827X50 (ASPH) S-8
RWY 07: P-line **RWY 25:** Thld dspicd 140'. P-line.
AIRPORT REMARKS: Unattended.
COMMUNICATIONS: CTAF 122.9
BILLINGS FSS (BIL) TF 1–800–WX–BRIEF. NOTAM FILE BIL.
RADIO AIDS TO NAVIGATION: NOTAM FILE BIL.
BILLINGS (H) VORTAC 114.5 BIL Chan 92 N45°48'31" W108°37'26" 118° 41.4 NM to fld. 3800/17E.

Figure 8-50. *Airport/Facility Directory* listings include the associated FSS and NOTAM file identifiers. At Fort Smith Landing Strip, the FSS is Billings and the airport NOTAM file identifier is "BIL." The same NOTAM identifier is used for radio aids.

Service A capability have access to the entire NATCOM database of NOTAMs. These NOTAMs remain available via Service A for the duration of their validity, or until published. [Figure 8-50]

NOTAM(L) information includes data such as taxiway closures, personnel and equipment near or crossing runways, airport rotating beacon outages, and airport lighting aids that do not affect instrument approach criteria, such as VASI. This information is distributed locally only and is not attached to the hourly weather reports. A separate file of local NOTAMs is maintained at each FSS for facilities in their area. NOTAM(L) information for other FSS areas must be specifically requested directly from the FSS that has responsibility for the airport concerned.

FDC NOTAMs are issued by the National Flight Data Center. They contain regulatory information such as temporary flight restrictions or amendments to instrument approach procedures and other current aeronautical charts. FDC NOTAMs are available through all air traffic facilities with telecommunications access.

An important part of your preflight planning should be a review of the **Notices to Airmen** publication. It is issued every 28 days and contains all current NOTAM(D)s and FDC NOTAMs (except FDC NOTAMs for temporary flight restrictions) available for publication. Airway changes are carried as Center Area NOTAMs (CANs) on the NOTAM(D) circuit, and are included. When NOTAM(D) information is published, it will not be provided during pilot briefings unless requested. Data of a permanent nature are sometimes printed in the NOTAM publication as an interim step prior to publication on the appropriate aeronautical chart or in the A/FD. [Figure 8-51]

You should always check the Notices to Airmen publication prior to flight.

U.S. Department of Transportation
Federal Aviation Administration

NOTICES TO AIRMEN

January 9,

Figure 8-51. In addition to alerting you to changes in the airway system, the NOTAM publication details information about individual airports and is alphabetized by state, city, and airport name.

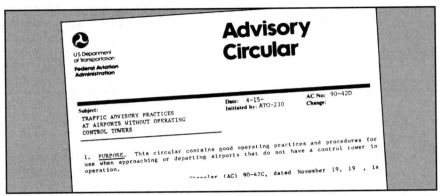

Figure 8-52. The subject of this advisory circular is identified in the heading. This AC defines the concept of a common traffic advisory frequency (CTAF).

ADVISORY CIRCULARS

ACs are informational in nature and present non-regulatory material of interest to pilots.

The Federal Aviation Administration has developed a systematic means of providing pilots with nonregulatory information of interest. These **advisory circulars** (ACs) are normally issued to provide you with guidance and information in a variety of subject areas, or to show a method acceptable to the Administrator for complying with Federal Aviation Regulations. Unless incorporated into a regulation by reference, the contents are not binding. [Figure 8-52]

Advisory circulars are divided into subjects by numbers. For example, ACs covering Airspace are issued under subject number 70.

Advisory circulars are divided into a variety of subjects, and are identified by numbers corresponding to the different part numbers of the Federal Aviation Regulations. Some of the subject areas are:

00	General
10	Procedural Rules
20	Aircraft
60	Airmen
70	Airspace
90	Air Traffic Control and General Operating Rules
150	Airports

FAA advisory circulars are available to all pilots. They may be ordered through the Department of Transportation, U.S. Government Printing Office.

You may find that a series of circulars exists for a given subject. When this happens, the general area of information is subdivided into specific areas. For example, within the 150 series pertaining to airports, *Advisory Circular 150/5340-1E* describes marking of paved areas on airports. Periodically, the *Advisory Circular Checklist (AC-00-2)* is revised and reissued to inform you of the current status of ACs. The checklist also provides you with pricing and ordering information. Some ACs are free and others are available at cost. You can order either type through the Department of Transportation, U.S. Government Printing Office.

JEPPESEN PILOT RESOURCE SERVICES

In addition to government publications, comparable commercial publications are available. As an example, the **Jeppesen Pilot Resource Services** include the Jeppesen Aeronautical Information Manual (AIM), Pilot FARs, the Jeppesen Airport Directory, and the GPS/Loran Coordinate Directory. The AIM, Pilot FARs, and Airport Directory are printed in loose-leaf format for ease of revision.

JEPPESEN AIM

The AIM Service contains all of the information published in the government edition, plus extra Tables and Codes, as well as Entry Requirements. It includes the full Pilot/Controller Glossary, and it is updated on a 112-day cycle. Because of the comprehensive coverage of the material and the frequency of revision, FAR Part 135.81 authorizes air taxi and commercial operators to use the Jeppesen AIM as a substitute for the FAA AIM.

JEPPESEN PILOT FARS

The FAR Service is particularly useful for pilots who need up-to-date regulations. Revisions are available as required, normally about eight times each year. The revised paragraphs, which are actually amendments to the regulations, are clearly indicated by arrows or brackets in the margin of the affected pages. [Figure 8-53]

PILOT FAR SERVICE – TABLE OF CONTENTS	
FAR-1	– Definitions and Abbreviations
FAR-43	– Maintenance, Preventive Maintenance, Rebuilding, and Alteration
FAR-61	– Certification: Pilots and Flight Instructors
FAR-67	– Medical Standards and Certification
FAR-91	– General Operating and Flight Rules
FAR-119	– Certification: Air Carriers and Commercial Operators
FAR-121	– Operating Requirements: Domestic, Flag, and Supplemental Operations
FAR-125	– Certification and Operations: Airplanes having a seating capacity of 20 or more passengers or a maximum payload capacity of 6,000 pounds or more
FAR-135	– Operating Requirements: Commuter and On-Demand Operations
FAR-141	– Pilot Schools
FAR-142	– Training Centers
HMR-175	– Hazardous Materials Regulations (HMR) — Carriage by Aircraft
NTSB-830	– Rules Pertaining to the Notification and Reporting of Aircraft Accidents or Incidents and Overdue Aircraft, and Preservation of Aircraft Wreckage, Mail, Cargo, and Records
SFAR	– Special Federal Aviation Regulations

Figure 8-53. Federal Aviation Regulations published in the Jeppesen Pilot FARs include all of the most commonly used Parts of interest to pilots, as well as the Hazardous Materials Regulations (HMR), National Transportation Safety Board (NTSB) Part 830, and current Special FARs.

JEPPESEN AIRPORT DIRECTORY

The Airport Directory Service includes a choice of regional coverages such as Northwest, North Central, Great Lakes, and so forth. Each regional coverage is updated twice a year. Full U.S. coverage is also provided.

To avoid duplication of diagrams on IFR approach charts, only VFR airport diagrams are published in these directories. However, pertinent airport data are included for both IFR and VFR airports. When appropriate, general operational information, airport remarks, fixed base operator (FBO) services, car rental services, and lodging and restaurant availability are noted. Airports within each state are listed by city name, followed by the airport name, when different. [Figure 8-54]

GPS/LORAN COORDINATE DIRECTORY

This directory contains coordinates for all public-use airports, navaids, and waypoints within the contiguous 48 states. This is an important reference document for users of GPS and LORAN equipment. Airports are

JENISON (RIVERVIEW) 08C ➜ VFR
603'. N42 56.1 W085 48.3 GRR 304°/16.3nm.
TPA 1500' (897'). LT +5(+4DT)=UTC.
Rwys: 14/32 3761'x46' (ASPHALT) MIRL. 32: LDA 2771'.

Communications: Traffic ©122.9.
Services: Fuel: 100LL, available 24 hrs w/notice. Repairs: small airframe, recip engine. Misc: tiedown, deicing, acft parts, refreshments, courtesy car, 24 hr phone, preheat, pilot lounge, conference room, daytime parking, overnight parking. Rental Cars: thru Riverview Aviation, Advantage. Lodging: Best Western, La Grande Motel, Lands Inn.
DODGEN AIRCRAFT, (616) 457-0820, Credit Cards: MC, VISA, Discover, Phillips.
DOGEN AIRCRAFT REFINISHING, (616) 457-1020.

KALAMAZOO (-BATTLE CREEK INTL)
AZO   IFR
874'. N42 14.1 W085 33.1 AZO on apt. ➜
TPA 1674' (800'). ARFF Index B. Lndg Rights Apt. LT +5(+4DT)=UTC.
Rwys: 05/23 3999'x100' (ASPHALT-GRVD) MIRL. 05: LDA 3436'; REIL, PAPI-L. 23: REIL, VASI-L. 09/27 3351'x150' (ASPHALT) MIRL. 09: LDA 3036'. 27: LDA 3136'.
17/35 6499'x150' (ASPHALT-GRVD) HIRL. 17: REIL, VASI-L. 35: MALSR.
Remarks: Birds and deer in vicinity of apt. General aviation parking not authorized on air carrier ramp. Twys F and G restricted to aircraft less than 12,500 lbs. PCL - 118.3, when twr closed: HIRL Rwy 17/35; MIRL Rwys 05/23, 09/27; MALSR Rwy 35, REIL Rwy 05/23 and Rwy 17, PAPI Rwy 05, VASI Rwy 17 and Rwy 23.
Communications: *ATIS 127.25. *KALAMAZOO App ®119.2 (353°-172°). *App ®121.2 (173°-352°). *Dep ®119.2 (353°-172°). *Dep ®121.2 (173°-352°). *CHICAGO Ctr ®127.55. *KALAMAZOO Tower ©118.3. *Ground 121.9. Unicom 122.95.
Services: Fuel: 100LL, Jet A, available 24 hrs. Repairs: 24 hr emerg svc, small airframe, recip engine. Misc: tiedown, hangar, deicing, oxygen, refreshments, courtesy car, 24 hr phone, preheat, APU, pilot lounge, conference room, daytime parking, overnight parking. Restaurants: on field, nearby. Rental Cars: Thrifty, Budget . Lodging: Holiday Inn, Radison, Lee's Inn.
KAL-AERO, INC, (616) 343-2548, unicom-122.95, Credit Cards: MC, VISA, Amex, U.S. Govt., MS, Discover, Avfuel, Amoco, Boron, Avcard, Mobil, Exon, Chevron, Sohio.

Figure 8-54. Since Rivervew is a VFR airport, the airport diagram is provided; Battle Creek International is an IFR airport and the diagram is omitted. As shown for both airports, information includes coordinates, traffic pattern altitudes, runway data, communications, and services.

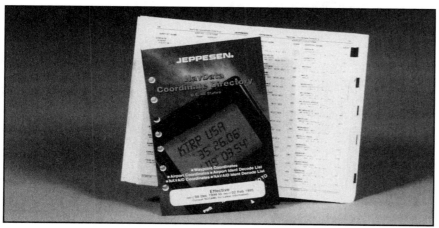

Figure 8-55. Unlike the other Pilot Resource Services, the Coordinate Directory is published in a bound book (5-1/2″ × 8-1/2″). It is updated and reissued on the FAA's 56-day cycle.

arranged by state, city, and airport name. An FAA identifier is included, as well as the airport reference point (ARP) coordinates. The ARP is usually located in the center of the airport. Another listing gives airports by the three-letter identifier. Navaids are also listed by name and identifier. Waypoints are listed by name. Each listing is indicated by an edge-marked tab. [Figure 8-55]

CHECKLIST

After studying this section, you should have a basic understanding of:

✓ **Airport/Facility Directory** — How it is used in conjunction with aeronautical charts, and how to interpret the information contained in each regional volume.

✓ **Aeronautical Information Manual** — What basic flight information and ATC procedures it contains.

✓ **Notices to Airmen** — How NOTAM(D)s, NOTAM(L)s, and FDC NOTAMs are used to update changes to information contained in the *Airport/Facility Directory*, the *Aeronautical Information Manual*, and aeronautical charts.

✓ **Advisory circulars** — What they are, how they are indexed, and how you can obtain them.

✓ **Jeppesen Pilot Resource Services** — The variety of information alvailable, and how it provides you with current aeronautical and airport data.

MAXIMUM PERFORMANCE TAKEOFFS AND LANDINGS

Typically you learn to fly at airports with relatively long, paved runways. However, not all airports have long runways, and many runways are made of dirt, grass, or sod. It is important that you learn how to perform short-field and soft-field takeoffs, climbs, approaches, and landings. These manuevers, also referred to as maximum performance takeoffs and landings, are designed to allow you to operate safely into and out of unimproved airports.

Before presenting the techniques you will use in maximum performance takeoffs and landings, let's review some important terms. The **best angle-of-climb** speed provides the greatest altitude gain for a given distance over the ground. Many manufacturers also specify an **obstacle clearance** speed. This speed is used immediately after lift-off when the airplane is in the takeoff configuration and you must clear an obstacle located in the departure path.

Obstacle clearance, best angle-of-climb, and best rate-of-climb are three important speeds used during the initial climb.

Typically, you use the best angle-of-climb speed or the obstacle clearance speed, as appropriate to your airplane, until all obstacles in the takeoff path have been cleared. Next, you accelerate to the **best rate-of-climb** speed. This speed provides the greatest gain in altitude in a given period of time. Since optimum performance is achieved by maintaining each speed precisely, you should make every effort to hold the best angle-of-climb, obstacle clearance, and best rate-of-climb speeds as precisely as possible.

SHORT-FIELD TAKEOFF AND CLIMB

During short-field practice sessions it is usually assumed that, in addition to a short runway, there is an obstruction that you must clear on each end of the runway. The obstructions are considered to be approximately 50 feet in height. [Figure 8-56]

The pretakeoff checklist is the same as that used for normal takeoff procedures, except that you set the flaps as recommended by the airplane manufacturer. The recommended flap setting varies between airplanes and can range from no flaps to approximately one-half flaps.

Check to determine that the engine is functioning properly before you release the brakes for takeoff.

Initiate the short-field takeoff by taxiing into position as close as possible to the end of the runway. Hold the brakes, apply full power, and then release the brakes. This procedure enables you to determine that the engine is functioning properly before you take off from a field where power availability is critical. As you begin the takeoff roll, maintain directional control with rudder pressure. A running, turning

Figure 8-56. Trees and powerlines are common types of obstructions. However, during flight training, your instructor will usually simulate the existence of obstacles if none are present.

takeoff is not recommended, especially at high speeds, because this technique does not permit stabilization of fuel levels in the tanks of some airplanes. [Figure 8-57]

Take care to avoid raising the nose prior to the recommended rotation speed. A premature nose-high attitude during the takeoff ground run produces more drag and causes a longer takeoff roll. After you have cleared the obstacle, lower the nose and accelerate to the best rate-of-climb speed. If you used flaps, retract them only after you have cleared the obstacle, established the best rate-of-climb speed, and climbed to a safe altitude.

Figure 8-57. The initial takeoff roll involves little or no use of elevator (or stabilator) control beyond permitting it to assume a neutral position (position 1). As you reach the recommended rotation speed (position 2), apply prompt, positive back pressure to establish the proper takeoff attitude (position 3). Hold this attitude until the best angle-of-climb speed (or obstacle clearance speed) is established, then maintain this speed until the obstacle is cleared (position 4).

SHORT-FIELD LANDING

During short-field landing practice, assume you are making the approach and landing over a 50-foot obstacle. Perform the landing from a full-flap stabilized approach and execute the touchdown with power off. By incorporating this technique, you can maneuver the airplane safely and accurately over the obstacle to a landing touchdown at the slowest possible groundspeed, producing the shortest possible ground roll.

The early part of the approach on the downwind leg and through the turn to base leg is very similar to a normal approach. You may extend approximately one-third of the available flaps during the latter portion of the downwind leg, two-thirds on base, and the remaining flaps on final approach, while progressively reducing the airspeed. Use the trim to remove control pressure.

FINAL APPROACH

The final approach path used for a short-field landing is somewhat steeper than the one used for a normal approach. It allows you to clear an obstacle located near the approach end of the runway. The use of full flaps during the approach allows a descent at a steeper angle without an increase in airspeed. This results in an overall decrease in the distance required to bring the airplane to a full stop. [Figure 8-58]

LANDING FLARE AND TOUCHDOWN

During the landing flare, reduce power smoothly to idle and allow the airplane to touch down in a full-stall attitude. When the airplane is firmly on

Figure 8-58. Two types of approach paths are shown here: the normal approach and the short-field approach. Notice when an obstacle is present how the short-field approach allows you to descend at a steeper angle and touch down closer to the end of the runway.

the runway, lower the nose and apply the brakes, as necessary, to further shorten the landing roll. As your training progresses, your goal will be to touch down beyond and within 200 feet of a point specified by your instructor.

SOFT-FIELD TAKEOFF

The objective of the soft-field takeoff is to transfer the weight of the airplane from the landing gear to the wings as quickly and smoothly as possible. The soft-field takeoff procedure requires you to accelerate the airplane in a nose-high attitude, keeping the nosewheel clear of the surface during most of the takeoff ground run. This technique keeps the nosewheel from sinking into the soft runway surface and allows the airplane to become airborne as soon as possible.

PRETAKEOFF CONSIDERATIONS

You actually begin the soft-field takeoff procedure during the taxi phase of the operation. If the taxi area is soft, you should use full-up elevator (or stabilator) deflection with a slight amount of power to help keep the airplane moving. This technique transfers some of the weight of the airplane from the nosewheel to the main wheels, resulting in lower power requirements and greater ease in taxiing. If practical, the pretakeoff check should be completed on a paved or firm-surfaced portion of the airport. This helps avoid propeller damage and the possibility of becoming stuck. After you complete the pretakeoff checklist, clear the approach and departure areas and the traffic pattern prior to taxiing onto the runway. In this manner, when there is no conflicting traffic, you can transition the airplane from the taxi phase to the takeoff roll without stopping. This technique allows the airplane to maintain momentum as you taxi over the soft surface.

While taxiing, maintain full back pressure on the control wheel.

USE OF RUDDER

As you taxi the airplane into position for takeoff and align it with the center of the runway, apply the remaining power smoothly and maintain full back pressure on the control wheel. When you apply takeoff power, you may need right rudder pressure to maintain directional control due to the effects of torque, P-factor, and spiraling slipstream. When the nosewheel is clear of the runway surface, nosewheel steering becomes ineffective. However, due to the increasing air flow, the rudder becomes sufficiently effective for maintaining directional control.

PITCH CONTROL

As you apply power and initiate the takeoff roll, maintain full back pressure to raise the nosewheel from the soft surface. As you increase speed and the elevator (or stabilator) becomes more effective, you will need to

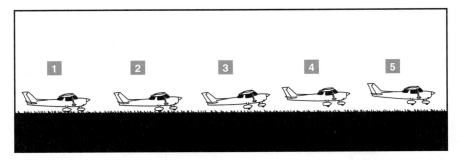

Figure 8-59. If you establish the proper pitch attitude during acceleration (position 1), the nosewheel will be clear of the surface during much of the ground run (position 2), and the airplane will lift off at or slightly below the power-off stall speed (position 3). After liftoff, reduce the pitch attitude gradually to level flight (position 4), allowing the airplane to accelerate within ground effect to the normal climb airspeed (position 5).

It is important to raise the nosewheel clear of the runway as soon as practical, but do not allow the tail to come in contact with the ground.

reduce back pressure slightly. If you do not reduce back pressure, the airplane may assume an extremely nose-high attitude, which can cause the tail skid to come in contact with the runway. [Figure 8-59]

GROUND EFFECT

During the takeoff, you will be aided by a phenomenon called **ground effect**. This is an increase in lift during flight, which is due primarily to the redirection of the air between the wings of the airplane and the surface of the earth. Ground effect allows the airplane to sustain flight at very low airspeeds and altitudes. However, this phenomenon is limited to a height above the ground which is about equal to the airplane's wingspan. For example, if the wingspan of the airplane is 40 feet, ground effect ends at approximately 40 feet above ground level. Since the intensity of ground effect decreases with height, you should fly the airplane as low as safety will permit until you have achieved the best angle-of-climb airspeed if obstacles must be cleared. If no obstacles are present in the departure path, or after clearing any obstacles, accelerate to the best rate-of-climb airspeed. Additional information on ground effect is included earlier in the text.

LIFTOFF AND FLAP RETRACTION

Be sure to accelerate to the best angle-of-climb speed before climbing out of ground effect.

As the airplane lifts from the runway surface, reduce back pressure to achieve a level flight attitude. You must then accelerate the airplane in level flight, within ground effect, to the best angle-of-climb airspeed before starting a climb. Do not retract the flaps, since the resultant loss of lift may cause the airplane to settle back onto the runway.

On a rough surface, it is possible for the airplane to skip or bounce into the air before its full weight can be supported aerodynamically. Therefore, it is important to hold the pitch attitude as constant as possible (an important application of maneuvering during slow flight). If you permit the nose to lower after a bounce, it may cause the nosewheel to strike the ground with resulting damage. On the other hand, sharply increasing the pitch attitude after a bounce may cause the airplane to stall.

OBSERVATION OF PROPER AIRSPEEDS

Throughout the takeoff procedure, observe the proper airspeeds and plan the necessary climb segments accordingly. After the airplane is airborne, accelerate to the best angle-of-climb speed if obstacles must be cleared as quickly as possible. At this point, you may begin your climb out of ground effect. Once all obstacles are cleared, accelerate to the best rate-of-climb speed and continue the climb. You should retract the flaps once you have attained a safe altitude and airspeed.

SOFT-FIELD LANDING

Conduct the soft-field landing from a normal full-flap approach. Touch down with a high angle of attack while applying necessary power for a soft touchdown. The objective is to ease the weight of the airplane from the wings to the main wheels as gently and slowly as possible while keeping the nosewheel clear of the runway. If you execute the landing properly, the total weight of the airplane rests on the main wheels with the nosewheel free of the soft surface during most of the landing roll. This technique prevents the nosewheel from sinking into the soft surface and reduces the possibility of an abrupt stop during the landing roll.

Hold the nose clear of the runway as long as possible.

PITCH AND POWER CONTROL DURING LANDING

Proper pitch and power control are important during the entire approach and landing, but become most critical during the landing flare and touchdown segments. Change the pitch smoothly from an approach to a touchdown attitude. Normally, you will maintain a small amount of power during the touchdown to facilitate a nose-high, soft touchdown. The amount of power required varies with weight and density altitude. When you maintain power, the slipstream flow over the empennage makes the elevator (or stabilator) more effective. As the airspeed decreases on the rollout, the slipstream becomes less effective. Allow the nosewheel to contact the runway surface gradually and smoothly.

CHECKLIST _____

After studying this section, you should have a basic understanding of:

✓   **Climb speeds** — When best angle-of-climb, obstacle clearance climb, and best rate-of-climb speeds are used.

✓   **Short-field takeoff** — What the procedures are to ensure a takeoff using the least amount of runway.

✓   **Short-field landing** — How to execute the short-field landing.

✓   **Soft-field takeoff** — How to execute a takeoff when departing an airport with unimproved runways and why these procedures are necessary.

✓   **Soft-field landing** — How to land on unimproved runways and why the nosewheel is held clear of the runway.

flight prep 9

VHF OMNIDIRECTIONAL RANGE

Of the many types of navigation systems available to you, the **very high frequency omnidirectional range** (VOR) system is the one you will probably use most frequently. A basic VOR system provides course guidance, automatic wind correction, and magnetic headings. The VOR system actually uses three different types of ground facilities to help you navigate through the sky. The basic VOR station provides you with course guidance, while VOR/DME and VORTAC facilities provide both course and distance information. Since all three of these facilities help you follow a course, your first step will be to learn how to use this feature.

PRINCIPLES OF OPERATION

A VOR station transmits radio beams, called **radials**, outward in every direction. Actually, there is an infinite number of radials, but you will be concerned with the 360 which are numbered clockwise from magnetic north. [Figure 9-1]

VORs are depicted on sectional charts, as discussed in Chapter 6. The compass rose surrounding the station helps you to visualize the radials as

Figure 9-1. The ground-based component of the VOR system is the VOR station shown on the left. It transmits radials throughout 360° of azimuth starting at magnetic north. During flight, you will use these radials to determine your position relative to the station.

Figure 9-2. Victor 12 connects the Otto VOR and the Anton Chico VORTAC. The airway is defined by the 074° radial of Otto and the 255° radial of Anton Chico. When navigating between two stations you typically change from one station to the next at the midpoint.

they travel outward. Many VOR stations are connected by specific radials, which form direct routes called Victor airways. [Figure 9-2]

The VOR signals are transmitted in the very high frequency range of 108.00 through 117.95 MHz. They travel on a line-of-sight basis. Any obstacle, such as a mountain or the curvature of the earth, can reduce the reception distance of the signal. In certain situations, terrain features can render the signals unusable for navigation purposes. You can find these exceptions published in the *Airport/Facility Directory* under the individual VOR listings. The reception range also varies with altitude. At low altitudes you must be very close to the station to receive the signal. As your altitude increases, you can use the VOR at greater distances from the station.

Reception range for VOR signals is limited by line of sight.

VOR AIRBORNE EQUIPMENT

Your airborne equipment consists of an antenna, a receiver, and an indicator. VOR signals are received through the antenna. Next, they are relayed to the VOR receiver, which interprets the signals and sends the information to the VOR indicator. Although most airborne VOR equipment is similar in appearance and operation, you should familiarize

Figure 9-3. The VOR antenna is shaped like a "V" and is normally located on the vertical stabilizer or on top of the fuselage. The VOR indicator displays course information required for navigation. This VOR receiver has 50 kHz spacing which provides 200 navigation channels. By pulling the volume control knob out, you access the ident feature which permits you to identify the station.

yourself with the particular make and model you are using. Information normally is available in the POH or in separate publications from the radio manufacturer. [Figure 9-3]

VOR NAVIGATION

VOR is simple to use once you understand its basic principles. To navigate effectively with it, you must complete certain preliminary steps. The first is to obtain the VOR frequency from the appropriate aeronautical chart and enter it into the VOR receiver with the frequency selector. Next, you need to identify the station to ensure that you have picked the right frequency. You must also determine that the station is operating properly, and that you have a reliable navigation signal.

The VOR indicator has three different components which give you related navigation information. The components are the course deviation indicator

Figure 9-4. The CDI needle shows you whether you are on or off course. When it is centered, you are on course. If it swings to either side, you are off course. The TO-FROM indicator tells you whether your selected course will take you to or from the station. The course selector, also called the omnibearing selector (OBS), allows you to choose a particular radial by setting it under the course index.

(CDI), the TO-FROM indicator, and the course selector. They work together to help you navigate along the course you have selected. [Figure 9-4]

COURSE INFORMATION

It is important to remember that radials travel outward from the VOR station. If you are flying away from the VOR on a given radial, your heading and the VOR course will be approximately the same. If you are going to the station, your heading will be 180° different than the radial you are following. Of course, wind can cause some heading variation, but assume a no-wind condition for this example. [Figure 9-5]

Figure 9-5. When you are flying away from a VOR station on the 030° radial (in a no-wind condition), your heading indicator will read 030°. On the other hand, if you fly inbound to the station on the 030° radial, your heading will be 210°.

If you wish to follow a particular radial to or from the station, simply set the desired course under the index at the top of the indicator. The reciprocal, or reverse course, appears under the index at the bottom of the indicator. When you are off course, the CDI points toward the desired course. The scale underneath the needle shows how far you are off course, with each dot on the scale representing a course deviation of two degrees. For example, if your CDI is deflected two dots to the left of center, your desired course is four degrees to your left. [Figure 9-6]

You should always identify a VOR station before using it for navigation.

In order to receive reliable course information, you must always identify a station before using it for navigation. A station may be identified by a three-letter Morse code signal or by a combination of code and a repetitive voice transmission that gives the name of the VOR. You can monitor the station identifier by selecting the ident feature on the VOR receiver. If you don't hear the identifier, it may mean that the station is not operating or that you are out of range of the facility. When a station is shut down for maintenance, it may radiate a T-E-S-T code (– · ··· –), or the identifier may be removed. In any case, do not use a station for navigation unless you can identify it.

TO-FROM INDICATIONS

The TO-FROM indicator helps you maintain your sense of orientation with respect to the station. With the course selector properly set, a FROM indication is shown when you are flying away from the station. When you are flying toward the station, it shows TO.

The TO-FROM indicator can also help you determine which course will provide the most direct route to a VOR station. For example, assume you are in the vicinity of a VOR and would like to fly directly to the station. After you tune and identify the station, simply turn the course selector until the TO-FROM indicator shows TO. Continue turning the selector

Figure 9-6. To aid in orientation, picture your airplane at the bottom of the VOR indicator. If the CDI overlaps the airplane, as it does on the left, you are on the selected course. If your airplane and the CDI are not aligned, you are off course, as shown on the right side of the illustration.

Figure 9-7. Besides signaling your position over the station, the OFF or NAV indication appears briefly when you are abeam, or 90° to either side of, your desired course. The FROM indication appears as you continue past the abeam position, even if you don't pass directly over the station.

until the CDI centers. The reading under the index is your magnetic course to the station. As you fly over the station, the TO indication disappears, and is replaced briefly by an OFF or NAV indication. On some equipment, a red flag is displayed momentarily. If these indications appear at times other than station passage, it means the VOR signal is too weak for reliable navigation. As you leave the station behind, the indicator reads FROM, meaning you are traveling away from the station. [Figure 9-7]

It is important for you to remember that the aircraft's heading has no direct relationship to the course selected in the VOR indicator. The VOR indicator reflects your position relative to the station you are receiving, regardless of the direction you are flying. However, when you actually navigate with VOR, the headings you fly will be in general agreement with your selected course. [Figure 9-8]

You can have many different magnetic headings for a single set of VOR indications.

Figure 9-8. Even though the aircraft are heading in three different directions, they are all located on the 090° radial (inbound course of 270°) and have the same VOR indications. However, only the airplane nearest the station will remain on the 090° radial, provided wind is not a factor. The headings of the other two airplanes will carry them away from the course selected.

Figure 9-9. Since you are flying to the station, a magnetic course of 090° is entered in the course selector, and a TO indication is displayed. As you fly left or right of course, the CDI is deflected accordingly. When you have passed over or abeam the station, the TO indication switches to FROM.

PRACTICE PROBLEM

As an example, assume you are on a cross-country flight and want to travel to a VOR, which you will approach from the west. You intend to fly inbound on the 270° radial. Your first step is to tune and identify the station using the frequency from the sectional chart. [Figure 9-9]

If you are flying away from the station in a no-wind situation, your aircraft heading will be the same as the course selected on the VOR indicator. However, if you experience wind, your wind correction will make your heading different from the selected course.

USING VOR NAVIGATION

Wind correction is normally required to maintain course and fly a straight line to or from a VOR station.

The most common VOR navigation you will perform is flying from one station to another during cross-country flights. You will use a process called tracking to accomplish this. Tracking involves entering a course in the course selector and maintaining that course by keeping the CDI centered. To stay on track if you are experiencing a crosswind, you will use a technique called bracketing. In a crosswind situation, the wind causes you to drift off course, so you need to make a series of corrections to regain your desired course and then maintain it. [Figure 9-10]

VOR ORIENTATION

Determining your position with respect to VOR navaids is called **VOR orientation**. You have learned how to determine the magnetic course to a

Figure 9-10. While tracking inbound to the Ashland VORTAC on the 180° radial, assume you begin to drift right of course due to a crosswind. This example shows the bracketing procedure required to regain the course and determine a heading that will compensate for wind.

Figure 9-11. First, draw a line from Otto, following the 120° radial. After tuning and identifying the Anton Chico VORTAC, turn the course selector until you get a FROM indication and the CDI centers. In this case, the VOR indicator shows that you are located on the 210° from Anton Chico. By plotting that radial on the chart, you can see that your position is the point where the lines intersect.

You can determine your exact position on a chart using two VOR stations.

station using the VOR indicator. This places you somewhere on a particular radial. One of the ways you can tell your distance from the station on that radial is to cross-check it with a second VOR. When you use two VOR stations to determine your location, you should select radials that are nearly perpendicular to each other. That way, they will intersect at a 90° angle, and you can locate your position more accurately. For example, assume you are tracking inbound on the 120° radial of the Otto VOR, and would like to know your exact location. [Figure 9-11]

INTERCEPTING RADIALS

In some situations, you may want to navigate on a different radial than the one you have been following. Essentially, you must fly from one radial to another. This is called intercepting. Intercepts are used for a variety of reasons. An intercept will help you get established on an airway following departure for a cross-country trip. Another example is when you need to position your aircraft over a VFR checkpoint for initial callup to enter Class B or C airspace. To use an intercept, you must visualize where you are from the station, and where you want to go. The intercept angle you use depends on how close you are to the station. It may range from 20° through 90°, depending on your position. The radials are closest together at the facility, much as spokes are closest together at the hub of a wheel. [Figure 9-12]

VOR CAUTIONS

There are two aspects of VOR navigation with which you should exercise caution. The first concerns unusual CDI fluctuations. Certain propeller r.p.m. settings can cause the CDI to fluctuate as much as six degrees. By varying the propeller r.p.m. slightly, you normally will eliminate this problem. The second aspect concerns a situation called reverse sensing.

The CDI may fluctuate with certain propeller r.p.m. settings.

Reverse Sensing

When your course selector is in general agreement with your heading indicator in an off-course situation, the CDI will be deflected toward the selected course. Therefore, if you want to get on course, all you need to do is correct toward the CDI. However, if you mistakenly set your course selector to the reciprocal of the desired course, your CDI will be deflected away from the course you want to follow. This situation is known as **reverse sensing**. It can be very confusing, because following the normal procedure of correcting toward the needle will actually take you farther off course. When you track to the station, you must set the VOR course selector to the reciprocal (180° opposite) of the radial you want to follow inbound.

If the course selected in your VOR indicator is in general agreement with your heading indicator, the CDI off-course indication will be in the direction of the desired course.

To illustrate this point, assume you want to track inbound on the 090° radial. In the course selector, you mistakenly enter a course of 090° and then take up a magnetic heading of 270° to get to the station. Your heading indicator now differs from the course selected by about 180°. In addition, you have a FROM indication, even though you are inbound to the station. This is a reverse sensing situation. [Figure 9-13]

Figure 9-12. While tracking inbound on the 250° radial with a course of 070°, you decide to intercept the 270° radial inbound. After turning left to establish an intercept angle, enter the new inbound course (090°) into the course selector. When the CDI begins to center, turn right and track inbound.

Figure 9-13. Your CDI is deflected toward the left, indicating that a turn to the left will bring you on course. However, with reverse sensing, this will take you farther from course. In this situation, you should enter the desired course of 270° into the course selector so you will have a TO indication and correct sensing.

VOR ADVANTAGES

VOR has many advantages that make it popular and easy to use. Its frequency range is relatively free from precipitation static and other annoying interference caused by storms and various weather occurrences. Since it is omnidirectional (radiates in all directions), you have many possible courses to choose from. The VOR is accurate to plus or minus one degree. By keeping the needle centered, you automatically compensate for wind drift during flight. Since VOR compass roses on sectional charts are oriented toward magnetic north, you can use magnetic headings to maintain course. The following illustration provides a review of the principles of VOR navigation. [Figure 9-14]

VOR TEST SIGNALS

Before you navigate using VOR, you should check your equipment to ensure it is functioning accurately. **VOR test facilities** (VOTs) enable you to make VOR accuracy checks regardless of your position in relation to the VOT. This is possible because they broadcast the signal for only one specific radial — 360°. The first step is to get the frequency for the check from the *Airport/Facility Directory* and set it in the VOR receiver. You should also note if the VOT is for ground or airborne checks, or both. Next, check the VOT for proper operation by verifying the aural signal, which should be a series of dots or a continuous tone.

A VOT check using a course of 180° should center the CDI and give you a TO indication. Using 0° should center the CDI and give you a FROM indication.

Now you are ready to set a course of either 0° or 180° in the VOR indicator. If the course selector is set at 0°, the CDI should center and the TO-FROM indicator should read FROM. If the course selector is set at 180°, the CDI should center and the TO-FROM indicator should read TO. If the CDI doesn't center, determine the magnitude of error by rotating the course selector until the needle does center. The new course should not vary from the test course (0° or 180°) by more than four degrees.

OTHER VOR CHECKS

You can also determine the accuracy of your VOR using ground or airborne checkpoints. On the ground, you can taxi your aircraft to a specific point on the airport designated in the "VOR Receiver Check" section of the *Airport/Facility Directory* and check your VOR course reading. Then, compare this reading to the published course. The maximum permissible error is plus or minus four degrees.

Airborne checkpoints are also listed in the directory and are usually located in the immediate vicinity of airports. These checkpoints are usually placed over easily identifiable terrain or man-made features on the ground. With this type of check, the maximum permissible course error is plus or minus six degrees.

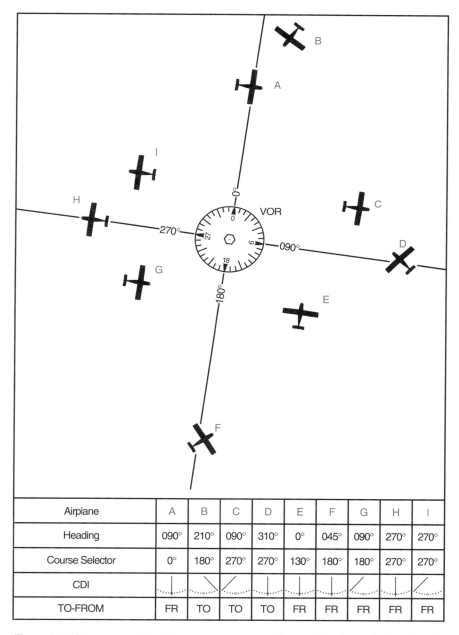

Airplane	A	B	C	D	E	F	G	H	I
Heading	090°	210°	090°	310°	0°	045°	090°	270°	270°
Course Selector	0°	180°	270°	270°	130°	180°	180°	270°	270°
CDI									
TO-FROM	FR	TO	TO	TO	FR	FR	FR	FR	FR

Figure 9-14. You can see that there are many possible combinations of aircraft position, heading, and VOR indications. For example, airplane A is directly north of the station on the zero degree radial with a magnetic heading of 090°. With zero degrees set in the VOR indicator, the CDI will be centered with a FROM indication. Study the other airplane positions, headings, and CDI indications so you are sure you understand VOR navigation.

Another airborne check uses the VOR airways. Because the VOR airway system is tested to plus or minus one degree, you can obtain a very accurate test of your VOR. To do this, select a VOR radial that defines the centerline of a VOR airway. On this route, select a prominent terrain feature, preferably 20 miles or more from the VOR facility. Maneuver your aircraft directly over the point and note the course reading on the VOR indicator. The permissible difference between the published radial and the indicated course is six degrees. You can also conduct a VOR check by using two VOR systems which are independent of each other. If your aircraft is equipped with two VOR radios, set both to the same VOR facility and note the indicated readings on each. When you check one against the other, the maximum difference should not be greater than four degrees.

The tolerances that have been discussed regarding VOR accuracy actually are specified for IFR operations in FAR Part 91. Although regulations do not require specific VOR accuracy for VFR operations, it is appropriate to follow the IFR guidelines.

CLASSES OF VOR FACILITIES

During your flying career, you will use three classes of VOR facilities. They are the **terminal VOR** (TVOR), the **low altitude VOR** (LVOR), and **high altitude VOR** (HVOR). Each class has a different function for navigation purposes. The TVOR provides terminal guidance and, as such, should not be used farther than 25 n.m. from the station or above 12,000 feet AGL. You may use an LVOR reliably up to 40 n.m. from the station at altitudes between 1,000 and 18,000 feet AGL. At altitudes above 18,000 feet AGL, interference from other VORs with the same frequency may exist. HVOR is effective to various ranges, depending on the altitude. Many of the airways you will fly on are defined by HVORs that have a maximum reception range of 130 n.m. The class designation of a VOR facility can be found in the *Airport/Facility Directory*.

DISTANCE MEASURING EQUIPMENT (DME)

DME provides distance information in nautical miles.

VOR/DME and VORTAC facilities provide you with an added capability to course guidance — distance. **Distance measuring equipment** (DME) provides a distance reading in nautical miles from a VOR/DME or VORTAC site. Without DME, the only way to get an accurate position is to use two VOR facilities and plot your location on a chart. With DME, you need only one navaid to achieve the same result. [Figure 9-15]

DME THEORY

DME operates on a UHF frequency band of 962-1213 MHz and, like VOR, is subject to line-of-sight restrictions. Your aircraft first transmits an interrogation signal to the station. The ground station receives this signal and transmits a reply back to the aircraft. The airborne DME records the round trip time of this signal exchange and computes distance values in terms of nautical miles and groundspeed values in knots. Many DME units also provide **time to station**, which is the time it will take you to reach the station at the computed groundspeed. These values are displayed on your cockpit indicator. With enough altitude, you should be able to receive reliable signals at 199 n.m. DME normally is accurate to less than one-half a mile or three percent of the distance, whichever is greater.

USING DME

There are two things you need to be cautious about when using DME. The groundspeed reading is accurate only when you are traveling directly to or from the station. Flight in any other direction will give you an unreliable reading. Also, DME measures slant range distance, not horizontal distance. Slant range distance is the result of two components, the horizontal distance and the vertical distance. Slant range error is not considered significant if the aircraft is one mile or more from the station for every 1,000 feet of altitude. [Figure 9-16]

Slant range error is greatest when you are at a high altitude and close to the station.

DME IDENTIFICATION

When you are using both VOR and DME, it is important to ensure both systems are working properly. This is done by first entering the navigation frequency of the VORTAC into the VOR receiver. Most general aviation VOR and DME receivers have paired frequencies. When you tune the

The absence of the single-coded identification signal every 30 seconds means the DME is not operational.

Figure 9-15. The airborne DME equipment consists of a transceiver and a "shark's fin" antenna. You will usually find the antenna on the underside of the aircraft.

Figure 9-16. If you are flying at an altitude of 1 n.m. at a horizontal distance of 1.7 n.m. from the station, your DME will register a distance of 2 n.m. The difference is due to slant range error which is greatest directly over the station.

VORTAC frequency, you will automatically receive DME information. Then, listen for the synchronized coded signals or voice identifications. The VOR identifier is repeated three or four times for each DME identifier If one of the systems is not working, you will notice a gap in transmissions. A single-coded identification transmitted approximately every 30 seconds indicates the VOR is inoperative. The absence of the single-coded identification every 30 seconds indicates the DME is inoperative.

CHECKLIST

After studying this section, you should have a basic understanding of:

✓   **VOR operation** — How it works and what advantages it offers.

✓   **VOR components** — What the air and ground components are and how to check them.

✓   **VOR indicator** — What it is and the information it provides.

✓   **VOR navigation** — How to set up your equipment for proper operation, how to track by bracketing, and how to intercept radials.

✓   **Reverse sensing** — What it is, when it occurs, and how to avoid it.

✓   **DME** — What it is, how it works, and the information it provides.

✓   **Slant range error** — How it affects you and when it is greatest.

AUTOMATIC DIRECTION FINDER

Another navigation system, and one which you could use as a backup to VOR, is the **automatic direction finder** (ADF). Unlike VOR, ADF does not rely on line-of-sight transmissions. This allows reliable navigation at lower altitudes than VOR and, depending on the facility, may also provide greater reception range. Your airborne ADF equipment is capable of receiving radio signals from ground facilities called **nondirectional radio beacons** (NDBs), as well as commercial broadcast stations.

ADF equipment allows you to navigate using NDBs and commercial broadcast stations.

ADF EQUIPMENT

ADF equipment in the aircraft permits L/MF signals to be received through the antenna, relayed to the ADF receiver where they are processed, and then sent to the ADF indicator. Although most automatic direction finders have similarities in appearance and operation, you should familiarize yourself with the make and model installed in the airplane you plan to use. Consult the POH or other publication provided by the radio manufacturer. [Figure 9-17]

Figure 9-17. The ADF airborne equipment consists of a combined loop and sense antenna, a receiver, and an indicator. When properly tuned, the bearing pointer of the ADF indicator points to the station selected.

ADF RECEIVER

Your ADF receiver has an on/off/volume control, selectors for entering the station frequency, and several function or mode selectors. The ANT, ADF, and BFO modes are typical of most ADF receivers. Normally, you tune and identify a station with the ANT mode, since it provides maximum sensitivity to radio signals. After you enter the charted NDB or broadcast station frequency into the receiver, you typically increase the volume until you can hear background noise, then readjust it for comfortable listening volume. Always identify the station positively by listening to the Morse code identification. You may also use the ANT mode to monitor voice transmissions such as weather broadcasts. The bearing pointer of the ADF indicator does not function in this mode.

The BFO (beat frequency oscillator) mode is for tuning and identifying CW (continuous wave) signals. CW signals are unmodulated compared to normal NDB signals. While tuning in the BFO mode, you determine maximum signal reception by the strength of the audio tone; that is, a maximum signal provides the strongest audio. Within the conterminous U.S., the BFO system usually is not required for station identification.

Always use the test function to verify that the bearing pointer is responding to a reliable signal.

Once you have tuned and identified the station, place the switch in the ADF mode, which allows the receiver to send navigation information to the ADF indicator. You should then notice the needle on the bearing indicator starting to move as it searches for the station's relative position. Once a strong signal from the station is found, the needle will stop searching and steady itself. At this time, you should use the ADF test function to ensure the signal is reliable. Check your operator's handbook to see how this function works on the ADF you will be using.

NDBs transmit ground and sky waves in the low and medium frequency ranges.

NDBs are shown on aeronautical charts and can be used for either VFR or IFR operations. They transmit low/medium frequency (L/MF) signals in the frequency range of 190 to 535 kHz. These signals travel both as ground waves that penetrate obstacles and as sky waves that are refracted by the ionosphere. These characteristics are the reason L/MF waves can be received over great distances, even at lower altitudes.

Selected commercial broadcast stations of the AM class are also shown on aeronautical charts. AM radio stations use the frequency range from 535 to 1605 kHz. However, their use is restricted to VFR operations, since they are required to identify themselves only once each hour.

ADF BEARING INDICATORS

An ADF bearing reflects the horizontal direction, or angle, between your aircraft and the station.

With L/MF facilities, bearings are used to describe your position rather than radials. A **bearing** is the horizontal direction to or from any point, which is measured clockwise through 360° from magnetic north. A bearing indicator gives you the horizontal direction, or angle, between your aircraft and the L/MF station. Actually, there are two types of bearing indicators — the fixed card and the movable card. Initially, we will discuss the fixed-card indicator. You will learn more about the movable card later in this section.

The fixed-card bearing indicator measures **relative bearing** — the angular difference between the airplane's longitudinal axis and a straight line drawn from the airplane to the station. This value is measured clockwise from the airplane's nose. If you wish to fly directly to the station, you must add your magnetic heading to your relative bearing. This value is called **magnetic bearing**; it will take you directly to the station. Stated in formula terms, magnetic heading (MH) + relative bearing (RB) = magnetic bearing (MB). If the total is more than 360°, you will need to subtract 360° to find the magnetic bearing to the station. [Figure 9-18]

> According to the ADF formula, MH + RB = MB, or RB = MB − MH (if this value is negative, add 360°).

HOMING

A procedure where you always keep the nose of the aircraft pointing directly to the station is called **homing** to the station. You do this by keeping the fixed-card bearing pointer on the aircraft's nose, or at 0°. In a no-wind situation, the magnetic heading will remain constant as you fly inbound to the station. However, in a crosswind situation, the wind will push you off course, and you must adjust the magnetic heading to keep the nose of the aircraft pointing toward the station. [Figure 9-19]

> Homing to the station results in a curved flight path in crosswind condition.

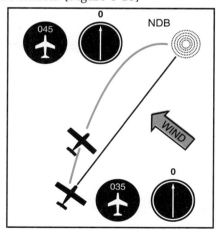

Figure 9-18. In this sample problem, the ADF bearing indicator is pointing 020° to the right of the aircraft's nose. This is a 020° relative bearing. To find the magnetic bearing to the station, read the magnetic heading of 070° from the heading indicator, then use the formula to determine the magnetic bearing: MH (070°) + RB (020°) = MB (090°). This means you should maintain a course of 90° to get to the station.

Figure 9-19. The curved, blue line represents your flight path while homing to the station in a right crosswind. When using this method, your flight path over the ground is uncertain; and the distance you travel can vary greatly, depending on the wind velocity and the distance to the station. In a no-wind situation, your flight path would follow the black line.

ORIENTATION

Assume you want to locate your position on a chart. To do this, you will need to determine the **reciprocal bearing**, which is the bearing from the station. First, add your relative bearing and your magnetic heading to determine your magnetic bearing to the station. Next, you will need to find the reciprocal bearing by adding 180° to or subtracting 180° from the magnetic bearing. If the magnetic bearing is less than 180°, add 180°; if it is more than 180°, subtract 180° to get the reciprocal. For example, if your magnetic bearing to the station is 090°, the reciprocal bearing is 270° (090° + 180° = 270°). If your magnetic bearing is 210°, the reciprocal is 30° (210° − 180° = 30°).

Some people find it easier to determine the reciprocal of the magnetic bearing by using the 200/20 rule. If the magnetic bearing is less than 180°, add 200 to the number and subtract 20. If the number is greater than 180°, subtract 200 and add 20 to find the reciprocal of the magnetic bearing.

To plot your position on a chart, convert the magnetic bearing to true bearing.

The magnetic bearing reciprocal would be easy to plot if the station on the chart had a magnetic compass rose surrounding it. However, since a chart depiction of an NDB does not have a compass rose, you will have to plot your azimuth with reference to grid lines. Since grid lines are referenced to true north instead of magnetic north, you will have to convert your magnetic values to true values. If you remember from Chapter 6, this is accomplished by adding or subtracting variation. However, when you convert magnetic values to true values, you add easterly variation and subtract westerly variation. After you have made this final computation, the result is called **true bearing**, which is your horizontal direction from the station with respect to true north. Now, plot this line by placing the edge of your plotter on the NDB and rotating it until the compass rose intersects a line of longitude at the same angle as your true bearing. By drawing this line on the chart, you will have narrowed your position down to some point on that line. To find your exact location, you can use a second navaid, as discussed in the VOR section. You may also locate your position with respect to identifiable landmarks or terrain beneath you.

TRACKING

The best way for you to get to or from a station is in a straight line, which requires tracking if any wind is present. The tracking procedure you learned in VOR is similar to the procedure used for ADF. It involves flying into the wind to compensate for its effect on your flight path. However, fixed-card ADF does not provide an automatic wind correction angle. Bracketing is required to determine the WCA, and then a corresponding bearing is used to maintain a steady track. [Figure 9-20]

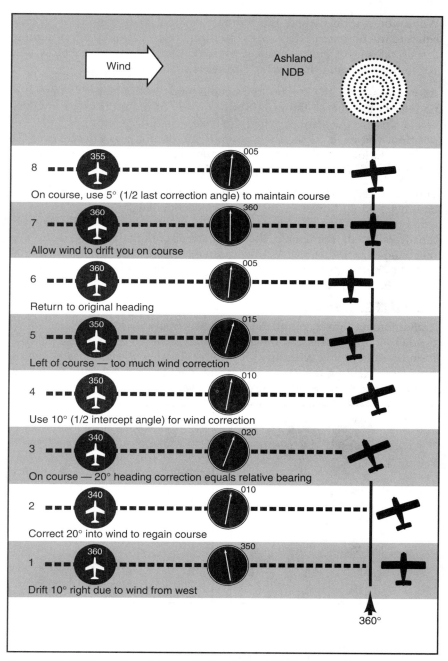

Figure 9-20. While tracking inbound to the Ashland NDB on the 360° bearing to the station, assume you begin to drift right of course due to a crosswind. This example shows the bracketing procedures necessary to regain course and determine a heading that will correct for wind.

When you are on course, the wind correction angle should be exactly equal to the number of degrees the bearing indicator points left or right of the aircraft's nose. For example, if your WCA is 10° left, the station will be 10° to the right, and the bearing pointer will also indicate 10°.

As you pass over the station, the needle tends to fluctuate. You are cautioned not to "chase" the needle, since many of the indications are erroneous close to the station. When the needle stabilizes at or near the 180° position, you have passed the station. If you do not pass directly over the facility, station passage occurs when the needle is steady and points to either wingtip position.

You can track outbound the same way you tracked inbound. With outbound tracking, however, the wind correction angle should be exactly equal to the number of degrees the station is located to the left or right of the aircraft's tail. Remember, the tail of the aircraft is the 180° position on the fixed-card indicator. As an example, assume you are tracking outbound from a station on the 090° bearing and experience a crosswind from the north. [Figure 9-21]

ADF INTERCEPTS

ADF intercepts are accomplished in a manner similar to those required for bracketing procedures, but the angles used are much greater. Use the ADF formula to help you with this procedure. Assume you are located southwest of an NDB on the 250° bearing and want to track inbound to the station on the 270° bearing. [Figure 9-22]

Figure 9-21. After you regain the course, take up a heading of 080° and notice the relative bearing remains at 190°. Use the ADF formula to determine the magnetic bearing to the station (80° + 190° = 270°). This means that 80° should result in a straight line course outbound from the station.

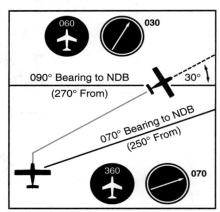

Figure 9-22. A heading of 060° will give you an intercept angle of 30° to the 090° bearing to the station (270° from). When the bearing pointer indicates 30°, you will know you have intercepted the 90° bearing to the station (270° from), and you can turn inbound.

MOVABLE-CARD INDICATORS

The movable-card bearing indicator is almost identical to the fixed-card indicator. The only difference is that you can rotate the movable card manually to reflect the aircraft heading at the top of the instrument. By putting the magnetic heading value under the top index of the ADF indicator, the bearing pointer will directly indicate magnetic bearing to a station. In addition, the number under the tail of the needle indicates magnetic bearing from the station.

The movable card reduces your workload in the cockpit, since it does not require you to use the ADF formula to find the magnetic bearing. In the next section, you will see that movable-card indicators have some of the same capabilities as the radio magnetic indicator (RMI).

ADF CAUTIONS

You should be aware of the limitations concerning L/MF navigation. First of all, the VFR reception range for L/MF facilities can vary greatly, depending on transmitter power, atmospheric conditions, and time of day. The ADF indicator does not have an OFF flag, so the tendency may be to use it when the signals are unreliable. A proper identification and test will counter this problem. You also should continuously monitor the station's ident feature, keeping in mind that commercial broadcast stations may not identify themselves regularly. The ident information for NDBs can be found in the associated frequency box on sectional charts. You also can find NDBs within the airport listings in the *Airport/Facility Directory*. These listings include the NDB name, power classification, and frequency.

The ADF indicator has no provision to warn you of unreliable signals.

You should also be aware that reliable ADF navigation is dependent upon the accuracy of the heading indicator. If the heading indicator has precessed 10°, tracking procedures and intercepts will be in error by 10°. Although this may not be very significant during inbound tracking, during outbound tracking over large distances, the error is multiplied. You can be miles off course and yet be completely unaware of your predicament. Be sure your heading indicator is in agreement with the magnetic compass.

The remaining limitations concern L/MF radio waves in general. Sometimes the signals are refracted by the ionosphere and return to earth 30 to 60 miles or more from the station. This leads to needle fluctuations on the ADF indicator. The phenomenon is called **twilight effect**, so named because the occurrence is most pronounced during the period just before and just after sunrise or sunset. To minimize the effect, you can average the fluctuations or fly higher. You also can select a station transmitting on frequencies lower than 350 kHz, since twilight effect has little impact on this portion of the frequency range.

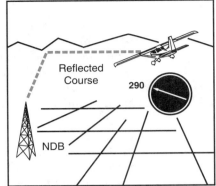

Figure 9-23. Shorelines can refract low frequency radio waves when they cross at small angles. However, radio waves that pass from land to water at angles greater than 30° have little or no shoreline effect. You can minimize this phenomenon by using stations where the signals cross the shoreline at angles greater than 30°. Terrain effect normally occurs in mountainous areas, since mountains have the ability to reflect radio waves. This can cause large fluctuations in bearing indications, as well as false courses. You should use only stations that give you strong steady signals while flying near mountainous areas.

Near thunderstorms, the bearing pointer may respond to lightning flashes. This is known as **thunderstorm effect**. You can compensate for it by disregarding the ADF indications during lightning flashes. Another problem can be interference from **precipitation static**, which is caused by a buildup of static electricity on an aircraft flying in rain, snow, or clouds. In severe cases, the bearing indicator may wander aimlessly, and you may not be able to identify the station properly. Two other problems associated with L/MF navigation include **shoreline effect** and **terrain effect**. [Figure 9-23]

CHECKLIST

After studying this section, you should have a basic understanding of:

✓ **L/MF facilities** — What types there are and the advantages they offer.

✓ **ADF components** — What the air and ground components are and how to use them.

✓ **Bearing** — What the different types are and how they are measured.

✓ **ADF navigation** — How to determine position, what the homing procedure is, how to bracket a bearing, and how to intercept a predetermined bearing and track inbound or outbound.

✓ **ADF cautions** — What they are and how to counter them.

As your flying career progresses, you will see more and more advanced navigation systems and equipment in the airplanes you fly. This discussion is designed to give you an overall view of the capabilities of some of these navigation systems; it is not intended to make you operationally proficient. If you need detailed information, refer to the POH or manufacturer's description for the particular equipment in question.

VORTAC-BASED RNAV

So far, you have become familiar with VOR and ADF, which are the systems you will probably use most frequently in the beginning. The next step for many pilots is area navigation. **Area navigation** (RNAV) allows you more lateral freedom in navigating, because it does not require you to track directly to or from navigation facilities. RNAV systems which utilize VOR/DME or VORTAC sites are referred to as VORTAC-based. **VORTAC-based area navigation** provides you with both course and distance information and allows you to fly to a predetermined point without overflying VOR/DME or VORTAC facilities. You benefit in many ways with this capability, since direct routing saves time, improves fuel economy, and lowers operating expenses. [Figure 9-24]

RNAV allows you to fly a straight path directly to your destination.

RNAV OPERATION

With RNAV, you have complete flexibility for determining the course you want to fly. VORTAC-based RNAV uses a **courseline computer** (CLC) which permits you to create "phantom stations" for use in navigation. Basically, the computer relocates, or offsets, the navigation aid to the desired radial and distance from the original location. You use a control panel to enter the amount of offset you want. The computer uses this

VORTAC-based RNAV allows you to offset a ground station to a specified distance along any desired radial from the facility.

Area Navigation Direct Route

Figure 9-24. With VOR routes, you typically travel from facility to facility. With RNAV capability, you can eliminate the zigzag flight path and fly in a straight line.

Figure 9-25. Your courseline computer compares the angle and distance between your aircraft and the VORTAC to the angle and distance between the VORTAC and the waypoint. By doing this, it knows two sides of a triangle and continuously solves for the third side, giving you angle and distance information from your position to the waypoint.

information to create the phantom stations, or **waypoints**. For a long cross-country flight, you will have a series of waypoints which collectively define an RNAV route. [Figure 9-25]

Another desirable RNAV feature is that you navigate using the VOR indicator. With RNAV, the needle deflections still indicate course displacement, but the deviation scale is in nautical miles and not degrees. Each dot on the horizontal scale represents a given value, such as .5 n.m. or 10 n.m., depending on what the manufacturer has set. When you are using RNAV, the DME will show the correct distance from you to the waypoint, but the groundspeed information also depends on the manufacturer. Some groundspeed readouts indicate the groundspeed in relation to the original facility, not the waypoint. Be sure to study the information supplied by the manufacturer for the RNAV equipment you are using.

LONG RANGE NAVIGATION

Long range navigation or LORAN is a leading navigation system. Advantages of modern LORAN-C systems include simplicity of operation and low cost. Older systems, referred to as LORAN-A, were used for maritime navigation. Early LORAN-A models were so heavy and cumbersome they were impractical for light aircraft, but technological advances in microprocessors and circuit miniaturization have led to lightweight LORAN-C equipment suitable for aviation. As a result, more and more LORAN receivers are being found in the general aviation aircraft of today, and chances are good you will fly a plane that has LORAN-C in it.

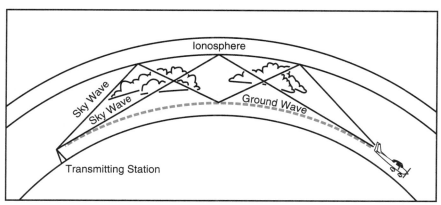

Figure 9-26. Since low frequency ground waves follow the contour of the earth, the reception range of LORAN signals is great (often 600 to 1,200 n.m. over land), and the transmitters can be located several hundred miles apart. Sky waves are also formed by LORAN signals but are not considered as reliable for navigation as ground waves.

The LORAN receiver you use will get its position information from a chain of low frequency (LF) transmitters. The chain transmits a synchronized signal on a frequency of 100 kHz in the form of ground and sky waves. [Figure 9-26]

You will find there are many types of LORAN receivers on the market with very different capabilities and operating requirements. The various receivers are differentiated primarily by the software programs or data bases they use. Generally, the more sophisticated a receiver is, the more capability it has, and the more extensive its data base. [Figure 9-27]

Figure 9-27. Although individual LORAN units vary considerably, this one has typical controls and display features and includes a major data base. Among other features, the data base contains the latitude, longitude, and identifier for over 2,500 waypoints, including all federally designated airports and VORs in the continental United States.

A typical LORAN receiver can compute bearing and distance from your present position to your intended destination. However, some data bases can give you navigation information, such as wind direction and velocity, fuel consumption, nearest airports in case of an in-flight emergency, audible warnings before you enter special use airspace, radio frequencies, and phone numbers. This is why it is so important to study the manufacturer's handbook to determine the capabilities of the particular LORAN set you are using.

LORAN OPERATION

In a typical LORAN chain, one transmitter is the master and two or more others are called secondaries. The master station transmits a group of coded pulses first; then, each secondary station transmits at a specific time interval after the master pulse. The time interval between one master pulse and the next is referred to as a **group repetition interval** (GRI). A GRI of 9940 means the master station pulses every 99,400 microseconds (millionths of a second). The GRI is unique to each chain and, in fact, identifies the chain. You use the GRI when you select a particular LORAN chain.

LORAN determines your postion by measuring differences in radio signal arrival time.

Next, you need to determine your location. Your LORAN receiver does this by measuring the **time difference** (TD) between a master station's signal and that of a secondary station. In other words, how long did it take for the master station's signal to reach you compared to the secondary signal? If this time difference were plotted on a chart, it would produce a **line of position** (LOP). [Figure 9-28]

The LORAN receiver automatically calculates your LOP fix, translates it into latitude and longitude values, and continuously updates your present position as you travel. Once the receiver has determined where you are, you can enter the coordinates of your destination, as well as other way-

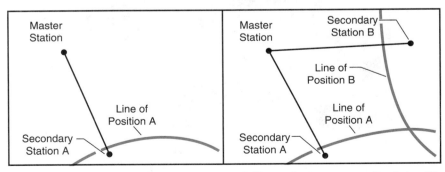

Figure 9-28. The line of position (LOP) in the left illustration represents all points with the same time difference (TD) between the master and one secondary. Your position is somewhere on this line. For the LORAN receiver to pinpoint your location, a second LOP needs to be determined using another secondary. Your present position is where the two LOPs intersect, as shown in the right illustration.

points. The receiver will calculate the course and distance to the point you specified, and continually update this information as you progress along your flight path. Most receivers will also give your groundspeed, as well as distance and time remaining to the destination.

LORAN CAUTIONS

Although LORAN is a popular navigation system, it does have some drawbacks. Since LORAN uses a low frequency AM radio signal, electrical disturbances such as thunderstorms and precipitation static can cause interference. It is not unusual to experience signal loss when you are flying in areas of electrical activity or heavy precipitation. An aircraft passing through rain, ice, or snow builds up a static charge which degrades signal reception. Static discharge wicks on airfoil trailing edges, fuselage grounding, and special antenna coatings are used to combat precipitation static.

A major limitation of LORAN deals with characteristics of the radio signals themselves. Even though they are very accurate (especially over water), they have a tendency to travel over land at different speeds. Surface type, foliage, seasonal changes, and weather can affect the speed of the radio waves and, consequently, their accuracy. You can use LORAN for enroute navigation, since this problem isn't significant. However, these problems and current specification requirements prohibit the use of LORAN as an instrument approach aid. Many LORAN receivers are classified as "VFR Only" because of these and other concerns.

Surface type, foliage, seasonal changes, and weather affect LORAN signals.

GLOBAL POSITIONING SYSTEM

The **global positioning system** or GPS is another type of radio aid that is well suited for aviation. GPS is a space based radio positioning, navigation, and time-transfer system developed by the Department of Defense. It provides highly accurate position, velocity, and time information on a global basis to an unlimited number of properly equipped users. The system is functional 24 hours a day, and is unaffected by weather. GPS also provides a worldwide common grid reference system. The concept is based on accurate and continuous knowledge of the spatial position of each satellite in the system with respect to the user. The GPS receiver automatically selects appropriate signals from the satellites in view and, through triangulation, translates these signals into a two or three-dimensional position fix with speed information. System accuracy for civil users is approximately 328 feet (100 meters) horizontally.

GPS is used for VFR and IFR navigation, and for designated instrument approaches. However, GPS receivers may be authorized for VFR operations only, or IFR navigation but not for IFR approaches, or for all types of operations. To determine the authorized operations for a particular GPS receiver, you will need to check the supplements section of the Airplane Flight Manual (AFM) or Pilot's Operating Handbook (POH). It is important to remember that when using GPS, or any other type of radio navigation system, you should also keep track of your position on a sectional chart.

ADVANCED NAVIGATION INDICATORS

You have already become familiar with the VOR and ADF systems and their associated navigation indicators. More advanced indicators have come into the marketplace, with the aim of simplifying navigation by providing more information on a single indicator. This is usually done by combining two or more instrument indicators into one. You will see these indicators more and more in the airplanes you fly. In the remaining discussion, you will become familiar with two of them.

RADIO MAGNETIC INDICATOR

The **radio magnetic indicator** combines the heading indicator with two bearing pointers. One functions like an ADF bearing indicator, while the other points to VOR stations. An RMI usually has a single-bar needle and a double-bar needle superimposed over a slaved compass card that is referenced to magnetic north. The single-bar needle normally points to a VOR station, while the double-bar needle may use either a VOR or an NDB facility, depending on the manufacturer. This provides you with constant position orientation, since the needles indicate magnetic bearing to their respective stations. The number under the tail of each needle indicates magnetic bearing from the appropriate station. Whereas the fixed-card ADF indicator requires you to use the ADF formula to find the magnetic bearing, the movable card in the RMI indicator displays magnetic bearings directly. This reduces your workload in the cockpit.

Navigating with RMI is much like navigating with VOR or ADF, depending on which needle and ground facility you use. The advantage of RMI is the combination of two navigation instruments on a properly oriented heading indicator. As you track inbound toward one facility, you can monitor your progress with the other indicator. Also, with two needles at your disposal, you can plot your position on a chart very easily. You should remember to consider variation when you plot your ADF bearing on sectional and WAC charts, since the charts are oriented toward true north. [Figure 9-29]

During a VOT check, the needle of an RMI should point to 180°, plus or minus four degrees.

Since the VOR pointer in the RMI depends on the VOR equipment, you need to check it for accuracy. The VOT check for an RMI is slightly different than the check for a VOR. When your VOR receiver is properly tuned to the VOT frequency, the RMI needle should indicate 180°, plus or minus four degrees.

HORIZONTAL SITUATION INDICATOR

You will find that many high-performance airplanes are equipped with a **horizontal situation indicator** (HSI). The HSI combines the functions of

VOR Needle Shows Magnetic Bearing to VOR Station

Magnetic Heading Under Index

ADF Needle Shows Magnetic Bearing to NDB Station

Wingtip Reference

Wingtip Reference

Magnetic Bearing From NDB Station

Compass Card

Magnetic Bearing From VOR Station

Figure 9-29. According to this RMI, you are located on the 235° radial of a VOR and are tracking inbound on a heading of 055°. You are also on the 105° bearing to an NDB facility. If you want to track inbound to the NDB, turn directly to the station (heading 105°) and apply wind correction, as needed.

the heading indicator and the VOR indicator in one display. This provides you with an accurate navigation picture on a single instrument. The HSI also presents glide slope information, which can be used by instrument pilots during ILS approaches. [Figure 9-30]

VOR course deviation, magnetic heading, and glide slope data are shown on an HSI.

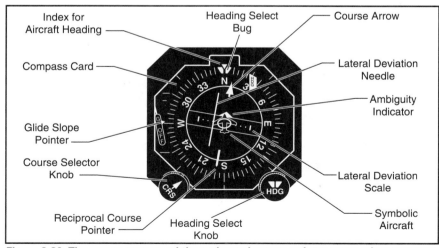

Index for Aircraft Heading

Heading Select Bug

Course Arrow

Compass Card

Lateral Deviation Needle

Ambiguity Indicator

Glide Slope Pointer

Course Selector Knob

Lateral Deviation Scale

Reciprocal Course Pointer

Heading Select Knob

Symbolic Aircraft

Figure 9-30. The course arrow and the reciprocal course pointer move when you turn the course selector knob. Notice the symbolic aircraft in the center, which represents your aircraft's position with respect to the desired course. Three OFF flags are usually incorporated in the HSI display to alert you to unreliable signals or equipment malfunctions.

The HSI has several components that help you navigate. The compass card provides you with the magnetic heading under the index at the top of the instrument. The heading select bug is used with an autopilot and automatically turns the aircraft to a newly selected heading. The HSI also incorporates the VOR course indications. The lateral deviation needle performs the same function as the CDI in a basic VOR indicator, depicting how far you are off course. When you are on course, the lateral deviation needle is aligned with the course arrow and the reciprocal course pointer.

The display shows the course selected, as well as its reciprocal. You will benefit from having a reverse course readily available during navigation. Another benefit for you is the ambiguity indicator, which does the same thing as the TO-FROM indicator on the conventional VOR. The arrowhead shifts to point rearward when you cross over a VOR station. Glide slope information is also displayed on the HSI. The glide slope pointer indicates aircraft position in relation to the ILS glide slope. If the pointer is above the center position, the aircraft is below the glide slope, and vice versa.

CHECKLIST

After studying this section, you should have a basic understanding of:

✓ **VORTAC-based RNAV** — What it is, how it operates, and the advantages of using it.

✓ **LORAN** — How it operates and what information it provides.

✓ **GPS** — What it is and how it operates.

✓ **RMI** — What it is, how it works, and the advantages it provides.

✓ **HSI** — What information you get from it and how it relates to VOR.

flight prep 10

VISION IN FLIGHT

Vision is by far the most important sense that we have, and flying is obviously impossible without it. Nearly everything that we perceive is visual or heavily supplemented by vision. The visual sense is especially important in collision avoidance and depth perception. Our vision sensors are our eyes, and they are not perfect in the way they function or see objects. Our eyes are not always able to see all things at all times: illusions and blindspots occur. The more you understand the eye and how it functions, the easier it will be to compensate for these illusions and blindspots.

THE EYE

Vision is primarily the result of light striking a photosensitive layer, called the **retina**, at the back of the eye. The retina is made of light-sensitive cones and rods. The cones in your eye perceive an image best when the light is bright, while the rods work best in low light. Your brain interprets what an image looks like by the pattern of light that strikes the cones and rods. Some information, such as movement and basic shapes, is actually processed on the retina itself, while other key features are sent by the optic nerve to the brain for processing there. [Figure 10-1]

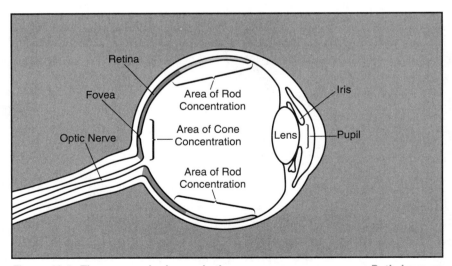

Figure 10-1. The eye works in much the same way as a camera. Both have an adjustable opening, or iris, to allow light in; a lens that focuses the image; and something to receive and record the image. The receptor in a camera is film; in the eye the receptors are rods and cones. These receptors instantly record the image and transmit it through the optic nerve to the brain for interpretation. Your eyes are like a camera with a never-ending roll of film.

CONES

Cones are concentrated around the center of the retina. They gradually diminish in number as the distance from the center increases. Cones allow you to perceive color by sensing red, blue, and green light. Directly behind the lens on the retina is a small, notched area called the **fovea**. This area contains only a high concentration of cone receptors. When you look directly at an object, the image is focused mainly on the fovea. The cones, however, do not function well in darkness, which explains why we cannot see color as vividly at night as we can during the day. [Figure 10-2]

RODS

The rods are our dim light and night receptors and are concentrated outside the fovea area. The number of rods increases as the distance from the fovea increases. Rods "see" only in black and white. Because the rods are not located directly behind the pupil, they are responsible for much of our peripheral vision. Images that move are perceived more easily by the rod areas than by the cones in the fovea. If you have ever seen something move out of the corner of your eye, it was most likely detected by your rod receptors.

Since the cones do not see well in the dark, you may not be able to see an object if you look directly at it. The concentration of cones in the fovea can make a night blindspot at the center of your vision. To see an object

Off-center viewing should be used at night. This helps compensate for the night blindspot in the center of your vision.

Figure 10-2. The best vision in daylight is obtained by looking directly at the object. This focuses the image on the fovea, which "sees" detail best.

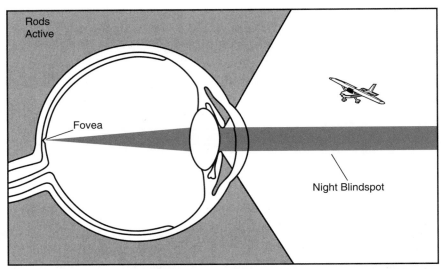

Figure 10-3. In low light, the cones lose much of their visual acuity, while rods become more receptive. The eye sacrifices sharpness for sensitivity. Your ability to see an object directly in front of you is reduced, and you lose much of your depth perception, as well as your judgment of size.

clearly, you must expose the rods to the image. This is accomplished by looking 5° to 10° off center of the object you want to see. You can try out this effect on a dim light in a darkened room. When you look directly at the light, it dims or disappears altogether. If you look slightly off center, it becomes clearer and brighter. [Figure 10-3]

How well you see at night is determined by the rods in your eyes, as well as the amount of light allowed into your eyes. The wider the pupil is open at night, the better your night vision becomes.

NIGHT VISION

The cones in your eyes adapt quite rapidly to changes in light intensities, but the rods do not. If you have ever walked from bright sunlight into a dark movie theater, you have experienced this dark adaptation period. The rods can take up to 30 minutes to fully adapt to the dark. A bright light can completely destroy your night adaptation and severely restrict your visual acuity.

Bright lights should be avoided for at least 30 minutes before a night flight.

There are several things you can do to keep your eyes adapted to the dark. The first is obvious; avoid bright lights before and during the flight. For 30 minutes before a night flight, avoid any bright light sources such as headlights, landing lights, strobe lights, or flashlights. If you encounter a bright light, close one eye to keep it light sensitive. This will allow you to see again once the light is gone. Light sensitivity also can be gained by using sunglasses if you will be flying from daylight into an area of increasing darkness.

Red cockpit lighting also helps preserve your night vision. But, red light severely distorts some colors, especially those found on aeronautical charts. A dim white light or carefully directed flashlight can enhance your night reading ability. While flying at night, keep the instrument panel and interior lights turned up no higher than necessary. This helps you see outside visual references more easily. If your eyes become blurry, blinking more frequently will often help.

Your diet and general physical health have an impact on how well you can see in the dark. Deficiencies in vitamins A and C have been shown to reduce night acuity. Other factors, such as carbon monoxide poisoning, smoking, alcohol, certain drugs, and a lack of oxygen also can greatly decrease your night vision.

Red cockpit lighting enhances dark adaptation, while regular white light, such as that from a flashlight, impairs your night adaptation.

NIGHT SCANNING

Good night visual acuity also is needed for collision avoidance. Night scanning is much like the day scanning technique discussed in Flight Prep 3. Unlike day scanning, however, off-center viewing is used to focus objects on the rods rather than the fovea blindspot.

When you look at an object, avoid staring at it too long. If you stare at an object without moving your eyes, the retina becomes accustomed to the light intensity and the image begins to fade. To keep it clearly visible, new areas in the retina must be exposed to the image. Small, circular eye movements help eliminate the fading. You also need to move your eyes more slowly from sector to sector than during the day to prevent blurring.

When scanning for traffic at night, move your eyes slowly and in small sectors. Use off-center viewing and avoid staring in one place for too long.

AIRCRAFT LIGHTING

In order for us to see other aircraft more clearly, regulations require that all aircraft operated during the night hours have special lights and equipment. The requirements for operating at night are found in FAR Part 91. In addition to aircraft lighting, the regulations also provide a definition of nighttime, currency requirements, fuel reserves, and necessary electrical systems.

Position lights enable you to see where an aircraft is, as well as its direction of flight. The approved aircraft lights for night operations are a green light on the right wingtip, a red light on the left wingtip, and a white position light on the tail. In addition, flashing aviation red or white anticollision

Figure 10-4. By interpreting the position lights on other aircraft, you can determine whether the aircraft is flying away from you or is on a collision course. If you see a red position light to the right of a green light, such as shown by aircraft number 1, it is flying toward you. You should watch this aircraft closely and be ready to change course. Aircraft number 2, on the other hand, is flying away from you, as indicated by the white position light.

lights are required for night flights. These flashing lights can be in a number of locations, but are most commonly found on the wingtips or tail. [Figure 10-4]

VISUAL ILLUSIONS

There are many different types of visual illusions. You can experience them at any time, day or night. The next few paragraphs cover some of the illusions that commonly occur at night and some that you may encounter during the approach and landing.

AUTOKINESIS

Autokinesis is caused by staring at a single point of light against a dark background, such as a ground light or bright star, for more than a few seconds. After a few moments, the light will appear to move on its own. If you attempt to align the aircraft in sole relation to the light, you can lose control of the airplane. Guard against this situation by keeping a normal visual scan and referring frequently to the instruments.

NIGHT MYOPIA

Another problem associated with night flying is night myopia, or night-induced nearsightedness. It is similar to empty field myopia, but is more pronounced because of the lack of visual references. With nothing to focus on, your eyes automatically focus on a point three to six feet in front of you. This happens less frequently to pilots who are more than 40 years old. Searching out and focusing on distant light sources, no matter how dim, will help prevent the onset of night myopia.

LANDING ILLUSIONS

Landing illusions occur in many forms. Above featureless terrain or at night, there is a natural tendency to fly a lower-than-normal approach. Elements that cause any type of visual obscuration such as rain, haze, or a dark runway environment also can cause low approaches. Bright runway lights, steep surrounding terrain, and a wide runway can produce the illusion of being too low, and there is the tendency to fly a higher-than-normal approach. [Figure 10-5]

Another type of landing illusion is produced by a sloping runway. It's not uncommon to find public airports that have runways with a grade, or slope, of three percent or more. On a 6,000-foot runway, a three percent grade means a 180-foot elevation difference between the approach and departure ends. There are many private airports that have even more grade. These runways appear very steep and give a very strong landing illusion. If you are aware of the contributing factors that lead to these types of visual illusions you will be able to identify them long before they become problems. For advance warning of conditions that could cause visual illusions, consult the aeronautical chart and *Airport/Facility Directory* for your destination airport. When available, take advantage of a visual approach slope indicator system to verify your landing approach. In

Your landing approaches at night should be made the same as during daytime to reduce the possibility of landing illusions.

Using the information supplied by a visual approach slope indicator system helps to verify approach height and descent rate and eliminates many of the visual landing illusions.

APPROACH ILLUSIONS		
Situation	**Illusion**	**Result**
Upsloping Runway or Terrain	Greater Height	Lower Approaches
Narrower-Than-Usual Runway	Greater Height	Lower Approaches
Featureless Terrain	Greater Height	Lower Approaches
Rain on Windscreen	Greater Height	Lower Approaches
Haze	Greater Height	Lower Approaches
Downsloping Runway or Terrain	Less Height	Higher Approaches
Wider-Than-Usual Runway	Less Height	Higher Approaches
Bright Runway and Approach Lights	Less Distance	Higher Approaches
Penetration of Fog	Pitching Up	Steeper Approaches

Figure 10-5. A variety of atmospheric and terrain conditions can produce visual illusions. When you encounter these situations, you must be able to recognize them and use all the resources available to counteract them.

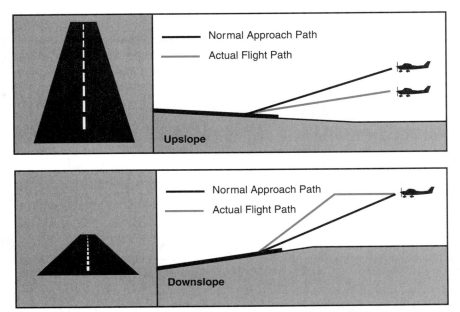

Figure 10-6. When approaching a sloped runway, the tendency is to position the airplane so the runway appears as it would for a normal, flat runway. On a runway that
slopes uphill, this produces a dangerously low approach. For a downhill runway, it
produces a high approach with the possibility of overshooting the runway. The runways depicted to the left show how normal three-degree approaches might look for
upslope and downslope runways.

addition, look for other clues, such as steep or featureless surrounding terrain. If you suspect an illusion, fly a normal traffic pattern and avoid long,
straight-in approaches. [Figure 10-6]

As a pilot, you will not always be able to eliminate the visual illusions that
you may encounter. Understanding the various types and how they occur,
and taking preventative measures when appropriate, will go a long way
toward making a safer flight.

CHECKLIST _____

After studying this section, you should have a basic understanding of:

✓   **The eye** — The structure and the components, and how day and
    night vision differ.

✓   **Blindspots** — Where they are, when they occur, and what methods
    can be used to counteract them.

✓   **Night vision** — How night scanning is used and what factors can
    increase night visual acuity.

✓   **Dark adaptation** — The amount of time required for the adaptation and what you can do to preserve it.

✓   **Aircraft position lights** — What color they are, where they are located, and how they are used in collision avoidance.

✓   **Visual illusions** — What the different types are and what causes them. What the effects of each illusion are and how they are avoided.

SPATIAL DISORIENTATION

Your body is designed to live and work in a one-G environment. Orientation with the world around you is easily maintained when your feet are planted firmly on the ground. However, when you enter the three-dimensional realm of flight, your body can be put into positions that are totally in conflict with what you see and feel. To deal effectively with these unrealistic sensations, you must know how they are created and what illusions are produced. Your awareness of your body's position is a result of input from three main senses: visual, vestibular, and kinesthetic.

VISUAL SENSE

As you have seen in Section A, vision helps you maintain balance and your position relative to objects around you. When other sensory input is contradictory or confusing, the brain relies primarily upon sight to determine orientation. In darkness or limited visibility, when few outside visual references are available, you need to rely heavily on your visual sense to interpret the flight instruments for accurate information.

VESTIBULAR SENSE

The semicircular canals and the vestibule (sometimes referred to as the static organ), located in your inner ear, are primarily responsible for your vestibular sense. This sense tells you when you are turning, climbing, descending, speeding up, or slowing down. It also senses gravity and G-loads created by centrifugal force. The **semicircular canals** sense angular acceleration such as roll, pitch, and yaw. The three semicircular canals are filled with fluid and are located so that each canal lies along a specific axis. At the base of each canal are small hair cells that detect movement when they are displaced. When you maneuver the airplane or move your head, the semicircular canals move too, while the fluid remains temporarily stationary. This deflects the sensory hairs and sends a nerve impulse to the brain, which interprets the "movement" as motion around an axis. [Figure 10-7]

The vestibular organs in the inner ear are easily deceived by slow or gradual movement.

The semicircular canals may not be able to sense a slow rate of rotation. They also are unable to sense movement after prolonged periods of uniform movement. If you maintain a prolonged turn without outside visual reference, it will seem normal after a while. This feeling is a result of fluid in the inner ear "catching up" to the rest of the ear; movement is no longer perceived by the small hairs.

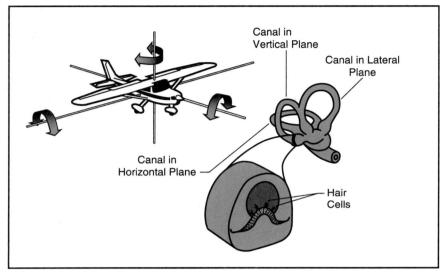

Figure 10-7. The semicircular canals lie in three planes that correspond approximately to those of an airplane. As you change the pitch attitude, an angular acceleration is created in the canal lying along the vertical axis. The brain interprets this acceleration by the deflection of tiny hair cells located at the base of the vertical canal. A roll into a turn is detected by the lateral canal, and a yawing movement is sensed by the horizontal canal.

The **utricle** and **saccule** organs within the **vestibule** are responsible for the perception of linear acceleration, which is movement forward and back, side to side, and up and down. One of the major problems with this sensory organ is its inability to tell the difference between gravity caused by the earth and G-loads caused by centrifugal force. [Figure 10-8]

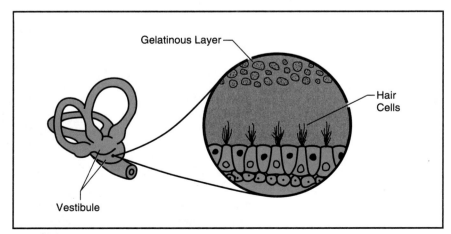

Figure 10-8. A gelatinous layer within the vestibule responds to linear acceleration forces. This, in turn, moves small hair cells that create the sensation of movement.

KINESTHETIC SENSE

When your awareness of position is obtained from the nerves in your skin, joints, and muscles, it is called the kinesthetic sense. Using this sense is sometimes called "flying by the seat of your pants," and this is literally what you are doing. Kinesthetic sense is unreliable, however, because the brain cannot tell the difference between input caused by gravity and that of maneuvering G-loads.

DISORIENTATION

When the brain receives conflicting messages from your sensory organs, a confused condition called spatial disorientation can occur. **Spatial disorientation** is an incorrect mental image of your position, attitude, or movement in relation to what is actually happening to your airplane.

Vertigo is the feeling that you are spinning, or that the world is spinning or tumbling about you. It is usually caused by a physical disorder in the inner ear, and can be completely incapacitating. Vertigo should not be confused with spatial disorientation. Although they are sometimes used interchangeably, spatial disorientation normally is caused by misinterpretation of outside stimuli, while vertigo is the result of a physiological problem.

Spatial disorientation is most common at night and during times of restricted visibility.

In good weather and daylight, you obtain your orientation primarily through your vision. Because of this, spatial disorientation rarely occurs during the day in good weather conditions. At night or in marginal weather conditions, visual cues are fewer, and you rely upon the vestibular and kinesthetic senses to supplement your visual sense. However, neither of these senses is as reliable for perceiving motion, and they can give false cues about your orientation. The probability of spatial disorientation occurring is quite high during these times. Correctly interpreting your flight instruments is extremely important, because they are your only sources of accurate information under these conditions.

Relying on the instruments and believing what they tell you, regardless of "how it feels," are the keys to maintaining spatial orientation.

Everyone is subject to spatial disorientation; even experienced pilots have felt its effects in one form or another and in varying degrees. Some situations are more disorienting than others. An awareness of the conditions that are more likely to produce spatial disorientation and the illusions they create will help you guard against their occurrence. Remember, you can avoid misinterpreting visual and spatial information by referring frequently to the flight instruments.

SPATIAL ILLUSIONS

The majority of the illusions presented here have one thing in common; they occur when visibility is restricted, either by darkness or by weather. Weather conditions can change very rapidly, and what was marginal VFR (MVFR) one moment can be IFR the next. Predicting when this change will occur can be difficult, if not impossible. It takes many hours of training and experience before a pilot is competent to fly an aircraft solely by reference to instruments. Each year, many fatalities result from non-instrument rated pilots continuing flight into deteriorating weather conditions.

GRAVEYARD SPIRAL

A prolonged, constant-rate turn may produce a graveyard spiral. During this type of turn, the fluid in the semicircular canals eventually stops moving. This can create the illusion that you are no longer turning. A loss of altitude in this situation may be interpreted as a wings-level descent, which can lead you to increase elevator back pressure. This action only tightens the turn and increases the altitude loss. A recovery to wings-level flight may produce the illusion that the airplane is in a turn in the opposite direction, resulting in a reentry of the spiral. This "feeling" must be fought until the fluid in your semicircular canals quits moving again.

CORIOLIS ILLUSION

Another illusion that occurs in a prolonged, constant-rate turn is the Coriolis illusion. If you tilt your head down to change a fuel tank or pick up a pencil, the rapid head movement puts the fluid in motion in more than one semicircular canal. This creates an overwhelming sensation of rotating, turning, or accelerating along an entirely different plane. An attempt to stop the sensation by maneuvering the airplane may put it into a dangerous attitude. Because this type of illusion is so overwhelming, it is considered to be one of the most deadly. To avoid it, do not move your head too fast in limited visibility or darkness. A simple wing-leveling autopilot can help overcome the temporary and sometimes overpowering feelings of spatial disorientation.

Since spatial disorientation can occur along more than one axis, use slow, deliberate head movements when performing cockpit functions.

LEANS

One of the most common types of spatial disorientation is called the leans. It occurs when an abrupt recovery or a rapid correction is made to a bank. If you make such a recovery, your semicircular canals sense a roll in the opposite direction. This may cause you to reenter the original attitude. When you return the aircraft to a wings-level condition, you will tend to lean in the direction of the incorrect bank until the semicircular canal fluids return to normal. Maintaining a level attitude for a minute or two generally will stop the leans.

SOMATOGRAVIC ILLUSION

A rapid acceleration or deceleration can cause a somatogravic illusion. An acceleration can produce the illusion that you are in a nose-high attitude, even though you are still in straight-and-level flight. This may prompt you to lower the nose and enter a dive. A deceleration, such as rapidly retarding the throttle, produces the opposite effect. You may think you're in a dive and raise the nose. If you raise the nose too far, a stall may be produced.

INVERSION ILLUSION

An abrupt change from a climb to straight-and-level flight can produce an inversion illusion. This illusion creates the feeling that you are tumbling backward. The effect may cause you to lower the nose abruptly, which may intensify the illusion.

FALSE HORIZONS

Another illusion, that of a false horizon, occurs when the natural horizon is obscured or not readily apparent. It can be generated by confusing bright stars and city lights. [Figure 10-9]

A false horizon can occur while you are flying toward the shore of an ocean or a large lake. Because of the relative darkness of the water, the lights along the shoreline can be mistaken for the stars in the sky. [Figure 10-10]

Flying above a sloping cloud deck can produce another illusion of a false horizon. The natural tendency, in this case, is to level the aircraft with the clouds.

FLICKER VERTIGO

A light flickering at a frequency of 4 to 20 flashes per second can produce flicker vertigo. Although rare, it can lead to convulsions, nausea, or

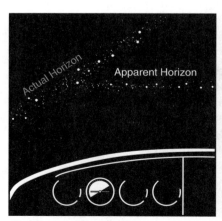

Figure 10-9. You can place your aircraft in an extremely dangerous flight attitude if you align the aircraft with the wrong lights. Here, the aircraft is aligned with a road and not the horizon.

Figure 10-10. In this illusion, the shoreline is mistaken for the horizon. To correct for the apparent nose-high attitude, you may lower the nose of the aircraft and attempt to fly "beneath the shore."

unconsciousness. It most frequently occurs when you are looking through a slow-moving propeller (240-1,200 r.p.m.) toward the sun. It can also happen when the sun is behind you, reflecting off the propeller. This situation can occur during descent, while landing, or while taxiing. The best way to prevent flicker vertigo is to avoid looking at a light source through a propeller for any length of time. Making frequent but minor changes in propeller r.p.m. can also decrease your susceptibility to flicker vertigo.

Fatigue, anxiety, heavy pilot workloads, and the intake of alcohol or other drugs increase your susceptibility to spatial disorientation and visual illusions. These factors increase response times, inhibit decision-making abilities, and cause a breakdown in scanning techniques and night vision. Reducing your workload with the use of a simple autopilot and improving your cockpit management skills help prevent "pilot overload" and the possibility of spatial disorientation.

The effects of spatial disorientation can be duplicated with the use of a vertigo simulator. All you need is a blindfold, a swivel chair, and some friends. With the blindfold on, tilt your head to one side. Then, have someone spin the chair at a constant rate for 30 to 60 seconds. The chair should then be brought to a gradual stop. When the chair has stopped, you will be told to raise your head. This action should produce the illusion of spinning or rotating. The simulation of spatial disorientation is so realistic that you should have someone close by to catch you if you fall out of the chair.

MOTION SICKNESS

Motion sickness, or airsickness, is caused by the brain receiving conflicting messages about the state of the body. The same types of factors that cause spatial disorientation also bring on airsickness. Passengers are more susceptible to motion sickness than pilots, because they often focus their attention inside the aircraft rather than outside. Airsickness comes in many forms. The most common symptoms are dizziness, nausea, and sweating. Other symptoms include general discomfort, paleness, and vomiting.

Specific remedies for airsickness can vary among people, but there are some actions that generally seem to help. You can suggest that your passengers put their heads back and attempt to relax. Most people are susceptible to the up-and-down motion common to flying in turbulent air. With the head reclined, passengers are better able to tolerate this up-and-down motion. Since anxiety and stress can contribute to motion sickness, keep unsure or nervous passengers informed on how the flight is progressing, and explain unusual noises such as flap or landing gear retraction and power changes. Opening the fresh-air vents and allowing cool, fresh air into the cabin also can improve the comfort level of your passengers.

Another suggestion that can reduce the possibility of airsickness is having passengers focus on objects outside the plane. A common road map can be very useful in this situation. Have passengers "follow along" and pick out various landmarks they can recognize. Avoiding warm, turbulent air and using earplugs also can reduce the likelihood of motion sickness. Keep in mind that most passengers are not used to steep banks or quick maneuvers, so be gentle.

CHECKLIST

After studying this section, you should have a basic understanding of:

✓ **Visual sense** — What information it provides and its limitations.

✓ **Vestibular sense** — What parts of the body provide this sense, how it functions, and its limitations.

✓ **Kinesthetic sense** — Where this sense comes from and its limitations.

✓ **Spatial disorientation** — How it is produced, where it is most frequently encountered, and how it differs from vertigo.

✓ **Spatial illusions** — What types of illusions are created, where they are frequently encountered, and how you can prevent them from occurring.

✓ **Flicker vertigo** — What causes it, and when does it occur. What precautionary measures can be taken to guard against it.

✓ **Motion sickness** — What causes it, and what can be done to prevent or reduce it.

RESPIRATION AND ALTITUDE

Your body needs energy to survive. We all know the body begins to deteriorate when it is deprived of food and water for very long, but we rarely consider the energy obtained from the oxygen we breathe. Since the body cannot store oxygen as easily as it does food energy, changes begin to occur rapidly when you are deprived of oxygen. This section covers the normal respiration cycle and looks at what happens when this process is interrupted or breaks down. It also includes a discussion of the effects on your body of changing atmospheric pressure.

RESPIRATION

To understand the respiration cycle, it is important to know how the atmosphere is constructed as it relates to the air you breathe. Each breath you inhale is a fairly uniform mixture of gasses. Life-sustaining oxygen makes up only about 21% of each breath, while 78% is nitrogen and 1% is other gasses, such as carbon dioxide and argon.

Your body uses only the oxygen in the air. Inhaled oxygen is diffused through the lungs into the bloodstream, where it attaches to hemoglobin. When the oxygen reaches individual cells, it acts upon certain compounds in the cells and causes them to release energy. This process creates a waste product called carbon dioxide (CO_2). Carbon dioxide is returned through the bloodstream to the lungs, where it is exhaled back into the atmosphere.

Although the mixture of air you breathe remains relatively uniform as altitude increases, the pressure or density of the air is less. This means there is less oxygen reaching the cells in your body as you climb. The altitude at which your body becomes starved for oxygen depends upon your level of activity. The higher the activity level, the lower the altitude.

HYPOXIA

Hypoxia occurs when the tissues in the body do not receive enough oxygen, regardless of the cause. There are two types of hypoxia that are common to flying: hypoxic hypoxia and anemic hypoxia.

Hypoxia is a state of oxygen deficiency in the body.

HYPOXIC HYPOXIA

Hypoxic hypoxia occurs when there is a lack of available oxygen in the atmosphere. It is considered to be the most lethal factor of all physiological causes of accidents. It can occur very suddenly at high altitudes during rapid decompression, or it can occur slowly at lower altitudes when you are exposed to insufficient oxygen over an extended period of time.

The symptoms of hypoxia vary with the individual. Some of the common symptoms include:

1. An increase in breathing rate
2. Lightheaded or dizzy sensation
3. Headache
4. Sweating
5. Tingling or warm sensation
6. Blue fingernails and lips
7. Reduced visual field
8. Sleepiness or frequent yawning
9. Impaired judgment
10. A slowing of decision-making processes
11. A feeling of euphoria
12. Changes in personality traits

Impaired judgment is an early symptom of hypoxia. It can occur at lower altitudes as well as at higher altitudes. Don't wait for the symptoms; anticipate them and use supplemental oxygen.

Your individual response to hypoxia can be safely experienced in an altitude chamber; however, some pilots have the misconception that it is possible to learn the early symptoms of hypoxia so they can take corrective action whenever they occur. This is an extremely dangerous assumption, because an early symptom is impaired judgment. When the onset of hypoxia is rapid, your judgment may be impaired before you have a chance to recognize other symptoms. Normally, the part of the body that is first affected by oxygen deprivation is the retina of the eye. The effectiveness of the retina begins to show signs of a loss of night visual acuity as low as 5,000 feet MSL. At higher altitudes, though, pilot performance can deteriorate rapidly, leading to unconsciousness.

Susceptibility to hypoxia can be increased by a number of factors. The oxygen-carrying capacity of the blood can be reduced by carbon-monoxide from smoking or exhaust fumes. Alcohol and certain medicines can also hasten the onset of hypoxia.

USEFUL CONSCIOUSNESS

When you fly on an airliner and listen to the flight attendant's announcement concerning the sudden loss of cabin pressure, do you wonder just how long you really have to get the oxygen mask over your face, or what will happen if the mask doesn't come down? Life expectancy at high altitudes without oxygen is a matter of minutes, and the time of useful consciousness is even less. The **time of useful consciousness** is the maximum time you have to make a rational, life-saving decision and carry it out following a lack of oxygen at a given altitude. If you go beyond this time, you may not be able to place an oxygen mask over your face, even if you try. [Figure 10-11]

TIME OF USEFUL CONSCIOUSNESS		
Altitude	**While Sitting Quietly**	**During Moderate Activity**
40,000 Ft.	30 Sec.	18 Sec.
35,000 Ft.	45 Sec.	30 Sec.
30,000 Ft.	1 Min. and 15 Sec.	45 Sec.
25,000 Ft.	3 Min.	2 Min.
22,000 Ft.	10 Min.	5 Min.
20,000 Ft.	12 Min.	5 Min.

Figure 10-11. Your amount of exertion can dramatically affect the time of useful consciousness. Although you may remain conscious for three or four minutes at 35,000 feet, you are receiving less than 30% of the oxygen your body needs, and you will be able to function less than a minute without supplemental oxygen.

Recovery from hypoxia usually occurs rapidly after a person has been given oxygen. If you have suffered severe hypoxia, your mental and physical performance may be reduced for several hours.

ANEMIC HYPOXIA

When your blood is not able to carry a sufficient amount of oxygen to the cells in your body, a condition called anemic hypoxia occurs. As the name implies, this type of hypoxia is a result of a deficiency in the blood (anemia), rather than a lack of inhaled oxygen. Anemia can occur as a result of excessive bleeding, a stomach ulcer, or a diet deficiency. It also can occur when oxygen is not able to attach itself to hemoglobin.

CARBON MONOXIDE

The most common cases of anemic hypoxia come from carbon monoxide poisoning. Carbon monoxide (CO) attaches itself to the hemoglobin about 200 times more easily than does oxygen. In fact, carbon monoxide prevents oxygen from attaching to the hemoglobin and can produce anemic hypoxia. It can take up to 48 hours for the body to dispose of carbon monoxide. The symptoms are very similar to hypoxic hypoxia, and can produce the loss of muscle power, a headache, and dizziness. If the poisoning is severe enough, it can result in death.

Carbon monoxide robs the body of oxygen by attaching to the hemoglobin and reducing the oxygen-carrying capacity of the blood. Large accumulations of CO result in a loss of muscular power.

Because carbon monoxide poisoning is a form of hypoxia, you are more susceptible to its effects as altitude increases. Carbon monoxide poisoning can result from a faulty aircraft heater. If you suspect carbon monoxide poisoning, you should turn off the heater immediately, open the fresh air vents or windows, and use supplemental oxygen if it is available.

Susceptibility to carbon monoxide poisoning increases as altitude increases.

Smoking also causes a mild case of CO poisoning. The effects of cigarette smoke are especially apparent by a reduction in visual acuity during a night flight. Smoking three cigarettes during a night flight can dramatically reduce the sharpness of your vision.

BLOOD DONATION

Another type of anemic hypoxia can be caused by the loss of blood that occurs during a blood donation. Your blood can take several weeks to return to normal following a donation. Although the effects of the blood loss are slight at ground level, there are risks when flying during this time. Therefore, you are advised not to give blood prior to flying.

SUPPLEMENTAL OXYGEN

To avoid the effects of hypoxia, do not fly for prolonged periods above 10,000 feet MSL during the day or 5,000 feet MSL at night without breathing supplemental oxygen.

Since judgment and rationality can be impaired when you are suffering from hypoxia, prevention is the best approach. There are two ways to prevent hypoxia. First, you can fly at low altitudes where hypoxia will not be a factor. This, of course, is not always practical. The most effective way to prevent hypoxia is through the use of supplemental oxygen.

Federal regulations specify when you must use supplemental oxygen. If you are planning a flight with a cruise altitude over 12,000 feet, you should consult these regulations. As a general rule, consider using supplemental oxygen when you fly above 10,000 feet during the day or above 5,000 feet at night.

Use only aviator's breathing oxygen to fill aircraft oxygen cylinders.

Aircraft oxygen systems should always be filled with aviator's breathing oxygen. Medical oxygen contains too much moisture, which can collect in the valves and lines of the system and freeze. This may stop the flow of oxygen.

HYPERVENTILATION

Rapid or extra deep breathing can cause hyperventilation. It can occur even while breathing supplemental oxygen.

Hyperventilation is the term used to describe a breathing rate that is too rapid and too deep. This process forces too much carbon dioxide from your body and creates a chemical imbalance in the blood. In severe cases it can lead to unconsciousness. It is possible to suffer from hyperventilation even if you are using supplemental oxygen.

Hyperventilation is most likely to result when you are experiencing emotional tension, anxiety, or fear.

Hyperventilation usually is an involuntary response to a stressful situation. Your body's natural attempt to maintain a normal breathing rate can be overcome when you are tense, anxious, apprehensive, fearful, or overworked. Since many of the symptoms of hyperventilation are similar to those of hypoxia, it is important to correctly diagnose and treat the proper condition. If you are using supplemental oxygen, check the equipment and flow rate to ensure you are not suffering from hypoxia. Some of the symptoms of hyperventilation include:

1. Dizziness
2. Tingling of the fingers and toes
3. Muscle spasms
4. Coolness
5. Drowsiness
6. Weakness or numbness
7. Rapid heart rate
8. Apprehension and mental confusion
9. Finally, loss of consciousness

The treatment for hyperventilation involves restoring the proper carbon dioxide level in the body. Breathing normally is both the best prevention and the best cure for hyperventilation. In addition to slowing the breathing rate, you also can breathe into a paper bag or talk aloud to overcome hyperventilation. Recovery is usually rapid when the breathing rate is returned to normal.

PRESSURE EFFECTS

As you climb or descend, changes in atmospheric pressure affect many parts of your body. Since half of the atmospheric pressure lies below 18,000 feet, you can experience a fairly large pressure change within this realm. Air trapped in the ears, sinus cavities, gastrointestinal tract, and teeth can cause pain and discomfort as the outside pressure changes. [Figure 10-12]

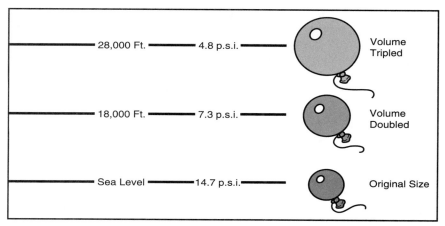

Figure 10-12. As a balloon ascends, atmospheric pressure decreases and the air within the balloon expands in an attempt to equalize itself with the surrounding pressure. The same thing happens with the air trapped in your body.

Figure 10-13. Normally, the eustachian tube keeps the pressure equalized between the ear canal and the middle ear. When the pressure is equal, the eardrum is not distended.

EARS

The ears are probably the most common area affected by changes in pressure. The pain you feel generally is the result of air trapped in the middle ear. When the air pressure in the middle ear is equal to the pressure in the ear canal there is no plugged feeling or pain. [Figure 10-13]

When you ascend, the pressure in the ear canal decreases. Usually, the increased pressure in the middle ear will open the eustachian tube and escape, thus equalizing the pressure in the middle ear. If the tube does not open, you may feel a fullness in the ear and experience a slight hearing loss and discomfort. This is because the eardrum is distended and cannot vibrate as freely as before. [Figure 10-14]

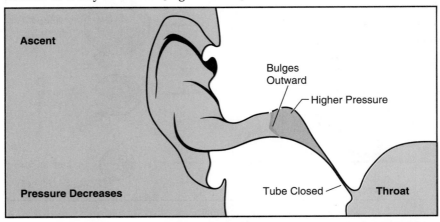

Figure 10-14. When the eustachian tube does not open during an ascent, the positive air pressure in the middle ear pushes the eardrum outward toward the ear canal.

Figure 10-15. During a descent, the pressure inside the ear canal increases, while lower pressure air remains in the middle ear. If the eustachian tube remains closed, the eardrum bulges inward causing severe pain.

During a descent, the opposite condition exists. The outside pressure in the ear canal will become higher than the pressure in the middle ear. This situation is harder to correct, because the eustachian tube opens more easily to let positive pressure out than it does to allow air back into the middle ear. Because of this, your ears seem to "plug" more easily when descending. [Figure 10-15]

Most people are aware of the pressure imbalance during descent. Sometimes you can open the eustachian tube by yawning, swallowing, or chewing. Air can also be forced into the middle ear by holding your nose and mouth shut and attempting to blow air gently into your nostrils. This is called the Valsalva technique, and it forces positive pressure into the eustachian tube and middle ear. This equalizes the pressure in the middle ear. [Figure 10-16]

Clearing your ears is more difficult when you are descending into higher pressure. You may have to gently force the eustachian tube open if an imbalance in pressure exists.

Figure 10-16. During times of descent, the inner ear may have to be reinflated manually to allow the pressure to equalize between the middle ear and the throat.

When the eardrum is pushed too far by the pressure imbalance, it can become very painful. If you have a cold, an ear infection, or a sore throat, you may not be able to equalize the pressure in your ears. A flight in this condition can be extremely painful, as well as very dangerous. You should avoid flying when you cannot clear your ears.

If you are experiencing minor congestion, nose drops or nasal sprays may reduce the chance of a painful ear blockage. Before you use any medication, check with an aviation medical examiner to make sure it will not affect your ability to fly. Slow descent rates can also help prevent or reduce the severity of ear problems.

Another preventive measure is associated with long-term hearing loss. Your ability to hear gradually diminishes with prolonged exposure to excessive noise levels. Most older pilots have experienced some loss of hearing, especially in the higher frequency ranges. The damaging exposure to noise is cumulative, but it can be minimized by the simple preventive measure of wearing noise attenuating headsets or ear plugs.

SINUSES

Your sinus cavities can sometimes cause problems during pressure changes. If you have an inflammation of the sinuses or nose from an allergy or a cold, you may experience discomfort from trapped air. As with the ears, using the Valsalva technique can help equalize the pressure.

TEETH

Trapped air in a cavity can expand and cause pain. Imperfect fillings, damaged root canals, and abscesses also can produce pain at altitude. A descent to a lower altitude may bring relief, but good dental care is the best way to prevent problems such as these.

GASTROINTESTINAL TRACT

At any given time, your gastrointestinal tract contains about one quart of gas. Most of this is swallowed air, and the rest is gas caused by the digestion process. As altitude increases, this gas expands and can cause abdominal pain. You are less likely to have this problem if you avoid foods that produce excess gas, such as onions, cabbage, raw apples, radishes, beans, cucumbers, melons, and any food that tends to "disagree" with you. A good diet and regular eating habits are important in avoiding this type of problem.

SCUBA DIVING

The reduction of atmospheric pressure that accompanies flying can produce a number of physical problems for scuba divers. Probably the most well known is decompression sickness, more commonly referred to as the "bends." Decompression sickness occurs when the nitrogen absorbed during a scuba dive comes out of solution and forms bubbles in the tissues and bloodstream, much like uncapping a bottle of soda. The condition is very serious and can produce extreme pain, paralysis and, if severe enough, death. Even though you may finish a dive well within the no-decompression limits, the reduced atmospheric pressure of flying can cause the onset of decompression sickness. If you or a passenger plan on flying after scuba diving, it is important that enough time is allowed for the body to rid itself of excess nitrogen absorbed during diving. The recommended waiting time before going up to 8,000 feet MSL is at least 12 hours after a dive which has not required a controlled ascent (nondecompression stop diving), and at least 24 hours after a dive which has required a controlled ascent (decompression stop diving). The waiting time before going to flight altitudes above 8,000 feet MSL should be at least 24 hours after any scuba dive.

Flying and scuba diving don't mix well. Decompression sickness can develop in those who fly too soon after diving.

CHECKLIST

After studying this section, you should have a basic understanding of:

✓ **Respiration** — What the normal respiration processes are, how oxygen is used, and how carbon dioxide is produced.

✓ **Hypoxia** — What the types of hypoxia are, how they are caused, and what the symptoms are.

✓ **Time of useful consciousness** — What it represents, and how it is affected by activity level and altitude.

✓ **Carbon monoxide** — Where it comes from, and how it affects the body.

✓ **Supplemental oxygen** — What type of oxygen should be used and when you should use it.

✓ **Hyperventilation** — What it is and how it affects your body.

✓ **The effects of pressure** — How the body is affected by pressure changes and what can be done to minimize the effects.

ALCOHOL, DRUGS, AND PERFORMANCE

Good health and safe flying go hand-in-hand. Your physical and mental skills must be in top shape when you are at the controls. Alcohol dulls these senses and can reduce your performance to a dangerous level. Illness and disease also can affect the functioning and performance of your body, as can the drugs that are meant to fight these illnesses. Unless specifically prescribed by a physician, do not take more than one drug at a time and, especially, do not mix drugs and alcohol. The effects are often unpredictable. The purpose of this section is to explain the hazardous effects of alcohol and the way seemingly harmless drugs can sometimes cause serious problems in the flying environment.

Various drugs are used to help fight illnesses, diseases, or to reduce the severity of their symptoms. A drug is a substance that is used to promote health or to treat a disease. It is not a food, but a chemical that alters the structure or function of the body. Among other things, drugs are used to eliminate pain (aspirin), satisfy a habit (nicotine), and produce "good feelings" (alcohol). In this section, alcohol is treated as a drug, since its effects are similar to depressant drugs.

One of the most complicated aspects of drugs is that they can produce side effects that can be completely unexpected or unrelated. Because of this, many of them cannot be used while flying. There are thousands of drug compounds available to the public. This section, obviously, cannot look at them all, but there are several common drugs, both prescription and over-the-counter, that we will examine as they relate to flying.

Either the use of a drug or the illness itself can prohibit safe flight. Both these factors need to be considered before you fly.

There are two things you should consider before flying while using a drug. First, what is the condition you are treating and, second, what are the side effects of the drug used to treat the condition. Some conditions are serious enough to prohibit flying, even if the illness is being treated successfully with drugs. When you take a drug, it is an indication that you are not well. Your main concern is whether the illness itself is severe enough to influence flight safety. In many cases, your decision to fly will end with the answer to these questions. In addition, many doctors prescribe medication without knowing that you are a pilot. Always let your physician know you are a pilot and ask about the side effects of the medication. You should also consult an aviation medical examiner (AME) about any medication that you suspect will adversely affect your ability to pilot an aircraft.

In this section, we have divided some common drugs into three basic categories according to their primary use or potential side effects. These are depressants, stimulants, and analgesics. Although all the drugs listed under each category may not be manufactured primarily for that purpose, they may have side effects that produce those responses.

DEPRESSANTS

Depressants are drugs that reduce the body's functioning in many areas. They lower blood pressure, reduce mental processing, and slow motor and reaction responses. There are several types of drugs that can cause a depressing effect on the body. The most common of these is alcohol.

Depressants slow your motor responses and mental processes.

ALCOHOL

Ethyl alcohol is the most widely used and abused drug. Although some alcohol is used for medicinal purposes, the majority of it is consumed as a beverage.

When you drink alcohol, it is not digested the same way as food; rather, it passes through your liver and is absorbed into your bloodstream. This produces a depressing effect on your nervous system and acts like a general anesthetic. The rate at which alcohol is absorbed into the body varies with the percentage of alcohol in the drink, the rate at which it is consumed, the amount and type of foods you have eaten, and the length of time you have been drinking.

Unlike many depressants, alcohol may increase your heart rate and blood pressure while depressing your central nervous system. Shortly after consumption, the blood vessels in the skin dilate, which increases the blood flow to the skin. When combined with the stimulant reaction on the heart, a sensation of warmth and stimulation is created. Under the influence of alcohol, you experience a dulling of the senses, a decrease in good judgment, and a reduced sense of responsibility. You begin to feel less fatigued and may experience a feeling of emotional and physical well-being. Sensory perception is diminished, as well as skilled responses, intellectual functioning, memory, and vision.

ALCOHOL AND ALTITUDE

Alcohol reduces the amount of oxygen absorbed into your bloodstream. It affects you in much the same way as a climb to a higher altitude. Therefore, when you drink, your "physiological altitude" is much higher than your actual altitude. The effect of alcohol on physiological altitude is much greater than that of smoking. Also, the body cannot metabolize alcohol as easily at higher altitudes. At sea level, the average person takes about three hours to metabolize an ounce of alcohol. After consuming one ounce of alcohol at 12,000 feet, the average person will take nearly four times longer to metabolize it as compared to sea level.

BLOOD ALCOHOL

Federal regulations require that your blood alcohol level be below .04% and that at least eight hours pass between "bottle and throttle."

Intoxication is determined by the amount of alcohol in the bloodstream. This is usually measured as a percentage by weight in the blood. The FARs require that your blood alcohol be less than .04% and that eight hours pass between drinking alcohol and piloting an aircraft. If you have a blood alcohol level of .04% or greater after eight hours, you cannot fly until your blood alcohol falls below that amount. Even though your blood alcohol may be well below .04%, you cannot fly sooner than eight hours after drinking alcohol. Although the regulations are quite specific, it is a good idea to be more conservative than the FARs. Most pilots allow a minimum of 12 hours from the last drink to flying; commercial airlines generally require their pilots to wait 24 hours.

There are several regulations that apply to offenses involving alcohol. You should be familiar with the regulations in Parts 61 and 91 that relate to alcohol violations and testing requirements. Any violation or refusal to submit to an alcohol test may result in the denial of the application for a pilot certificate or the suspension or revocation of a pilot certificate.

HANGOVER

If you have a hangover, you are still under the influence of the drug. Flying with a hangover is just as dangerous as flying while intoxicated.

A greatly underestimated hazard is the hangover. When you have a hangover, you are still under the influence of alcohol, even though you may think that you are functioning normally. The degrading effects on motor and mental responses still remain. The possibility of committing errors while under the influence of a hangover is increased. Considerable amounts of alcohol can remain in the body for over 16 hours, so you should be cautious about flying too soon after drinking.

TRANQUILIZERS

Taking tranquilizers or relaxants is extremely hazardous when you are flying. Sleeping pills and other types of tranquilizers, whether prescription or nonprescription, can greatly reduce motor response, coordination, attentiveness, and judgment. Decision making is inhibited to a point where risks and information are not appropriately weighed. The effects of tranquilizers increase as altitude increases. In no case should they be used in conjunction with flying activities unless you have gotten the approval of an aviation medical examiner.

MOTION SICKNESS MEDICATION

Although Dramamine and other types of motion sickness remedies can be very helpful for airsick passengers, you should not use them when piloting an aircraft. These types of drugs often contain sedatives that can cause drowsiness and decreased alertness. You should not fly for at least 24 hours after taking them.

STOMACH MEDICATION

The antacids used for minor indigestion or an upset stomach are generally considered safe to use when flying. If repeated or painful indigestion occurs for more than a few weeks, you should stop using antacids and see a physician. You may have a more serious condition that would affect your ability to safely pilot an aircraft.

Drugs that help alleviate the stomach problems associated with a nervous or hyperactive digestive tract usually contain anticholinergics. These drugs reduce the activity of the nervous system that controls the levels of acid and digestive fluid going to the stomach and small intestine. This helps reduce stomach distress and the growth of ulcers. Many of these drugs contain sedatives which can cause blurred vision and reduce your ability to respond and function in a fully alert state. You should consult an aviation medical examiner for specific information about any drug you may be taking for this and related purposes. In many cases, if you suffer from a peptic ulcer, you are considered unfit to fly.

DECONGESTANTS AND ANTIHISTAMINES

There are many forms of decongestants and antihistamines available over the counter. Most are designed to alleviate cold and allergy symptoms. These drugs often cause drowsiness and slowed motor response, and can be very hazardous to use when flying. Antihistamines can also cause a stimulant reaction in some people. Nasal decongestants that are taken for clearing sinuses and ears should be used in moderation. You can get a good idea of whether a specific antihistamine produces side effects by looking at the precautions printed on the container. If you are in doubt, ask an AME about taking the drug before flying. A cold or allergy, whether treated or not, may be severe enough to preclude safe flying. When using any drug, always familiarize yourself with its effects before you fly.

STIMULANTS

Stimulants are drugs that stimulate the central nervous system and produce an increase in alertness and activity. Some of the common uses of these drugs include appetite suppression, fatigue reduction, and mood elevation. These drugs can produce anxiety and drastic mood swings, both of which are very dangerous when you fly. Some drugs cause a stimulant reaction, even though this reaction is not their primary function. Amphetamines, caffeine, and nicotine are all forms of stimulants.

Stimulants generally excite the central nervous system and can be hazardous when mixed inappropriately with flying. Amphetamines, caffeine, and nicotine are all stimulant drugs.

AMPHETAMINES

Amphetamines may be used in the form of pep pills, uppers, and appetite suppressants. Some common brand names include Dexedrin, Benzedrine, Methedrine, and Drinamyl. Flying under the influence of amphetamines can be very dangerous. They can produce restlessness, anxiety, mood swings, panic, cardiac disturbances, paranoia, hallucinations, convulsions, and coma. Consult an aviation medical examiner for information concerning the specific drug and its side effects.

CAFFEINE

Caffeine is a very common stimulant. It is found in soda, coffee, tea, some pain killers, and some antihistamines. Caffeine is used every day by millions of people as a quick "pick-me-up." It begins to show up in the bloodstream within five minutes of ingestion, and its effects can last for as long as 14 hours. Too much caffeine can lead to nervousness and sleep disturbances. Other symptoms of a caffeine overdose are increased mental fatigue, muscle tremors, and occasional stomach irritation. Although caffeine use is not prohibited by the FARs, you should use it in moderation to avoid the side effects.

NICOTINE

Nicotine, which is the active ingredient in tobacco, has several side effects that are hazardous to your health. It stimulates the nervous system and can cause a sensation of lessened fatigue and euphoria in some people. Within 20 to 30 minutes after taking nicotine, it begins to wear off and the user experiences feelings of fatigue and of slowing down. Nicotine withdrawal may produce irritability, aggression, or hostility. Although nicotine and cigarette smoking are addictive, they are not prohibited under Part 67 of the FARs. However, many of the long-term health conditions caused by smoking are medically disqualifying. Your aviation medical examiner can give you the details on the risks and effects of smoking and flying.

Smoking increases the level of carbon monoxide in your bloodstream and increases the chance of hypoxia.

If you are a regular smoker, you carry a carbon monoxide level of about five percent in your bloodstream. This raises your physiological altitude from sea level to about 7,000 feet. A smoker is much more susceptible to hypoxia and will feel the effects of hypoxia at lower altitudes.

PASSIVE SMOKING

Cigarette smoke is also hazardous to others flying with you. Smoke from the lit end of a cigarette has twice the amount of carbon monoxide as does exhaled smoke. This can cause hypoxia in passengers and can increase their overall discomfort and susceptibility to air sickness. Smoking can harm your aircraft as well. The gyroscopic instruments have sensitive bearings and filters which can become gummed by tar and other chemicals contained in cigarette smoke. This tar also clogs outflow valve movement in aircraft pressurization systems and is the most common cause of pressurization system failure.

PAIN KILLERS

Pain killers can be grouped into two broad classes: analgesics and anesthetics. Analgesics are drugs that decrease pain such as aspirin and codeine. Anesthetics are drugs that deaden pain or cause a loss of consciousness. These drugs are commonly used for dental and surgical procedures.

ANALGESICS

There are many over-the-counter analgesics available for the relief of pain. The majority of the drugs that contain acetylsalicylic acid (Aspirin), acetaminophen (Tylenol), and ibuprofen (Advil) have few side effects when taken in the correct dosage. Flying usually is not restricted when you take these drugs. However, some people are allergic to these analgesics or may suffer from stomach irritation. Other drugs, such as an antihistamine, may be added to relieve other symptoms. These additives may restrict flying because of their side effects.

Prescription analgesics, such as Darvon, Percodan, Demerol, and codeine, have a wide variety of side effects that usually preclude flying while using them. They are used for the reduction of moderate to severe pain and can be prescribed for extensive dental and surgical procedures. Codeine is also found in several types of cough syrups. These prescription drugs may cause mental confusion, dizziness, a headache, nausea, and vision problems. You should consult an aviation medical examiner before using any prescription drug when you are flying.

LOCAL ANESTHETICS

Most local anesthetics used for minor dental and outpatient procedures wear off within a relatively short period of time. The anesthetic itself may not limit flying so much as the actual procedure and subsequent pain. You should carefully weigh all factors when determining whether to fly soon after any procedure requiring a local anesthetic. Your physician and AME can assist you in making an informed decision concerning your specific case.

OTHER PROBLEM DRUGS

Other types of drugs can also have adverse effects on flying. These drugs can neither be classified as stimulants nor depressants; however, they can produce perceptual errors in balance and vision.

ANTIBIOTICS

Some forms of antibiotics can produce dangerous side effects, such as balance disorders, hearing loss, nausea, and vomiting. Other antibiotics are safe for use while flying. As a general rule, you should consult your aviation medical examiner before using an antibiotic. Certain infections require specific antibiotics, and the infection itself often will prohibit safe flight. Generally, at least two days should elapse between last taking these antibiotics and flying.

When you are not feeling well or are taking medication, you should ask yourself several key questions to determine your flying status. If you have an illness, does the condition present a hazard to safe flight? If you are taking a drug for an illness and it wears off during a flight, will it cause an unsafe condition? If you are taking a drug, can the drug produce any side effect that would influence your motor, perceptual, or psychological condition? If the answer to any of these questions is "Yes" or "I don't know," consult with an AME before flying.

CHECKLIST

After reading this section, you should have an understanding of:

✓ **Drugs** — What they are and how they can present hazards to flight.

✓ **Depressants** — What they are and what effects they have on the body's system. What different types of drugs fit into this category.

✓ **Alcohol** — What the effects of alcohol on the body are, what blood alcohol is, and what regulations pertain to alcohol use and flying.

✓ **Stimulants** — What the different types are and what effects they have on the body.

✓ **Smoking** — What the hazards of smoking are and its ill effects on the pilot, the passengers, and the aircraft.

✓ **Pain Medicine** — What the general rule of use is, and the different types available.

In many respects, night flight is easier and more pleasant than daytime flying. Traffic is usually easier to locate at night, and the air is generally smoother and cooler, resulting in more comfortable flight and better airplane performance. Furthermore, at night the pilot experiences less airport traffic pattern congestion and often finds less competition when using communication frequencies. However, because visual acuity is reduced at night, you must consider additional factors and exercise extra caution.

NIGHT FLIGHT CONSIDERATIONS

On a bright, moonlit evening, when the visibility is good and the wind is calm, night flying is not a great deal different than flying during the day. However, you must consider the following factors carefully before making a night flight.

1. Visibility

2. Amount of outside light available

3. Surface winds

4. General weather situation

5. Availability of lighted airports enroute

6. Proper functioning of the airplane and its systems

7. Equipment in the airplane for night flying

8. Your recent night flying experience

PREFLIGHT INSPECTION

Perform the preflight inspection in the usual manner, preferably in a well-lighted area with the aid of a flashlight. Be sure a spare set of fuses is aboard the airplane or, if the airplane is equipped with circuit breakers, check them to see that they are not tripped. A tripped circuit breaker may be an indication of an equipment malfunction, since most circuit breakers cannot be tripped manually. When you discover a tripped circuit breaker during the preflight, reset it and test the associated equipment for proper operation prior to flight.

Check the windshield for dirt that may interfere with vision. Although this is a good preflight procedure anytime, it is especially important before a night flight.

AIRCRAFT LIGHTS

All aircraft operating between sunset and sunrise are required to have operable navigation lights, or **position lights**. You should turn these on during the preflight inspection so you can check them visually to ensure proper operation, then immediately turn them off to avoid excessive drain on the battery. Many airplanes allow you to check for proper operation of the lights from inside the airplane through use of position light detectors. These plastic attachments for the navigation lights convey light above or below the surface of the wing. [Figure 10-17]

All aircraft must have an **anticollision light** system for night operation. A common type is the rotating beacon, which usually is located at the top of the tail and emits red flashes of light. An increasing number of airplanes, however, are being equipped with brilliant, flashing, white strobe lights that can be seen for many miles at night. These lights can also be used in poor visibility conditions during the day. Check the anticollision lighting system during the preflight inspection.

Most airplanes have **landing lights**, and some have **taxi lights** to illuminate the runway and taxiway. These lights may be mounted behind a common lens in the leading edge of the wing or in the cowling. Another installation which usually is restricted to high-performance airplanes is described as a retractable gear-mounted light.

Although you must visually check both the landing light and the taxi light for correct operation during the preflight inspection, do not allow these lights to operate for any length of time with the engine shut down, because of the high electrical drain on the battery. Your preflight check should include inspection for illumination, cracks in the lens, and the correct aiming angle of each light. However, take care when you are operating the landing and taxi lights to avoid shining them in the direction of another aircraft, since this can impair the other pilot's night vision.

> All aircraft operated at night are required to display position lights.

Figure 10-17. A red position light is located on the left wingtip, a white light on the tail, and a green light on the right wingtip.

All modern airplanes are equipped with a system for lighting the instrument panel and instruments. Prior to any night flight, check the panel lighting system to determine that it is operating satisfactorily. Carry a flashlight on night flights to provide an alternate source of light if interior lights malfunction.

Panel lighting generally is controlled by a rheostat switch which allows you to select the intensity of light that best satisfies your needs. There may be separate rheostats for the flight instruments, engine instruments, and radios. The light intensity should be adjusted just bright enough so you are able to read the instrument indications. If the lighting is too bright, a glare results and your night vision suffers.

Flood lighting is a common method of illuminating the entire instrument panel with one light source. This system uses a single ceiling-mounted light with a rheostat to regulate its intensity. Its beam is directed over both the flight and engine instruments. Flood lighting seems to produce the most glare if the intensity is too high.

Post lighting provides each instrument with its own light source, which is adjacent to the instrument. Each post light beam is directed at the instrument and is shaded from your eyes. Generally, there are two or more rheostats for this lighting system — one for the flight instruments, another for the engine instruments. In addition, there may be controls for illumination of fuel tank selectors, switch panels, radios, and convenience lighting.

Internal instrument lighting is similar to post lighting, except that the light source is located inside the instrument itself. The magnetic compass and radios generally utilize internal lighting. Luminescent lettering is often used with internal lighting to permit instrument interpretation with less light. This type of lighting normally produces the least amount of glare.

CABIN FAMILIARIZATION

As part of the preflight inspection, you should become thoroughly familiar with the airplane's cabin, instrumentation, and control layout. You should practice locating each instrument, control, and switch, both with and without cabin lights. Since some switches and circuit breaker panels may be hard to see at night, be sure that you are able to locate them in poor lighting conditions.

VISUAL IMPRESSIONS

During early training in night flight, you will probably find the initial visual impressions after traffic pattern departure to be strikingly different than those you are accustomed to during daytime flying. Therefore,

> A flashlight is a necessity for any night flight.

orientation in the local flying area will help you relate chart information to actual terrain and landmarks under night conditions.

Usually, the outlines of major cities and towns are clearly discernible at night. Major metropolitan areas are visible during favorable weather from distances up to 100 miles or more, depending upon the flight altitude. Major highways tend to stand out at night because of the presence of numerous automobile headlights. Less traveled roads are usually not seen easily at night unless the moonlight is bright enough to reveal them.

On clear, moonlit nights, outlines of the terrain and other surface features are dimly visible. For example, you can often discern the outlines of bodies of water by noting the reflection of the moonlight. However, on extremely dark nights, terrain features are nearly invisible, except in brightly lighted, populated areas.

ENGINE STARTUP

Use caution in the engine startup procedure at night, since it is difficult for other persons to determine that you intend to start the engine. In the daytime you shout, "Clear!" At night, in addition to this, turning on the position lights or momentarily flashing other aircraft lights helps warn others that the propeller is about to rotate.

TAXI TECHNIQUE

After you have started the engine and checked the oil pressure, turn on other necessary electrical equipment, including the rotating beacon. However, the taxi light normally should be left off until you are actually ready to taxi.

Airplane taxi and landing lights usually cast a beam that is narrow and concentrated. Because of this fact, taxi light illumination to the side is minimal and taxi speed should be slower at night, especially in congested ramp areas. Initially, it is more difficult to judge distances, and it takes some adaptation to taxi within the limitations of the area covered by the taxi light.

PRETAKEOFF CHECK

When you stop the airplane at the runup area, turn off the taxi and landing lights until you complete the runup. In addition to the usual checklist procedures, check the radios carefully for operation. During the runup, watch for a drop in the intensity of the lighting equipment when you reduce power to idle. A pronounced drop in intensity may indicate a problem. To check the system, add power and check the ammeter, or loadmeter, for proper indications.

TAKEOFF

You can minimize the differences between day and night flight by scheduling a night checkout which begins at twilight. When you use this procedure, the takeoffs, landings, and traffic pattern work begin in the more familiar daylight environment and, as darkness increases, you make the transition to night operation gradually. This procedure is highly recommended.

As you initiate the takeoff roll, select a reference point down the runway, such as the point where the runway edge lights seem to converge. If you look directly toward the lights near the airplane, you will experience an illusion of speed. However, you can use these lights to keep the airplane properly aligned during the takeoff roll.

During your first night takeoff, you may notice the lack of reliable outside visual references after you are airborne. This is particularly true at small airports located in sparsely populated areas. To compensate for this effect, use the flight instruments in conjunction with available outside visual references. Immediately after liftoff, maintain a normal climb attitude on the attitude indicator. The vertical speed indicator and altimeter also should indicate a climb. Include the airspeed indicator in the cross-check as well. The first 500 feet of altitude gain after takeoff is considered to be the critical period in transitioning from the comparatively well-lighted airport area into what sometimes appears as total darkness.

Use the attitude indicator for pitch and bank reference after takeoff at night.

NIGHT MANEUVERS

In many ways, night flight is similar to flying in marginal VFR conditions. There are times when you need the discipline of an instrument-rated pilot, because your senses may urge you to believe your physical sensations rather than the instrument indications. Some of the illusions you may experience at night were covered earlier in this Flight Prep.

Preparation for night flying should include a review of basic instrument flight techniques. Your instructor may conduct a simulated instrument session which includes straight-and-level flight, turns, climbs, climbing turns, descents, descending turns, and unusual attitude recoveries.

COLLISION AVOIDANCE AT NIGHT

Due to the reduction in outside visual references, you may have a tendency to spend too much time looking at the flight instruments. Therefore, you must make a special effort to devote enough time to scan for traffic. You can determine the position of other aircraft at night by scanning for position lights and anticollision lights. As discussed earlier, the placement of position lights helps you determine another aircraft's direction of flight.

ENROUTE PROCEDURES

High cruising altitudes provide improved margins of safety, especially for night flights. There are several reasons for this. First, range is usually greater at higher altitudes. Second, gliding distance is greater in the event of engine failure. Third, pilotage is less difficult, because you usually can see lighted landmarks at greater distances. The reception range of many navigation aids is also greater.

You should use a subdued white cabin light for reading charts, since considerable information on charts is printed in red and disappears under red cabin lighting. If a map reading light is not available in the airplane, use your flashlight for reading the charts. Place special emphasis on the terrain elevations provided on the charts to ensure adequate obstruction clearance.

WEATHER

It is relatively easy to fly into undetected clouds or fog at night.

When you are operating at night, you must be especially attentive to signs of changing weather conditions. It is extremely easy to fly into an overcast at night, because you cannot detect the clouds easily by direct visual observation. There are several guidelines that will assist you at night if you inadvertently fly into heavy haze, patches of clouds, or an overcast.

If you are approaching an overcast, you can sometimes detect the presence of the clouds because the lights in the distance disappear. In addition, a luminous glow, or halo, around the position lights indicates imminent or actual penetration of IFR weather conditions.

You can get another indirect visual cue by turning on the landing light for a short period of time. On a very clear night, the beam of a landing light is barely scattered by particles in the air. However, if there is considerable haze or the temperature and dewpoint are converging rapidly and cloud formation is imminent, you will notice some scattering of the beam. If actual penetration of a cloud layer occurs, the light beam will be dispersed in all directions. If inadvertent penetration of IFR conditions occurs, you should calmly, but immediately, initiate a 180° standard-rate turn, using the flight instruments to fly out of the weather conditions.

Before you fly at night, obtain a thorough weather briefing. Give special attention to any information in the weather briefing that indicates possible formation of clouds, overcast, fog, or precipitation.

NORMAL LANDINGS AT NIGHT

In some respects, night landings are actually easier than daytime landings, since the air is generally smooth and the disrupting effects of turbulence and excessive crosswinds usually are absent. However, there are a few special considerations and techniques that apply to landings at night.

Many pilots have a tendency to make higher or lower approaches at night than during the daytime. Therefore, give careful consideration to traffic pattern procedures and to the factors that enable you to maintain the proper glide angle on final approach. Fly a standardized approach pattern using the altimeter and vertical speed indicator to monitor the rate of descent.

You should fly the same "standard" approach at night that you use during the day.

The runway lights provide an effective peripheral vision cue for beginning the landing flare. Runway lights, when you see them with peripheral vision, seem to rise and spread laterally as you near the proper touchdown point.

It is standard operating procedure to use your landing lights for night landings, even though they may cause an illusion of runway height. The portion of the runway illuminated by the landing lights seems higher than the dark area surrounding it. This effect tends to cause you to flare high. In addition, focusing your attention on the area immediately in front of the airplane is poor practice, but the arrangement of most landing lights tends to encourage this technique. When using landing lights, your sighting point should be near the forward limit of the lighted area.

Proper preparation for night flight should include landings made both with and without the aid of the landing lights. As previously discussed, the cues for the proper maintenance of the approach profile are derived from the altimeter indications and, when on final, from the perspective created by the size, shape, and patterns of the runway lights. Check the altimeter and the vertical speed indicator against your position in the pattern to monitor the approach.

You can make a no-light landing in the manner described or modify it slightly in the flare and touchdown phases. Hold a normal approach until you are over the threshold where the flare normally begins. At this point, slow the airplane by using a slightly higher-than-normal pitch attitude. This attitude should remain constant until touchdown. With your hand on the throttle, adjust power as needed and lower the plane to the runway by maintaining a very shallow sink rate. Be careful to avoid an increasing sink rate or the approach of a stall.

Good landings without landing lights require practice. After the first few approaches and touchdowns, you will be able to execute them accurately. Familiarity with the technique allows you to make a safe night landing with the landing lights inoperative.

EMERGENCY LANDINGS

If it is necessary for you to make a forced landing at night, use the same procedures as those recommended for daytime emergency landings. If it is available, turn on the landing light during the final approach to assist you in avoiding obstacles in the approach path. Highways may be used as emergency landing strips at night, but you must exercise extreme caution to avoid any powerlines crossing the highway.

Prudent pilots select routes for night flights that keep them within reach of airports as much of the time as possible. For example, a course comprised of a series of 25° zigzags in the direction of various airports is only 10% longer than a straight course. Higher cruising altitudes also are advantageous. At 10,000 feet AGL, a light airplane with a glide ratio of 8 to 1 may glide 13 miles. This distance may place the airplane within range of an airport.

CHECKLIST

After studying this section, you should have a basic understanding of:

✓   **Special considerations** — What the differences are between daylight and night operations and the additional factors that should be considered before starting a flight at night.

✓   **Aircraft lighting** — What lights are required to be displayed on an airplane operated at night and how these lights are used to assist you in collision avoidance.

✓   **Airplane operation** — How the various phases of night flight are conducted from preflight to shutdown.

✓   **Night emergencies** — What some of the procedures are that minimize the hazards of an engine failure or other emergency at night.

flight prep 11

PLANNING AND ORGANIZING FLIGHTS

By now you should have a good idea of what the flight planning process involves. This section brings together several subject areas from previous sections, including aeronautical charts, flight publications, weather, navigation, communications, performance, and regulations. Preflight planning puts all of this information to practical use and helps to build an extra margin of safety into every flight you make. It is important to develop a definite pattern of preflight activities so you will not omit essential items. As you gain experience, you should also strive to refine your planning skills. To provide an overview of the process, we have selected a cross-country flight between two small airports in Nebraska. Although the route selected is intentionally short for purposes of illustration, it requires the same steps you would use for longer cross-country flights.

INITIAL PLANNING

Normally, you should make a preliminary check of the weather ahead of time to see if the planned flight is feasible. Unfortunately, an FSS usually is unable to issue a detailed forecast beyond 24 to 36 hours. You can, however, assess the current national weather situation in terms of pressure systems and fronts and decide if adverse weather is likely. When you need a long-range forecast, it is best to contact the NWS. Forecasters there can provide reasonably accurate predictions of general weather patterns up to five days into the future. They also can provide a 6- to 10-day outlook, but keep in mind that the longer the forecast period, the less accurate the information.

There are several other sources that you can use for getting an overall picture. In many areas, there are local cable channels that are devoted to weather; major networks and local TV stations also provide useful weather information. Regardless of what preliminary source you use, be sure to get a standard weather briefing from an FSS specialist before you complete your flight planning on the day of the flight.

Another preliminary step is selecting current sectional charts for the trip. The Omaha Sectional covers the area of the planned flight from York Municipal to Stefan Memorial Airport at Norfolk, Nebraska. [Figure 11-1]

After drawing the course line on the chart, you should select checkpoints which will be easy to identify. In this example, they are Stromsburg Airport, the road and railroad near the town of Oconee that intersect with the 272° radial from the Columbus VOR/DME, and the town of Humphrey. Don't forget to look over the surrounding area for other prominent landmarks that will help you maintain your orientation.

Figure 11-1. For this flight, you will follow a direct route between York and Norfolk. You may want to refer back to this excerpt during the following discussion.

Keep in mind that terrain, special use airspace, or the availability of checkpoints may influence your route selection. Sometimes, a direct course may not be the best choice because of terrain, performance limitations, or navigation equipment. Although a longer route may take more time, it may be the most practical choice. Another factor you should consider is the necessity for an intermediate fuel stop. A direct route is appropriate for this example, since the terrain is relatively flat and the available fuel is adequate. Note the checkpoints on the navigation log as individual legs. Remember that a leg may be any segment of a cross-country flight, such as the distance between checkpoints, intermediate stops, or course changes. Since this flight is direct, your estimates of heading, groundspeed, and wind correction angle will be the same for each leg.

Take the time to study your route of flight carefully. You can begin by looking at the different types of airspace in the area. IR507, an MTR, crosses your course just north of the Stromsburg Airport. Remember that a three-digit identifier means the MTR has segments which may be flown above 1,500 feet AGL. When receiving the standard weather briefing on the day of the flight, ask the weather briefer if it will be in use. Also, make a mental note to be especially alert for traffic arriving at or departing from the airport at Columbus when you pass through the area.

Since the flight to Stefan Memorial will be conducted in controlled airspace, appropriate VFR cloud clearance and visibility requirements will be considerations the day of the flight. Three statute miles visibility and a 1,000-foot ceiling are required for landing at Stefan Memorial because of the Class E airspace surrounding the airport. As you can see by the special use airspace boundary, there is an MOA to the west of Norfolk. This could become a factor if you needed to make a diversion to the west. When you receive your preflight weather briefing, check to see if the MOA will be active. If so, you may need to consider other alternatives if a diversion becomes necessary.

This is a good time to consider your options in the event you need to make a diversion. Take note of airfields along your route, especially those with services available, and check for navaids that you could use during a diversion.

Use the plotter to determine the total distance, the distance between checkpoints, and the true course. The distance between York Municipal and Stefan Memorial Airport is 66 nautical miles, with legs of 14, 21, 13, and 18 nautical miles. The true course is 7°. The isogonic line just west of York shows that the magnetic variation is 7° east. Note these items on the nav log.

You can also give some consideration to your cruising altitude ahead of time. After checking the terrain and obstruction heights, select an approximate altitude, considering FAR requirements for minimum safe altitudes and VFR weather minimums. Remember that the VFR cruising altitudes are based on your magnetic course. For the example, the true course minus the variation is 0°. This makes a cruising altitude of 5,500 feet appropriate, although winds aloft and cloud cover the day of the flight will be the final determining factors.

Above 3,000 feet AGL, use odd thousands plus 500 feet cruising altitudes for magnetic courses from 0° to 179°.

This is an appropriate time to check pertinent flight publications, such as the *Airport/Facility Directory* and NOTAMs. Along with the airport elevation and a description of services available, you should note the runway information, such as surface type, length, and width. Also, look for any pertinent special notices. In addition, the A/FD gives valuable data about communications facilities and radio aids to navigation. [Figure 11-2]

AIRPORT/FACILITY DIRECTORY

NORFOLK
 KARL STEFAN MEM (OFK) 3 SW UTC-6(-5DT) N41°59'08" W97°26'05"   **OMAHA**
  1572 B S4 FUEL 100LL, JET A CFR Index Ltd   **H-1D, 3A, L-11B**
 RWY 01-19: H5800X150 (ASPH-PFC) S-75, D-192, DT-360 HIRL .7% up S   **IAP**
  RWY 01: MALSR. Tree.
  RWY 19: VASI(V4L)—GA 3.0°TCH 39.3'. Antenna.
 RWY 13-3: H5800X150 (ASPH-PFC) S-75, D-192, DT-400 + MIRL .4% up SE
  RWY 13: VASI(V4L)—GA 3.0°TCH 39.3'. Railroad   **RWY 31:** VASI(V2L)—GA 3.0°TCH 27'. Ground.
 AIRPORT REMARKS: Attended Nov-May 1400-2400Z‡, May-Nov 1400-0200Z‡, other times call 371-1783.
  ACTIVATE MALSR Rwy 01, VASI Rwy 19, 13 and 31—122.7. Ultralight activity on and in vicinity of arpt. CLOSED
  to air carrier ops with more than 30 passenger seats except PPR call arpt manager 402-371-7210.
 COMMUNICATIONS: CTAF/UNICOM 122.7
  COLUMBUS FSS (OLU) Toll free call Dial 1-800-WX-BRIEF. NOTAM FILE OFK.
  NORFOLK RCO 122.15 (COLUMBUS FSS)
 AIRSPACE: CLASS E svc effective continuous
 RADIO AIDS TO NAVIGATION: NOTAM FILE OLU.
  WOLBACH (H) VORTAC 114.8 OBH Chan 95 N41°22'33" W98°21'12" 038°55.2 NM to fld. 2010/10E.
  NORFOLK (L) VORW 109.6 OFK Chan 33 N41°59'17" W97°26'03" at fld. NOTAM FILE OFK.
   VOR unusable beyond 35 NM below 3000' and 200°-230° beyond 35 NM below 3400'.
  ILS 111.5 I-OFK Rwy 01 Unmonitored.

NOTAMS

NORFOLK

Karl Stefan Memorial

FDC 6/3418 /OFK/KARL STEFAN MEMORIAL, NORFOLK, NE.
ILS RWY 1 AMDT 1 ALTERNATE MINIMUMS NA.

Norfolk VOR/DME

(OFK) DME UNUSABLE 130-190 BYD 25 NM BLO 4000 FT; 190-240 BYD 20 NM BLO 5000 FT; 240-255 BYD 25 NM BLO 4000 FT; 280-130 BYD 30 NM BLO 3500 FT. (6/)

Figure 11-2. The A/FD excerpt shows that the Norfolk VOR/DME has several restrictions, depending on your altitude and distance from the station. From this, you can conclude that the VOR signals may not be reliable during the descent into the Norfolk area. In addition, NOTAMs issued since the last A/FD issue indicate further restrictions involving the DME portion of the navaid. This demonstrates the importance of checking all available information for the flight.

Another item to check in the A/FD is the aeronautical chart bulletin to see if there are any changes to the Omaha Sectional since its publication date. You can also use a map in the back of the A/FD to locate flight watch facilities. This check reveals the Columbus FSS does not provide EFAS, but Grand Island has a remote flight watch outlet from Minneapolis, Minnesota. You can use this facility for an enroute weather update on your way to Norfolk.

To complete your navigation log, enter the appropriate radio frequencies and use the pilot's operating handbook cruise performance table or chart to find the fuel flow, true airspeed, and power setting for the cruise portion of the flight. These should be entered on the navigation log in the appropriate spaces. [Figure 11-3]

Be sure you have the necessary equipment and supplies gathered up in advance. Having a well-equipped flight case can aid in cockpit management during cross-country flights. Typical items you may want to include are a fuel sampler, clipboard, flight computer, plotter, charts, a flashlight, and a small first aid kit. No one likes to consider that the airplane may develop mechanical problems or that an emergency landing will have to be made. In fact, these occurrences are rare. As a precautionary measure, however, you should have on board appropriate emergency equipment and survival gear, particularly for long flights, flights over remote areas, or flights over large bodies of water.

FINAL PLANNING STAGE

Always obtain a weather briefing prior to departure.

An hour or so before you are scheduled to leave, call the FSS and get a complete weather briefing. For the flight to Norfolk, the standard weather briefing is obtained through the Columbus Flight Service Station. FSS phone numbers are usually included in the communications section of airport listings in the A/FD. They are also listed in the back of the A/FD in a section called "FAA and NWS Telephone Numbers."

Check Points (Fixes)	VOR Ident	Course (Route)	Altitude	Wind Dir.	Vel.	CAS	TC	TH	MH	CH	Dist. Leg	GS Est.	Time Off	GPH
	Freq.			Temp.	TAS	-L +R WCA	-E +W Var.	±Dev.			Rem.	Act.	ETE ETA / ATE ATA	Fuel Rem.
YORK		▷ 5,500					07°				14		66	
STROMSBURG AIRPORT								07°			52			
272° RADIAL	OLU			114			07°	07°			21			
COLUMBUS VOR	112.2						07°	07°			31			
HUMPHREY				114			07°	07°			13			
STEFAN MEMORIAL	OFK 109.6	↓	↓	114			07°	07°			18 18 0			

Figure 11-3. As you complete your advanced planning, your navigation log will look similar to this. After you receive your weather briefing on the day of the flight, the remaining calculations will take a relatively small amount of time.

When you call for your standard briefing, you should tell the FSS special-ist that you are a student or private pilot, as appropriate, and that you will be flying VFR. Include the type and registration number of the plane you will be flying, your intended cruising altitude, and your estimated time of departure. The weather section on the back of a navigation log can serve as a guide as you write down the information given to you by the briefer. It enables you to record the weather with the rest of your flight planning information. It also helps you to locate specific weather data needed for your remaining calculations or for later in-flight references. [Figure 11-4]

After receiving the briefing, you may have unanswered questions. If you need more detailed information, don't hesitate to ask for it. For example, an inquiry about special use airspace and MTRs reveals that IR507 is in use until 10 p.m., and the O'Neill MOA will be active during the after-noon. You may also need weather for any alternate airports that you have chosen. Planning for a diversion to an alternate should always be part of your preflight planning.

With the information from the weather briefing, you can finish the nav-igation log by computing your wind correction angles, magnetic head-ings, groundspeed, estimated time enroute, estimated time of arrival, and the total fuel requirements. You should also calculate your takeoff distance; the time, fuel and distance to climb; cruise performance fig-ures; and performance data for the destination airport. Although it is not a requirement, it is highly recommended that you file a flight plan with

WEATHER LOG

| | Ceiling, Visibility, and Precipitation | | Winds Aloft | Icing and |
	Reported	Forecast		
Departure	70 SCT 120 SCT VIS. 20 WIND 220/7	120 SCT VIS. 20 TRW AFTN	270/10 TEMP +14	N/A
En Route	60 SCT 120 SCT VIS. 20	120 SCT VIS. 20 TRW AFTN		
Destination	50 SCT 100 SCT VIS. 20 WIND 330/10	120 SCT VIS. 20 TRW AFTN		
Alternate				

Figure 11-4. This weather log excerpt reflects the information from the briefing. Generally, current conditions show scattered clouds at 5,000 to 12,000 feet with vis-ibilities 20 miles throughout the area. The forecast shows no adverse weather except for some thundershower activity by late afternoon or evening. Winds at 6,000 feet are expected to be from 270° at 10 knots.

FLIGHT PLAN						
1. TYPE ☑ VFR IFR DVFR	2. AIRCRAFT IDENTIFICATION *N773PR*	3. AIRCRAFT TYPE/ SPECIAL EQUIPMENT *C-172 /A*	4. TRUE AIRSPEED *115* KNOTS	5. DEPARTURE POINT *YORK MUNI (JYR)*	6. DEPARTURE TIME PROPOSED (Z) *1700Z* ACTUAL (Z)	7. CRUISING ALTITUDE *5,500*

8. ROUTE OF FLIGHT
DIRECT

9. DESTINATION (Name of airport and city) *STEFAN MEMORIAL NORFOLK (OFK)*	10. EST. TIME EN ROUTE HOURS *0* MINUTES *40*	11. REMARKS *STUDENT PILOT*

12. FUEL ON BOARD HOURS *5* MINUTES *0*	13. ALTERNATE AIRPORT(S) *NONE*	14. PILOT'S NAME, ADDRESS, TEL. NO. & AIRCRAFT HOME BASE *B. BRAND, 614 COWEN ST., YORK, NE* *(402) 362-1234, YORK MUNI*	15. NUMBER ABOARD *1*

16. COLOR OF AIRCRAFT *GREEN ON WHITE*	17. DESTINATION CONTACT/TELEPHONE (OPTIONAL) *(402) 371-4321*

CLOSE VFR FLIGHT PLAN WITH   *COLUMBUS*   FSS ON ARRIVAL

Special Equipment Suffix
X - No Transponder
T - Transponder With No Altitude Encoding Capability
U - Transponder With Altitude Encoding Capability
D - DME, No Transponder
B - DME, Transponder With No Altitude Encoding Capability
A - DME, Transponder With Altitude Encoding Capability

C - RNAV, Transponder With No Altitude Encoding Capability
R - RNAV, Transponder With Altitude Encoding Capability
W - RNAV, No Transponder
G - Flight Management System (FMS) and Electronic Flight Instrument System (EFIS) equipped aircraft with /R capability having a "Special" Aircraft and Aircrew Authorization" issued by the FAA.

Figure 11-5. After completing the flight plan, call and file it with Columbus FSS. You may use the "Fast File" system, which records the information from your flight plan as you give it. Normally, the flight service specialist transmits essential parts of the flight plan to the destination FSS. For this flight, however, Columbus FSS serves both departure and destination airports.

an FSS before departure. All of the information that you need to file can be taken from the navigation log. [Figure 11-5]

Remember, if you do not open your flight plan within one hour of the departure time you gave to the FSS, they will usually delete it from the system. In the event of an unexpected delay, be sure to call the FSS and amend your departure time.

Always perform a walk-around inspection using a written checklist before you fly an airplane.

Before any flight, you should always perform a walk-around inspection of the airplane. Using the appropriate checklist for the preflight and other operations is highly recommended to ensure that all necessary items are checked in a logical sequence. During the preflight, it is extremely important to verify that the airplane has been serviced with the correct grade and amount of fuel for the flight. Don't assume the oil level has been checked just because the airplane was refueled. If the oil quantity is low, have it filled too. You may even want to take an extra quart or two with you so that, if you need to add oil, you will be using the same type. If any portion of the trip will be taken at night, make a visual inspection of the position, anti-collision, and landing lights.

Check for damage caused by animals, birds, or insects when you pre-flight an airplane coming out of storage.

Even if the airplane was hangared and ready to fly the night before, a pre-flight inspection will allow you to check on possible fuel contamination from condensation or other conditions that may have changed overnight. In cases where an aircraft has been stored for an extended period of time, be especially alert for damage or obstructions caused by animals, birds, or insects.

As pilot-in-command, you are responsible for determining the airworthiness of the airplane. One of the factors involved with this is ensuring that the maintenance for the airplane is up to date. Remember, the airworthiness certificate for the airplane remains valid only so long as the airplane is maintained and operated according to FARs.

An airworthiness certificate is not valid unless the aircraft is maintained according to FARs.

CHECKLIST

After studying this section, you should have a basic understanding of:

✓ **The planning process** — What it entails and what sequence to follow.

✓ **Route consideration** — How to select a route based on airplane performance, terrain, and weather conditions.

✓ **Weather briefing** — How to assess weather conditions in advance and determine the feasibility of the flight.

✓ **Navigation log** — Why it is essential and how it helps you complete the flight plan.

FACTORS AFFECTING DECISION MAKING

In recent years, the FAA, General Aviation Manufacturer's Association, and Transport Canada have conducted studies concerning decision making. Various other aviation groups also participated in or contributed to these studies. The following section is a summary of the results of this research.

THE DECISION-MAKING PROCESS

Flying requires a continuous stream of decisions about yourself, your airplane, and the environment.

Flying is a combination of events which requires you to make a continuous stream of decisions. The events in this process are interrelations between people, the aircraft, and the environment which occur over time. They can be placed in five subject areas:

1. **Pilot** — As a pilot, you are continually making decisions about your own competency, state of health, level of fatigue, and many other variables.

2. **Aircraft** — Your decisions are frequently based on evaluations of the aircraft, such as its power, equipment, or airworthiness.

3. **Environment** — This encompasses many of the items not included in the two previous categories. It can include such things as weather, air traffic control, and runway length or surface.

4. **Operation** — The interaction of you, your aircraft, and the environment is influenced by the purpose of each flight operation. You must evaluate the three previous areas to decide on the desirability of undertaking or continuing the flight as planned. Is the trip worth the risks?

5. **Situation** — Situational awareness is the accurate perception of the conditions affecting you and your aircraft during a specific period of time. More simply, it is knowing what is going on around you. [Figure 11-6]

Figure 11-6. Any given situation is affected by the pilot, aircraft, environment, and operation subject areas. There is a direct relationship between your awareness of the situation and safety. The higher your situational awareness, the safer you are as a pilot.

In conventional decision making, the need for a decision is normally triggered by the recognition that something has changed or that an expected change did not occur. Once you have recognized the need for a decision, your selection of the proper response depends on several elements. Your level of skill, knowledge, experience, and training all influence your ability to make the best choice. If you fail to search for and recognize the change, you reduce your chance of controlling it. As time passes, your available alternatives may decrease. For example, if you have already entered an area of hazardous weather, your alternative to circumnavigate the weather is automatically lost.

It is important to recognize a change, then take action to control it.

Aeronautical decision making (ADM) builds on the foundation of the conventional process, but enhances it to decrease the probability of pilot error. It can be defined as:

- The ability to search for and establish the relevance of all available information regarding a flight situation, to specify alternative courses of action, and to determine expected outcomes from each alternative
- The motivation to choose and authoritatively execute a suitable course of action within the time frame permitted by the situation

The first portion of this definition refers to intellectual capabilities. It relies on your abilities to sense, store, retrieve, and integrate information. This part of decision making is purely rational. If used alone, it would allow problem solving in much the same manner as a computer. The second portion implies that, in part, your decisions are based on tendencies to use other than safety-related information when choosing courses of action. For example, you might consider such items as job demands, convenience, monetary gain, and self-esteem before taking action. Ideally, this non-safety information can be eliminated and your decisions can be directed by a more rational process.

The decision-making process is quite complex; however, it can be condensed into six elements, using the acronym DECIDE. The steps in the DECIDE process are as follows:

The steps in the DECIDE process are detect, estimate, choose, identify, do, and evaluate.

- **D**etect the fact that a change has occurred.
- **E**stimate the need to counter or react to the change.
- **C**hoose a desirable outcome for the success of the flight.
- **I**dentify actions which could successfully control the change.
- **D**o the necessary action to adapt to the change.
- **E**valuate the effect of the action.

Several elements are involved in good decision making. These include: identifying personal attitudes which are hazards to safe flight, developing risk assessment skills, learning to recognize and cope with stress, learning behavior-modification techniques, and evaluating the effectiveness of your ADM skills. First, lets look at the role your attitudes play in decision making.

HAZARDOUS ATTITUDES

The five hazardous atti-
tudes are anti-authority,
impulsivity, invulner-
ability, macho, and
resignation.

There are five hazardous attitudes which affect pilot decision making. It is important to understand them as they apply to your flying. The *Private Pilot Workbook* contains a self-assessment inventory to give you personal insight into these attitudes.

1. **Anti-authority:** "Don't tell me!" — People with this attitude may resent having someone tell them what to do, or they may just regard rules, regulations, and procedures as silly or unnecessary. (Remember, though, it is always your prerogative to question authority if you feel it is in error.)

2. **Impulsivity:** "Do something — quickly!" — This is the thought pattern of people who frequently feel the need to do something — anything — immediately. They do not stop to consider what they are about to do so they can select the best alternative; they do the first thing that comes to mind.

3. **Invulnerability:** "It won't happen to me!" — Many people feel that accidents happen to others but never to them. Pilots who think this way are more likely to take chances and run unnecessary risks.

4. **Macho:** "I can do it." — These people are always trying to prove that they are better than anyone else by taking risks and by trying to impress others. While this pattern is thought to be a male characteristic, women are equally susceptible.

5. **Resignation:** "What's the use?" — People with this attitude do not see themselves as making a great deal of difference in what happens to them. When things go well, they think, "That's good luck." When things go badly, they attribute it to bad luck or feel that someone is "out to get them." They leave the action to others — for better or worse. Sometimes, such an individual will even go along with unreasonable requests just to be a "nice guy."

ANTIDOTES FOR HAZARDOUS ATTITUDES

There are ways to overcome the five major hazardous attitudes which contribute to poor pilot decision making. One way is to become thoroughly aware of them by studying the preceding paragraphs and completing the self-assessment inventory in the *Workbook*. Another is to use **antidotes**. By telling yourself something to counteract the hazardous attitude, you're "taking an antidote." Learn to recognize a hazardous attitude, correctly label the thought, and then say its antidote to yourself. [Figure 11-7]

RISK ASSESSMENT

To enjoy safe flying, you
must learn to identify
and deal with the ele-
ments of risk.

Every aspect of life involves some element of risk, regardless of whether you drive a car, ride a motorcycle, or fly an airplane. You must learn to cope with the risks associated with flying to ensure years of safe flying. The five subject areas discussed earlier — pilot, aircraft, environment,

HAZARDOUS ATTITUDE	ANTIDOTE
Anti-authority: "Don't tell me!"	"Follow the rules. They are usually right."
Impulsivity: "Do something—quickly!"	"Not so fast. Think first."
Invulnerability: "It won't happen to me!"	"It could happen to me."
Macho: "I can do it."	"Taking chances is foolish."
Resignation: "What's the use?"	"I'm not helpless. I can make the difference."

Figure 11-7. To overcome hazardous attitudes, you must memorize the antidotes for each of them. Know them so well that they will automatically come to mind when you need them.

operation, situation — are also the five elements of risk. Let's look at each of these separately.

As a pilot, your performance may be affected in many ways during a flight. The risk raisers, or things that affect you by raising the degree of risk, are called **stressors**. The three types of pilot stressors are:

1. **Physical stress** — Conditions associated with the environment, such as temperature and humidity extremes, noise, vibration, and lack of oxygen

2. **Physiological stress** — Your physical condition, such as fatigue, lack of physical fitness, sleep loss, missed meals (leading to low blood sugar levels), and illness

3. **Psychological stress** — Social or emotional factors, such as a death in the family, a divorce, a sick child, a demotion at work, or the mental workload of in-flight situations

The risk element of the aircraft focuses on its equipment, condition, and suitability for the intended purpose of the flight. The best time to make this assessment is on the ground during preflight planning. However, it also needs to be done continuously during flight, since conditions can change at any time. For example, winds aloft may increase your anticipated flight time, making available fuel a factor to be analyzed.

The environment is a far-reaching risk element which includes situations outside the aircraft that might limit, modify, or affect the aircraft, pilot, and operational elements. Weather is a common environmental risk raiser.

Density altitude, runway length, obstacles, and related factors can also create environmental concerns.

In terms of the purpose of the flight operation, you must evaluate the interaction of you, your aircraft, and the environment. When determining the desirability of undertaking or continuing the flight as planned, be sure to consider all available information.

The combination of these first four risk elements leads into the fifth — the overall situation which you must evaluate continuously. Remember, to become a safer pilot, you should increase your situational awareness.

To assess risk effectively, you must be aware of risk raisers and the possibilities for risk accumulation so you can determine the need to neutralize or balance these factors. One way to become aware of risk is to look at statistics to see what types of flight activities are most likely to result in accidents. The National Transportation Safety Board (NTSB) has conducted studies of accident rates for the various types of flying in general aviation (1982 data). They reveal that aerial application operations have the highest accident rate, followed by personal and business flying.

Poor decision-making skills are often a factor in aircraft accidents.

You should also be aware that the accident rate for single-engine airplanes is the highest for all general aviation airplane operations. More importantly, studies of the most common cause/factors of accidents in fixed-wing aircraft show that most accidents were the result of an unsafe outcome of the pilot's decision-making process. In fact, 85% of all general aviation accidents can be attributed, at least in part, to pilot error. Some common causes were: failure to maintain directional control, failure to maintain airspeed, misjudged distance, fuel exhaustion, inadequate preflight preparation and/or planning, selection of unsuitable terrain, and inadequate visual lookout.

The NTSB also evaluated the phase of operation in which accidents occurred. The results indicate that the largest number (27.1%) occurred during landing, while 21.5% occurred during takeoff.

Other statistics concern accident rates for pilots without instrument ratings flying single-engine airplanes at night in VFR conditions. The night VFR accident rate is high for pilots with less than 51 hours. [Figure 11-8]

Unless all five risk elements indicate "go," you should reconsider your decision to make a flight.

Good aeronautical decision making requires a continuous assessment of whether to start a particular flight or to continue a flight as planned. You can use the five risk elements to help you make a "go/no go" decision. Unless all five indicate "go," you should reevaluate your decision to make a flight. A good decision maker in aviation does not act hastily upon "gut"

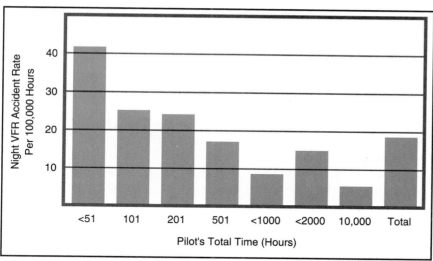

Figure 11-8. The accident rate decreases by nearly 50% once a pilot obtains 100 hours, and continues to decrease until the 1,000-hour level. The data suggest that, for the first 500 hours, pilots flying VFR at night should establish higher personal limits than are required by the regulations and apply instrument flying skills in this environment.

feelings. With an accurate assessment of the risks associated with each of the five elements, you are best able to arrive at decisions that ensure a safe conclusion to a flight, even if it means not taking off.

STRESS REDUCTION

Stress can be defined as the body's response to any demand made on it by physical, physiological, or psychological factors known as stressors. Anything that is perceived as a threat to the body's equilibrium causes a reaction as the body marshals its resources to cope with it. These reactions include the release of chemical hormones (such as adrenaline) into the blood and the speeding of the metabolism to provide energy to the muscles. Blood is shunted away from the stomach and digestive tract to supply the muscles in the arms and legs with more oxygen. Blood sugar is increased. Heart rate, respiration, blood pressure, and perspiration all increase. Other hormones improve the blood's ability to clot. The result prepares the body to fight or flee.

The factors that may cause this type of stress are also the five elements of risk discussed in "Risk Assessment." During flight, it is common to have to deal with many stressors simultaneously. For instance, on a cross-country flight, you realize you are much lower on fuel than you expected. The clouds ahead appear to be building. Static is interfering with your radio. You are off course and can't locate your current position on the sectional chart. On top of all this, you are tired, and hungry. The cabin heater

Stress is the body's reaction to demands.

isn't working, and you have to contend with turbulence. You begin to worry about arriving at your destination on time and missing an important appointment. You contemplate a forced landing and begin to worry about damaging your aircraft. What if your insurance won't cover it? Can you afford the deductible? What about injury to yourself or your passengers? Your palms are sweating, your mouth is dry, and your heart is pounding! At this point, you feel growing sense of urgency and tension. You may give too much attention to "what if" questions which should be ignored. You are reaching (or have reached) a state of stress overload. You begin to use poor judgment that results in a series of bad decisions, such as pressing on into deteriorating weather or overflying good landing areas, until you are almost out of fuel. The stage is set for panic and disaster.

Your performance level decreases rapidly when stress levels exceed your ability to cope.

A certain amount of stress is good for you. It keeps you on your toes and prevents complacency. However, stress effects are cumulative and can eventually add up to an intolerable burden, unless you cope with them adequately. Performance generally increases with the onset of stress, but peaks and then begins to fall off rapidly as stress levels exceed your ability to cope. [Figure 11-9]

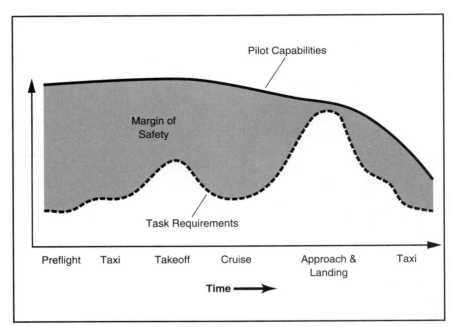

Figure 11-9. Accidents often occur when flying task requirements exceed pilot capabilities. The difference between these two factors is called the margin of safety. Note that in this idealized example, the margin of safety is minimal during the approach and landing. At this point, an emergency or distraction could overtax pilot capabilities, causing an accident.

Stress-handling techniques vary considerably. An individual's personal strategies for dealing with stress may be healthy and adequate, or they may be inappropriate and lead to an increased burden through self-imposed stress. Individuals who are not coping with stress adequately often show symptoms in three ways: emotional, physical, and behavioral. These symptoms differ, depending upon whether aggression is focused inward or outward.

Those individuals who typically turn their aggressive feelings inward often demonstrate the emotional symptoms of depression, preoccupation, sadness, and withdrawal. Physical symptoms may show up as headaches, insomnia, appetite changes, weight gain or loss, indigestion, and so on. Behavioral symptoms can include hypochondria, self-medication, a reluctance to accept responsibility, tardiness, absenteeism, and poor personal appearance.

On the other hand, those individuals who typically take out their frustrations on other people or objects will show few physical symptoms. However, emotional symptoms may show up as overcompensation, denial, suspicion, paranoia, agitation, restlessness, defensiveness, excess sensitivity to criticism, argumentativeness, arrogance, and hostility. The behavioral symptoms can include episodes of desperate acting out or temper tantrums.

You need to be able to recognize the symptoms of stress overload in yourself and to learn how to manage your stress. There are several techniques which can be applied to help prevent the accumulation of life stresses. The first involves a program of physical fitness. Second, learn to recognize and avoid the heavy pressures imposed by getting behind schedule and not meeting deadlines. Plan your schedule to accomplish those tasks that are important and necessary, and don't worry about those that are not. Allow time in your schedule for relaxation. Third, take a realistic assessment of yourself. What are your capabilities and limitations? Strengths and weaknesses? Set your goals accordingly. Fourth, whenever possible, avoid stressful situations and encounters. If driving in traffic raises your blood pressure, join a car pool or ride the bus. If crowds add to your frustration, avoid them whenever possible. Finally, be aware of other, more specialized techniques that can help you cope with stress, such as biofeedback and meditation. Most are designed to evoke what psychologists call the relaxation response. These techniques have been used successfully by athletes, businessmen, and others in high tension professions to maximize performance and minimize the effects of stress.

Learn to recognize the signs of stress overload in yourself and develop techniques for dealing with stress.

The "I'm Safe" Checklist	
Illness?	Do I have any symptoms?
Medication?	Have I been taking prescription or over-the-counter drugs?
Stress?	Am I under psychological pressure from the job? Worried about financial matters, health problems, or family discord?
Alcohol?	Have I been drinking within eight hours? Within 24 hours?
Fatigue?	Am I tired and not adequately rested?
Eating?	Am I adequately nourished?

Figure 11-10. Check yourself as carefully as you check your airplane before flight. If in doubt, don't go.

SELF-ASSESSMENT

Use the "I'm Safe" checklist before each flight.

Most pilots give their aircraft a thorough preflight, yet many forget to preflight themselves. You should use the "I'm Safe" checklist before you decide to fly. [Figure 11-10]

If an emergency occurs, stay calm and maintain a safe airspeed.

If an emergency does occur, be calm — think for a moment, weigh the alternatives, then act. Remember that fear and panic are your greatest enemies during an in-flight emergency. Be sure you maintain a safe airspeed as you determine your course of action. Don't hesitate to declare an emergency, when necessary, or to let other people (including passengers) know about your situation. Don't delay until it is too late.

Your greatest tool for combating fear and panic is to familiarize yourself thoroughly with your aircraft, its systems, and emergency procedures, along with the navigation/communications frequencies along your route of flight. Above all, maintain proficiency in your aircraft, because proficiency builds confidence. Know and respect your own personal limits. Always have a plan and an alternate plan — leave yourself an out! Finally, if flying is adding to your stress, then you had better quit. But, if it helps you cope with your life by providing an enjoyable means of earning a living or a hobby that takes your mind off everyday cares, then relax and enjoy.

CHECKLIST _____

After studying this section, you should have a basic understanding of:

✓   **The decision-making process** — What it is and what factors influence it.

✓   **Hazardous attitudes** — What they are and how you can combat them.

✓   **Risk** — How to assess it and reduce it.

✓   **Stress** — What its symptoms are and how you can relieve them.

COCKPIT RESOURCE MANAGEMENT

Cockpit resource management (CRM) was originally developed to address airline accidents where lack of crew coordination and pilot error were considered to be contributing factors. As CRM training developed, it became apparent that many of the concepts applied to general aviation single-pilot operations as well. Today, the thrust of CRM training is specialized in two areas: crew resource management for the airlines and corporate flying, and cockpit resource management for general aviation single-pilot operations. This section will focus on the general aviation aspects of CRM training.

PRIMARY RESOURCES

Your own knowledge, skills, and abilities are your most valuable cockpit resources.

To begin with, just what are the primary resources available in single-pilot operations? If you really stop and think about this question, there are a number of resources readily available to you every time you fly. The three most valuable resources include your own knowledge, skills, and abilities. As basic as these items may seem, they are by far your most powerful resources.

While knowledge involves knowing and understanding, skill involves the application of knowledge through training. For example, map reading and using a flight computer are considered skills. However, use of these skills to plan a flight or compute the ETA is considered an ability. Another example is the ability to determine that the anticipated flight can be conducted safely. In other words, you need the ability to make a sound go/no-go decision. The following scenario shows how you can apply CRM principles to a cross-country flight.

PREPARATION

Cockpit resource management begins when you start preparing for a flight.

CRM should begin long before you arrive at the airport. Begin by observing the weather on the local news or A.M. Weather broadcast. This preliminary weather check can save a lot of time and effort. If the weather looks favorable, make a note of the weather systems and fronts. Note their direction and speed, as well as any areas of poor weather. With this step completed, you will be better prepared for the planning portion of the flight.

Planning is, of course, the most important aspect of any flight. The degree of planning required for local flights is not as extensive as it is for cross-country flights. However, most of the information presented here is applicable to all flights including local flights. During cross-country flight planning, you should determine each of the following.

1.   Route of flight

2.   Distance to destination

3.   Fuel requirements

4.   Availability of fuel and services

5.   Runway lengths

Also ensure you have all of the charts you need to make the flight. It is a good idea to carry the charts that border those needed, just in case a deviation from your planned route becomes necessary. [Figure 11-11]

Fill in the navlog as much as possible *before* you get your weather briefing. The more you know about the route and airports along your flight path, the more information you can extract from the weather briefing. The weather briefer is able to be specific about the weather if you are able to be specific about your route of flight. Write down the pertinent information during the weather briefing and, where practical, draw in the fronts and weather systems on the back of the navlog.

It's best to fill out your navlog before you contact the weather briefer because it will help you obtain more from the briefing.

Based on the weather, regulations, and your own personal limitations (as well as those set by your instructor during training), you can make the go/no-go decision with confidence and safety. If, after due consideration, a no-go decision is made, you have enough information to consider alternatives such as rescheduling the flight for another day, changing the route of flight, leaving earlier, or leaving later.

After a go decision is made, complete the navlog by calculating the required headings, true airspeeds, groundspeeds, time between checkpoints,

Deciding whether a fuel stop is necessary is an important resource management issue.

Figure 11-11. Marking your route of flight on the charts and selecting prominent checkpoints is an important preflight activity which enhances the usefulness of your charts during cross-country flight.

and fuel required for the flight. If you cannot carry enough fuel to make the trip nonstop, you'll have to plan a fuel stop enroute. Now is the time to determine if a fuel stop will be required and, if it is, where you will stop. It is a good operating practice to ensure your fuel stop has the services you need. Once the navlog is complete, file a flight plan, and keep one copy as a record for yourself.

When the planning is completed, collect everything you need for the flight such as charts, navlogs, pencils, a flight computer, and plotter. Sunglasses, a flashlight, kneeboard, and a first-aid kit are good items to include. Pack your flight case or tote bag carefully so you can locate each item. [Figure 11-12]

PREFLIGHT

The first thing to check when you arrive at the aircraft is whether it is legal for the flight. Check that all required documentation is on board and ensure the aircraft has been properly maintained.

Another important check is to ensure the aircraft has the necessary avionics for the flight. If the destination airport is located within Class C airspace, for example, your aircraft will need to be equipped with a functioning two-way communications radio, and a 4096-code transponder with automatic altitude reporting. The transponder must have been checked within the preceding 24 calendar months. This inspection should be noted in the aircraft maintenance records.

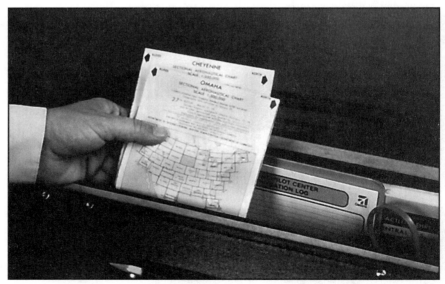

Figure 11-12. It is a good practice to pack your charts so they can be removed in the order in which they will be used.

The final steps prior to loading the aircraft are to use the pilot's operating handbook to check the weight and balance, compute performance data, and preflight the aircraft. When you unpack your flight case, remove only those items you will need during the first portion of the flight. Do not place anything on the glareshield that can block your field of vision or interfere with the magnetic compass. Certain items, such as plastic flight computers or plotters, warp when left in the sun.

A final check of the aircraft's weight and balance condition and performance data require use of a primary cockpit resource, the POH.

Once certified as a private pilot, you will be permitted to carry passengers. As pilot-in- command, you will be responsible for the safety and comfort of each passenger you carry. Take time to explain how to operate the doors, seats, and the seat belts. If oxygen will be required on the flight, explain how the oxygen masks are to be used. It is a good idea to occasionally practice briefing your instructor.

An important cockpit resource management task is to become familiar with all the instruments and controls in your aircraft. Know the location of every switch and its function. This step is particularly important if you do not fly the same aircraft every time. The aircraft checklists, are extremely important items. [Figure 11-13]

Figure 11-13. Checklists are excellent cockpit resources for verifying the instruments and systems on the aircraft are checked, set, and operating properly. It is a recommended procedure to verbalize each checklist item and to touch or move the item, as appropriate, to make sure the checklist item is performed instead of just read.

In addition to check-lists, common sense is another important cock-pit resource.

As good as checklists are, they are *not* all inclusive. You should use common sense in addition to the checklist. For example, just before starting the engine with the master switch on, you should check to see that the ammeter shows a slight discharge. After starting, the ammeter should be showing a charge. In addition, the gyros for the attitude and heading indicators should be spinning up to operating speed. Another example might be the RADIOS — ON check. Common sense would tell you to turn on *all* the radios you expect to use. In addition, you should select the standby mode for avionics equipment such as the transponder.

It is important to test the aircraft brakes as soon as the aircraft starts to move. Observe the flight instrument indications as you taxi to see if they agree with the movements of the aircraft. After completing the aircraft runup, make sure all seatbelts are fastened. Get in the habit of checking to see if your instructor's seat belt is fastened, and don't forget to tell the examiner on your checkride to buckle up.

Before departure, it is a good practice to set up your radios. For example, you should tune each navigation radio and set the selectors for the proper courses based upon the initial departure routing. [Figure 11-14]

Figure 11-14. The tower frequency should be set in one radio, and either the departure frequency or the flight service station in the other. The management of radios is as important as any other aspect of the flight. Keeping the radios set up well in advance of when they will be required will help eliminate a hurried search for a frequency on a chart.

DEPARTURE

Pick a point along the runway where the aircraft should become airborne based upon the performance computations made earlier. This will help you judge how the aircraft is accelerating during the takeoff roll. If the departure airport has an operating control tower, obtain a clearance for takeoff. Generally, clearances should be read back to provide a means of acknowledgement and verification. Just before you taxi onto the runway for takeoff, record the time for later use on the navlog. Also, remember to turn on the transponder.

Monitor the aircraft's acceleration throughout the takeoff roll. If it is not accelerating normally, discontinue the takeoff. Keep in mind that a high density altitude will *decrease* engine output, *decrease* acceleration, and *increase* the takeoff roll. Knowing what to expect can help eliminate unwanted surprises.

ENROUTE

Your enroute cockpit management duties involve monitoring the systems in the aircraft, navigating, and maintaining a continual watch for other traffic. Systems monitoring is greatly enhanced by using the appropriate checklist for the enroute climb and cruise. You should scan *all* the instruments at regular intervals so any problems can be noted before they become serious.

NAVIGATION

One of the first things you should do after departure is open your flight plan. Since you wrote down your time off, it won't have to be estimated. Another important use for your time off is to estimate your arrival over the first checkpoint. As you pass each checkpoint, note and record the time on your navlog. Having the estimated time enroute and estimated groundspeed agree with the actual values will confirm your planning. However, if the estimates and actual numbers vary, it is important to determine the reason so a correction can be applied to the following legs.

The navigation log becomes a valuable resource when you record the progress of your flight.

You should determine if the actual true airspeed agrees with your estimate. A 10-knot difference on a 500-mile trip could result in an extra 30 minutes of flight time. You also should compute the actual winds aloft. If they differ from the forecast, not only should you revise your navlog, but you also should advise Flight Watch. In fact, anytime you encounter weather that is different than forecast, or that was not forecast at all, you should advise Flight Watch.

As you proceed from one flight chart to the next, place the chart you were using out of the way, but keep it located within arm's reach in case you need it again. Another important cockpit resource management task is to monitor the aircraft's fuel consumption. During the planning phase, you assumed a certain fuel consumption rate. If you are consuming fuel at a higher rate, you may run out before you reach your destination.

Keeping track of the fuel consumption rate and your remaining fuel requirements is a primary cockpit management task for any flight.

On cross-country flights, you are required by FARs to obtain altimeter settings of stations along the route of flight and within 100 nautical miles of the aircraft. As you do this, you should obtain updated weather reports for the route and for your destination. Keeping track of the weather can prevent you from flying into an area of deteriorating weather conditions.

SEE AND AVOID

Although all pilots are required to see and avoid each other, the use of departure, enroute, or arrival radar services can help you with this critical task. It is important to remember, however, that radar service does not relieve you of basic see-and-avoid responsibilities. Even when operating under positive radar control, such as in Class B airspace, you are still required to see and avoid *all* other aircraft.

ARRIVAL

The approach to your destination is an appropriate place to apply cockpit resource management by properly planning the descent. Generally, you should avoid descending at more than 500 feet per minute. Assume you are flying at 8,000 above the elevation of your destination airport. If a 500 foot per minute descent is used, it will take about 14 minutes to descend to the pattern altitude of 1,000 feet AGL. If the groundspeed during the descent is 110 knots, the descent should be started about 26 miles out. If you wait until you get closer, you will either be too high, or have to descend at a higher rate.

As you approach the airport, monitor the ATIS, if available, and the tower frequency before you call. By listening in, you should be able to get a good idea of what to expect. This, also, is an excellent procedure for local flights.

If the destination airport is equipped with approach radar, it makes common sense to use this service. Not only will controllers point out traffic, but they also will provide radar vectors to your destination. You should not, however, rely on this service to locate an unfamiliar airport. Like traffic advisories, radar vectors are available on a workload-permitting basis only.

As you enter the traffic pattern, start planning your approach, but keep your planning flexible. Remember, you may have to extend or shorten your downwind leg for another aircraft. On final, always be ready for a go-around. Decide long before you get near the runway what you will do if you must execute a go-around.

ON THE RAMP

Once on the ground, taxi at a low power setting to allow the engine time to cool. This cool-down period is particularly important with a turbocharged engine. When you're ready to shut down, follow the appropriate checklists. Securely tie down the aircraft and collect all of your equipment before you leave. As you enter the terminal, get in the habit of closing your flight plan first. Then, go back to the flight counter to place a fuel order and fill out any required paperwork.

EXPANDING YOUR RESOURCES

As mentioned previously, some of the most valuable resources are your own knowledge, skills, and abilities. Obviously, if you can improve your own capabilities, you will expand your cockpit resources immensely. An important way to do this is to continue training after your obtain your private pilot certificate.

ADDITIONAL CERTIFICATES AND RATINGS

An instrument rating provides a substantial increase in cockpit resources and has direct carry over to VFR flying. If you obtain a multi-engine rating, commercial, flight instructor, or airline transport pilot certificate, each new step enhances your cockpit resources.

Acquiring additional certificates and ratings is an effective way of increasing your knowledge, skills, and abilities.

CURRENCY AND PROFICIENCY

Don't forget that currency and proficiency also are valuable resources because they promote familiarity with the aircraft, its operating procedures, and flying in general. Pilots who maintain their currency are actually strengthening their resources.

Consider your currency and proficiency as key resources.

IMPROVING WEATHER KNOWLEDGE

Another resource that falls into the basic category includes the ability to access weather information. Of course, this also involves knowledge and skills — the knowledge of what is available and the skill to obtain it. The use of computerized equipment has revolutionized flight service stations and the way they operate. More and more, you need specialized knowledge not just for interpreting weather data, but for obtaining it through new automated systems and methods of dissemination.

Improving your weather knowledge helps you access, analyze, and interpret available weather information.

One of the implications of these new systems is that you now have more ways to access weather information, but less help in analyzing and interpreting weather data. So, this is one more knowledge and ability resource you need — acquiring, analyzing, and interpreting weather data. Your Cessna Private Pilot *Manual of Flight* contains the information you need to develop this important resource.

FLIGHT INFORMATION PUBLICATIONS

Flight information publications are other valuable resources that are sometimes overlooked. During training, if you have ever flown beyond the boundary of the chart or become lost, you know the value of current aeronautical charts. Since aeronautical charts are dynamic documents, you will need to keep up with chart enhancements and symbology changes. When considering the resource value of publications, don't forget the importance of a current airport directory as well as the *Aeronautical Information Manual*. Any pilot who has a thorough working knowledge of the AIM can't help but have expanded resource capabilities over someone with only passing familiarity.

Flight information publications can expand your resource capabilities when planning, as well as conducting, a flight.

AIR TRAFFIC CONTROL

Pilots usually associate ATC with IFR flight plans. When not on an IFR flight plan, they tend to forget ATC until they are approaching a large terminal area. The fact is that ATC has incredible on-request resources for VFR, as well as IFR pilots. Some good examples include radar traffic information service, safety alerts, radar assistance to VFR aircraft, and terminal radar programs for VFR aircraft. Radar flight following is another service which has wide application to VFR aircraft. In emergencies, radar-equipped approach control facilities, as well as centers, can provide a wide range of assistance to VFR and IFR aircraft alike.

ATC services are often overlooked during VFR flight operations, yet they can be a valuable resource.

PILOT'S OPERATING HANDBOOK

Other important resources pertain to the particular aircraft you are flying. Obviously, the pilot's operating handbook is one of the most essential cockpit resources. It contains the operating and performance limitations, as well as the systems descriptions. Not only is it a regulatory requirement that the POH (or approved Airplane Flight Manual, markings, and placards as prescribed in FAR Part 91) be in the airplane, accurate flight planning is not possible without it. In addition, resolution of in-flight instrument or system malfunctions is very dependent on the POH.

The POH is one of your most essential cockpit resources.

AIRCRAFT EQUIPMENT

The equipment on a particular aircraft also may provide some additional resources which can be to your benefit. Avionics and autopilots are two areas which are particularly significant during single-pilot operations. Environmental systems, such as oxygen or pressurization, are other resources which give you an option of climbing to higher altitudes.

As you can see, cockpit resource management involves a working knowledge of all available resources, the skills to use these resources, and the ability to apply your knowledge and skills when conducting flight operations. Good CRM has many benefits including improved in-flight organizational skills and the capability to handle heavy workload situations. These skills translate directly to better decision making and flight safety.

Good cockpit resource management skills enhance your piloting efficiency and competence.

CHECKLIST _____

After studying this section, you should have a basic understanding of:

✓ **CRM** — What it means and how it applies to general aviation single-pilot operations.

✓ **Primary resources** — What they are and how they are used.

✓ **Flight preparation** — How cockpit resource management applies and what your resources are.

✓ **Enroute cockpit management** — What your duties are and what additional resources are available.

✓ **Expanding your resources** — How to accomplish this by improving your own capabilities.

GLOSSARY

A

ABSOLUTE ALTITUDE — Actual height above the surface of the earth, either land or water.

ABSOLUTE CEILING — The altitude where a particular airplane's climb rate reaches zero.

ADVECTION FOG — Fog resulting from the movement of warm, humid air over a cold surface.

AGONIC LINE — Line along which no magnetic variation occurs.

AIR DENSITY — The density of the air in terms of mass per unit volume. Dense air has more molecules per unit volume than less dense air. The density of air decreases with altitude above the surface of the earth and with increasing temperature.

AIR ROUTE TRAFFIC CONTROL CENTER (ARTCC) — A facility established to provide air traffic control service to aircraft operating on IFR flight plans within controlled airspace, principally during the enroute phase of flight.

AIR TRAFFIC CONTROL (ATC) — A service provided by the FAA to promote the safe, orderly, and expeditious flow of air traffic.

AIR TRAFFIC SERVICE — A generic term referring to Flight Information Service, Alerting Service, or ATC Services.

AIRMASS — An extensive body of air having fairly uniform properties of temperature and moisture within a horizontal plane.

AIRMET — In-flight weather advisory concerning moderate icing, moderate turbulence, sustained winds of 30 knots or more at the surface, and widespread areas of ceilings less than 1,000 feet and/or visibilities less than three miles.

AIRPORT ADVISORY AREA — The area within 10 statute miles of an airport where a flight service station is located, but where there is no control tower in operation.

AIRPORT SURVEILLANCE RADAR (ASR) — Approach and departure control radar used to detect and display an aircraft's position in the terminal area and to provide aircraft with range and azimuth information.

ALERT AREA — Special use airspace which may contain a high volume of pilot training activities or an unusual type of aerial activity.

ALTIMETER — The instrument that indicates flight altitude by sensing pressure changes and displaying altitude in feet.

ALTIMETER SETTING — The barometric pressure setting used to adjust a pressure altimeter for variations in existing atmospheric pressure and temperature.

ALTITUDE — Height expressed in units of distance above a reference plane, usually above mean sea level or above ground level.

ANGLE OF ATTACK — The angle between the airfoil's chord line and the relative wind.

ANGLE OF INCIDENCE — The angle between the chord line of the wing and the longitudinal axis of the airplane.

APPROACH CONTROL — A terminal air traffic control facility providing approach control service.

AUTOMATIC DIRECTION FINDER (ADF) — An aircraft radio navigation system which senses and indicates the direction to an L/MF nondirectional radio beacon (NDB) or commercial broadcast station.

AUTOMATIC TERMINAL INFORMATION SERVICE (ATIS) — The continuous broadcast of recorded noncontrol information in selected terminal areas. Its purpose is to improve controller effectiveness and to relieve frequency congestion by automating the repetitive transmission of essential but routine information.

AUTOMATED SURFACE OBSERVATION SYSTEM (ASOS) — Weather reporting system which provides surface observations every minute via digitized voice broadcasts and printed reports.

AUTOMATED WEATHER OBSERVING SYSTEM (AWOS) — Automated weather reporting system consisting of various sensors, a processor, a computer-generated voice subsystem, and a transmitter to broadcast local, minute-by-minute weather data directly to the pilot.

B

BEARING — The horizontal direction to or from any point, usually measured clockwise from true north (true bearing), magnetic north (magnetic bearing), or some other reference point, through 360°.

BEST ANGLE-OF-CLIMB AIRSPEED — The best angle-of-climb airspeed (V_X) will produce the greatest gain in altitude for horizontal distance traveled.

BEST RATE-OF-CLIMB AIRSPEED — The best rate-of-climb airspeed (V_Y) produces the maximum gain in altitude per unit of time.

C

CALIBRATED AIRSPEED (CAS) — Indicated airspeed of an aircraft, corrected for installation and instrument errors.

CAMBER — The curve of an airfoil section from the leading edge to the trailing edge.

CATEGORY — (1) As used with respect to the certification, ratings, privileges, and limitations of airmen, means a broad classification of aircraft (airplane, rotorcraft, glider, and lighter-than-air). (2) As used with respect to the certification of aircraft, means a grouping of aircraft by intended use or operating limitations (transport, normal, utility, acrobatic, limited, restricted, and provisional).

CEILING — The height above the earth's surface of the lowest layer of clouds or obscuring phenomena that is reported as broken, overcast, or obscuration and not classified as thin or partial.

CENTER OF GRAVITY (CG) — The theoretical point where the entire weight of the airplane is considered to be concentrated.

CHORD — An imaginary straight line between the leading and trailing edges of an airfoil section.

CLASS — (1) As used with respect to the certification, ratings, privileges, and limitations of airmen, means a classification of aircraft within a category having similar operating characteristics (single engine, multi-engine, land, water, gyroplane, helicopter, airship, and free balloon). (2) As used with respect to certification of aircraft means a broad grouping of aircraft having similar characteristics of propulsion, flight, or landing (airplane, rotorcraft, glider, balloon, landplane, and seaplane).

CLASS A AIRSPACE — Controlled airspace covering the 48 contiguous United States and Alaska east of 160° West longitude, and out to 12 nautical miles from the coasts, from 18,000 feet MSL up to and including FL600, but not including airspace less than 1,500 feet AGL.

CLASS B AIRSPACE — Controlled airspace designated around certain major airports, extending from the surface or higher to specified altitudes. For operations in Class B areas, all aircraft are subject to the rules and pilot/equipment requirements listed in FAR Part 91.

CLASS C AIRSPACE — Controlled airspace surrounding designated airports where ATC provides radar vectoring and sequencing on a full-time basis for all IFR and VFR aircraft. Participation is mandatory, and all aircraft must establish and maintain radio contact with ATC.

CLASS D AIRSPACE — Controlled airspace around at least one primary airport which has an operating control tower. Aircraft operators are subject to the rules and equipment requirements specified in FAR Part 91.

CLASS E AIRSPACE — Controlled airspace which covers the 48 contiguous United States and Alaska east of 160° West longitude, and out to 12 nautical miles from the coasts, from 14,500 feet MSL up to but not including 18,000 feet MSL. Exceptions are restricted and prohibited areas, and airspace less than 1,500 feet AGL. Class E airspace also includes Federal airways, with a floor of 1,200 feet AGL or higher, as well as the airspace from 700 feet or more above the surface designated in conjunction with an airport which has an approved instrument approach procedure.

CLASS G AIRSPACE — Airspace that has not been designated as Class A, B, C, D, or E, and within which air traffic control is not exercised.

CLEAR AIR TURBULENCE — Turbulence that occurs in clear air, and is commonly applied to high-level turbulence associated with wind shear. It is often encountered near the jet stream, and it is not the same as turbulence associated with cumuliform clouds or thunderstorms.

COLD FRONT — The boundary between two airmasses where cold air is replacing warm air.

COMMON TRAFFIC ADVISORY FREQUENCY (CTAF) — A frequency designed for the purpose of carrying out airport advisory practices while operating to or from an uncontrolled airport. The CTAF may be a UNICOM, MULTICOM, FSS, or tower frequency and it is identified in appropriate aeronautical publications.

COMPASS HEADING — A compass reading that will make good the desired course. It is the desired course (true course) corrected for variation, deviation, and wind.

CONDENSATION — A change of state of water from a gas (water vapor) to a liquid.

CONTROLLED AIRSPACE — Airspace designated as Class A, B, C, D, or E, within which some or all aircraft may be subject to air traffic control.

CONVECTION — The circular motion of air that results when warm air rises and is replaced by cooler air. These motions are predominantly vertical, resulting in vertical transport and mixing of atmospheric properties; distinguished from advection.

CONVECTIVE SIGMET — In-flight weather advisory concerning tornadoes, lines of thunderstorms, embedded thunderstorms, areas of thunderstorms, and/or hail greater than or equal to 3/4 inch in diameter.

CORIOLIS FORCE — A deflective force that is created by the difference in rotational velocity between the equator and the poles of the earth. It deflects air to the right in the northern hemisphere and to the left in the southern hemisphere.

COURSE — The intended or desired direction of flight in the horizontal plane measured in degrees from true or magnetic north.

CROSSWIND — A wind which is not parallel to a runway or the path of an aircraft.

CROSSWIND COMPONENT — A wind component which is at a right angle to the runway or the flight path of an aircraft.

D

DENSITY ALTITUDE — Pressure altitude corrected for nonstandard temperature variations. Performance charts for many older airplanes are based on this value.

DEVIATION — A compass error caused by magnetic disturbances from electrical and metal components in the airplane. The correction for this error is displayed on a compass correction card placed near the magnetic compass in the airplane.

DEWPOINT — The temperature to which air must be cooled to become saturated.

DISPLACED THRESHOLD — When the landing area begins at a point on the runway other than the designated beginning of the runway.

DISTANCE MEASURING EQUIPMENT (DME) — Equipment (airborne and ground) to measure, in nautical miles, the slant range distance of an aircraft from the DME navigation aid.

DOWNBURST — A strong downdraft which induces an outburst of damaging winds on or near the ground. Damaging winds, either straight or curved, are highly divergent. The sizes of downbursts vary from 1/2 mile or less to more than 10 miles. An intense downburst often causes widespread damage. Damaging winds, lasting 5 to 30 minutes, could reach speeds as high as 120 knots.

E

EMERGENCY LOCATOR TRANSMITTER (ELT) — A radio transmitter attached to the aircraft structure which operates from its own power source on 121.5 Mhz and 243.0 Mhz. It aids in locating downed aircraft by radiating a downward-sweeping audio tone.

EVAPORATION — The transformation of a liquid to the gaseous state, such as the change of water to water vapor.

F

FINAL APPROACH — A flight path of a landing aircraft in the direction of landing along the extended runway centerline from the base leg or straight in to the runway.

FLIGHT PLAN AREA — The geographical area assigned by regional air traffic divisions to a flight service station for the purpose of search and rescue for VFR aircraft, issuance of NOTAMs, pilot briefings, in-flight services, broadcasts, emergency services, flight data processing, international operations, and aviation weather services. Three letter identifiers are assigned to every flight service station and are annotated in the A/FD.

FLIGHT SERVICE STATION — Air traffic service facilities that provide a variety of services to pilots, including weather briefings, opening and closing flight plans, and search and rescue operations.

FREEZING LEVEL — A level in the atmosphere at which the temperature is 32°F (0°C).

FRONT — The boundary between two different airmasses.

G

GLOBAL POSITIONING SYSTEM (GPS) — A satellite-based radio positioning, navigation, and time-transfer system.

GROUND EFFECT — A usually beneficial influence on aircraft performance which occurs while you are flying close to the ground. It results from a reduction in upwash, downwash, and wingtip vortices which provide a corresponding decrease in induced drag.

GROUNDSPEED — Speed of the aircraft in relation to the ground.

H

HAZARDOUS INFLIGHT WEATHER ADVISORY SERVICE (HIWAS) — Recordings of hazardous inflight weather forecasts broadcast over selected VORs.

HEADING — The direction in which the longitudinal axis of the airplane points with respect to true or magnetic north. Heading is equal to course plus or minus any wind correction angle.

HUMIDITY — Water vapor content in the air.

HYPERVENTILATION — The excessive ventilation of the lungs caused by very rapid and deep breathing which results in an excessive loss of carbon dioxide from the body.

HYPOXIA — The effects on the human body of an insufficient supply of oxygen.

I

IDENT — Request by ATC for a pilot to activate the aircraft transponder identification feature to help the controller identify the aircraft.

INDICATED AIRSPEED — The speed of an aircraft as shown on the airspeed indicator.

INDICATED ALTITUDE — The altitude shown by an altimeter set to the current altimeter setting.

INDUCED DRAG — That part of total drag which is created by the production of lift.

INSTRUMENT FLIGHT RULES (IFR) — Rules that govern the procedure for conducting flight in instrument weather conditions. When weather conditions are below the minimums prescribed for VFR, only instrument-rated pilots may fly in accordance with IFR.

INVERSION — An increase in temperature with altitude — a reversal of the normal decrease of temperature with altitude in the troposphere.

ISOBAR — A line of equal or constant barometric pressure.

ISOGONIC LINES — Lines on charts that connect points of equal magnetic variation.

ISOTACH — A line of equal or constant wind speed.

ISOTHERM — A line of equal or constant temperature.

J

JET STREAM — A narrow band of winds with speeds of 50 knots and greater embedded in the westerlies in the high troposphere.

L

LAND BREEZE — A coastal breeze blowing from land to sea caused by temperature difference when the sea surface is warmer than the adjacent land; usually blows at night and alternates with a sea breeze which blows in the opposite direction by day.

LAPSE RATE — The rate of decrease of an atmospheric variable with altitude; commonly refers to a decrease of temperature or pressure with altitude.

LATITUDE — Measurement north or south of the equator in degrees, minutes, and seconds.

LOAD FACTOR — The ratio of the load supported by the airplane's wings to the actual weight of the aircraft and its contents.

LOCAL AIRPORT ADVISORY (LAA) — Advisory service provided to pilots by FSS or the military at airports without an operating control tower. Information includes known traffic and weather conditions.

LONGITUDE — Measurement east or west of the Prime Meridian in degrees, minutes, and seconds.

LONG RANGE NAVIGATION (LORAN) — An electronic navigational system by which lines of position are determined by measuring the difference in the time of reception of synchronized pulse signals from fixed transmitters. LORAN - C operates in the 100 - 110 kHz frequency band.

M

MAGNETIC COURSE — True course corrected for magnetic variation.

MANEUVERING SPEED (V_A) — The maximum speed at which full and abrupt control movements will not overstress the airplane.

MAYDAY — International radio distress signal. When repeated three times, it indicates imminent and grave danger and that immediate assistance is requested.

MEAN SEA LEVEL (MSL) — The average height of the surface of the sea for all stages of tide; used as a reference for elevations throughout the U.S.

MICROBURST — A small downburst with outbursts of damaging winds extending 2.5 miles or less. In spite of its small horizontal scale, an intense microburst could induce wind speeds as high as 150 knots.

MILITARY OPERATIONS AREA (MOA) — Special use airspace of defined vertical and lateral limits established to help VFR traffic identify locations where military activities are conducted.

MILITARY TRAINING ROUTE (MTR) — Route depicted on an aeronautical chart for the conduct of military flight training at speeds above 250 knots.

MILLIBAR — A unit of atmospheric pressure equal to a force of 1,000 dynes per square centimeter.

MOVEMENT AREA — Runways, taxiways, and other areas of an airport used by aircraft for taxi, take-off, and landing, excluding ramps and parking areas. When a control tower is operational, approval from ATC must be obtained prior to entering the movement area.

N

NIGHT — The time between the end of evening civil twilight and the beginning of morning civil twilight, as published in the American Air Almanac.

NOTICE TO AIRMEN (NOTAM) — A notice containing a recent change to any component in the National Airspace System which is considered essential to persons concerned with flight operations.

O

OBSTRUCTION LIGHT — A light, or one of a group of lights, usually red or white, mounted on a surface structure or natural terrain to warn pilots of the presence of a flight hazard.

OROGRAPHIC — Associated with or induced by the presence of mountains, such as orographic lift or orographic clouds.

OUTER AREA — Airspace surrounding a Class C airspace area, extending out to a radius of 20 n.m. ATC provides radar vectoring and sequencing for all IFR aircraft and participating VFR aircraft.

P

PARASITE DRAG — That part of total drag created by the form or shape of airplane parts.

PILOT IN COMMAND (PIC) — The pilot responsible for the operation and safety of an aircraft.

PILOT WEATHER REPORT — A PIREP is a report of meteorological phenomena encountered by aircraft in flight.

PRESSURE ALTITUDE — Height above the standard pressure level of 29.92 in. Hg. Obtained by setting 29.92 in the barometric pressure window and reading the altimeter.

PREVAILING VISIBILITY — The greatest horizontal visibility throughout at least half the horizon circle. The half circle does not need to be continuous.

PREVAILING WIND — The wind direction most frequently observed during a given period.

PROGRESSIVE TAXI — Precise taxi instructions issued to a pilot unfamiliar with an airport, usually issued in stages as the aircraft proceeds along the route.

PROHIBITED AREA — Airspace of defined dimensions identified by an area on the surface of the earth within which the flight of aircraft is prohibited.

R

RADAR ADVISORY — Information or advice provided to pilots based on radar observations.

RADAR CONTACT — Term used by ATC to advise a pilot that the aircraft is identified on radar.

RADAR VECTOR — A heading issued by a radar controller to the pilot of an aircraft to provide navigational guidance.

RADIAL — A navigational signal generated by a VOR or VORTAC, measured as a magnetic bearing from the station.

RECIPROCAL — A reverse bearing, opposite in direction by 180°.

RELATIVE BEARING — Angular difference between the airplane's longitudinal axis and a straight line drawn from the airplane to the station. It is measured clockwise from the airplane's nose.

RESTRICTED AREA — Designated special use airspace within which aircraft flight, while not prohibited, is subject to restrictions.

RUNWAY HEADING — The magnetic direction that corresponds with the runway centerline extended, not the painted runway number. When cleared to "fly or maintain runway heading," pilots are expected to fly or maintain the heading that corresponds with the extended centerline of the departure runway. Drift correction shall not be applied; e.g., Runway 4, actual magnetic heading of the runway centerline 044, fly 044.

RUNWAY SAFETY AREA — A defined surface area surrounding the runway which is prepared or suitable for minimizing damage to aircraft which undershoot, overshoot, or run off the runway.

RUNWAY VISIBILITY VALUE — Visibility determined by a transmissometer for a particular runway.

RUNWAY VISUAL RANGE — An instrumentally derived value representing the horizontal distance a pilot will see down the runway from the approach end, based on either the sighting of high intensity runway lights or on the visual contrast of other targets, whichever yields the greatest visual range.

S

SATURATED AIR — Air containing the maximum amount of water vapor it can hold at a given temperature (100% relative humidity).

SEA BREEZE — A coastal breeze blowing from sea to land, caused by the temperature difference when the land surface is warmer than the sea surface.

SEGMENTED CIRCLE — A set of visual indicators which provide traffic pattern information at airports without operating control towers.

SERVICE CEILING — The maximum height above mean sea level, under normal conditions, at which a given airplane is able to maintain a rate of climb of 100 feet per minute.

SIGMET — An in-flight advisory concerning severe icing, severe and extreme turbulence, widespread duststorms, sandstorms, or volcanic ash lowering visibility to less than three miles.

SPECIAL USE AIRSPACE — Defined airspace areas where aircraft operations may be limited. Examples include: alert area, controlled firing area, military operations area, prohibited area, restricted area, and warning area.

SPECIAL VFR CONDITIONS — Weather conditions which are less than basic VFR weather conditions, but permit flight under VFR within the lateral boundaries of the surface areas of Class B, C, D, or E airspace designated for an airport. ATC authorization must be received.

SQUALL LINE — Any nonfrontal or narrow band of active thunderstorms.

STANDARD ALTIMETER SETTING — Altimeter set to the standard pressure of 29.92 in. Hg, or 1013.2 Mb.

STANDARD ATMOSPHERE — A hypothetical atmosphere based on averages in which the surface temperature is 59°F (15°C), the surface pressure is 29.92 in. Hg (1013.2 Mb) at sea level, and the temperature lapse rate is approximately 2°C per 1,000 feet.

STOPWAY — An area beyond the takeoff runway which is designed to support an airplane during an aborted takeoff without causing structural damage to the airplane.

STRAIGHT-IN APPROACH-VFR — Entry into the traffic pattern by interception of the extended runway centerline (final approach course) without executing any other portion of the traffic pattern. (See Traffic Pattern)

SUBLIMATION — Process by which a gas is changed to a solid or a solid to a gas without going through the liquid state.

SUPERCOOLED WATER — Water that has been cooled below the freezing point, but is still in a liquid state.

T

TAILWIND — Any wind more than 90 degrees from the magnetic heading of the runway.

TAXI INTO POSITION AND HOLD — Used by ATC to inform a pilot to taxi onto the departure runway in takeoff position and hold. It is not authorization for takeoff. It is used when takeoff clearance cannot immediately be issued because of traffic or other reasons.

TELEPHONE INFORMATION BRIEFING SERVICE (TIBS) — Telephone recording of weather and/or aeronautical information.

TERMINAL RADAR SERVICE AREA (TRSA) — Airspace surrounding designated airports in which ATC provides TRSA service: radar vectoring, sequencing, and separation for all IFR aircraft and participating VFR aircraft.

TETRAHEDRON — Device used as a landing direction indicator, usually at nontower airports. The small end points into the wind, or in the general direction of landing.

THRESHOLD — The beginning of the landing area of the runway.

TRACK — The actual flight path of an aircraft over the ground.

TRAFFIC ADVISORIES — Advisories issued to alert a pilot to other known or observed air traffic which may be in such proximity to their position or intended route of flight as to warrant their attention.

TRAFFIC PATTERN — The traffic flow that is prescribed for aircraft landing and taking off from an airport. The usual components are the upwind, crosswind, downwind, and base legs; and the final approach.

TRANSCRIBED WEATHER BROADCAST (TWEB) — A continuous recording of weather and aeronautical information broadcast over L/MF or VOR stations.

TRANSPONDER — An electronic device aboard the airplane that enhances an aircraft's identity on an ATC radar screen.

TRUE AIRSPEED (TAS) — The speed at which an aircraft is moving relative to the surrounding air.

TRUE ALTITUDE — The actual height of an object above mean sea level.

TRUE COURSE (TC) — The intended or desired direction of flight as measured on a chart clockwise from true north.

TRUE HEADING — The direction the longitudinal axis of the airplane points with respect to true north. True heading is equal to true course plus or minus any wind correction angle.

U

UNCONTROLLED AIRSPACE — Class G airspace.

UNICOM — A nongovernment communications facility which may provide airport information at certain airports.

V

VARIATION — The angular difference between true north and magnetic north; indicated on charts by isogonic lines.

VICTOR AIRWAY — An airway system based on the use of VOR facilities. The north-south airways have odd numbers (Victor 11), and the east-west airways have even numbers (Victor 14).

VISIBILITY — The distance one can see and identify prominent unlighted objects by day and prominent lighted objects by night.

VISUAL FLIGHT RULES (VFR) — Rules that govern the procedures for conducting flight in visual conditions. The term "VFR" is also used to indicate weather conditions that comply with specified VFR requirements.

VOR — Ground-based navigational system consisting of very high frequency omnidirectional range (VOR) stations which provide course guidance. VORTAC provides both VOR and TACAN course guidance plus distance (DME) information.

W

WARM FRONT — The boundary between two airmasses where warm air is replacing cold air.

WARNING AREA — Airspace of defined dimensions, extending from three nautical miles outward from the coast of the United States, that contains activity that may be hazardous to nonparticipating aircraft.

WIND CORRECTION ANGLE (WCA) — The angular difference between the heading of the airplane and the course.

WIND SHEAR — A sudden, drastic shift in wind speed, direction, or both that may occur in the vertical or horizontal plane.

WINGTIP VORTICES — Circular patterns of air created by an airfoil when generating lift. Vortices from medium to heavy aircraft may be extremely hazardous to small aircraft.

ABBREVIATIONS

A

A/FD — Airport/Facility Directory
AC — Advisory Circular
ADF — automatic direction finder
ADIZ — air defense identification zone
ADM — aeronautical decision making
AFSS — automated flight service station
AGL — above ground level
AIM — Aeronautical Information Manual
AIP — Aeronautical Information Publication
AIRMET — Airman's Meteorological Information
ALS — approach light system
ARSR — air route surveillance radar
ARTCC — air route traffic control center
ARTS — automated radar terminal system
ASOS — automated surface observation system
ASR — airport surveillance radar
ATA — actual time of arrival
ATC — Air Traffic Control
ATCRBS — ATC radar beacon system
ATD — actual time of departure
ATE — actual time enroute
ATIS — automatic terminal information service
AWOS — automated weather observing system
AWW — severe weather forecast alert

B

BFO — beat frequency oscillator mode of ADF
BHP — brake horsepower

C

CAP — Civil Air Patrol
CAS — calibrated airspeed
CAT — clear air turbulence
CDI — course deviation indicator
CFI — certified flight instructor
CG — center of gravity
CIG — ceiling
C_L — coefficient of lift
CLC — courseline computer
CO — carbon monoxide
CO_2 — carbon dioxide
CRT — cathode ray tube
CSG — slide graphic computer
CTAF — common traffic advisory frequency
CW — continuous wave NDB signals
CWA — center weather advisory

D

DA — density altitude
DC — direct current
DEWIZ — distant early warning identification zone
DF — direction finder
DG — directional gyro
DME — distance measuring equipment
DR — dead reckoning
DUATS — direct user access terminal system
DVFR — defense visual flight rules

E

EAS — equivalent airspeed
EFAS — enroute flight advisory service
EFC — expect further clearance (time)
ELT — emergency locator transmitter
ETA — estimated time of arrival
ETD — estimated time of departure
ETE — estimated time enroute

F

f.p.m. — feet per minute
f.p.s. — feet per second
FA — area forecast
FAA — Federal Aviation Administration
FARs — Federal Aviation Regulations
FBO — fixed base operator
FCC — Federal Communications Commission
FDC — Flight Data Center
FD — winds and temperatures aloft forecast
FL — flight level
FM — frequency modulation
FREQ — frequency
FSDO — Flight Standards District Office
FSS — flight service station

G

g.p.h. — gallons per hour
GADO — General Aviation District Office
GAMA — General Aviation Manufacturers' Association
GPS — Global Positioning System
GS — groundspeed

H

HF — high frequency
HIRLs — high intensity runway lights
HIWAS — hazardous inflight weather advisory service
HSI — horizontal situation indicator
HVOR — high altitude VOR
Hz — Hertz

I

IAS — indicated airspeed
ICAO — International Civil Aviation Organization
IFR — instrument flight rules
ILS — instrument landing system
IMC — instrument meteorological conditions
in. HG — inches of mercury
IOAT — indicated outside air temperature

IR — IFR military training route
ISA — International Standard Atmosphere

K

kHz — kiloHertz
KIAS — knots indicated airspeed
KTAS — knots true airspeed

L

L/MF — low/medium frequency
LAA — local airport advisory
LAT — latitude
LF — low frequency
LIFR — low IFR
LIRLs — low intensity runway lights
LLWAS — low level wind shear alert system
LONG — longitude
LOP — line of position
LORAN — long range navigation
LVOR — low altitude VOR

M

mb — millibars
MB — magnetic bearing
MEF — maximum elevation figure
METAR — aviation routine weather report
MH — magnetic heading
MHz — MegaHertz
MIRLs — medium intensity runway lights
MOA — military operations area
MSAW — minimum safe altitude warning
MSL — mean sea level
MTR — military training route
MULTICOM — frequency used at airports without a tower, FSS, or UNICOM
MVFR — marginal VFR

N

n.m. — nautical miles
NAS — National Airspace System

NAVAID — navigational aid
NDB — nondirectional radio beacon
NFCT — non-federal control tower
NOAA — National Oceanic and Atmospheric Administration
NORDO — no radio, in reference to lost communications
NOS — National Ocean Service
NOTAM — notice to airmen
NTSB — National Transportation Safety Board
NWS — National Weather Service

O

OAT — outside air temperature
OBS — omnibearing selector
OTS — out-of-service

P

p.s.i. — pounds per square inch
P-factor — an element of asymmetrical thrust
PA — pressure altitude
PAPI — precision approach path indicator
PAR — precision approach radar
PCL — pilot controlled lighting
PIC — pilot in command
PIREP — pilot report
POH — Pilot's Operating Handbook
PTS — Practical Test Standard

R

r.p.m. — revolutions per minute
RAIL — runway alignment indicator lights
RAREP — radar weather report
RB — relative bearing
RCO — remote communications outlet
REIL — runway end identifier lights
RMI — radio magnetic indicator
RMK — remark
RNAV — area navigation
RRWDS — radar remote weather display system

RSC — runway surface condition
RVR — runway visual range
RVV — runway visibility value
rwy — runway

S

s.m. — statute mile
SA — surface aviation weather report
SAR — search and rescue
SCATANA — Security Control of Air Traffic and Air Navigation Aids
SDF — simplified directional facility
sfc — surface
SFL — sequenced flashing lights
SHF — super high frequency
SIGMET — significant meteorological information
SPECI — aviation selected special weather report
SR—SS — sunrise — sunset
STC — sensitivity time control
STOL — Short Takeoff and Landing
SVFR — special VFR

T

TACAN — tactical air navigation
TAF — terminal aerodrome forecast
TAS — true airspeed
TC — true course
TEL—TWEB — telephone access to TWEB
TIBS — telephone information briefing service
TRSA — terminal radar service area
TVOR — terminal VOR
TWEB — transcribed weather broadcast

U

UFN — until further notice
UHF — ultra high frequency
UNICOM — aeronautical advisory station
UTC — Coordinated Universal Time (Zulu time)
UWS — urgent weather SIGMET

V

VASI — visual approach slope
indicator
VFR — visual flight rules
VHF — very high frequency
VHF/DF — VHF direction finder
VMC — visual meteorological
conditions
VOR — VHF omnidirectional
receiver
VOR/DME — collocated VOR and
DME navaids
VORTAC — VOR and TACAN
collocated
VOT — VOR test facility
VR — VFR military training route
VSI — vertical speed indicator

W

WA — AIRMET
WAC — World Aeronautical Chart
WCA — wind correction angle
WILCO — understand and will
comply
WP — waypoint
WS — SIGMET
WSO — Weather Service Office
WST — convective SIGMET
WW — severe weather watch
bulletin

INDEX

The NOTAMs Section is designed to inform you of recent developments that could affect your training.

AERONAUTICAL KNOWLEDGE AREAS

The following information pertains to areas of increased or new emphasis in aeronautical knowledge requirements for private pilot applicants.

AIRCRAFT MAINTENANCE

Rules pertaining to aircraft maintenance are covered in the Federal Aviation Regulations. Specific maintenance-related regulations include FAR Part 43 and FAR Part 91, Subpart E. Definitions which apply to maintenance, preventive maintenance, and alterations or repairs are listed in FAR Part 1.

PART 1

Maintenance means inspection, overhaul, repair, preservation, and the replacement of parts, but excludes preventive maintenance. Overhauling an engine or replacing a propeller are examples of maintenance.

Preventive maintenance means simple or minor preservation operations and the replacement of small standard parts not involving complex assembly operations. Servicing landing gear wheel bearings or replenishing hydraulic fluid are examples of preventive maintenance.

Alterations are classified as major or minor. A **major alteration** means an alteration not listed in the aircraft, aircraft engine, or propeller specifications that might appreciably affect weight, balance, flight characteristics, or other qualities of airworthiness; or that is not done according to accepted practices or cannot be done by elementary operations. **Minor alteration** means an alteration other than a major alteration. Major and minor repairs have definitions similar to major and minor alterations.

PART 43

Detailed maintenance procedures are prescribed in FAR Part 43. These rules govern the maintenance, preventive maintenance, rebuilding and alteration of civil aircraft. Generally, Part 43 applies to maintenance personnel; however, owners, operators, and pilots should be familiar with the basic requirements. As an example, anytime preventive maintenance has been performed on an aircraft, specific procedures must be followed. The signature, certificate number, kind of certificate held by the person approving the work, and a description of the work done must be entered in the aircraft maintenance records.

PART 91, SUBPART E

According to FAR Part 91, Subpart E, the owner or operator of an aircraft is primarily responsible for maintaining that aircraft in an airworthy condition. No person may perform maintenance, preventive maintenance, or alterations on an aircraft other than as prescribed in this Subpart and other regulations, including FAR Part 43. Each owner or operator of an aircraft shall have that aircraft inspected as required. When maintenance is completed, the owner/operator responsibilities include ensuring that maintenance personnel make appropriate entries in aircraft maintenance records indicating the aircraft has been approved for return to service. If alteration or repair substantially affects the aircraft's operation in flight, that aircraft must be test flown by an appropriately rated pilot with at least a private pilot certificate and approved for return to service before being operated with passengers aboard.

PRACTICAL TEST STANDARDS

The FAA's Private Pilot Practical Test Standards (PTS) were revised in 1995. The accompanying table shows a comparison of the old areas of operation and tasks to the new ones. Changes are highlighted by bold type. For example, under area of operation, Preflight Preparation, new tasks include National Airspace System and Minimum Equipment List. Notice that Imminent Stalls — Power On and Power Off have been deleted, and new areas of operation, Performance Maneuver and Postflight Procedures, have been added. The revised PTS stresses safety-related items such as collision and runway incursion avoidance, crew resource management, and checklist usage. [Figure N-1]

PRIVATE PILOT PRACTICAL TEST STANDARDS — AIRPLANE (SEL)	
Old	New

I. PREFLIGHT PREPARATION
  A. Certificates and Documents
  B. Obtaining Weather Information
  C. Determining Performance and Limitations
  D. Cross-Country Flight Planning
  E. Airplane Systems
  F. Aeromedical Factors
	I. PREFLIGHT PREPARATION
	  A. Certificates and Documents
	  B. Weather Information
	  C. Cross-Country Flight Planning
	  D. **National Airspace System**
	  E. Performance and Limitations
	  F. Operation of Systems
	  G. **Minimum Equipment List**
	  H. Aeromedical Factors

II. GROUND OPERATIONS
  A. Visual Inspection
  B. Cockpit Management
  C. Starting Engine
  D. Taxiing
  E. Pretakeoff Check
  F. Postflight Procedures **(new Area XII)**
	II. **PREFLIGHT PROCEDURES**
	  A. Preflight Inspection
	  B. Cockpit Management
	  C. Engine Starting
	  D. Taxiing
	  E. Before Takeoff Check

Figure N-1. FAA Private Pilot Practical Test Standards

III.	AIRPORT AND TRAFFIC PATTERN OPERATIONS A. Radio Communications and ATC Light Signals B. Traffic Pattern Operations C. Airport and Runway Marking and Lighting	III.	**AIRPORT OPERATIONS** A. Radio Communications and ATC Light Signals B. Traffic Patterns C. Airport and Runway Markings and Lighting
IV. XI.	TAKEOFFS AND CLIMBS A. Normal and Crosswind Takeoffs and Climbs B. Short-Field Takeoff and Climb C. Soft-Field Takeoff and Climb APPROACHES AND LANDINGS **(now included in Area IV)** A. Normal and Crosswind Approaches and Landings B. Forward Slips to Landing C. Go-Around D. Short-Field Approach and Landing E. Soft-Field Approach and Landing	IV.	TAKEOFFS, LANDINGS, **AND GO-AROUNDS** A. Normal and Crosswind Takeoff and Climb B. Normal and Crosswind Approach and Landing C. Soft-Field Takeoff and Climb D. Soft-Field Approach and Landing E. Short-Field Takeoff and Climb F. Short-Field Approach and Landing G. Forward Slip to a Landing H. Go-Around
		V.	**PERFORMANCE MANEUVER** A. **Steep Turns**
VIII.	FLIGHT MANEUVERING BY REFERENCE TO GROUND OBJECTS A. Rectangular Course B. S-Turns Across a Road C. Turns Around a Point	VI.	**GROUND REFERENCE MANEUVERS** A. Rectangular Course B. S-Turns C. Turns Around a Point
V.	CROSS-COUNTRY FLYING A. Pilotage and Dead Reckoning B. Radio Navigation C. Diversion D. Lost Procedures	VII.	**NAVIGATION** A. Pilotage and Dead Reckoning B. Radio Navigation C. Diversion D. Lost Procedures
VII.	FLIGHT AT CRITICALLY SLOW AIRSPEEDS A. Full Stalls — Power Off B. Full Stalls — Power On C. Imminent Stalls — Power On and Power Off **(deleted)** D. Maneuvering at Critically Slow Airspeed E. Constant Altitude Turns	VIII.	**SLOW FLIGHT and STALLS** A. Maneuvering During Slow Flight B. **Power‑Off** Stalls C. **Power‑On** Stalls D. **Spin Awareness**
VI.	FLIGHT BY REFERENCE TO INSTRUMENTS A. Straight-and-Level Flight B. Straight, Constant Airspeed Climbs C. Straight, Constant Airspeed Descents D. Turns to Headings E. Unusual Flight Attitudes F. Radio Aids and Radar Services	IX.	**BASIC INSTRUMENT MANEUVERS** A. Straight-and-Level Flight B. Constant Airspeed Climbs C. Constant Airspeed Descents D. Turns to Headings E. **Recovery from** Unusual Attitudes F. **Radio Communications, Navigation Systems/Facilities**, and Radar Services
X.	EMERGENCY OPERATIONS A. Emergency Approach and Landing (Simulated) B. System and Equipment Malfunctions	X.	EMERGENCY OPERATIONS A. **Emergency Descent** B. Emergency Approach and Landing C. Systems and Equipment Malfunctions D. **Emergency Equipment and Survival Gear**
IX.	NIGHT FLIGHT OPERATIONS A. Night Flight	XI.	**NIGHT OPERATIONS** A. **Night Preparation** B. **Night Flight**
		XII.	**POSTFLIGHT PROCEDURES** A. **After Landing** B. **Parking and Securing**

Figure N-1. (Continued)

NOTICES TO AIRMEN

For many years the *Notices to Airmen* publication was published on a bi-weekly schedule (every 14 days). Beginning September 12, 1996, *Notices to Airmen* publication cycle changed from 14 days to 28 days. The change to the four-week cycle was a cost savings measure that was supported by a customer survey.